Understanding Foodservice Cost Control

An Operational Text for Food, Beverage, and Labor Costs

THIRD EDITION

Edward E. Sanders

Timothy H. Hill

Donna J. Faria

PEARSON

Prentice Hall

Upper Saddle River, NJ 07458

Library of Congress Cataloging-in-Publication Data

Sanders, Edward E.
   Understanding foodservice cost control: an operational text for food, beverage, and labor costs/Edward E. Sanders, Timothy H. Hill, Donna J. Faria–3rd ed.
      p. cm.
   Previously published under title: Foodservice profitability, 2nd ed., 2001.
   Includes index.
   ISBN-13: 978-0-13-171487-8
   ISBN-10: 0-13-171487-2
   1. Foodservice–Cost control.   I. Hill, Timothy H.   II. Faria, Donna J.   III. Sanders, Edward
E. Foodservice profitability.   IV. Title.
   TX911.3.C65S26 2008
   647.95–dc22

2007013719

Editor-in-Chief: Vernon R. Anthony
Senior Editor: William Lawrensen
Managing Editor—Editorial: Judith Casillo
Managing Editor—Production: Mary Carnis
Production Liaison: Jane Bonnell
Production Editor: Shelley Creager, Aptara, Inc.
Manufacturing Manager: Ilene Sanford
Manufacturing Buyer: Cathleen Petersen
Senior Marketing Manager: Leigh Ann Sims
Marketing Coordinator: Alicia Dysert
Marketing Assistant: Les Roberts

Senior Design Coordinator:
   Miguel Ortiz
Interior Design: Aptara, Inc.
Cover Designer: Linda Punskovsky
Cover Image: Burke/Triolo Productions,
   Jupiter Images/FoodPix
Composition: Aptara, Inc.
Media Production Project Manager:
   Lisa Rinaldi
Printer/Binder: Bind-Rite Graphics
Cover Printer: Coral Graphics

Previous editions published under the title *Foodservice Profitability: A Control Approach* by Edward E. Sanders and Timothy H. Hill.

Text photo credits appear on page 599, which constitutes a continuation of the copyright page.

Pearson Education LTD.
Pearson Education Singapore, Pte. Ltd.
Pearson Education Canada, Ltd.
Pearson Education—Japan
Pearson Education Australia PTY, Limited
Pearson Education North Asia, Ltd.
Pearson Educación de Mexico, S.A. de C.V.
Pearson Education Malaysia, Pte. Ltd.

10 9 8 7 6 5 4
ISBN-13: 978-0-13-171487-8
ISBN-10:   0-13-171487-2

Brief Contents

Contents

Perspective

A primary function of management that affects the level of success of any food-service operation is an ability to control costs. We believe that to talk in generalities about systems, without at least presenting the components of a system, would be a disservice to the reader. Therefore, this book will refer to forms that have been developed to illustrate specific control principles, strategies, or tactics. We are not suggesting that the way that these forms illustrate control methods is applicable in all foodservice situations, but if exemplary systems or forms are not used to teach principles, the student reader will be unable to understand the concepts being taught. The reader must exercise his or her own judgment in the use and design of control systems and reporting forms so that what is used ultimately provides the necessary information for making good decisions.

The book will demonstrate how to arrive at the right financial numbers and percentages and ways in which the wise manager can prevent problems or correct them once they occur. Examples of forms and reports used in this text demonstrate what can be accomplished manually or with the help of a computer.

In an industry of expanding growth and opportunity, employers increasingly seek to recruit prospective managers whose education will allow them to quickly become involved and productive in foodservice operations. Crucial to this situation on the part of the new foodservice manager is an appreciation and thorough comprehension of the competitive and unpredictable climate of the industry and how internal control procedures represent management's most effective way to maximize the opportunity for and extent of success and profits.

With this in mind, this text presents very detailed technical explanations and justifications for the use of these control systems. One of the primary goals of this project from the beginning has been to create a volume that can be used both as a textbook in an academic setting and a technical guide and manual in an industry setting. Students who seriously consider and become aware of the importance of these concepts will be in an advantageous position when being considered for industry recruitment. They will also be impressive in their positions as they implement these concerns and get results.

Edward E. Sanders
Timothy H. Hill
Donna J. Faria

Note: This book is designed to provide accurate and authoritative information with regard to the subject matter covered. It is provided with the understanding that the authors are not engaged in rendering legal, accounting, or other professional services. If legal advice or other expert assistance is required, the services of a competent professional should be sought.

An Expression of Appreciation

The authors would like to acknowledge several individuals who reviewed the manuscript during its development and some faculty members within their respective departments and schools who also reviewed text materials. The evaluations and suggestions were outstanding and have enhanced the quality of the final text.

- Paul Bagdan, Ph.D.
- Patt Bowman
- H. Andy Divine, Ph.D., CHA, FMP
- Erna Harris, Ph.D.
- Ray R. Kavanaugh, Ed.D., CHA
- Steven V. Moll
- Matt Samel
- W. Terry Umbreit, Ph.D.

Robin Baliszewski, who recognized the need for the book; Vern Anthony, who challenged the authors to bring forth their best.

Harland L. Hill, DPA, for editorial contributions to the first chapter. In memory of Andrea Hill, who influenced her son to enter the foodservice industry.

Many thanks to Nick Drossos, executive chef, restaurant general manager, restaurant owner, mentor, and loyal friend to Ed Sanders, who took a personal interest in his career as a young restaurant manager and rigorously taught him the skills he had learned over a successful 40-year career in the foodservice industry.

Laura Faria for all her wonderful design work—some of it spur of the moment: the Farfalle Arrabbiata logo, menu design and layout, Chef Farfalle banner and Chef Farfalle caricature, the Operating Cycle of Control design, and a number of other graphics.

Beth and Laura Faria for developing the name of the model restaurant, *Farfalle Arrabbiata* ("the angry bowtie"), one fine summer day while hanging around the house with some college friends.

Sandra Lindblom for her wonderful technical expertise. Sandra was always willing to untangle some computer glitch or file mix-up or explain the vagaries of importing a table and making it presentable. Her advice was invaluable.

Professors Matt Samel, Paul Bagdan, Patt Bowman, Erna Harris—all faculty at the Center for Foodservice Management at Johnson & Wales University, Providence Campus. These fine folks read, critiqued, and offered up sage advice for this project.

Special thanks and kudos to Professor Matt Samel for all his help with this project—especially the design of the Triangle of Enlightenment, and for his endless reading, reading, and more reading.

Professors Alexander (Sandy) Turchetta and Donna Degnan of the Department of Accountancy at Johnson & Wales University, Providence, who read a number of chapters and assisted with materials and advice.

Personal Notes

Ed Sanders and Tim Hill wish to express heartfelt appreciation for the support of their families during the long writing process: their wives, Linda A. Sanders and Judith D. Hill, and, of course, their children.

Donna Faria wishes to express heartfelt appreciation to her family for their support during this project: her husband, Fred T., and her children, Laura and Beth Faria. Thanks, Fred, for putting up with this—now we can get back to bike riding.

Organization of Text

This textbook is written so that the chapters flow in a logical sequence that builds a cumulative understanding of foodservice cost controls. This flow or control cycle divides any food and beverage operation into a series of activities—necessary to profitably and efficiently supply food and beverage products and services to guests. This system, known as the Cycle of Control, is the foundation for the organization of each chapter. To illustrate the concepts found in the Cycle, a restaurant profile has been developed. Chapter content and end-of-chapter exercises have been designed around the restaurant model. The chapters are also self-contained so that the reader can go directly to any chapter for specific information. The text is thus very versatile. It can be used as a guide for thorough, overall comprehension of managing cost controls or as an easily referenced manual for specific industry concerns. The following is a brief overview of the content of each chapter.

Chapter 1—About Operating Controls in the Foodservice Industry provides a general explanation of the control process, the operating environment of a foodservice operation, functions that generally occur, and cost relationships between the menu, the level of service, labor, and technology. The aspects of the internal and external environments that influence how management and employees perform their duties are introduced. The evaluation of controls, the value of information, and the type of information available to manage a foodservice establishment is also discussed. The Operating Cycle of Control is introduced here. A graphic model is used to explain the common activities and systems necessary for food operations to profitably and efficiently supply food and beverage products and services to guests. Farfalle Arrabbiata, the model restaurant used in the text, is also introduced in this chapter.

Chapter 2—About Recipes covers the art of creating standardized recipes. Recipe yield, portion sizes, and weights and measures are carefully studied.

Chapter 3—About the Portion Cost thoroughly discusses the practice of portion costing for all types of menu items. Recipe costs, yield percentages, and butcher and cooking loss tests are covered.

Chapter 4—About Purchasing overviews the five steps or functions involved in the purchasing process. This chapter covers specifications and make-or-buy analysis.

Chapter 5—About Purchasing the "Right Quantity" covers computing order quantities for food items through the use of par inventory levels. Sales history, popularity percentages, yield percentages, requisitions, and yield analysis are discussed.

Chapter 6—About the "Right Supplier" covers the process of selecting the right supplier for food products and services. Developing a supplier specification is demonstrated.

Chapter 7—About Receiving & Storing Products & Processing Invoices covers the knowledge and accountability required to document the receiving process and to record the invoices for tracking and timely payment.

Chapter 8—About Inventory & Inventory Control covers the process of keeping enough inventory to meet customers' needs without investing more money than necessary. How to properly account for and assess the value of inventory is discussed. The use of inventory turnover rate for tracking inventory is demonstrated.

Chapter 9—About Food Production Control covers the use of sales history and kitchen production schedules to control back-of-house production by determining the right quantity of menu items to produce.

Chapter 10—About Food Cost & Food Cost Percentage includes more detailed purposes and functions of cost control. The examples and explanations provide comprehensive applications for every type of foodservice operation.

Chapter 11—About Monitoring Sales explains how to monitor sales by cash, check, and credit or debit cards, together with proper control of customer guest checks, either manually or electronically. Accounting for accuracy, theft prevention, measuring productivity, sales tracking, inventory control, and waste prevention are also discussed.

Chapter 12—About Menus, Menu Pricing, Sales Forecasts, & Sales Analysis describes the process of using sales history to analyze menu sales and make decisions about menu selection. Menu items are categorized by profitability and popularity, and subsequent menu decisions are made.

Chapter 13—About Beverage Production Control & Service starts with standardized recipes and management decisions regarding pouring and other procedures. This chapter shows how employee theft can be prevented by using systems that account for the number of drinks sold and by properly managing inventory. Complying with state laws and posting house policies that both employees and patrons can read and understand are also essential.

Chapter 14—About Beverage Cost & Beverage Cost Percentage discusses all the ingredient costs for preparing alcohol beverages. The principles of control for menu development, purchasing and receiving, tracking product movement, producing, and serving are similar to those for foodservice operations.

Chapter 15—About Bar & Inventory Control covers efficient receiving, storage, and usage, beginning with the liquor storeroom inventory and ending with customer pouring and cash accountability. Also, the application of automated bar systems is considered.

Chapter 16—About Controlling Payroll Costs & Employee Turnover discusses a primary concern of foodservice owners and managers, beginning with payroll cost, which may be controlled by establishing budgets, using work schedules, and monitoring actual costs. The process can be accomplished either manually or electronically. Employee turnover, together with reasons and solutions, is discussed.

Chapter 17—About Measuring Staff Performance & Productivity describes methods of examining the quantity, efficiency, and quality of work, as well as the dependability and responsibility of employees. Sales per hour; covers per hour; person hours; mishaps per hour; and shift, month, and annual production charts are discussed.

Chapter 18—About Operating Statements explains the use of income statements in understanding the financial position of an operation. Income statements and cost behavior are explained. Two methods of analyzing income statements—Common Size and Comparative Analysis—are discussed.

Chapter 19—About Preparing Income Statements continues with the study of income statements by using the concepts of income statement analysis developed in Chapter 18 to prepare operating statements for future operating periods.

Glossary—A full glossary of all major terms used in the text is included in this edition.

Index—A detailed index of all major terms and topics is included in this edition.

Component CD—Select questions from the Discussion Questions and Exercises have been formatted into Excel for use by faculty and students. Questions included on the CD are marked with a CD graphic in the text. The exercises on the CD have multiple uses: students can work the problems manually, they can try their hand at writing cell formulas or they can add data to the spreadsheets and watch the answers unfold. All questions on the CD include an answer key. An instruction file is also included.

About the Authors

Edward E. Sanders
Restaurateur/Associate Professor/Publisher (Emeritus)
Ed was the Founder/CEO of *Hospitality News*, a trade journal for foodservice entrepreneurs. His prior experience as chief operating officer for a regional chain of restaurants, a restaurant owner, food buyer, and associate professor of business, uniquely qualified him for the task—knowing what operators wanted to read. Along the way he earned the Certified Food Executive and Certified Purchasing Manager credentials. Ed has a Master's Degree in international management from Thunderbird School of Global Management and a doctor of business administration degree in management and organization. He also co-founded with the President of Southern Oregon University, the Hotel, Restaurant, and Resort Management program within the University's School of Business. Ed is a recognized Pearson Prentice Hall author, being the lead coauthor for textbooks on cost controls, catering, and professional table service.

Timothy H. Hill
Restaurateur/Associate Professor/Consultant and Trainer
Tim is a certified Foodservice Management Professional, with experience in managing restaurants and lodging operations, and has owned two restaurants. He earned his Ph.D. from Washington State University. He founded the Hotel Management program at Brigham Young University–Hawaii Campus and the Hospitality, Tourism, and Recreation Management program at Central Oregon Community College. He also was a partner in founding the Cascade Culinary Institute at Central Oregon Community College. Further, he has been a consultant in customer service and human resource management for resorts, hotel chains, independent restaurants, and lodging operations.

Donna J. Faria
Associate Professor, The Hospitality College,
The Center for Foodservice Management
Johnson & Wales University, Providence Campus
Donna has been on the faculty at Johnson & Wales University for more than 19 years, where she teaches foodservice management courses in The Hospitality College. She is a Certified Hospitality Educator (CHE) and is ServeSafe certified. She earned an Associate in Culinary Arts, a Bachelor in Foodservice Management, and a Masters in Hospitality Administration, all from Johnson & Wales. Prior to her career as a college-level instructor, she worked as assistant to the foodservice director for a local managed services company, owned and operated an off-premise catering service, and cooked at a variety of foodservice operations during her college years. She got her start in foodservice cooking in a 125-bed skilled nursing facility.

Chapter One

About Operating Controls in the Foodservice Industry

Chapter Objective

To relate traditional management principles to managing a foodservice operation using the Operating Cycle of Control.

Learning Objectives

After reading this chapter and completing the discussion questions and exercises, you should be able to:

1. Define control.
2. Identify the internal environments in a foodservice operation and the external environments that affect all foodservice organizations.
3. Recognize the interrelationship between front-of-the-house operations and back-of-the-house operations.
4. Identify the steps of a basic management control system.
5. Relate the steps in the basic management control system to the steps in the Operating Cycle of Control.
6. Use the Operating Cycle of Control to trace the coordinated procedures involved in managing a foodservice operation.
7. Identify the variety of sources of information required to manage a foodservice operation.
8. Be familiar with the elements of the restaurant profile designed for this text.

Chapter Map

About the Control Process, or, Why Control Is So Important
- Control Versus Cost Control

Internal Foodservice Environments
- Front-of-House Functions
- Back-of-House Functions
- Management Functions

External Foodservice Environments
- Government Regulations
- Local Market Conditions
- Labor Force Demographics
- National, Regional, & Local Economic Conditions
- Supplier Relations
- New Technology
- Media

The Need for Control Processes & Procedures
- Perspective for Control
- Causes of Excess Cost in Foodservice Operations

The Purpose of Controls

The Basic Control Procedure
- Set Standards
- Measure Performance
- Determine Whether Standards Have Been Met
- Take Corrective Action
- Recycle Through the Process
- The Nature of a Control

The Operating Cycle of Control
- About the Operating Cycle of Control

Prepurchase Functions
- The Menu
- Paperwork and Procedures

Chapter Map   (Continued)

Back-of-House Functions

- Receiving
- Invoice Management
- Storage Practices, Inventory Management, and Issuing
- Kitchen Production

Front-of-House Functions

- Guests
- Guest Check

Manager's Role

- Control & Labor Costs, & Technology

- Service & Labor
- New Technology

The Value of Information

- Menu Concepts
- Food Cost
- Beverage Cost
- Labor Cost
- Sales

Farfalle Arrabbiata

- Restaurant Profile

Chapter ✓

Check the chapter content for the answers to the following questions:

1. What are internal environments?
2. How do external environments affect foodservice operations?
3. How do managers control internal environments?
4. What is an Operating Cycle of Control?
5. Why do managers of foodservice operations need an Operating Cycle of Control?
6. What are the four greatest causes of excess cost in a foodservice operation?

---

*A*bout the Control Process, or, Why Control Is So Important

The control process affects every part of the foodservice operation. To understand this process, one must be familiar with the following:

- The internal and external operating environments
- The need for standard control processes and procedures
- The purpose of controls
- The basic control process
- The control process applied to costs and technology
- The reliability and validity of control measures
- The evaluation of management controls
- The value of information
- The types of information

The control process within a foodservice operation sets forth efficient control techniques that are designed to serve several important functions:

1. Maximize food and beverage sales
2. Control expenses

3. Manage employees

4. Maximize profits

These four areas of control are the heart and soul of the foodservice manager's work. They are the *key operating points for an establishment*. The importance of standard controls in each of these central areas cannot be emphasized enough—they are key to a profitable operation. Without control in each of these areas, a business may fail.

This first chapter describes the way managers use information to operate foodservice operations effectively and profitably. A general understanding of the control process and the internal and external operating environments is needed in order to understand the setting in which foodservice operations take place.

At the end of this chapter, the model foodservice establishment designed for this textbook will be introduced. In subsequent chapters, this restaurant is used to demonstrate, clarify, and model the practical importance of many of the concepts in the Operating Cycle of Control. The importance of an adequate information system that supports the operational and management control functions will be outlined. An **information system** is *a formal method of processing information used for management purposes and functions.*

Control Versus Cost Control

To **control** means *to exercise authority over, regulate, verify, or check some function.* It implies *a method, device, or system that accomplishes one or more of these purposes.* In the foodservice industry, the term **cost control** has come to mean the following:

- Control over all items of income
- Control over all items of expense
- Control over the flow of products and services (internal and external to a foodservice operation)

Every foodservice operation, regardless of its size, type, or method of service must have some system of cost control. A **system** is *a collection of things that work together to create a specified outcome.*

DEFINITIONS

To **control** is to exercise authority over, regulate, verify or check some function through a method, device or system.

Cost control is the process of regulating, checking, and exercising authority over income, expenses, and the flow of products and services internal or external to a foodservice operation.

A **system** is a collection of things that work together to create a specified outcome.

An **internal environment** consists of functions carried on within the organization to achieve organizational objectives.

An **external environment** includes factors such as government regulations, local market conditions, labor force demographics, national economic conditions, supplier relations, new technology, and the media.

Internal Foodservice Environments

All businesses operate within an **internal environment** and an **external environment**. The internal environment consists of *functions carried on within the organization to achieve organizational objectives.* The following three functional areas constitute

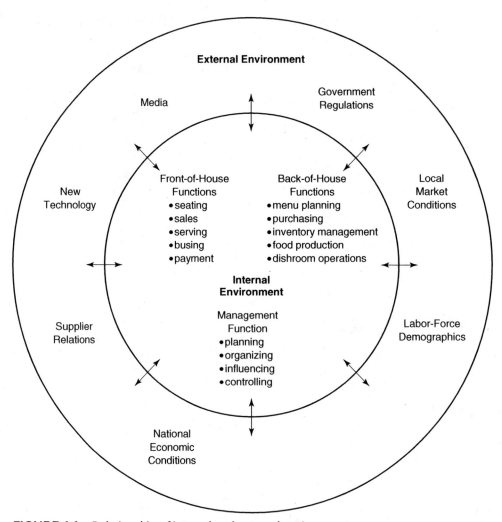

FIGURE 1.1   Relationship of internal and external environments.

the internal environment of a foodservice operation and directly influence how managers and employees perform their duties:

1. Front-of-house functions (FOH)
2. Back-of-house functions (BOH)
3. Management functions

The manager of a foodservice operation must recognize that these two environments exist and that the controls described later in this book are designed to help the foodservice operation succeed within these environments. Figure 1.1 shows these two environments and their relationship to each other. A brief overview may be helpful.

Front-of-House Functions

Within the internal environment, five basic cost control functions occur in the front of the house (FOH). The **front-of-house** includes *all of the guest contact areas of a foodservice operation*. These functions occur in different ways, depending on the type of customer and **foodservice concept**, or *the way the restaurant wants to market itself*. They are:

1. ***Seating.*** This refers to managing the customer experience from the moment of entry. In addition, it includes managing the customer flow through the operation, regardless of whether it is a fine-dining, family, or fast-food takeout

operation. A facility layout and design that allows for ease in service and customer movement consistent with the foodservice concept is critical.

2. *Sales.* Customers order food and beverage items. They may select these items in a variety of ways, ranging from a handheld printed menu, to a lighted menu board behind a takeout counter, to a verbal presentation by servers. In any case, any menu must be regarded as a marketing tool and be so designed as to influence customer selection.

3. *Serving.* This is the delivery of food and beverage items to the customer, with all related foodservice needs also being fulfilled. Specifically, the food and beverage items are served at the proper temperature, with appropriate condiments and other accompaniments. The specific restaurant concept will dictate the service style, which can include full-table styles such as American, French, buffet, self-service; and so on.

4. *Busing.* Simply noted, all the dishes, glasses, and flatware required for service are removed from the table when not needed. In fast-food operations, customers may clear their own tables, and busing may simply mean monitoring the dining room, restrooms, and public areas for cleanliness, wiping off tables and chairs as needed.

5. *Payment.* Collecting payment from the customer can be accomplished by the servers, fast-food counter person, or a cashier using a variety of payment methods: cash, credit cards, house accounts, and so on.

FRONT-OF-HOUSE COST-CONTROL FUNCTIONS
1. Seating
2. Sales
3. Serving
4. Busing
5. Payment

Back-of-House Functions

The five basic cost control functions in the back of the house (BOH) will also vary according to the type of customer and foodservice concept. The **back-of-house** areas are all *the non-customer-contact areas in the foodservice operation.* The back-of-house cost control functions are as follows:

1. *Menu planning.* Developing the food items to be offered via information gathered from sales records, guest comment cards, demographics, and industry trends. This is a critical step in the success of an operation.

2. *Purchasing.* Ordering the correct quality and quantity of food, beverage, and nonfood items and services needed to adequately supply the foodservice operation.

3. *Receiving, storing, inventory management.* Receiving what has been purchased, placing it in the appropriate storage areas, and managing the use of these items for food production.

4. *Food production.* The actual preparation of the food to be served, using established standards and procedures designed by management. These standards and procedures support the restaurant concept.

5. *Dishroom operations.* The maintenance of all food preparation equipment, smallwares, utensils, china, glasses, flatware, and other items used to prepare and serve the food. Maintenance includes washing, sanitizing, storing, and keeping enough items in inventory to successfully serve maximum customer levels.

BACK-OF-HOUSE COST-CONTROL FUNCTIONS

1. Menu planning
2. Purchasing
3. Receiving, storing, and inventory management
4. Food production
5. Dishroom operations

Management Functions

Management functions *enable the front- and back-of-house departments to operate successfully.* The management functions include the following:

- Planning, organizing, influencing, and controlling all the internal functions
- Assessing external factors to determine their impact on internal operations

---

MANAGEMENT FUNCTIONS

1. **Planning**
2. Organizing and influencing
3. Controlling

Planning   This is the key activity. An operation will rarely succeed unless its owner or manager does adequate planning. (Henceforth, both owner and manager will be referred to as "manager.") It starts with the manager's basic assumption that customers targeted in a population area will, over an extended period of time, repetitively purchase an adequate number of specified menu items, and that these will be delivered at a specific level of service via a particular foodservice concept within a price range that will generate a satisfactory level of profit. Within the constraints of the menu, price range, service level, and foodservice concept, the manager must develop a plan to create sufficient product demand (marketing) as well as to ensure the necessary production to meet that demand, thus attaining the organization's profit goal. In general, the plan must do the following:

1. Specify the physical facility and equipment needed to implement the concept.
2. Assign the responsibilities and duties associated with each of the previously discussed internal functions to FOH and BOH positions, and specify the relationships between these positions. This defines the overall organizational structure of the operation.
3. Design standard operating procedures for both the FOH and the BOH that agree with management goals. **Standard operating procedures (SOPs)** are *methods by which management requires certain processes to be completed.* Detailed methods for the performance and evaluation of these procedures must also be developed.
4. Specify the necessary personnel, in numbers and qualifications, and develop recruitment and training plans.
5. Set forth a financial plan for the start-up and ongoing operation, including projected cash flow and **budgets** (*estimates of expenditures and proposals for financing them*), to ensure that funds are available to meet obligations on a timely basis. A **financial plan** is *a plan for how money will be spent in an operation.*
6. Identify the management controls needed to ensure that production and financial goals are met. **Management controls** are *methods of comparing and exercising authority over a foodservice operation's performance to attain established operating goals.* These plans must also include a menu management

system that managers utilize in their daily work. These systems should be so designed as to allow managers to monitor actual results and take corrective action quickly once variances are detected.

MANAGEMENT FUNCTIONS

1. Planning
2. Organizing and Influencing
3. Controlling

Organizing and Influencing   This effort is directed toward putting the plan into action. It involves the following:

- Obtaining the necessary financing
- Acquiring facilities
- Purchasing and installing equipment
- Hiring and training personnel
- Directing personnel
- Providing for the flow of information
- Exerting the influence necessary to meet the goals of the organization

This is accomplished through a strong organizational culture, whereby employees know how to perform and what is expected of them. The **organizational culture** is *the shared values, beliefs, attitudes, and norms that help to direct employee behavior by creating a sense of purpose.*

MANAGEMENT FUNCTIONS

1. Planning
2. Organizing and Influencing
3. Controlling

Controlling   When operations are ongoing, management must determine, either directly through observation or indirectly through management reports, whether the organization is achieving expected progress toward its financial goals. If expected progress cannot be quantified, management must consider some form of planned intervention. This evaluation and intervention may lead to one of several actions:

- Improving or changing operational procedures
- Identifying and eliminating nonfunctional procedures
- Changing or eliminating goals

A detailed discussion of all these functions is beyond the scope of this text. The focus of this book *is,* however, to delve more deeply into the cost-control functions as they are applied to all areas of the foodservice operation.

External Foodservice Environments

Factors in the external environment also influence how managers and employees perform their duties. The following are some primary external environment factors:

- Government regulations
- Local market conditions

- Labor force demographics
- National, regional, and local economic conditions
- Supplier relations
- New technology
- Media

Foodservice operations exist within an external environment. Monitoring this environment is critical, given the potential impact of changes on business volume. This is especially true for chain or franchise businesses operating in a global marketplace. The external environment of a foodservice operation embraces several areas:

Government Regulations

Federal, state, and local governments require timely compliance with a variety of licensing, inspection, and reporting requirements. This can be time consuming for the foodservice manager. Managers may also want to establish contacts with local, state, and national professional associations, as well as with political action groups, which may have an influence over the development of regulations and reporting requirements.

Local Market Conditions

Keeping informed of changes in local market conditions is essential. A manager should be aware of business openings, closings, or expansions; demographic changes; tourism efforts; competitors' efforts to attract and keep business; street improvements; changes in traffic patterns; and competitors starting up or discontinuing business.

Labor Force Demographics

Recruiting and hiring practices are influenced by local labor market conditions. Although a foodservice manager can do little to determine labor force demographics, he or she can use certain control techniques to hire qualified people.

National, Regional, and Local Economic Conditions

National economic conditions affect everyone. Managers must watch for changes, to predict their impact on internal operations as well as on the external environment. Related activities include reading foodservice and other trade publications; being involved with local, state, and national restaurant and other professional associations; and keeping informed of local economic conditions that could have a direct impact upon business.

Supplier Relations

Although purchasing is considered part of the internal environment, it also involves interacting with the external environment. Suppliers are a major source of information useful to managers when developing menus and monitoring the marketing environment. In addition, suppliers sponsor food and equipment shows to provide an opportunity for foodservice managers to sample new food and beverage products and learn about advancements in foodservice equipment.

New Technology

New developments in kitchen equipment and design technology enable kitchens and equipment to be more energy efficient, cost effective, and labor saving. Also, information system software and hardware exemplify how new technology continues to advance foodservice operations.

Media

Television, radio, newspapers, and the Internet not only provide information regarding external factors, but they are also excellent resources for reaching the target population the foodservice manager desires to serve through promotional advertising. Without a doubt, development of Web sites by foodservice operations for doing everything from marketing the restaurant and specialty products to making reservations remains one of the major marketing breakthroughs of this millennium.

EXTERNAL ENVIRONMENTAL FACTORS

- Government regulations
- Local market conditions
- Labor force demographics
- National, regional, and local economic conditions
- Supplier relations
- New technology
- Media

The Need for Control Processes and Procedures

Perspective for Control

In the early days of foodservice operations, the types of controls needed and the records maintained were relatively simple. The cash went into the cash box (register), and daily expenses were taken care of by a transfer of cash out of the cash register. Envelopes may have been used for weekly and monthly expenses, as money was reserved for payroll, rent, utilities, and so on. At the end of the week or month, whatever was left over was the profit.

In today's business environment, however, with its various taxes, business, and license fees; credit cards; accounts payable schedules; payroll taxes; pension plans; vacation plans; health plans; and innumerable other items, individual entrepreneurs, as well as corporations of all sizes, need more detailed information. Complex situations require sophisticated systems. Today, many foodservice operations are run by absentee management or community public-service agencies, such as healthcare providers and schools. Additional controls and reports are necessary in these situations. Even healthcare providers, schools, and other traditionally "nonprofit" organizations must avoid losses and are viewed as revenue centers for their host businesses.

Federal, state, and local governments require monthly, quarterly, and yearly reports concerning the financial status of a business. At the same time, businesses have become agents of the government—collecting taxes on sales, withholding payroll taxes from employees, and paying these sums to the government, according to a structured time schedule.

In less complicated times, the decision to purchase equipment or to construct a building might have been based exclusively on the production needs of the organization. Today, however, this decision is often influenced by several factors:

- Type of business ownership
- Depreciation allowed by the government

- Local, state, or federal regulations
- Leasing options versus ownership
- Obsolescence of the equipment, building, or location.

Working and ownership arrangements have changed markedly over the years. Today, chains and franchises dominate the marketplace, bringing their standardized operating systems with them. The sales volume and size of food and beverage operations reach millions of dollars. These operations are likely to employ a large number of people who must be controlled by a system that will assure management that all income is being received and that all products are either sold or properly utilized. A business may own one or more establishments, yet the owner may not necessarily be personally involved in supervising day-to-day operations at any of them. When this is the case, authority must be delegated to other responsible people. In turn, systems must be devised to determine who bears the responsibility if deviations from owner-manager expectations occur.

Causes of Excess Cost in Foodservice Operations

4 CAUSES OF EXCESS COST

1. Inefficiency
2. Fraud
3. Errors
4. Waste

In any business, every error has an effect. Having clear, precise standards in place eliminates **inefficiency, fraud, errors, and waste (IFEW)**, the four greatest causes of excess costs in a foodservice operation. (Remember this acronym as: **I** will have **FEW** profits if these elements are not controlled.) Employers and employees have a vital interest in ensuring that control systems are reliable and effective. Managers use cost-control systems to help pinpoint responsibility for inefficiency, fraud, errors, and waste. Employees should be aware that control systems can protect them and reward them for good performance. If an employee is doing an outstanding job, management should be able to detect this and reward or possibly advance the employee. If theft occurs, innocent employees have a substantial interest in the control system. An efficient system will be able to identify the source of the theft, which will both deter such occurrences and minimize damage to employee morale caused by unsubstantiated suspicion.

*T*he Purpose of Controls

The primary responsibility for safeguarding the assets of foodservice establishments and preventing and detecting inefficiencies, errors, and fraud rests on management. Thus, cost control systems for the foodservice industry are designed for three primary purposes:

1. To establish an efficient operation
2. To prevent fraud or theft by employees or guests. (Unlike in the retail industry, nearly all theft in foodservice organizations can be attributed to employees.)
3. To ensure that the operation functions in a manner that complies with the goals of management

Whatever the type of food served, the particular function of the foodservice operation, the method of service, and the type of ownership and organization structure, the control system should cover every facet of the operation. The primary objective of a control system may differ for various types of foodservice operations. For a restaurant operator, the first concern is to increase profits. For a school foodservice director or other nonprofit operator, it may be to lower operating costs or increase participation. Each must approach his or her task with a control system tailored to the needs of the organization. The types of systems used in food and beverage operations will differ. What may be effective in one organization may be useless in another.

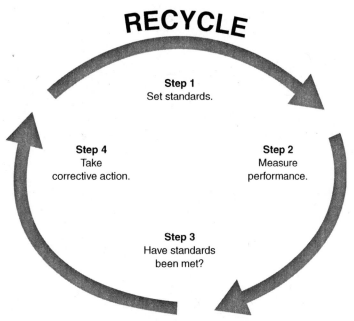

FIGURE 1.2 The basic management control procedure. *Courtesy of Laura Faria.*

The Basic Control Procedure

Managers control the various aspects of the foodservice operation. Simply expressed, the manager knows that something should be done in a specific way, observes whether what is actually occurring is what should be occurring, and corrects the situation as needed. Figure 1.2 illustrates how this process works. Management control consists of the following set of procedures:

A BASIC MANAGEMENT CONTROL PROCEDURE

1. Set standards.
2. Measure performance.
3. Determine whether standards have been met.
4. Take corrective action.
5. Recycle through the process.

Set Standards

Management sets a standard, based on specific criteria, to be achieved or maintained for a specified condition, with or without tolerance for deviation from that standard. *What does this mean to a manager?* It simply means that management determines who, what, when, where, how, and why for all aspects of the operation. "All aspects" simply means that everything from the workplace to the employees to the financial objectives must have descriptive standards and accompanying measurable criteria. These standards must be based on sound business practices and industry norms and must be reasonable for the business one is in. Table 1.1 shows how to use the Cycle of Control for a variety of businesses.

Measure Performance

An ongoing or periodic measurement of the condition for which the standard is set occurs, using the same measures that defined the standard. *What Does This Mean to a Manager?* This means the operating systems in place collect timely information about

Table 1.1   Using the Control Procedure for a Variety of Businesses

Business Example	Description of Situation	Establishing a Standard	Measuring Performance	How to Determine if Standard Was Met	Taking Corrective Action	Recycling
Quick-Service Restaurant	Control the amount of time it takes to service a customer at the counter.	All customers will order, pay for, and receive their orders within 2 minutes of approaching counter.	Timer on point-of-sale terminal tracks service time. End-of-shift manager's reports summarize shift activity.	Manager evaluates information from performance measures to determine compliance.	Employees identified as not meeting standard are retrained or moved to another position.	Monitor reports after every shift.
Full-Menu Table-Service Restaurant	Monitor the temperatures of all equipment.	Prep cooks record walk-in temps every 2 hours; line cooks record hot line temps every 2 hours.	Responsible employees complete and sign time–temperature logs.	Manager or chef monitors logs during and after each shift.	Incomplete or falsified logs will trigger retraining by manager or chef.	Consistently monitor all logs every day.
Housekeeping Department of Hotel	Target turnover time of rooms to be made up.	Staff will turn a standard room in 30 minutes or less.	Start/finish time logs. Time room is turned over to front desk. Number of rooms staff complete in a shift.	Manager monitors housekeeping reports and records from front desk.	Staff not completing room turnover on time will be retrained or replaced.	Consistently monitor logs every day.
Department Store	Staff incentive program to increase sales of accessories.	Floor staff suggest accessories to customers during shopping experience; cashier suggests accessories at close of sale.	Manager's observation; sales records for each shift; sales records for each employee.	Sales records meeting forecasts; manager's observation of employees; employee incentive program.	Employees not in compliance will be retrained, reminded or replaced.	Consistently monitor staff and sales records throughout the program.
Movie Theater	Monitor employees for compliance with snack bar upselling.	Secret shoppers randomly select employees to purchase snacks from using scripted dialogue.	Secret shoppers complete survey responses and submit to management.	Manager receives information; identifies employees needing retraining, reminding or replacement.	Employees consistently identified as not in compliance will be retrained, reminded, or replaced.	Consistently monitor reports from secret shopper program.

Standards guarantee quality.

what has actually occurred. Reports to managers allow them to compare actual results to established standards. Generally, this is easiest to understand when evaluating financial results. However, the same activity transpires when evaluating daily work taking place by employees. The managers know the standard and observe what is actually occurring. The evaluative tool becomes the managers' eyes.

Determine Whether Standards Have Been Met

Synthesize information, making comparisons of actual results to standards. *What Does This Mean to a Manager?* In Steps 1 and 2, setting standards and measuring performance, the stage is set to give managers tools to "manage." In this step, comparison takes place. Managers know the standards and criteria (what is supposed to happen). They know what did happen. Using this information, managers determine whether or not things are on track.

Take Corrective Action

A specific planned intervention is triggered whenever the ongoing or periodic measurement of the standard-related condition exceeds or falls below the standard or its specified tolerances, if any. *What Does This Mean to a Manager?* Simply stated, look at what happened, look at what was supposed to happen, identify those things that need attention, and determine what to do about it. This is what managers do—find a solution for problems revealed through this evaluation process.

Recycle Through the Process

Failure to achieve a standard may mean that the standard, or the criteria used to set the standard, needs to be lowered or abandoned, or it could mean that operational procedures need to be replanned to attain the unmet standard. If the standard was easily attained, it may need to be raised to a higher level, and replanning may be necessary to achieve the higher standard. Careful observations throughout normal business operations may also suggest better procedural methods and evaluation techniques, so that the standard is accurately measured.

What Does This Mean to a Manager? If reports indicate the standard is repeatedly not being met, the *Why* question must be invoked. Why are we not on target? There are two possible answers: The standard is too difficult to achieve, or it is too easy to achieve and is not an acceptable measure. In either situation, the standard needs to be reevaluated and possibly reestablished. Recycling is constantly occurring in any business, if that business is monitoring its results carefully. Recycling fosters change.

The Nature of a Control

A thermostat is a good metaphor to illustrate the nature of a control. Suppose the manager, based on management criteria, decides the air temperature in the restaurant should be maintained at 70°F and sets the thermostat accordingly. A measuring device (a column of mercury) constantly measures the temperature. When the temperature falls below 70°F, the heating unit to which the thermostat is attached is automatically triggered to send heat to the area. When the desired temperature is reached, an automatic message is sent to the heating unit, shutting it off. In actual practice, the control unit may delay sending signals to the heating unit until the temperature reaches a full degree or more above or below 70°F. A two-degree tolerance prevents the heating unit from turning off and on continually, as this could be annoying to patrons and cause excessive wear on equipment.

In this example, the manager set a standard, 70°F, for the temperature of the restaurant. A standard usually reflects a subgoal or subobjective related to attaining an overall goal or a higher subobjective. For example, the manager's overall goal is to make a profit from the restaurant. A subgoal might be to make budget on the Utility Expense line item. In order to do so, the manager must keep the restaurant full of paying customers. To accomplish that, the temperature level must satisfy the comfort level of the patrons. Thus, one of the criteria for setting the standard is the temperature comfort level of the patrons.

More than one criterion is likely to be operative in setting a standard. In the interest of making a profit, the manager undoubtedly used cost as a second criterion by selecting the lowest temperature that will achieve the first criterion. Thus, the standard was set at 70°F, not 72°F. Many criteria may be used in setting a single standard, and many standards are normally involved in a single business. Notice that the standard in this example is stated not as "a comfortable temperature" but in measurable terms, that is, 70°F. No margin should be left for interpretation of the standard. An effective standard should have the same meaning to all concerned. It should be set forth in measurable terms whenever possible.

The Operating Cycle of Control

The basic control procedure for a foodservice operation is the Operating Cycle of Control (OCC). The OCC model was developed with the concepts of a management control system in mind. Figure 1.3 is a visual interpretation of a basic management control system for a foodservice operation. The first three steps in the control process—Establish Standards, Measure Performance, and Determine Whether Standards Have Been Met—are easily accomplished in a foodservice operation using some form of this control model. The last two steps—Taking Corrective Action and Recycling—together are a natural by-product of the first three steps and ones that all trained managers use while monitoring their operations. The following discussion briefly describes each step in the Operating Cycle of Control process.

About the Operating Cycle of Control

All businesses execute a series of *precise* activities that are the heart of what it is that they "do." From these activities, revenue is generated and, hopefully, profit. The restaurant business is no different. Each day, as the doors are unlocked, employees and managers begin a very specific series of activities to fire up the restaurant, prepare menu items, service guests as they purchase food and beverages, and ultimately close the operation at the end of the day. These steps vary slightly from one operation to the next, but no matter what, they all will occur at some point.

The Menu

Pre-Purchase Functions

GUEST CHECK
Sales history, turnover,
average check, cash management,
revenue forecasting & budgeting,
menu item analysis

STANDARDIZED RECIPES
Standard ingredients, portion size,
quality, consistency, quantity, purchasing

COST CARDS
Portion costs, yield factors, sell prices

GUESTS
Greeting, seating, sales,
serving, busing, payment,
comment cards

SPECIFICATIONS
Product descriptions

FOH Functions

PAR STOCK
Inventory levels, order building

KITCHEN PRODUCTION
Production schedules, portion tracking,
recipe control, serving controls, food safety

REQUISITION
Order building, purchasing

PRODUCT ISSUING
Requisitions, transfers, daily & monthly costs,
food cost percentage

SHOPPING LISTS
Call sheets, bid sheets,
suppliers, bidding

**STORAGE PRACTICES &
INVENTORY MANAGEMENT**
Best practices, sanitation,
security, inventory methods

PURCHASE ORDERS
Security, ship order,
price guarantee, contract

INVOICE MANAGEMENT
Payment, price checking, security

BOH Functions

RECEIVING ACTIVITIES
Best practices, invoices, security, sanitation

FIGURE 1.3 Operating Cycle of Control. *Courtesy of Laura Faria.*

All of these activities together are called the Operating Cycle of Control or the OCC. It is a basic control procedure. The **Operating Cycle of Control** is defined as *a control cycle that divides any food and beverage operation into a series of coordinated procedures that are necessary to profitably and efficiently supply food and beverage products and services to guests, given an acceptable volume of business.* These steps include all the basic activities, procedures, and paperwork needed to operate a restaurant every single day.

THE OPERATING CYCLE OF CONTROL

A control cycle that divides any food and beverage operation into a series of coordinated procedures that are necessary to profitably and efficiently supply food and beverage products and services to guests, given an acceptable volume of business.

Earlier in the chapter, cost-control systems were identified as *the way* to control for inefficiency, fraud, errors, and waste in an operation. The steps in the Cycle of Control represent a cost control system of industry "best practices" (Figure 1.3). These activities are the "best" things to do to successfully operate a profitable foodservice operation. Each step in the model represents a "tool" in a manager's toolbox to effectively and efficiently manage a foodservice operation.

What do you observe about the Cycle of Control shown in Figure 1.3? Did you notice the cycle is separated into FOH and BOH sections? Did you notice the distinct steps spelled out in both the FOH and BOH sections? Did you notice the prepurchase functions? Did you wonder why these steps are first? Given that most independent table service operations spend close to 30 percent of their food sales buying food and beverage products, these prepurchasing steps are nonnegotiable—they outline the homework the managers or chefs must do before ordering even the salt and pepper!

Observe that once the prepurchase functions are complete and orders are placed, the receiving, storing, and issuing procedures automatically follow. It is worth noting that this part of the cycle is where most operations fail to plan properly and the most likely place where profit will be lost. It is where inefficiency, fraud, error, and waste can wreak havoc on profit if adequate controls and procedures are not in place.

Kitchen production is the final segment under BOH functions. Basically, let the cooking begin. At this point, the raw products are in-house and ready for action. The BOH staff is set, ready to prepare, and ready to serve, according to anticipated sales. All that's missing are the actual orders from the FOH staff.

Prepurchase Functions

On first review of the Operating Cycle of Control, one notices that the cycle is broken down into front-of-house (FOH) and back-of-house (BOH) areas. Then, the details in each of these sections becomes more apparent, beginning with the back-of-house functions. Notice that the **menu**, *which lists the establishment's food and beverages, is the key element that drives the cycle.* Following the menu come the broad steps and the most common paperwork and procedures used by foodservice operators.

It is likely that many operations have additional specialized paperwork developed for their use. This would be evident in the chains and franchises so common today. Others, such as small, low-volume operations, may not have a need for every procedure in the cycle. What follows is a general explanation of each step in the cycle, together with a brief description of the controls related to that step. Note that the specifics of each element will be thoroughly covered in the subsequent text chapters, using the restaurant model as a backdrop for explanations and examples.

The Menu

The menu starts the cycle. Without one, no work can take place. It can be presented to the customer on a menu board (sign) on a wall or on a handheld document. Management's decisions regarding menu content are the most important decisions made in a foodservice operation. Developing the menu concept and specific selections will be covered in greater detail in a later chapter. For this conversation, it is fair to say that if an item makes it onto a written menu as a selection, there must be customer demand or at least anticipated demand and the item must generate profit.

All of the following have to be considered when developing menu selections:

- The targeted customer population to be served
- The restaurant concept
- Food quality
- Financial backing and cash flow
- Guest preferences
- Level of service offered

- Management financial goals
- Staff abilities
- Availability and capacity of facilities and equipment
- Availability of products

The point here is that the menu drives all other steps because it identifies what is to be sold. Buyers cannot buy, cooks cannot cook, managers cannot manage, and servers cannot serve unless there is a carefully crafted menu with appropriate food and beverage selections.

Paperwork and Procedures

Standardized Recipes   If the menu drives the cycle, then standardized recipes are like the gas for the cycle. Each and every menu item sold—be it food or beverage—must have a standardized recipe. Why? Because without standardized recipes for every single food and beverage item on the menu, buyers cannot buy. If buyers cannot buy, then cooks cannot cook and servers cannot serve, and so on. Why, again? Because **standardized recipes** *identify menu item ingredients* (these would be the "gas"). They *list what needs to be purchased*. If it's not on the recipe card, the product will not and should not be purchased. From this ingredient list and an accurate sales history, buyers know how much to purchase.

STANDARDIZED RECIPES
✓ Control how the product is to be made.
✓ Describe how the item is to be presented on the plate.
✓ Provide for total consistency each and every time the item is sold.
✓ Should guarantee consistency in cost.

Recipe Cost Cards   **Recipe cost cards** are the backbone of *the financial controls for all menu items.* Their accuracy and value are solely dependent on the consistent use of standardized recipes by all staff, both FOH and BOH. Whereas BOH staff obviously work daily with recipes and have maximum responsibility for the end product, FOH staff are accountable for identifying plating errors (portion sizes and presentation), communicating guest comments, and being knowledgeable of menu selections.

Specifications   **Specifications** are *comprehensive product and service descriptions used to make the purchasing job easier.* Although developing specs is often tedious work, once completed, they become a wonderful purchasing tool. Because they completely describe what is and is not acceptable, there should be no chance of receiving product that is not correct. For this to be true, receivers must be carefully trained and suppliers must have accurate updated copies. Well-written specifications reduce costs and receiving errors.

Par Stock   A **par stock** is *the average amount of inventory needed for a specific period of time.* This period of time is typically the longest time between deliveries. Calculating this level of inventory and using the information to compile orders simplifies the ordering process.

Establishing and using pars is an important tool in the manager's toolbox to accurately and efficiently order the correct amount of product. Given the perishable nature of most product used in a restaurant, taking the time to establish par inventory levels is time well spent.

Requisitions   **Requisitions** are *forms used to request that the purchaser order a specific product or service.* Typically, managers or chefs fill out requisitions in advance of needing products or services. These documents are a means by which purchasers develop orders for suppliers. They are especially useful in operations with multiple departments and revenue centers. It is not unusual, however, for operators, even fairly large ones, to effectively purchase goods and services without the use of requisitions.

Shopping Lists   In this next step, lists of products needed are compiled, usually by product type. Next, a standardized procedure is used to check prices, product availability, and delivery time. In some operations, a bidding process will be employed for select products or even for all products. **Bidding** is *a process businesses use to compare supplier prices, services, and other criteria prior to making purchasing decisions.* Oftentimes, an **approved supplier list** has been developed to make purchasing easier. These are *suppliers with whom a relationship has been established and agreements put in place regarding products, quality, pricing, delivery, billing, and so on.*

In the chain or franchise industry, purchasing is typically arranged through purchasing contracts negotiated and managed at the corporate level. Foodservice managers working in this forum purchase products and services from approved suppliers, who meet corporate specifications for product quality, quantity, price, and so on. Smaller operations may accomplish much of their purchasing through food clubs.

Purchase Orders   Shopping lists beget orders and orders beget purchase orders! A **purchase order (PO)** is *used to initiate the exchange of goods between operator and supplier.* POs are used in every business and are not particular to the foodservice or hospitality industry.

*B*ack-of-House Functions

Receiving

Once POs are enlisted to initiate the exchange, products will be delivered. **Receiving** is one of the most important control steps in a foodservice operation. It is at this point that errors should be caught and corrected. Skillful employees employing excellent **standard receiving practices** *ensure that the correct product is received at the correct price and in the correct quantity.* Larger operations may employ bar-code readers to speed the receiving process and to control product. In addition, receiving practices should follow accepted industry practices for sanitation.

Invoice Management

Establishing accounts with suppliers; matching POs with invoices; charging purchases and transfers to departments; checking invoices for errors and proper signatures; validating product ordered was received, paid for, and used on premises; paying invoices on time—all these activities and more fall under the umbrella of invoice management. **Invoice management** is *the financial file cabinet for the operation.*

Storage Practices, Inventory Management, and Issuing

Excellent **storage practices** follow excellent receiving practices. Once received, product must be quickly stored using accepted industry practices. The following are some examples of acceptable practices: standard sanitation procedures, stock rotation, product dating, physical inventory, storage area organization, and security. Unfortunately, in the foodservice business, it is more likely that employees, rather than customers, are stealing. Consequently, limiting access to storage areas and employing locks with limited key distribution are common industry practices.

Once product is in storage, it must eventually get into prep and production areas. Here is where requisitions come back into play. Originally, requisitions assisted the buyer in determining what to order. Now the product is in-house and must move to where it is needed. Requisitions completed at the start of the cycle listing necessary products or services are now filled. **Requisitions** are *a means of charging departments for product ordered* as well as assisting buyers in ordering. **Transfers** are similar to requisitions in that *they move product and its associated cost from one department or store to another.* Charging requisition and transfer costs to departments is a means to accurately determine departmental costs, necessary for calculating daily and monthly cost of goods and for other reports. It is obvious that these forms are required in large operations with multiple food outlets. Small operators may not employ requisitions or transfers, because all products are charged to one area.

Kitchen Production

Controlling exactly how much and what is to be prepared is the goal of **kitchen production**, and the kitchen production schedule is the tool that makes this happen. Accurately **forecasting**, *or predicting,* guest counts and employing popularity indexes should reduce overproduction and keep waste to a minimum in the kitchen. Standard recipes control food quality and consistency. In addition, managers and chefs monitor portion sizes, plating and cooking errors, kitchen portion prep, and actual portion sales.

ℱront-of-House Functions

The model in Figure 1.3 shows front-of-house (FOH) operations as distinct from the back-of-house (BOH). Imagine that the imaginary line on the graphic separating the two is like the door between the kitchen and the dining room. Although the two departments are separate, they clearly work in concert. There are only two stages in the FOH area. The disparity in the number of steps in the FOH section is not an indication that the FOH is not important or is of lesser importance. On the contrary, operating controls in the front of the house are crucial to a profitable operation. After all, this is the "front line" of contact with the guest. The importance of the FOH is not predicated on the number of steps in the control cycle.

Front-of-house action is completely dependent on customers deciding from among many options to dine at a particular foodservice operation. Restaurants do not have **captive audiences**, or *people on the premises whom they must feed because they have no other place to go.* Rather, management develops multiple strategies to attract guests. Once guests arrive, SOPs automatically kick in. Simply stated, these are as follows:

- Guests are greeted and seated.
- Servers take orders and deliver food.
- Guests ultimately pay the check.

The guest check is the primary FOH tool from which critical operating data is generated. Consider this: What activities can the back-of-house staff engage in without the historical data collected from this document? In reality, not very much. Food should not be purchased, received, stored, or prepared before the sales data are studied. Employees should not be scheduled without referring to it. Budgets and forecasting just can't be done without analyzing this information.

Once the check is paid, the model shows the cycle starting over again. It is not to say that as each guest leaves, the cycle automatically repeats—that would not make sense. The parts of the cycle represent *activities that occur over a period of time*. Some things happen daily, some weekly, and some only monthly. No matter what, though, at some point, all those steps happen in every foodservice operation.

Guests

The goal of the previous steps were to guarantee that adequate amounts of product are on hand and ready for when the guests arrive to enjoy a meal. It seems like a lot of "before" work, and it is. Everyone is in place in anticipation of the guests' arrival. Once they are seated, the real action begins . . .

- Guests are greeted and seated.
- Menus are delivered.
- Orders are taken.
- Food and beverages are delivered.

In due course, tables are cleared, comments are solicited, checks are paid, and, hopefully, out goes another satisfied customer, who will give the establishment their repeat business. What remains of that guest's experience is his or her "memory," good or bad. This "memory" is the most powerful advertising tool on earth. It is invaluable to a business when it is positive, but it can absolutely crush a business if it is negative. We all know it as "word of mouth." Every employee is accountable and responsible for the guest's total experience.

Guest Check

The final step in the cycle is the **guest check**. The guest check is discussed as a separate step because so much important information is gathered from this document. Consider what one learns from the guest check:

- Number of guests served
- Identity of the server
- Food and beverage items ordered
- Start and end time of guest's visit
- Amount of money guest has spent
- Table number and section
- Method of payment
- Sales tax

What happens to this information? It is tabulated, accumulated, manipulated, and otherwise turned into reports for management. Here are some of the more common examples of the information a manager can glean from the guest checks:

- Average check per shift, day, week, month, overall
- Seat turnover per meal period, daily, overall
- Menu item popularity
- Server statistics
- Meal period sales—dollars and customers

Managers can, in turn, use this information to do the following:

- Generate cash reports—daily, weekly, and more
- Create sales forecasts—daily, weekly, monthly, in both guests and dollars
- Create expense forecasts—daily, weekly, monthly
- Create employee schedules
- Create revenue forecasts and budgets

- Measure marketing program successes and failures
- Create floor layout charts
- Identify "best and worst" tables and sections

The importance of the information gathered from the guest check is evident by the numerous calculations that originate from it. Managers use this information on a daily basis to plan and organize the work of the FOH and BOH staff. Today, using available technology (the **point-of-sale, or POS, systems**) makes the work of the restaurant manager much easier than it was in the past.

_M_anager's Role

Essentially, the manager's mission is to interpret the information through various reports. It is in interpreting this information that managers employ their skills and training to make competent decisions about how to achieve management's goals—the last two steps in the control process. This, in turn, brings us around to the original notion that managers use all these "tools" in their "manager's toolbox" to manage effectively, efficiently, and most important, profitably, in order to eliminate inefficiency, fraud, error, and waste.

Control and Labor Costs, and Technology

The foodservice business is undoubtedly labor intensive. So much so that labor cost is right behind food and beverage costs in terms of budget expenditures. Because of this, labor costs deserve as much of management's attention as food and beverage costs. Today, technology in the form of computerized menu management systems and labor scheduling programs are designed to increase efficiency, decrease waste, eliminate errors, and control for fraud in food, beverage, and labor cost (IFEW). A brief consideration of the costs related to service and labor and new technology follows.

Service and Labor

Service and labor costs are one of the "big three costs" (prime costs) in the foodservice business. The _amount of money spent on labor_ is referred to as the **labor cost**. Labor cost is largely dependent on the level of service rendered by the FOH and BOH staff. Labor cost combined with food cost and beverage cost (the "Big Three") often consume as much as 60 percent of a restaurant's income. Hence, these three costs—_labor cost, food cost, and beverage cost_—are referred to as **prime costs**. These three expenses demand special attention because of their potential impact on the overall profitability of a restaurant.

PRIME COSTS—THE "BIG THREE" IN FOODSERVICE OPERATIONS
1. **Food cost:** The cost of the food products used to generate sales.
2. **Beverage cost:** The cost of the alcohol beverage products used to generate alcohol beverage sales.
3. **Labor cost:** The cost of payroll and benefits needed to generate sales.

The more complicated the menu, the greater the skill needed by those preparing the food items. Thus, a more complicated menu requires higher labor costs to prepare the menu items. The inverse relationship is also true—the less complicated the menu, the less it costs to prepare menu items.

The relationship is the same in the case of service. Generally, a limited-service foodservice establishment requires less skilled and therefore less expensive labor. As staff services are reduced, customer self-service usually increases. Consequently, labor costs are reduced. Customer self-service increases when customers elect to dine from a salad bar, carry their own trays, and clear their own tables in a cafeteria or a fast-food establishment, or to serve themselves in a buffet setting. In the latter case, however, management loses control of portion size. The trade-off is reduced server costs for potentially increased food costs, unless control of portion size is maintained.

Conversely, full service requires additional skill and training with often increased numbers of those rendering the skill. This means labor costs will be higher. A full-service operation requires servers to secure the order, deliver all food and beverages to the customer, and present the guest check.

New Technology

New technology affects costs and operating efficiencies. For example:

- *Old Paradigm:* In a full-service setting, the customer's order is taken by a server and transmitted either verbally or on a handwritten guest check to the kitchen staff. The costs of time elapsed and staff time spent depend on the distances between the serving and preparation areas.
- *New Paradigm:* With the advent of new technology, servers in many operations no longer use guest checks as a way to send orders to the kitchen but rather utilize a handheld touch-screen (Figure 1.4) or a fixed-position point-of-sale (POS) terminal with a touch-screen (Figure 1.5). Using this new technology, service and communications are improved between servers and kitchen staff, which reduces costs.

Likewise, current technology includes silent vibrating pocket pagers that notify servers that orders are ready. As a result, the servers no longer need to check the kitchen for the status of their orders. The time saved enables servers to serve food faster, serve a greater number of tables, and spend more time on the floor servicing guests. This means increased **table turnover** (or, **seat turnover**—*the number of times a table is used during the service hours*). Thus, not only is there greater productivity, but the potential is there for servers to increase their personal earnings by netting more tips per shift.

New technology is also elbowing its way into production via automated kitchen equipment and more sophisticated information systems. These new developments

FIGURE 1.4   Handheld touch screen. *Courtesy of Micros.*

FIGURE 1.5   Point-of-sale (POS) terminal. *Courtesy of Micros.*

enable rapid and frequent changes of menus by changing recipes stored in a database. A **database** is *a collection of information that has been identified and arranged so that it can be retrieved from a computer.* Similarly, other technologies are causing changes in purchasing, inventory control, sales, and payment functions. A seamless integrated information system using a point-of-sale (POS) terminal can trace the impact of activities that produce **data** (*factual information*) using an in-store network (see Figure 1.5). For example, the effect of a single sales order on inventory, purchasing, production, labor costs, and so on can be recorded, summarized, and, when desired, presented to management at any terminal throughout the foodservice operation.

Development of Internet Web sites for restaurants, suppliers, and other related businesses has changed how we "do" business. Restaurant Web sites include photos of menu selections and the property, menu listings, company history, employment opportunities, and property descriptions. These sites are being used to market mail-order products, such as specialty clothing, packaged specialty items, decorations, and food items.

Researching food and beverage products using the Internet has opened up the product world to every existing restaurant with a computer and Internet access. Foodservice suppliers use Internet hookups that allow operators to input their own orders at a remote location—their restaurants.

The new technology is here, and more is coming (see, for example, Figure 1.6). Each new development has its costs and its savings. Each offers the opportunity for changes in organization, procedures, and management, which translates into a more efficient foodservice operation through improved methods and new habits.

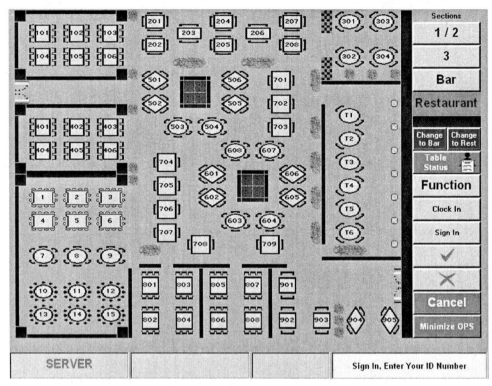

FIGURE 1.6   Table Service Management. Touch-screen flow management system designed to maximize a restaurant's customer service efficiency. This system reduces customer wait times by shortening the time a table remains empty between departing and arriving customers. *Courtesy of Micros.*

NEW TECHNOLOGY THAT HAS CHANGED "DOING" IN THE FOODSERVICE BUSINESS

1. Point-of-sales systems.
2. Touch screens for server ordering.
3. Customer and server pager systems.
4. Automated kitchen systems.
5. Internet Web sites for restaurants, suppliers, and other related businesses.

The Value of Information

In every business, an underlying information system (Operating Cycle of Control) supports its operation and management. The information may be communicated verbally, in writing, electronically, or with a combination of methods. The quality of the system will vary, depending on the skill of its designer and the resources available to implement it. Ideally, the information system will support the business operation with timely, accurate data to help it operate efficiently. Much of the necessary information will be generated as transactions occur during the course of business operations. Some management information, such as local market conditions, will originate outside the confines of the business—in the external environment.

In the foodservice industry, the operational information system should serve each of the functions and factors described in the external and internal environments. In addition, information available to managers must help them do several things:

- Set goals
- Plan strategies
- Implement procedures
- Evaluate results

The operational information system should include all the information required to implement management controls, set standards, determine progress toward those standards, and evaluate a standard's impact on goal achievement.

All foodservice managers must decide what information they need to operate their establishment and the format in which they wish to receive it. The following chapters, however, will suggest the forms and procedures needed to support specific management controls, following the steps in the Operating Cycle of Control. Whether the data should be presented manually or electronically is a decision best left to those implementing an information system designed for a specific foodservice operation. These forms and procedures accomplish the immediate objective of demonstrating efficient food, beverage, and labor cost-control techniques.

The following are some specific subject areas of information that are relevant to a foodservice operation:

- Menu concept
- Food cost
- Beverage cost
- Labor cost
- Other operating costs
- Revenue

Although other operating costs exist in foodservice operations, the primary costs (the Big Three) to a foodservice operator are food cost, beverage cost, and labor cost. Nearly two-thirds of a restaurant's total revenue can be spent in just these three areas alone. Consequently, the need for standards and controls is greatest in these areas.

Menu Concepts

The menu provides the customer with essential information for making a choice. It is designed to reflect the foodservice concept. Chosen by the manager or owner, this concept depends on the type of service and food to be offered. Examples of foodservice concepts are shown in the sidebar.

EXAMPLES OF FOODSERVICE CONCEPTS

All-you-can-eat buffet	Mexican theme restaurant
Upscale hamburgers	Continental fine dining
Seafood restaurant	Old-fashioned pizza parlor
Fifties diner	Asian cuisine
College dorm foodservice	Italian theme restaurant
Healthcare foodservice	Soup and delicatessen
School foodservice	Steak house
Fast casual	Eatertainment (eating + entertainment)

Today, there are literally hundreds of foodservice concepts. Each concept conjures up a mental picture of a specific foodservice establishment.

𝒩et Work

Check out the following food service companies and concepts:

www.aramark.com—See About Aramark; Who We Serve; Services We Provide; Careers

www.backbayrestaurant-group.com

www.brinker.com

www.capitalrestaurants.com

www.compass-group.com—See About Us; Marketplace; Services; Strategy & Mission; Working With Us & Service Sectors

www.darden.com

www.eatnpark.com

www.leye.com

www.mcdonalds.com—See Corporate: About McDonalds; Franchising; Careers

www.panerabread.com

www.rarehospitality.com

www.sodexhousa.com

www.starbucks.com

www.subway.com

www.tacobell.com—Franchise Information

www.yum.com

Food Cost

The recipe determines the ingredients needed to produce meals. **Food ingredients** are all the food product items used to produce meals. The information needed to control food purchasing, receiving, storage, and preparation costs may be presented manually or electronically. Traditionally, this information has been presented on forms such as those listed in the following table:

Types of Food-Cost Reports

Bid sheets	Other inventory reports
Food-cost percentage reports	Plate cost charts
Food-cost reports	Portion-control charts
Food-mishap reports	Recipe-cost charts
Food production charts	Requisitions and transfers
Inventory forms	Service system charts
Invoice payment schedules	Standardized recipes
Menu-analysis charts	Yield charts
Order sheets	

All of the information that these forms collect can be used as needed for successfully managing a foodservice operation.

𝒩et Work

Explore the following Web site:

www.restaurant.org—National Restaurant Association

Explore these sites for an overview of automated restaurant menu management systems:

www.squirrelsystems.com

www.chefdesk.com—See Management Guides

www.cbord.com

www.costgenie.com

Beverage Cost

As with food costs, beverage costs must be controlled. Many of the techniques used for controlling beverage costs are the same as for controlling food costs. Techniques for ordering, paying for, transferring, and requisitioning beverages are the same as for food. Data that is unique to beverage control are collected using the forms in the accompanying table:

Types of Beverage-Cost Reports

Alcohol use reports	Beverage recipes
Bar- and inventory-control reports	Liquor storeroom inventory reports
Beverage-cost percentage reports	Pour cost charts
Beverage-cost reports	Sample house policy
Beverage-mishap reports	

Labor Cost

Besides the ingredients, all foodservice establishments must use labor and facilities to accomplish their service goals. Labor and productivity information can be collected and evaluated using the following forms:

Types of Labor Cost Reports

Daily work sheets	Productivity charts
Job descriptions	Server production charts
Kitchen production charts	Time cards
Labor cost forms	Tip-reporting forms
Labor-cost percentage reports	Work schedules
Payroll cost estimates	Workers' Compensation reports
Payroll-cost reports	

Managers who use these forms faithfully find that they help them operate their foodservice establishments efficiently, within projected costs, and within the law.

Sales

Information related to the sale and service of menu items to customers is referred to as sales information. This information also relates to collecting money and measuring how satisfied customers are with their experience. Sales information is collected and monitored using several types of reports.

Types of Sales Reports

Cashier's reports	Guest checks
Customer count and table turnover reports	Marketing program analysis
Daily, monthly and annual reports	Server shift reports
Guest check daily reports	Work flow charts

The presented lists of forms in each category are not to be considered all-inclusive but cover most of the situations a foodservice manager may encounter. You will find that the subsequent chapters in this text demonstrate the use of many of these forms to control a foodservice operation. The underlying organization of chapters and content will follow the flow of the Operating Cycle of Control.

Net Work

Explore the following Web sites:

www.restaurant.org—Web site of the National Restaurant Association
www.toolkit.cch.com—Click Business Tools and browse.
www.restaurantowner.com

WHAT'S FARFALLE ARRABBIATA?

The objective of Chapter 1 was to relate traditional management principles to managing a foodservice operation using the functions of the Operating Cycle of Control (OCC). Chapters 2 through 15 tease out many of the details of the OCC by applying all the steps to a conceptual restaurant named Farfalle Arrabbiata, located in Anywhere, USA. A restaurant profile has been developed for Farfalle Arrabbiata to illustrate using the control system. The profile thoroughly describes everything, from the corporate philosophy to, of course, the food! Chapter discussions, as well as end-of-chapter problems, are designed using this operation as the model, which provides continuity between the operating system and its actual application and use in a restaurant setting. A partial description of Farfalle Arrabbiata's operations is included here. See Appendix A for the restaurant's full profile, including the menu.

Restaurant Profile

The restaurant created for this text is named _Farfalle Arrabbiata,_ which means "the angry bow tie." A southern Italian theme has been selected for the operation. Southern Italy is well known for its spectacular scenery, favorable (hot and dry) climate, abundant wheat fields, and rich cuisine. Olive groves and vineyards grace the hillsides, and the area boasts the finest olive oils, as well as wineries that produce exceptional vintages. The coastal Mediterranean location means fresh seafood is abundant and a natural part of the local cuisine. Pastas of all shapes are still made by hand from family recipes handed down through generations. These timeless dishes are typically served with rich vegetable sauces. Calzone, pizza, and Bruschetta are classic luncheon selections, often served with fresh seafood and vegetables. Traditional dinner dishes naturally feature pasta, seafood, and vegetables.

Farfalle Arrabbiata is a full-menu table-service restaurant serving authentic southern Italian food. Menu selections have been developed through meticulous research of the area and its cuisine. Professional relationships have been developed with some of the oldest continuously operating restaurants in the area.

Traditional preparation methods have been adapted to the modern kitchen facilities at Farfalle Arrabbiata. Pastas are produced by hand in-house, using time-honored methods. Menu items are prepared fresh from the best ingredients available. Specialty suppliers are used to procure authentic ingredients. There is minimal use of convenience items.

Sound interesting? Review the rest of the profile, including the menu, in Appendix A.

Net Work

Explore these restaurant concepts on the Web:
www.applebees.com
www.bahamabreeze.com
www.banderarestaurants.com
www.bugaboocreek.com
www.chilis.com
www.mccormickand-schmicks.com
www.nathansfamous.com
www.olivegarden.com
www.outback.com
www.redlobster.com
www.coldstonecreamery.com
www.hooters.com
www.jalexanders.com
www.jaspersrestaurants.com
www.longhornsteakhouse.com
www.rockbottom.com
www.ruby-Tuesday.com
www.ruthschris.com
www.smokeybones.com
www.thecheesecake-factory.com

Chapter Wrap

The Chapter ✓ at the beginning of the chapter posed several questions. Review the questions and compare your responses with the following answers:

1. **What are internal environments?**

    All businesses operate within two environments: internal and external. The internal environment consists of functions carried on within the organization to achieve organizational objectives. Aspects of the internal environment that influence how management and employees perform their duties are front-of-house, back-of-house and management functions.

2. **How do external environments affect foodservice operations?**

    Factors in the external environment also influence how managers and employees perform their duties. Some external environment factors are government regulations, local market conditions, supplier relations, new technology and media.

3. **How do managers control internal environments?**

    Internal environments are controlled by the basic management principles of setting standards, measuring performance against the standards, determining whether or not standards have been met, taking corrective action and recycling through the process.

4. What is an Operating Cycle of Control?

All businesses execute a series of *precise* activities that are the heart of what it is that they "do." From these activities, revenue is generated and, hopefully, so is profit. All of these activities together are called the Operating Cycle of Control, or the OCC. It is a basic control procedure. The Operating Cycle of Control is defined as *a control cycle that divides any food and beverage operation into a series of coordinated procedures that are necessary to profitably and efficiently supply food and beverage products and services to guests given an acceptable volume of business.* These steps include all the basic activities, procedures, and paperwork needed to operate a restaurant every single day.

5. Why do managers of foodservice operations need an Operating Cycle of Control?

Without these coordinated procedures, the foodservice operation would be unable to serve guests and thus would not generate revenue or profit. These steps have developed over time and are industry best practices. They are important tools in a manager's toolbox.

6. What are the four greatest causes of excess cost in a foodservice operation?

There is an effect to every error in any business. Having clear precise standards in place eliminates inefficiency, fraud, errors, and waste (IFEW)—four of the greatest causes of excess costs. Employers and employees have a vital interest in ensuring that control systems are reliable and effective. Managers use cost control systems to help *pinpoint responsibility for inefficiency, fraud, errors, and waste.*

$\mathcal{K}$ey Terminology and Concepts in This Chapter

Approved supplier list	Labor cost
Bidding	Management controls
BOH (back-of-house) functions	Management functions
Budgets	Menu
Captive audiences	Operating Cycle of Control (OCC)
Control	Organizational culture
Cost control	Par stock
Data	Point-of-sale (POS) systems
Database	Prime costs
External environment	Purchase order (PO)
Financial plan	Receiving
FOH (front-of-house) functions	Recipe cost cards
Food ingredients	Requisitions
Foodservice concept	Seat turnover
Forecasting	Specifications
Guest check	Standardized recipes
IFEW (inefficiency, fraud, errors, and waste)	Standard operating procedures (SOPs)
	Standard receiving practices
Information system	Storage practices
Internal environment	System
Invoice management	Table turnover
Kitchen production	Transfers

Discussion Questions and Exercises

1. Name the internal environments of a foodservice operation; a hotel; a retail clothing operation; your college or university; a bank.

2. What external environments affect each of the establishments named in Exercise 1?

3. What sources of information would management use to monitor the external environment of each of the establishments named in Exercise 1? Why is it important to understand the factors related to the external environment of a business?

4. Using the four management functions, design a plan to implement a new server incentive program to increase sales of appetizers.

5. Create an example of the control process from your personal work experience or from some other activity that you have been involved with that fits into the model. Be comprehensive in your response.

6. What are the four leading causes of excess cost in the foodservice industry?

7. Visit a fast-food foodservice operation. Note how technology is being used to cook, hold, and serve food to customers. Write a brief paper on what you have discovered.

8. A prep cook uses a recipe from the standardized recipe file to prepare Black Bean Salsa. A different prep cook prepares the same item using a personal recipe. You are managing this foodservice operation and are evaluating the quality of the Black Bean Salsa. What is your criterion for measuring the flavor of the salsa? How should the situation be handled?

9. Define OCC.

10. You are the manager of The Macarena Restaurant. You have been searching everywhere for a recipe for Chocolate Tofu Cheesecake. Your hostess screams into work today and excitedly hands you a recipe for Chocolate Tofu Cheesecake that she found flipping through a magazine in the checkout aisle of the local supermarket. She is hoping you will offer it as a special dessert tonight. From a management perspective, explain why this will not be possible. Use the OCC model to help with your answer.

11. Assume you have adopted the recipe for the Chocolate Tofu Cheesecake and will be offering it on your menu. Using the OCC model, follow the recipe through the steps to get the item ready for service.

12. What information will the guest check give you about the cheesecake? What will analysis of the sales information tell you about the cheesecake?

13. Name six different kinds of foodservice concepts in which you have had the experience of dining.

14. Name six different types of documents related to FOH operations.

15. Name six different types of documents related to BOH operations.

16. Name six different types of documents related to sales information.

17. The National Restaurant Association is the premier professional organization representing foodservice operators. Their Web site, www.restaurant.org, provides a wealth of information about the restaurant industry. Visit their site. Select the Policy & Politics tab. Go to the State & Local Issues menu selection on the sidebar. Select three issues from the list that are of interest to you. Read the Latest News, Background, and NRA Update. Research the topics further by studying any other information/resources listed. Then, do the following:

    a. Summarize the effect of this issue on the industry. What is the NRA's position on each? What action, if any, is the NRA suggesting members take? Include any other pertinent information you may have found about these topics.

    b. What are the possible outcomes for each situation? What impact would each have? Report your findings to your classmates.

18. The long-time and beloved general manager of Farfalle Arrabbiata has suddenly taken ill and is forced to retire. You, as the restaurant's owner, have an interest in the "hot shot" general manager at a competitor's operation. You would love for her to come and join the team at Farfalle Arrabbiata. Her reputation is impeccable. In addition, you know her personally, as you both graduated from college together and originally started your careers with the same restaurant group. As luck would have it, you spot her at the monthly meeting of the local Hospitality Association. You know she is quite successful and happy in her current position. Given you only have 3 minutes of her undivided attention before anyone else spots her, devise a sales pitch to encourage her to seriously consider joining your staff. Use the information from the profile. Consider carefully what you will say—what information will likely pique her attention, given her career and reputation? (Salary, benefits, working conditions, etc., are not a part of the discussion points at this stage.) Remember to read the complete profile of Farfalle Arrabbiata in Appendix A before answering this question.

## Chapter Two

About Recipes

Learning Objectives

After reading this chapter and completing the discussion questions and exercises, you should be able to:

1. Explain the purpose of standardized recipes and plate cards in a foodservice operation.
2. Identify the elements of standardized recipes.
3. Develop standardized recipes and plate cards for menu items.
4. Correctly express a recipe yield.
5. Recognize the role of the recipe yield in controlling portion sizes and portion costs.
6. Recognize the difference between weights and measures in relation to recipes, portion costs, and purchasing.
7. Calculate multipliers to size recipes for a range of sales levels.

The Menu

Pre-Purchase Functions

STANDARDIZED RECIPES
Standard ingredients, portion size, quality, consistency, quantity, purchasing

GUEST CHECK
Sales history, turnover, average check, cash management, revenue forecasting & budgeting, menu item analysis

COST CARDS
Portion costs, yield factors, sell prices

GUESTS
Greeting, seating, sales, serving, busing, payment, comment cards

SPECIFICATIONS
Product descriptions

FOH Functions

PAR STOCK
Inventory levels, order building

KITCHEN PRODUCTION
Production schedules, portion tracking, recipe control, serving controls, food safety

REQUISITION
Order building, purchasing

PRODUCT ISSUING
Requisitions, transfers, daily & monthly costs, food cost percentage

SHOPPING LISTS
Call sheets, bid sheets, suppliers, bidding

STORAGE PRACTICES & INVENTORY MANAGEMENT
Best practices, sanitation, security, inventory methods

PURCHASE ORDERS
Security, ship order, price guarantee, contract

INVOICE MANAGEMENT
Payment, price checking, security

BOH Functions

RECEIVING ACTIVITIES
Best practices, invoices, security, sanitation

Chapter Map

About Those Recipes

- What Is a Standardized Recipe?
- How to Standardize a Recipe
- The Nuts and Bolts of a Standardized HACCP Recipe
- Standardized Recipes and Plate Cards

Elements of a Standardized HACCP Recipe and Plate Card

- Recipe Name and File Number
- Recipe Yield
- Equipment
- Prep Time
- Cook Time
- Hot & Cold Holding Temperatures & Times

Chapter Map   (Continued)

Chapter ✓

Check the chapter content for the answers to the following questions:

1. Why a recipe?

2. Why a standardized recipe?

3. What does a standardized recipe look like?

4. What is the difference between weights and measures?

*A*bout Those Recipes

In this chapter, we begin to navigate the steps in the Operating Cycle of Control. Once the menu is selected (see Chapter 10), recipes need to be developed for each menu item. This is a critical step in the control process. Developing standardized recipes is the first step to *controlling product quality and cost*. Instituting a workplace attitude that says using these recipes is a standard operating procedure is the second step. Without these two practices in place (creating recipes and requiring the use of them), a foodservice operation is probably destined to fail. From the standardized recipe comes all the costing and control activity crucial to the financial success of an operation.

These concepts can be stated simply as follows:

- If management cannot control how much food is served each time the item is produced, then management cannot control the cost of producing the item.
- If management cannot control the portion cost, then management does not have a sound basis on which to compute the selling price.

Developing and using standardized recipes for all menu offerings is an indication of sound management.

What Is a Standardized Recipe?

The idea of a **recipe**—*producing something from a variety of ingredients*—is a very general definition. So much so that the term is even used in a popular metaphor—think of the saying "a recipe for disaster." What does this mean? It means that a variety of events (ingredients) are conspiring to produce a bad result (something). In the food-service business, recipes are the backbone of the operation. They are the gold standard of control. Because of the enormous impact they have on the success or failure of an operation, recipes used in foodservice organizations are commonly referred to as standardized recipes. Why? Because a **standardized recipe** *is one that has been tested, adjusted, and retested again and again until it produces a menu item as management wants the item produced.* A standardized recipe has to fit management's plan for quality, taste, portion size, cost, selling price, purchasing, production, profitability, and appearance on the plate. Moreover, the guests have to like it!

A STANDARDIZED RECIPE

A recipe that has been tested, adjusted, and retested again and again until it produces a menu item as management wants the item produced.

How to Standardize a Recipe

1. Work on one recipe at a time.
2. Produce the item exactly as the recipe is written, without changing or adjusting anything.
3. Analyze the outcome for the following:
   - Overall taste (ingredients and their proportions, seasonings)
   - Appearance (color, texture, overall appearance)
   - Method of prep (clarity of steps, accuracy of cooking times, temperatures during all phases of production, proportions of ingredients, and so on)
   - Portion size
   - Cost per portion for the item as prepared
   - Menu fit
4. Adjust the recipe according to the evaluation. Rewrite the recipe as needed.
5. Produce the item again and analyze according to the same criteria.
6. Analyze the item again as in Step 3, recording all changes and modifications.
7. Produce the item again.
8. Analyze and record again. Repeat this process until satisfied with the results.

Each time the process is repeated, any changes and revisions are recorded. A recipe is standardized when it is produced three consecutive times with the same result. Note that a recipe has to be retested any time the ingredients or equipment change.

Historically, standardized recipes were often carried only in the memory of the chef. Today this is not likely to happen. If the foodservice operation employs more than one chef or cook, then it is imperative that standardized recipes are used. The practice of using standardized recipes allows foodservice managers to deliver a consistent product to the customer, regardless of who is in the kitchen.

The Nuts and Bolts of a Standardized HACCP Recipe

Did you notice the addition of the term *HACCP* into the heading for this section? **HACCP** stands for **Hazard Analysis Critical Control Point**. For those certified through the National Restaurant Association's ServeSafe program, this is a familiar term. Watch for the HACCP principles as they are integrated into the content. For those who are not certified, examples of time, temperature, and procedural terminology used in the explanations and models are examples of HACCP principles as applied to Standardized HACCP recipes. Food safety training is an important aspect of understanding the elements of HACCP in a recipe.

Developing any recipe into a standardized HACCP recipe is a major investment of time and energy. The exact format used is not important. What is important is that the recipe is

- Consistent.
- Easy to use.
- Developed with easy-to-follow, written instructions.
- Comprehensive—it includes all necessary information.
- Readily available at all times.
- Correct.

Standardized recipes must be designed while keeping in mind that employees must work with this document every day. Poor recipe format and development creates a good excuse for employees to "forget" to use the recipe. These problems can also explain inconsistent product, guest dissatisfaction, and high food, beverage, and labor costs.

NONSTANDARDIZED RECIPES
- Cause confusion because they leave out essential information.
- Bury time and temperature settings and other important details of the method of prep.
- Neglect to specify the sizes of pots and pans or list other equipment needed for the quantity of food being prepared.
- Neglect to specify portion sizes, leaving employees to guess how much to serve on a plate.
- Use unfamiliar terminology.
- Have a poorly written method of prep that could lead to inconsistent product.
- Wastes employees' and management's time. (Remember, labor cost is one of the Big Three Costs.)

It should be obvious that using standardized recipes is non-negotiable. If you are still not convinced, the next list should clear up any resistance. Figure 2.1 lists how poor recipe development contributes to problems for employees who must use them. Realize that the impact of this mistake radiates to people and places beyond the kitchen door, through

- Increased labor cost and food cost.
- Inconsistent product.
- Inaccurate recipe yields.
- Inaccurate portion costs.
- Server confusion.
- Guest dissatisfaction.
- Potential health code violations and fines.

Standardized Recipes and Plate Cards

The following is a list of information needed for each item offered on the menu. Traditionally, this information was included as part of a standard recipe form. Today, with the widespread use of convenience products that require little or no preparation,

---

THE TOP 10 REASONS TO USE STANDARDIZED HACCP RECIPES

1. "Chef, I put the ribs in the slow cooker at 4:30. They should be done in time for the 5:30 function, right?"

2. "I can't believe this 2-gallon stock pot isn't big enough for 400 servings of soup."

3. "I need seven pieces of pie for my table. I can get that many out of this whole pie, can't I?"

4. "Does anyone remember how to make menu item number 131?"

5. "The chicken seems to be done. It feels warm." "Yes, sir, we are the restaurant where all those people got sick."

6. "Chef, do you measure or weigh salt? I can't remember." "Chef, do you mise en place the mirepoix or mirepoix the mise en place?" "Chef, what's a mirepoix, anyhow?"

7. "We need 150 portions of mashed potatoes. How many potatoes is that per plate, so I can order them for tomorrow?"

8. "I have a customer who wants to know if there are any peanuts or almonds in the Green Bean Amandine casserole special. Anybody have any idea?

9. "Mary says she ordered the same sandwich yesterday and it came with two slices of bread."

And the top reason for using standardized HACCP recipes . . .

10. **"Well, the Chef isn't here today and he's the only one who knows the recipes. I guess we'll have to start your training tomorrow. Can you come back then?"**

FIGURE 2.1   Top 10 reasons to use standardized HACCP recipes.

plate cards function as a hybrid form of a recipe and often act as the primary control tool. These cards *describe one complete menu item as management wishes it to be served.* They are best used for items that utilize convenience products that require little or no prep. They can include many of the details listed in the following discussion and also incorporate general HACCP principles.

Most operations that prepare items from scratch and thus use traditional recipes also use plate cards as *a control tool on the line for servers and cooks.* These cards *serve as a plating guide and do not include any preparation information.* Plate cards serve as important training tools. Some examples of plate cards will be given after the recipe section, in this chapter.

A STANDARDIZED RECIPE OR PLATE CARD INCLUDES

- The recipe name and file number.
- The recipe yield.
- Equipment.
- Prep time.
- Cook time.
- Hot and cold holding temperatures and times.
- Food safety statement.
- The ingredients, including garnish.
- The quantities of ingredients in both weight and measures.
- The method of prep, using HACCP terminology.
- Plating and garnish instructions.
- Cutting instructions.
- Cooling and storage of leftovers.
- Nutritional analysis.
- Alternatives to reduce fat and calories.
- Photos of the item plated.

Elements of a Standardized HACCP Recipe and Plate Card

Recipe Name and File Number

Typically, recipe file systems are organized by menu category (appetizers, soups, salads, entrées, etc.), and recipes are filed alphabetically or numerically within the group. Depending on the complexity of the menu selection and the number of items on the menu, categories can be further expanded to include subgroups. An example of this would be the entrée menu category. This category can be further broken down by product type to—beef, veal, seafood, poultry, and vegetarian selections. Soups might be categorized into clear soups, cream soups, thickened soups, seasonal, and so on. **Subrecipes** can also be created. These are *recipes for products used within a number of other recipes.* (Think Marinara Sauce in an Italian restaurant or Pomodoro Sauce at Farfalle Arrabbiata.) Sauces, stocks, and thickeners are good candidates for this category.

Recipe Yield

The most important information on the recipe card is the recipe *yield,* because it is the control for portion size and portion cost. A **recipe yield** is the *standard number of servings and the serving size.* It may also include the total amount a recipe produces. The yield is written using three separate notations or descriptions: the number of servings, the serving size, and the total quantity the recipe produces.

HOW TO EXPRESS A RECIPE YIELD

1. Number of servings
2. Serving size
3. Total quantity the recipe produces

Of these three items, the first two—the **number of servings** and the **serving size**—are an absolute must. *No recipe is complete or correct unless the portion size is included with the recipe yield.* Why? Because the staff will not know how much of the product to serve. Guessing is not acceptable in portioning, for several reasons:

- It affects the product's portion cost.
- It can seriously affect purchasing.
- It affects the guest who regularly orders the same dish and expects the same taste, look, and portion size each time.

The third item, **total recipe quantity**, is best *used for recipes where there is a total measurable quantity produced, such as soup, sauces, or other batch-type items.*

The following is an example of a correctly expressed recipe yield that uses all three descriptors:

Minestrone Soup   **File Code:** S-16
Yield: 16 - 8 oz. servings   **Total Recipe Quantity:** 1 gal.

Notice that the Minestrone Soup recipe includes all three notations because it is a "batch"-type item. The total quantity (1 gallon) is helpful to know. Suppose a function is planned at which a 6-ounce serving of soup is to be served. Knowing that the recipe produces 1 gallon enables the chef to quickly determine how many 6-ounce servings the recipe will yield.

TOTAL RECIPE QUANTITY/DESIRED PORTION SIZE =
NUMBER OF SERVINGS

128 oz. (1 gal.)/6 oz. (desired serving size) =
21 - 6 oz. servings

The following is an example of a correctly expressed recipe yield using just two descriptors:

Salmon a la Griglia   E-25
Yield: 24 - 6 oz. servings

The Salmon a la Griglia does not need a total recipe quantity because it is prepared one serving at a time and cooked to order.

Expressing Serving Sizes Correctly Using Active and Passive Portioning Methods   Serving sizes must also be expressed using very specific measures. **Active portioning** measures are so named because they *leave little or no room for error or employee interpretation as to the correct amount to serve.* Active expressions of portion sizes are as follows:

1. An exact weight → (use accurate portion scales; see Figure 2.2)
2. An exact measure → (use sized ladles, scoops, measures, etc.; see Figures 2.3, 2.4, and 2.5)

FIGURE 2.2   Portion control scales. *Courtesy of Pelouze.*

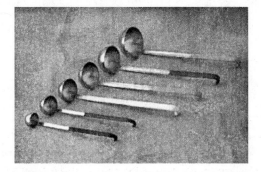

CAPACITY	COLOR
1 oz.	Black
2 oz.	Blue
3 oz.	Ivory
4 oz.	Gray
5 oz.	Teal
6 oz.	Orange

FIGURE 2.3   Ladle sizes. *Courtesy of the Vollrath Company.*

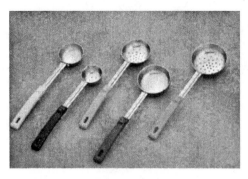

CAPACITY	COLOR
2 oz.	Blue
3 oz.	Ivory
4 oz.	Gray
6 oz.	Teal
8 oz.	Orange

FIGURE 2.4   Spoodle sizes. *Courtesy of Vollrath Company.*

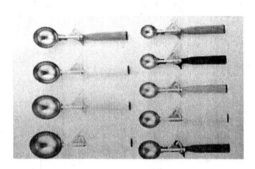

CAPACITY	MEASURE	SIZE	COLOR
5⅓ oz.	⅔ c.	6	White
4 oz.	½ c.	8	Gray
3¼ oz.	⅓ c.	10	Ivory
2⅔ oz.	5 Tbsp.	12	Green
2 oz.	4 Tbsp.	16	Dark Blue
1⅝ oz.	3 Tbsp.	20	Yellow
1⅓ oz.	2⅔ Tbsp.	24	Red
1 oz.	2 Tbsp.	30	Black
¾ oz.	1 Tbsp.	40	Orchid

FIGURE 2.5   Scoop sizes. *Courtesy of Vollrath Company.*

3. An exact count → (6 chicken nuggets per order)
4. Even division or pan cuts → References cutting pans of product into specific sizes. This method is typically used for baked goods or other menu items prepared in hotel pans or sheet pans. Purchasing scored sheet pans and pie or cake scorers will decrease errors when portioning these products. Preportioned frozen desserts eliminate all possibility of portioning error.

EXAMPLES OF ACTIVE PORTION METHODS

Portion Size:
- Exact weight
- Exact measure
- Exact count
- Even division or pan cut

Correctly Written Example:
- 24 - 6 oz. servings of salmon
- 24 - 12 oz. servings of Cream of Mushroom and Chive Bisque
- 5 grilled shrimp per order
- 9-in. pecan pie, cut into 8 slices

The following examples demonstrate proper yields for portioning other kinds of baked goods.

Brownies   **File Code:** D-4
Yield: 4 sheet pans (48 brownies each)   **Pan Cut:** 6 × 8

Death by Chocolate Cake   **File Code:** D-1
Yield: 1 - 16″ cake   **Cut:** 16 slices per cake

Passive portioning methods are *ambiguous descriptions of how much to serve* and are to be avoided at all costs. From a control perspective, they do not fit in. These expressions are called *passive* because they *leave room for interpretation on the part of employees as to how much to serve.* See sidebar for a few examples of passive portioning instructions.

EXAMPLES OF PASSIVE PORTIONING METHODS

- Fill compote dish ¾ full of pudding.
- Serve one spoonful of broccoli on each plate.
- Serve a heaping mound of mashed potatoes on each plate.
- Ladle enough sauce to cover the entrée.

Remember that it is quite possible that some employees may not understand what ¾ means, and they may be too embarrassed to ask. Overportioning the pudding in the example just given will not likely cause financial ruin, but as scholars of cost control, we must think more broadly. What if the menu item was Lobster Bisque, and the recipe simply stated, "Fill bowl ¾ full"? Guessing here is a much more costly error. Pulled lobster meat can cost as much as $30.00 a pound. If Lobster Bisque is "the" signature dish, and gallons and gallons are produced each week, overportioning could amount to quite a loss. Guesswork and portioning must never ever be an option in the restaurant business.

Lobster Bisque	**File Code:** S-8
Yield: 32 - 8 oz. servings	2 gal.

Finding the Portion Size When It Is Not Given   The rule just discussed states that a portion size must be given on the standard recipe. However, many recipes list the number of servings but not the serving size. This is especially true when using the Internet, popular periodicals, the food section of the newspaper, and other nonprofessional sources. If you are feeding four people, it's easy to visually divide the food into four equal servings. If you are feeding 400, however, not having the serving size certainly becomes an issue. Guessing is not a good thing, either. Overportioning means you will run out before all 400 guests are served. The plates will already have gone out, so you cannot adjust the serving size, and you will be stuck. On the other hand, underportioning means you will be likely to have leftovers that may be wasted—not to mention that the plates may have looked a little "lean" to the guests.

What's a manager to do when a portion size is not given?

Produce the recipe as is and serve the portion size you *think* is correct.

OR

Put your cost-control skills to work!

Here's how to find the portion side, when it is not given:

1. Determine the **total number of ounces** the entire recipe's ingredients produces, in either weight or volume. Do this by converting each ingredient's recipe quantity into total ounces and adding them all up. (Check out the following

example.) Be sure to work with the unit of measure in which the item is most commonly served or measured. Soups and liquids would be converted into liquid ounces. Meats and similar solid products would be converted into scaled ounces. Use the solid ingredients only. Do not include spices, herbs, or garnishes.

2. Divide the total ounces the recipe produces by the number of servings given. This will be the portion size.

TO FIND THE PORTION SIZE

$$\frac{\text{TOTAL NUMBER OF OUNCES THE RECIPE PRODUCES}}{\text{NUMBER OF SERVINGS THE RECIPE PRODUCES}} = \text{PORTION SIZE}$$

This method will get you an initial approximation of the portion size that can be refined once the recipe is actually produced. Once the portion size is known, it can be evaluated for conformity with other similar menu items.

(Note: The following recipe shows all ingredients converted into weight and measure equivalencies, regardless of the normal purchasing or serving unit, except for spices and seasonings. Good standardized recipes will appear this way. This concept is discussed in more detail later in this chapter.)

FINDING TOTAL RECIPE YIELD

Recipe for Chicken Noodle Soup

Yield: 25 portions

Ingredients	Weight	Measure	Ounces Per Unit	Total Recipe Ounces
Chicken stock	12 lb.	1½ gal.	× 128 (oz. per gal.)	192 oz.
Chicken breast meat	1½ lb.	4 c.	× 8 (oz. per c.)	32 oz.
Noodles, egg, narrow	1¼ lb.	5 c.	× 8 (oz. per c.)	40 oz.
Onions, ¼ dice	½ lb.	6 oz.		6 oz.
Bay leave		2 each		
Salt		To taste		
Pepper		To taste		
			Total Recipe Ounces	270

There are approximately 270 ounces of **Chicken Noodle Soup**. Given the soup will simmer out and reduce and the onions, noodles, and ingredients will cook down, it is fair to say that the recipe will probably yield about 250 servable ounces.

TO FIND THE PORTION SIZE OF THE SOUP

TOTAL NUMBER OF OUNCES	/	NUMBER OF SERVINGS	=	PORTION SIZE
RECIPE PRODUCES		RECIPE PRODUCES		
250	/	25	=	10 oz.

The same process can be applied to any recipe to quickly find the serving size when it is not given.

See the sidebar for a reminder of the elements of a good standardized recipe.

ELEMENTS OF A STANDARDIZED HACCP RECIPE OR PLATE CARD

- The recipe name and file number.
- The recipe yield.
- Equipment.
- Prep time.
- Cook time.
- Hot and cold holding temperatures and times.
- Food safety statement.
- The ingredients, including garnish.
- The quantities of ingredients, in both weight and measures.
- The method of prep using HACCP terminology.
- Plating and garnish instructions.
- Cutting instructions.
- Cooling and storage of leftovers.
- Nutritional analysis.
- Alternatives to reduce fat and calories.
- Photos of finished item.

Equipment

List on the standardized HACCP recipe or plate card the pots, pans, and smallwares necessary to produce the item. Do not include large equipment, such as stove, walk-in, broiler, and so on. Listing the smallwares and tools allows the staff to *prepare* or **"mise en place"** their work station before pulling product to work on. The goal is to eliminate wasted time and energy with multiple trips to retrieve pots, pans, knives, and so on. Failure to include this information results in frustration on the part of the employee and increases labor cost. This information should be at the top of the card in an easily identified location, so staff can quickly and easily access it. It should not be buried in the method of prep.

Prep Time

Indicate the approximate amount of time needed to prep the item. This is easily determined during the recipe-testing phase. This notation allows staff to time out their prep so menu items are ready for service when needed. Kitchen production schedules should also incorporate the prep time. This information should not be buried in the method of prep. It should also be easy to find.

Cook Time

This information goes hand in hand with prep time. It should convey the amount of time required to finish cooking the item. This is, of course, relative to what is being prepared. Some menu items are cooked to order and others require longer finish times. This information is especially important for items that require roasting, simmering, or reducing. Prep times and cook times should be located near each other on the recipe.

Hot and Cold Holding Temperatures and Times

Since we are designing standardized HACCP recipes and not just standardized recipes, we must include this crucial information on the recipe card. This information must conform to accepted industry standards. Hot holding equipment must hold food at 135°F degrees or higher. Cold holding equipment must hold at 41°F or lower. The length of time an item can be held before quality is compromised should also be included on the recipe. Monitoring and tracking the time and temp of products must be a part of an establishment's SOPs. Temp logs should be employed to control for this. Improper holding times and temps can result in food-borne illness. Vigilance in complying with this standard operating procedure is critical.

Food Safety Statement

Each standardized recipe must have a **food safety statement** incorporated into its format. This is a statement used to *outline basic sanitation procedures employees must carry out before commencing production*. It should include

- Hand washing instructions.
- Tool sanitation instructions.
- Work station set-up and sanitation procedures.
- Any other information the employee may need for a particular item.

The following is an example of a food safety statement.

FOOD SAFETY STATEMENT

Before beginning this recipe, clean and sanitize your work station. Wash your hands, paying attention to the fingers and the nails. Gather all equipment needed to complete the recipe. To avoid the possibility of spoilage, only work on as much food product as you can process in 30 minutes or less. Be sure all equipment and tools are cleaned and sanitized before proceeding.

Ingredients, Including Garnish

Recipes usually list the ingredients with the largest quantities first. Depending on the format, some recipes group ingredients that are combined or worked on together with the method of prep listed on the right side of the card. In other formats, all ingredients and their quantities will be listed first, and the method of prep will be printed below.

About Recording Ingredients Correctly   There are two terms with which scholars of foodservice cost control should become intimately familiar. They are:

1. ***AP (as purchased).***   This is the acronym for *all products received at the door*. It is the total *amount of raw product purchased from the supplier*.
2. ***EP (edible portion; also AS [as served]).***   This acronym represents *a food product that has been processed in some way, shape, or form. It has been peeled, trimmed, cooked, and portioned*. EP is used to describe *the portion of food as served to the guest*. EP will be the primary reference used in this text for this concept.

It is important to know whether a recipe is recorded in AP, EP, or AS quantities. These designations carry with them cost and purchasing implications, especially in high-volume operations. These concepts are covered in detail in Chapter 5.

A standardized recipe will also include specific instructions on how ingredients are to be prepared before inclusion in the recipe. A specific size measurement must be included for any ingredients that are to be cut in any way (diced, sliced, cubed, etc.). For instance, "Onions, ½″ dice." See the following box for more examples.

Incorrect Item Description	Correct Item Description
• Chickens, cut into pieces	• Chickens, whole, quartered
• Milk	• Milk, 2% fat
• Eggs	• Whole-shell eggs, large
• Ground beef	• Ground beef, 90/10 mix

It is important to write the ingredients in "food friendly" language (Chickens, whole, quartered). Because the recipe is used as reference when procuring products, incorrect terminology may cause the wrong product to be purchased.

Recording Quantities of Ingredients   To aid further in purchasing, a recipe should show quantities of ingredients. Good standardized recipes record each ingredient in both **weight** (*a measure of density or heaviness*) and **measure** (equivalencies, so a recipe card should have a column for weights and measures. This *enables staff to correctly measure everything regardless of the measuring instrument on hand.* From a costing standpoint, all recipe quantities must, as a minimum, be recorded in the same unit the item is purchased in. Chapter 3 covers recipe costing.

EXAMPLES OF INCORRECT RECIPE QUANTITIES

Ingredients

• Onions	3 each
• Peppers, green	4 c.
• Parmesan cheese	2 c.
• Parsley, fresh	2 c.
• Chicken, diced	6 c.

There are a number of problems with the quantities as listed in this recipe:

- Because onions are purchased by the pound, recording "3 each" is useless information. Consider that "foodservice-size" onions (very large) are different from "supermarket size" (relatively small) onions. If the recipe were a homemaker's recipe, then "3 foodservice-size" onions would, without a doubt, overwhelm the recipe.
- Peppers are purchased by the pound and are not uniform in size, so recording "4 cups" is inaccurate. Many nonprofessional recipes record vegetable quantities in volume measures. From a costing point of view, however, these have to be converted to a purchasing equivalency in order to accurately compute the cost per portion.
- Parmesan cheese is purchased by the pound. Because an ounce volume is not equivalent to an ounce scaled, this item cannot be costed correctly from the information given. (See later discussion for explanation.) This kind of error accounts for many instances of inaccurate portion costs and can affect purchasing.
- Fresh parsley is purchased by the bunch. For costing purposes, this should be written on the recipe as a proportion of a bunch.

CORRECTLY WRITTEN RECIPE QUANTITIES

Ingredients
- Onions   1 lb.
- Peppers, green   1¼ lb.
- Parmesan cheese   ¾ lb.
- Parsley, fresh   ½ bunch
- Chicken, diced   2 lb.

When preparing a recipe, making conversions to quantities useful for purchasing is quite easy to do. *The Book of Yields* by Francis T. Lynch (New York: Wiley) is the tool to use to convert any product into weight and measure equivalencies. This book is an excellent resource and is a must for any serious restaurant operator.

Writing the Method of Prep   The **method of prep** *records the procedural steps to produce the menu item.* If the method of prep is written according to HACCP principles, then the steps must be written in such a way that there is little or no room for interpretation, especially where misinterpretation could lead to a contamination of the ingredients or the final product. The method of prep should include CP (Control Point) and CCP (Critical Control Point), where applicable.

BEST PRACTICES FOR WRITING RECIPE INSTRUCTIONS
- Use terminology the staff understands. If you have highly trained chefs and cooks, using food-preparation-related terminology such as roux, mirepoix, brunoise, and béchamel without explanation would probably be acceptable. If the majority of the staff are high-school students, however, this language will not work. Staff skill level is very important.
- Embed HACCP principles and language into the steps.
- Consider language. If necessary, translate recipes and other paperwork into the language your staff understands.
- Use precise descriptions. See the table "Creating Acceptable Wording for Procedural Steps in a Recipe" on the following page.
- Do not write in paragraph form. Numerically step out the procedures.
- Use HACCP language and include proper food safety procedures within the context of the method of prep. Include proper temperatures and times, when to wear gloves, and so on.
- Write clearly and concisely. The method of prep is not the latest epic novel out on the *New York Times* Best Seller's list!.
- Follow the steps yourself to see if they make sense. Edit appropriately. Ask other employees with different skill sets to test the recipe. Use their feedback to perfect the steps. This is how a recipe is standardized.
- Use photos to demonstrate complicated procedures, show how the product should look during different stages of preparation, and show how the final plate should look. Digital cameras make this work easy.
- Include corrective actions for procedures. Some examples include *continue cooking, increase cooking time, increase cooking temperature, continue to reduce,* and so on.

Writing steps that are clear and accurate takes time and energy. The goal should be a method of prep so clear that any employee using the recipe could produce the item with the same results the cooks have. For that to happen, though, procedural steps must be written out and tested time and time again until they are absolutely foolproof.

Creating Acceptable Wording for Procedural Steps in a Recipe

Wording for Procedural Steps That May Lead to Misinterpretation	Rephrased Wording for Procedural Steps
• Stir until well blended.	• Stir until uniform consistency, with no streaks.
• Lightly brown.	• Cook until light brown in color, about 3 to 5 minutes.
• Steam, bake, boil *until done* (ambiguous term).	• Steam, bake, boil for ____ (a specific length of time).
• Slightly undercook.	• Cook a maximum of __ minutes. Product should remain firm to the bite.
• Reduce slightly.	• Sauce should be cooked to a consistency that will fully coat the back of a spoon.
• Adjust seasonings.	• Phrasing is fine if a minimum quantity for each seasoning is stated.
• Hold in a warm spot.	• Place food in a warming oven or steam table set at 140°F.
• Pierce the skin.	• Using a paring knife, make ¼-inch cuts in the surface of the product.
• Toss lightly.	• Toss ingredients together until the product is well coated with dressing or sauce mixture.

Plating Instructions

Plating instructions are a description of the actual placement of the item onto the serviceware. This direction can be incorporated onto the plate card.

Garnish Instructions

This, too, is included in the recipe, as well as on the plate card. For accurate purchasing and preparation, the garnish needs to be included in the ingredient list of the recipe. If the garnish is not on the recipe, it will not make it onto a purchasing list, and from a production standpoint, it may not get prepped.

Cutting Instructions

Include precise cutting instructions for plating where appropriate.

Cooling and Storing Leftovers

A standardized recipe will include a description of how to properly cool and store **leftovers**. Instructions must include time, temperature, and procedural standards. Labeling and dating the leftovers are a must. If items are to be discarded after service, this should be so noted.

Nutritional Analysis

Good standardized recipes include a **nutritional analysis** of the product. This is typically found at the bottom of the recipe card. Information on nutritional analysis commonly includes the number of calories, as well as the amount of protein, fat, cholesterol, carbohydrates, fiber, and sodium content in one serving. More and more, from the guest's perspective, this is becoming an important piece of information. Some foodservice operators are incorporating this information into item descriptions on menus and Web sites.

Reducing Fat and Calories

Analyzing ingredients and prep methods to reduce a recipe's fat and calories can be a convenience for the guest. In operations that cater to a population for which this is an issue (senior citizens come to mind), doing this work on the recipe card will enable the staff to respond to a request effectively and without guesswork. In addition, noting this information on the menu can be an excellent marketing tool.

Photos

Including a photo of the finished plate on the recipe card or the plate card can eliminate any confusion as to how the dish is to be presented. Photos can also be used to illustrate complicated food items in various states of finish during the method of prep. They are an invaluable tool to assist employees in production. Further, with the development of digital camera technology, this work no longer has to be done by a professional photographer. All preparation and presentation work can be done on the premises, photographed and reproduced on photo paper using an in-house computer.

A Standardized HACCP Recipe

The following box gives an example of a standard HACCP recipe:

STANDARDIZED HACCP RECIPE FOR BAKED POTATOES

Name: Baked Potatoes   **File Code:** Sides—10

Yield: 8 - 16 oz. potatoes   1 each per person

Oven Temperature: 400 degrees

Prep Time: 15 minutes   **Cook Time:** 45–50 minutes

Holding Temperature/Time: Min. 135°F or higher/1 hour

Equipment: half sheet pan, paring knife, measuring spoons, vegetable brush, measuring cup, gloves

Ingredients	Weight	Measure
Russet potatoes, 16 oz.	8 lb.	8 each
Vegetable oil	2 oz.	3 Tbsp.
Kosher salt	1½ oz.	3 Tbsp.
Sour cream	18 oz.	1 pt.
Butter pats		16 each, or as needed

Food Safety Statement:
Before beginning this recipe, clean and sanitize your workstation. Wash your hands, paying attention to the fingers and the nails. Gather all equipment needed to complete the recipe. Avoid the possibility of spoilage by only working on as much food product as you can process in 30 minutes or less. Be sure all equipment and tools are cleaned and sanitized before proceeding.

Method of Prep:
1. Preheat the oven to 400°F.
2. Using the vegetable sink, scrub each potato with the vegetable brush, using cool running water. (Scrubbing too hard will damage the skin.) After removing all visible dirt, use the paring knife to make ¼" slices into the surface.
3. Using gloved hands, rub the surface of the potato with the vegetable oil. Place the oiled potatoes on the half sheet pan. Sprinkle each potato with the Kosher salt. *Note:* Salt should cover all sides of the potato.
4. Remove the potatoes from the sheet pan and place on the oven rack.
5. Bake at 400°F for approximately 50 minutes. Test by inserting a paring knife or metal skewer into the center of the potato. The knife or skewer will slide in and out easily, and the potato will be soft at the center. If the potato is not soft, return to oven and recheck at 5-minute intervals.
6. Serve at 135°F or higher.
7. Potatoes can be held uncovered in the warming oven at 140 degrees. Discard after 1 hour.
8. CP service: With gloved hands, score the top of the potato with an "X" and squeeze potato slightly to open it up. Serve with 1 oz. sour cream if requested by guest.
9. Leftover potatoes (on the hot line for less than 1 hour) can be placed on a rack set inside a ½ sheet pan (leave space between potatoes) and allowed to cool in the walk-in refrigerator. Potatoes should be cooled below 70°F within 2 hours, and to below 41°F in four more hours. After cooling, potatoes should be covered, labeled, and dated.

Did you notice the following important information in the sample?

- Use of times and temperatures throughout the recipe for baking, holding, and so on
- Conversion of ingredients into weights and measures
- When to use gloved hands
- How to determine doneness
- Corrective action if item is not done in the recommended time frame
- Where to clean potatoes and what water temperature to use
- Discard time—this is when quality is considered to be compromised
- Leftover potatoes—how to cool them, good storage practices for covering, dating, labeling
- Procedures steps that are numerically stepped out
- Tailored food safety statement

𝒩et Work
Explore www.costgenie.com—Click on Recipes and download the demo.

The World of Weights and Measures

The foodservice industry in the United States uses two units of measure—weight and volume. These two ways of measuring ingredients cause untold amounts of confusion to most cost-control students. The following is an attempt to clarify the world of weights and measures.

Weights and Volume—Those Two Infamous Units of Measure

It is important to remember when dealing with units of measure that **weight** *measures density or heaviness.* The standard unit of measure for weight is a pound. A pound can be further broken down into smaller units called ounces. There are 16 ounces in a pound. A scale is the common measuring tool for weight.

The next important thing to remember is that **volume** simply *measures space.* Everything from teaspoons and tablespoons to quarts and pints and gallons are common units of measure for volume. When we say we have a quart of milk, we simply mean we have a quart-sized (32-ounce) container filled with milk.

Unfortunately, volume measurements, like weight measures, also use the term ounce to describe smaller units of measure, and herein lies the ultimate confusion: *an ounce volume and an ounce scaled (a weighed ounce) are not the same.* Volume measures *space,* weight measures *density or heaviness.* They are not equivalent to each other.

The following example illustrates the difference between volume and weight. When measuring volume, one gallon is one gallon, regardless of what type of substance is placed in the gallon measure. **One gallon** always contains **128 ounces**, so anytime you have a gallon of something, you have 128 ounces. There could be chocolate fudge topping or milk or popcorn or cheese or shampoo or cotton balls or anything inside the gallon measure. And how much of each product is there? There are 128 ounces of each item.

From a weight perspective, however, the story is different. Each item scaled (weighed) will not equal 128 ounces. To know the **weight equivalency** of each product, a scale would be used to *weigh one gallon of each product,* so the actual weight can be determined. Here are the results, if you "do the math":

- One gallon of popcorn will weigh 8 ounces (according to a recent "hi-tech" test conducted by one of the authors late one night, with a measuring cup and a big bag of ready-made Smartfood popcorn).
- Chocolate fudge topping will weigh 12 pounds, according to the conversion chart found in *The Book of Yields*.

CHECK IT OUT

	Measured Amount	Scaled Amount
Popcorn	128 oz.	8 oz. (less than 1 lb.)
Chocolate fudge topping	128 oz.	12 lb.
		(12 lb. × 16 oz. = 192 oz. scaled)

Neither product is 128 ounces scaled, because their scaled measure (density) is different from their volume measure.

Remember: 1 oz. volume ≠ 1 oz. scaled. Because of this fact, there is *almost* no truth to the old saying: *"A pint is a pound the world around,"* because it depends on what is being measured. Be aware that there are a number of products for which 1 ounce volume is, in fact, 1 ounce scaled. Flour happens to be one of them, and so are milk, water, and other liquids of similar density.

The difference between these two entirely different units of measure is of particular importance when costing out recipes and purchasing products. Help is available, though: Tables can be found that convert weight and measure equivalencies for just about any product needed. Many professional foodservice books include conversion tables for the most common products. Once again, refer to *The Book of Yields* for complete conversion charts.

♪ℓet Work

Explore www.Chefdesk.com—Click on *The Book of Yields* tab. Go to Free Online Foodservice Calculators and try out the measurement calculator.

Standard Weights and Measures

See below for a general table of standard weights and measures.

TABLE OF STANDARD WEIGHTS AND MEASURES

Weight	Measures (common units)
Pound (lb.) = 16 ounces (oz.)	1 gallon (gal.) = 128 oz.
	½ gal. = 64 oz.
	1 quart (qt.) = 32 oz.
	1 pint (pt.) = 16 oz., or 2 c.
	1 cup (c.) = 8 oz.
	3 teaspoons (1 tsp.) = 1 tablespoon (Tbsp.)
	1 tablespoon (Tbsp.) = ½ oz. liquid
	2 tablespoons (Tbsp.) = 1 oz. liquid
	16 tablespoons (Tbsp.) = 1 c.
	16 cups (c.) = 1 gal.

A Hot Tip for Remembering Measures

An easy way to remember liquid measures (which seem to cause the most confusion) is to start at gallons or cups and either divide the ounces in half (if starting with gallons) or double the ounces (if starting with cups), to get to the next unit.

Think about the method shown in the following box:

WHEN DIVIDING IN HALF	WHEN DOUBLING UP
Start with 1 gallon (128 ounces)	**Start with 1 cup (8 ounces)**
1 gallon 128 oz./2 = 64 oz. (½ gal.)	1 cup 8 oz. × 2 = 16 oz. (1 pt.)
½ gallon 64 oz./2 = 32 oz. (1 qt.)	1 pint 16 oz. × 2 = 32 oz. (1 qt.)
1 quart 32 oz./2 = 16 oz. (1 pt.)	1 quart 32 oz. × 2 = 64 oz. (½ gal.)
1 pint 16 oz./2 = 8 oz. (1 c.)	½ gallon 64 oz. × 2 = 128 oz. (1 gal.)
1 cup 8 oz.	1 gallon = 128 oz.

Plate Cards: Another Form for a "Recipe"

Restaurants that focus on very precise production, with the majority of items made from scratch, will undoubtedly use recipes in a form with which most of us are already familiar. In addition to the recipe, most operations develop plate cards for use on the line and in the kitchen.

A **plate card** is used to *describe one complete menu item as management wishes it to be served. It breaks down a specific menu item into a plate presentation.* The plate card describes each item on the plate, the portion sizes of each, the placement and positioning of the food, the garnish, the serviceware, and any other detail management desires. It also provides a photo of menu item, as finished on the plate. Plate cards should be developed for all menu items (including beverages) and assembled in a binder for use on the service line by line cooks, expediters, and servers. These books are the standard for plate presentation, and they safeguard against mistakes. They are invaluable training tools.

WHAT IS INCLUDED ON A PLATE CARD?

1. Each item on a plate
2. The portion size of each item on the plate
3. The placement and positioning of the food on the plate
4. The garnish
5. The serviceware
6. A photo
7. The cooking and preparation instruction, if appropriate
8. Any other detail needed

In operations where convenience items are primarily used, the plate card may include the cooking and preparation instruction and will actually serve as the "recipe." This application is acceptable, as it provides the standard needed to control for taste, portion size, and so on, and it also allows for portion costing. In operations where recipes are the norm, plate cards are still used on the service line as a control tool for portioning and presenting the item to the guest. In this case, they are descriptive only and usually will not include preparation instruction.

Whether standardized recipes or plate cards, or a combination of both, are used is not important. What is important is that all of the necessary information discussed earlier is found on either one or the other. The goal is to control exactly

- What goes on the plate.
- How it looks.

- How it tastes.
- How it is prepared.
- How much it costs to produce.

Sizing Recipes

At times, it is necessary to **size** or convert *recipes for a different number of servings.* Computer software programs for the foodservice industry often have this feature built in. However, many times it is necessary to size recipes by hand, so it is good to know how to do so. The process is not difficult. A recipe conversion form, such as the one shown in Figure 2.6, is the tool to use to convert recipes to a quantity that differs from the original. To practice sizing a recipe, assume that a small function has been booked at Farfalle Arrabbiata for 15 people. Those attending have selected the Chicken Noodle Soup as one of their courses. The original recipe serves 25 people.

STEPS TO SIZING RECIPES

1. **Determine the recipe multiplier.**
2. Convert each ingredient's recipe amount into ounces.
3. Multiply each recipe ingredient's quantity by the multiplier to get the new recipe amount needed.
4. Convert to a common unit of measure.

Step 1: Determine the Multiplier

Use the following formula to determine the recipe multiplier:

NEW RECIPE YIELD/ORIGINAL RECIPE YIELD = RECIPE MULTIPLIER

15 servings/25 servings = .6 (recipe multiplier)

Recipe Name: Chicken Noodle Soup

Conversion Factor Calculation

New Yield: __15__ /Original Yield: __25__ = __.6__ **Recipe Multiplier**

Recipe Ingredients	Ingredient Amounts From Original Recipe In Ounces	Recipe Multiplier	Raw Conversion	New Amount Needed for New Yield in Common Measure
Chicken stock	1.5 gal. × 128 = 192 oz.	.6	116 oz.	3 qt. + 3 c.
Chicken (breast meat)	1½ lb. × 16 = 24 oz.	.6	15 oz.	15 oz.
Noodles (egg, narrow)	1¼ lb. × 16 = 20 oz.	.6	12 oz.	12 oz.
Onions, ¼" dice	½ lb. × 16 = 8 oz.	.6	5 oz.	5 oz.
Bay leaf	2 each	.6	1 bay leaf.	1 bay leaf
Salt and pepper	To taste			
	A	× B	=	C

FIGURE 2.6   Recipe conversion sheet.

Remember these Hot Tips about multipliers:

- If you are making **more than the original number of servings**, the *multiplier will be a whole number first, followed by a decimal point and other digits.*
- If you are making **less than the original number of servings**, the *multiplier will have a decimal point first, followed by the digits,* because you are making a fraction of the original quantity.

STEPS TO SIZING RECIPES

1. Determine the recipe multiplier.

2. **Convert each ingredient's recipe amount into ounces.**

3. Multiply each recipe ingredient's quantity by the multiplier to get the new recipe amount needed.

4. Convert to a common unit of measure.

Step 2: Convert Each Ingredient's Recipe Quantitiy into Ounces

Each ingredient should be converted into total ounces to make working with the multiplier easier. Once the recipe is sized, the new recipe quantity must be returned to a standard unit of measure used in the kitchen (Step 4). For instance, the original recipe calls for 1½ gallons of Chicken Stock. This amount is converted into total ounces as follows:

$$1\frac{1}{2} \text{ gal.} \times 128 \text{ oz. per gal.} = 192 \text{ oz.}$$

STEPS TO SIZING RECIPES

1. Determine the recipe multiplier.

2. Convert each ingredient's recipe amount into ounces.

3. **Multiply each recipe ingredient's quantity by the multiplier to get the new recipe amount needed.**

4. Convert to a common unit of measure.

Step 3: Multiply the Quantity By the Multiplier to Get the New Recipe Amount Needed

Notice that the factor used to resize the original quantity to the new quantity is called a **recipe multiplier**. That is a hint to help you remember how to work with it. Simply *multiply each recipe ingredient's quantity by the multiplier to get the new quantity to produce.* It is easier to work with the recipe multiplier if each ingredient's amount is converted into ounces before converting into a new measure. Be sure to remember to convert the new quantity back to a usable measure:

RECIPE INGREDIENT QUANTITY $\times$ MULTIPLIER = RAW CONVERSION

192 oz. of chicken stock $\times$ .6 (multiplier)

= 116 oz. of stock for 15 servings

STEPS TO SIZING RECIPES

1. Determine the recipe multiplier.

2. Convert each ingredient's recipe amount into ounces.

3. Multiply each recipe ingredient's quantity by the multiplier to get the new recipe amount needed.

4. **Convert to a common unit of measure.**

Step 4: Convert to a Common Unit of Measure

The Golden Rule of sizing recipes is as follows: Never leave converted ingredients in total ounces. They must be converted back to a standard unit of measure used in the kitchen. Continuing with the chicken stock, we convert back to a standard unit of measure (quarts and cups):

NEW AMOUNT NEEDED IN COMMON MEASURE

116 oz. = 3 qt. + 3 c.

The standard recipe amount would read 3 quarts and 3 cups of chicken stock. The recipe conversion sheet below shows all of the ingredients converted for 15 servings of Chicken Noodle Soup.

Now, try your hand at sizing the Chicken Noodle Soup recipe for 215 servings for a function that has just been booked. Use the following recipe conversion sheet.

Recipe Name: Chicken Noodle Soup

Conversion Factor Calculation

New Yield: __215__ /**Original Yield:** __25__ = ____ **Recipe Multiplier**

Recipe Ingredients	Ingredient Amounts from Original Recipe in Ounces	Recipe Multiplier	Raw Conversion	New Amount Needed for New Yield in Common Measure
Chicken stock	1.5 gal. × 128 = 192 oz.			
Chicken (breast meat)	1½ lb. × 16 = 24 oz.			
Noodles (egg, narrow)	1¼ lb. × 16 = 20 oz.			
Onions, ¼″ dice	½ lb. × 16 = 8 oz.			
Bay leaf	2 each			
Salt and pepper	To taste			

Here are the answers:

Recipe Name: Chicken Noodle Soup

Conversion Factor Calculation

New Yield: __215__ /**Original Yield:** __25__ = _8.6_ **Recipe Multiplier**

Recipe Ingredients	Ingredient Amounts from Original Recipe in Ounces	Recipe Multiplier	Raw Conversion	New Amount Needed for New Yield in Common Measure
Chicken stock	1.5 gal. × 128 = 192 oz.	8.6	1651 oz.	12 gal. + 3½ qt.
Chicken (breast meat)	1½ lb. × 16 = 24 oz.	8.6	206 oz.	12 lb. + 14 oz.
Noodles (egg, narrow)	1¼ lb. × 16 = 20 oz.	8.6	172 oz.	10 lb. + 12 oz.
Onions, ¼″ dice	½ lb. × 16 = 8 oz.	8.6	69 oz.	4 lb. + 5 oz.
Bay leaf	2 each	8.6	17 bay leaves	See the Chef!
Salt and pepper	To taste	8.6		

Best Practices When Converting Recipes

The following rules of thumb will make converting recipes even easier:

1. Notice when checking the math in the examples just discussed that some rounding of numbers has taken place in order to make the measured amounts easier to work with. This rounding will not significantly affect the end product or the cost, though, and that is how the situation should be approached.

2. Obviously, it would not be very realistic to record the information in the Raw Conversion column on a recipe card. This is especially true when sizing a recipe up (increasing the size of the recipe). (Picture the BOH staff attempting to measure 1,651 ounces of chicken stock!) Whatever you do, *the final amounts for all ingredients must be converted into user-friendly quantities.*

3. Realize that increasing standardized recipes to many times the original quantity (suppose the recipe yield is 8 servings, and you want to make 80 servings) will cause some odd results, specifically in relation to spices and herbs. Care must be taken during preparation to be sure the seasoning is correct. This is also true of baked items that use a leavening agent, because these rely on precise interactions with other ingredients to achieve the proper chemical reactions.

Calculating a Multiplier When the Required Portion Size Is Different from the Original Portion Size

There are 25 ten-ounce servings in the original recipe for the Chicken Noodle Soup. Assume a function has been booked for 250 people. The serving size for the function is only 6 ounces. In order to determine the correct multiplier to use to size the recipe for 250 six-ounce servings, start by determining the ounces of soup produced in the original recipe. In this case, the original yield was 25 ten-ounce servings, or 250 ounces. Next, divide this total by the new portion size, to find the number of 6-ounce portions in the original recipe. Last, revert back to the mulitplier formula to determine the new multiplier.

CALCULATING A MULTIPLIER WITH A NEW PORTION SIZE

1. Determine the total number of ounces in the original recipe by multiplying the original number of servings by the original serving size:

   Determine the Total Number of Ounces in the Original Recipe:
   25 servings $\times$ 10 oz. = 250 oz.

2. Divide the total ounces in the original recipe by the desired portion size. This determines the number of servings in the original recipe at the desired portion size:

   Divide Total Ounces by the New Portion Size:
   250 oz./6 oz. = 41.6 - 6 oz. servings

3. Find the new recipe multiplier by dividing the new quantity to produce by the number of servings determined in Step 2.

$$\frac{\text{NEW QUANTITY TO PRODUCE}}{\text{RECIPE QUANTITY AT THE NEW SERVING SIZE}} = \text{MULTIPLIER}$$

$$\frac{250 \text{ servings}}{41.6 \text{ servings}} = 6.009 \text{ or } 6$$

Standardized Recipes and Plate Cards at Farfalle Arrabbiata

The following are partial recipe samples and a plate card for Farfalle Arrabbiata, the signature dish at Farfalle Arrabbiata. The example demonstrates using subrecipes within a recipe. These recipe samples combined, with the plate card for Farfalle Arrabbiata, are the primary control tools for this menu item and will contain all of the information needed to produce the item consistently each and every time it is ordered. Because this item is finished on the line to order, the recipe will involve prepping the necessary quantities of products to stock the hot line according to the sales forecast. The subrecipes are for the pasta and the Pomodoro Sauce. Each of these is an independent production because they are cross-utilized within a number of other menu selections. Each menu item at Farfalle Arrabbiata would have a similar set of documents. *Note:* These are intentionally presented as partial recipes.

STANDARD RECIPE FOR SIGNATURE DISH "FARFALLE ARRABBIATA"

Name: Farfalle Arrabbiata   **File Code:** Pasta-4

Yield: 20 servings

   10 oz. cooked pasta, 8 oz. Pomodoro Sauce, 3 oz. vegetable mix, 5 each shrimp

Prep Time: 20 minutes   **Cook Time:** To order on line

Holding Time/Temperature: Hold on hot line for service minimum 135°F or higher

Equipment: Vegetable cutting board, French knife, ½-sheet pans, cheese grater

Ingredients	Weight	Measure
Bowtie pasta, fresh (subrecipe: Pasta)	5½ lb.	11 qt.
Pomodoro Sauce (subrecipe: Sauces)	6½ lb.	1½ gal.
Peppers, red, sliced ¼"	1¾	8½ c.
Peppers, green, sliced ¼"	1¾	8½ c.
Calamata olives	1 lb.	2¼ c.
Button mushrooms, whole	2½ lb.	12 c.
Parmesan cheese	5½ oz.	1½ c.
Shrimp, 16/20 count, deveined, tail on	5 lb.	100 each

Food Safety Statement:
Before beginning this recipe, clean and sanitize your work station. Wash your hands, paying attention to the fingers and the nails. Gather all equipment needed to complete the recipe. Avoid the possibility of spoilage by working on only as much food product as you can process in 30 minutes or less. Pay particular attention to the temperature of the shrimp. Be sure all equipment and tools are cleaned and sanitized before proceeding.

Method of Prep:

STANDARD RECIPE FOR SIGNATURE PASTA RECIPE AT FARFALLE ARRABBIATA

Name: Pasta Dough   **File Code:** Fresh Pasta

Yield: 4 lb.

Prep Time: 20 minutes   **Cook Time:** Finished on line

Holding Time/Temperature: N/A

Equipment: Scale, measuring cups, 10-quart mixing bowl, pasta machine

Ingredients	Weight	Measure
Flour (semolina)	2 lb. 8 oz.	5 c.
Olive oil	1½ oz.	1 Tbsp.
Salt	½ oz.	1 Tbsp.
Eggs (whole, shell, large)	27 oz.	15 each

Food Safety Statement:

Before beginning this recipe, clean and sanitize your workstation. Wash your hands, paying attention to the fingers and the nails. Gather all equipment needed to complete the recipe. Avoid the possibility of spoilage by working on only as much food product as you can process in 30 minutes or less. Be sure all equipment and tools are cleaned and sanitized before proceeding.

Method of Prep:

STANDARD RECIPE FOR SIGNATURE POMODORO SAUCE FOR FARFALLE ARRABBIATA

Name: Pomodoro Sauce   **File Code:** Sauce-10

Yield: 1½ gal.

Prep Time: 30 minutes   **Cook Time:** 1 hour to simmer

Holding Time/Temperature: On hot line during service minimum 135°F or higher

Equipment: 10-quart stock pot, scale, measuring spoons, vegetable cutting board, French knife, 1½ sheet pan

Ingredients	Weight	Measure
Roma tomatoes	10 lb.	7 qt.
Brown stock	½ lb.	1 c.
White wine	½ lb.	1 c.
Garlic infused olive oil	¾ oz.	2 Tbsp.
Garlic (browned)	1¾ oz.	1 head
Salt	¼ oz.	1½ tsp.
Black pepper (fresh ground)	¼ oz.	1½ tsp.
Bay leaf		3 each
Basil (fresh, minced)	¾ oz.	1 Tbsp.
Chili flakes	⅓ oz.	1 Tbsp.
Parsley (fresh, minced)	1½ oz.	2 Tbsp.

Food Safety Statement:

Before beginning this recipe, clean and sanitize your work station. Wash your hands, paying attention to the fingers and the nails. Gather all equipment needed to complete the recipe. Avoid the possibility of spoilage by working on only as much food product as you can process in 30 minutes or less. Be sure all equipment and tools are cleaned and sanitized before proceeding.

Method of Prep:

PLATE CARD EXAMPLE FOR ONE SERVING OF FARFALLE ARRABBIATA

Menu Item: Farfalle Arrabbiata

Serviceware: 10-inch rimmed salad bowl, warmed

Plate Presentation	Quantity	Directions
Bowtie pasta	10 oz.	In a 6-qt. sauce pan on the line, place 5 oz. of fresh bowtie pasta in small strainer and immerse into boiling water for 30 seconds. Drain and transfer to sauté pan. Sauté the pasta with ½ oz. of olive oil for 30 seconds. Transfer pasta to center of service bowl. Pasta should be heaped into the center.
Pomodoro Sauce	8 oz.	Ladled over center of pasta with vegetable mix
Grilled shrimp	3 oz.	Arrange shrimp in a pinwheel arrangement with tails set into the center of the pasta. Shrimp backs face up.
Garnish:	1 oz. chopped fresh parsley	Sprinkle around rim of bowl and over shrimp in center.
	2 - 10" thin breadsticks	Insert the breadsticks into the pasta at the 2 o'clock and 10 o'clock positions. Breadsticks will cross at the top of the bowl (12 o'clock position). Insert at pick-up to avoid soggy breadsticks.
Utensil:		Serve with large serving spoon inserted at the 9 o'clock position.

Plate Card Example for a Convenience Item with Little Prep

This example combines the recipe format with the plate card format for a convenience item with limited preparation. This format can be adapted to many different types of menu items (sandwiches, desserts, appetizers) that do not require complicated preparation steps.

Menu Item: Chili Dog   **Hot Sandwiches:** 5

Yield: 1 serving

Serviceware: 8" Warmed dinner plate

Ingredients	Quantity	Directions
All beef hot dog (8/lb.)	1 each	Simmer 3" of water in a 10-qt. stock pot. Place hot dogs in simmering water for 1 minute. Remove and place in ½ hotel pan with 1" of hot water on the hot line at 140°F. Hold for service. Discard leftovers.
Rolls, hot dog (8/pkg.)	1 each	Place rolls in warming unit 1 hour before service. Discard unused rolls.
Chili sauce (#10 can)	2 oz.	Heat chili sauce to 160°F on stovetop. Transfer to hot line and hold at 140°F. Ladle 2 oz. of chili sauce over hot dog.
Pickle chips (gallons)	6 each chips	
French fries	6 oz.	Serve 6 ounces from fry station.
		Plating
		With gloved hands and tongs, place one hot dog in warm roll. Ladle 2 oz. of chili sauce over the top. Place across the top half of the plate, just below 12 o'clock. Heap fries on bottom ½ of plate between 3 o'clock and 9 o'clock. Place pickle chips at 3 o'clock. Serve immediately with condiment tray.

So What About Farfalle Arrabbiata?

Since its inception, Farfalle Arrabbiata has operated using sound standard operating procedures. Standard HACCP recipes and plate cards are a part of daily operations. A standard HACCP recipe and a plate card have been developed for every menu item. Plate cards are assembled in menu books located for reference on the hot line and in the pick-up area. Plate cards are descriptive in nature because most of the menu items require complex procedures to produce.

FARFALLE ARRABBIATA MENU SELECTIONS

The following is a sample of some of the current menu selections for Farfalle Arrabbiata. The restaurant is open for lunch and dinner, 7 days a week, from 11:00 a.m. until 10:00 p.m. The bar is open until 1:00 a.m., and after 10:00 p.m., only desserts are served. Check Appendix A for Farfalle Arrabbiata's complete offerings.

Appetizers
- Mozzarella in Carrozza Arrabbiata (house specialty)—Fresh homemade mozzarella stuffed with Prosciutto di Parma and fresh basil. Breaded and pan-fried. Served with a side of house specialty Pomodoro Sauce.
- Bruschetta con Portobello e Manzo—Grilled Tuscan bread topped with a seared Portobello mushroom and pan-seared tenderloin tips in a Madeira wine and fresh thyme cream sauce.
- Antipasti—Mixed selection of fresh mozzarella, Roma tomatoes, black and green olives, fresh Parmesan, sliced Prosciutto di Parma, salami, roasted peppers, sautéed eggplant, Auricchio provolone and grilled polenta.

Soups
- Pasta e Fagioli—A classic straight from the shores of Italy—Bean soup prepared from fresh chicken stock, pancetta, tomatoes, garlic, and fresh herbs.
- Minestrone—Another of the Tuscan classics, with a medley of vegetables, fresh chicken, Prosciutto and herbs.
- Chicken Noodle—Mama's own special family recipe. A house favorite.

Salads (Lunch and Dinner)
- Insalata Cesare—Classic romaine, Grana Parmesan, fresh black pepper, croutons, and special house anchovy dressing.
- Insalata Mista—Traditional mix of radicchio, endive, frisee, romaine, red onion, and tomatoes. Seasoned with extra virgin olive oil, aged balsamic vinegar, and garlic.

Panino—Sandwiches (Lunch Only)
- Calzone Melanzane Arrabbiata (house specialty)—Classic Eggplant Parmesan, with a twist. Pomodoro Sauce, breaded eggplant, and Parmesan cheese.
- Calzone Spinacchio (Spinach Calzone)—Pizza dough with marinated spinach, sliced Roma tomatoes, Calamata olives, fresh Mozzarella.

- Panino Panzanella—Grilled Portobello mushrooms, Roma tomatoes, red onions, cucumbers, fresh Mozzarella, green olives, fresh basil, extra virgin olive oil, and balsamic vinegar.

Wood-Grilled Pizzas (Lunch and Dinner)
- Pizza Arrabbiata (house specialty)—Pomodoro Sauce made with browned garlic, chili flakes, extra virgin olive oil, white wine, and parsley. Topped with hot pepperoncini, roasted peppers and onions, artichokes, eggplant, Prosciutto di Parma, and Parmesan cheese.
- Pizza Picante—Picante sauce, pepperoni, sweet sausage, Mozzarella.
- Pizza Pomodoro Caprese—Pizza with Pomodoro Sauce, porcini mushrooms, vine-ripened tomatoes, fresh Mozzarella cheese.

Entrées (Dinner Only)
- Cioppino Classic dish with fresh squid, fish, lobster, shrimp, clams, sea scallops, Gaeta olives, simmered in freshly prepared fish stock
- Scallopine di Vitello—Tender veal scallopine, roasted red peppers, asparagus and artichoke hearts in lemon white wine butter sauce
- Salmon a la Griglia—Norwegian salmon marinated in extra virgin olive oil, white wine, garlic, and fresh thyme
- Bistecca—12 oz. N.Y. sirloin grilled to spec

Pastas (Lunch and Dinner)
- Farfalle Arrabbiata (house specialty)—Bowtie pasta served with house specialty Pomodoro Sauce, fire-roasted tomatoes and peppers, Calamata olives, fresh button mushrooms, our secret herb blend, and grilled shrimp. Topped with fresh Parmesan.
- Spaghetti Bolognese—Spaghetti tossed with house Pomodoro Sauce, ground veal, pancetta, mushrooms, red wine, and heavy cream.
- Risotto Alla Pescatora—Arborio rice, little neck clams, shrimp, scallops, mussels, squid, fresh fish, in a light plum tomato sauce and fresh herbs.

Desserts (Lunch and Dinner)
- Crema Fritta Con Salsa di Cioccolato (house specialty)—Fried custard with chocolate sauce.
- Tira Misu—Mascarpone and cream cheese mixture, layered between Lady Finger cookies soaked in Myers dark rum. Topped with slightly bitter powdered cocoa and strawberries.
- Gellato (house specialty)—Gellato prepared fresh daily in-house.

farfalle arrabbiata!

_/l/et Work

Explore the following Web sites:

www.costgenie.com

www.micros.com

www.calcmenu.com

www.foodsafety.gov

www.pelouze.com

www.edlundco.com—Click on the product clips.

Check these Web sites for recipe examples:

www.tyson.com

www.venturafoods.com—Click Menu Planning and Recipe Search

Chapter Wrap

The Chapter ✓ at the beginning of the chapter posed several questions. Review the questions and compare your responses with the following answers:

1. **Why a recipe?**

   Developing good standardized recipes that work is key to _controlling product quality and cost_. Simply stated, if we don't know how much food goes on the plate each time the item is produced, than we don't know the cost. If we don't know the actual cost, we don't have a basis upon which to compute a selling price.

2. **Why a standardized recipe?**

   A **standardized recipe** is one that has been tested, adjusted, and retested again and again until it produces a menu item as management wants the item produced. It has to fit management's plan for quality, taste, plate appearance, portion size, cost, selling price, purchasing, production, and profitability. Moreover, the guests have to like it, so they order it! From the standardized recipe comes all the costing and control activity that is crucial to the financial success of an operation. Developing and using standardized recipes for all menu offerings is an indication of sound management.

3. **What does a standardize recipe look like?**

   Review the examples in the text for an example of a user-friendly format, as well as the lists for standard recipe content. Be sure to check the 'Net Work Web sites listed within the chapter.

4. **What is the difference between weights and measures?**

   Weight measures density or heaviness. The standard unit of measure is a pound. Volume simply measures space. Everything from teaspoons and tablespoons to quarts and pints and gallons are common units of measure for volume. Unfortunately, volume and weight measurements each use the term "ounce" to describe smaller units of measure. It is important to remember that an ounce volume and an ounce scaled are not the same. _The Book of Yields_ is an excellent resource to assist with solving weight and measure problems.

$\mathcal{K}$ey Terminology and Concepts in This Chapter

Active portioning	Passive portioning
As purchased (AP)	Plate card
As served (AS)	Recipe
Edible portion (EP)	Recipe multiplier
Food safety statement	Recipe yield
HACCP (Hazard Analysis Critical	Serving size
Control Point)	Size sizing recipes
Leftovers	Standardized recipe
Measure	Subrecipes
Method of prep	*The Book of Yields*
Mise en place	Total recipe quantity
Number of servings	Volume
Nutritional analysis	Weight
Ounces (volume)	Weight equivalency
Ounces (weight)	

$\mathcal{D}$iscussion Questions and Exercises

1. After studying this chapter, create your own definition for a standardized recipe and a plate card. Explain why you defined them the way you did.

2. Farfalle Arrabbiata uses a combination of standardized recipes and plate cards as a normal part of daily operations. Production at that establishment is such that menu items are prepared from scratch. Review the list of elements for standardized recipes and plate cards and respond to the following questions.

   a. Sort the information into standardized recipe information and plate card information based on Farfalle Arrabbiata's type of operation.

   b. Should any information be on both? Which elements? Why?

3. Explain how a standardized recipe and plate card system would differ for a hot dog kiosk at a mall. What might their system look like?

4. Farfalle Arrabbiata's menu offers Minestrone Soup. The recipe produces 64 servings of soup. The total recipe yield is 4 gallons. What is the portion size?

5. How many 4-ounce servings are there in the 4 gallons of Minestrone Soup?

6. How many gallons of Minestrone Soup would need to be prepared for 120 guests for a function tomorrow? Serving size is 8 ounces.

7. Salmon a la Griglia is a popular menu selection at Farfalle Arrabbiata. The serving size is 6 ounces. Sixty orders are forecasted for Friday night's production. Assuming 100 percent yield, how many pounds of salmon should be ordered?

8. Totanetti Agli Asparagi e Menta (Squid Sauteed with Asparagus and Mint) is one of the most popular appetizers served at Farfalle Arrabbiata. The original recipe is from one of the oldest restaurants in Southern Italy. It was converted into U.S. measures while being tested and standardized. The original recipe did not show a portion size. Given the following ingredients, determine the portion size in weight. Remember, you are only concerned with the solid ingredients or those that will be served on the plate. Serving size = 8 oz.

   How many servings?

Name: Totanetti Agli Asparagi e Menta	Description of Item: Squid sautéed in extra virgin olive oil, dry white wine, black pepper, and mint.	
Ingredients	**Weight**	**Measure**
Squid rings	12½ lb.	
Olive oil		2 c.
Dry white wine		2 c.
Asparagus tips	4½ lb.	
Cracked black pepper		2 oz.
Mint		½ bunch

9. Cioppino, a classic Italian dish, is very popular at Farfalle Arrabbiata. Read the description for this item in the Entrée section of the menu sample selections listed earlier. Modify the sample food safety statement in the chapter for Cioppino. Take special note of the need to carefully handle seafood. Before you write this statement, research seafood safety on www.foodsafety.gov. Click Consumer Advice and Seafood or enter Seafood into the search.

10. What are AP and EP? Why do we, as cost control wizards, care about these? What is the relationship of AP and EP to recipes? Portion costing? Purchasing?

11. In the chapter, the saying, "A pint is a pound the world around," is debunked as a myth. Horror of horrors—homemakers and cooks alike have been singing this rhyme since the beginning of time! Defend the saying. When is it true and when it is not true?

12. If a pint could be a pound, as you defended in the previous question, then explain just how many pints there are in the 64 pounds of high-test gas I put in my hot red two-seater Spyder convertible. How many gallons would this be?

13. You are the manager on duty today, and Larry, one of the cooks at Farfalle Arrabbiata, is glaring at you. The office assistant has just handed him a recipe for Tortellini Alla Nero to prep for a function tonight. Here are the results of the conversion. Why is Larry so upset? You are the manager—fix it quick.

Convert to metric

Name: Tortolini Alla Nero	Yield: 120 servings	
Ingredients	**Weight**	**Measure**
Tortolini	720 oz.	
Red peppers	240 oz.	
Red onion	180 oz.	
Zucchini	270 oz.	
White wine		120 oz.
Tomatoes	210 oz.	
Portobello mushroom	120 oz.	
Garlic (minced)		35 tsp.
Basil		45 tsp.
Oregano		15 Tbsp.

in weight

What is the approximate serving size of one order of Tortolini?

14. Larry needs to prep the Ziti al Tonno Fresco (Ziti with Fresh Tuna) for dinner service tonight. Unfortunately, the recipe yield is for 20 servings, the sales forecast is

for 68 servings, and the computer in the office has crashed. The recipe must be manually sized. You don't want to delay Larry, so you quickly get to work converting it for him.

Name: Ziti with Fresh Tuna Sauce		Yield: 20 servings	Conversion Factor:	
Ingredients	**Weight**	**Measure**	**New Weight**	**New Measures**
Ziti	10 lb.			
Fresh tuna	5 lb. 12 oz.			
Olive oil		1 qt		
Dry white wine		3½ c.		
Tomatoes	2½ lb.			
Calamata olives	1¼ lb.			
Oregano		2 oz.		

15. Review the elements of a standardized recipe. Using your quick wits and imagination as a scholar of cost control, create a standardized recipe and plate card using the following information. Create a method of prep as best you can. Be creative and have fun. Feel free to embellish the recipe and take liberties where you wish.

Elephant Stew **Yield:** 3,800 servings

1 - 3,000 lb. elephant (50% yield)

900 gal. of elephant stock

900 lb. potatoes

700 lb. onions (diced)

700 lb. celery (diced)

700 lb. carrots (diced)

Flour for roux—200 lb.

Oil for roux—200 gal.

Salt 25 lb.

Pepper 15 lb.

Secret elephant stew seasoning—30 lb.

Parsley sprigs for garnish

Procedure: Cut elephant into bite size pieces. Boil to tenderize. Prepare vegetables. Heat stock and add elephant meat, vegetables, and seasonings. Prepare roux and thicken when vegetables are tender. Serve in very large bowl with a big spoon. Garnish with chopped parsley.

We would like to serve an elephant-size serving of 32 ounces.

Approximately how much elephant meat should each bowl contain?

16. The church ladies are having their annual dinner next month. You have graciously agreed to prepare the meal for them. In anticipation of the dinner, the ladies have given you a few of their *very favorite* recipes, which they insist you must use for the dinner. They have been serving these items for the past 20 years. This event is the talk of town.

Critique each recipe with your "standardized recipe eye." What information is missing? Where is more detail needed? Can you straighten them out? Give it a try. The party is next week, and you have to order the food. First, check some of the Web site samples in the 'Net Work box at the end of the chapter for ideas.

Harvest Casserole

1 pkg. broad noodles

1 can cream of mushroom soup

1 onion (medium)

1 lb. hamburger

1 lb. Velveeta cheese

1 can evaporated milk

1 can mushrooms (sliced)

Cook noodles. Drain. Dice onion. Add onion and cream of mushroom soup to noodles. Fry hamburger. Drain and add to noodle mixture. Add evaporated milk. Cube cheese and add to mixture. Stir well. Spoon into 13″ × 9″ pan. Bake at 350°F for 35 to 45 minutes, until cheese is melted and top is very light brown.

Chicken Stir Fry

1 pkg. chicken breasts (skinless)

1 head of cauliflower

3–5 stalks of celery

3 carrots

1 can chicken broth

Mushrooms

Peppers

Onions

Bean sprouts

Soy sauce to taste

In a large fry pan, place sliced chicken and soy sauce. Heat until all sides of chicken are white. Add chopped vegetables and cook for 3 minutes to allow juices to escape. Add can of broth and ½ can of water. Simmer until vegetables are tender. Add soy sauce to taste.

Tuna Macaroni Salad

1 lb. box of elbow macaroni

2 cans of tuna

3–5 stalks of celery

4 scoops of mayonnaise

4 scoops of sour cream

Garlic salt to taste

2 pinches of dill

2 pinches of parsley

3 pickles

½ cup of pickle juice

Cook elbow macaroni until tender. Drain completely. In a large mixing bowl, combine drained tuna, chopped celery, mayonnaise, sour cream, garlic salt, dill, parsley, chopped pickles, and pickle juice. Mix until tuna is broken apart and all ingredients are mixed well. Add drained macaroni and fold into the mixture; stir completely. Chill for at least one hour.

## Chapter Three

Chapter Objective

To calculate the Cost per Portion for various types of menu items.

Learning Objectives

After reading this chapter and completing the discussion questions and exercises, you should be able to:

1. Calculate the Cost per Portion for Recipes and Plate Cards.
2. Use Butcher Tests and Cooking Loss Tests to calculate the Cost per Portion for menu items with shrinkage and trim.
3. Determine Q Factors and Spice Factors for menu items.
4. Use the Menu Pricing Formula to perfect portion costs.
5. Use the Triangle of Enlightenment to calculate food cost percentages, determine sell prices, and compute product costs.

The Menu

Pre-Purchase Functions

GUEST CHECK
Sales history, turnover, average check, cash management, revenue forecasting & budgeting, menu item analysis

STANDARDIZED RECIPES
Standard ingredients, portion size, quality, consistency, quantity, purchasing

COST CARDS
Portion costs, yield factors, sell prices

GUESTS
Greeting, seating, sales, serving, busing, payment, comment cards

SPECIFICATIONS
Product descriptions

FOH Functions

PAR STOCK
Inventory levels, order building

KITCHEN PRODUCTION
Production schedules, portion tracking, recipe control, serving controls, food safety

REQUISITION
Order building, purchasing

PRODUCT ISSUING
Requisitions, transfers, daily & monthly costs, food cost percentage

SHOPPING LISTS
Call sheets, bid sheets, suppliers, bidding

STORAGE PRACTICES & INVENTORY MANAGEMENT
Best practices, sanitation, security, inventory methods

PURCHASE ORDERS
Security, ship order, price guarantee, contract

INVOICE MANAGEMENT
Payment, price checking, security

BOH Functions

RECEIVING ACTIVITIES
Best practices, invoices, security, sanitation

Chapter Map

About Portion Costing

- Portion Costing Options

Recipes and Recipe Cost Cards

- Recipe Cost Card Information
- The Cost Card Form
- Basic Cost Card Math
- Sample Cost Card for Chicken Noodle Soup
- Total Recipe Cost and Calculating the Cost per Portion
- As Purchased, Edible Portion, Recipes, and Costing
- Chicken Noodle Soup Cost Card

Chapter Map   (Continued)

Costing for Plate Cards

The Menu Pricing Formula

- The Spice Factor
- The Q Factor
- The Q Factor and the Spice Factor in Action
- Minimum Menu Price
- What About the Chili Dog?

Butcher Tests and Cooking Loss Tests

- How to Use a Butcher Test
- Yield Percentages
- What's Next?—The Cooking Loss Test

The Triangle of Enlightenment

- Working with the Triangle

Chapter ✓

Check the chapter content for the answers to these questions:

1. How are portion costs for menu items determined?
2. Why use a Butcher Test? A Cooking Loss Test?
3. What is a yield percentage (%)? A waste percentage (%)?
4. How can high portion costs be managed?
5. What are the primary uses for the formulas in the Triangle of Enlightenment?

*A*bout Portion Costing

Portion costing is the next step to navigate through in the **Operating Cycle of Control**. This task can be tedious to do by hand. Fortunately, computerized menu management systems integrate purchasing functions, recipes, and Cost Cards electronically, which eliminates the need for hand calculations. Frequently, however, it is necessary to calculate portion costs manually, so one must be prepared to do so.

As a manager, you will be likely to run into various situations that require different costing approaches. The complexity of the menu selection and preparation will ultimately determine how many of these methods will need to be used in an operation. Portion cost is the basis for determining the selling price. Consequently, the result of an inaccurate portion cost may be that the selling price is not set high enough to cover the cost for that dish and its fair share of other budgeted expenses. What if this mispriced item represents the majority of your sales because it's your signature dish? This situation is the crux of many a restaurant failure. The following list shows eight reasons for inaccurate portion costs:

CAUSES OF INACCURATE PORTION COSTS

1. No standardized recipes, or recipes exist, but they are not used
2. Poorly written standard recipes
3. No standard portion size on recipe
4. Inadequate equipment to portion correctly
5. Lack of or improper equipment
6. Not a management priority
7. Supplier price increases
8. Poor purchasing—lack of research of costs

The only item in this list beyond the control of management is supplier price increases. Every other item is a *control issue,* going back to developing and using standard operating procedures (SOPs). In other words, it is *fixable* by examining the Operating Cycle of Control to determine where an operating procedure seems not to be working or is not in place. Furthermore, although price increases are not directly under management's control, good supplier relationships and communication can minimize the effect of this situation, or at the very least, create an environment where changes in prices won't be a surprise.

Portion Costing Options

Four **portion costing** options are available to a manager: Recipes, Plate Cards, Butcher Tests, and Cooking Loss Tests. The complexity of the menu, staff skill level, purchasing decisions, and management preference will determine how many will be employed.

PORTION COSTING OPTIONS

1. *Recipes*—Used for menu items with multiple ingredients and little or no shrinkage or trim. Menu items are portioned after completing the recipe. Recipe yields are not subject to additional shrinkage or loss from cooking. The final recorded number of servings is accurate as long as ingredients are measured properly and procedures are followed as recorded on the recipe.
2. *Plate Cost Cards*—Used to cost one completed meal as it is served to the guest. This is best used for operations using convenience items that are not prepared in the same way as a recipe item is prepared. A good example of this is the Chili Dog Plate Card in Chapter 2.
3. *Butcher Test*—Used for costing menu items that have loss because of trimming. These menu items may be portioned, cooked, and served, or the item may be roasted and only portioned after cooking. If the item is only portioned after cooking, a Cooking Loss Test would be used to calculate the final Cost per Portion.
4. *Cooking Loss Test*—Used for menu items that will experience shrinkage and final trimming during the cooking process. These items are only portioned after cooking. There may be some additional trimming. Roast Prime Rib of Beef is a good candidate for a Cooking Loss Test.

$\mathcal{R}$ecipes and Recipe Cost Cards

As discussed in Chapter 2, *each and every menu item should have a Recipe or Plate Card and, as such, a corresponding portion cost.* So, in addition to using standardized recipes, managers should have a very complete understanding of the costs of every recipe. A **Recipe Cost Card** is *a form used to calculate the cost of one serving of a specific menu item using the approved standardized recipe to produce it.* The key to this work is having accurate standardized recipes. As soon as employees start to take liberties in interpreting the quantities of ingredients to use or in procedures, actual recipe yields will be affected, and portion costs will not be accurate. As repetitious as it might sound, *if portion costs are not accurate, then menu selling prices are probably not adequate to cover expenses and produce profit.*

A further repercussion is in the purchasing area. Products are ordered based on standard portions sizes and controlled production. If ingredients are not measured accurately or food is not portioned correctly, there is a risk of either running out of a product or throwing out the product because it was not used. Losing product or sales for either of these reasons is not acceptable.

To keep costs current, it is critical to update the pricing on the Recipe Cost Cards frequently because prices from suppliers change often. Use the most recent prices, and take them directly from current invoices. Although you can do this by hand, a computer application generates the results the fastest. Follow the recipe costing ground rules for best results.

RECIPE COSTING GROUND RULES

1. For a manager to cost accurately, recipe units must agree with purchasing units. If you purchase something by the pound and the recipe calls for that item to be measured in cups, you cannot do so without converting the measure into a weight equivalency. Refer to Chapter 2 and the discussion on Weights and Measures.
2. When costing, always round up to the next penny.
3. Rounding should only be done at the end of an equation rather than at every breakdown. (Reasons for this practice will be demonstrated later.)
4. Ignore spices, herbs, and ingredients that are difficult to cost out. These will be accounted for in the "Spice Factor," to be discussed later in this chapter.

Recipe Cost Card Information

In addition to ingredients and invoice costs, a Recipe Cost Card includes other information that is used to ultimately find the **Minimum Menu Price (MMP)**, or *minimum selling price,* for each item.

ADDITIONAL COST CARD INFORMATION

- Recipe name
- Date when priced
- Number of portions
- Portion size
- Type of recipe

- File code reference
- Cost per Portion
- Spice Factor percentage
- Q Factor, if used.
- Standard food cost percentage

The Cost Card Form

The **Cost Card** form was designed with cost control students in mind. It works well in teaching the mechanics of recipe costing. It is used specifically because it teaches the concept of breaking down purchasing units into recipe units. The format forces one to do several things:

1. Record invoice purchasing units
2. Break these purchasing units down into a unit that agrees with the recipe quantity

Most costing forms record the purchasing units already in agreement with recipe units. However, most students have no idea where those costs came from or how they were calculated.

𝒩et Work

Check these sites for examples of Cost Cards as part of software menu management systems:

www.costgenie.com
www.micros.com

Basic Cost Card Math

The work you are about to do is called extending a recipe. It determines the cost of each ingredient needed to produce a menu item. The basic mathematical formulas used to extend the cost of the ingredients in a recipe are as follows:

(1) QUANTITY $\times$ UNIT PRICE = EXTENDED PRICE
(2) EXTENDED PRICE/YIELD   = COST PER _____

These two formulas are used extensively in portion costing for recipes, Butcher Tests, and Cooking Loss Tests. These will appear time and again in the following pages.

Sample Cost Card for Chicken Noodle Soup

The Chicken Noodle Soup recipe from Chapter 2 will be used to demonstrate use of the recipe ingredient costing formulas. Later on, the work will be expanded to other recipes used at Farfalle Arrabbiata. The information at the top of the form is taken primarily from the recipe card. Next, observe that there are three column headings: Recipe, Invoice, and Recipe (again). Notice that beneath each heading, the columns are shaded and are split into two subcolumns, where the appropriate information is recorded. See page 72 to learn how to correctly use this form.

Sample Cost Card for Chicken Noodle Soup

Recipe Name: Chicken Noodle Soup			Type of Recipe: Soup				Spice Factor % =	
Date: 8/2XXX			File Code: Soup – 6				Q Factor =	
# of Servings: 25			Cost per Portion (CPP):				FC% =	
Portion Size: 10 oz.								
Recipe		Ingredients	Invoice		Recipe		Extension	
Amount	Unit		Cost	Unit	Cost	Unit		
1½	gal.	Chicken stock	$ .50	qt.	$2.00	gal.		
1½	lb.	Chicken breast meat	2.25	lb.	$2.25	lb.		
1¼	lb.	Egg noodles, narrow	17.00	Case/10 lb.	$1.70	lb.		
½	lb.	Onions	15.00	Bag/50 lb.	.30 per lb. or .01875 per oz.	lb.		
2	each	Bay leaves	SF					
To taste		Salt	SF					
To taste		Pepper	SF					
25	each	Oyster crackers, pkg.	10.65	Case/200	.05325	each		
½	oz.	Parsley, chopped, garnish	SF					
					Rec. Cost / # of Servings			
					CPP			
					CPP + Q			
					CPD × 1.SF%			
					TCPD/FC% = MMP			
A	B	C	D	E	F	G	H	I

Recipe Columns (A, B, C)   These columns are completed by transferring the recipe quantities and ingredient names from the standardized recipe to the first three columns on the Cost Card. The Recipe Amount column is for the quantity of ingredients. The Recipe Unit column records the measuring unit. The Ingredients column records each ingredient.

Invoice Columns (D & E)   The first column in this section (Cost) transfers the **invoice cost** of the purchasing unit to the form. *This number comes from inventory files or invoices.* Normally, it will come from inventory records. The second column (Unit) records the unit of measure. Make note of several important things while reviewing the Invoice column:

- Assume the chicken stock is produced in-house and is the result of costing a subrecipe for stock. This cost would be found in the inventory file under stocks. Other options would be to purchase canned chicken stock or to use a stock base to prepare the stock.
- Notice the notation of SF (Spice Factor) for salt, pepper, and parsley. Spices, herbs, garnish components, and other ingredients would be noted with SF in place of an invoice cost. Look for a discussion of the Spice Factor later in this chapter.

Notice the format for the invoice prices for egg noodles, onions, and crackers. This format is how prices actually appear on invoices. It is important to know how to read these and break them down.

Recipe Columns (F & C)   This column is where the calculator comes into play. The process is simple—*break down the invoice cost into a unit that agrees with the recipe cost.* Your knowledge of measurements is tested in this work. (Remember the measurements from Chapter 2.)

The four ingredients we have pricing issues with are:

- The stock
- The egg noodles
- The onions
- The crackers

Each of these is purchased in a different unit (usually larger) than the recipe is calling for. To remedy the situation, *break the cost down into a unit that is compatible with the units called for in the recipe.* Watch how to calculate the recipe cost for each ingredient used, starting with the stock.

RECIPE COSTING HOT TIP #1

When the recipe unit and the purchasing unit are not compatible, break the purchasing cost down into a unit that is compatible with the units called for in the recipe.

Chicken Stock   The recipe calls for 1½ gallons. The invoice cost is .50 per quart. One of two things can happen. Either:

1. Convert the quart cost to a gallon cost, and record that in the recipe cost column. The math: 4 (quarts per gallon) $\times$ .50 (unit price) = \$2.00 per gallon

Or,

2. Convert 1½ gallons into quarts and use .50 per quart in the recipe cost column. The math: 1½ gallons = 6 quarts

Use these conversions in the way that makes the most sense to you. A mastery of volume measures is needed to do this work. Remember to reference the table in Chapter 2 as a refresher.

Chicken Breast   Any time the recipe unit and the **invoice unit** are in harmony—as in the case of the chicken—the task is quite simple. The purchasing unit and the recipe unit match. *The invoice cost simply transfers to the recipe cost column with no further manipulation or breakdown needed.*

TO FIND THE COST PER PURCHASING UNIT
EXTENDED PRICE/YIELD = COST PER _____

FIGURE 3.1   Finding the cost per purchasing unit.

RECIPE COSTING HOT TIP #2

When the recipe unit and the invoice unit match, simply transfer the cost information to the recipe cost column. No further manipulation or breakdown is needed.

Egg Noodles   Egg noodles are purchased in a 10-pound case. That is the **purchasing unit**. The recipe calls for a *portion of the case*. The task here is to *compute a unit cost for the egg noodles that agrees with the recipe units*. Here is the formula (Figure 3.1):

$$\text{EXTENDED PRICE/YIELD} = \text{COST PER} _____$$

The **extended price** is the *invoice cost* for the full case of egg noodles. Think of the **yield** as being *what is inside the case*—in this case, it is 10 pounds of egg noodles. The end of the formula is left blank because this will change, depending on the product you are working with. For the egg noodles, the outcome is **cost per pound**. Do the math:

$$\text{EXTENDED PRICE/YIELD} = \text{COST PER} _____$$
$$\$17.00/10 \text{ lb.} = \$1.70 \text{ per pound}$$

You would enter **$1.70** under the **Recipe Cost** for the egg noodles. Be sure to include the units.

Onions   The process is the same as for the egg noodles, but with a little twist. The onions are purchased in 50-pound bags, so the first task is to *break the cost down to the cost per pound*. Do the math:

$$\text{EXTENDED PRICE/YIELD} = \text{COST PER} _____$$
$$\$15.00/50 \text{ lb.} = \$.30 \text{ per pound}$$

Because only .5 pound is needed, you must use the same formula one more time, to find the cost per ounce. In other words, do the math again:

$$\text{EXTENDED PRICE/YIELD} = \text{COST PER} _____$$

$$.30/16 \text{ (ounces in a pound)} = .01875 \text{ per ounce}$$

The next step is to *multiply the 8 ounces needed in the recipe by .01875 to get the final cost for 8 ounces*. (This is actually the last step in the process and since we are in the middle of it, it makes good sense to just continue the equation and finish the job.) The cost recorded in the invoice cost column can be recorded in either the cost per pound or cost per ounce notation. Now you can find the recipe cost for the onion:

$$.01875 \text{ (cost per ounce)} \times 8 \text{ (recipe ounces)} = .15 \text{ (cost for ½ pound)}$$

(Note: Do all the steps one after another. Round only at the end.)

As scholars of cost control and measurements, it is obvious that there is a quicker way to calculate the cost of the onions. Eight ounces is one half of a pound. Just divide .30 in half and get the answer quickly. Be aware that there is no "rule" that recipes have to record ingredients in such convenient units. In fact, most are not that easy to do.

Oyster Crackers   The procedure for the oyster crackers is exactly the same:.

$$\text{EXTENDED PRICE/YIELD} = \text{COST PER PACKAGE OF CRACKERS}$$
$$\$10.65/200 = .05325$$

Because, ultimately, 25 packages are needed—1 for each serving of soup—the final extension will be:

EXTENDED PRICE/YIELD = COST PER PACKAGE OF CRACKERS
$10.65/200 = .05325

COST PER PACKAGE OF CRACKERS × 25 = TOTAL EXTENDED PRICE
.05325 × 25 = $1.33125, OR $1.34

Rounding should take place at this point rather than rounding at the per-package cost and then rounding again at the end.

Take care not to fall into the trap of over-rounding figures. Calculations like the one just used should be carried through on your calculator all the way to the final answer without rounding between steps. Following this rule will give you the most accurate result.

RECIPE COSTING HOT TIP #3

Rounding should take place at the end of the work; do not round at every step of the way. Carry the calculation through on your calculator all the way to the final answer, then round up.

Practice a Few Calculations   Practice breaking down the following examples into a recipe cost.

Recipe Calls For	Invoice Cost	Recipe Cost
8 lb. of carrots	$17.50/25 lb. bag of carrots	
2 pt. of half & half	$3.69/½ gal. of half & half	
1 c. of milk	$2.25/1 gal. of milk	
20 lb. of potatoes	$14.50/50 lb. bag of potatoes	
4 lb. of butter	$81.00/36 lb. case of butter	
2 - #10 cans of tomatoes	$36.50/6 - #10 cans of tomatoes	

Answers

Carrots	$17.50/25 = .70 per pound
Half & half	$3.69/2 (quarts) = $1.85 per quart
	or
	$3.69/64 (oz. per ½ gallon) = .0576 per ounce
	.0576 × 32 oz. (ounces per quart) = $1.85
Milk	$2.25/16 (cups per gallon) = .1406 per cup
	(If sticking to the rule of always rounding costs up, this would be recorded as .15)
Potatoes	$14.50/50 lb. = .29 per pound
Tomatoes	$36.50/6 cans = $6.0833 per can, or $6.09

Finishing the Costing Job   The work in the cost card on page 71 established agreement between **recipe units** and **purchasing units**. The last step is to **compute the extensions**. Do this by *multiplying the recipe quantities and the recipe cost together*. This is called **extending the recipe**. The formula for this work is as follows.

FORMULA TO EXTEND A RECIPE

RECIPE QUANTITY × RECIPE UNIT PRICE = EXTENDED PRICE

or

QUANTITY × UNIT PRICE = EXTENDED PRICE

Now you can complete the Cost Card for the Chicken Noodle Soup.

Recipe Name: Chicken Noodle Soup			Type of Recipe: Soup				Spice Factor % =	
Date: 8/2XXX			File Code: Soup – 6				Q Factor =	
# of Servings: 25			Cost per Portion:				FC% =	
Portion Size: 10 oz.								
Recipe		*Ingredients*	*Invoice*		*Recipe*		*Extension*	
Amount	**Unit**		**Cost**	**Unit**	**Cost**	**Unit**		
1½	gal.	Chicken stock	$ .50	qt.	$2.00	gal.	$3.00	
1½	lb.	Chicken breast meat	2.25	lb.	$2.25	lb.	3.38	
1¼	lb.	Egg noodles, narrow	17.00	Case/10 lb.	$1.70	lb.	2.13	
½	lb.	Onions	15.00	Bag/50 lb.	.30 per lb./ .01875 per oz.	lb.	.15	
2	each	Bay leaves	SF				SF	
To taste		Salt	SF				SF	
To taste		Pepper	SF				SF	
25	each	Oyster crackers, pkg.	10.65	Case/200	.05325	each	1.34	
½	ounce	Parsley, chopped, garnish	SF				SF	
					Rec. Cost/# of Servings			
					Cost per Portion (CPP)			
					CPP + Q = CPD			
					CPD × 1.SF% = TCPD			
					TCPD/FC% = MMP			
A	B	C	D	E	F	G	H	I

Here's the math for the extensions:

Column: A × F = H

Stock: 1½ gals. × $2.00 per gallon = $3.00

Chicken breast: 1½ lb. × $2.25 per pound = $3.375 or $3.38

Egg noodles: 1¼ lb. × $1.70 per pound = $2.125 or $2.13

Onions: ½ lb. × .30 per pound = .15

When costing, always round up to the next penny if the extension is not exact. Doing this will give an accurate result.

Total Recipe Cost and Calculating the Cost per Portion

To determine the total recipe cost, add all the extensions together. This result tells what it costs to produce the full recipe. This is nice to know, but more important, we would need to know what it costs for just one serving. This is easy to do using a formula we used earlier.

$$\text{EXTENDED PRICE/YIELD} = \text{COST PER} _____$$
$$\$10.00/25 = .40$$

The *total recipe cost* for the Chicken Noodle Soup is $10.00. This is the **extended price**. The recipe's yield is 25. Now let's complete the Cost Card and calculate the Cost per Portion (CPP).

Completed Cost Card for Chicken Noodle Soup

Recipe Name: Chicken Noodle Soup			Type of Recipe: Soup				Spice Factor % = 10%
Date: 8/2XXX			File Code: Soup – 6				Q Factor =
# of Servings: 25			Cost per Portion: $.40				FC% = 30%
Portion Size: 10 oz.							

Recipe		Ingredients	Invoice		Recipe		Extension	
Amount	Unit		Cost	Unit	Cost	Unit		
1½	gal.	Chicken stock	$ .50	qt.	$2.00	gal.	$3.00	
1½	lb.	Chicken breast meat	2.25	lb.	$2.25	lb.	$3.38	
1¼	lb.	Egg noodles, narrow	17.00	Case/10 lb.	$1.70	lb.	$2.13	
½	lb.	Onions	15.00	Bag/50 lb.	.30 per lb. or .01875 per oz.	lb.	.15	
2	each	Bay leaves	SF				SF	
To taste		Salt	SF				SF	
To taste		Pepper	SF				SF	
25	each	Oyster crackers, pkg.	10.65	Case/200	.05325	each	$1.34	
½	oz.	Parsley, chopped, garnish	SF				SF	
					Recipe Cost/ # of Servings		$10.00/25	
					Cost per Portion (CPP)		.40	
					CPP + Q = CPD			
					CPD × 1.SF% = TCPD			
					TCPD/FC% = MMP			
A	B	C	D	E	F	G	H	I

As Purchased, Edible Portion, Recipes, and Costing

In Chapter 2, we defined the concepts "as purchased" (AP) and "edible portion" (EP). We will now discuss these concepts in more detail. To refresh our memories, here are the definitions of these two terms:

AP—As Purchased. This is the acronym for *all products received at the door. It is the total amount of raw product purchased from the supplier.*

EP—Edible Portion. This acronym represents *a food product that has been processed in some way. It has been peeled, trimmed, cooked, and portioned.* EP is used to describe *the portion of food as served to the guest.*

Generally speaking, recipes are recorded in EP quantities. What this means is the amount of product needed to produce the requisite number of servings is the *processed amount of product (EP)*. It is not the AP amount of product. The AP amount is the quantity needed to end up with the EP amount called for in the recipe. As such, the cost of the item must be based on this AP amount of product and not just the end amount (EP). Failure to account for the EP cost of product affects

- Portion costs.
- Selling prices.
- Purchasing quantities.

What This Means for the Chicken Noodle Soup Cost Card

Technically, the Chicken Noodle Soup cost is not accurate. Why? Look at the list of ingredients from the recipe. Which ingredient(s) have this AP/EP issue? If the chicken breast had to be skinned, boned, and trimmed, it would certainly fall under this category. Assume it was purchased ready-to-serve. How about the onions? The recipe calls for ½ pound of onions. In order to get a half pound EP for the recipe, a larger quantity would have to be used (AP). How much more? Onions have a standard yield of 87 percent. By dividing the recipe of onions amount by their yield percentage, the AP amount is easily determined.

$$EP\ AMOUNT/YIELD\ \% = AP\ AMOUNT$$
$$8\ ounces/87\% = 9.19\ ounces$$

How to Correct This Problem   Some Cost Card versions include a Yield Percentage column to account for this problem. It might look something like this:

Example of Cost Card With Yield Percentage Column

Chicken Noodle Soup				
Recipe				*Ingredients*
Amount	Unit	Yield %	New Amount	
1½	gal.			Chicken stock
1½	lb.			Chicken breast meat
1¼	lb.			Egg noodles, narrow
½	lb.	87%	9.19 oz.	Onions
2	each			Bay leaves
To taste				Salt
To taste				Pepper
25	each			Oyster crackers, pkg.
½	oz.			Parsley, chopped, garnish

Notice that in order to end up with 8 ounces of onions EP, the cooks need to start with 9.19 ounces AP. In this example, the cost difference is minimal because the recipe calls for only 8 ounces of onions and onions are not expensive. Imagine, however, businesses that serve thousands of meals per day—perhaps your school is an example! What are the cost implications? The purchasing implications? Calculate the cost and purchasing implications if the kitchen needed to make 5,000 servings of Chicken Noodle Soup!

⁄*Net* Work

Check www.chefdesk. com for *The Book of Yields.* Check the site for useful information
about product yield.

Costing for Plate Cards

Recipe costing for plate cards is quite simple. Some formats include the costing directly
on the card itself. The plate card example for the Chili Dog in Chapter 2 will be adapted
into a Cost Card format.

Menu Item: Chili Dog   **Hot Sand. #5**   **Cost per Portion:** .71
Yield: 1 serving   **Spice Factor:** 10%   **True Cost per Dish:**
Date: 8/2XXX   **Food Cost %:** 30   **Minimum Menu Price:**

Ingredients	Quantity	Unit Price	Extension
All beef hot dog (8/lb.)	1 each	$1.92/lb (8/lb.)	.24
Rolls, hot dog	1 each	$1.25/pkg. (8/pkg.)	.16
Chili sauce (#10 can)	2 oz.	$20.22/6 #10 cans	.07
Pickle chips (gal.)	6 each chips	SF	SF
French fries	6 oz.	$12.50/20 lb. case	.24
		Total	**.71**

Do the Math

(Ext. Price/Yield = Cost per _____)

Hot dogs	$1.92/8 (per pound) = **.24 per dog**
Roll	$1.25/8 (per package) = **.156, or .16 per roll**
Chili sauce	$20.22/6 cans per case = $3.37 per can $3.37/104 ounces per can = .0324 per oz. .0324 × 2 ounces per dog = **.064, or .07**
French fries	$12.50/20 = .625 per pound .625/16 ounces per pound = .039 per ounce .039 × 6 = **.2343, or .24**
	Add all the component extensions together: .24 + .16 + .07 + .24 = .71
	Total Plate Card Cost = .71

Congratulations! You have successfully completed finding the **Cost per Portion** (*the
raw food cost for one standard serving*) for a standardized recipe item and a plate card
menu item. Your work is yet to be finished, however! For a number of ingredients on
the Cost Card and the plate card, a notation of SF, or Spice Factor, was entered. To
complete the costing process, the Spice Factor must be added onto the Cost per
Portion so the cost of all of the food used to produce the item is accounted for.

The Menu Pricing Formula

The work completed thus far is part of a larger formula used to ultimately calculate the
Minimum Menu Price (MMP). The first two lines of the formula are used to work with
recipe and plate Cost Cards and are the ones used in the work we did earlier.

RECIPE AND PLATE CARD INGREDIENT COSTING FORMULAS
QUANTITY $\times$ UNIT PRICE = EXTENDED PRICE
EXTENDED PRICE/YIELD = COST PER _____

Once the Cost per Portion is determined, it has to be perfected so that the selling price covers all raw food costs plus other budgeted expenses and profit. *Costing is not complete until every ingredient purchased is accounted for in some part of the costing formula.* The rest of the formula looks like this:

MINIMUM MENU PRICE FORMULA
COST PER PORTION + Q FACTOR = **COST PER DISH** (CPD)

COST PER DISH $\times$ 1.SF% = **TRUE COST PER DISH** (TCPD)

TRUE COST PER DISH/STANDARD FOOD COST % = MINIMUM MENU PRICE
(MMP)

Notice that this part of the formula adds a few other factors to the Cost per Portion. The two factors are:

- The Q Factor
- The Spice Factor

The Q Factor addresses side dishes offered with entrees. Consequently, it is added to entrees that are sold using a semi-à-la-carte pricing structure. If the item you are costing is not an entrée, this line is ignored. Simply jump down to the Spice Factor line. Since the Spice Factor covers spices, herbs, and so on, it is added to everything on the menu. The Spice Factor will be explained first because it is added to the portion cost of all menu items.

OTHER FACTORS NEEDED TO ARRIVE AT AN ACCURATE MINIMUM MENU PRICE
Q Factor—Used for side dishes offered with entrees using a semi-à-la-carte pricing system
Spice Factor—Factor used on all menu items for spices, herbs, and so forth

---

The Spice Factor

Remember that a number of ingredients in the examples discussed earlier were not costed out but were simply marked **SF** or **Spice Factor**. Those ingredients are indeed purchased, so they must be accounted for somewhere in the costing process. Because trying to determine the recipe cost for those items would be difficult or even impossible, and we have better things to do with our time, one solution is to lump these products into one category and use one factor to cover it all.

What Is the Spice Factor? The **Spice Factor** is *a percentage that is added to every menu item to account for things such as spices, herbs, garnishes, and waste.* The Spice Factor is like a tax—just as everyone pays taxes, the Spice Factor is charged to every menu item. It is nondiscriminatory in that *it is tacked on to the portion cost of every menu item without regard to what the item is.* If it's cake, use the Spice Factor. If it's soup, use the Spice Factor.

What Does It Cover?   The Spice Factor accounts for the following in each recipe:

1. Spices, herbs, and seasonings used in quantities that are difficult to cost out

2. Garnish cost

3. Waste—every operation allows a certain amount of waste. This waste is considered the cost of doing business. It is the product left in a can or jar or small amounts of food that is spilled or dripped. The perishable nature of food makes it necessary to allow for waste. The amount considered acceptable is a management decision.

4. Very expensive ingredients. Rather than cost very expensive ingredients into a recipe, the cost can be placed in this category and spread over all items sold. For example, remember the Chicken Noodle Soup discussed earlier? Suppose we decided for some reason to turn it into Saffron Chicken Noodle Soup. Saffron is extremely expensive (to the tune of several hundred dollars per pound). If the cost of the saffron is added into the recipe cost for the chicken soup, the portion cost of one serving will be too high. (Recall that currently the cost is only .40 for one serving.) The saffron disproportionately skews the Cost per Portion of the soup. Because the selling price is determined by the portion cost, including the saffron in the recipe cost will produce a selling price so high that no one will order it. By adding the cost of the saffron into the Spice Factor category, however, the soup can now be sold at a price customers are willing to pay.

5. Whatever else management chooses. When it comes to costing, it is really management's decision as to what items should fall under this umbrella. The more ingredients placed in this category, however, the higher the percentage will be.

How Is It Determined?   You can determine the Spice Factor using these easy steps:

1. Identify from recipes and inventory lists which products belong in this category.

2. Determine the cost of purchasing these items over a period of time, showing usage or turnover. Because spices and herbs represent the bulk of these items, looking at one week's worth of purchases will not give the most accurate picture. Several weeks or a month's worth of records may be needed to get a representative sum.

3. Determine the total food purchased for the same period of time.

TO DETERMINE THE SPICE FACTOR PERCENTAGE

$$\frac{\text{COST OF SPICE FACTOR ITEMS}}{\text{TOTAL FOOD PURCHASES}} = \text{SPICE FACTOR \%}$$

(The **percentage** represents *the proportion of total food purchases that these items represent.*)

Using the Spice Factor   Using the Spice Factor is quite simple. Each item's Cost per Portion is increased by this percentage. To demonstrate this concept, return to the bottom portion of the Chicken Noodle Soup Cost Card. It was determined that the soup cost .40 to produce. Since the soup is not an entrée, the next line (**Q Factor**) is skipped. Assume the Spice Factor for this operation is 10%. Simply multiply the Cost per Portion by 1.10 (110%) to get the new Cost per Portion (Figure 3.2).

Recipe Cost/# of Servings	$10.00/25
Cost per Portion (CPP)	.40
CPP + Q = CPD	
CPD × 1.SF% = TCPD	**.44**
.40 × 1.10 = .44	
TCPD/FC% = MMP	

FIGURE 3.2   Adding the Spice Factor to the Cost per Portion.

What Does This Mean?   The Cost per Portion has now jumped to **.44**. This means that .04 is added on to cover the spices, herbs, garnish, waste, and so on, for this bowl of soup. Looking back at the recipe, this would be the bay leaves, salt, pepper, and parsley. This would also include allowable waste for this product.

When using the Spice Factor, resist the temptation to just multiply the .40 by .10 (10 percent) and add the .04 to the .40. By using the formula above, steps are eliminated and the answer is computed in one shot. Many a student has recorded the new TCPD as .04, a major error.

RECIPE COSTING HOT TIP #4

Be sure to write the Spice Factor line like this:

COST PER PORTION × 1.SF% = TRUE COST PER DISH

The Q Factor

The **Q Factor** is defined as *the Cost per Portion of the surrounding items included in a meal.* It is used to address the portion cost of side dishes offered with an entrée. The Q Factor is used specifically with the **semi-à-la-carte menu pricing format** commonly used in most restaurants. Unlike **à la carte pricing**, *where all menu selections are priced individually,* semi-à-la-carte pricing *is a combination method, where several courses or selections are grouped together and sold for one price.*

Since the Q Factor is a Cost per Portion, it is a *dollar and cents value* versus a percentage (such as the Spice Factor). When the Q Factor is in use, it must be added to the entrée cost prior to adding on the Spice Factor because spices, herbs, waste, and so on, are also used in these items. It is also quite likely that there is more than one Q Factor in effect. For example, because our signature dish, Farfalle Arrabbiata, includes pasta, we would not need to serve an additional starch with it. Consequently, the Q Factor for this dish and all the other pasta items would be adjusted to reflect this. All selections would have to be examined to determine exactly which sides accompany each entrée.

Determining the Q Factor   To determine the Q Factor in a recipe, follow these steps:

1. Identify selections to be included with the entrée. The most common are a side salad and dressing, starch, vegetable, and roll and butter.
2. Develop a standardized HACCP recipe and Cost Card for each. (This is non-negotiable.)
3. Create a summary card (**Q Card**) for all the portion costs.
4. Select the most expensive portion cost from each category.
5. Sum the Cost per Portions for these elements. The sum is the Q Factor.

Example: Farfalle Arrabbiata   Figure 3.3 shows a Q Card for Farfalle Arrabbiata.

In Figure 3.3, the total cost of the surrounding items offered with the meal is $1.13.

Salad		Vegetables	
House salad	.18	Asparagus	**.27**
Small Caesars	**.21**	Seasonal Medley	.17
Dressings		**Starches**	
House dressing	.11	Baked potato	**.24**
Blue Cheese	**.16**	Spanish rice	.08
Creamy Parmesan	.07	Garlic smashed	.18
Raspberry vinaigrette	.06	Oven roasted new potatoes	.10
		Foccacia bread **.20**	
		Herbed butter **.05**	
TOTAL Q FACTOR = $1.13			

FIGURE 3.3   Q Card for Farfalle Arrabbiata.

The Q Factor is like a picture—a picture of a meal. The Cost per Portion is the cost of the entrée on the plate. The Q Factor fills in the empty spots on the plate and on the table—the starch, the vegetable, the salad and dressing, and the roll and butter. The Spice Factor is the garnish! Figure 3.4 illustrates these concepts.

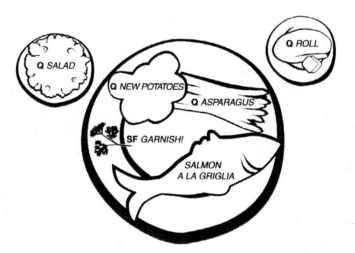

FIGURE 3.4   A complete costing meal: Entrée, Q Factor, and Spice Factor.

Using the most expensive selections builds a cushion into the pricing structure. Every time a guest selects Spanish Rice or the Seasonal Vegetables or the House Salad, give a cheer, because these are the least expensive side dishes, and pricing was set on the more expensive items. If supplier prices increase (as they will), the menu prices will still reflect a selling price that is accurate to costs and budget. At some point, new menu prices will have to be set. This is usually done in conjunction with a reprinting of the menu. Any time menus are reprinted, all recipes, portion sizes, portion costs, and sales records are evaluated.

How to Remember When to Use the Q   Let's rename the Q Factor the Smashed Potato Factor. When costing a dish, ask this question: Would I serve smashed potatoes with this item? If the answer is "Yes," add the Q in and continue on your way. If the answer is "No," then skip over the line and move to the Spice Factor.

RECIPE COSTING HOT TIP #5

Rename the Q Factor the Smashed Potato Factor to remember to only add the Q Factor to entrée items offered with the semi-à-la-carte pricing structure.

The Q Factor and the Spice Factor in Action

To demonstrate using both factors, we will need an entrée cost. Let's assume the recipe cost for Salmon a La Griglia served at Farfalle Arrabbiata is $68.75, and the number of servings is 25. Using the Spice Factor percentage (10%) and the Q Factor ($1.13) found earlier, we work through the minimum menu pricing (MMP) formula. Figure 3.5 demonstrates the work.

Extended Price/Yield = Cost per Portion (CPP)
$68.75/25 = **$2.75** (Salmon a la Griglia)

Cost per Portion + **Q Factor** = Cost per Dish (CPD)
$2.75 + **$1.13** = **$3.88**

Cost per Dish × **1.SF%** = True Cost per Dish (TCPD)
$3.88 × **1.10** = **$4.268**

True Cost per Dish/Standard Food Cost % = Minimum Menu Price (MMP)
$4.268/.30 = **$14.226**

FIGURE 3.5   Using the MMP formula to find the MMP for Salmon a la Griglia.

Minimum Menu Price

Notice that the last line is completed in this example. When the **True Cost Per Dish (TCPD)** is divided by the standard (budgeted) food cost percentage, the result is a **Minimum Menu Price (MMP)**. This is a starting point to determine actual menu prices. Using the food cost percentage to determine sell prices is a very common menu pricing method. We will discuss menu pricing methods further in a later chapter.

Back to the Chicken Noodle Soup

The Chicken Noodle Soup recipe can be used to demonstrate the menu pricing formula for an item with no Q Factor added. The end of the Cost Card is presented here, with the MMP added (Figure 3.6):

Recipe Cost/# of Servings	**$10.00/25**
Cost per Portion (CPP)	**.40**
CPP+ Q = CPD	
CPD × 1.SF% × TCPD	**.44**
.40 × 1.10 = .44	
TCPD / FC% = MMP .44 / .30 = $1.47	**$1.47**

FIGURE 3.6   Chicken Noodle Soup Cost Card, with no Q Factor added.

Figure 3.7 follows this information in the formula format. Notice that there is no Q Factor added in. The line is simply skipped. In the box just shown, the Q Factor line is left blank.

$$\text{Extended Price/Yield} = \text{Cost per Portion (CPP)}$$
$$\$10.00/25 = \textbf{\$.40}$$

$$\text{Cost per Dish} \times \textbf{1.SF\%} = \text{True Cost per Dish (TCPD)}$$
$$\$.40 \times \textbf{1.10} = \textbf{\$.44}$$

$$\textbf{True Cost per Dish/Standard Food Cost \%} = \textbf{Minimum Menu Price (MMP)}$$
$$\$.44/.30 = \$1.4666, \text{ or } \$1.47$$

FIGURE 3.7   Using the MMP formula to find the MMP for the Chicken Noodle Soup.

What About the Chili Dog?

The portion cost for the Chili Dog was found by using a plate card. The MMP formula works the same way. The Chili Dog as a complete meal has a plate cost of .71. Because all the plated items are included in the plate cost, there is no need to use the Q Factor here. We use the same method we used for the Chicken Noodle Soup.

In Figure 3.8, .07 (the difference between the Cost per Portion and the True Cost Per Dish) is allocated for Spice Factor items. This would cover the cost of condiments, onions, and everything else served with the hot dog, as well as waste.

Menu Item: Chili Dog		Hot Sand. # 5	
Yield: 1 serving		Cost per Portion: .71	
Date: 8/2XXX		Spice Factor: 10%	True Cost per Dish: .781
		Food Cost %: 30%	Min. Menu Price: $2.37
Ingredients	Quantity	Unit Price	Extension
All-beef hot dog (8/lb.)	1 each	$1.92/lb. (8/lb.)	$.24
Rolls, hot dog	1 each	$1.25/pkg. (8/pkg.)	.16
Chili sauce (#10 can)	2 oz.	$20.22/6 - #10 cans	.07
Pickle chips (gal.)	6 each chips	SF	SF
French fries	6 oz.	$12.50/20 lb. cs.	.24
		Total	$.71

FIGURE 3.8   Calculating the MMP for the Chili Dog.

Here is the same information presented in the MMP formula format:

USING THE MMP FORMULA TO FIND THE MMP FOR THE CHILI DOG

COST PER DISH $\times$ 1.SF% = TRUE COST PER DISH (TCPD)

.71 $\times$ 1.10 = $.781

TRUE COST PER DISH/STANDARD FOOD COST % = MINIMUM MENU PRICE (MMP)

.781/.30 = $2.366, or $2.37

Refer to Hot Tips #6–10 for a group of pointers to use when doing this kind of work. They should help prevent errors in costing that could lead to incorrect selling prices.

RECIPE COSTING HOT TIPS #6–10

6. Cost is always going up. If at any time you are using this formula and your new answer is less than the previous line—**STOP**. This is impossible. If we keep adding on factors to increase the cost, then the answers should demonstrate that fact. Recheck your work.
7. The Q Factor has to be added on before the Spice Factor. Those recipes use seasonings, herbs, and so on.
8. Always write out the formula line-by-line, as demonstrated. You don't need to write out all the letters, just the math work. Doing so means you can easily check your work and you can spot errors quickly. Resist the temptation to write the computation in one string. When you do so, you cannot check your work or spot errors. Only use shortcuts after you have completely mastered the formula and its elements.
9. The beauty of the formula is that one line takes you right to the next one. There is no need to clear numbers out of calculators after each calculation.
10. For the most accurate results, run the figures through the calculator without rounding at each line. The final answer is the place to round.

---

*B*utcher Tests and Cooking Loss Tests

The costing methods just discussed tend to be the most widely used. There are situations, however, in which Butcher Tests or Cooking Loss Tests can be useful.

With the availability of high-quality convenience items and changing skill levels in the back of the house, the need to butcher meat and fish in-house has decreased significantly. Although in recent years there has been some resurgence in the practice of cutting meat in-house, the general trend has been to purchase meat and fish in more ready-to-use forms. Even if full-scale butchering is not in practice, however, Butcher Tests are still used to

- Analyze product yield.
- Calculate waste percentages.
- Calculate portion costs.
- Compare supplier costs.

The **Butcher Test** *determines what is actually servable after trimming.* The **Cooking Loss Test** *measures what is servable after the cooking process has taken place.* The point of it all is to determine accurate portion costs for menu items that experience trimming and shrinkage somewhere along the way. Butcher Tests are especially useful in making purchasing decisions.

Butcher Tests and Yield Analysis   To determine accurate portion costs, it is first necessary to do a yield analysis of the item. The first method used for doing a yield analysis is a Butcher Test (sometimes called a **Yield Test**). Using the Butcher Test, it is possible to make several determinations:

- The final amount of usable raw product
- The cost of the product (both in portion cost and pound cost)
- Yield percentages

From this point, the product can be either:

1. Portioned, cooked, and served to the guest (as in a steak or an order of fish)

or

2. Cooked, then portioned only after the cooking process is completed (as in Prime Rib or some other roasted product). In this case, the roasted product would also go through a Cooking Loss Test, to determine final cooked yields, final portion costs, and so on.

How to Use a Butcher Test

The Butcher Test can be used for any food product that can be measured for a set quality standard and quantity yield. This is true for meats such as beef, pork, lamb, veal, and fish—before the meat item is purchased already cut, the usable product was an entire animal. Butcher Tests are also appropriate to use in operations that clean and cut their own fish, but the primary usage is for meat products.

Figure 3.9 demonstrates the use of a Butcher Test and Cooking Loss Test for a meat product that traditionally has loss from trimming fat, bones, and other unservable pieces, as well as shrinkage after cooking. What is removed (unservable) does have value if it is used in some other product. With this in mind, the value of that trimmed piece must also be taken into consideration in either of two ways when computing the actual product cost:

- Trimmed parts that end up in the trash because there is no other use for them are charged to the portion cost of the menu item being prepared.
- Trimmed parts that end up as something else (used for another menu item) are not charged to the portion cost of the item being prepared.

We will use a Butcher Test to analyze the yield in preparing and cooking a NAMP #109C, oven-ready rib roast, USDA Choice. The purchase weight is 26 pounds. Invoice cost is $3.45 per pound. The task is to determine just how much of the 26 pounds purchased is saleable as the menu item "Rib" to a guest. The first step is to work from the raw state. Once the rib is trimmed and ready, it will be roasted following a standard procedure. Next, it will be measured for shrinkage and any other remaining trimming will be done, so a final yield and portion cost can be determined. Butcher Tests and Cooking Loss Tests are used to determine yield percentages for everything trimmed off and for making purchasing decisions. Figure 3.9 shows what the Butcher Test chart would look like.

BUTCHER TEST			Prepared By:		Date:	
Item: NAMP 109C USDA Choice Rib						
A. Amount Purchased: 26 lb.			Invoice Cost: $3.45 lb.			
Item	Yield %	Quantity	×	Unit Price	=	Extended Price
Rib, #109	100%	26 lb.	×	$3.45/lb.		$89.70
B. **Raw Trims**						
Fat	7.6%	2 lb.	×	.20/lb. Fair market value		40 (Subtract from $89.70)
Scrap	5.7%	1 lb. 8 oz.		No value		0
C. **Total Trimmed Wt. = 3½ lbs.**						
Raw trimmed Oven Ready Rib	87.6%	22 lb. 8 oz. (26 lb. – 3½ lb. = 22½)		$3.97/lb. ($89.30/22.5 = $3.97)		$89.30 ($89.70 – .40 = $89.30)

FIGURE 3.9   Butcher Test for Rib.

What This Chart Shows

It seems that of the 26 pounds purchased, after trimming, only 22 pounds 8 ounces is left to be put in the oven. It also appears that the cost per pound has gone up some because of the loss of the trimmed product. See line C in Figure 3.9.

How the Chart Works   Notice what is familiar in the chart:

QUANTITY × UNIT PRICE = EXTENDED PRICE
EXTENDED PRICE/YIELD = COST PER POUND

A. *Amount Purchased and Invoice Cost*   This is right off the invoice for the product. In this case, the product is the 109C Rib. The invoice indicates that 26 pounds were received at a cost of $3.45 per pound. See line C in Figure 3.9.

Item Description   Record the item, quantity purchased, unit price, and extension.

26 lb. × $3.45 = $89.70

B. *Raw Trims*   List all trimmed product that is not servable to the guest as the menu item Rib. The trimmed product is identified and weighed. See line B in Figure 3.9. This product can be:

1. *Used for something else.* The unit price for these trimmed products is determined by the fair market value of that product. In other words, if this item were purchased through a supplier, what would the unit cost (fair market value) be? Because the fat in this example is given a value, it must be used in some other menu item. (Perhaps they grind their own meat for hamburgers.) The .20 represents what a supplier would have charged for the beef fat, if it were ordered on invoice.

Fat   2 lb. × .20 = .40

2. *Discarded as scrap.* Anything that is not usable is considered scrap. The cost of the scrap is absorbed by the Cost per Portion of the rib, and there is no value recorded in the Unit Price column.

C. *Raw Trimmed Rib*   *Subtracting the raw trimmed products from the original rib* determines what is oven-ready. (**Oven-ready** means it is *ready to be cooked using a standard cooking procedure.*) See line C in Figure 3.9. Here's how it's done:

AS PURCHASED RIB − RAW TRIM = OVEN-READY RIB
26 lb. − $3\frac{1}{2}$ lb. = $22\frac{1}{2}$ lb. (Ready for the oven)

The **monetary value of the trimmed rib** is determined by *subtracting the dollar values of the trims from the original cost.* In this case:

INVOICE COST − VALUE OF TRIM = VALUE OF TRIMMED RIB
$89.70 − $.40 = $89.30

The **unit price** for the rib is calculated by *dividing the final value of the oven-ready rib by its weight.* See line C in Figure 3.9.

VALUE OF OVEN-READY RIB/EP WEIGHT OF RIB = UNIT PRICE

$89.30/22½ pounds = $3.97 per pound

This value ($3.97) is important because it is the true cost per pound of the rib versus the invoice cost per pound. On invoice, the rib cost is $3.45 per pound. After trimming, the actual cost is $3.97 per pound. This is helpful when comparing supplier prices, portion costs, and yield percentages, and when evaluating alternative products.

Yield Percentages

The **yield percentage** is determined by *dividing the part by the whole* (Part/Whole). Sometimes, this is written as **EP/AP** or **edible portion divided by as purchased**. The **part** is *the weight of the specific item trimmed.* The **whole** is *the weight of the entire rib (100%) as purchased.* The yield percentage tells *how much of the whole product (100%) is left to sell to a guest as the menu item Rib and thus generate dining room sales.* The difference (100% − YIELD%) is called the **waste percentage**.

YIELD CONCEPTS

- The YIELD % is determined by:

Part/Whole

- The PART is the weight of the specific item trimmed.
- The WHOLE is the weight of the entire item as purchased.
- The YIELD % tells how much of the whole is left to sell.
- The WASTE % tells how much of the whole is not saleable.

Yield percentages are critically important when evaluating identical cuts from different meat packers. The following are the calculations for the yield percentages for each of the trimmed items from the Butcher Test just performed:

YIELD PERCENTAGE CALCULATIONS FOR THE RIB

$$\text{Fat. } \frac{2 \text{ lb.}}{\text{Rib (AP) } 26 \text{ lb.}} = 7.6\% \qquad \text{Scrap } \frac{1½ \text{ lb.}}{\text{Rib (AP) } 26 \text{ lb.}} = 5.7\% \qquad \text{Raw Trimmed Rib } \frac{22½ \text{ lb.}}{\text{Rib (AP) } 26 \text{ lb.}} = 87.6\%$$

A supplier may quote a lower AP price for the same product, but unless final yields—both raw and cooked—are evaluated, the buyer must beware. The cheapest invoice price is not necessarily the cheapest price when it comes to meat.

What's Next?—The Cooking Loss Test

It's obvious that the rib can't be served raw, so the next step is to follow standard procedures (the standardized HACCP recipe) for roasting the rib. The importance of following the procedure during cooking is especially important here. Portion costs are determined by the final cooked weight. You want to be able to sell every possible ounce.

Remember, this product has already been paid for. Some of it has been lost because of trimming. The goal now is *to control the cooking process so there is minimal shrinkage and moisture loss during cooking.* Using an inappropriate cooking method or not carefully controlling the internal temperature of the rib will change the final yield and leave fewer servings of rib to sell.

After the rib is cooked, it is weighed. The weight is recorded on the **Cooking Loss Test form**. This form looks mysteriously like the Butcher Test form, except that the name and a few of the terms have been changed. The Cooking Loss Test form is handled in exactly the same way as the Butcher Test form, except *the meat is now cooked instead of raw.* The bottom of the form will reveal the *final servable amount of rib available to generate dining-room sales:*

COOKING LOSS TEST		Prepared By:		Date:	
Item: NAMP 109C USDA Choice Rib—Cooked					
Amount Available: 22 lb. 8 oz. (Raw Weight)				**Cost per Pound:** $5.82 lb. **Cost per Portion:** $4.37	
Cooked Weight: 17 lb.				**Portion Size:** 12 oz.	

Item	Yield %	Quantity	×	Unit Price	=	Extended Price
Cooked Rib	100%	17 lb. Weight after cooking		$5.25 ($89.30/17 = $5.25)		$89.30 (From Butcher Test)
Cooked Trims						
Scrap	5.8%	1 lb.		No value		0
Trimmings for soup	5.8%	1 lb.	×	$2.00/lb.		$2.00 (subtract) from $89.30)
Servable Rib (Edible portion)	88.2%	**15 lb.** (17 lbs. − 2 lbs = 15 lbs.)		**$5.82/lb.** ($87.30/15 = $5.82)		$87.30 ($89.30 − $2.00 = $87.30)

When all is said and done, there are **15 pounds** of product available to generate revenue as the menu item Roast Prime Rib. This is 100% servable. No more loss is expected. This 15 pounds has a per-pound cost of **$5.82**. What about the portion cost? How is that determined? Check the standard recipe. The recipe identifies the portion size. Suppose the recipe and menu description state a 12-ounce portion. Knowing the cost per pound makes it very easy to determine the portion cost (Figure 3.10).

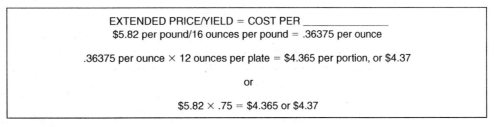

EXTENDED PRICE/YIELD = COST PER _____
$5.82 per pound/16 ounces per pound = .36375 per ounce

.36375 per ounce × 12 ounces per plate = $4.365 per portion, or $4.37

or

$5.82 × .75 = $4.365 or $4.37

FIGURE 3.10   Using the MMP formula to determine the portion cost.

By now you may recognize that 12 ounces is ¾ of a pound, and this alternative method can be used to determine the portion cost.

Using the **Q Factor** ($1.13) and **Spice Factor** (10%) and **food cost percentage** (30%) from the previous examples, continue on to determine the **Minimum Menu Price** for this rib dinner:

USING THE MMP FORMULA TO DETERMINE THE MINIMUM MENU PRICE FOR THE RIB

COST PER PORTION + Q = COST PER DISH

$4.37 + $1.13 = $5.50

(Rib)

COST PER DISH × 1.SF% = TRUE COST PER DISH

$5.50 × 1.10 = $6.05

TRUE COST PER DISH/FC% = MINIMUM MENU PRICE

$6.05/.30 = $20.17

Some Butcher Test and Cooking Loss Test forms also have a space to record the **cost per ounce**. This is handy when finding sell prices for different portion sizes of rib.

The Cost per Portion Is Too High!   A high portion cost will calculate out to a high selling price. This price may not fit the profile of the operation. Here are some options, but as always, care must be taken.

1. Study the recipe or plate card for product substitutions or new products that decrease the portion cost but do not significantly change the item. Suppliers are very good resources. The rule here is not to change the taste or appearance of the item.

2. Decrease the portion size. This approach is always dangerous, especially if this is a signature dish or the operation's reputation is about large portion sizes.

3. Rearrange the plate presentation with new sides (and portion sizes), while decreasing the portion size. Then, give the item a new name. This can work well but must be done very carefully. In the case of a signature dish, this may not be an effective strategy.

4. Purchase a lower quality product. Generally, this is not in the best interest of the business unless the ingredient is chopped up and mixed into something else or the level of quality purchased is too high for the product being produced. Good sleuthing as to the correct product to purchase for the menu item should eliminate the need to pursue this option. Purchasing a lower quality rib in the example just discussed would probably not work or be cost effective, as the yield of the alternative product would probably be less than the original product. **A GENERAL RULE:** If the item is the primary taste sensation, don't touch the quality! If it is a product that is mixed in, research possibilities that include purchasing a substitute of lower quality.

5. Confer with employees. Use your staff as a resource. Their input may be valuable in identifying ways to eliminate waste or change a procedure that increases yield or decreases cost.

Congratulations again! You have now learned how to find the portion cost and subsequent selling price for all types of menu items.

The Triangle of Enlightenment

We will complete our work in this chapter by covering one last topic. Many a cost control student has been stymied by the next three formulas. These are important, however, because they are used almost daily. The **Triangle of Enlightenment** is a great way to remember them. The Triangle is aptly named because many a cost control scholar has proclaimed profound enlightenment in dealing with these formulas once exposed to the triangle model. The three formulas are shown in Figure 3.11.

COST $$/COST % = SALES $$ OR SELL PRICE

COST $$/SALES $$ = COST %

SALES $$ × COST % = COST $$

FIGURE 3.11   Triangle of Enlightenment formulas.

These universal formulas are used by foodservice managers near and far. As a matter of fact, one of these formulas was used within the Minimum Menu Price (MMP) formula you saw earlier. Recall that in order to generate the MMP, the true Cost per Portion was divided by the Food Cost %. That formula is the first one in Figure 3.11.

In the Triangle, Cost $$ is at the top because it is the numerator in two of the equations. The lower part, or denominator, shows Sales and Cost %. By positioning these 3 elements as shown in Figure 3.12, you can work the Triangle to get an answer to any problem. As long as you remember that Costs are on top, the rest is easy.

Net Work

Check Chef Desk at www.chefdesk.com. Click *The Book of Yields* and view some sample screens. Click on Online Foodservice Calculators and try the costing calculator.

Working with the Triangle

To use the Triangle, put your hand over what you are looking for, and the Triangle will reveal the answer! Notice that *the two factors that are a part of the equation generate the third factor, which is left.* Follow the pattern around the Triangle (Figure 3.12).

PUT YOUR HAND OVER WHAT YOU ARE LOOKING FOR AND THE TRIANGLE WILL REVEAL THE ANSWER!

COST $$/SALES $$ = COST %
SALES $$ × COST % = COST $$
COST $$/COST % = SALES $$

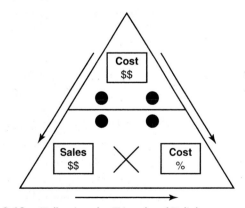

FIGURE 3.12   Following the Triangle of Enlightenment.

The First Equation: COST $$/SALES $$ = COST %

Consider the first equation in the Triangle of Enlightenment. It is used to determine cost percentages for a multitude of situations:

$$COST \ \$\$/SALES \ \$\$ = COST \ \%$$

This determines the part of all the sales dollars needed to pay for whatever it is that is being measured. One use of this equation is to measure an expense's proportion of sales. Another use is to determine a plates' actual food cost percentage. Yet another is to determine actual cost percentages for expenses versus budget. To a manager, this simple equation reveals the overall health of a business through reports such as profit and loss statements. It is one of the most widely used equations in any business.

Examples   According to the calculations done earlier, Salmon a la Griglia should sell for $14.23. Assume the actual menu price is $16.95. We know from the costing work we've done that the TCPD is $4.27. Using the Triangle of Enlightenment, calculate the **actual food cost percentage** for this dish:

COST $$/SALES $$ = COST %
$4.27/$16.95 = 25.19%

What does this mean? It means that it takes 25.19% (about ¼) of the *sales dollars generated by this dish* to pay for the *raw food product needed to produce this food item.* Here's another way to look at it: It takes about .25 instead of the budgeted .30 from each dollar of the sales price to cover the cost of the food to produce this dish.

In the costing examples discussed earlier, **30%** was determined to be *the budgeted food cost percentage,* and that was the percent used to generate the Minimum Menu Price. This means that management has determined that 30% of the dollar sales from a product is to be budgeted to provide the raw food product for a menu item. Management has also determined that this 30% is *adequate to purchase the quantity and quality of product that distinguishes that operation's dining experience from a competitor's.*

A reduced food cost percentage means it takes a lesser proportion of the sales dollars to pay for the food needed to produce the item. What this really means is that management likes it when guests choose Salmon a la Griglia because it is priced higher than the minimum, thus reducing its per plate cost percentage! Because this item can be sold for more than the calculated Minimum Menu Price, there will automatically be more dollars available for profit, as long as all other expenses remain in line with the budget.

Practice a few:

Menu Item	TCPD	Actual Sell Price	Cost %
Chicken Noodle Soup	$ .44	$ 1.50	
Pizza	1.89	8.95	
Farfalle Arrabbiata	3.10	17.95	
Cioppino	7.24	22.95	

Note: Remember two rules when recording cost percentages:

1. Do not round cost percentages up or down. They are what they are.

2. Record two places after the decimal and stop.

Here are the answers:

Menu Item	TCPD	Actual Sell Price	Cost %
Chicken Noodle Soup	$ .44	$ 1.50	29.33
Pizza	1.89	8.95	21.11
Farfalle Arrabbiata	3.10	17.95	17.27
Cioppino	7.24	22.95	31.54

You can also use this formula to interpret income statement information. Although budgets and income statements are covered later, a short demonstration of the use of the formula is included here.

Suppose the labor cost for Farfalle Arrabbiata was $30,000 for the month. Sales for the month were $100,000. Using the formula, the labor cost percentage for the month is:

$$\text{COST \$\$/SALES \$\$} = \text{COST \%}$$

$$\$30,000/\$100,000 = 30\%$$

What this reveals is that *30% of all the dollars brought in were needed to cover just the payroll for this month.* Now a manager would want to know what the budgeted labor cost percentage is. Knowing the budgeted percentage allows management to compare budget to actual and determine if there is a problem.

Assume that the budgeted labor cost percentage for Farfalle Arrabbiata is 28%. If that were the case, too much money was spent on labor—2% more. Because every expense has a standard, overspending in one area while spending to budget in all others means that in order to pay all the bills, profit dollars will have to be used.

Percentages are used because they show proportion and give meaning to the dollars. Knowing you spent $30,000 on payroll this month, $35,000 last month, and $33,000 the month before is almost meaningless. They are just dollar values. Until these values are compared with the sales dollars for each month, there is not much that can be said other than payroll was $30,000 this month. Management doesn't know if this is good or bad.

By turning the data into percentages, however, seemingly unrelated values can be compared and evaluated. By this we mean that each month's labor cost percentage can be calculated, and meaningful comparisons can be made.

Practice a few:

Expense	Expense Dollars	Sales Dollars	Cost %
Rent	$ 5,650	$100,000	
Food & Beverage	30,525	100,000	
Utilities	4,575	100,000	
Repair & Maintenance	2,830	100,000	

Here are the answers:

Expense	Expense Dollars	Sales Dollars	Cost %
Rent	$ 5,650	$100,000	5.65
Food & Beverage	30,525	100,000	30.52
Utilities	4,575	100,000	4.57
Repair & Maintenance	2,830	100,000	2.83

The Second Equation: SALES $$ × COST % = COST $$

Let's look at the second equation in the Triangle of Enlightenment:

$$\text{SALES \$\$} \times \text{COST \%} = \text{COST \$\$}$$

This equation helps managers determine:

1. How much money is available for something—usually an expense.

2. How much should be spent on raw food cost.

Examples

Management has identified the following cost percentages as budget targets for this month. Assume monthly sales are forecasted at $100,000. Using the formula, it is easy to determine how much money is allocated for each.

Expense	Sales	Cost %	Cost $
Rent	$100,000	5.25	
Food & Beverage	100,000	32	
Utilities	100,000	4.25	
Repair & Maintenance	100,000	2.28	
Payroll	100,000	30	

Here are the answers:

Expense	Sales	Cost %	Cost $
Rent	$100,000	5.25	$ 5,250
Food & Beverage	100,000	32	32,000
Utilities	100,000	4.25	4,250
Repair & Maintenance	100,000	2.28	2,280
Payroll	100,000	30	30,000

Try these:

Menu Item	Actual Sell Price	Standard Food Cost %	Cost $
Chicken Noodle Soup	$ 1.50	30	
Pizza Al Forno	8.95	30	
Farfalle Arrabbiata	17.95	30	
Cioppino	22.95	30	

Here are the answers:

Menu Item	Actual Sell Price	Standard Food Cost %	Cost $
Chicken Noodle Soup	$ 1.50	30	$ .45
Pizza Al Forno	8.95	30	2.69
Farfalle Arrabbiata	17.95	30	5.39
Cioppino	22.95	30	6.89

The Third Equation: COST $$/COST % = SALES $$

The last formula is familiar. It is the last line of the **Minimum Menu Price** formula. It is used to *determine a sell price based on the standard food cost percentage.* Other menu pricing methods, and there are a few, will be covered in a later chapter.

Practice these, using a variety of cost percentages:

Menu Item	TCPD	Cost %	Sell Price
Minestrone Soup	$ .55	30	
Calzone Luna	.62	25	
Insalata Gorgonzola	.83	31	
Rack of Lamb	5.52	29	

Here are the answers:

Menu Item	TCPD	Cost %	Sell Price
Minestrone Soup	$ .55	30	$ 1.84
Calzone Luna	.62	25	2.48
Insalata Gorgonzola	.83	31	2.68
Rack of Lamb	5.52	29	19.03

These formulas are used repeatedly throughout the remaining chapters. Mastering them here will make your work easier later on.

*N*et Work

Explore the following Web sites:
www.phoenixscale.com
www.advancedhospitality.com
www.calcmenu.com
www.micros.com
www.cbord.com
www.squirrelsystem.com

Chapter Wrap

The Chapter ✓ at the beginning of the chapter posed several questions. Review the questions and compare your responses with the following answers:

1. **How are portion costs for menu items determined?**

   Standardized recipes are used for menu items with multiple ingredients and little or no shrinkage or trim. The portion cost for these menu items is found by using a standard Cost Card to calculate the cost of one serving using the approved standardized recipe. Plate Cost Cards are used to cost one completed meal as it is served to the guest. A Butcher Test and Cooking Loss Test may be used to find portion costs for items with trim and cooking loss before portioning.

2. **Why use a Butcher Test? A Cooking Loss Test?**

   A Butcher Test is used to find the Cost per Portion for menu items that have loss due to trimming. The concept of butchering is to determine what is actually servable after trimming. These menu items may be portioned, cooked, and served, or the item may be roasted and only portioned after final cooking. The concept of cooking loss is to measure what is left after the cooking process has taken place. A Cooking Loss Test is used for menu items that will experience shrinkage, trimming, and other loss during the cooking process. These items are only portioned after cooking. Using these tools to determine Cost per Portion will ensure that product lost through trimming, cooking, and portioning are calculated into the selling price.

3. **What is a yield percentage (%)? A waste percentage (%)?**

   The yield percentage tells how much of a whole product (100%) is left to sell to a guest as a specific menu item. It is calculated by the following formula: PART/WHOLE = YIELD %. The difference (100% − YIELD %) is called the waste percentage (%). Waste is not servable to a guest and is factored into the portion cost.

4. How high can portion costs be managed?

There are several approaches to solving this problem: Study the Recipe and/or Plate Card for product substitutions or new products that will decrease the portion cost but will not significantly change the item. Decrease the portion size. (This is always dangerous, however, especially if this is the signature dish or the operation's reputation is for the portion sizes.) Rearrange the plate picture with new sides (and portion sizes), and decrease the portion size. Then, give the item a new name. This can work well but must be done very carefully. In the case of a signature dish, however, this may not be an effective strategy. Purchase a lower quality product. Generally, this is not in the best interest of the business unless the ingredient is chopped up and mixed into something else, or the level of quality you are purchasing is too high for the product being produced. Confer with employees. Use your staff as a resource. Their input may be valuable in identifying ways that waste can be eliminated or a procedure can be changed to increase yield, and so on.

5. What are the primary uses for the formulas in the Triangle of Enlightenment?

- COST \$\$/SALES \$\$ = COST %

This equation is used to determine cost percentages for a multitude of situations. The equation determines what part of all the sales dollars are needed to pay for whatever it is that is being measured. One way to use this equation is to measure expenses' proportion of sales. Another use is to determine a plate's actual food cost percentage. Yet another is to determine actual cost percentages for expenses versus budget. This simple equation reveals the overall health of a business to a manager through reports like profit and loss statements. It is one of the most widely used equations in any business.

- COST \$\$/COST % = SELLING PRICE \$\$

This equation is one of the most common ways to determine menu sales prices. Of all the possible menu pricing formulas, this one is the most widely used.

- SALES \$\$ × COST % = COST \$\$

This formula is used to determine cost parameters for menu items. It is also used on income statements.

Key Terminology and Concepts in This Chapter

à la carte
à la carte pricing
AP (as purchased)
Butchering
Butcher Test
Computing extensions
Cooking loss
Cooking Loss (Test) form
Cooking Loss Test
Cost Card
Cost \$\$/Cost % = Sales \$\$
Cost per ounce
Cost \$\$/Sales \$\$ = Cost %
Cost per dish
Cost per Portion

Cost per pound
EP (edible portion)
EP/AP = Yield %
Extended price
Extending the recipe
Food cost percentage (%)
Invoice cost
Invoice unit
Minimum Menu Price (MMP)
Operating Cycle of Control
Oven-ready
Portion costing
Purchasing units
Q Card
Q Factor

Recipe Cost Card
Recipe extension
Recipe units
Sales $$ × Cost % = Cost $$
Semi-à-la-carte pricing
Spice Factor (SF)
Triangle of Enlightenment

True Cost Per Dish (TCPD)
Unit price
Yield
Yield percentage (%)
Yield test
Waste percentage (%)

Discussion Questions and Exercises

1. Discuss the connection between standardized recipes and standardized portion costs.

2. Describe the implications of inaccurate portion sizes.

3. Explain the distinction between recipe units and purchasing (invoice) units.

4. This is your first function as a new manager at Farfalle Arrabbiata. The event is not too complicated. Dinner and speakers are lined up. There are 300 diners from the Association of Split Pea Soup Makers. You have been working on the details with Mr. Peter Soup. The first course is—Chicken Noodle Soup, of course! The soup is an award-winning favorite at Farfalle Arrabbiata. A server inadvertently retrieved the wrong size ladle to serve the soup. A 12-ounce ladle was used instead of the 10-ounce ladle. The original recipe/Cost Card combo makes 25 ten-ounce servings, at a total recipe cost of $10.00. According to the costing work earlier in the chapter, this serving size costs $.40. Adding the Spice Factor of 10%, the TCPD jumped to $.44 per serving.

   a. At about what point or guest count during the service do you realize you have a problem?

   b. How many people aren't getting Chicken Noodle Soup?

   c. Per the original recipe, how many 12-ounce bowls can be portioned out of the approximately 2 gallons of soup?

   d. What will the portion cost be for the 12-ounce bowl, including the 10% Spice Factor?

   e. Assume you were able to dig up enough soup to ultimately feed all 300 guests. (You have to continue serving the 12-ounce serving sizes.) Determine the overall financial implications of this error in terms of actual cost versus standard cost. What is the cost difference per bowl?

   f. As a manager, develop SOPs to prevent this from happening again.

   g. Suppose you could not dig up more Chicken Noodle Soup and you had to substitute Minestrone Soup. How would you explain this situation to the affected guests. What would you say to Mr. Soup?

   h. What are the cost implications when you realize that Minestrone has a TCPD of $.62 per serving?

   i. Mrs. Soup (Mr. Soup's wife) had her heart set on the Chicken Noodle Soup. She had read rave reviews in the food section of the local paper, and all of her friends were talking about it. She was seated at one of the tables that did not get Chicken Noodle Soup. As a manager, what would you do?

   j. The pricing for this function was à la carte—every course was priced separately. The soup was quoted at a sell price of $1.50. What was the actual food cost percentage for the soup, given the 12-ounce serving?

   k. If Farfalle Arrabbiata operates at a standard 30% food cost, what should the sell price have been, given the 12-ounce portion size?

5. Cost out the following recipes and determine the portion cost and sell price for Farfalle Arrabbiata. The Q Factor for this dish is $.42, because no starch is needed. The Spice Factor is 10%. The food cost percentage is 33.6%.

Recipe Name: Pasta Dough			Type of Recipe: Fresh Pasta			Spice Factor % = NA
Date: 8/2XXX			File Code: Pasta 1			Q Factor = NA
# of Servings: 4 lb.			Cost per Portion:			FC% = NA
Portion Size: NA						
Recipe		*Ingredients*	*Invoice*		*Recipe*	*Extension*
Amount	Unit		Cost	Unit	Cost	Unit	
2½	lb.	Semolina flour	$13.92	50 lb.			
1	Tbsp.	Olive oil	12.80	qt.	SF		
½	oz.	Salt	.34	lb.	SF		
15	each	Eggs, whole	40.50	30 doz.			
					Recipe Cost		
					Cost per Pound (CPP)		
					CPP + Q = CPD		NA
					CPD × 1.SF% = TCPD		NA
					TCPD/FC% = MMP		**NA**

Recipe Name: Pomodoro Sauce			Type of Recipe: Sauce			Spice Factor % = NA
Date: 8/2XXX			File Code: Sauces – 15			Q Factor = NA
# of Servings: 1½ gal.			Cost per Portion:			FC% = NA
Portion Size: NA						
Recipe		*Ingredients*	*Invoice*		*Recipe*	*Extension*
Amount	Unit		Cost	Unit	Cost	Unit	
10	lb.	Roma tomatoes	$14.96	10 lb.			
1	c.	Brown stock	1.50	gal.			
1	c.	White wine	4.75	25 oz.			
2	Tbsp.	Garlic oil	4.69	qt.	SF		SF
1	head	Garlic, fresh	1.10	lb./12 hd.	SF		SF
1½	tsp.	Salt	1.10	24 oz.	SF		SF
1½	tsp.	Pepper, black	2.69	lb.	SF		SF
3	each	Bay leaves	5.89	lb.	SF		SF
1	Tbsp.	Basil, fresh	18.75	12 bunches	SF		SF
⅓	oz.	Chili flakes	4.69	lb.	SF		SF
2	Tbsp.	Parsley, fresh	16.80	24 bunches	SF		SF
					Recipe Cost		
					Cost per Gallon		
					CPP + Q = CPD		NA
					CPD × 1.SF% = TCPD		NA
					TCPD/FC% = MMP		**NA**

Recipe Name: Farfalle Arrabbiata			Type of Recipe: Entrée				Spice Factor % = 10%
Date: 8/2XXX			File Code: Entrée – 8				Q Factor = .42
# of Servings: 20			Cost per Portion:				FC% = 33.6
Portion Size: 10 ounces							

Recipe		Ingredients	Invoice		Recipe		Extension
Amount	**Unit**		**Cost**	**Unit**	**Cost**	**Unit**	
5½	lb.	Bowtie pasta (Pasta recipe above)					
1½	gal.	Pomodoro Sauce (Sauce recipe above)					
1¾	lb.	Peppers, green	$ 31.50	22 lb.			
1¾	lb.	Peppers, red	29.85	11 lb.			
1	12 oz. bottle	Olives, Calamata	39.84	12-12 oz. bottles			
2½	lb.	Mushrooms, button	17.80	10 lb.			
5½	oz.	Cheese, Parmesan	45.40	10 lb.			
6¼	lb.	Shrimp, 16/20 count	412.50	50 lb.			
½	bunch	Parsley	16.80	24 bunches			
40	each	Bread sticks	.02	each			
					Rec. Cost/# of Servings		
					Cost per Portion (CPP)		
					CPP + Q = CPD		
					CPD × 1.SF% = TCPD		
					TCPD/FC% = MMP		

 6. Chef Raoul purchases whole beef tenderloins, NAMP #189. The most recent invoice shows one tenderloin weighed 7½ pounds. Invoice cost was $7.85. Three pounds of fat was removed and thrown away. Using the Butcher Test form below, compute the cost per pound for the tenderloin after trimming. Comment on your findings.

BUTCHER TEST			**Prepared By:**			**Date:**
Item: NAMP 189 Whole Tenderloin		**Invoice Cost:** $7.85 lb.				
Amount Purchased: 7½ lb.						
Item	**Yield %**	**Quantity**	×	**Unit Price**	=	**Extended Price**
Tenderloin	100%	7½ lb.	×	$7.85	=	$
Raw Trims						
Total trimmed wt. =						
Raw trimmed tenderloin						

7. Compute the Cost per Portion and subsequent selling price for the tenderloin using the following information.

    Portion size = 9 ounce

    Q Factor = $1.13

    Spice Factor = 10%

    Food cost percentage = 33.6

8. Chef Raoul has been doing some research on tenderloins. He has purchased the following item and is performing a Butcher Test in order to compare this item to the product just discussed. The product purchased was a 7-pound Pismo Tenderloin. There was ¾ of a pound of fat that was thrown away. He has given you the following information because he doesn't like to fill out forms. Compute the cost per pound, evaluate both items, and recommend the best item to purchase.

BUTCHER TEST		Prepared By:				Date:
Item: NAMP Whole Tenderloin—Pismo, defatted						
Amount Purchased: 7 lb.		**Invoice Cost:** $9.95 per lb.				
Item	**Yield %**	**Quantity**	**×**	**Unit Price**	**=**	**Extended Price**
Tenderloin	100%	7 lbs.	×	$9.95		$
Raw Trims						
Total trimmed wt. =						
Raw trimmed tenderloin						

Compute the Cost per Portion and subsequent selling price for this product using the following information.

Portion size = 9 ounces

Q Factor = $1.13

Spice Factor = 10%

Food cost percentage = 33.6

9. Chef Raoul has also been busy working on rib costs. He purchased a forequarter that he is getting ready to butcher into usable products. The final product removed from this item will be an oven-ready rib. He is going to compare this item to an Oven-Ready 109 Rib, which is what he normally purchases. Chef has a use for all the trimmed products from the forequarter. He is interested in seeing which is the better purchase. The following is a list of raw trims and unit prices for the forequarter. Complete the form for Chef and determine the amount, unit price, and yield percentage for the Oven-Ready Rib.

    Forequarter 81 lb.   Invoice cost = $4.50

Raw Trims

Ground beef	18 lb. @ $1.89 lb.
Stew meat	13 lb. @ $2.25 lb.

Fat	10 lb. @ $.20 lb.
Briskets	12 lb. @ $1.95 lb.
Scrap	4 lb.

BUTCHER TEST		**Prepared By:**				**Date:**
Item: Forequarter						
Amount Purchased: 81 lb.		**Invoice Cost:** $4.50 lb.				
Item	**Yield %**	**Quantity**	**×**	**Unit Price**	**=**	**Extended Price**
Forequarter	100 %	81 lb.		$4.50		
Raw Trims						
Total trimmed wt. =						
Oven-ready rib						

10. Chef removed 4 pounds of scrap from the Oven-Ready 109 Rib discussed on the following Butcher Test form. Determine the yield and cost per pound for this product.

BUTCHER TEST		**Prepared By:**				**Date:**
Item: NAMP 109 Oven-Ready Rib						
Amount Purchased: 25 lb.		**Invoice Cost:** $9.95 lb.				
Item	**Yield %**	**Quantity**	**×**	**Unit Price**	**=**	**Extended Price**
Rib	100%	25 lb.	×	$9.95		$
Raw trims						
Total trimmed wt. =						
Oven-ready rib						

11. Which of the two items is the better purchase?

12. Why is it not really possible to say which is the better purchase at this point?

13. To completely analyze each product, a Cooking Loss Test has to be performed on each item. Chef Raoul is not fond of forms, so you volunteer to fill out the Cooking Loss charts for him. He has given you the following information. Compute the cost for each product after roasting. Each was roasted under the same conditions. Remember to bring down the final Extended Price from the Butcher Tests used in Exercises 9 and 10. Calculate the yield percentage of raw to cooked for each product.

COOKING LOSS TEST		Prepared By:				Date:
Item: Butchered Rib from Forequarter						
Amount Available: 24 lb. (Raw Weight from Butcher Test)		**Cost per Pound:** **Cost per Portion:**				
Cooked Weight: 22 lb.		**Portion Size:** 12 oz.				
Item	**Yield %**	**Quantity**	**×**	**Unit Price**	**=**	**Extended Price**
Cooked Rib	100 %	22 lb.				
Cooked Trims						
Fat – Scrap		2 lb.				
Servable Rib						

COOKING LOSS TEST		Prepared By:				Date:
Item: NAMP 109C USDA Choice Rib—Cooked						
Amount Available: 21 lb. (Raw Weight)		**Cost per Pound:** **Cost per Portion:**				
Cooked Weight: 17 lb.		**Portion Size:** 12 oz.				
Item	**Yield %**	**Quantity**	**×**	**Unit Price**	**=**	**Extended Price**
Cooked Rib	100%	17 lb.				
Cooked Trims						
Fat – Scrap		1 lb.				
Servable Rib						

14. Which is the better purchase now?

15. Compute the Cost per Portion and Minimum Menu Price for each item after cooking (Q Factor = $1.13; Spice Factor = 10%; Food cost percentage = 33.6).

Triangle of Enlightenment Exercises

16. Annual sales at Farfalle Arrabbiata were $1,522,000. Targeted labor cost percentage is 30%. How much was the labor budget for this year?

17. Actual labor cost for Farfalle Arrabbiata came in at $486,000. What is the actual labor cost percentage at the level of sales listed in Exercise 16?

18. Cioppino sells for $22.95 on the menu. Food cost is 28%. How much should it cost to produce this item?

19. You have been recosting recipes and realize that the actual TCPD for this dish is $6.85. What is the actual food cost percentage for the Cioppino?

20. Calculate what the real sell price for the Cioppino should be, given its actual TCPD and the current selling price.

21. Cioppino is wildly popular at Farfalle Arrabbiata. What is the financial impact of this situation? As a manager, how will you address this? What are some possible solutions?

Learning Objectives

After reading this chapter and completing the discussion questions and exercises, you should be able to:

1. Describe the purchasing functions (the Five Rights) integral to any foodservice operation.

2. Recognize the role the purchasing functions play in the Cycle of Control.

3. Define quality in terms of products and services used in foodservice operations.

4. Write detailed specifications for products and services.

5. Recognize the complexity in selecting the correct food products for an operation.

6. Select the correct product to purchase by completing a Make-or-Buy Analysis (MOBA).

About Purchasing

The Menu

Pre-Purchase Functions

GUEST CHECK
Sales history, turnover, average check, cash management, revenue forecasting & budgeting, menu item analysis

STANDARDIZED RECIPES
Standard ingredients, portion size, quality, consistency, quantity, purchasing

GUESTS
Greeting, seating, sales, serving, busing, payment, comment cards

COST CARDS
Portion costs, yield factors, sell prices

SPECIFICATIONS
Product descriptions

FOH Functions

KITCHEN PRODUCTION
Production schedules, portion tracking, recipe control, serving controls, food safety

PAR STOCK
Inventory levels, order building

REQUISITION
Order building, purchasing

PRODUCT ISSUING
Requisitions, transfers, daily & monthly costs, food cost percentage

SHOPPING LISTS
Call sheets, bid sheets, suppliers, bidding

STORAGE PRACTICES & INVENTORY MANAGEMENT
Best practices, sanitation, security, inventory methods

PURCHASE ORDERS
Security, ship order, price guarantee, contract

INVOICE MANAGEMENT
Payment, price checking, security

BOH Functions

RECEIVING ACTIVITIES
Best practices, invoices, security, sanitation

Chapter Map

About Purchasing

The Purchasing Functions, or "The Five Rights"

- Purchasing the Right Product
- In the Right Quantity
- From the Right Supplier
- At the Right Price
- Delivered at the Right Time

Chapter Map (Continued)

About Purchasing the Right Quality

- Decide the Menu Concept
- Create an Inventory List
- Develop Product Specifications

Bidding & Specifications

- Why Write Specifications?
- Writing a Specification
- Where to Get Information for Writing Product Specs

- Writing Sample Product Specs
- Specifying Services for a Foodservice Operation

Make or Buy? The Make-or-Buy Analysis

- Outcomes of Using Value-Added Foods
- How to Do a Make-or-Buy Analysis
- Evaluating Portion Costs
- One Last Alternative: Outsourcing

Chapter ✓

Check the chapter content for the answers to these questions:

1. What does purchasing mean?
2. How does a buyer determine product quality?
3. Why are specifications written for services?
4. How can a buyer compare similar products?

About Purchasing

For some foodservice operations, the primary role of the buyer is to ensure that the operation has all the food, beverage, and nonfood items required. This role, however, is only part of the function of the buyer. In addition to being the purchasing agent, it's quite likely the buyer is also the unit manager or even the owner. As such, a comprehensive purchasing system is needed to get the job done effectively and efficiently. Who actually does the buying in an operation depends on the organizational size and sales volume of the foodservice operation.

In the past, the buyer (who could have been the steward, chef, dietician, food and beverage manager, or owner) had little choice when buying products. Not so in today's marketplace. Today's buyer is faced with the challenge of sifting through all the different options available and deciding which to actually use in an operation. Improvements in technology, including the use of the Internet, product availability and variety, and improved distribution systems all play a role in how foodservice operators go about their purchasing responsibilities. The *financial plan for the operation, guest expectations,* and *final EP cost* are always in the forefront of the buyer's mind when it comes to purchasing decisions.

If you add the following considerations, the job becomes even more complicated:

- The desired quality of the final product
- The skill level of employees
- The cost of the product
- The overall cost of production
- Storage space allocation
- Equipment required
- Building costs
- Labor costs
- Customer acceptance
- Selling price and average check

Each of these influences affect product selection. Buyers weigh the impact of each in order to select the best product for the job at hand.

Every day, the average foodservice establishment uses hundreds of products. The buyer is charged with making product decisions based on obtaining the best-quality product as defined by operating standards at the lowest possible price. The next steps in the Operating Cycle of Control (Chapter 1) navigate through these principles.

The Purchasing Functions, or "The Five Rights"

Once the menu selection is set and the recipes are standardized, the next task in the Operational Cycle of Control becomes purchasing. The mission for the chef, manager, buyer, or owner is this:

> *To purchase the right product (or service), in the right quantity, from the right supplier, at the right price, and have it delivered at the right time.*

These are known as the **"Five Rights"** (Figure 4.1) and as simplistic as the displayed sentence may sound, the essence of purchasing boils down to these five activities. Anyone actively engaged in purchasing products and services knows that getting all of these elements to work together like a well-oiled machine is an art.

Figure 4.2 displays the content of the "Five Rights" as they will be covered in this chapter and the next two chapters. Once complete, the next step in purchasing is to receive, store, issue, and process invoices. These topics follow in Chapter 7.

The first function, **Purchasing the Right Product**, is covered in this chapter. A discussion of functions 2 through 5 follow, in Chapters 5 and 6. To set the stage, however, a brief description of each function is offered here.

Purchasing the Right Product

Purchasing the right product depends on the purchaser's ability to define precisely the qualities of the product. In order to accomplish this, a specification or "spec" is developed for each product that needs to be purchased. **Specifications** *describe the precise characteristics of each product used in an operation.* These descriptions enable suppliers

THE FIVE *RIGHTS*

TO PURCHASE:
1. THE *RIGHT PRODUCT* IN
2. THE *RIGHT QUANTITY* FROM
3. THE *RIGHT SUPPLIER* AT
4. THE *RIGHT PRICE* AT
5. THE *RIGHT TIME*

FIGURE 4.1 The Five Rights of purchasing.

THE "FIVE RIGHTS," OR THE PURCHASING FUNCTIONS		
CHAPTER 4	**CHAPTER 5**	**CHAPTER 6**
THE RIGHT PRODUCT	THE RIGHT QUANTITY	THE RIGHT SUPPLIER, PRICE, & TIME
1. Specifications 2. Make-or-Buy Analysis	1. Popularity % 2. Par Stock 3. Order Sheets 4. Requisitions 5. Orders for Functions 6. Yield Analysis	1. Distribution Systems 2. Selecting a Supplier 3. Bid Systems 4. Bid/Call Sheets 5. Placing Orders 6. Purchase Orders 7. Supplier Prices 8. Yield Factors

FIGURE 4.2 Chapter content distribution for the purchasing functions.

to correctly fill orders. Without a specification, there is no guarantee that what was ordered is, in fact, the correct product for the menu item.

In the Right Quantity

Determining the **"right order size"** is the purchaser's next task. Numerous models exist to accomplish this. To find the correct order size, use some *methodology to determine the correct amount of product to order to carry the production from one delivery date to the next*. A system is needed to avoid over- or underordering. Find proper order levels by referring to accurate sales records and standard portion sizes (recipes).

From the Right Supplier

Reputable suppliers work with foodservice operators and see the relationship as a partnership. Finding suppliers who share this view requires fortitude and perseverance. It is critical to purchase from suppliers who provide quality products and services. To find the **"right supplier,"** management must "do its homework."

At the Right Price

Purchasing at the **"right price"** may not mean purchasing at the lowest price. The right price is the price that buys the desired level of quality in products and supplier services necessary to meet guest expectations and management goals. It is a function of many variables.

Delivered at the Right Time

Timely delivery of products is essential, to assure inventory levels are adequate to serve the expected level of customers. Generally, reputable suppliers will be regarded as such because they are reliable in delivery time, price, and overall service.

About Purchasing the Right Quality

To purchase a product of the **right quality**, you will need to follow three simple steps: *Decide the menu concept, create an inventory list or file, and develop product specifications*.

Step 1—Decide the Menu Concept

Quality is a perceived value. People often confuse quality with status. Thus, a fast-food hamburger chain is perceived as offering a certain level of quality and service, and an upscale fine-dining restaurant is perceived as offering another level of food quality and service. In reality, both deliver good-quality food and service *for the price paid*. The difference is in the quality of food each can afford to offer, the level of service each can afford to deliver, and the atmosphere each can provide for its guests' dining experience.

STEPS TO BUYING THE "RIGHT QUALITY"

1. **Decide the menu concept.**
2. Create an inventory list or file.
3. Develop product specifications.

The first step in developing **quality standards** is to *decide the type of food to be offered*. This decision is connected with understanding the foodservice concept that has been or will be chosen. For example, an operation designed to appeal to families with children that includes table service and a broad menu is logically a "family restaurant concept." Examples of this type of operation include Denny's, IHOP (International House of Pancakes), and Bickfords. Prices on the menu will be at a level that appeals to family clientele. The target market for Farfalle Arrabbiata is clearly the mid- to upscale customer. This is evidenced by the menu selections, menu prices, décor and ambiance, and level of service.

Regardless of the foodservice concept—Bickfords versus Farfalle Arrabbiata—a "quality food experience" is distinguished from a "nonquality food experience" by guest satisfaction in several areas:

- Product taste
- Quality of ingredients
- Portion size
- Methods of preparation
- Level of service
- Overall guest experience

A nonquality experience occurs when too many of these elements are violated, affecting the guests' experience. This problem is not a function of check average—we all know spending a lot of money dining out does not guarantee a quality experience. It just hurts more if the experience is nonquality!

Low cost does not necessarily mean low quality. It means the items served fit a specific cost parameter—the operation is purchasing the best product available for the budget. With most foodservice operations, food quality is a function of budgeted ingredient cost, combined with the cost of preparation (labor cost), or at least it should be.

All foodservice operations should strive to offer the highest quality menu items at a price that is appropriate for the quality and amount of food being served. This may seem like a paradox. After all, how can high quality be associated with moderately priced foods, such as those available at a Denny's or IHOP?

The answer is that the food offered should be as high a quality as possible in relationship to the menu price of the food. To achieve high quality, foodservice managers need to buy the highest quality ingredients they can afford and carefully control how each is handled once in-house. Standardized recipes and corresponding comprehensive ingredient specifications are two key control "tools" in the manager's toolbox.

Step 2—Create an Inventory List

The second step in the quest to develop quality standards is to realize that *standardized recipes create a comprehensive "shopping list" or inventory of all ingredients that need to be purchased.* This step can be called developing an **inventory list** or **inventory file**. Once this list is set, specifications can be written for each item needing to be purchased.

STEPS TO BUYING THE "RIGHT QUALITY"

1. Decide the menu concept.
2. **Create an inventory list or file.**
3. Develop product specifications.

The True Cost per Dish (TCPD), or plate cost, represents the final cost of the food served to each customer. This cost includes every ingredient listed on the standardized recipe. Every one of these products—from the main ingredients to herbs, spices, and garnishes (the Spice Factor) and side selections (the Q Factor)—has to be purchased. The place to start to assemble the inventory list is with standardized recipes.

Step 3—Develop Product Specifications

The third step is writing product specifications. **Specifications** are *detailed descriptions of products and services written to assist the buyer and the supplier in getting the right product (or service) to the operation.* Specifications describe a product that is the best fit from a quality and cost perspective. The product is not necessarily the most expensive or the least expensive or the best or the worst. It is simply the best fit, given the parameters a buyer has to work within.

STEPS TO BUYING THE "RIGHT QUALITY"

1. Decide the menu concept.
2. Create an inventory list or file.
3. **Develop product specifications.**

Specifications can have a number of different formats. They can be simple lists or complicated and lengthy biographies! For many operations, a simple list organized into a book format will get the job done. **Specification books**, or "spec books," *organize the inventory into traditional food categories: meats, poultry, seafood, produce, dairy, grocery, baked,* and so on. Tabbed sections sort the categories. Within each tab, items are alphabetized and then described. Subcategories are used when the inventory and menu selection is extensive. An example of using subcategories would be organizing the meat section into beef, veal, lamb, pork, and so on. Descriptions as used in spec books are generally referred to as **product specifications**. Today, computerized menu management systems have built-in programs to assist with specification development.

*B*idding and Specifications

If an operation uses a **bid process** to secure products and services, specifications will provide more than just product information. They will include the product description, plus very detailed information about payment terms, ship dates, delivery dates, cost, trade association standards, substitutions, delivery procedures, and much more. Normally, corporate purchasing staff develop this type of specification before negotiating complex national contracts to supply products to hundreds if not thousands of units. This is common in the chain and franchise business. The **bid procedure** at this level *ensures consistent supply levels of products at all locations at all times at an agreed upon price.*

Bids are usually written for a specific period of time (several months or a year) versus for a day or a week. During the bidding process, a buyer writes a detailed specification, commonly called an **RFP**, or **request for proposal**, which includes all necessary information, and circulates the bid via advertising, or his or her own supply network. Interested suppliers submit a proposal in answer to the RFP. The buyer then reviews the submissions and selects the supplier(s) who best meet the criteria. This process takes time. Large foodservice operators (e.g., multiunits, chains, and franchises), as well as many noncommercial foodservice operations such as school systems, healthcare facilities, and government foodservice programs, utilize this procedure to procure products. Buyers can also use less complicated versions of this process to secure products, services, and prices. Any business, regardless of size, can develop bid specs as a part of its purchasing activities and use the bid process to purchase products and services.

Why Write Specifications?

Without a doubt, *specifications are one of the primary control tools used to purchase products and services.* Creating them is time consuming and tedious, but given their usefulness, they are well worth the investment. Consider how useful such a tool can be when the buyer is unexpectedly out and an order for produce must be placed. Anybody can pick up the specification book, review the par sheets (to be discussed in Chapter 5), and know exactly what to order. This is one of the most valuable uses of a spec book.

Writing specs forces the chef or manager to consider the exact requirements for each product to be purchased. From a cost and quality perspective, specs force buyers to thoroughly research all possible choices in their quest to select the best possible product. Good research can lead to products that can be cross-utilized or products that are more cost effective from an EP and labor cost perspective. Specs speed up the ordering process—suppliers with your specifications always know exactly what is being ordered. Buyers spend less time chasing down items. It is also easy to see that specs eliminate mistakes and confusion between the supplier and the operator (Figure 4.3). From a receiving standpoint, specs reduce back-door errors and the amount of time staff spend keeping track of and returning products that are not right.

FIGURE 4.3 Specifications get the right product to an operation.

TOP 10 REASONS TO DEVELOP SPECIFICATIONS

1. "Chef, I had to use those funny green apples in the walk-in to make the apple pies for the banquet tonight. I couldn't find any of the red ones we usually use. I don't think anyone will notice since we peel the skin off."
2. "I said I needed 100 pounds of sliced onions, not sponges."
3. "Has anyone seen those 10 cases of Beluga caviar we received by mistake last week? The driver is here and has a slip to pick them up."
4. "Oh no. We've got a big problem in the restrooms. Wasn't the septic tank pumped out just last week? Don't we have 500 guests coming for a wedding this afternoon?"
5. "Chef, how many of those little tiny cans of tuna does it take to make up one of the great big cans of tuna that we usually use?"
6. "Chef, the produce driver tried to pull a fast one on me but I didn't fall for it. He wanted to deliver red leaf lettuce today. Imagine—red leaf lettuce. Everyone knows lettuce is green. Don't worry, though. I made him take it back. Who ever heard of red leaf lettuce? Do we have enough of the green stuff for the banquet this afternoon?"
7. "Chef, the meat guy called and said he was substituting a side of beef instead of one all cut up like you usually order. I said it was OK because I heard you say we were getting low on meat. I think Mary knows how to cut it up."
8. "Boy, these sure are little onions—it's going to take me all day to peel them. What happened to those big ones we usually get?"
9. "Boy, these sure are big pieces of cheese. It's going to take me all day to slice them. What happened to the presliced cheese we usually get?"
10. Your significant other showed up and wants to "help"!

Writing a Specification

Many pieces of information *could* be included in the spec, but what *should* be included is *all the information the supplier needs in order to ship the right product.* In an effort to keep it simple, write specs from that point of view—What does the supplier need to know to fill the order? If in doubt, ask the supplier directly. Suppliers can and should be used as resources to assist in preparing accurate specifications.

When writing specs, take care to be neither too specific nor not specific enough. This is sometimes referred to as having specs that are too "tight" or too "loose." Being too specific or tight would be including details that don't increase the value of the item sought but add cost. In other words, you are asking for something that the supplier will have to expend additional labor and effort on in order to meet your requirements. Of course, this cost will be passed directly on to you.

Too-Tight Specs   Suppose fresh sliced green beans are used on the house salad. The purchasing spec was written with the following requirement: Each green bean will be between 3″ and 3¼″ long. In order to meet this requirement, a supplier would have to appoint an employee with a ruler to measure out green beans just for you. Imagine the cost this requirement will add to an otherwise ordinary request for green beans. Not only does this request add cost, but it does not add any special value. The 3″ beans will not taste any different than 2½″ beans. It's obvious that this requirement is not necessary.

Too-Loose Specs   Likewise, the reverse situation can occur. Not being specific enough (too loose) means too many products can meet spec, none of which may be what is actually needed. Specifying that beans are needed, without giving an intended use or a color or variety, will net you any old beans the supplier has on hand, and he or she would not be wrong in shipping them.

Common Information on a Product Specification The following is the most common information found on a product specification.

COMMON INFORMATION ON A PRODUCT SPECIFICATION

- Name
- Intended use
- Quality characteristics
- Allowable substitutions
- Form
- Expiration dates
- Unit size
- Packaging information
- Cost parameters
- Trade association requirements
- Receiving procedures

Name The **name of the item** *should include all information that identifies the item to be purchased.* For example, if apples are to be used, the name of the item would be Apples, Red Delicious. The type or variety is always listed, as specifically as possible. The exact name can also include brand names. See the following examples:

- Lettuce, Romaine
- Onions, Vidalia
- Cheese, Mozzarella, fresh
- Bread, French
- Cracker, Oyster
- Flour, Semolina
- Ketchup, Heinz
- Cookies, Oreos
- Soup, Chicken Noodle, Campbell's
- Chicken, Purdue

Intended Use One of the most important lines on the spec—and the first piece of information after the item's name—is that item's **intended use**. This crucial piece of information *enables a supplier to consider usage of the item and to perhaps suggest an alternative product that will perform better and be more cost effective.* Check the examples below:

- Lettuce, Romaine–Intended use: Caesar Salad
- Onions, Vidalia–Intended use: Meatballs for Panino Polpetta
- Cheese, Mozzarella, fresh–Intended use: Antipasti (fresh mozzarella, Roma tomatoes, Calamata olives, Provolone, etc.)

A professional sales rep working closely with a buyer should notice the intended use for the Vidalia onions. A less expensive alternative—all-purpose Spanish onions—would do nicely for the meatballs. The onions are to be diced and mixed into the meatball mix and cooked in sauce, so there is no need to purchase this more expensive onion. There is only one exception: If the menu description notes that the meatballs are made with Vidalia onions, then they must, in fact, be used. In this case, Truth-in-Menu laws require that Vidalia onions be used in the meatballs.

Quality Characteristics   This is a very broad descriptor. Each product purchased has *quality descriptions that identify it.* Here are some ways that quality can be described:

- *Desired appearance,* such as crispness
- *Variety.* This is especially important and commonly used with fruits and vegetables (e.g., Rome apples, Valencia oranges, shitake mushrooms, Bosc pears, Beefeater tomatoes, Spanish onions).
- *Color*
- *Age*
- *Size*
- *U.S. quality grades.* **Quality grades** are *standards used by the United States Department of Agriculture (USDA).* Fruits, vegetables, meats (except fish), and many canned and processed food products are graded by the USDA. These standards may be obtained from regional offices of the U.S. Government Printing Office and are available in various pamphlets and books on food purchasing.
- *U.S. yield grades (meats).* These grades describe the fat/lean ratio of a product. Yield grades are important as the final yield impacts the EP cost of the product. Yield grades are described fully in the North American Meat Processors Guide. See below for information on this guide.
- *Point of origin.* It is important to include this to avoid issues with Truth in Menu laws (examples of point-of-origin information: Maine lobsters, Alaskan king crab, Australian beef, Gulf shrimp, etc.).
- *Ripeness*
- *Packing mediums.* Applies primarily to canned fruits, vegetables, tuna
- *Firmness*
- *Brand name or packer brand name.* Indicating a brand name or a packer's name is in and of itself an indication of quality. It also means that you accept this product's quality, and as such, spec writing becomes that much easier. Most broad-line foodservice distributors have their own label for most products. Using these products is usually more cost effective than specifying a brand name. A comparison analysis of similar products with different brand names will reveal which is the better purchase.

Allowable Substitutions   Suppliers find it helpful if management includes products deemed an *acceptable substitute* for the item on the spec. This information enables a supplier to ship an order with the substitute if the original product is unavailable, eliminating a potential backorder or shortage for the operation. This is particularly helpful when specifying brand-name items.

Form   **Form** *describes the product in some way other than how it is ordinarily packaged or bought.* Generally, describing a product with an alternative form means that someone else has processed the product in some way to make it easier to use. As such, expect that product form to cost more when purchased (it will have a higher **AP**, or *as purchased,* unit price). The additional cost covers the labor, packaging, or equipment needed to process the item. Buyers evaluate product form carefully to determine the best product to use. Often, small operators will use a processed form rather than spending funds to hire new staff to provide labor to process the larger, more economically priced form on the premises.

EXAMPLES OF FORM

- Cheese: Wheels, blocks, cubes, sliced, shredded, grated
- Juice: Fresh squeezed, made from concentrate, frozen, powdered, canned from concentrate, bottled, shelf-stable, or refrigerated
- Fruit: Fresh, sliced, diced, cubed, frozen, canned, dried
- Shrimp: Head on or off, shell on or off, easy peel and deveined, peeled, raw or cooked, fresh or frozen—IQF
- Ketchup: #10 cans, bottles (various sizes), portion-control pack—PC
- Carrots: Whole (various sizes), fresh (bunches, sticks, shredded, baby peeled), canned (various cuts and forms), frozen (various cuts and forms)
- Hamburgers: Bulk ground beef, fresh patties, frozen raw patties, frozen cooked patties
- Bread and rolls: Fresh (fully baked), frozen (fully baked), fresh-made dough, frozen dough, dough shaped into breads or rolls (ready to bake)

Expiration Dates   Expiration dates are especially important on dairy products and baked goods. Specs should include the minimum amount of time acceptable to serve the item to guests. Here are some examples:

- Yogurt: Minimum 2 weeks
- Cheeses: Minimum 30 days
- Milk and milk products: 2 weeks

Unit Size   **Unit size** is the *size of the purchasing unit*. Every product purchased has a unit size that is correct for the production volume. Contrary to popular belief, this is not necessarily the largest purchasing unit available, even if the AP price appears to be so. Because of the perishable nature of food, it is most cost effective to buy in a unit size that can be quickly turned over before it has to be thrown out. Here are a few examples of purchasing with unit size in mind:

- Purchasing a 25-pound wheel of cheddar cheese is more cost effective than purchasing only the number of pounds needed each time it is ordered. However, if the bulk of the cheese is lost because that quantity cannot be used before it spoils, then the purchasing unit was not right for that level of production.
- Buyers must be familiar with can sizes and purchase the correct can size for the item's usage (Figure 4.4). Only buying #10 cans because they are less expensive is a mistake if the product cannot be turned over before it spoils. Likewise,

FIGURE 4.4   Example of a #10 can (left) and a #303 can (right).

purchasing a unit that is too small for the production volume will increase final portion cost and the labor cost needed to work with the product.

Common Foodservice Can Sizes

Can Size	Equivalency in Volume	Case Pack
#300	1¾ c. (13½ fluid oz.)	24 - #300
#303	2 c. (15 fluid oz.)	24 - #303
#2	2½ c. (19 fluid oz.)	24 - #2
#2½	3½ c. (27 fluid oz.)	24 - #2½
#5	5¾ c. (46 oz.)	12 - #5
#5 squat	5¾ c. (46 oz.)	6 - #5 squat
#10	12 c. (101 fluid oz.)	6 - #10

Packaging Information   The **packaging information** describes *how the product is packaged*. Packaging materials are especially important for produce, frozen products, fish and seafood, and meats and poultry. Poor packaging may affect the quality and taste of the ingredients. Buyers need to familiarize themselves with all the packaging options available and select the best one for the product they are purchasing. Here are some things to consider when choosing packaging options:

- Packaging for **fresh produce**—especially fruits—must be such that the product is not damaged from bumping during shipping and handling. Individually wrapping fruit and using cardboard nesting trays between layers are two common packaging procedures for fruit and some vegetables.
- Packaging for **frozen goods** must protect the products inside from the extremes of temperature on the outside. The quality and strength of the container will be most important with frozen products.
- Packaging for **fish and seafood** varies. Fresh seafood and fish may come packed on ice, or wrapped in seaweed and on ice. Fresh fish is commonly packed in plastic fish buckets. The perishable and delicate nature of the product demands special attention in shipping and receiving.
- **Raw and fresh meat** is typically boxed and wrapped in some type of Cryovac packaging. This method protects the product from spoilage and is standard in the industry.
- **Fresh poultry** is bagged, packed in ice, and boxed. Parts may also come bagged, iced, and packed in boxes.
- Packaging for **processed foods** depends entirely on the product. Processed foods include canned items, frozen items, dried items, dry goods such as flour and sugar, and so on. The choices are almost endless. Suppliers will carry the same product packed in a variety of ways. Research on the part of management will determine which is best.

The best packaging is the method that gets every item ordered to the buyer in perfect condition. This could mean paying a higher **AP** (as purchased) price in return for maximum yield and lower final **EP** (edible portion) cost.

Cost Parameters   Some operators will include *a price range that identifies the maximum unit price* they will pay. If prices rise beyond this, the supplier notifies the buyer.

Trade Association Requirements   These are especially important when purchasing equipment or services. They might include requirements from the NSF International (National Sanitation Foundation), UL (Underwriters Laboratories, Inc., for electrical requirements), AGA (American Gas Association, for gas equipment), or NFPA (National Fire Protection Association, for fire safety).

Receiving Procedures, Including Acceptable Temperatures Standard receiving procedures for all products should be described. Acceptable product temperature readings should be a part of the specification. Likewise, you need to include your standard practices, such as how everything received should be counted and weighed. This is important to note so the supplier and driver will know what to expect. Standard HACCP guidelines should be the norm.

Where to Get Information for Writing Product Specs

Meats Purchasing the correct meat product is critical from a cost and customer perspective. To help with this, the **North American Meat Processors Association (NAMP)** has created a meat specification book called ***The Meat Buyers Guide***. Meat specifications for beef, veal, lamb, pork, and other meat products are described in this guide (Figures 4.5–4.8). This book recommends that products be specified by the corresponding NAMP item number, product name, and weight range to be purchased. For example, to order a rib roast, the foodservice manager would specify Item #109: rib, roast ready, netted, weight range 11 to 13 pounds. In addition, quality and yield grades would be included. The Web site for the National Pork Producer's Council (www.nppc.org) is another source of product information.

In addition, suppliers may have their own particular method of specifying meat. This is not uncommon. Buyers purchasing from a supplier that uses its own specs for meat products would have to become familiar with that company's grading criteria and jargon when ordering. The supplier will be the best resource for information in this case. The following is an example of how to order sirloin steaks from Foodservice of America, a regional full-service supplier: Top Sirloin Choice, N/R, 12/up 1/83# avg, UPC #712AC. The codes represent a method of tracking and ordering the specified item.

Further information on writing meat specs can be found through the NAMP organization. Their contact information is: North American Meat Processors Association (NAMP), *The Guide,* 1920 Association Drive, Suite #400, Reston, VA 20191-1547. They may also be reached by phone at 703-758-1900, by fax at 703-758-8001, or via the Internet at www.namp.com.

Fresh Produce Fresh produce specs are easily written using standard USDA specifications as a guide. Given the wonderful selection available to operators, it is helpful to use these tools as an aid to procuring the right product. These guides are especially helpful to operators new to the spec-writing task. The USDA's Agricultural Marketing Service can be resourced for help with writing specs for produce, milk, poultry, meat, fresh produce, and processed products. They can be reached by mail at 14 Independence Ave., S.W., Washington DC, 20250; by telephone at 202-720-8998; or via the Internet at www.ams.usda.gov. Another excellent source of information is the Produce Marketing Association. Their Web site is www.pma.com.

The National Restaurant Association's Educational Foundation, Information Service, and Library, is located at 250 South Wacker Drive, Chicago, IL 60606. They may be reached by phone at 800-765-2122; the Educational Foundation's Internet address is www.edfound.org. The National Restaurant Association has a Web page that contains information pertinent to the foodservice industry: www.restaurant.org.

Convenience Products Purchasing brand-name convenience items makes the spec-writing job very easy. Essentially, the buyer accepts the manufacturer's specification. Suppose managers at Farfalle Arrabbiata elected to purchase fresh bowtie pasta rather than make it by hand. Assume their research of different brands of pasta revealed that La Pastina brand of pasta was equal to or even better than the in-house product. By specifying that particular brand, Farfalle Arrabbiata, in effect, accepts the manufacturer's product and description as their spec.

Sales reps for food distributors carry product specification sheets created by the manufacturers. These product sheets are a manufacturer's spec, but they in effect become the

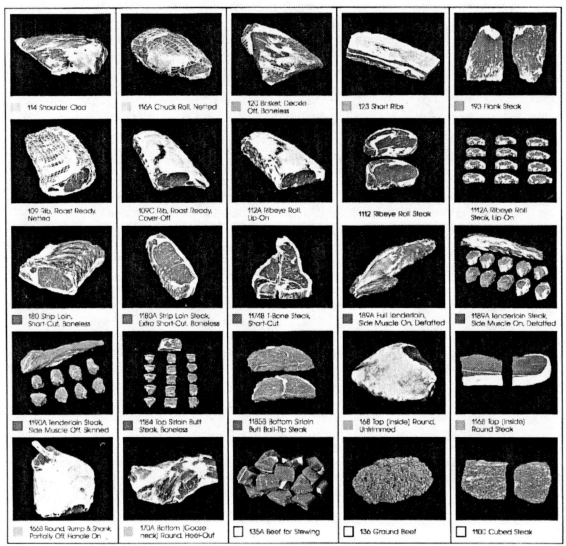

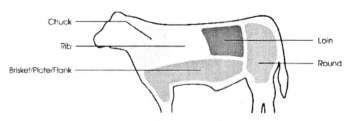

NAMP/IMPS Number (National Association of Meat Purveyors/Institutional Meat Purchase Specifications)

FIGURE 4.5   Purchase Specifications—Beef. *Courtesy of National Cattlemen's Beef Association.*

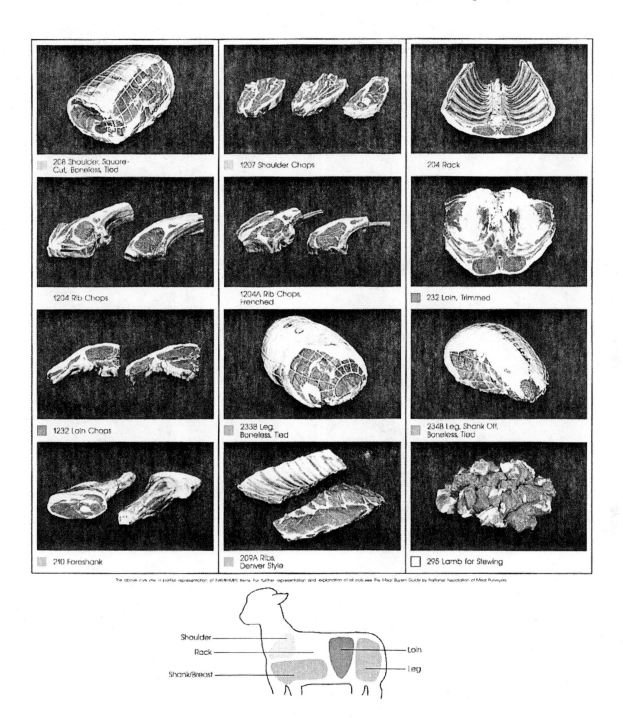

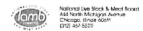

FIGURE 4.6 Purchase Specifications—Lamb. *Courtesy of National Cattlemen's Beef Association.*

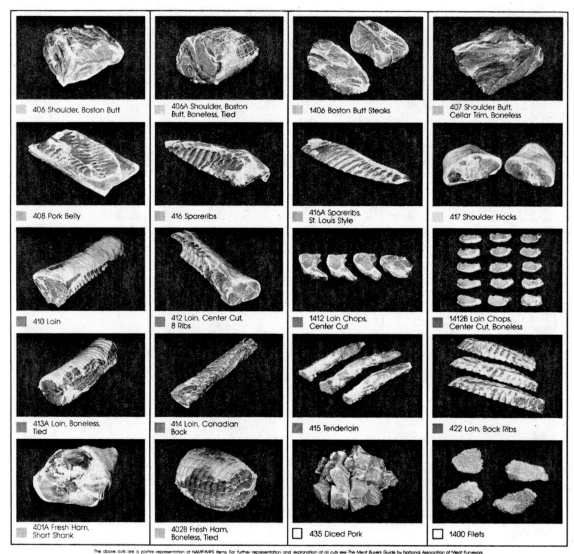

406 Shoulder, Boston Butt

406A Shoulder, Boston Butt, Boneless, Tied

1406 Boston Butt Steaks

407 Shoulder Butt, Cellar Trim, Boneless

408 Pork Belly

416 Spareribs

416A Spareribs, St. Louis Style

417 Shoulder Hocks

410 Loin

412 Loin, Center Cut, 8 Ribs

1412 Loin Chops, Center Cut

1412B Loin Chops, Center Cut, Boneless

413A Loin, Boneless, Tied

414 Loin, Canadian Back

415 Tenderloin

422 Loin, Back Ribs

401A Fresh Ham, Short Shank

402B Fresh Ham, Boneless, Tied

435 Diced Pork

1400 Filets

The above cuts are a partial representation of NAMP/IMPS items. For further representation and explanation of all cuts see The Meat Buyers Guide by National Association of Meat Purveyors.

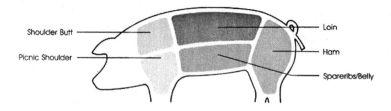

NAMP/IMPS Number (National Association of Meat Purveyors/Institutional Meat Purchase Specifications)

National Association of Meat Purveyors
8365-B Greensboro Drive
McLean, Virginia 22102
(703) 827-5754

©1988 National Association of Meat Purveyors

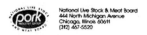

National Live Stock & Meat Board
444 North Michigan Avenue
Chicago, Illinois 60611
(312) 467-5520

FIGURE 4.7   Purchase Specifications—Pork. *Courtesy of National Cattlemen's Beef Association.*

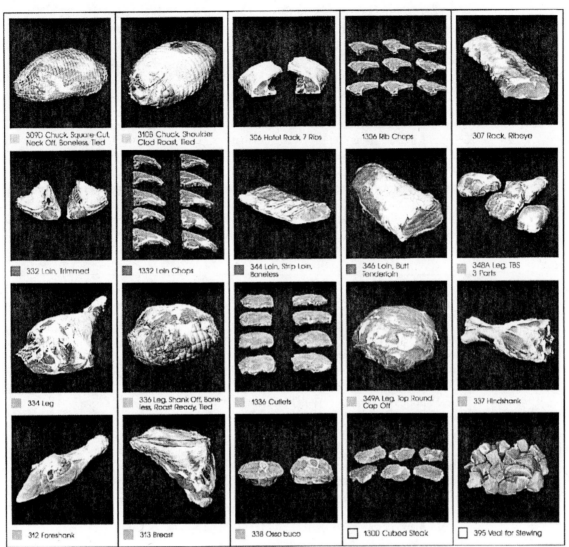

3090 Chuck, Square Cut, Neck Off, Boneless, Tied

310B Chuck, Shoulder Clod Roast, Tied

306 Hotel Rack, 7 Ribs

1306 Rib Chops

307 Rack, Ribeye

332 Loin, Trimmed

1332 Loin Chops

344 Loin, Strip Loin, Boneless

346 Loin, Butt Tenderloin

348A Leg, TBS 3 Parts

334 Leg

336 Leg, Shank Off, Boneless, Roast Ready, Tied

1336 Cutlets

349A Leg, Top Round, Cap Off

337 Hindshank

312 Foreshank

313 Breast

338 Osso buco

1300 Cubed Steak

395 Veal for Stewing

The above cuts are a partial representation of NAMP/IMPS items. For further representation and explanation of all cuts see The Meat Buyers Guide by National Association of Meat Purveyors

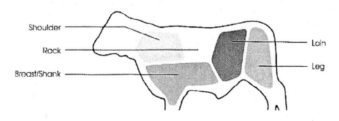

Shoulder
Rack
Breast/Shank
Loin
Leg

NAMP/IMPS Number (National Association of Meat Purveyors/Institutional Meat Purchase Specifications)

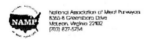

National Association of Meat Purveyors
8365-B Greensboro Drive
McLean, Virginia 22102
(703) 827-5754

©1988 National Association of Meat Purveyors

National Live Stock & Meat Board
444 North Michigan Avenue
Chicago, Illinois 60611
(312) 467-5520

FIGURE 4.8   Purchase Specifications—Veal. *Courtesy of National Cattlemen's Beef Association.*

operators', should he or she opt to purchase that item. These materials will include pictures of the product, purchasing options in reference to portion sizes, case pack, quantity purchases, and even recipe and menu ideas. Sales reps use these as marketing tools to promote a manufacturer's products. Most suppliers and sales reps are very interested in helping foodservice managers learn about their products and generally have a wealth of product information readily available.

Restaurants USA (published by the National Restaurant Association) and *The National Culinary Review* (published by the National Culinary Federation) are excellent publications for product information. Among the most widely read foodservice publications is *Nation's Restaurant News*, a weekly trade journal.

Other objective information may be obtained from national associations, councils, and commissions that represent producers of products, such as the National Meat Council or the (Oregon) Bartlett Pear Commission. These groups offer product information and recipes that can be used in any foodservice operation. Most libraries have a directory of state and national associations and commissions.

Net Work
WEB SITES HELPFUL IN RESEARCHING PRODUCTS

Meats
www.aamp.com—North American Meat Processors Association
www.aamp.com—American Association of Meat Processors
www.beef.org—National Cattlemen's Beef Association
www.nppc.org—National Pork Producers Council
www.meatami.org—American Meat Institute

Fish and Shellfish
www.seafoodhandbook.com—Seafood Handbook
www.alaskaseafood.com—Alaska Seafood Marketing Institute

Poultry
www.namp.com—North American Meat Processors Association
www.aeb.org—American Egg Board

Fresh Produce
www.ams.usda.gov—Agricultural Marketing Service at USDA
www.PMA.com—Produce Marketing Association
www.nffa.org—National Frozen and Refrigerated Food Association
www.primoproduce.com

Dairy
www.nationaldairycouncil.org—National Dairy Council
www.milk.org—Dairy Farmers of Ontario
www.idfa.org—International Dairy Foods Association

Equipment
www.nsf.org—NSF International (formerly the National Sanitation Foundation)
www.nafem.org—National American Association of Food Equipment Manufacturers

Services
www.pestworld.org—National Pest Management Association
www.ecolab.com—Ecolab
www.terminix.com—Terminix

Writing Sample Product Specs

Remember in previous chapters, when a number of menu items were used for recipe samples and cost cards? Well, continuing here with these same items, we will develop sample product specs for a number of the main ingredients.

Chicken Noodle Soup   Remember the Chicken Noodle Soup recipe created in Chapter 2? The following is a list of the recipe's ingredients. From this list, specifications will be developed so the buyer communicates precisely to the supplier exactly what is needed to produce the soup. For the sake of this example, only the primary ingredients are being used.

Chicken Noodle Soup

Ingredients
Chicken breast meat
Noodles, egg, narrow
Onions, Spanish
Celery
Carrots

The following are samples of specs written for the chicken noodle soup ingredients.

Exact Name:	Chicken, breast
Intended Use:	Chicken Noodle Soup
Grade:	A
Brand Name:	Sysco
Form:	Boneless, skinless
Size:	Whole, random
Pack:	Cryovac, 4 - 10 lb. per case
Receiving Procedure:	Under refrigeration; ice pack or chill pack; 28–29°F

FIGURE 4.9   Chicken breast.

Exact Name:	Egg Noodles
Intended Use:	Chicken Noodle Soup
Brand Name:	LaBella
Size:	Fine
Pack:	2 - 5 lb. per case
Receiving:	Cases are dry and free of debris

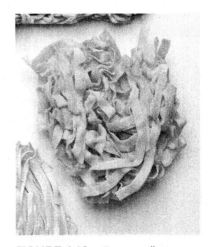

FIGURE 4.10   Egg noodles.

Exact Name:	Onions, Spanish, yellow globe
Intended Use:	Various menu items
Grade:	USDA #1
Form:	Whole
Variety:	Spanish
Size:	Large, foodservice
Pack:	50 lb. mesh bags
Receiving:	Under refrigeration; below 41°F

FIGURE 4.11   Spanish onion.

Exact Name:	Celery
Intended Use:	Various menu items
Grade:	USDA #1
Variety:	Pascal
Pack:	24/bunches per case
Receiving:	Under refrigeration; below 41°F

FIGURE 4.12   Pascal celery.

Exact Name:	Carrots
Intended Use:	Various menu items
Grade:	USDA #1
Size:	Jumbo, foodservice
Pack:	50 lb. bag
Receiving:	Under refrigeration; below 41°F

FIGURE 4.13   Foodservice carrot.

Baked Potato   Remember the baked potato recipe from Chapter 2? Here are specs for each of the ingredients:

Baked Potato

Ingredients
Baked potatoes
Vegetable oil
Sour cream
Butter pats

Exact Name:	Baked Potatoes
Intended Use:	Side dish
Grade:	US #1
Variety:	Russet/Burbank
Form:	Fresh
Size:	90 count
Pack:	50 lb. case
Receiving:	Under refrigeration; below 41°F

Exact Name:	Oil, Vegetable
Intended Use:	Various menu items
Brand Name:	Wesson
Pack:	6 - 1 gal./case

Exact Name:	Cream, Sour
Intended Use:	Garnish for Baked Potato
Brand Name:	Cabot, Vermont
Grade:	USDA "A"
Expiration Date:	2 weeks from delivery date
Pack:	6 - 5 lb. containers/case
Receiving:	Under refrigeration; below 41°F

Exact Name:	Butter, Pats
Intended Use:	With Baked Potato
Brand Name:	Land O'Lakes
Grade:	USDA AA
Form:	Pats
Count:	90 count
Pack:	6 - 5 lb. boxes per case
Receiving:	Under refrigeration; below 41°F

Chili Dog   Try the Chili Dog from Chapters 2 and 3:

Chili Dog

Ingredients
Hot Dog, All Beef
Chili Sauce
Pickle Slices
French Fries

Exact Name:	Hot Dogs, All Beef
Intended Use:	Lunch selection
Brand Name:	Hebrew National
Size:	8 × 1, 8 in.
Form:	Skinless
Pack:	2 - 5 lb. per case
Receiving:	Frozen; 0–10°F

FIGURE 4.14   Hot dog.

Exact Name:	Sauce, Chili
Intended Use:	Chili Dog
Brand Name:	Hunts
Pack:	6 - #10 cans per case

FIGURE 4.15   Chili sauce.

Exact Name:	Pickle Spears, Kosher
Intended Use:	Chili Dog
Count:	215–265
Brand Name:	Vlasic
Pack	1 - 5 gal. pail
Receiving:	Under refrigeration; below 41°F

FIGURE 4.16   Pickles.

Exact Name:	French Fries
Intended Use:	With Chili Dog
Brand Name:	Simplot
Grade:	A
Form:	Krinkle Kut
Size:	3/8"
Pack:	6 - 5 lb. boxes per case
Receiving:	Frozen; 0–10°F

FIGURE 4.17   French fries.

Bowtie Pasta   Last, let's look at the Bowtie Pasta, from Chapter 2:

Bowtie Pasta

Ingredients
Semolina Flour
Olive Oil
Eggs

FIGURE 4.18   Bowtie pasta.

Exact Name:	Flour, Semolina
Intended Use:	Bowtie Pasta
Brand Name:	Gold Medal
Form:	Unbleached
Pack:	50 lb. bags
Receiving:	Bags are dry and free from excess soil

FIGURE 4.19   Semolina flour.

Exact Name:	Oil, Olive, Extra Virgin
Intended Use:	Pasta dough
Brand Name:	Colvito
Grade:	Extra virgin
Pack:	6 - 17 oz. bottles

FIGURE 4.20   Olive oil.

Exact Name:	Eggs, Fresh
Intended Use:	Pasta dough
Brand Name:	Sysco
Grade:	USDA AA
Form:	Whole
Color:	Brown
Size:	Large
Pack:	2½ doz. per flat
	30 doz. per case
Receiving:	Under refrigeration; below 41°F

FIGURE 4.21   Large brown eggs.

And there you have it—specifications for a number of the menu items from Chapters 2 and 3! To wrap up our discussion, the following is basic specification information for primary foodservice products:

Meat	Poultry	Fish/Shellfish	Produce	Dairy	Grocery
BASIC SPECIFICATION INFORMATION FOR PRIMARY FOODSERVICE PRODUCTS					
Name & Intended Use	→				
NAMPS # or supplier number					
USDA Quality Grade	USDA Quality Grade	USDA Quality Grade where applicable	USDA Quality Grade	USDA Quality Grade	USDA Quality Grade
Yield Grade	Size	Size	Size	Size	Product size
Yield %	Yield %	Yield	Yield/trim		Pack
Packer/Brand Name	Packer/Brand Name	Packer/Brand Name	Packer/Brand Name	Packer/Brand Name	Packer/Brand Name
Weight range	Weight range	Weight range/size	Point of origin	Fat content	Case pack/ Can size
Color	Color	Color	Color	Color	Color
Trim/waste	Trim/waste	Trim	Ripeness	Flavor	Drained weight
Cost parameters	Cost parameters	Cost parameters	Cost parameters	Cost parameters	Cost parameters
Feed	Feed	Point of Origin	Preservation & Packaging		Packing medium
Form	Form	Form	Form	Form	Form
Pack	Pack	Pack	Pack	Pack	
		Fresh/farm raised	Case weight range		
Receiving procedures	Receiving procedures	Receiving procedures	Receiving procedures	Receiving procedures	Receiving procedures

Specifying Services for a Foodservice Operation

Much attention is given to writing specs for food products. What about services, though? Many operations outsource a variety of tasks. There are a number of reasons to do this, including:

- Cost effectiveness.
- Expertise—some things are just best left to the professionals.
- Lower labor costs.
- Lack of specialty equipment and the staff to operate it
- Can be regularly scheduled.
- Need for special skills.
- Eliminates legal problems
- Guarantees quality
- Saves time

The same techniques used to develop food specs apply to writing specs for services. Managers use service specs for exactly the same reasons they are used for food products. The Five Rights still apply: Purchase the right services, in the right quantities, from the right supplier, at the right price, delivered at the right time. There are a myriad of services an operator might contract for. Here are some of them:

- Trash removal and recycling
- Payroll
- Other financial services, such as benefit administration
- Landscaping and snow removal
- Parking lot maintenance or valet service
- Pest control
- Advertising
- General kitchen cleaning: knives, floor mats, vents, and ducts
- Maintenance of plants and supply of floral arrangements
- Deep cleaning: drapes, upholstery, carpets, walls
- Electric and gas equipment maintenance
- Insurance
- Laundry and linen service
- Maintenance of fire systems and extinguishers
- Music or entertainment
- Septic tank maintenance

As always, when writing a specification for a service, be as specific as possible. In many cases, poorly written service specs could lead to some very serious consequences—a fire, an injured employee or guest, ruined equipment, and so on. And *always inspect to be sure the work was completed*. Do not leave to chance or goodwill that a contracted service was performed, even if the invoice is waiting to be paid. Validate that the work was completed, that quality products were used, that the service is being performed according to scheduled frequency, and so on.

The format for a service spec would be similar to that of a food spec. It, too, will be a list. A more complicated service—say, a construction project—will require a much more sophisticated spec. Specs for basic services such as rubbish removal and pest control services can be written easily by working with the supplier. So you don't get biased information, research supplier options with a number of companies before drafting your final spec. Look to other industry professionals for information about reliable service providers. Word-of-mouth endorsements by these associates can eliminate a lot of wasted time and energy.

Tips for Writing Service Specs

Tips for Writing Service Specs When writing service specs, always do the following:

- Use precise language. Do not be ambiguous.
- Include an intended use, just as you do for a food product
- Require references—current and past customers, professional references, and professional organizations such as the Better Business Bureau and the local Chamber of Commerce
- Include completion dates
- Note frequency of service
- Note licenses or qualifications required
- Outline payment terms and conditions
- Inspect work
- Check quality of materials or products to be used
- Note the skill level of employees used to deliver the service

Here is a sample service spec for waste and recycling removal:

Sample Service Spec	
Service	Waste and recycling removal
Intended Use	Remove waste and recycling materials
References	3 current customers, member of Better Business Bureau; fully insured
Pick-Up	Twice weekly: Mondays and Fridays
Time	Before 10:00 a.m.
Required Service	Empty disposal container, including any materials outside of container; remove recycling materials
Equipment	Provide 10 yard waste container, recycling containers, and driveway pad
Inspection	Manager will inspect at each pick-up
Billing	Monthly

Make or Buy? The Make-or-Buy Analysis

One of the more important tasks managers and chefs have to take on is to decide whether it is best to make an item from scratch or to purchase a **convenience** or **value-added** item. The choices available in the value-added market are so diverse that it makes good sense to research and consider the possibility that there is a complete product or an individual ingredient available that can work for even the most intricate menu item. Sometimes an entire menu item can be found; Sometimes it's just a specific recipe ingredient.

Outcomes of Using Value-Added Foods

Prepared foods can have several positive outcomes:

- They can reduce labor cost and overall portion cost.
- They can improve the end product.
- They can reduce receiving, storage, and inventory costs.
- They can significantly increase the consistency of an end product—taste, cost, portion size, and so on.
- They usually have very little waste. Often, yield is 100%.
- They can afford an operator the option of offering menu items that would not otherwise be feasible, given the skills of the existing staff and the existing production equipment.
- They can reduce the workload on existing equipment.
- They can increase customer interest in the operation and overall satisfaction.
- They can enable flexibility of labor hours.

So what could be wrong with them? Using value-added foods can also do the following:

- Increase overall portion cost
- Limit ordering options with suppliers—the supplier you have to deal with may not be one you like dealing with
- Affect supplier delivery schedules or minimum order amounts (other pricing issues may be more costly)
- Affect overall availability of product (value-added foods may not be as readily available)

- Cause backorders and shortages
- Run out during a service period
- Increase customer demand for "home-made" foods vs. pre-prepared foods.
- Affect reputation of operation.
- Affect supplier price increases.
- Be difficult to find a substitute for.

Researching new products and ingredients is an interesting and exciting activity. The opportunity to interact with sales reps and new suppliers is an eye-opening experience—a new buyer can learn a lot! Smart suppliers train their sales staff in product knowledge to better service their customers. Smart operators and buyers challenge sales reps when it comes to product research. Suppliers and sales reps should be a valued resource to operators regarding products.

Another option for researching product is to attend hotel and restaurant trade shows. These shows showcase vendors of every conceivable hospitality-related product on the market. The array of products is astounding: furniture, fixtures, equipment, food and beverage products, technology, and so much more makes a trip through one an education in itself.

How to Do a Make-or-Buy Analysis

Our description of Farfalle Arrabbiata revealed that skilled professional staff prepare all menu items from scratch. Reviewing the menu, it is clear there are a number of items where a **Make-or-Buy-Analysis (MOBA)**, or *research of the facts needed to decide to make an item from scratch or to use a convenience or value added item,* should be explored. Assume that a production problem has developed at Farfalle Arrabbiata. Because of increased volume, Chef Raoul is having difficulties with equipment capacity and load. He has studied the situation and is interested in learning if a value-added item would reduce the amount of stove time currently used to prepare the Chicken Noodle Soup from scratch. You, the buyer, have been asked to assist Raoul by researching possibilities.

Remember that the Chicken Noodle Soup is a major favorite at Farfalle Arrabbiata. The original recipe has been handed down through the owner's family for many generations. To top it off, the recipe has been featured a number of times in the food section of the local newspaper.

The steps presented here are the first part of the job when making a decision to make or buy. They simply help identify potential value-added items that could be used as they are, or with some enhancement, in place of preparing the Chicken Noodle Soup from scratch. After the initial testing, a more complex analysis will reveal the answer, and the process will be complete.

STEPS IN THE MOBA PROCESS
1. Identify product contenders.
2. Eliminate possibilities based on obvious factors.
3. Prepare the products to be considered according to direction and without changing anything.
4. Evaluate for taste, appearance, and match to original product.

Step 1—Identify Product Contenders   The first task is to identify product contenders. In this case, assume you, the buyer, have found through your research, four possible value-added items that potentially match the original Chicken Noodle Soup.

One choice is a dried or dehydrated product that would need to be reconstituted. The next choice is a canned soup, also needing to be reconstituted. Another is a canned product that is simply reheated without reconstitution (called **ready to use,** or **RTU**). The fourth and last is a frozen product.

Step 2—Eliminate Contenders Based on Obvious Factors   Next, you and Chef Raoul will eliminate any contender that is not deemed viable. The reasons to eliminate at this stage are usually very obvious (e.g., the taste, overall quality, or appearance is too far off the original menu item). In this case, assume the dried/dehydrated product is out of the running. From an overall taste, quality, and appearance standard, it is not acceptable. In this step, any item that does not produce an acceptable substitute is immediately eliminated.

Step 3—Prepare the Products to Be Considered According to the Directions, Without Changing Anything   Now, we have two canned products and a frozen product to evaluate. Each would be prepared according to standard preparation instructions. Nothing would be added or left out. Each is prepared according to instructions.

Step 4—Evaluate for Taste, Appearance, and Potential Match to the Original Product   Each contender would be further evaluated for taste and overall appearance. Any contender that is deemed not a close enough match is eliminated at this point. Those that are left will have to undergo further transforming in order to really make a comparison with the original item.

It is highly unlikely that a value-added product will be a perfect match in taste and appearance right out of the box, especially in the case of a more specialized production, as would be found at Farfalle Arrabbiata. Assume that in this case, you and Chef Raoul agree that the three contenders have potential but each will need to be "enhanced" to more closely match the original soup. This means Chef Raoul will have to play around with each by adding extra seasonings, ingredients, and so on, to create a match. As he goes through this process, he will keep careful notes of everything he has added—seasonings and extra ingredients, as well as all cooking times and preparation methodologies. The most important criteria at this point will be how closely each modified value-added sample can be made to match the original Chicken Noodle Soup.

DEVELOPING A MATCH WITH VALUE-ADDED PRODUCTS

1. Prepare each product independently, adding other ingredients, seasonings, and so on, to produce a sample that matches as closely as possible the original menu item being replicated.
2. Record all additions, deletions, and changes—in effect, create a "recipe" for the altered products.

   a. Any additional ingredients, spices, herbs, seasonings, and so on, used to "fix" the samples must be carefully measured and recorded.

   b. Any additional preparation steps, simmering times, and so on, have to be recorded.

   c. Essentially create a "recipe" for each contender.

3. Evaluate and critique the final products.
4. Make a decision.

The samples are adjusted and tested over and over until a comparable product is developed, with the convenience item as the base. After the last bit of tinkering, a decision has to be made as to the compatibility with the original product. At this point, though, the decision is based solely on taste and appearance.

After the taste and appearance hurdle is crossed, other factors must be considered. These are:

1. Final portion cost including labor.
2. Production.
3. Availability of value-added product.
4. Customer satisfaction.
5. Is it worth it?

Evaluating Portion Costs

We will need to evaluate portion costs. Let's start with evaluating the cost of the three pre-prepared products for Farfalle Arrabbiata. In order to compare "apples with apples," let's first look at the original recipe for the signature Chicken Noodle Soup, as it is made at Farfalle Arrabbiata:

CHICKEN NOODLE SOUP

Yield: 25 portions   **Portion Size:** 10 oz.

Ingredients	Weight	Measure
Chicken stock	12 lb.	1½ gal.
Chicken breast meat	1½ lb.	4 c.
Noodles, egg, narrow	1¼ lb.	5 c.
Onions, ¼" dice	½ lb.	6 oz.
Celery	½ bunch	2 c.
Carrots	½ lb.	¾ c.
Bay leaf		2 each
Salt		To taste
Pepper		To taste

Next, we need the purchasing unit of the pre-prepared items. Assume the canned soup product was purchased in #5 cans and was reconstituted with one equal can of water. The second canned product is **ready to serve (RTS)**. The frozen product is simply reheated.

To do a full analysis, we will assess labor costs for both the original soup recipe and the three contenders. Assume a labor cost of $14.00 per hour. The portion size is 10 ounces, as per the original recipe. We will include the invoice cost for each product. The goal is to calculate the cost per portion, including labor, for each product. After we complete that process, we make our final decision—to make it or buy it—following the guidelines outlined earlier. The following table presents the analysis.

	Original Recipe	Canned Reconstituted Soup	Ready to Use Soup	Frozen Soup
Portion Size	10 oz.	10 oz.	10 oz.	10 oz.
Purchasing Unit	Recipe	Case 12 - #5 cans	Case 12 - #5 cans	Case 4/1 gal.
Cost	$10.00/25 servings	$39.00/case	$37.20/case	$27/case
Purchasing Unit Yield	25 servings	1 can soup base = 46 oz. 1 can water = 46 oz. 92 oz. total	46 oz. per can	128 oz.
No. of Servings Per Unit	25	92 oz./10 oz. = 9.2	46 oz./10 = 4.6	128/10 = 12.8
Cost of Additional Ingredients		Chicken stock .10 Carrots ¼ lb. .08 Onions ¼ lb. .06 Celery ¼ bunch .20 Noodles ¼ lb. .04 Add'l. cost = .48	Carrots ¼ lb. = .08 Noodles ½ lb. = .08 Add'l. cost = .16	
Cost Per Portion	10.00/25 = .40 .40 × 1.04 = .42 (Spice Factor) .42	$39.00/12 = $3.25 $3.25 + .48 = $3.73 $3.73/9.2 = .41 .41 × 1.04 = .43 .43	$37.20/12 = $3.10 $3.10 + .16 = $3.26 $3.26/4.6 = .67 .67 × 1.04 = .70 .70	$27/4 = $6.75 $6.75/12.8 = .53 .53 × 1.04 = .56 .56
Labor Cost @ $14.00 per Hour	30 minutes $7.00/25 = .28 per serv.	25 minutes $5.83/9.2 = .63 per serv.	15 minutes $3.50/4.6 = .76 per serv.	10 minutes $2.33/12.8 = .18 per serv.
Total Food and Labor Cost	.42 + .28 = .70	.43 + .63 = $1.06	.70 + .76 = $1.46	.56 + .18 = .74

The results are in! Looking at portion costs alone, it initially appeared that the reconstituted soup is in contention with the original recipe. After figuring in the labor, though, the picture is changed. The frozen soup and the original recipe come in at about the same total cost per portion. Surprisingly, the reconstituted soup and the ready to use soup come in significantly higher. The labor is the deciding factor in this case.

Assuming all the alternatives produced an end product that was very similar to the original, any decision to make a change would involve further analysis. The criteria listed earlier now come into play:

- Final portion cost, including labor
- Production
- Availability of value-added product
- Customer satisfaction
- Is it worth it?

You and Chef Raoul, in consultation with management, will have to decide whether or not it is in the best interest of Farfalle Arrabbiata to make a change. Given that the soup is a favorite and highly regarded by customers, it might not be best to change the way it is produced.. Because Chef Raoul embarked on this analysis due to an equipment capacity or production issue, it may be that a change in that area is in order. Management would, of course, need to monitor sales closely. Care must always be taken with special menu items—customers must not detect the change

If management decided it was not best to change the product, Chef Raoul's work was not in vain. Knowing that the frozen soup is a viable alternative gives Raoul some flexibility in production and purchasing.

One Last Alternative: Outsourcing

There is one last alternative. Many times, operations **outsource** the production of some "recipe" products to *food manufacturing firms that specialize in producing customized restaurant products to restaurant specifications.* This practice is quite common with chains and multiunit operations. These items are proprietary to the restaurant, so the item is not marketed to any other operators. Farfalle Arrabbiata could look to this concept as another possibility of solving the production problem. Outsourcing production makes sense when an operation is short on kitchen space, storage space, and skilled staff.

⁄Net Work

Explore the following Web sites for information about specs:
www.namp.com—North American Meat Processors Association
www.aamp.com—American Association of Meat Processors
www.beef.org—National Cattlemen's Beef Association
www.nppc.org—National Pork Producers Council
www.meatami.org—American Meat Institute
www.seafoodhandbook.com—Seafood Handbook
www.alaskaseafood.org—Alaska Seafood Marketing Institute
www.aeb.org—American Egg Board
www.ams.usda.gov—Agricultural Marketing Service at USDA
www.PMA.com—Produce Marketing Association
www.nffa.org—National Frozen and Refrigerated Foods Association
www.nationaldairycouncil.org—National Dairy Council
www.milk.org—Dairy Farmers of Ontario
www.idfa.org—International Dairy Foods Association
www.nsf.com—NSF International (formerly the National Sanitation Foundation)
www.nafem.org—North American Association Food Equipment Manufacturers
www.pestworld.org—National Pest Management Association
www.realcaliforniacheese.com—Real California Cheese
Check out this additional site:
www.preparedfoods.com—Prepared Foods

Chapter Wrap

The Chapter ✓ at the beginning of the chapter posed several questions. Review the questions and compare your responses with the following answers:

1. **What does purchasing mean?**

   For some foodservice operations, the primary role of the buyer is to ensure that the operation has all the food, beverage, and nonfood items required. This role, however, is only part of the function of the buyer. A comprehensive purchasing system gets the job done effectively and efficiently. The mission for the chef, manager, buyer, or owner is this: ***To purchase the right product (or service), in the right quantity, from the right supplier, at the right price, all delivered at the right time***. These are known as the "Five Rights," or purchasing functions, and as simplistic as the sentence may sound, the essence of purchasing boils down to these five activities. Anyone who is actively engaged in purchasing products and services knows that getting all these elements to work together like a well-oiled machine is an art.

2. How does a buyer determine product quality?

Purchasing the best product starts with defining the quality of that product. This definition is shaped by the financial plan for the operation, guest expectations, and final EP cost. In other words, the buyers' challenge is to purchase the best possible product, given the institutional constraints that they manage.

Food products, by their very nature, have varying degrees of quality and yield. They are also subject to price fluctuations, as market conditions often cause increases or decreases in prices. Hence, it is extremely important to define quality standards through the development of specifications for all ingredients used in standardized recipes. Using specifications to procure products and services ensures production consistency and customer satisfaction. Specifications are detailed descriptions of products and services written to assist the buyer and the supplier in getting the right product (or service) to the operation. Specifications describe a product that is the best fit from a quality and cost perspective. The product is not necessarily the most expensive or the least expensive or the best or the worst. It is simply the best fit, given the parameters a buyer has to work within.

3. Why are specifications written for services?

Service specifications are written for all the same reasons that product specifications are written: Management wants the right services, in the right quantities, from the right supplier, at the right price, delivered at the right time.

4. How can a buyer compare similar products?

One of the more important tasks left to managers and chefs is deciding whether it is best to make an item from scratch or to purchase a convenience or value-added item instead. The choices available in the value-added market are so diverse that it makes good sense to research and consider the possibility of using a complete product or an individual ingredient in even the most intricate menu item.

Key Terminology and Concepts in This Chapter

AP (as purchased)
Bid process/procedure
Convenience food
EP (edible portion)
Expiration date
Five Rights
Form
Intended use
Inventory file
Make-or-Buy Analysis (MOBA)
NAMP (North American Meat Processors Association)
National Culinary Review
Nation's Restaurant News
Operating Cycle of Control
Outsource
Packaging information
Product specifications

Quality grades
Quality standards
RFP (request for proposal)
Restaurants USA
Right order size
Right price
Right product
Right quality
Right quantity
Right supplier
Right time
RTS (ready to serve)
RTU (ready to use)
Specifications
Specification books
The Meat Buyers Guide
Unit size
Value-added food

Discussion Questions and Exercises

1. Which operational factors have the greatest impact on a buyer's purchasing decision? Why did you select these?

2. Define quality as it pertains to food served in a commercial foodservice operation.

3. Explain the difference between a quality food experience and a nonquality food experience.

4. According to the text, "Food quality is a function of budgeted ingredient cost and the cost of preparation." Do you agree with this statement? Why? Why not?

5. What should quality standards define?

6. Define the term *specification*. How do specifications create quality standards?

7. You just got an email from the folks. They are so excited—you are finally graduating from college! To show you how proud they are of your accomplishment, THEY ARE GOING TO BUY YOU A BRAND NEW CAR! They want to know what kind you want. Amazingly, they didn't mention a thing about budget. You're dreaming—a hot red convertible sports car! (Or whatever you would like if you had such an offer.) Develop a "specification" for your new toy, so you can go haggle over price at the local dealership. Here are a few areas to consider when writing the details for your spec: Price (best to have all the facts and figures—it's going to come up), safety, maintenance and upkeep, tune-ups, warranty, gas mileage, special packages, and options (those " 'gotta have it!" things).

8. Review the spec you wrote for your dream car. Examine it for details that might be too specific or not specific enough. How would you have to change the language? What could be the result if you don't make these changes?

9. The car was delivered last week, and *it looks great* sitting in the driveway. You and a few friends are going on a road trip to test it out. The plan is to take a leisurely cruise along the infamous Route 1, along the California coast. You estimate the trip will take 2½ weeks. You have a dog, tropical fish, and 10 exotic plants that you need to arrange care for during your absence.

   - The fish need to be fed twice a day and the tank has to be cleaned every 7 days.
   - The dog needs to be walked twice a day and has a weekly appointment at the Froo Froo Poodle Parlor down the street. She is box trained.
   - The plants need to be watered at precisely 5:00 p.m. daily and require a special vitamin treatment every 5 days.

   Write a specification for services for the dog, the fish, and the plants for the duration of your road trip. Obvious needs not listed, such as feeding, grooming, clean up, and so on, also have to be taken into consideration.

10. Review the menu for Farfalle Arrabbiata in Appendix A. Which menu items or ingredients (refer to item descriptions) would be good candidates to research using a value-added food as a substitute? (Do not use Chicken Noodle Soup!)

11. Review the pro and con lists for using value-added food. From your list in Exercise 10, select five items that you think deserve further research as a substitute product. Why do you think a value-added product is a viable option for your selections? Defend your choices. Your arguments should reference the restaurant profile in Chapter 1 and Appendix A.

12. Chef Raoul has been experimenting with some new specials for Farfalle Arrabbiata. He needs duck, apples, and Asiago cheese for one of the recipes. Marcel, who is still out of town, can't help. You must write the spec and research the products available for Chef Raoul. Chef Raoul is not known for his patience— he wants it now! Where would you go to start your research? Using some of the Web sites noted in the chapter, draft the elements and any details needed for a spec for each of these products.

13. Currently, the Tira Misu served at Farfalle Arrabbiata is made in-house. It is the second most popular dessert. Business has increased, and right now kitchen equipment is maxed out in production. You have been researching purchasing options for a number of menu items to relieve some of the equipment and production problems. You have prepared a product spec for the Tira Misu. A bakery in the next town has submitted a test sample. Following is the data you have for both the in-house product and the test sample.

In-House Tira Misu: It currently costs $22.72 to produce. One cake is cut into 12 portions. There is a 5% Spice Factor. Labor cost is $1.75 per slice.

Test Product: This product costs $38.64 per cake. It is pre-cut into 12 portions. The Spice Factor is 5%. Labor cost is $.93 per slice. The supplier only ships once every 2 weeks. There is a minimum order of 20 cases. It is comparable in size and taste.

- Develop a test form for analyzing value-added products against the original recipe. Use the pro and con list to complete your form.
- Complete a cost per portion analysis for each option.
- What are your recommendations from a cost perspective? From a pro and con and cost perspective?

## Chapter Five

Chapter Objective

To determine the right quantity of products to order for all menu items.

Learning Objectives

After reading this chapter and completing the discussion questions and exercises, you should be able to:

1. Employ sales histories, sales forecasts, and menu item popularity percentages to assist with determining order quantities.
2. Establish par inventory levels using a variety of methods.
3. Determine order quantities using pars and requisitions.
4. Determine order quantities for functions.
5. Determine order quantities for products with yield or waste factors.

About Purchasing the "Right Quantity"

The Menu

Pre-Purchase Functions

GUEST CHECK
Sales history, turnover, average check, cash management, revenue forecasting & budgeting, menu item analysis

STANDARDIZED RECIPES
Standard ingredients, portion size, quality, consistency, quantity, purchasing

GUESTS
Greeting, seating, sales, serving, busing, payment, comment cards

COST CARDS
Portion costs, yield factors, sell prices

SPECIFICATIONS
Product descriptions

FOH Functions

PAR STOCK
Inventory levels, order building

KITCHEN PRODUCTION
Production schedules, portion tracking, recipe control, serving controls, food safety

REQUISITION
Order building, purchasing

PRODUCT ISSUING
Requisitions, transfers, daily & monthly costs, food cost percentage

SHOPPING LISTS
Call sheets, bid sheets, suppliers, bidding

STORAGE PRACTICES & INVENTORY MANAGEMENT
Best practices, sanitation, security, inventory methods

PURCHASE ORDERS
Security, ship order, price guarantee, contract

INVOICE MANAGEMENT
Payment, price checking, security

BOH Functions

RECEIVING ACTIVITIES
Best practices, invoices, security, sanitation

Chapter Map

About Ordering Products

Ordering the Right Quantity

- Sales History, Sales Forecasts, & Popularity Percentages
- Sales History
- Sales Forecasts
- Popularity Percentage (Index)

Chapter Map   (Continued)

Par Stock

- How a Manager Uses this Information
- Setting Par Using Common Usage Patterns
- Using Formulas to Calculate Par

Using Par Inventory Amounts with Order Sheets to Order Product

- Using Order Sheets
- Order Form Details

Requisitions

- The Requisition Process
- So What Exactly Is a Requisition?

Types of Requisitions
- Par Amount Requisitions
- Blank Requisitions

Ordering for Functions

- Using the Par Formula to Calculate Order Amounts
- Using the Par Formula to Calculate Number of Portions, Portion Size, & Yield Percentage
- Amount Purchased Equivalency

Performing a Yield Analysis for Canned Products

Chapter ✓

Check the chapter content for the answers to these questions:

1. What data is used to determine order quantity?
2. What is a par stock?
3. How are food orders prepared using a par?
4. How are requisitions used to prepare orders?
5. How are orders prepared for functions?
6. How are canned products analyzed for yield?

---

*A*bout Ordering Products

Looking back at the "**Five Rights**" (the right product, quantity, supplier, price, and time) from Chapter 4, it's easy to see what is next—**ordering the right quantity**. This topic—the Right Quantity—is a critical step in the purchasing process. This chapter covers the methods used to calculate order size and generate orders for a number of different purchasing situations.

THE FIVE RIGHTS, OF PURCHASING FUNCTIONS		
CHAPTER 4	**CHAPTER 5**	**CHAPTER 6**
THE RIGHT PRODUCT	THE RIGHT QUANTITY	THE RIGHT SUPPLIER, PRICE, & TIME
1. Specifications	1. Popularity %	1. Distribution Systems
2. Make-or-Buy Analysis	2. Par Stock	2. Selecting a Supplier
	3. Order Sheets	3. Bid Systems
	4. Requisitions	4. Bid/Call Sheets
	5. Orders for Functions	5. Placing Orders
	6. Yield Analysis	6. Purchase Orders
		7. Supplier Prices
		8. Yield Factors

Note in Figure 5.1 where we are in the purchasing functions content.

THE FIVE *RIGHTS*

To Purchase:
1. The *Right Product* in
2. The *Right Quantity* from
3. The *Right Supplier* at
4. The *Right Price* at
5. The *Right Time*

FIGURE 5.1   The Five Rights of purchasing.

Correct ordering begins with a thorough understanding of inventory management. The concept is pretty simple:

1. Don't run out of product.
2. Don't have too much product on hand.

Picture these two statements as though they are the goal posts in the end zones at either end of a football field. The objective of ordering is to *stay out of the end zones*! Ideally, order at levels that are about "mid-field" (neither too much nor too little), in order to maximize the purchasing dollar while minimizing waste and cost.

Any time a foodservice operation is out of a product (failure to obey Rule No. 1), the result is often a loss in potential profit because a customer may order either something of lesser value (and possibly less profitable) or nothing at all. Consider the customer who orders Farfalle Arrabbiata, the signature dish, and the Tira Misu for dessert, only to have the server say, "Sorry, we are out of Farfalle Arrabbiata this evening and we just served our last order of Tira Misu." The customer may decide to go to another restaurant or perhaps just order a dinner salad with the thought of never returning again. The customer wants what they want when they want it, to be satisfied.

On the other hand, any time a foodservice operation is not managing inventory levels, the result will be excessive waste and cost. The nature of the "beast" (the food) is that it is highly perishable and "If you don't use it, you will lose it." As such, having too much perishable product on hand will result in waste that inevitably leads to high food costs (and a failure to obey Rule No. 2). Consider, too, the costs associated with the time and energy of the buyer and other staff to order, receive, track, and store these products.

Ordering the Right Quantity

The following discussion is about calculating order quantity. In the list of the Five Rights, the **Right Quantity** is No. 2.

Sales History, Sales Forecasts, and Popularity Percentages

These three sources of data—sales history, sales forecasts and popularity percentages—are used to develop accurate order quantities. Watch for these three concepts as they are developed further in later chapters. The next three statements frame the discussion that follows:

1. **Sales histories** *tell what happened in the past* and are used to develop sales forecasts. The history can be organized by day, week, month, or year. Look for examples in the discussion about popularity percent.

2. **Sales forecasts** *predict what will occur in the near future* and are used to purchase products, plan for menu production, and schedule staff. Look for examples in the discussion about popularity percent.

3. **Popularity percentages or indexes** (developed from historical data) *track guests' menu preferences.*

Why Track Them? Imagine managing a high-volume, full-menu, table service restaurant. Imagine that high volume translates to 4 million dollars in sales annually, with an average guest check of $18.00. The restaurant is open for lunch and dinner and seats 280 people. This calculates to an annual customer count of 222,222 guests, which converts to a mean average of 617 customers per day. Since this is a mean average, on some days more than 617 arrive for a meal and other days fewer than 617 arrive. Imagine that you are responsible for ordering all food, beverage, and nonfood supplies, as well as directing the kitchen production and schedule staff—in both front and back of house. The questions before you are:

- How much food and other supplies should be ordered?
- How many portions of each menu item should be prepared?
- How many servers, cooks, and other staff need to be scheduled?

The problem would best be solved by using past history to forecast or predict the number of customers and their menu preferences—which is exactly what any manager would do. With the data in hand, a manager can accurately order all food and supplies, direct kitchen production, and staff appropriately for the level of business anticipated.

Without an accurate sales history and sales forecast, life in the kitchen and dining room would be utter chaos. Guest satisfaction would be inconsistent. On some days enough servers and cooks will be scheduled, and on some days they will not. On some days enough food will be prepped, and some days it will not. In today's competitive restaurant world, there is no room and no reason for this level of guessing. Success begins with capturing information and using it to strategically plan, organize, and direct operations.

Sales History

A sales history records the "business history" of an operation. Each time a guest check is entered into the POS (point-of-sale) system, a detailed record of the day's business is recorded. All these details accumulated together create a story line: How many customers came in last week? Last month? What menu items did they select? Managers read and study the "business story line" via a Manager's Report—a summary report printed at the end of every shift. This report is a tool in the manager's toolbox that is used for the daily tasks of purchasing, forecasting sales, scheduling staff, and managing kitchen production.

Sales Forecasts

Sales forecasts—developed from the sales history—predict how many customers are expected. The forecast is generated electronically by the POS system, using sales data collected from guest checks. With a sales forecast, management is able to estimate the number of guests expected for any meal period.

Popularity Percentage (Index)

Armed with the sales forecast, the next step is to break down the forecasted guest count into estimates of which menu items guests will be likely to select. It is reasonable to conclude that the same proportion (percentage) of guests who normally consume a particular item will continue to do so unless there is some extenuating circumstance to say otherwise. This proportion (percentage) is known as the popularity percentage. The **popularity percentage**, or **popularity index**, is defined *as the frequency with which each menu item is selected as it competes with other menu items.* As long as the selection pattern shown via the sales history is stable, it is logical to use the popularity index to:

- Determine menu item counts.
- Determine order quantities.

How It's Computed   In Figure 5.2, the sales data for a one-week period is used to determine the popularity percentages for the soup selections at Farfalle Arrabbiata. Popularity indexes can be computed using sales information for a day, a week, a month, or any other time period. Popularity percentages (POP. % in the figure) can also be rolling—computed by adding the most recent day's sales information on to the existing data, while dropping the oldest data. The exact length of time to use for this is best determined by management. It should be a period of time that reflects the most current consumer purchase pattern.

To calculate the popularity percentage, divide each item's total number sold by the total number of items sold. Rounding up or down to the next whole number is acceptable. To check your work, add up the percentages. They should equal 100%. Over or under by less than one is a rounding issue. Anything more than that means there is a mathematical error. Here is what the equation should look like:

$$\frac{\text{EACH ITEM'S TOTAL NUMBER SOLD}}{\text{TOTAL NUMBER OF ITEMS SOLD}} = \text{POPULARITY \%}$$

This example can easily be turned into a rolling popularity percentage example by simply inserting the most current day's sales information into the appropriate day's spot. By dropping the old information, the popularity percentage reflects the most current sales information for the period identified. See Figure 5.3; the shaded areas show the new sales, new Sunday count, and new percentages.

Although calculating the percentages for one day or one week may not give a clear enough indication of just how popular an item is, using 6 months or a year's worth of data

SALES REPORT			WEEK OF: 2/14						
ITEM	**MON.**	**TUES.**	**WED.**	**THU.**	**FRI.**	**SAT.**	**SUN.**	**TOTAL**	**POP. %**
Chicken Noodle Soup	25	39	33	41	37	40	32	247/610 =	40
Pasta e Fagioli	35	25	32	15	28	31	29	195/610 =	32
Minestrone	15	27	14	25	36	21	30	168/610 =	28
TOTAL	75	91	79	81	101	92	91	610	100

FIGURE 5.2   Sales data for a one-week period, showing popularity percentages.

SALES REPORT			WEEK OF: 2/21						
ITEM	MON.	TUES.	WED.	THU.	FRI.	SAT.	SUN.	TOTAL	POP. %
Chicken Noodle Soup	25	39	33	41	37	40	42	257/630 =	41
Pasta e Fagioli	35	25	32	15	28	31	24	190/630 =	30
Minestrone	15	27	14	25	36	21	45	183/630 =	29
TOTAL	75	91	79	81	101	92	111	630	100

FIGURE 5.3 Sales data for a one-week period, calculating a rolling popularity percentage. The shaded show the new percentages.

is overkill. The goal is to find the relative popularity of an item in the business climate in which it is currently selling. To do this, choose a time frame with enough history to show a true pattern. If customer counts stay relatively steady, then a week or two is probably reasonable. If there is any doubt, increase the time frame accordingly.

Using the Popularity Percent to Determine Menu Counts   Once the popularity percent is known, using it with sales forecasts is quite easy. Here is an example:

Suppose the manager of Farfalle Arrabbiata is working on ordering product and completing production schedules for the end of the week. The sales forecast calls for

- 100 orders of soup for Friday
- 200 for Saturday
- 90 for Sunday

Altogether, 390 servings of soup are forecasted for the weekend.

The popularity indexes calculated in Figure 5.3 can be used to determine how many orders of *each kind of soup* will be needed for the weekend:

POPULARITY % × ITEM SALES FORECAST = NUMBER OF ITEMS
FORECAST TO BE SOLD

Here is what the forecast for soup, by type, will look like:

USING THE POPULARITY PERCENTAGE TO DETERMINE PORTION FORECASTS

	POP. %	Friday Forecast	Saturday Forecast	Sunday Forecast
Covers Forecast: 390		100	200	90
Chicken Noodle	40	100 × 40% = 40	200 × 40% = 80	90 × 40% = 36
Pasta e Fagioli	32	100 × 32% = 32	200 × 32% = 64	90 × 32% = 29
Minestrone	28	100 × 28% = 28	200 × 28% = 56	90 × 28% = 25

The work shown in the box reveals:

- A total of 156 orders of Chicken Noodle Soup are needed (40 + 80 + 36 = 156).
- A total of 125 orders of Pasta e Fagioli are needed (32 + 64 + 29 = 125).
- A total of 109 orders of Minestrone are needed (28 + 56 + 25 = 109).

Note the following as you work through these calculations:

- Always cross-check your work: 156 + 125 + 109 = 390 orders of soup. This matches the original forecast. Being off by one is simply rounding. Anything more than that is a math error.
- The result should always be in whole numbers. These are full orders of soup.

Be aware that popularity percentages will fluctuate, so it is best to base percentages on the most recent sales data. Some of the reasons for fluctuation are:

- Seasons—demand for soups, salads, and hearty/light foods will fluctuate by season.
- Weather events
- Food trends
- BOH inconsistencies—a management problem.
- Changes in the economic environment. Remember the internal and external environments discussed in Chapter 1.
- Menu changes
- Positioning on the menu
- Specials
- Special events
- Health or diet trends

The truth of the matter is that popularity percentages and sales history only go so far in predicting sales and customer preferences. They are not an absolute indicator of either, but using them is better than just taking a guess. These on-paper forecasts are not aware of external issues that could affect business on a day-to-day basis, however. For this reason, managers have to use their knowledge of external events and make adjustments accordingly.

Popularity indexes are often used to help identify consumer preferences for specific types of product (e.g., seafood, beef, or poultry). This information can then be used to develop menu selections that cross-utilize these products. This practice can lead to reduced purchasing costs and increased customer satisfaction.

Using Popularity Indexes to Build Order Quantities   Refer to Figure 5.1. We will now use popularity indexes to build order quantities: No. 2 in the Five Rights of Purchasing. Remember the goal posts on the football field: Don't run out and don't have too much on hand. Aim for mid-field! While a football team will never win a game by always being mid-field, a purchaser will. Ordering at "mid-field levels" means management is ordering enough product to carry production between order dates.

Par Stock

The key to determining what to order is knowing how much of any given item should be on hand in inventory. It is recommended that a par stock be set for all merchandise purchased. A **par stock**, or **par amount**, is *the minimum level of inventory needed to carry production between delivery dates*. The idea is not to have too much or too little of any item in inventory. Par amounts are used for several good reasons. For one, a par stock

- Enables any employee to determine order amounts if the buyer is not available.
- Reduces the possibility of spoilage through good inventory rotation.
- Eliminates the need for greater storage space and facilities.
- Reduces the temptation of theft.
- Reduces the dollar investment in inventory.
- Provides an adequate supply of food items to meet the expected product demand.

Par stock levels can be determined using a number of different approaches. Our discussion involves two methods:

1. Setting par stock levels using common usage patterns.
2. Setting par stock levels using formulas.

How a Manager Uses this Information

Once par stock levels are set, the information is transferred onto **order sheets**, which have been created from the inventory list. Order sheets are used to determine orders. Essentially, the order sheets create a **master grocery list** for the operation—*a list of every item used in production*. These forms are organized by product type: meats, poultry, fish and shellfish, dairy, produce, baked goods, and grocery. See Figures 5.4 through 5.9 for examples of order sheets.

Setting Par Using Common Usage Patterns

In operations with a limited inventory, a limited menu selection, and where a majority of the food is pre-prepared (i.e., not much cooking is done from recipe), it is easy to set pars by evaluating common usage patterns. What this means is *through observation, experience, and knowledge of the business, the chef or manager "knows" how much product is regularly used*. Thus, the par *is set by the working knowledge of these staff members*. This system works quite well in any operation but is easiest to apply in:

- Small businesses with a limited menu.
- Operations serving primarily pre-prepared foods and stocking a limited inventory.

An Example of Par Using Common Usage Patterns   Assume that Farfalle Arrabbiata uses diced Roma tomatoes for preparing the tomato sauce for the grilled pizzas and a number of other menu items. The specification calls for the tomatoes to be purchased in #10 cans, which are packed 6 per case. Chef Raoul has determined that every day at least 8 cans are used, and some days up to 11 cans may be used. This would be the **common usage pattern**. It evolved through Chef Raoul's *observation of the amount of product typically used over a period of time*. To be certain that there are enough tomatoes on hand, Chef Raoul should have at least 12 cans (one more than the highest usage amount) in inventory at all times. So the *per day* par amount is 12 - #10 cans. The par amount for between deliveries depends on how often deliveries take place. If deliveries occur twice a week, then the par amount that needs to be on the shelf is the *maximum number of days between deliveries multiplied by the maximum number of items used*. In this example it would be calculated as follows:

- Maximum number of items used per day: 12 - #10 cans
- Maximum number of days between deliveries: 3.5 days (7 days/2, or twice per week)
- Inventory par amount: 42 - #10 cans ($12 \times 3.5 = 42$)

A par amount of 42 cans means that Farfalle Arrabbiata should have a minimum of 42 - #10 cans of Roma tomatoes on the shelf on the day after delivery. The par amount may be adjusted to accommodate how the product is packed. As luck would have it, $42/6 = 7$ cases, so seven cases would be the par level of inventory needed for this particular item.

Ordering Tomatoes Using the Par Calculation   Determining how many cases of Roma diced tomatoes to order at any given time will depend on the number of cans currently on the shelf. If there are only four cans on the shelf and delivery is expected

ITEM: MEATS

Description	Pur. Unit	Monday Par	Monday On Hand	Monday Order	Tuesday Par	Tuesday On Hand	Tuesday Order	Wednesday Par	Wednesday On Hand	Wednesday Order	Thursday Par	Thursday On Hand	Thursday Order	Friday Par	Friday On Hand	Friday Order	Saturday Par	Saturday On Hand	Saturday Order	Sunday Par	Sunday On Hand	Sunday Order
Veal	10 lb. – 12 lb.	20 lb.	8 lb.	12 lb.						0	35 lb.	10 lb.	25 lb.			0			0			0
NY Sirloin	22 lb. – 25 lb.	25 lb.	5 lb.	20 lb.						0	45 lb.	15 lb.	30 lb.			0			0			0

FIGURE 5.4 Order sheets organized by product types: meat items.

ITEM: POULTRY		Monday			Tuesday			Wednesday			Thursday			Friday			Saturday			Sunday		
Description	Pur. Unit	Par	On Hand	Order	Par	On Hand	Order	Par	On Hand	Order	Par	On Hand	Order	Par	On Hand	Order	Par	On Hand	Order	Par	On Hand	Order
Chix Breast	10 lb.	30 lb.	15 lb.	15 lb.				35 lb.	10 lb.	25 lb.			0	40 lb.	15 lb.	25 lb.			0			0
Chix Tenders	10 lb.	15 lb.	5 lb.	10 lb.				20 lb.	6 lb.	14 lb.			0	35 lb.	10 lb.	25 lb.			0			0

FIGURE 5.5 Order sheets organized by product types: poultry items.

ITEM: SEAFOOD

Description	Purchasing Unit	Monday			Tuesday			Wednesday			Thursday			Friday			Saturday			Sunday		
		Par	On Hand	Order	Par	On Hand	Order	Par	On Hand	Order	Par	On Hand	Order	Par	On Hand	Order	Par	On Hand	Order	Par	On Hand	Order
Salmon	10 – 12 lb.	15 lb.	5 lb.	10 lb.				30 lb.	5 lb.	25 lb.			0	45 lb.	10 lb.	35 lb.			0			0
Shrimp	5 lb. bags	15 lb.	5 lb.	10 lb.						0			0	25 lb.	5 lb.	20 lb.			0			0
Squid	5 lb. bx.	60 lb.	10 lb.	20 lb.						0			0	85 lb.	15 lb.	70 lb.			0			0

FIGURE 5.6 Order sheets organized by product types: seafood items.

ITEM: DAIRY

Description	Purchasing Unit	Monday			Tuesday			Wednesday			Thursday			Friday			Saturday			Sunday		
		Par	On Hand	Order	Par	On Hand	Order	Par	On Hand	Order	Par	On Hand	Order	Par	On Hand	Order	Par	On Hand	Order	Par	On Hand	Order
Cream Cheese	3 lb. blk.	30 lb.	10 lb.	20 lb.						0			0	35 lb.	15 lb.	25 lb.			0			0
Sour Cream	½ gal.	4	1	3				8½'s	3	5			0	16½'s	5	9			0			0
Butter Pats	6 – 5 lb. cs.	1 cs.	5 lb.	1 cs.						0			0			0			0			0

FIGURE 5.7 Order sheets organized by product types: dairy items.

ITEM: GROCERY		Monday			Tuesday			Wednesday			Thursday			Friday			Saturday			Sunday		
Description	Pur. Unit	Par	On Hand	Order	Par	On Hand	Order	Par	On Hand	Order	Par	On Hand	Order	Par	On Hand	Order	Par	On Hand	Order	Par	On Hand	Order
Cr. Tomato	6/#10's cs.	46	6 cn.	40 cn.						0			0			0			0			0
Egg Noodles	2/5 lb. cs.	30 #	0 #	30 #						0			0			0			0			0
Veg. Oil	6 gal./cs.	2 cs.	2 g.	2 cs.						0			0			0			0			0

FIGURE 5.8 Order sheets organized by product types: grocery items.

ITEM: PRODUCE Description	Pur. Unit	Monday Par	On Hand	Order	Tuesday Par	On Hand	Order	Wednesday Par	On Hand	Order	Thursday Par	On Hand	Order	Friday Par	On Hand	Order	Saturday Par	On Hand	Order	Sunday Par	On Hand	Order
Romaine	24/cs.	2 cs.	1 cs.	1 cs.	3 cs.	1 cs.	2 cs.	3 cs.	1 cs.	2 cs.	4 cs.	1 cs.	3	8 cs.	1 cs.	7			0			0
Carrots	50 # bg.	1 bg.	½ bg.	1 bg.				1 bg.	0	1bg.			0	2 bg.	½ bg.	2 bg.			0			0
Span. Onion	50 # bg.	1 bg.	10 #	1 bg.							1 bg.	½ bg.	1 bg.						0			0
Celery	24/cs.	2 cs.	1 cs.	1 cs.				2 cs.	1 cs.	1 cs.				3 cs.	1 cs.	2 cs.			0			0

FIGURE 5.9 Order sheets organized by product types: produce items.

the following afternoon, the amount of tomatoes to be ordered would be determined as follows:

PAR AMOUNT − AMOUNT ON HAND = AMOUNT TO ORDER

Par amount of #10 cans of tomatoes needed	42
−Number of #10 cans of tomatoes on hand	− 4
Total number of #10 cans of tomatoes to be ordered	38

In this example, because there are six cans per case, 38 cans divided by 6 cans equals 6.33 cases. Chef Raoul should order 7 cases.

$$38 \text{ cans}/6 \text{ cans per case} = 6.33 \text{ cases}$$
$$\text{Order 7 cases}$$

Using Formulas to Calculate Par

Another method of determining par involves the use of a formula. The formula uses a number of variables to determine a par. These variables are

- The number of forecasted servings.
- The portion size expressed as a decimal or part of the purchasing unit.
- Yield percentage.

The beauty of this formula is that it can be used with each week's sales forecast to set pars for all items. The not-so-beautiful thing about it is that it is not realistic to sit down each week with pen and paper and determine a par for every item in inventory. A computer programmed to perform this function is the solution. Using technology, a foodservice manager simply drops the sales data into the computer and par amounts are determined quickly and efficiently in a matter of minutes. In other words, don't try this by hand!

Interestingly, the following formula can also be used to calculate par amounts as well as to order amounts for different situations. By rearranging the variables, we can solve for a number of other factors. Watch for further discussion of this issue a little later on in the chapter. Here's the formula:

$$\text{PAR AMOUNT} = \frac{\text{NUMBER OF SERVINGS DESIRED} \times \text{PORTION SIZE (as a decimal)}}{\text{YIELD \%}}$$

Remember that **yield percentage** tells *how much of the whole product (100%) is left to sell to a guest as a menu item.* Let's determine the par for the week for the Filetto di Maiale (pork tenderloin) marinated in honey Dijon mustard and fresh herbs. Assume whole pork tenderloins are purchased and trimmed by the staff. What information is needed to do the computation? Check the formula and the following table

VARIABLE	WHERE IS THE INFO FROM?	RESULT
# of servings	Current sales forecast.	240 orders
Portion size	Standard recipe	12 oz.
Yield %	Butcher Test or supplier	86%

$$\text{PAR AMOUNT} = \frac{\text{NO. OF SERVINGS DESIRED} \times \text{PORTION SIZE (as a decimal)}}{\text{YIELD \%}}$$

$$209.3 \text{ pounds, or 210 pounds} = \frac{240 \text{ servings} \times .75 \ (12/16)}{86\%}$$

The par for the pork tenderloin for this week is 210 pounds.

What About Other Types of Products?   The same formula can be adapted to just about anything ordered, as long as the portion size, yield percentage, and purchasing unit are known. Let's try a few examples; but first, make note of a few caveats:

1. In this work, the portion size is expressed as a decimal, or percentage amount of the **purchasing unit**.
2. The yield percentage will be the servable amount of the purchasing unit. It can be found in the usual ways: Calculate it yourself or refer to *The Book of Yields*.

Tomato sauce for the pizzas served at Farfalle Arrabbiata is ordered from a specialty sauce maker. One case contains 2 - 1 gallon bags. Pizza sales for this week are forecast at 500 orders.

PAR AMOUNT =

$$24.67, \text{ or } 25 \text{ gallons} = \frac{\text{NO. OF SERVINGS DESIRED} \times \text{PORTION SIZE (\% of purchasing unit)}}{\text{YIELD \% (\% of purchasing unit)}}$$

$$24.67, \text{ or } 25 \text{ gallons} = \frac{500 \times .046875 \text{ (6 ounces/128 ounces per gallon)}}{95\% \text{ (Yield \%)}}$$

Because the sauce is purchased at 2 bags per case, the number of cases for the par for this week would be:

$$25 \text{ bags}/2 = 12.5, \text{ or } 13 \text{ cases}$$

Let's try an example with produce. Mista mix is used in a number of salads. Let's say the sales forecast for salads incorporating Mista mix for the week is 320 orders. Standard portion size is 4 ounces of greens. The yield is 98%. Mista mix is purchased in 10 pound cases.

PAR AMOUNT =

$$76.53, \text{ or } 77 \text{ pounds} = \frac{\text{NO. OF SERVINGS DESIRED} \times \text{PORTION SIZE (\% OF PURCHASING UNIT)}}{\text{YIELD \% (\% of purchasing unit)}}$$

$$76.53, \text{ or } 77 \text{ pounds} = \frac{300 \times .25 \text{ (4 ounces/16 ounces per pound)}}{98\% \text{ (Yield \%)}}$$

The par for the Mista mix for this week is 77 pounds. The number of cases can be found by dividing this amount by the case weight.

$$77 \text{ pounds}/10 \text{ pounds per case} = 7.7, \text{ or } 8 \text{ cases}$$

Once the par is calculated, the amount is transferred to the par sheet and the buyer goes about his or her business creating the order for the week. Of course, this is all based on the ease of availability. At certain times, a product may not be readily available or will be increasing in price. This is when advance buying may be the most economical decision. Buying enough when products are available and when significant price increases are expected will save money and ensure that supplies remain in stock. If the par amount is maintained, there should always be an adequate amount of products available. The manager must keep in mind that the par must be continually adjusted as sales increase or decrease.

A par amount is set for every item kept in inventory. Once par amounts have been calculated, the first step in determining what to order is complete.

*U*sing Par Inventory Amounts with Order Sheets to Order Product

The **order sheet** represents a systematic approach to controlling what to buy from suppliers (see Figures 5.4 through 5.9 for examples). As mentioned, all products in inventory should have an established par, set either by common usage patterns or formulas as described previously.

HOW TO SET UP AND USE ORDER SHEETS

1. Create order sheets for all product categories.

Meats
Poultry
Fish and shellfish
Produce
Dairy
Baked
Groceries
Sundries

2. List all inventory items on the appropriate **order sheet**. (This list is created from inventory lists.) You have now created the **order book**!

3. Enter Par Inventory Levels for all products on the order sheets.

4. When getting ready to place an order, enter the number of units into the Amount on Hand column. Subtract this amount from the Par amount. This is the order amount needed for the next delivery.

The order sheets are organized to follow normal product ordering categories: meats, poultry, seafood, dairy, baked goods, grocery, and so on. The next step (Step 2 in the Orders Sheets box) is to list all the products and their par (Step 3) onto the sheets, creating an **order book**. Product inventory lists such as the one used to take a physical inventory are the database for this information. These lists are a result of standardized recipes. Computerized menu management systems simplify this task. Step 4 determines the order amount.

An order sheet may be set up to accommodate ordering on a daily, semiweekly, weekly, semimonthly, or monthly basis. The **order sheet** starts with the name of the product and its inventory number. It also asks for an item description and order unit. The remaining boxes on the form show how to go about establishing par amounts and determining the amount to be ordered. Check out the example of order sheets for Figures 5.4 through 5.9.

Notice the ingredients on the order sheets match the recipes for the Chicken Noodle Soup and for the Bowtie Pasta. A few other examples are included. The par amounts would have been computed using one of the methods discussed.

Order Form Details

The first column, **Item Description**, should include the *name of the product to be ordered*, an identifiable variety, brand name, grade, and identification number or some other description of the product in terms of standard and quality.

The next column, **Unit**, is used to indicate the *purchasing unit* of the item being ordered. The purchasing unit represents *how items are packaged for delivery*. In the example, lettuce is delivered by the case.

After the unit column, the next 14 columns identify, alternately, the Day and Order. In the Day column, indicated by the day of the week, the par amount, or,

Par, is recorded in the left part of the box. The **on-hand amount** is *the actual product amount in inventory* and is written in the next part of the box. The difference between what is written is on the left and to the right of it is the amount to be ordered. This figure is recorded in the adjacent Order column to the right of the Day column.

For perishable items, the par can be set at varying levels during the week. Nonperishables do not need this type of adjustment. Note on the sample order sheet that the par for the Romaine is higher toward the end of the week, reflecting the normal business pattern for a restaurant—peak business at the end of the week. Because of the perishable nature of the Romaine (and lots of other items!), it makes sense to vary the par from day to day.

Notice on the sample order sheet that the **par** for Romaine on Monday is two cases. See Figure 5.9, this represents the par amount needed for a scheduled Tuesday delivery. The actual amount of Romaine on hand is one case. The order amount is the difference between two cases and one case of lettuce, which is one case.

PAR FOR ROMAINE − ON HAND = AMOUNT TO ORDER
2 cases − 1 case on hand = 1 case to order

One case of Romaine needs to be ordered for the Tuesday delivery. This amount is written in the Order column. An order for a Tuesday delivery would normally be prepared late in the day or at the close of business on Monday and telephoned, faxed, or e-mailed to the supplier for next-day delivery. Suppliers may start processing orders as early as 1:00 a.m. for early-morning deliveries. Note that the par amounts increase as the week goes on to accommodate the weekend business.

This system exercises tight control of inventory, ensuring proper rotation and reducing the possibility of spoilage as the older items are used first. Items that are supplied on a contract basis (as is common with produce, dairy, or baked products) rather than daily or weekly may be organized on order sheets by supplier name versus product type.

*R*equisitions

There's another way to order products: Use requisitions. Requisitions are a simple way of preparing a grocery list. Think of it this way: A family member is sent to the supermarket with a list of items to purchase for dinner. If he or she is going to the market to buy items for two different people, then two lists are needed, along with two receipts and separate cash envelopes to keep the change separate.

A requisition system accomplishes the same goal—shopping for more than one department—and is best suited for *large foodservice operations with multiple revenue centers* (for example, a hotel with several restaurants, a coffee shop, a lounge or bar, and event or meeting space). The function of the requisition system is to

1. Assist the purchaser in the timely ordering of adequate supplies for all departments.
2. Identify costs directly associated with each department, so they can be accurately charged back.
3. Assist in tracking departmental costs, so a Food Cost Report can be prepared. (Food Cost Reports will be covered in a later chapter.)

The Requisition Process

The following shows how the requisition works:

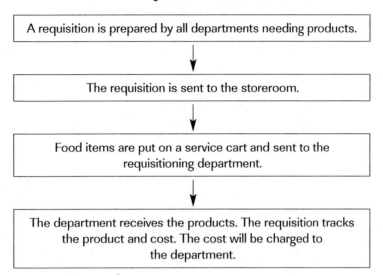

THE REQUISITION PROCESS

A requisition is prepared by all departments needing products.

↓

The requisition is sent to the storeroom.

↓

Food items are put on a service cart and sent to the requisitioning department.

↓

The department receives the products. The requisition tracks the product and cost. The cost will be charged to the department.

So What Exactly Is a Requisition?

A **requisition** is, simply, *a request*. It is *a request from individual departments to the purchaser for food, nonfood, and beverage products needed for production*. The requisition is an in-house form, with several characteristics:

- It is completed and signed by a manager or chef or other authorized individual.
- It works as a control tool and a security tool.
- It is used by the buyer to compile orders for suppliers.
- It is used to issue these ordered products to each respective department.
- It is used to charge the cost of these products to the requisitioning department.

A **requisition** can also be thought of as *a written order to obtain products from the shelves of the storeroom, the walk-in refrigerator, or the freezer*.

A requisition system controls and tracks the movement and use of all products within a foodservice operation. Requisitions are typically used in high-volume foodservice operations with units that are part of hotels, resorts, healthcare providers, large country clubs, and other organizations with multiple foodservice locations. These operations have multiple departments, such as a coffee shop, multiple dining rooms, a catering service, a snack bar, a lounge, and so on.

The manner in which requisitions are used depends on the size of the operation:

- In smaller foodservice operations, requisitions are usually completed by the executive chef or kitchen manager and turned in to the manager or owner.
- In larger foodservice operations, requisitions may be filled out by line cooks, sous chefs, or executive chefs and turned in to a storeroom manager. The **storeroom manager** is *in charge of all stores, both food and nonfood, and will issue the items to the requesting department*.
- In many operations, the purchasing function is executed effectively without the use of requisitions at all.

Types of Requisitions

A requisition can be prepared in two basic formats. The first is called a par amount requisition. The second is a blank requisition. A blank requisition is just that—blank. It is filled out with product requests as needed.

TYPES OF REQUISITIONS

1. **Par Amount Requisition:** A preprinted requisition sheet with par amounts assigned to each inventory in regular use.
2. Blank Requisition: A requisition form that is filled out by staff.

Par Amount Requisitions

The **par amount requisition** is a *preprinted requisition sheet with par amounts (a predetermined level or numbers of an item kept in inventory) assigned to each inventory item in regular use.* It marries the concept of establishing par inventory levels with a requisition system to compute order amounts.

Par amount requisitions work best when dealing with a department such as a snack bar with a fixed, limited menu, or a unit within a department that uses a fixed amount of products.

A good example would be a coffee shop that repeatedly uses juices, post mix (a method of dispensing carbonated beverages), and premade pies.

The par amount requisition lists all the products that the department uses and can be thought of as a **master grocery list**—*a list of all products used in that department.* The form lists:

- The stock number
- The item description
- The unit size
- The par amount
- The On Hand and To Order columns
- The current price
- The extension.

The par amount is established on the basis of a common usage pattern and in anticipation of sales. It is important to note, however, that if there is a large banquet or a special event in the community, sales will be higher than normal and the par amounts will have to be temporarily increased. Conversely, bad weather and other circumstances will negatively affect sales, and par amounts will have to be adjusted down.

If the par amount is maintained, there should always be an adequate amount of products available for the anticipated level of sales. The manager must keep in mind that the par amount must be continually adjusted as sales increase or decrease. Also, the manager should make adjustments for certain days of the week that may be busier than others. The par amount requisition can be one page or several pages in length. It can also be used in conjunction with blank requisitions.

The beauty of the par amount requisition is that it *reduces the risk of forgetting items used during the peak periods such as breakfast, lunch, or dinner.* By avoiding shortages or stockouts during the rush hours, employees will experience less stress, and customer satisfaction is further assured.

Example of a Par Amount Requisition   The restaurant profile described Farfalle Arrabbiata as being located in a building that housed offices as well as several small businesses selling food. Assume that Farfalle Arrabbiata operates a coffee shop as a kiosk in the building. In essence, this operation is a satellite operation. Because the menu is limited and the same items are sold daily, a preprinted par amount requisition would work nicely in ensuring that this outlet is always properly stocked. Figure 5.10 shows a number of stock items that the kiosk would typically replenish daily at 10:00 a.m., a slow period following breakfast and preceding lunch. As shown in the example, juices are to be restocked after the morning commuters are well into their workday. The juice will thus be in place and properly chilled for the next morning. Post mix and fresh pies will be in place for lunch. This will keep up a balance of product quality, freshness, and ready availability.

PAR AMOUNT REQUISITION					
Date: 2/14/2XXX			Transfer Number: 524		
Time: 10 A.M.			Priced By: ABC		
Prepared By: DJF			Extended By: DEF		
Delivered By: JC			Approved By: GHI		
Received By: LARRY					
ITEM DESCRIPTION	PAR	ON HAND	ORDER	PRICE	EXTENSION
JUICES					
Apple (46 oz.)	2	2	0	$1.49	$0
Grapefruit (46 oz.)	3	½	2	1.17	2.34
Pineapple (46 oz.)	2	1½	0	1.17	0
Tomato (46 oz.)	3	1	2	.96	1.92
V-8 (5.5 oz.)	6	2	4	.27	1.08
POST MIX					
Cola	2	½	2	33.00	66.00
Diet Cola	1	½	0	33.00	0
Root Beer	1	¼	1	33.00	33.00
Orange	1	½	0	33.00	0
PIES					
Apple (10 inch)	2	0	2	3.60	7.20
Blueberry (10 inch)	1	0	1	4.85	4.85
Cherry (10 inch)	3	0	3	5.05	15.15
Chocolate (10 inch)	1	0	1	4.25	4.25
Lemon (10 inch)	2	0	2	4.25	8.50
Boston Crème	1	0	1	5.25	5.25
TOTAL					$149.54

Original Copy: To remain with issuing department
Duplicate Copy: To be sent to the receiving department

FIGURE 5.10   A par amount requisition.

The on-hand amount on the par amount requisition is the physical count of the item kept in the appropriate storage area. To determine the order, as in the previous discussion of using par, subtract the on-hand number from the par to get the amount to order. The unit price for each item is taken directly from the most recent invoice, so current pricing is always maintained. Extensions are calculated by multiplying the price by the order.

Blank Requisitions

TYPES OF REQUISITIONS

1. **Par Amount Requisition**—A preprinted requisition sheet with par amounts assigned to each inventory in regular use.
2. **Blank Requisition**—A requisition form filled out by staff.

The second requisition format is a **blank requisition**. The only difference between a par amount requisition and a blank requisition is that the blank one *does not have the product items and par amounts preprinted on the form.* The manager must fill in the requisition with the items needed, each time they are needed. Operations using a requisition system can use preprinted forms or blank forms, or both types. If preprinted forms are used, blank requisitions are still a part of the system. Because preprinted forms are used for items implemented on a daily or regular basis, blank requisitions are used for items that are not needed on a daily basis. A blank requisition is shown in Figure 5.11. Some operations do not use preprinted forms at all; blank requisitions are used for all ordering. It's obvious to see that preprinted forms are more efficient.

Requisitions should be printed with sequential numbers, in the same manner as personal checks. The requisition is like a check written to the storeroom for products. The **sequential numbering system** *allows the manager to track requisitions and see*

A BLANK REQUISITION

Dept.:				
Date:		Transfer Number:		
Time:		Priced By:		
Prepared By:		Extended By:		
Delivered By:		Approved By:		
Received By:				
ITEM	**UNIT**	**QUANTITY**	**PRICE**	**EXTENSION**
TOTAL				

Original Copy: To remain with issuing department
Duplicate Copy: To be sent to the receiving department

FIGURE 5.11   A blank requisition.

how they are used, which makes it easy to account for every requisition, in case the potential for mishandling or misuse existed. If a mistake is ever made, as with a bank check, the requisition can be voided, the error recorded, and the next number used. If the potential for mishandling does not exist, preprinted numbers are not necessary. Finally, all requisitions should identify by name and signature the person preparing, delivering, and receiving the products. Sign-offs will tighten the physical control when theft or sloppy order filling may be a problem.

Note about this form:

1. Prepared By, Delivered By, Received By, Approved By—These are sign-offs that work as a control.

The sign-offs validate that

- The product ordered was needed by the department.
- The product was actually delivered.
- The product was actually received.

2. Transfer Number—This number tracks and charges the product from the storage areas to the receiving department. Each department will have a department number.

3. Priced By, Extended By—These sign-offs ensure proper charging to departments.

Example of When to Use a Blank Requisition   Suppose the coffee kiosk had a request from a good customer for some fresh fruit needed for an office meeting. These items are not normally stocked at the kiosk and are not in inventory in the restaurant. The server or supervisor would fill out a blank requisition to request the product. The buyer, Marcel, would receive the requisition, order the necessary product, and deliver it to the kiosk. The kiosk staff, in turn, would sell the products to customers. The requisition would tip off Marcel that something different was being ordered. The requisition would track the product and the cost, enabling Marcel to properly charge the kiosk for the product. The following is a fully completed blank requisition:

COMPLETED REQUISITION

Dept.: Kitchen					
Date: 2/14/2XXX			Transfer Number: 1234		
Time: 10:00 A.M.			Priced By: Marcel		
Prepared By: DJF			Extended By: Jackie		
Delivered By: Zach			Approved By: JR		
Received By: Stacey					
	REC.				
ITEM		UNIT	QUANTITY	PRICE	EXTENSION
Mangoes		each	25	$1.00 each	$25.00
Pineapples		each	4	$2.00 each	8.00
Peaches		each	25	$1.00 each	25.00
TOTAL					$58.00

Original Copy: To remain with issuing department
Duplicate Copy: To be sent to the receiving department

Ordering for Functions

The work we have done thus far deals with ordering product for a restaurant where a sales history and customer preferences are, for the most part, known. These order quantities do not take into account ordering for functions, however. Because functions change constantly, product ordering has to be done on a function-by-function basis. These products will then be added on to the restaurant orders. This scenario assumes a limited amount of function space, and both restaurant and function ordering are combined.

Ordering for functions follows the same pattern as ordering for the restaurant menu: standardized recipes identify product to be ordered and specifications define the quality. The next step is calculating how much to purchase. This, of course, depends on the guarantee guest count for each function. Let's assume that Farfalle Arrabbiata has a function for the upcoming weekend. Remember the 300 diners from the Association of Split Pea Soup Makers in the exercises for Chapter 3? Assume Mr. Peter Soup (the director of the Association) has booked their closing function at Farfalle Arrabbiata. They are guaranteeing 300 guests and have selected the following as their menu:

- Shrimp Cocktail Appetizer
- Chicken Noodle Soup
- Caesar's Salad
- Roast Sirloin of Beef, or Grilled Salmon with Dill Sauce
- Roasted Rosemary Potatoes
- Honey Glazed Parsley Carrots
- Strawberry Cheesecake

To prepare the order, recipe quantities for the ingredients are identified. The goal is to determine the bulk amount of product to order, so it can be added to the restaurant order. This example demonstrates setting the order quantity for the main entrée plate. The items on the plate have a yield percent. If you order products without taking the yield into account, you may run short during plating. Plating is not the time to realize this mistake. See Figure 5.12 for an example of ordering for a function.

CALCULATING THE FUNCTION ORDER

Menu Item	A Guest Count	B POP. %	C No. to Produce	D Portion Size on Plate	E Raw Ounces Needed	F Yield %	G Adjusted Ounces (will be more than column E)	H Divided by 16 (ounces per pound)	I Amount to Purchase
Roast Sirloin	300	60	180	9 oz.	1620 oz.	70%	2315 oz.	144.68 lb.	145 lb.
Grilled Salmon	300	40	120	8 oz.	960 oz.	95%	1011 oz.	63.18 lb.	64 lb.
Roasted Potatoes	300	100	300	5 oz.	1500 oz.	97%	1547 oz.	96.68 lb.	97 lb.
Honey Carrots	300	100	300	4 oz.	1200 oz.	87%	1380 oz.	86.25 lb.	87 lb.
THE MATH:	A × B	=	C	× D	= E	/ F	= G	/ 16	= I

FIGURE 5.12 Calculating the function order.

Note: The yield percentage for products can be learned from suppliers, by performing yield tests in-house, or by referencing industry publications like *The Book of Yields.*

Using the Par Formula to Calculate Order Amounts

Once the concepts we just discussed are mastered, it is easy to see that it is quicker and more efficient to use a formula to do the same work. A chart is useful because of the visual picture it creates. Once the concept is mastered, however, using a simple manipulation of the par formula explained earlier will give the same result more quickly.

Interestingly, the variables in the par formula can be adapted to solve for a number of other factors. First, let's demonstrate how to use the formula to determine an order amount for a banquet. Start with the information from the Roast Sirloin example in Figure 5.12.

AMOUNT TO ORDER =

$$\frac{\text{NO. OF SERVINGS DESIRED} \times \text{PORTION SIZE (as a decimal)}}{\text{YIELD \%}}$$

The amount of Roast Sirloin to order for the function above can be found as follows:

$$145 \text{ pounds} = \frac{180 \text{ servings} \times .5625 \text{ (9 ounces/16 ounces)}}{70 \%}$$

The amount calculated exactly matches the amount of roast sirloin calculated on the chart. The amount to purchase (145 pounds) can then be turned into an order amount by dividing the amount needed by the amount per case. In this example, the order would most likely be placed using the total poundage needed versus case weight.

Using the Par Formula to Calculate Number of Portions, Portion Size, and Yield Percentage

The same formula can be used to solve for other desired results. The variables can be manipulated in three additional ways:

1. The number of portions from a quantity of meat can be calculated if the portion size and yield percentage is known.

$$\text{NUMBER OF PORTIONS} = \frac{\text{QUANTITY OF MEAT} \times \text{YIELD \%}}{\text{PORTION SIZE (as a decimal)}}$$

$$180 = \frac{145 \times .70}{.5625}$$

2. The portion size can be calculated if the number of servings, yield percentage, and quantity of meat are known.

$$\text{PORTION SIZE} = \frac{\text{QUANTITY OF MEAT} \times \text{YIELD \%}}{\text{NUMBER OF SERVINGS}}$$

$$9 \text{ ounces} = \frac{145 \times .70}{180}$$

Note: The answer is .5638 and represents the portion size as a decimal. This is close to the variable of .5625 and represents the portion size as a decimal as originally calculated. The difference between the two is simply rounding. Here's how to calculate the portion size: 16 (ounces per pound) × .5638 = 9 ounces. This matches the original portion size on the chart.

COST PER PORTION CALCULATION FOR FUNCTION ORDER					
Item	Amount to Purchase	AP Price	Total AP Cost	No. of Servings	Cost Per Portion
Roast Sirloin	145 lb.	$4.45/lb.	$645.25	180	$3.59
Grilled Salmon	64 lb.	5.50/lb.	352.00	120	2.94
Roasted Potatoes	97 lb.	.98/lb.	95.06	300	.32
Honey Carrots	87 lb.	.65/lb.	56.55	300	.19
THE MATH:	A ×	B	= C	/ E	= F

FIGURE 5.13 Cost per portion calculation for function order.

3. The yield percentage can be calculated if the number of servings, the portion size, and the original quantity of meat is known.

$$\text{YIELD \%} = \frac{\text{NUMBER OF SERVINGS} \times \text{PORTION SIZE (as a decimal)}}{\text{QUANTITY OF MEAT}}$$

$$70\% = \frac{180 \times .5625}{145}$$

Amount Purchased Equivalency

The **Amount Purchased Equivalency** is *the ratio of portion size to the yield percentage.* By calculating this factor, you can quickly calculate the cost per portion for menu items where the portion size and the yield percentage are known. Here is the formula. You then have the **Amount Purchased Equivalency (APE)**.

PORTION SIZE/16 (OUNCES PER 1 POUND)/STANDARD YIELD % =
AMOUNT PURCHASED EQUIVALENCY (APE)

AMOUNT PURCHASED EQUIVALENCY × INVOICE PRICE =
COST PER PORTION

Test this on the Roast Sirloin example:

$$9/16 = .5625$$
$$.5625/.70 = .8035$$
$$.8035 \times \$4.45 = \$3.58$$

Compare the answer, $3.58, with the chart in Figure 5.13. They match. Initially, because it is visual, the chart version of this work may be easier to understand. After working with these formulas, you should find them faster and easier than filling out a chart.

Performing a Yield Analysis for Canned Products

Another important task in identifying and controlling portion costs is determining yields for canned products. This activity, called **can cutting**, is helpful in determining how much to order because it identifies exactly how much servable product is in a can (EP–edible portion). It also assists in making purchasing decisions by identifying the best EP price by specific brand name.

Yield analysis may be used to check net weight and drained weight claims made by manufacturers. **Net weight** is *the total weight of the product and the packing* *medium.* The **packing medium** is the *fluid in which the product is packed.* This is usually water or a type of syrup. **Drained weight** represents *what is left after the packing medium is removed.*

The following represents how the yield of a #10 can of fruit is checked according to the traditional procedure:

PROCEDURE FOR PERFORMING A CAN CUTTING

1. *Note the net weight.* The net weight is the weight of all the contents of the can; it is listed on the can. All manufacturers of food products are required to list the net weight.
2. *Note the drained weight.* Drained weight is the weight of the items in the can after the medium has been poured off. This will be the servable weight and is what is important to know for portion costing. Not all manufacturers list drained weight. If it is listed, then it is usually printed under the net weight. Even if this information is listed on the can, it is best to check the accuracy of this information.
3. *Note the product count.* The **product count** is the *number or range of items in the container.* The product count is usually listed on the label next to the description of the items in the can—for example, Elberta peach halves, 30 to 35 count per #10 can.
4. *Open the can and empty the contents.* How this is done depends on what is in the can. If the contents of the can fill up the can, they should be poured into a bowl. Prior to pouring out the contents, the bowl should be weighed so the bowl weight can be subtracted later. After pouring the contents into the bowl, the bowl and its contents are weighed. If the product is packed in a medium, then two bowls will be needed: one bowl to separate the product from the medium and one bowl in which to weigh the product.
5. *Compare the net weight, drained weight, or count with what is listed on the can.* If a discrepancy is found, the chef or manager should talk to the supplier about obtaining a credit.

Regardless of how the product is packaged, a cost should be assigned to the usable food. If peach halves, 30 to 35 count, packed in light syrup, are used and the can of peaches costs $4.36, the cost of one peach half at most is $.145 ($4.36/30 = $.1453). If Chef Raoul decides to use canned peaches for a menu item, he now knows exactly the cost for the product.

Can cutting will also allow the buyer to find out which brands yield the best final EP cost. It is not enough to simply look at the invoice cost of canned products and make a selection based on price alone. Savvy buyers and chefs calculate the true cost and yield of the product inside the purchasing unit. Always remember: AP is not EP. It is a fact of life that the lowest AP price will not necessarily work out to the lowest EP cost. Because selling prices are set on EP, management must do their homework by determining the effect of product yield on final EP cost.

₋*Ν*et Work

Explore the following Web sites:
www.farmersmarket.com—Farmer's Market
www.nrn.com—Nation's Restaurant News
www.rimag.com—Restaurants and Institutions

Chapter Wrap

The Chapter ✓ at the beginning of the chapter posed several questions. Review the questions and compare your responses with the following answers:

1. **What data is used to determine order quantity?**

   Sales history, sales forecasts, and popularity percentages are key data used to formulate order quantities. The sales history tells what happened in the past. Sales forecasts predict what is likely to occur in the future. Popularity percentages track guest menu preferences.

2. **What is a par stock?**

   One key in determining what to order is knowing how much of any given item should be on hand in inventory. It is recommended that a par stock or par amount be set for all merchandise purchased. A par stock or amount is the minimum level of inventory needed to carry production between delivery dates. The idea is not to have too much or too little of any item in inventory.

3. **How are food orders prepared using a par?**

   Par stock levels can be determined using a number of different approaches. Two methods are:

   1. Setting par stock levels using common usage patterns.
   2. Setting par stock levels using standardized recipes.

   Once the par stock levels are set, the information is transferred onto order sheets created from the inventory list. Essentially, the order sheets create a master grocery list for the operation—a list of every item used in production. These forms are organized by product type for ease in ordering: meats, poultry, fish and shellfish, dairy, produce, baked, and grocery.

4. **How are requisitions used to prepare orders?**

   A requisition is, simply, *a request*. It is a request from individual departments to the purchaser for food, nonfood, and beverage products needed for production. The requisition is an in-house form. A requisition system controls and tracks the movement and use of all products within a foodservice operation. It can be prepared in two basic formats. The first is called a par amount requisition. The second is a blank requisition.

   The par amount requisition is a *preprinted requisition sheet with par amounts (a predetermined level or numbers of an item kept in inventory) assigned to each inventory item in regular use*. It marries the concept of establishing par inventory levels with a requisition system to compute order amounts. A blank requisition is filled out with product requests, as needed.

5. **How are orders prepared for functions?**

   Ordering for functions follows the same pattern as ordering for the restaurant menu: Standardized recipes identify product to be ordered and the portions size. The specs define the quality. The next step is calculating how much to purchase. Bulk products with less than 100% yield have to have this loss accounted for before purchasing.

6. **How are canned products analyzed for yield?**

   Another important task in identifying and controlling portion costs is determining yields for canned products. This activity is helpful in determining how much to order because it identifies exactly how much servable product is in a can (EP—edible portion). It also assists in making purchasing decisions by identifying the best EP price by specific brand name.

Yield analysis may be used to check net weight and drained weight claims made by manufacturers. Net weight is the total weight of the product and the packing medium. The packing medium is the fluid in which the product is packed. This is usually water or a type of syrup. Drained weight represents what is left after the packing medium is removed.

$\mathcal{K}$ey Terminology and Concepts in This Chapter

Amount Purchased Equivalency (APE)	Par stock/amount
Blank requisition	Popularity percentage (popularity index)
Can cutting	Product count
Common usage pattern	Purchasing unit
Drained weight	Requisition
Master grocery list	Sales forecasts
Net weight	Sales history
On-hand amount	Sequential numbering system
Order book	Storeroom manager
Order sheets	Yield analysis
Packing medium	Yield percentage
Par amount requisition	

$\mathcal{D}$iscussion Questions and Exercises

1. How does a sales history assist management with the ordering process?
2. How is a sales forecast used by managers and chefs to plan for daily production?
3. Define popularity percentage.
4. The following sales record was retrieved from the POS system at Farfalle Arrabbiata. Calculate the popularity percentage for each item.

ITEM	10/1	10/2	10/3	10/4	TOTAL	POP %
Insalata Cesare	35	28	46	30		
Insalata Mista	47	43	55	41		
Portobello, Prosciutto, and Vegetables	29	23	20	26		
Insalata Gorgonzola	23	18	25	12		
Total						

Following is the forecast for next weekend. Using the popularity percentages you just calculated, determine how many orders of each Chef Raoul and Marcel, the buyer, should plan for.

FORECAST	POP %	FRI 148	SAT 165	SUN 125
Item				
Insalata Cesare				
Insalata Mista				
Portobello, Prosciutto, and Vegetables				
Insalata Gorgonzola				
Total				

5. The produce order has to be called in by 3:00 p.m. today. Marcel, the buyer, is off today, so the job falls to you. The following is a list of the greens and produce used for the salad selections. Marcel has developed a par for each, using the common usage pattern. Determine how much of each must be ordered.

GREENS	PAR	ON-HAND	TO ORDER
Romaine	8 cases	3 cases	
Mista Mix	3 cases	1 case	
Peppers, Red	3 cases	2 cases	
Arugula	2 cases	2 cases	
Onions, Spanish	4 bags	2 bags	
Portobello Mushrooms	2 cases	.5 case	

6. As manager, one of your responsibilities is to monitor food orders so that you stay out of the proverbial "end zones." You have been looking over food orders with Chef Raoul and Marcel, and you notice the invoices for the olive oil. What should you do about the order amounts? What is the ramification of the inventory levels of the olive oil?

DATE	ORDER AMOUNT
10/1	19 cases
10/8	17 cases
10/15	15 cases
10/22	9 cases
10/29	11 cases
11/4	7 cases

7. Chef Raoul is very perplexed. After adjusting the par for the Colvita Olive Oil down because of the ordering situation revealed by the analysis above, the kitchen is suddenly running short. There isn't enough for the weekend. With a once-a-week delivery, it won't be in until next Tuesday. How could this situation have been avoided? What clues did management miss that should have been a tip off that inventory levels needed adjusting again? What operating information should management watch more closely to prevent this situation from occurring again?

8. The sales rep for Farfalle Arrabbiata has brought in a new brand of canned pineapple chunks. Chef Raoul is performing a can cutting to compare the yield to the brand he currently uses. Describe the procedure he should use to determine the best yield. In addition to the yield, what else should Chef evaluate?

9. The Rock, Scissors, Paper Association has booked a function for Saturday night. The food for this event must be added to the regular food orders. Marcel is still out of town, so it has fallen on you to figure the amounts needed for the function. Guests have been given the following choices; compute the bulk order quantities for each item. The guarantee is for 400.

BULK ORDER CHART

Menu Item	A Guest Count	B POP. %	C No. to Produce	D Portion Size on Plate	E Raw Ounces Needed	F Yield %	G Adjusted Ounces (will be more than column E)	H Divided by 16 (ounces per pound)	I Amount to Purchase
Insalata Cesare	400	60		6 oz.	170	85			
Insalata Gorgonzola	400	40		6 oz.	170	95			
Scallopine Di Vitello	400	25		8 oz.	227	92			
Salmon a la Criglia	400	30		8 oz.	227	96			
Bistecca	400	45		10 oz.	284	85			
Fettucini Fontina	400	100		5 oz.	142	100			
Fresh Asparagus	400	100		4 oz.	113	90			

10. Determine the total quantity of greens needed for this produce order by adding in the Romaine needed for the function in Question 9. Assume Romaine is needed for both the Insalata Cesare and Insalata Gorgonzola.

ORDER SHEET

Item	Purchasing Unit	Par Amount	Function Amount	Total to Order
Romaine	10 lb. case 4.5 kg	4 cases		
Raddicchio	12 count per case/10 lb. 4.5 kg	1 case		
Endive	11 lb. case 5 kg	2 cases		
Frisee	3 lb. case 1.36	1 case		
Misto Mix	3 lb. case 1.36	1 case		
Arugula	3 lb. case 1.36	2 cases		

11. Marcel purchases Colvita Extra Virgin Olive Oil for the restaurant. It is packed as 6 - 17 ounce bottles per case. This olive oil is used for specific recipe items and is very expensive. A less expensive kind is used for general cooking. Chef Raoul and Marcel have agreed that on a daily basis the restaurant uses between 8 and 17 bottles of olive oil. To get a better price, the olive oil is only ordered once a week from a specialty vendor who gives a quantity discount for the order size. Establish the par for the olive oil using the common usage method.

12. Marcel checked the inventory today to determine how many cases of olive oil to order. There were 12 bottles on the shelf. How many cases are needed to bring the supply up to par? Show your work.

13. It's Monday afternoon, and Peter Soup (remember him?) has just called. An emergency meeting of the Split Pea Soup Association has been called for Wednesday, and he was hoping you could accommodate the group for dinner. He is guaranteeing 180 on the spot. You have no functions booked for that night, so you say yes. The menu is as follows:

	Portion Size	Yield %	AP Price	
Insalata Cesare	6 oz. 170	85%	.85/lb.	45
Salmon Criglia (40%)	8 oz. 227	97%	$6.49/lb.	45
Bistecca (60%)	10 oz. 283	80%	$5.25/lb.	.45
Asparagus	4 oz. 113	92%	$2.59/lb.	.45
Baked Potato	1 each	90 count per case	$40.50/cs.	
Cheesecake	1 slice each	16 slices per cake	$24.00/cake	

Because the function is so soon, there is no time to fill out a form to get to the order quantities. Fortunately, you are familiar with those nifty formulas from a few pages back that are used for just such an occasion. Go to it! The suppliers await your call!

14. Mr. Soup will be looking for a price quote soon. You decide to quickly rough out a cost. Using the APE formula, calculate the portion costs for the salad, the salmon, the steak, and the asparagus. Add in the portion cost for the potato and cheesecake. See Question 13.

15. Determine a sell price based on these costs using the MMP formula (from Chapter 4). Use a Q factor of $1.75, a Spice Factor of 10%, and a Food Cost Percentage of 30%. How much revenue will be generated for this function?

16. Chef Raoul found 30 pounds of Bistecca in the freezer that could be used for the function. How many servings would this yield? How many pounds of fresh steak would need to be ordered now?

17. Surprise! Thirty members of the Garden Club showed up begging Chef Raoul to cook up something special for them. He came up with Pork di Maile. He had 24 pounds of pork tenderloin. The pork has a yield of 86%. What was the portion size?

## Chapter Six

Chapter Objective

To use a supplier specification to select the right supplier for products and services for an operation.

Learning Objectives

After reading this chapter and completing the discussion questions and exercises, you should be able to:

1. Explain how foodservice distribution systems move products into the marketplace.
2. Identify services commonly offered by suppliers.
3. Develop "supplier specifications" to evaluate prospective suppliers.
4. Complete paperwork to evaluate supplier prices (bid sheets) and place orders (purchase orders).
5. Explain supplier pricing methods.
6. Evaluate the impact of yield percentages on AP and EP prices.
7. Recognize purchasing and supplier services terminology.

About the "Right Supplier"

The Menu

Pre-Purchase Functions

GUEST CHECK
Sales history, turnover, average check, cash management, revenue forecasting & budgeting, menu item analysis

GUESTS
Greeting, seating, sales, serving, busing, payment, comment cards

FOH Functions

KITCHEN PRODUCTION
Production schedules, portion tracking, recipe control, serving controls, food safety

PRODUCT ISSUING
Requisitions, transfers, daily & monthly costs, food cost percentage

STORAGE PRACTICES & INVENTORY MANAGEMENT
Best practices, sanitation, security, inventory methods

INVOICE MANAGEMENT
Payment, price checking, security

STANDARDIZED RECIPES
Standard ingredients, portion size, quality, consistency, quantity, purchasing

COST CARDS
Portion costs, yield factors, sell prices

SPECIFICATIONS
Product descriptions

PAR STOCK
Inventory levels, order building

REQUISITION
Order building, purchasing

SHOPPING LISTS
Call sheets, bid sheets, suppliers, bidding

PURCHASE ORDERS
Security, ship order, price guarantee, contract

BOH Functions

RECEIVING ACTIVITIES
Best practices, invoices, security, sanitation

Chapter Map

Take a Look at Where We've Been

- About the Last of the "Five Rights" of Purchasing

About Foodservice Distribution Systems

- Sources
- Manufacturers, or Processors
- Foodservice Distributors
- Other Intermediaries: Brokers
- "eProcurement," or B2B Purchasing

Chapter Map   (Continued)

Researching & Selecting Suppliers
- Supplier Selection Criteria
- Developing a Supplier "Specification"
- Evaluating a Supplier Using Specifications
- Approved Supplier Lists
- Other Buyer Responsibilities
- One-Stop Shopping

Purchasing Plans
- The Informal Purchasing Method
- The Formal Purchasing Method
- Choosing the Appropriate Supplier(s)
- Using Order Sheets & Bid Sheets: An Example

Placing an Order
- Purchase Orders
- Delivering the Purchase Order to a Supplier
- Information Included on the Purchase Order

Supplier Pricing
- Methods of Markup
- Getting the Best Price

As-Purchased Prices, Yield Factors, & Portion Costs
- Calculating As-Purchased Prices Using Yield Percentages
- Calculating Portion Costs
- Comparing Vendor Prices

Conclusion: The "Five Rights" of Purchasing, Revisited

Chapter ✓

Check the chapter content for the answers to these questions:

1. What is a distribution system?
2. How are suppliers selected?
3. How is bidding used to procure product?
4. What is a purchase order?
5. How do suppliers set prices?

*T*ake a Look at Where We've Been

You will recall that Chapter 4 introduced the "Five Rights" as a model for the basic purchasing functions used by most foodservice operators. A quick review of the box that follows will show that this chapter wraps up our discussion of these concepts.

THE "FIVE RIGHTS," OR THE PURCHASING FUNCTIONS		
CHAPTER 4	**CHAPTER 5**	**CHAPTER 6**
THE RIGHT PRODUCT	THE RIGHT QUANTITY	THE RIGHT SUPPLIER, PRICE, & TIME
1. Specifications 2. Make-or-Buy Analysis	1. Popularity % 2. Par Stock 3. Order Sheets 4. Requisitions 5. Orders for Functions 6. Yield Analysis	1. Distribution Systems 2. Selecting a Supplier 3. Bid Systems 4. Bid/Call Sheets 5. Placing Orders 6. Purchase Orders 7. Supplier Prices 8. Yield Factors

THE FIVE *RIGHTS*

TO PURCHASE:

1. THE *RIGHT PRODUCT* IN

2. THE *RIGHT QUANTITY* FROM

3. THE *RIGHT SUPPLIER* AT

4. THE *RIGHT PRICE* AT

5. THE *RIGHT TIME*

FIGURE 6.1   The Five Rights of purchasing.

About the Last of the "Five Rights" of Purchasing

This chapter covers the last three topics in the "Five Rights" series:

- Researching and selecting the right supplier
- Negotiating the right price
- Understanding the importance of delivery times

Before we begin, a brief discussion of distribution systems will help clarify how products make it to market. Industry terminology used in general purchasing practices will also be introduced.

About Foodservice Distribution Systems

The process for the distribution of food and nonalcoholic beverage products in the United States is fairly sophisticated. Compared to not so many years ago, the choices are almost endless in terms of suppliers and product availability. With today's improved distribution systems and the ability to use the Internet to research buying options, buyers have alternatives like never before. Hence, it seems fitting that practitioners of cost control first understand the distribution picture before tackling selecting suppliers. Understanding how product moves through channels to get to the loading dock is especially important.

Let's set the stage ...

1. Imagine for a moment, a garlic farmer in Gilroy, California. Why Gilroy? Because Gilroy is *the Garlic Capital of the World.* (Check their Web site: www.Gilroy.org.) Gilroy is so into garlic that the city sports the annual Gilroy Garlic Festival. What better place is there to have a garlic farm? This imaginary garlic farm produces acres and acres of the stuff! It also specializes in exotic varieties of garlic. This farm grows lots and lots of garlic.

2. Why Garlic? Well, why not? Garlic might just get your attention. Feel free to substitute any product if garlic doesn't suit your fancy!

3. Imagine now that that there is a fabulously popular chain of 600 Italian eateries across the United States that specializes in Italian dishes featuring garlic!! These restaurants purchase fresh garlic, minced garlic, garlic paste, whole cloves in oil, and every imaginable form of garlic available. Not only do these restaurants use all those forms of garlic—they use *many different varieties, as well.* (Remember form from Chapter 4?) Those 600 restaurants use a lot of garlic.

At this point, we have just two simple questions:

1. How does the garlic farmer move garlic to the marketplaces across the United States?

2. How does the restaurant chain get all the garlic needed in all its different forms to all the different restaurant locations?

And in response, we have one simple answer: They use a distribution system.

Sources

The garlic farmer has expertise growing fresh garlic. Businesses that produce raw products such as farms, ranches, coal producers, wood-processing plants, and so on, all share this characteristic. These businesses can be thought of as **sources** because they are *sources of raw products.* Products in this raw state are a valuable commodity but are not necessarily useful to the everyday foodservice operator. Imagine a feed-lot full of cattle that a rancher has raised. Restaurants need beef, but not in this form! Generally, businesses at this level produce large amounts of raw product and are located in areas with natural characteristics suitable for the production of these products. For this reason, sources are not going to be located right next door to all the restaurants and businesses that need the product. For example:

- California, with its mild climate and good soil, is home to farms that grow every conceivable type of produce on the market. Foodservice operators across the United States rely on California produce year round.
- Florida is known for oranges, lemons, limes, and grapefruits. Operators in all parts of the United States rely on their production for these citrus products year round.
- Corn and wheat are native to the West and Midwest.
- Ranches tend to be in the West and Midwest, where open land to raise animals is found. Not coincidentally, this is where most of the corn and wheat is grown and where the granaries are located to process these products.
- Sawmills and wood-processing plants tend to be in the West, upper Midwest, and parts of the south, close to the source.

Manufacturers, or Processors

So what happens to the hundreds of acres of tomatoes or the thousands of head of cattle that a farmer or rancher has available? Why, another group of businesses purchases these goods and makes these raw products more "user friendly." These businesses are known broadly as types of **intermediaries**, or **middlemen**, and more specifically as **manufacturers**, or **processors**.

EXAMPLES OF MANUFACTURERS OR PROCESSORS

- *Food processing plants and canneries*—purchase farm goods and process them into value-added foods. (Think canned vegetables, fruit, or soup.) Take a walk down any supermarket aisle and imagine that many of these products—fresh, frozen, refrigerated, or processed—started out in a field somewhere.
- *Graineries*—mill flour and corn into products for bakeries and food processors.

- *Meat-processing plants*—purchase animals from ranchers to process into meat products for foodservice operations and supermarkets.
- *Steel mills*—make the products necessary to build equipment (think ranges, walk-ins, mixers, dishwashers) of all sizes, tools, etc.
- *Sawmills and wood-manufacturing plants*—harvest trees and process into tables, chairs, paneling, flooring, etc.
- *Specialty producers*—make proprietary items for restaurant chains.

Remember that processors are usually close to the sources— hence, canneries and food-processing plants are generally located in close proximity to the farms from which they purchase raw products. Graineries (flour-milling plants) are located near corn and wheat crops. Meat-packing houses are located close to the ranches where the animals are raised. This makes sense.

Businesses at this level (processors and manufacturers) are not very interested in selling their products to individual operations like the Italian restaurants discussed earlier. This is not their function. Their function is *to process raw product into a more useful form.* At this stage, some of these products will be "finished" and are ready for distribution. Other products will go on to other processors where they will be combined with additional ingredients to produce even more **value-added products**.

- Think of a grainery milling wheat into a variety of types of flour. This flour might be shipped to a processor for ready-mix cake mixes that will be purchased through a supermarket chain, to a bakery with a national distribution, or to a national chain for doughnuts.
- The garlic farmer from Gilroy probably shipped some fresh garlic through produce distribution companies and sold the rest to a processing plant where it was peeled and processed into a variety of products: Remember all the forms of garlic that are needed by the Italian restaurant chain: whole, minced, paste, and fresh.

Now the very raw products purchased from farmers, ranchers, and other sources have moved to large businesses that process and pack these goods into more user-friendly forms. These products are still nowhere near the restaurants and stores that need them, however. They need someone else to move them there.

_Net Work

Explore the following Web sites:

www.conagrafoods.com

www.mccormick.com—Search Products & Promotions, My McCormick, All About Spices

www.simplotfoods.com

www.beeffoodservice.com

www.hormel.com

www.internationalmultifoods.com

www.primoproduce.com

Foodservice Distributors

Finished products move from processors to the distribution warehouses of suppliers across the country. These businesses, called **foodservice distributors**, are also considered intermediaries, or middlemen. Some of these companies are so large that they distribute nationally and even internationally. Some are regional businesses. Some distribute product in just a few states. Small businesses may distribute in just a specific area. Others will have a niche, handling only specialty products. The process of moving product through these channels adds value and cost to the product. It is through these distributors that product gets to a foodservice operation and ultimately, the guest. Remember the garlic processing plant: After the garlic was processed and packaged, it was picked up by distributors to be sold later to foodservice operators of every type.

Foodservice distributors are classified by the product lines they carry:

- **Broadline distributors**—*carry food, nonfood, nonalcohol beverages, small-wares, large kitchen equipment, dining room equipment. They work with operators on just about any need.* Some even offer various services: architectural, installation, payroll, printing, advertising and marketing, training, and much more.
- **Full-line distributors**—*carry only food, nonfood, and nonalcohol beverages.* They may offer limited services.
- **Specialty product distributors**—*carry specialty product lines;* these businesses specialize in a limited line of specialty products. These suppliers may offer limited, extra services to their customers.
- **Commissaries**—*part of the distribution system used by large national chains to supply products to individual stores.* Warehouses and plants are regionally located and service stores in a specific area. Commissaries may *purchase raw product and produce finished goods in kitchens, using company recipes, or purchase already processed goods for distribution.* These chains use local suppliers for a limited amount of product.

Processors and manufacturers are only interested in shipping large quantities of product, usually by truck or train. Foodservice operators would also like to purchase at this level (and not through distributors) because pricing is very attractive. It is obvious, however, that the average foodservice operator does not have the business volume to support purchasing these quantities, no matter how good the price looks. At this volume, only distributors have the resources to transport, warehouse, and distribute these goods. Large foodservice chains, franchises, and some multiunits *are* able to purchase from processors by doing one or more of the following:

- Working through a distributor.
- Hiring a trucking firm.
- Using their own trucks to move product to regionally located distribution centers that ship to individual units as it is ordered.

In essence, these large foodservice operations act as their own "distributor."

Net Work

Explore the following Web sites of broadline distributors:
www.sysco.com—Search About Us, Products, Services, Employment Opportunities
www.usfoodservice.com—Search About Us, Products, Services, Careers
www.kraftfoodservice.com
www.pfgc.com Search About Us, Our Brands, Careers
www.fooddude.com—This is a search engine for food and beverage exporters.
www.foodprocessing.com

To learn more about e-commerce:
www.instill.com
www.efoodcommerce.com—Check the Tour and Demo in the menu bar at left.
www.efr-central.com
www.menulink.com Click on Learn More Under Commissary, Quick Service Restaurants, and Menu Modeling and examine sample reports and data sheets.

So How About the Italian Restaurant Chain?   Management decided to contract with a national distributor to service all 600 units. The distributor orders the garlic products from the processor and stocks the inventory in its warehouses across the United States. Each store orders garlic on an as-needed basis from the contracted supplier. The price is guaranteed; the supply is guaranteed; the delivery is guaranteed. What more could a buyer ask for?

Note that the restaurant chain probably contracts with the distributor to handle a variety of products (maybe even all products) and not just the garlic. In return for all this business, AP pricing to the chain would be very favorable as compared to pricing offered to an independent operator (a single restaurant). This is the purchasing power of volume! The distributor could also market the garlic products to its existing customer base, assuming there were no proprietary provisions in the contract. Figure 6.2 illustrates the distribution system.

Other Intermediaries: Brokers

A **broker** is another type of intermediary in the channel of distribution. Brokers deal exclusively with food products. Their role is to do the following:

- Assist sources, or processors or manufacturers, in moving new and existing products into distribution.
- Develop a market for new products.
- Link end users (foodservice operators) with processors.

Brokers occupy an interesting place in the distribution system:

- They neither buy nor sell product.
- They don't deliver or take orders.
- They never physically handle the product they are marketing.

So What Do Brokers Do?   Brokers are *an independent marketing team contracted to link interested parties together:* a processor or manufacturer, a distributor, and an end user (foodservice operation).

- A broker is hired by a source, or processor or manufacturer.
- Brokers specialize in specific types of products.
- Brokers provide an external marketing force for sources or processors who do not have an internal marketing team.
- Brokerage firms range in size from very small businesses specializing in limited product types to large firms, complete with test kitchens and many reps.
- Brokers receive a commission from source on the amount of product sold.

Here's an Example of a Broker at Work   Suppose our research and development team at the garlic-processing company develops a new, high-energy Garlic Tart targeted to the college/university student market. Company research and product testing shows strong demand for this type of product. The task now is to:

- Generate interest for the product within the target market.
- Get the product into normal distribution channels.

The garlic-processing firm decides to contract with a **brokerage firm** with expertise in the college/university market.

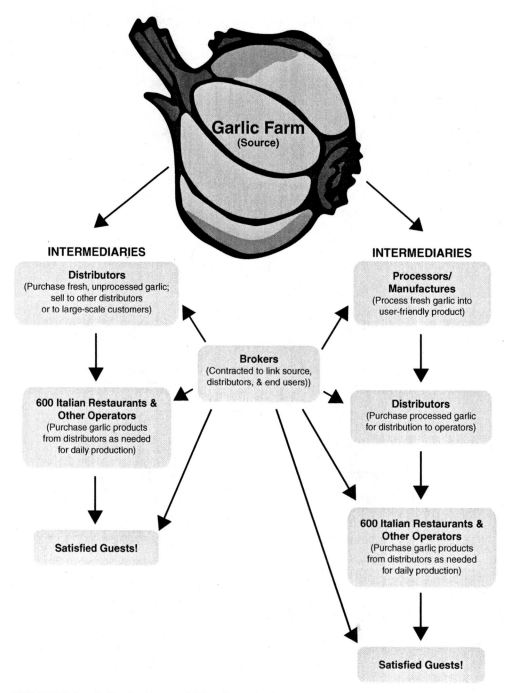

FIGURE 6.2   A distribution model for the garlic farm.

Other than the processor, there are three other parties who need to become interested if the high-energy Garlic Tart is going to make it into distribution:

- The first is the end user or customer—*the student*.
- The second is the *foodservice business that ultimately sells this item*.
- The third is the *distributor* who stocks the product.

The broker's task is to develop demand for the product to such a degree that distributors will be convinced to warehouse the product. Since the broker's role is to link interested parties together, he or she works with both foodservice buyers and distributors, all at the same time. To introduce the product, brokers carry marketing materials and samples for tasting as part of their marketing bag of tricks.

Distributors are in a very precarious position. These intermediaries purchase large quantities of products that they hold in warehouses, refrigerators, and freezers and distribute a little at a time as their customers place orders. They also wait for payment after shipping these goods to customers. These are the folks that will be glad to send you one pound of garlic or 10 pounds of ground beef, even though they purchased a truckload full. Remember that most distributors carry hundreds if not thousands of different products. Adding another item to the product line requires warehouse space and adds inventory cost. Distributors need assurance the product will move. The broker's job is to provide that assurance.

To Summarize

Brokers are Marketing Specialists—In the case of the new Garlic Tart, the broker's first challenge is to develop interest in the product. The firm would develop a marketing plan targeting the college/university system. Because brokers tend to handle specific products or markets, the brokerage house would use its existing contact base. Other research would reveal additional outlets and clients. Figure 6.3 shows the scope of a broker's job.

Armed with this marketing information, brokers make their pitch to distributors. Once distributors agree to carry the product and foodservice buyers order it, the broker's work is essentially done—picture the marriage between processor, distributor, and end user as complete.

"eProcurement," or B2B Purchasing

eProcurement, or **B2B purchasing**, is the latest in technology applied to foodservice purchasing. It is the *exchange of products or services from one business to another (B2B)* rather than between a business and a consumer (B2C). It is a method of purchasing, whereby a foodservice operation contracts with a Web, or online, supplier for their purchasing needs. These businesses provide comprehensive products and services to foodservice operators. Although their use is not yet widespread, many independents as well as chain or franchise groups use B2B purchasing as their primary method of securing product and services. An exhaustive discussion of B2B purchasing is beyond the scope of this text. For more information, check www.efoodcommerce.com. Try the free tour and demo.

Brokers Work With	Brokers Work To
• Potential customers. • Foodservice buyers. • Foodservice directors and chefs. • Distributors and suppliers.	• Develop interest in products. • Develop a marketing plan. • Demonstrate marketing, sales, and profit potential to all interested parties. • Estimate demand and get the product into distribution channels.

FIGURE 6.3 The broker's job.

*R*esearching and Selecting Suppliers

Now that an understanding of how products get to market is complete, a discussion about selecting the right supplier can begin. Once the right product is known and the order amount determined, research begins to identify the best supplier for the order.

Supplier Selection Criteria

What makes one supplier preferable to another? It all comes down to supplier selection criteria, or **supplier specifications**. The criteria should *represent the most important needs of the operation* and should be considered non-negotiable—the supplier must be able to meet these needs 100% of the time. The buyer, in conjunction with management, is responsible for deciding which needs are most important. Buyers establish supplier selection criteria in much the same way that selection criteria for product are set. In fact, a supplier specification can be developed by borrowing from the theory of product specifications (refer to Chapter 4). Once buyer specs are established, the evaluation and selection process can begin.

It is important to remember that the supplier's main goal is to make a sale at the highest possible price while at the same time remaining competitive. Suppliers strive to build a relationship with their customers by

1. Being competitive, and
2. Providing good service.

They realize that foodservice managers want to buy product at the lowest possible price and receive all the items ordered in a timely manner.

By and large, most managers and buyers would agree that the four most important supplier selection criteria are:

1. *Competitive AP prices:* Suppliers should offer prices similar to those of their competition.
2. *Product quality:* Buyers depend on suppliers to provide product that consistently meets specification.
3. *Supplier services:* Suppliers and sales persons should provide information on products that enhance the foodservice operation's ability to compete for customers. Suppliers, at the minimum, should provide information on pricing, new products, price changes, and special sales, and help with menu ideas.
4. *Supplier dependability:* Suppliers should deliver ordered products courteously and on time. There should be a minimum of back orders, short orders, substitutions, and other errors. Dependability also infers a degree of trust and strong business ethics. The buyer trusts he or she is being dealt with fairly and honestly, and the supplier has a right to be treated fairly and honestly by the buyer.

The order does not indicate importance, necessarily, which may be based on the needs of individual foodservice operations. Many will argue that quality is more important than price!

Other Supplier Criteria The characteristics just discussed represent the "short list" of supplier criteria—the ones that most buyers consider most important. In addition to the short list, buyers develop a set of secondary supplier criteria and use them to further evaluate potential suppliers. At the least, buyers should know each potential suppliers' policy on many of these items. Figure 6.4 is the "long list" of supplemental supplier criteria.

```
┌─────────────────────────────────────────────────────┐
│  **Long List of Supplier Selection Criteria**        │
│                                                       │
│  • Online ordering procedure                          │
│  • Professional sales staff                           │
│  • Delivery schedule                                  │
│  • Minimum order size                                 │
│  • Breadth of product line                            │
│  • Lead time                                          │
│  • Credit terms and payment options                   │
│  • Returns policy and ease of returning goods         │
│  • Substitution policy and ability to substitute      │
│  • Discounts: cash, quantity, and volume              │
│  • Supplier facilities, vehicles, and professionalism of staff │
│  • Case-break pricing                                 │
│  • References                                         │
│  • Reputation                                         │
└─────────────────────────────────────────────────────┘
```

FIGURE 6.4   Long list of supplier selection criteria.

The buyer will need to be familiar with the concepts behind these supplemental supplier selection criteria:

- *Online ordering procedures:* The ability to **order online**, or electronically, through the Internet is a great improvement over the time-consuming task of physically calling in orders, meeting with sales reps, or filling out and faxing orders. This service is still in its infancy. Most broadline and full-line suppliers offer this service.

- *Professional sales staff:* In the past, sales representatives pounded the pavement, driving from account to account to take orders. This service is obviously costly to the supplier and is reserved for only the largest customers. Today, small accounts that do not qualify for sales rep appointments phone orders to in-house sales reps, fax in order sheets, or complete orders on-line. Sales reps service small accounts through phone contact, e-mail, and occasional visits. Developing a professional relationship with a sales rep is to the advantage of the foodservice manager or buyer. Occasionally, emergencies occur that require a special delivery or some other service. Based on a sound relationship with a client, a supplier usually responds in a timely manner in order to accommodate a good account. Good sales reps will alert buyers to new products, sales, and ways to save food-cost dollars.

- *Delivery schedule:* Generally, a buyer accepts the supplier's delivery schedule. When purchasing from out-of-state suppliers, the delivery can only be made on the day the truck is in the buyer's area. There is not a lot of wiggle room in this case.

- *Minimum order size:* Suppliers have a **minimum order size** that is either in dollars or number of pieces ordered. This is the minimum order size *to qualify for a delivery.* In the event an order does not meet the minimum for delivery, *the buyer can opt to pick up the order at the supplier's warehouse* (this is known as a **will-call order**) or pay an additional charge for delivery. Some suppliers offer **cash and carry** services to small operators or to the general public. "Cash and carry" means just that—*the buyer brings in cash and carries out the product.*

- *Breadth of product line:* **Broadline distributors** offer the most comprehensive product lines. Smaller suppliers, however, will offer limited options in product choice—they will carry only one brand of an item. The degree to which the buyer needs buying-broad options for product will determine whether a small supplier can meet the needs of a buyer.

- *Lead times for orders:* Buyers have call deadlines for ordering from suppliers in order for products to be delivered by a certain date and time. Lead times for orders placed with out-of-state suppliers are often longer than for those placed with local suppliers. Suppliers may either assign a specific day for accepting orders or specify a certain time of day as the latest hour that orders will be accepted to meet a certain delivery schedule.

- *Credit terms and payment options:* Buyers like to purchase **"on account."** What this means is *a buyer will order goods over the course of a period of time (usually a month), and the supplier bills at the end of the period.* In essence, the buyer is purchasing on credit and the supplier is waiting for payment. This is a privilege earned by a business. A good bill-paying reputation is important to a supplier. Operators without a good bill-paying history will be sold goods but probably on a **COD** basis only. COD means *cash on delivery*—the invoice is settled with the driver when the goods are delivered.

- *Returns policy and ease of returning goods:* It is common to have to return goods to suppliers. This can be a buyer's worst nightmare. A supplier who makes this process easy and efficient will earn high marks with a buyer. Returns are usually handled through the sales rep—either one who visits the client or an in-house rep. A pick-up slip authorized by the sales rep is issued to the driver, who signs for the goods as they are placed back on the truck. Tracking returns through the accounting system is important to ensure all credits due back to the operator are so given.

- *Substitution policy and ability to substitute:* Buyers have to consider the supplier's ability to substitute products in the event that an item on a buyer's order is not available. Good specifications will indicate which products are suitable substitutes. A supplier with a limited product line may not be able to offer acceptable substitutions for a back-ordered or out-of-stock item.

- *Discounts: cash, quantity, and volume:* **Cash discounts** are *discounts given for prompt payment of statements at the end of the accounting period.* Typically, this is read as 2%/10 days and will be so noted on the statement sent by the supplier at the end of the month. This means if the account is paid within 10 days, a 2% discount is earned on the order. A **quantity discount** is *a discount given when a certain quantity of the same product is ordered.* For example, a supplier may have a discount program for ordering 10 cases or more of a specific product. Ordering full pallets of one product is another example of qualifying for a quantity discount. **Volume discounts** are given for *invoices of more than a certain amount of money.* The discount is for all products—not just a specific product.

- *Supplier facilities, vehicles, and professionalism of staff:* At the top of the long list should be the cleanliness of the supplier's vehicles and plant. In addition, the professionalism of the drivers is another criterion. Buyers should have HACCP temperature requirements written into specifications to guarantee that products are stored and shipped properly—out of the temperature danger zone (41°F to 135°F). Suppliers should welcome a buyer to make either pre-arranged or surprise site inspections. Suppliers handling products for large chains or franchises are under strict sanitation requirements and are subject to constant inspection either by full-time inspectors working on-site or through regular surprise inspections conducted by trained professionals in the employ of the chains or franchises.

- *Case-break pricing:* *Ordering a partial case of a product* usually nets a unit price that is higher than the unit price of the item, had the full case been purchased. When this happens, the supplier has to "break" the case, and that full case is no longer available to ship as a whole unit. Now the supplier has to hold the items in the open case until single units are ordered again. This can be costly for the supplier. Not all suppliers will break cases because of their inability to move the leftover units. Some suppliers price at the case price and not at a higher AP price. Buyers should inquire as to supplier policy.

- *References:* Request references (current and past clients) from the supplier and carefully check each one.
- *Reputation:* The single most important piece of research a buyer can do when selecting a supplier is to check with other industry professionals. This is easy to do when the buyer is connected with other local industry professionals through professional organizations such as the American Culinary Federation, affiliates of the National Restaurant Association, the local Chamber of Commerce, and any other professional hospitality organizations active in the area. The Better Business Bureau is also another avenue to research.

Developing a Supplier "Specification"

In Chapter 4, a product specification was defined as *a detailed description of products and services written to assist the buyer and the supplier in getting the right product or service to the operation.* It's possible to apply this concept to the supplier selection process. A supplier specification is a *list detailing the selection criteria a buyer has created for potential suppliers.* It is a tool in the manager's toolbox that he or she can use to develop a pool of qualified suppliers able to meet the standards identified by the buyer as key to carrying out the purchasing job.

SUPPLIER SPECIFICATION
- A list detailing the selection criteria a buyer has created for potential suppliers.
- A tool in the manager's toolbox to use to develop a pool of qualified suppliers able to meet the standards identified by the buyer.

Evaluating a Supplier Using Specifications

With a spec, the buyer is able to evaluate each supplier and select the one or ones that best meet the needs of the operation. When a buyer evaluates the information in Figure 6.5, he or she may find that there may be no supplier that is clearly unacceptable, but there may be a strong enough case to choose one over the other. In addition, a buyer will often use more than one supplier and spread the buying around. This gives a lot of flexibility, particularly with delivery days and AP price.

DECISION-INFLUENCING CRITERIA (SEE FIGURE 6.5)
- If the buyer needed a supplier who could deliver small wares and equipment, then the ABC Company is the one to go with. If there were other equipment suppliers in the area, this would not necessarily be a deciding factor.
- If the buyer needed flexible or broad product options, the ABC Company or the LMNOP Company would be the better choice.
- If online ordering is important, then again, the availability of this service is identified, so the decision is quite easy.

A Supplier Specification			
Company Name:	ABC Co.	YYZ Co.	LMNOP Co.
Location: Notes:	500 Main Street Any City, USA	500 Main Street Another City, USA	500 Main Street Anywhere, USA
Phone/Fax/Email:	800-123-4567 jdoe@abc.com	576-345-6789 No 800; local call robin@yyz.com	800-987-6543 jsmith@lmnop.com
AP Prices: Notes:	Willing to negotiate a set % over supplier cost	Offering regular pricing schedule	Analyze order volume to negotiate pricing structure
Product Quality: Notes:	Brand names and self-branded products	Brand names only; no self-branding	Brand names and self-branded options
Supplier Dependability: Notes:	Other operators report good overall service; BBB report no complaints	BBB—no complaints; average report from other operators	Excellent reports from other operators and BBB
Online Ordering:	Available www.abcprepared1foods.com	Not available	Available w/in 6 mo
Sales Staff: Notes:	Sales rep visits weekly for order. Fax & phone in available	Call in order to main phone line; fax available	Sales rep calls for order; visits periodically; fax and phone
Minimum Order Size:	$500 or 15 pieces	$400 or 10 pieces	No minimum
Delivery Schedule:	Available daily Courteous drivers	Tue., Fri. Courteous drivers	Mon., Wed., Fri. Courteous drivers
Product Line: Notes:	Broadline distributor	Full-line distributor	Full-line distributor w/some small-wares
Credit/Payment Schedule:	On account with credit check	On account with credit check	On account with credit check
Returns: Notes:	Notify sales rep for driver pick-up with slip	Call in for OK. Driver pick-up with slip	Notify sales rep for driver pick-up with slip
Substitutions:	As per spec	As per spec	As per spec
Discounts: Cash, volume, quantity	Cash, volume, quantity	Cash, volume, quantity	Cash, volumes, quantity
Case Break:	Available at case price	Not available	Available at higher each price
Facility Inspection: Notes:	Excellent; relatively new trucks	Good to excellent; trucks in good condition	Good to excellent; trucks older
References: Notes:	Good customer references	Good customer references	Good customer references

FIGURE 6.5 A supplier specification.

Approved Supplier Lists

Many operations develop **approved supplier lists** for buyers. These lists are quite common in the chain and franchise market. With this arrangement, *the corporate purchasing department researches, evaluates, and negotiates terms with suppliers on behalf of the foodservice operation.* Approved supplier lists take the guesswork out of deciding from which supplier to order. Because the suppliers are preapproved, prices and other terms and services are already in place, having been negotiated by upper management. All management has to do is call in the order. Approved supplier lists can be created for any size operation.

Other Buyer Responsibilities

The objective of every buyer is to purchase the product of best quality for its intended purpose, at the lowest possible price. In order to accomplish this, the buyer must be aware of all factors outside the foodservice operation that influence the quality of the product. The buyer must also be alert to conditions within the operation that may alter or influence the quality of the end product to be served. It would be foolish for a buyer to purchase a whole side of beef if no one in the operation has the skills to cut and trim it into the correct cuts of meat. Nor should the buyer purchase unpeeled potatoes if the in-house equipment necessary for the operation (a potato peeler) is either inoperable or nonexistent.

Conditions in the general economic community that appear to have no direct bearing on a foodservice operation may greatly affect the products that are available for use. Consider the following:

- The buyer who is unaware of weather conditions in various parts of the country may suddenly find that the cost of produce has unexpectedly either risen or fallen because of a change in harvest conditions.
- The corn or grain harvest one year might affect the cost of beef the next year.
- The effect of governmental policies on price supports and other farm policies is a crucial factor in the overall costs of goods purchased.
- Transportation expenses are an integral part of the overall costs of raw products: A strike by transportation workers may cause a shortage or a complete absence of products from the market.
- The devaluation of the dollar causes a price increase for all imported products. The alert buyer may be able to stock up on some items just prior to price increases.

Efficient buyers must get their information from many sources. They must not become so preoccupied with the internal needs of their own organizations that they ignore some of the basic tools necessary to perform their tasks: To be aware of price changes, they should be knowledgeable of trade publications, product Web sites, government agricultural bulletins, stock market reports, commodity bulletins, wholesale daily reports, and food supplier and equipment Web sites.

The sales person of each supplying company should share with the buyer information on new products, price changes, and special sales. Too often, salespeople become merely order takers, either from a lack of foresight on their part or because the attitude of the buyers clearly demonstrates that they merely wish to place orders. This lack of interest on the part of both parties often creates undue costs for the operation because opportunities for discount buying or special purchases are overlooked. This does not mean that buyers need to devote a great deal of time to every salesperson who comes along, but they should indicate a willingness to listen and be receptive to new ideas and be interested in information on sales or other important changes.

In the course of doing business with various salespeople, buyers develop an awareness of which salespeople do indeed pass on information and which ones are merely trying to sell or take orders. Good salespeople are aware of the needs of the foodservice operation to which they are selling. They may have a number of products on sale during a given week, but they refrain from mentioning them because they realize that those products do not fit the needs of that particular foodservice operation. They save the buyer's time as well as their own and, in turn, earn the respect and appreciation of the buyer. When a product may be useful, buyers will listen more closely because they know the information is important to their operation.

One-Stop Shopping

One-stop shopping is the practice of *ordering all or most products from one supplier.* There is good argument for and against this system. Old-school purchasing practices

PROs To One-Stop Shoping	CONs To One-Stop Shoping
Reduces buyer's time spent ordering	Depends on reliability of one supplier
May reduce AP prices because of larger order size	AP prices on all items may not be the best price the buyer could find by using a variety of suppliers.
Reduces administrative costs associated with purchasing	May be difficult to resolve product quality issues without changing suppliers.
Reduces time because working with only one or two sales reps	Suppliers with limited product lines may not be able to substitute in case of back orders or short orders, causing supply issues with buyer.
Gives opportunity to build a strong relationship with supplier	Relational issues may develop, given the high turn of sales reps.
Reduces receiving costs because of fewer deliveries	In emergencies, outside vendors may not be willing to service the account.
Can benefit small operators that do not qualify for deliveries and volume discounts	

FIGURE 6.6   Pros and cons of one-stop shopping.

shunned such an idea; in fact, it was unheard of. Traditionally, buyers spread the purchasing dollars around in order to have leverage with suppliers and to ensure they could shop for the best prices. Today, there is a move toward centralizing the bulk of the purchases with one or two suppliers. See Figure 6.6 for the pros and cons of the concept.

Purchasing Plans

Buyers use two primary purchasing methods to procure products. One is the **informal purchasing** method; the second is the **formal purchasing** method. Both systems can be employed by an operation, and one method is not necessarily better than the other. Each has a place in a buyer's bag of purchasing tricks.

The Informal Purchasing Method

The informal purchasing method supposes a buyer has done his or her work regarding supplier selection and has a reliable list in place. The buyer, upon compiling the order, simply *calls the suppliers, receives a verbal price quote, and places the order*. The buyer may solicit prices from more than one vendor. This system has merit in a number of situations:

- There are only one or two qualified suppliers for the product.
- The product is needed immediately, and there is no time to place formal bids.
- Small operations ordering minimal quantities have no reason to bid out for prices; perhaps no suppliers will be interested in the business. In cases where there is a minimum dollar amount for a delivery, there is no choice to be made.

The Formal Purchasing Method

The formal purchasing method of purchasing involves using a **bid system** to *secure the right quantity and quality of products at the right price*. There are a number of variations on the bid process, and most buyers will use a combination of strategies to get the best pricing. Two versions of this system are the **fixed bid** and the **daily bid**.

FIXED BID PROCEDURE

1. Buyer prepares detailed specification (a Request for Bid, or RFB)
2. Spec is sent to qualified suppliers.
3. Sealed responses are delivered to the buyer.
4. Responses are evaluated.
5. The contract is awarded and a signing is scheduled.

The first and most formal type of bid is called the fixed bid. In this situation, *a buyer prepares very detailed specifications* (a **Request for Bid**) *that are sent only to qualified suppliers.* The key is that the supplier is deemed qualified. This is not a case of sending the bid to every supplier listed in the phone book. Next, the buyer waits to receive sealed responses to the Request for Bid. Once received, the responses are opened and evaluated, and a contract is awarded. Contracts are then signed by both parties, and the process is complete. Fixed bids are best used for guaranteeing a specific amount of product, at a set price, for a fairly long period of time. Most chains and franchises utilize this type of system to ensure all stores have all products on hand at all times at the negotiated price. Many school systems and other large-scale feeding institutions also use the fixed bid, particularly for canned and nonperishable products used in large quantities at multiple locations.

The second type of fixed bid is called the daily bid. There are a number of variations to this method. The daily bid is best used with products that have a quick turn—this would include produce, some dairy items, and baked goods. Think of these items as those the buyer would order on a daily or every-other-day basis.

DAILY BID PROCEDURE

1. Use order sheets to compile a list of products to be ordered.
2. Transfer information to bid sheets.
3. Research prices with vendors and record findings.
4. Highlight the best prices.
5. Determine the best buy.

The buyer inventories products using the order sheets and standard pars as discussed in Chapter 5. The **order sheets** *establish the products needed to be ordered on a particular day and their respective quantities.* From these sheets, the buyer prepares a **bid sheet**—*a form listing all the products needed* (Figure 6.7) A bid sheet is also known as a **call sheet**. The bid sheet or call sheet represents the most efficient way to document and compare price quotations. The order sheets (from Chapter 5) on the next page demonstrate using a bid sheet to get price quotes.

To determine the best price, the buyer must initially request price quotations. In most cases, suppliers will provide a **browse sheet**, or **product printout**—*a computer printout of the current prices for products.* This information is usually available on a daily or weekly basis. After receiving the pricing information, the buyer records the information on the bid sheet. Bid sheets can also be faxed to suppliers for quotes.

A browse sheet can be used as a resource for completing a bid sheet as long as it contains the following information:

1. A list of each item needed

2. Unit size as purchased

3. Minimum quantity to be ordered, if applicable

4. Current prices

BLANK BID SHEET				
Date:				
Item Description & Pack	**Purchasing Unit**	**Supplier's Name & Bid/Pur. Unit**		
TOTAL				

FIGURE 6.7   Example of a blank bid sheet.

Bid sheets can also be used by suppliers interested in submitting bids who do not provide browse sheets. These suppliers will quote prices through the salesperson calling on the foodservice operation. Nearly always, the salesperson carries a current price book and in some cases a laptop computer with direct hook-up to the supplier. The prices can then be verified and entered on the bid sheet. To save time, managers should prepare bid sheets that list the most common items they purchase on a regular basis. The buyer will be able to intelligently compare prices on an item-by-item basis with each supplier.

Choosing the Appropriate Supplier(s)

DAILY BID PROCEDURE

1. Use order sheets to compile a list of products to be ordered.
2. Transfer information to bid sheets.
3. Research prices with vendors and record findings.
4. Highlight the best prices.
5. Determine the best buy.

The next step is to *highlight the best price for each item, then total each supplier's product column and determine the best buy*. Buying the best-priced items from several, or even all, suppliers surveyed is appropriate if the quantities are large enough to meet each supplier's minimum delivery dollar amount, and the supplier services, including delivery date, meet the buyer's needs (look ahead for a moment at Figure 6.10). In fact, depending on just one supplier may be risky. On the other hand, a manager may pick the one supplier with the overall best prices. Speaking of best prices, care must be taken to carefully analyze supplier prices in order to be sure the overall cost is, indeed, the best price. Requesting weekly bids can be time consuming. Also, the increased complexity of scheduling and working with several suppliers may be impractical. Much must be considered when deciding to go with one or several suppliers.

Many successful foodservice operators request quarterly or annual supplier bids. This can save time and money, and it is a way to build supplier relationships. Bid sheets must also be compared to invoices at the time of delivery to verify that the price quoted was the price charged.

Using Order Sheets and Bid Sheets: An Example

Below are a few of the sample order sheets from Chapter 5. Remember that these items were organized by product type. They listed the product to be ordered, the par, the amount on hand, and the amount to order. In each of these cases, the product to be ordered would be listed on the bid sheet. Because the task is simply to secure price quotes, the quantity to be ordered is not necessary. The buyer would, if appropriate, inquire as to quantity discounts available in order to take advantage of any price breaks.

EXAMPLE OF ORDER SHEETS

Item: Dairy		Monday	Monday	Monday
Description	Pur. Unit	Par	On Hand	Order
Cream Cheese	3 lb. block	30 lb.	10 lb.	20 lb.
Half & Half	½ gal.	8–½ gal.	2	6
Butter Pats	6/5 lbs. cs.	60 lb.	5 lb.	55 lb.

Item: Grocery		Monday		
Description	Pur. Unit	Par	On Hand	Order
Cr. Tomato	6/#10's cs.	46	6 cans	40 cans
Lemon Jc.	12 qt./cs.	12	2	10 qt.
Olive Oil	12 qt./cs.	24	2	22 qt.

Item: Produce		Monday		
Description	Pur. Unit	Par	On Hand	Order
Romaine	24/cs.	2 cs.	1 cs.	1 cs.
Carrots	50 lb. cs.	1 cs.	½ cs.	1 cs.
Spanish onion	50 lb. bag	1 bag	10 lb.	1 bag
Celery	24/cs.	2 cs.	1 cs.	1 cs.

Item: Dairy		Monday	Monday	Monday
Description	**Pur. Unit**	**Par**	**On Hand**	**Order**
Cream Cheese	3 lb. block	30 lb.	10 lb.	20 lb.
Half & Half	½ gal.	8½'s	2	6
Butter Pats	6/5 lb. cs.	60 lb.	5 lb.	55 lb.

FIGURE 6.8   Completed order sheet for dairy.

The information from these order sheets has been transferred to the bid sheet in Figure 6.10. The buyer then contacts the suppliers listed for a price quote. Following the steps in the procedure, the best price is identified.

Because there are three product categories (Dairy, Groceries and Produce), three separate sheets may need to be filled out if different suppliers are used for each product type. When using broadline suppliers, this would not be necessary. For this example, the dairy and groceries will be purchased from one set of suppliers (Figures 6.8, 6.9, and 6.10). The produce will be ordered from a different set (Figures 6.11 and 6.12).

Item: Grocery		Monday		
Description	**Pur. Unit**	**Par**	**On Hand**	**Order**
Cr. Tomato	6/#10's cs.	46	6 cans	40 cans
Lemon Jc.	12 qt./cs.	12	2	10 qt.
Olive Oil	12 qt./cs.	24	2	22 qt.

FIGURE 6.9   Completed order sheet for groceries.

BID SHEET				
Date: 2/14/2XXX				
			Supplier's Name & Bid/Pur. Unit	
Item Description & Pack	**Purchasing Unit**	**ABC Co.**	**DEF Co.**	**GHI Co.**
Cream Cheese – 3 lb. block	3 lb. block	$ 3.74/block	**$ 3.54/block**	$ 3.68/block
Half & Half – ½ gal.	½ gal.	1.79/½ gal.	1.85/½ gal.	**1.75/½ gal.**
Butter – 30 lb. case	case	51.60/cs.	**49.50/cs.**	50.40/cs.
Crushed Tomatoes – 6/#10's	case	21.48/cs.	20.40/cs.	**20.34/cs.**
Lemon Juice – 12 qt.	case	45.00/cs.	**43.20/cs.**	45.00/cs.
Olive Oil – 12 qt.	case	62.32/cs.	**62.32/cs.**	62.65/cs.
TOTAL				

FIGURE 6.10   Order sheet and completed bid sheet for dairy and groceries.

Item: Produce		Monday		
Description	**Pur. Unit**	**Par**	**On Hand**	**Order**
Romaine	24/cs.	2 cs.	1 cs.	1 cs.
Carrots	50 lb./cs.	1 cs.	½ cs.	1 cs.
Spanish Onion	50 lb./bg.	1 bg.	10 lb.	1 bg.
Celery	24/cs.	2 cs.	1 cs.	1 cs.

FIGURE 6.11   Completed order sheet for produce.

BID SHEET				
Date: 2/14/2XXX				
		Supplier's Name & Bid/Pur. Unit		
Item Description & Pack	**Purchasing Unit**	**JKL Co.**	**MNO Co.**	**PQR Co.**
Romaine – 24 heads	case	$45.36/cs.	$46.80/cs.	$41.28/cs.
Carrots	case	19.00/cs.	18.00/cs.	20.50/cs.
Spanish Onion – 50 lb. bg.	50 lb. bg.	19.75/bg.	18.50/bg.	19.85/bg.
Celery	case	46.50/cs.	43.20/cs.	45.90/cs.
TOTAL				

FIGURE 6.12   Completed bid sheet for produce.

The information in Figure 6.10, seems to show that supplier DEF has the best prices for the majority of the dairy and groceries needed. In Figure 6.12, supplier MNO is quoting the best prices for most of the produce. The decision as to which supplier to order from based on price is quite clear! Complete produce and grocery orders would have many more items on it. When all items are quoted, it might work out that two suppliers could supply the products at the most reasonable prices. In that case, an order would be placed with both suppliers. In other cases, the order will be given to the supplier with the majority of products at the lowest price.

If an operation uses only one supplier for a particular product (let's say there is just one produce supplier), then there is no need to check around for prices; the order sheets will establish the products and quantities to order. The guesswork regarding supplier is removed, and the order is simply placed. Any time an operator uses more than one supplier with available product, the procedure is the same as just discussed: Order sheets establish what needs to be ordered, and bid sheets are used to evaluate prices and select the best buy.

Placing an Order

Let's count the ways to actually place that order! Placing the order with a supplier can be accomplished in a number of ways. Given advancements in technology, it can be as easy as the click of a mouse or as "old fashioned" as picking up the phone.

The following are the primary methods used to place orders with suppliers:

- Placing a phone call to in-house sales staff.
- Faxing the order to suppliers.
- Regularly scheduled appointment with sales staff (weekly, biweekly, monthly)
- E-mail.
- Online ordering, using the supplier's software.
- Online ordering services.

Purchase Orders

Each time an order is prepared and placed, a **purchase order** (or **PO**) is prepared. It is the next line of documentation needed to control the purchasing process and can be compared to a sales agreement. A purchase order *is a numbered form that identifies the item(s), the quantity ordered, the price, unit cost, extension, total, and authorization signatures.* It is a control tool used by most businesses that authorizes the exchange of goods and services and ensures payment to the supplier. It creates a legally binding contract when prepared and signed by a buyer and received by a supplier. Only authorized staff members can sign purchase orders thus they become an important control tool for both the buyer and the supplier.

Delivering the Purchase Order to a Supplier

A purchase order can be delivered to a supplier in a few different ways:

- A PO number is given to the supplier when the order is placed over the phone or fax.
- A hard copy can be mailed to the supplier. (This is less common.)
- A signed PO is faxed to the supplier.
- A standing PO is housed with the supplier, who accepts orders from authorized staff. A PIN (personal identification number) number is used by these employees to ensure there is no corruption of the ordering process. Issuing special account numbers for authorized employees is another method of controlling who can place orders with suppliers.

Buyers use purchase orders because POs

- Document the product, quantity, price, and delivery date of the items ordered.
- Include special instructions agreed on by the supplier.
- Clarify for the receiver exactly what deliveries are expected each day, exactly what has been ordered (according to spec) and exactly how much should be received.
- Clarify the exact terms of the sale.
- Verify the receipt of goods.

Suppliers require purchase orders because POs

- Authorize the exchange of goods.
- Document the product, quantity, price, and delivery date of the items ordered.
- Include authorized signatures guaranteeing the invoice will be paid.
- Clarify the exact terms of the sale.
- Verify the receipt of goods.

Both parties—the buyer and the supplier—have many of the same reasons to require the use of purchase orders. It should be clear from this discussion that the purchase order protects both parties by validating all terms of the sales agreement. It is worth noting that small operators do not use purchase orders, bid systems, requisitions, or even order sheets. Their purchasing model is different from that of a full-scale restaurant. The bulk of their products are probably purchased through food clubs and on a cash-and-carry basis with distributors.

The following is a completed purchase order for Farfalle Arrabbiata:

COMPLETED PURCHASE ORDER FOR FARFALLE ARRABBIATA

DATE: 2/14/2XXX

Purchase Order Number: 69421

Name: Farfalle Arrabbiata
567 West St.
Anytown, USA 12345

Authorized by:

Telephone: 567-890-1234

E-mail: DEF.com

Supplier

Company Name	DEF CO.	**Required Delivery Date:** 2/14/2XXX	
Street Address **City, State, Zip Code**	123 Main St. Anytown, USA 12345	**Terms:**	

Freight Charges:

❑ Cash

Telephone: 800-899-3456 | **Fax:** 500-456-7892 | ❑ FOB | ❑ Pre-paid

Contact Name: RM

Special Instructions:

STOCK #	QUANTITY	UNIT	ITEM DESCRIPTION	UNIT COST	EXTENSION
112345	7	3 lb. blk.	Cream Cheese–3 lb. block	$ 3.54	$ 24.78
059837	6	½ gal.	Half & Half–	1.85	11.11
945820	2	30 lb./cs.	Butter–	49.50	99.00
459061	5	6/#10's/cs.	Crushed Tomatoes–	20.40	102.00
273061	1	12/qt./cs.	Lemon Juice–	43.20	43.20
285402	2	12 qt/cs.	Olive Oil–	63.32	126.64

Ordered By: Marcel

Received By:

Manager OK:

Office OK:

TOTAL: 406.73

Copies to: Purchasing, Receiving, Accounts Payable

Information Included on the Purchase Order

The exact format of a purchase order will, of course, vary by business. Common elements on most forms, however, include the following.

Product Information	Vendor/Buyer Information
1. Item name	1. Name
2. Item size and pack information	2. Address
3. Stock number, if applicable	3. Phone, fax, e-mail
4. Specification reference	4. Purchase order number
5. Quantity	5. Order date and ordered by
6. Unit price	6. Delivery address and date
7. Extension	7. Special instructions
8. Special information or instructions, and any other agreements	8. Signatures: receiver, buyer, accounting office

With the completion of the purchase order, the buying process has come full circle. A quick review of the Cycle of Control (Chapter 1) reveals that all that is left to do is to wait for the deliveries to come in. In the next chapter, Chapter 7, we will discuss receiving, storing, and bill-issuing and bill-paying procedures.

Supplier Pricing

How did the supplier come up with that price quote? The supplier price is a function of the cost of the product to the supplier plus a degree of mark-up to cover shipping, handling, storage, and billing costs.

Methods of Markup

The degree of markup can be an agreed-upon dollar figure or a set percentage. In commercial foodservice pricing, the operator usually pays a set percentage over the suppliers' product cost. If the product cost increases, then the overall cost to the operator increases, because the cost to the operator is the cost of the item to the supplier, plus a percentage of markup over the supplier's cost. If the product cost decreases, then the overall cost to the operator will also decrease. The percentage or dollar amount of markup will vary with the size of the operation. Large operators usually enjoy a more favorable (lower) percentage of markup than do small, independent operators. For this reason, small operators may choose to opt for volume-based, one-stop shopping with a supplier, in return for a more favorable pricing structure.

The following is an example of pricing based on a percentage markup:

Item	Supplier Case Cost	% Markup	Operator Cost
Tomatoes, crushed, #10 cans	$15.96 per case	10%	$17.56/cs.

Let's assume that the supplier's cost for the crushed tomatoes decreases to $13.89 per case. The cost to the operator would also decrease:

$$\text{SUPPLIER CASE COST} \times \% \text{ OF MARKUP} = \text{OPERATOR COST}$$

Item	Supplier Case Cost × % Markup = Operator Cost		
Tomatoes, crushed, #10 cans	$13.89 per case	10%	$15.28/cs.

The second method is similar to this one, except that the markup is a set dollar figure added to each case to cover the suppliers' overhead. The operator would pay the suppliers' direct cost for products plus the agreed upon fee. This method is more commonly used for institutions and is usually a part of a contractual agreement for a period of time. Here's what the equation looks like:

$$\text{SUPPLIER CASE COST} + \$\$ \text{ MARKUP PER CASE} = \text{OPERATOR COST}$$

Item	Supplier Case Cost + $ Markup = Operator Cost		
Tomatoes, crushed, #10 cans	$15.96 per case	$2.50	$18.46/cs.

Getting the Best Price

Foodservice operations in large metropolitan areas have many suppliers from which to choose. As might be expected, operators located in small cities and towns have access to fewer suppliers. The competitiveness of the foodservice environment depends on the number of suppliers in relationship to the number of foodservice operations in a trading area. In most cities and towns, there is quite a bit of competition. Therefore, when a foodservice operation requests price quotations from competing suppliers, it is assured of getting the best possible price within the community.

Regardless of location—large metropolitan area or small town—the buyer is always in a position to negotiate price. The key to fair pricing is in developing a professional, working relationship with one's suppliers that is based on trust and an understanding that price is a function of more than just the numbers on the paper.

Emerging trends will dramatically streamline the purchasing process. Using the Internet to order directly from suppliers and using supplier-provided software to place orders are two of these—the objective being to make the process more timely and efficient for the foodservice operation and the supplier. This reduces the amount of labor and creates a better linkage with suppliers, which will improve response time and decrease the cost of transactions, thus reducing the cost of inventory management.

$\mathcal{A}$s-Purchased Prices, Yield Factors, and Portion Costs

Calculating As-Purchased Prices Using Yield Percentages

At times, a buyer needs to quickly assess the **AP** or *As-Purchased* **(AP)** price of an item using its known yield factor. To compare AP prices from different vendors for meat items with a yield factor, for example, simply divide the AP price on invoice by the yield percentage (written as a decimal)

$$\frac{\text{AP PRICE}}{\text{YIELD \%}} = \text{EP COST PER POUND}$$

Yield percentages for meat items used in an operation are normally found by performing on-site Butcher Tests. In the event that an operation does not perform Yield Tests, standard yield percentages are available through suppliers or through

The Book of Yields. It is best to validate yield percentages by cutting, preparing, and cooking the item with in-house equipment. This will give the most accurate yield factors.

Calculating Portion Costs

The result is the **EP** or **edible portion** (EP) cost per pound of the product. From this information, the cost per portion can be found easily:

$$\frac{\text{AP PRICE}}{\text{YIELD \%}} = \text{EP COST PER POUND}$$

Beef Tenderloin = \$4.69 on invoice

Standard Yield = 87%

$$\frac{\$4.69}{87\%} = \$5.39 \text{ per pound}$$

If the portion size for the tenderloin is 8 ounces, then the cost per portion would be:

\$5.39/2 (servings per pound) = \$2.70 per serving

Comparing Vendor Prices

A buyer can use this formula to quickly compare the EP price of an item, given different AP prices and meat packers (by brand name).

ABC Company	XYZ Company	LMNOP Company
Beef Tenderloin	Beef Tenderloin	Beef Tenderloin
Pismo – defatted	Pismo – defatted	Pismo – defatted
NAMPS: 189A	NAMPS: 189A	NAMPS: 189A
Brand: All American	Brand: American Beef	Brand: Beef USA
AP Price: \$6.39/lb.	AP Price: \$6.49/lb.	AP Price: \$6.41/lb.
Yield %: 85%	Yield %: 87.5%	Yield %: 88.5%
\$6.39/85 = \$7.52/lb.	\$6.49/875 = \$7.42/lb.	\$6.41/885 = \$7.24/lb.

The chart analysis shows that the tenderloin from the LMNOP Company will net the best EP price and ultimately, the lowest cost per portion. Strict attention to cutting and cooking is needed to ensure that the yield will hold. It is in the best interest of the operation to verify that the yields for the product are true. Performing a Yield Test, or Butcher Test (Chapter 3), is the only way to validate a supplier's yield percentage. Yield percentages should be checked periodically for accuracy.

Conclusion: The "Five Rights" of Purchasing, Revisited

The following is the purchasing model covered in Chapters 4 through 6. By this time, it should be as familiar and comfortable to you as an old hat.

Congratulations—you now know how . . .

THE FIVE *RIGHTS*

TO PURCHASE:

1. THE *RIGHT PRODUCT* IN

2. THE *RIGHT QUANTITY* FROM

3. THE *RIGHT SUPPLIER* AT

4. THE *RIGHT PRICE* AT

5. THE *RIGHT TIME*

Net Work

Explore the following Web sites:

www.tyson.com
www.tysonfoods.com
www.hersheyfoods.com
www.generalmills.com
www.venturafoods.com
www.ecolab.com
www.fooddude.com—This is a search engine for food and beverage exporters.
www.foodprocessing.com
www.foodcontact.com

Chapter Wrap

The Chapter ✓ at the beginning of the chapter posed several questions. Review the questions and compare your responses to the following answers:

1. **What is a distribution system?**

   The distribution of food and nonalcoholic beverage products in the United States is a fairly sophisticated process. Compared to not so many years ago, the choices are almost endless in terms of suppliers and product availability. With today's improved distribution systems and the ability to use the Internet to research purchasing options, buyers have alternatives like never before. Finished products are moved from processors to the distribution warehouses of intermediaries. From these warehouses, the product is sold to end-users—foodservice operators.

2. How are suppliers selected?

Suppliers are selected on their ability to meet the needs of the buyer. As such, a supplier specification should be developed to compare multiple suppliers. A supplier spec is a list detailing the selection criteria a buyer has created for potential suppliers.

3. How is bidding used to procure product?

Buyers use two primary purchasing methods to procure products. One is the informal method, the second is the formal method. Both systems can be employed by an operation, and one method is not better than the other. Each has a place in a buyer's bag of purchasing tricks. The informal method supposes a buyer has done his or her work regarding supplier selection and has a reliable list in place. The buyer, upon compiling the order, simply calls the suppliers, receives a verbal price quote, and places the order. The buyer may solicit prices from more than one vendor.

The first and most formal type of bid is called the *fixed bid*. In this situation, a buyer will prepare very detailed specifications (a *Request for Bid*) that are sent only to qualified suppliers. The key here is that the supplier is deemed qualified. Next, the buyer waits to receive sealed responses to the bid. Once received, the responses are opened and evaluated, and a contract is awarded. Contracts are then signed by both parties, and the process is complete. Fixed bids are best used for guaranteeing a specific amount of product, at a set price, for a fairly long period of time.

4. What is a purchase order?

Each time an order is prepared and placed, a purchase order (or PO) is prepared. This is the next line of documentation needed to control the purchasing process. It can be compared to a sales agreement. A purchase order is a numbered form that identifies the item(s), quantity ordered, price, unit cost, extension, total, and authorization signatures. It is a control tool used by most businesses that authorizes the exchange of goods and services and ensures payment to the supplier. It creates a legally binding contract when prepared and signed by a buyer and received by a supplier.

5. How do suppliers set prices?

The supplier price is a function of the cost of the product to the supplier, plus a degree of markup to cover shipping, handling, storage, and billing costs. The degree of markup can be an agreed-upon dollar figure or a set percentage. Commercial foodservice pricing is usually a function of the operator paying a set percentage over the supplier's product cost. If the product cost increases, then the overall cost to the operator increases, because it is a percentage of mark-up over the supplier's cost. If the product cost decreases, then the overall cost to the operator will also decrease. The percentage or dollar amount of markup will vary with the size of the operation. Large operators usually enjoy a more favorable percentage of markup than do small, independent operators.

*K*ey Terminology and Concepts in This Chapter

As-Purchased (AP)

Approved supplier lists

Bid sheet

Bid system

Broadline distributors

Broker

Brokerage firm

Browse sheet

B2B purchasing

Call sheet

Case-break pricing

Cash and carry

Cash discount

COD (cash on delivery)

Commissaries

Daily bid

Distribution edible portion (EP) cost

eProcurement

Fixed bid

Foodservice distributor

Formal purchasing

Full-line distributor

Informal purchasing

Intermediaries

Manufacturers

Marketing specialists

Middlemen

Minimum order size

One-stop shopping

Online ordering

Order sheets

Processors

Product printout

Product specification

Purchase order (PO)

Quantity discount

Request for Bid

Requisitions

Sources

Specialty product distributors

Supplier specifications

Value-added products

Volume discount

Will-call order

Discussion Questions and Exercises

1. Marcel, the buyer, has given notice that he will be leaving Farfalle Arrabbiata. You are responsible to hire a replacement. Develop a job description and a comprehensive list of duties that the new buyer will be expected to perform.

2. Chef Raoul, Larry the line cook, and a few other members of the cooking team have just returned from the National Restaurant Association's Hotel and Restaurant Trade Show in Chicago. They have collected information about products, equipment, and so on. Larry spent a lot of time chatting it up with the sales reps from the processor that makes the fresh mozzarella used in the restaurant. It is currently ordered through a local supplier. Larry has the sales brochures and price quotes. He's quite excited to see the quantity discounts available—especially for a tractor-trailer load. Explain to Larry why this won't work for Farfalle Arrabbiata.

3. Explain how Larry's information could be used to research or negotiate other purchasing options with the local supplier. With the processor.

4. What criteria would be needed to create a supplier spec for the mozzarella cheese?

5. Review the menu selections for Farfalle Arrabbiata (see Appendix A.) Through the descriptions, identify the ingredients that would most likely be purchased through a specialty supplier.

6. Review the menu descriptions for Farfalle Arrabbiata and identify five products that would be good candidates for the fixed bid procedure.

7. Current purchasing practices for Farfalle Arrabbiata involves using a number of suppliers. The general manager is hot to go to a one-stop shopping model. She is looking to you for an opinion. Create a pro and con list based on the background information, the knowledge you have of this operation (Appendix A), and the menu. Write a memo that gives your opinion on the matter.

8. Chef Raoul was informed of the function for 180 guests booked by Peter Soup (see Chapter 5, Exercise 13) for Wednesday night. Because it is Monday, the orders have to be called in immediately. Unfortunately, his usual meat supplier is unable to deliver the Bistecca, because he is located out of state, and the usual delivery days are Monday and Thursday. As a result, a secondary supplier was contacted. His price quote was $5.19 a pound—a better price than usual. Chef ordered 141 pounds of meat (as you would have determined in Chapter 5, Exercise 13). It was delivered

on Wednesday morning. As Raoul prepped the meat (trimming and cutting), he realized he was going to be short on steaks. Explain why and how this could happen.

9. Chef Raoul purchased 141 pounds of meat from the secondary supplier. He was only able to cut 165 steaks at 10 ounces each after final trimming. The function is guaranteed at 180 guests. How much was he short? What is the actual yield for this item? How much more meat is needed from this vendor for this function? What is the portion cost of this item? What is the cost of this error?

10. Look back at the pricing work for problems 14 and 15 in Chapter 5. Substitute the actual cost per portion for this steak into your equation and calculate what this meal should have sold for. What is the cost of this error?

11. The GM is not well-schooled in the concepts of EP/AP. She is questioning why broccoli crowns were purchased versus full heads of broccoli. Broccoli crowns are $1.69/lb. and have a standard yield of 92%. Heads of broccoli are $1.39/lb. and have a yield of 73%. Explain the concept and demonstrate the cost implications. Translate this into a portion cost. The portion size is 5 ounces.

BID SHEET

Date: 2/14/2XXX

Item Description & Pack	Purchasing Unit	Supplier's Name & Bid/Pur. Unit		
		ABC Co.	DEF Co.	GHI Co.
Ricotta Cheese	5/lb. tub	$17.50/tub	$16.50/tub	$16.00/tub
Semolina Flour	50 lb./bag	$22.50/bag	$23.45/bag	$22.75/bag
Red Wine Vinegar	4/1 gal./cs.	$11.00/cs.	$10.80/cs.	$10.25/cs.
Arborrio Rice	10 lb./bag	$28.00/bag	$31.00/bag	$30.50/bag
Granulated Sugar	25 lb./bag	$12.50/bag	$11.00/bag	$12.00/bag
Canola Oil	6/1 gal./cs.	$26.00/cs.	$27.00/cs.	$25.50/cs.
Heavy Cream		$4.80/qt.	$4.50/qt.	$4.05/qt.
Crushed Tomatoes	6/#10's cs.	$21.40/cs.	$22.00/cs.	$22.50/cs.
Butter	36/1 lb. cs.	$112/cs.	$110/cs.	$108/cs.
TOTAL				

---

12. Marcel has received prices for the products listed on the bid sheet from his suppliers. Determine the best purchase, given the following conditions.

Order quantities are as follows:

Ricotta Cheese	5 tubs
Semolina Flour	10 bags
Vinegar	1 case
Rice	8 bags
Sugar	2 bags
Oil	1 case
Heavy Cream	10 quarts
Crushed Tomatoes	12 cases
Butter	1 case

a. Circle the best prices for each item. From which supplier would you order?

b. Which supplier has the lowest total product cost? Explain why this answer differs from your answer in a.

c. What would all these supplies cost in total if you were able to split the order and order by price alone? What would these supplies cost if you split the order between the two best suppliers?

d. What does this exercise teach you about pricing?

BID SHEET

Date: 2/14/2XXX

Item Description & Pack	Purchasing Unit	Supplier's Name & Bid/Pur. Unit		
		ABC Co.	DEF Co.	GHI Co.
Cream Cheese – 3 lb. block	3 lb. block	$3.74/block	$3.54/block	$3.68/block
Half & Half – ½ gal.	½ gal.	$1.79/½ gal.	$1.85/½ gal.	$1.75/½ gal.
Butter – 30 lb.case	case	$51.60/cs.	$49.50/cs.	$50.40/cs.
Crushed Tomatoes – 6/10's	case	$21.48/cs.	$20.40/cs.	$20.34/cs.
Lemon Juice – 12 qts.	case	$45.00/cs.	$43.20/cs.	$45.00/cs.
Olive Oil – 12 qts.	case	$62.32/cs.	$62.32/cs.	$62.65/cs.
TOTAL				

---

13. Because of an ordering error, supplies are needed ASAP. The amounts are listed on the purchase order on page 191. Chef Raoul has a large function on Friday on top of the usual full house. Because of a concert in town, the dining room is expected to be at full tilt all weekend. It is now 5:00 p.m. on Thursday afternoon. Only supplier ABC is still open for orders. Marcel has no choice but to order from this supplier. Refer to the bid sheet above to answer the following:

• How much will this error cost Farfalle Arrabbiata?

• What would it cost to order all the supplies from supplier DEF?

• What would it cost to order the supplies with the best pricing for each item?

## Chapter Seven

About Receiving & Storing Products & Processing Invoices

Chapter Objective

To use standard operating procedures to receive, store, issue, and inventory products.

Learning Objectives

After reading this chapter and completing the discussion questions and exercises, you should be able to:

1. Apply standard receiving practices to the receiving process in an operation.
2. Complete Meat and Product Tags, receiving reports, requisitions, and other standard receiving paperwork.
3. Properly process invoices for payment.
4. Apply invoice management procedures to track received goods.
5. Apply standard storage management techniques to keep storage areas organized and secure.
6. Use standard operating procedures to issue products.

The Menu

Pre-Purchase Functions

GUEST CHECK
Sales history, turnover, average check, cash management, revenue forecasting & budgeting, menu item analysis

STANDARDIZED RECIPES
Standard ingredients, portion size, quality, consistency, quantity, purchasing

GUESTS
Greeting, seating, sales, serving, busing, payment, comment cards

COST CARDS
Portion costs, yield factors, sell prices

SPECIFICATIONS
Product descriptions

FOH Functions

KITCHEN PRODUCTION
Production schedules, portion tracking, recipe control, serving controls, food safety

PAR STOCK
Inventory levels, order building

REQUISITION
Order building, purchasing

PRODUCT ISSUING
Requisitions, transfers, daily & monthly costs, food cost percentage

SHOPPING LISTS
Call sheets, bid sheets, suppliers, bidding

STORAGE PRACTICES & INVENTORY MANAGEMENT
Best practices, sanitation, security, inventory methods

PURCHASE ORDERS
Security, ship order, price guarantee, contract

INVOICE MANAGEMENT
Payment, price checking, security

BOH Functions

RECEIVING ACTIVITIES
Best practices, invoices, security, sanitation

Chapter Map

About Receiving, Invoice Management, Storing, & Issuing

Elements of Good Receiving

- A Place
- A Person
- Paperwork

Chapter Map   (Continued)

- Equipment
- A Standard Procedure

Verifying Quantity, Quality, & Price

- Invoice Receiving
- Verifying Quantity
- Verifying Weight
- Verifying Count
- Verifying Volume
- Verifying Quality
- Verifying Price
- Wrapping Up Receiving an Order
- Documenting the Receiving Process
- Potential Problems in Receiving

Storage

- Refrigeration
- Freezers
- Dry Storage
- Chemical Storage
- Storage Area Control

Other Paperwork Used In Receiving

- Product or Meat Tags
- Receiver's Daily Report
- What Is the Receiving Report Used For?

Processing Invoices

- Working with Invoice Payment Schedule
- Electronic Invoice Processing

Chapter ✓

Check the chapter content for the answers to these questions:

1. What is needed to receive deliveries?
2. What is invoice receiving?
3. What are the mechanics of storing product?
4. What does it mean to process invoices?

*A*bout Receiving, Invoice Management, Storing, and Issuing

This chapter covers a host of activities that start once a delivery appears at the loading dock. Prior to this stage, we were consumed with determining what and how much to order. Now that orders have been placed, they are starting to arrive at the door. So what's next? Why, we receive them!

This chapter details receiving procedures, along with invoice processing and payment, a critical function to sound **inventory management**, or *keeping track of stock and costs*. In addition, the prompt and efficient manner in which a foodservice operation receives merchandise and pays the bills will go far to establish strong relationships with suppliers.

A lot of time and effort has been expended to determine what and how much to order. Reflect for a moment on the content of Chapters 2 through 6. Essentially, these chapters lead up to receiving. The objective of receiving for any operation should be:

- To receive the right product in the right quantity at the right price at the right time.

It's simply four of the Five Rights, revisited. **Receiving** is defined as *the process of comparing what was ordered against what is being delivered and either accepting or rejecting all or part of the order.*

Once an order is in-house, management's task is to secure and monitor these supplies so that all products purchased ultimately produce a sale. Any product purchased but not actually sold as a menu item represents a loss of revenue to the business. The reason(s) for product not to make it onto a plate can be many, but the majority of the time, there are just three: theft, waste, and spoilage. All of these are controllable with standardized receiving, storage, and inventory procedures.

PURCHASING AND RECEIVING NON-NEGOTIABLES

- Buyers never receive or pay bills, or issue product.
- Re-key locks and change padlocks when there is a staff change.
- Weigh and count everything.
- Keep receiving areas clear of nonreceiving personnel.
- Keep delivery personnel strictly in the receiving areas.
- Select reputable suppliers.

Elements of Good Receiving

So what is needed to receive goods? Five primary items are necessary: **a place, a person, paperwork, equipment, and a standard procedure**.

FIVE PRIMARY REQUIREMENTS NECESSARY TO RECEIVE GOODS

1. **A place**
2. A person
3. Paperwork
4. Equipment
5. A standard procedure

A Place

The first thing needed to receive goods is a place to receive them. The receiving area is a critical control point in the receiving process. Often, the receiving area is just the back door of the kitchen amidst all the hubbub of production. The message to drivers and suppliers is that receiving is not a valued activity at this place of business. Poor receiving space opens a business to theft, scams, and fraud. Dedicated space is very important to properly receive orders from suppliers.

Adequate receiving space is clean and easily cleaned. It has good lighting and temperature control, and it has an office (in large-scale operations) or space to process paperwork. The area should be easily secured when not in use. Access to receiving and production areas should be limited to authorized employees and delivery representatives. Unauthorized employees should not have access to receiving areas, and delivery personnel should not have access to production and storage areas.

Space and good lighting are needed to examine, count, and weigh all products; test for temperatures; and complete paperwork. Receiving areas should be free of any debris, empty boxes, paper, and so on. Businesses operating a recycling program should have adequate space indoors and outdoors to collect, then store, these goods. Receiving areas must be secure, especially after receiving hours.

FIVE PRIMARY REQUIREMENTS NECESSARY TO RECEIVE GOODS

1. A place
2. **A person**
3. Paperwork
4. Equipment
5. A standard procedure

A Person

The receiver is the second critical control point in the receiving process. The person assigned to receive the food, beverage, and nonfood products that have been ordered should be both knowledgeable and experienced. Receiving skill is acquired through training and experience, particularly with meat, poultry, and seafood items. The receiver also needs knowledge of proper handling and storage of food items.

Being able to recognize that the quality of the goods delivered is consistent with what was ordered is essential. For example, it would be extremely awkward and difficult to have someone who has little knowledge of fat content, marbling, color, and so on, receiving, inspecting, and checking in fresh and frozen meat products. Although most suppliers try their best to deliver the exact products that have been ordered, errors do occur, and dishonest suppliers will try to slip substandard products through to an operator. The importance of a thorough and complete receiving procedure conducted by a professional and knowledgeable person should be apparent.

RECEIVER'S JOB DESCRIPTION

- Manages paperwork.
- Manages storage facilities.
- Recognizes acceptable quality in all products ordered.
- Manages deliveries and drivers.
- Adheres to food safety protocols.
- Communicates errors, problems, and issues to management.
- Solves problems.

Who is best suited for this task? Employees who have been properly trained and have the right tools can do this job. The operative word is *training*. A receiver manages paperwork, recognizes acceptable quality in all products ordered, and manages the deliveries and drivers. He or she adheres to food safety protocols, solves problems, and communicates errors, problems and other issues to management. This is a tall order. Proper training is a must in order to avoid errors, mistakes, and confusion, all of which costs the operation money.

The complexity of the receiver's job is determined by

- The size of the operation.
- The extensiveness of the menu selection.
- The type of food production.

Operations purchasing mostly pre-prepared food have an easier job of receiving than do operations preparing menu items from scratch. More complex menu production requires more knowledge and training on the part of the receiver.

If several different people are receiving merchandise and they are not properly trained, the result can be loss of control over inventory. Unauthorized substitutions, receipt of poor-quality merchandise, incorrect weights, and other problems are more likely to occur when the receiver is whoever happens to be around at the moment a truck pulls up. The importance of training in the receiving area cannot be emphasized enough.

FIVE PRIMARY REQUIREMENTS NECESSARY TO RECEIVE GOODS

1. A place
2. A person
3. **Paperwork**
4. Equipment
5. A standard procedure

Paperwork

Paperwork, the third critical control point, is essential to successfully receiving and tracking products. A receiver needs

- Copies of POs, order sheets, and bid sheets as applicable.
- A copy of specifications.
- Receiving sheets.
- Product identification tags, such as Meat Tags or other forms used for this purpose.
- Basic office supplies: pens, paper, clipboards, a calculator, and so on. Larger operations may also have an office with a fax machine, computer, file cabinets, and other office equipment.

FIVE PRIMARY REQUIREMENTS NECESSARY TO RECEIVE GOODS

1. A place
2. A person
3. Paperwork
4. **Equipment**
5. A standard procedure

Equipment

Some standard pieces of product **receiving equipment**, or *equipment needed to receive products,* include

- Scales—heavy-duty pound scales accurate to a fraction of a pound and scales able to weigh to a fraction of an ounce, for portion-controlled products.
- Temperature probes (properly calibrated) and rulers (if applicable), as well as food handler gloves.
- Knives to cut product to spot-check for quality (primarily used for produce).
- Wheeled carts, dollies, and hand trucks, to efficiently move products into storage areas.
- Stainless steel work tables (if applicable), on which to place product for inspection; large bins in which to unpack cases to check for quality—especially important with produce.
- Pallet jack and forklift, if applicable.

Obviously, the exact equipment needed to receive will vary by size and type of operation. Smaller operations will manage with a minimum amount of equipment; larger operators will go so far as to need pallet jacks, forklifts, and skilled drivers.

FIVE PRIMARY REQUIREMENTS NECESSARY TO RECEIVE GOODS

1. A place
2. A person
3. Paperwork
4. Equipment
5. **A standard procedure**

A Standard Procedure

You've got the space, the trained person, the paperwork, and the equipment. All that's needed now is the **receiving procedure**. Picture a delivery truck pulled up to the loading dock. It is full of produce or some of that garlic from Chapter 6. Here's the procedure:

STANDARD RECEIVING PROCEDURE
1. **Verify the quantity, quality, and price.**
2. Remove products to designated secure storage areas.
3. Complete paperwork and forward to appropriate office.

This short and sweet list is anything but. Good receiving practices demand rigor at the loading dock as well as in office operations. Let's discuss each of these procedures in detail.

$\mathcal{V}$erify the Quantity, Quality, and Price

The most common procedure used to receive goods is called *invoice receiving*.

Invoice Receiving

An **invoice** is *a form that accompanies the products being delivered*. It provides an itemized list of what was delivered. It also serves as a bill or invoice for payment. During **invoice receiving**, *the quantity of product on the truck is verified against the invoice quantity and the PO quantity*.

Verifying Quantity

During invoice receiving, the first thing that needs to be done is to do a **quantity check**—*to verify the quantities in the order*. Checking quantities has two steps:

- Verify that the number of cases delivered matches the invoice and the PO,
- verify the weight, count, or volume of products delivered (as appropriate).

Once a truck arrives to deliver an order, the driver will remove the order from the delivery truck and move it to a designated area, where the receiver can, item by item, check the delivered amount against the invoice amount (Figure 7.1). Using a copy of the PO and the order sheets, the receiver compares three things: (1) the items that are physically present, (2) the items that are written on the invoice, and (3) the items that were ordered. Working down the list, the receiver reads the first item and the quantity ordered, then confirms by a case or item count that that amount is, in fact, present. As an item is verified, a checkmark is made next to that item. The receiver moves down the invoice and repeats the process until all items are accounted for. Items not found will not have a checkmark. Problems of missing items or quantities need to be resolved before the invoice is signed and the driver leaves.

Notice the sample invoice in Figure 7.2. A column is included for checking off the items as they are received. There are also signature lines for signing off by the receiver.

Using a check-off system makes it easy to see which items have been received, which have not yet been checked in, and whether something is missing. This is a common practice, one that aids the receiver and the driver in their efforts to be sure all items ordered are delivered.

FIGURE 7.1   A receiver checks in an order.

Verifying Weight

The second task under the "Quantity" umbrella is verifying the weight, count, or volume of received goods. Although all items must be verified, this is especially true for meats, poultry, fish, and shellfish, as well as dairy items, such as cheeses and produce.

There are two acceptable ways to check **weight**:

1. The first is to weigh each item individually. This is a time-consuming process, but it is especially important, because most of the items purchased in the weight category are the more expensive products purchased overall. (Businesses that do not, as a rule, weigh products will become "known" by suppliers for this practice and are more likely to be scammed because no one on the receiving end is paying attention.) The stricter an operation is in its receiving practices, the less likely a supplier is to try to "slip one by." Well-written specs communicate to the supplier exactly what the delivery procedures will be. There must be follow through—do what you say you are going to do.

   Some meat items come in with the weight of the item stamped on the box. You can accept this as true and not weigh individual items. As a rule, spot-checking is a good policy. Suppose there are 20 cases of cooked turkey breast in front of the receiver. Each has a weight stamped on the box. The following describes three methods to check in this type of product.

OPTIONS FOR CHECKING WEIGHTS OF INDIVIDUAL ITEMS
- The receiver can open each box and weigh each item to verify that the weight matches what is stamped on the box.
- Weigh the entire case, box and turkey together (it should weigh slightly more than the label to account for the weight of the box).
- Spot-check: Open and weigh every fifth box, or randomly pick out a few and check.

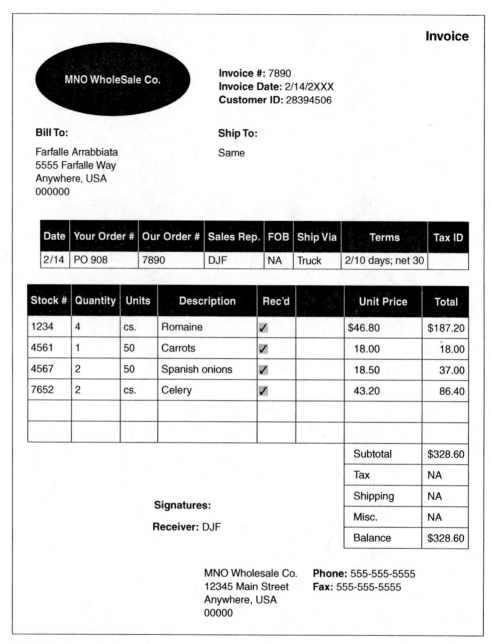

FIGURE 7.2 Sample invoice for Farfalle Arrabbiata.

Whatever the policy is, it must be adhered to consistently by whoever is doing the receiving.

2. Another easy way to check weights is to put all items sold by weight on the scale (Figure 7.3) After all items are put on the scale, compare the total weight of all items as reported by the scale to the total weight as reported by the invoice. Of course, a small discrepancy for packing materials should be allowed. If the discrepancy is reasonable, the order should be accepted. If the weight seems high or low, each individual item should be weighed. This practice, although not uncommon, has the potential for problems. It is possible that the total weight received is correct but the individual item weights are not exactly as ordered. Because of this, sharp receivers will *never* use this system exclusively to check in products. The preferred method is to weigh everything separately.

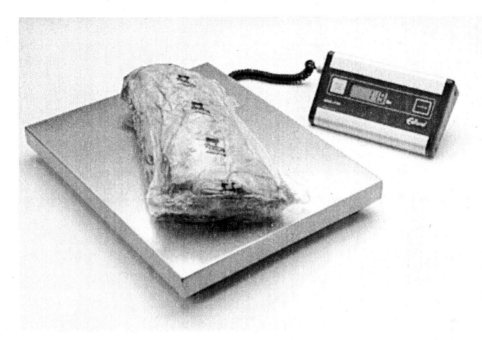

FIGURE 7.3   Product being weighed in. *Courtesy of Edlund Company, Inc.*

Verifying Count

Counting and verifying the case count is one form of counting. Purchasing items **"by the each"** is a purchasing term for *single units ordered*. The receiver verifies the individual counts of such products as lobsters, crabs, and other seafood purchased by the each, certain produce items purchased by the each, any broken cases, and miscellaneous items and any other things that need counting.

It is common practice to spec many produce items by a specific count per case. This count indicates a particular size the buyer needs. It also affects the cost per unit. Obviously, the lower the case count, the more expensive the individual item will be. Size also impacts total EP yield for the case.

EXAMPLES OF COUNT PER CASE
- Apples 56–252 per case; 113 per case is average.
- Pears 70–245 per case; 110 per case is average.
- Oranges 48–180 per case; 72 per case is average.
- Romaine 24 heads per case.

The amount of time it would take to verify the case count for produce makes it questionable as to whether or not to do this as a standard procedure. As a matter of practice, spot-checking might be enough to keep an unscrupulous supplier from short-counting cases of produce.

Receivers must also check for correct can size and case pack. Can sizes should be specified on the purchase order. Spec books are also used to verify can sizes.

Verifying Volume

The receiver will also want to verify the volume of products, particularly dairy items. The receiver is checking that the unit on the floor is correct to the unit ordered. If gallons of milk were ordered, then gallons should be in the case. Smaller purchasing units cost more on a per-ounce cost, which increases portion costs. The reverse can also be true. Accepting a larger purchasing unit—let's say half gallons of heavy cream versus pints—may increase spoilage that, in turn, increases food cost.

Verifying Quality

Next, receivers want *to be sure the quality of the product before them matches what is being charged on the invoice and was ordered on the PO*—they want to do a **quality check**. This activity is easily done at the same time that the quantity is being checked. The specification book is the tool in the toolbox for this work. Well-trained receivers will, in time, become expert at recognizing quality in all products. New or inexperienced receivers will need to refer to this document often.

The following chart is right out of Chapter 4. It is the list of common product specification criteria. It's useful as a quality control list for the receiver to use as an order is being received.

PRODUCT SPECIFICATION CRITERIA

Meat	Poultry	Fish/Shellfish	Produce	Dairy	Grocery
NAMPS # or supplier number					
USDA Quality Grade	USDA Quality Grade	USDA Quality Grade where applicable	USDA Quality Grade	USDA Quality Grade	USDA Quality Grade
Yield Grade	Size	Size	Size	Size	Product size
Yield %	Yield %	Yield	Yield/trim		Pack
Packer/Brand Name	Packer/Brand Name	Packer/Brand Name	Packer/Brand Name	Packer/Brand Name	Packer/Brand Name
Weight range	Weight range	Weight range/size	Point of origin	Fat content	Case pack/Can size
Color	Color	Color	Color	Color	Color
Trim/waste	Trim/waste	Trim	Ripeness	Flavor	Drained weight
Cost parameters	Cost parameters	Cost parameters	Cost parameters	Cost parameters	Cost parameters
Feed	Feed	Point of Origin	Preservation & Packaging		Packing medium
Form	Form	Form	Form	Form	Form
Pack	Pack	Pack Fresh/farm raised	Pack Case weight range	Pack	
Receiving procedures	Receiving procedures	Receiving procedures	Receiving procedures	Receiving procedures	Receiving procedures

Experienced receivers verify count and quality at the same time. This speeds the process along, especially when several deliveries are waiting to be checked.

Other Quality Checks the Receiver Should Make   After or while checking quantity and quality of the order, the receiver should make note of several other things:

1. Check the condition of the delivery vehicle—cleanliness, temperature, general condition.
2. Note the demeanor and professionalism of the driver.

3. Observe the general condition of the goods. Look for

- Wet or damp cases.
- Broken or torn boxes.
- Squashed cases, dented cans, other signs of mishandled goods.
- Drippings or spills on cases.
- Smell or odors of products or truck.

Verifying Price

Another responsibility of receiving is to verify invoice prices and extensions. This may fall on the receiver or on other staff. To verify price, the invoice is compared with the PO. Because one of the purposes of the PO is to guarantee price, the PO is the control tool the receiver relies on for this task. Discrepancies between the invoice price and the PO price should be marked on the invoice and brought to the attention of the buyer or manager, who will, in turn, consult with the supplier. All discrepancies should be investigated before the invoice is approved to be paid.

Once prices are verified, the extensions should also be checked for accuracy. This is especially important when a handwritten invoice accompanies the order. Computer-generated invoices are less likely to have mistakes. Once both of these tasks are complete, the invoice stamp sign-off lines can be signed. The invoice stamp is discussed in the next section.

Wrapping Up Receiving an Order

Once the order has been checked in, the receiver signs the invoice. There are always two copies of an invoice: the original and a duplicate. Once signed, the original goes back to the delivery person and the duplicate remains with the receiving person. It should be paired with the accompanying PO.

Documenting the Receiving Process

The next step is to **document the receiving process**. By documenting the process, *the receiver accepts responsibility for the order received.* The receiver will stamp the back of the invoice with an invoice stamp, which includes the information shown in Figures 7.4 and 7.5. This **invoice stamp** ensures that *all checks for quantity, quality, and price have been made and that payment of the invoice can move forward.* By using the stamp, the receiver and the personnel responsible for doing the price and extension checks are made accountable for their work. Also included are sign-offs for the buyer and for accounts payable, once the invoice has been paid. Invoices should not be paid unless the buyer or other authorized personnel approve the payment.

```
DATE: _____

REC'D BY: _____

PRICE ✓ _____

EXTENSION ✓ _____

BUYER ✓ _____

INVOICE PAID: _____
```

FIGURE 7.4   An invoice stamp.

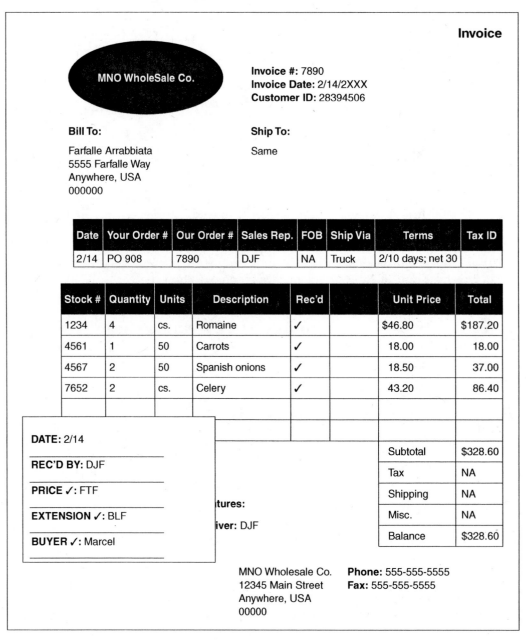

FIGURE 7.5   An invoice with stamp.

Potential Problems in Receiving

A Short Order   What if the order is short by one or more items? This is called a *short*. You are "short" on the order. A **short** is when *a different amount appears on the invoice than was actually delivered.* A correction should be made immediately by the delivery person and the receiver. He or she will cross off the incorrect amount, write in the correct amount, and initial the change. The invoice total is reduced on the spot.

Some suppliers prefer that the delivery person issues a credit memo for the difference instead of making any changes on the original invoice. A **credit memo** is *a form listing the name of the item(s), the quantity short, the unit price, and the extension.* A credit memo is also used for product that is not acceptable. The extension is the amount of credit due. The credit memo is then signed by the receiver and the driver as verification of the paperwork. The credit memo will make its way to the accounting

Date: 12/14			Invoice Number: 98734	
Supplier: ABC Co.			**Amount of Credit:** $42.28	
Receiver: DJF				
Item	**Unit**	**Quantity**	**Unit Price**	**Extension**
Romaine	cs.	1 cs.	$41.28	$41.28
Comments: Product was not acceptable				
Signed:	(Supplier)			
Signed:	(Receiver)		TOTAL	$41.28

FIGURE 7.6   A credit memo.

office, where it will be reconciled with billing statements at the end of the billing period. It is important for operators to track credit memos to be sure credit is actually received. Figure 7.6 is an example of a credit memo.

In some instances, shorted items will not appear on the invoice at all. Checking the invoice against the PO will reveal this "short" in the order. A well-trained receiver alerts managers before the shortage causes difficulties in production.

What if One or More Items Does Not Meet Specified Quality or Is Not Acceptable for Some Other Reason?   Once again, the credit memo is used to receive credit for the item from the supplier. The procedure would be the same as described earlier. (See the previous section, "A Short Order.") When this happens, the driver takes the unwanted items back at that moment. The receiver is left with a copy of the credit memo, which should be attached to the invoice (Figure 7.7).

One important reason an item can be refused is improper temperature. Receiving procedures and specifications should document acceptable receiving temperatures for products. The following is a summary of standard receiving temperatures for a variety of products:

Standard Receiving Temperatures

Meat, poultry, and fish	41°F or lower
Fresh shellfish and crustaceans	45°F or lower
Fresh eggs	45°F or lower

What Happens if an Item Is Received and Accepted but Is Found to Be Incorrect Later?   Generally, once the receiver receives the goods and signs the invoice, the merchandise becomes the operation's property. If an error is found later, credit is issued at the supplier's discretion. Most suppliers are in the customer service business, though, and will pick up goods delivered in error, even after they have been signed for. When this occurs, the buyer contacts the supplier, who issues a pick-up slip to the driver. The items will be picked up with the next delivery. Some suppliers will not pick up frozen or refrigerated products for food safety reasons—they cannot verify the product was handled properly at all times.

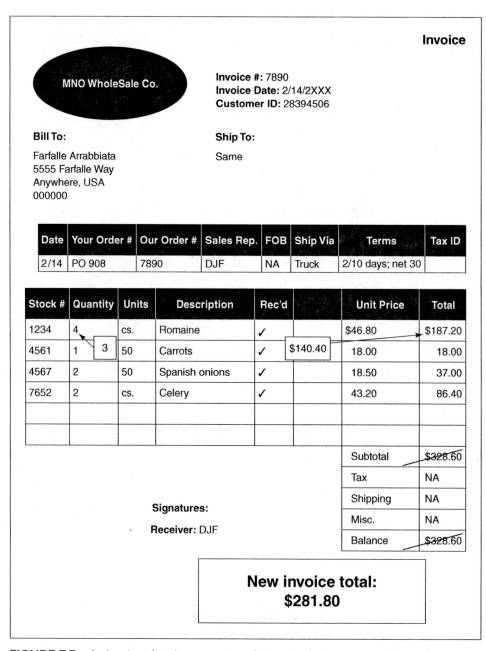

FIGURE 7.7 An invoice showing one case of Romaine lettuce returned.

The **pick-up slip** *lists the items to be retrieved, along with the case count, unit price, and extension.* This will be the amount credited to the account. This form requires the signatures of the driver and the receiver. It is similar in looks and function to a credit memo. The pick-up slip is attached to the invoice and sent to the accounting office.

STANDARD RECEIVING PROCEDURE

1. Verify the quantity, quality and price.

2. Remove products to designated secure storage areas.

3. Complete paperwork and forward to appropriate office.

Storage

Recall the second step of the Standard Receiving Procedure: Remove products to appropriate storage areas, or, put the groceries away!

Every piece of merchandise must be *placed somewhere and kept for a period of time*—it must be placed in storage. The orderly placement of merchandise is essential so that it can be easily found, retrieved, and issued. In some cases, the storage period may be only for a matter of hours. In other cases, it may be several months. The period of time and conditions for the storage of the product is governed by the characteristics of the product itself.

Once the products are checked in, they must be *quickly* moved to appropriate storage areas to reduce the chances of pilferage, theft, or spoilage. Proper food safety procedures specify that no perishable food item should be left at room temperature for more than 4 hours of cumulative time. With this in mind, a trained receiver knows that the product at the loading dock must go. So ... where does it "go"? Using carts, dollies, or pallet jacks, the products are moved into storage areas, where they become "inventory." They are moved into one of the following areas:

- Refrigeration units
- Freezer units
- Dry storage areas
- Chemical storage areas

The location of storage areas should be carefully thought out, to eliminate any chance of theft and contamination from garbage, chemicals, or other contaminants. They should be easily accessible to the receiving dock, food preparation areas, and cooking line. All storage areas should be secured with locks. Only authorized staff should have keys to storage areas. Large operations may use video surveillance to assist in monitoring and securing storage areas.

Storage areas are usually the last thing on management's mind, and, as such, they are often too small, poorly lit and ventilated, poorly located (in less-than-desirable places), and woefully inadequate. There is hardly a foodservice manager around who boasts of having too much storage space.

Refrigeration

Some of the standard types of **refrigeration** for storage include reach-in refrigerators, walk-in refrigerators, and under-counter refrigeration units. Units can stand alone or be built in, and they can range in size from small under-counter units to units large enough to accommodate forklifts and drivers. The size and variety of equipment is endless. Regardless of the type of equipment, however, all refrigeration units must meet the simple criteria of maintaining product at safe temperatures.

To adhere to refrigeration best practices, do the following:

- Use appropriate shelving, which allows for proper circulation of air. Shelving must be cleaned regularly. All shelving should be 6 inches from walls; the lowest shelf should be 6 inches from the floor.
- Maintain internal temperatures that are appropriate for each product requiring refrigeration. Monitor storage temperatures as part of standard operating procedures. Figure 7.8 shows temperatures appropriate for specific products.
- Don't overload refrigerators or obstruct fans or condenser units.
- Wrap, label, date, and rotate all foods in food-grade containers.
- Separate raw foods from cooked foods, whenever possible.
- Store raw foods below cooked foods.
- Store nothing on the floor.

Meats	41°F or below
Poultry	41°F or below
Fish	41°F or below
Shellfish	35–45°F
Eggs	45°F or below
Dairy	41°F or below
Fresh produce	41°F or below; varies by type of product

FIGURE 7.8   General refrigerated product storage temperatures.

- Regularly clean and sanitize every refrigeration unit. This includes floors, walls, shelves, and floor.
- Secure all refrigeration units with locks. Strict key control is an important security measure to safeguard against theft. Keys should only be issued to authorized employees.

Freezers

Many food products require **freezer storage**. Like refrigerators, there is an endless variety of freezer units to select from.

To adhere to freezer best practices, do the following:

- Use appropriate shelving, which allows for proper circulation of air. Typically, slatted metal shelving is used. The lowest shelf should be at least 6 inches from the floor.
- Maintain freezer temps at or below 0°F. Monitoring freezer temperatures should be a part of standard operating procedures.
- Receivers should immediately move frozen products into freezers and store appropriately. Inventory should be rotated, labeled, and dated.
- Don't overload freezers or obstruct fans or condenser units.
- Wrap, label, date, and rotate all foods in appropriate food-grade containers. Packaging materials should be sufficient to protect the contents from the extremes of freezer temperatures.
- Store all products off the floor.
- Supply appropriate clothing—coats, hats and gloves—for employees who spend significant amounts of time in freezers.
- Regularly clean and sanitize every freezer unit. This includes floors, walls, and shelves.
- Secure all freezer units with locks. Strict key control is an important security measure to safeguard against theft. Keys should only be issued to authorized employees.

Dry Storage

Dry storage areas often hold *unrefrigerated and unfrozen* food products for long periods of time. Products in dry storage may be organized by product type, in a way that mirrors inventory lists, to speed up checking inventory. Some operations use shelf labels to assist with organization (Figure 7.9).

FIGURE 7.9   Dry storage area shelving.

Dry storage best practices include the following:

- Dry storage areas should be just that—dry—with a humidity level of 50% to 60%.
- The air temperature should be between 50°F and 70°F.
- These storage areas should be easy to clean and be kept clean.
- As with refrigerators and freezers, shelving should be 6 inches from walls and 6 inches from the floor.
- No product should be stored directly on the floor.
- All product to be stored should be properly labeled, dated, and rotated.

Storage areas must be cleaned regularly and examined for evidence of rodent or insect infestations. In addition, walls, ceilings, and floors must be inspected for holes and cracks that could lead to problems with insects and rodents. Screening on doors and windows should be checked regularly for damage. An integrated pest management program should be in place in every foodservice operation. Pest management companies are the professionals to best assist in designing and implementing such a program.

Authorized employees should be the only staff with access to dry storage areas. These areas should be easily secured with limited distribution of keys. In some operations, video surveillance cameras are used to assist with security of the facilities.

Chemical Storage

Chemical storage best practices include the following:

- Chemicals used for cleaning, for equipment, or for any other use must be stored away from food products.
- Chemicals *never* share storage space with food.
- As with storage areas for food, these spaces must be kept clean and organized, and follow standard procedures for inventory and food safety.

- Chemical storage areas should be secured, just like any other storage space.
- Chemicals should be stored in their original containers and must never be transferred to empty food containers. Chemicals should always be clearly labeled.
- Material Safety Data Sheets (MSDS) provided by the manufacturer must be posted in a conspicuous place, so employees have easy access to the information.

Storage Area Control

Locking doors to stockrooms, refrigerators, and freezers, as well as controlling the keys, are forms of inventory control. Another method is leaving stock areas unlocked but controlling employee access. The challenge is to prevent spoilage, outright theft, and "inventory shrinkage." Although spoilage is controlled by ordering correct amounts, dating incoming products, and stock rotation, theft and inventory shrinkage are controlled by strictly monitoring employee access to storage areas. The following is a brief description of ways to manage access to storage areas. Savvy operators tailor a system that fits their workplace. What works in one operation may be ineffective in another.

TYPES OF STOREROOMS
- Open storerooms
- Closed storerooms

Open and Closed Storerooms   Storerooms can be open or closed. **Open storerooms** are "open" for employees to remove products as needed. In an open storeroom environment, *access is not restricted and employees remove products themselves.* This may sound like a lack of control, but open storerooms are common and work well in many operations. The control of the storeroom in this situation is close monitoring by the chef or manager. Even though access is not restricted, managers and chefs know who should or should not be in the storeroom. Their eyes and production knowledge "secure" the inventory.

There are many versions of an open storeroom. Some open storerooms use **storeroom requisitions**. Most do not. Some open storerooms are open all day long. Some are not. Those that are not may be "open" for a posted time period—perhaps for several hours in the morning, then again in the afternoon. During these times, employees retrieve products needed for the shift's production. After that, access is only through an authorized employee, such as a manager or chef, who has a set of keys and can let the employee in to retrieve what is needed.

Storeroom control in this "open" system is through a strong presence by either the manager or chef, who monitors those going in and out. Many operations, large and small, operate an open storeroom concept with excellent results. Good storeroom control suggests, however, that storage areas never be left open and unsupervised.

Closed storerooms are, as the name implies, closed. What this means is *access is limited to authorized employees only.* Staff members who need products from storage never physically enter the storeroom. They wait at a secure entrance while a storeroom employee retrieves the required goods. These storage areas will include dry storage, refrigeration, and freezers. A storeroom requisition is used to issue these products to the employee.

Issuing   The requisition is then used *to charge the cost of the items requested to the department ordering the products.* As a security measure, products are only issued to requisitions with authorized signatures. As with the invoice receiving procedure described earlier, the employee accepting the items will "sign" for the products at the time of delivery.

Dept.: Kitchen					
Date: 2/14/2XXX				Req. Number: 1234	
Time:	10:00 A.M.			*Priced By: Marcel*	
Prepared By:	DJF			*Extended By: DJF*	
Delivered By:	Zach			*Approved By: LEF*	
Received By:	Stacey				
	Rec.				
Item	✓	Unit	Quantity	Price	Extension
Mangoes	✓	each	25	$1.00 each	$25.00
Pineapples	✓	each	4	2.00 each	8.00
Peaches	✓	each	25	1.00 each	25.00
TOTAL					$58.00

Original Copy: To remain with issuing department.

Duplicate Copy: To be sent to the receiving department.

FIGURE 7.10   A sample filled requisition.

Figure 7.10 shows an example of a filled requisition. While looking at the sample requisition, note the following:

- The "Received" column is checked off.
- Authorized staff members have signed off in the appropriate places.

The process described here is called issuing. **Issuing** is a means of *tracking the movement of product from the receiving areas to production areas via the storeroom requisition.* As product is issued, the cost is then charged to the requesting department. Issuing to requisitions can be done with both an open and closed storeroom concept. Generally, though, most open storeroom operations do not utilize the requisition system for product retrieval.

It should be obvious that the average restaurant does not have a closed storeroom with staff to fill requisitions. High-volume operators such as resorts and hotels with multiple food and beverage distribution outlets, convention centers, casino hotels, theme parks and other recreational sites, colleges and universities (and many other venues)—manage their purchasing in this way. For the rest of the foodservice world, some version of an open storeroom with or without requisitions is the most sensible arrangement.

To adhere to storeroom best practices, do the following:

- Label all shelving.
- Rotate, label, and date all stock.
- Lock up all storage areas.
- Monitor who goes in and comes out of storage areas.
- Design storage facilities so they are easy to clean and easy to monitor and secure.

Regarding Theft   Most foods do not have high value, in relationship to weight or volume, with the exception of meats, some seafood products, and specialty items. Few people will bother to steal items of low dollar value, because the risk of being caught far outweighs the value of the product. Of the several thousand items kept in stock in many restaurants, only about 10 percent of them have high dollar values. Management's efforts to secure items from theft or pilferage should concentrate primarily on these items.

This does not mean that normal security should be ignored. Just as with liquors, though, key items should be stored in special locked areas, and a limited number of personnel should be allowed to have access to these areas. Because most items of high dollar value require similar storage conditions (refrigerated or frozen), or perhaps occupy limited space (as with jars of caviar), it becomes fairly simple to give priority ratings to this merchandise and to set up accurate control systems to account for all items. A separate freezer with locks and limited access should be maintained for high-value foods (meats, seafood, and specialty items), whereas a freezer with unlimited access is acceptable for items of low value, such as frozen French fries or vegetables.

Regarding Spoilage Foodservice managers should keep spoilage to a minimum by properly rotating goods, but natural spoilage and shrinkage does occur. The simplest method to document spoilage is to report an item spoiled or damaged on a separate Spoilage Report (see Chapter 8). The manager should watch this figure closely, to ensure that no excessive amounts of spoilage occur. Note that if spoilage of product occurs prematurely, this form may generate a request for credit to the appropriate supplier.

Other Paperwork Used in Receiving

**ADDITIONAL
RECEIVING
FORMS**

• Product or Meat
  Tags
• Receiver's Daily
  Report

In addition to invoices, POs, credit memos, and requisitions, some operations use other paperwork to control products even further, once they are in-house. Two such forms are Product or Meat Tags and receiver's daily reports.

These forms are more commonly used in larger operations. A brief discussion of each follows.

Product or Meat Tags

Product or Meat Tags are *special inventory control tools reserved for tracking high cost products from the point of receipt through production and final sale.* The receiver attaches the two-part tag to the product as it is placed in storage. The tag records product information from the invoice (Figure 7.11). After filling out the information on the tag, the receiver attaches one half of the tag to the product and sends the other half to the accounting office. In production, when the item is used, the tag is removed and sent to the accounting office, where it is paired with its other half. The item is then removed from the inventory, and the cost of the product is charged to food cost at that point. The accounting office is then able to accurately track product costs, validate daily production records with guest check sales, and fine-tune ordering, inventory, and par information.

Product Tags also function as a security tool. Office tags without a match within a specified period of time should trigger an inquiry as to the whereabouts of the item(s) in question. Since tagged products tend to be those that are highly perishable, all tags should rotate over a relatively short period of time.

It would be wonderful to tag every product and watch as it makes its way through the production and accounting processes; however, reality maintains that this is not feasible. The use of Product or Meat Tags is generally reserved for expensive and

Product Tag No.:	Product Tag No.:
Item Name:	Item Name:
Grade:	Grade:
Weight:	Weight:
Unit Price:	Unit Price:
Extension:	Extension:
Supplier:	Supplier:
Date Rec'd:	Date Rec'd:
Date Issued:	Date Issued:

FIGURE 7.11 Product or Meat Tag.

highly perishable items like meats (hence the name "Meat Tag"), fish, seafood, shell-fish, and other specialty products. These tags are used at the discretion of management and the buyer.

Receiver's Daily Report

A **Receiver's Daily Report**, or **Receiving Report**, is a *daily report of deliveries received*. The purpose of the report is to break down daily purchases into specific cost categories. This report assists operators with determining the daily cost of goods (Figure 7.12). Larger operations use the report to track and route products and costs to other departments. Receiving reports are completed each day for the deliveries received on that day. They are forwarded to the accounting office when completed.

Using the Receiving Form   Once a delivery is accepted, the receiver will use the invoice to classify the incoming food products into one of two cost categories: **directs** or **stores**. Next, the receiver will enter the items and their cost into the appropriate column on the receiving form. Some forms also include a column for nonfood purchases and distribution columns for other internal departments. The form designed for this text (Figure 7.12) is only distributed to directs, stores, and **nonfood items**.

Directs and Stores   **Directs** stands for **direct purchases**—*purchases that go directly into production*. These items are charged to daily food cost as soon as received. These products are those that are purchased daily and are used immediately. In theory, direct purchases are consumed on the day received, so they are charged to food cost on a daily basis. These items are considered "issued" the moment they are signed for by the receiver. The **Direct** column on the receiving form is used to identify the dollar value of these items.

   Stores refers to the storeroom and is used for *purchases that will be placed into storage areas* as described previously. These items will be used gradually over a period of time. Because they are used gradually, stores are only charged to food cost when they enter production. And guess what form is used to charge these costs to production areas? It would have to be the **requisitions** form, discussed earlier. "Stores" not only includes products placed in dry storage, but the category also includes products

Invoice Number		DATE: 2/14/2XXX		A	B	C				
	Supplier	Item Description	Quantity	Unit Price	Extension	Invoice Total	$$$ Directs	$$$ Stores	$$$ Non-food	Notes
98765	ABC Co.	Crushed tomato	1 cs.	$33.00	$33.00			$33.00		
		Butter	2 cs.	49.50	99.00			99.00		
		Cream cheese	5 each	3.54	17.70			17.70		
						$149.70				
76509	DEF Co.	Romaine	2 cs.	41.28	82.56					
		Carrots	1 bg.	20.50	20.50					
		Spanish onion	2 bg.	19.85	39.70					
		Celery	1 cs.	45.90	45.90		$188.66			
						188.66				
98435	LMN Co.	Paper napkins	4 cs.	15.00	60.00				$60.00	
			A ×	B =	C					

Column Descriptions:

Invoice Number:	Pulled from each invoice
Supplier:	Each supplier is listed
Item Description:	Each item is listed
Quantity:	Amount delivered on the invoice
Unit Price	Price per unit
Extension	Quantity × Unit Price = Extension

Supplier Total:	Invoice total
$$$ Directs:	$$ amount of direct purchases
$$$ Stores:	$$ amount of stores
Notes:	Receiver's notes on delivery

FIGURE 7.12 Receiver's Daily Report.

placed in refrigerators and freezers. Finally, stores also includes tagged items, discussed earlier.

CHARACTERISTICS OF DIRECTS AND STORES

Directs	Stores
• Purchased daily	• Purchased several times a week or even less frequently
• Used immediately	• Drawn out of storage areas as needed
• Charged to food cost immediately	• Charged to food cost only when used
• Requisition is not required—the invoice is the tracking tool.	• Requisition is the control tool that identifies costs.
• TYPE OF PRODUCTS: Produce, dairy, baked goods	• TYPE OF PRODUCTS: groceries, meats/poultry, seafood/fish, frozen goods

---

Nonfood Items **Nonfood items** include nonedible items, such as paper supplies, linens, smallwares, and cleaning supplies. These items are removed from the cost of goods and are accounted for under the expense category of Direct Operating Expenses on the income statement.

What Is the Receiving Report Used For?

Two big questions that should form in one's mind when thinking about the receiving report are:

1. Why do all that work sorting costs into categories and recording them on a form?
2. Who uses it, anyway?

Here are the answers:

1. The office staff, manager, or chef will use the information to determine the daily cost of goods and the daily food cost percentage. Stay tuned—daily food cost is covered in Chapter 10.
2. This information gives managers and chefs an idea of where they stand in their battle to stay on budget.

STANDARD RECEIVING PROCEDURE

1. Verify the quantity, quality, and price
2. Remove products to designated secure storage areas.
3. Complete paperwork and forward to appropriate office

---

*P*rocessing Invoices

It's taken a while, but we are finally to the last step in standardizing receiving procedures: Complete the paperwork and forward to appropriate office. This step allows us to process invoices for payment. **Processing invoices**, from the time products are delivered to final payments, can be a simple and efficient task when a basic procedure is established and followed. The receiving function *verifies that all the products that were* *ordered have been received.* Management develops control procedures to ensure that the quality of the product coming in is the same as what was ordered and that there have been no substitutions, changes, or deterioration in the products. Once the receiver verifies all of this, paperwork is completed and forwarded to accounting for payment.

PAPERWORK FORWARDED TO THE ACCOUNTING OFFICE

- Stamped and signed invoices
- Copies of accompanying POs
- Credit Memos
- Receiving Sheets
- Product and Meat Tags

This system of purchasing means that the supplier and the operator have established what is, in effect, a credit payment system. This type of payment plan is called an **invoice on account** plan. It is the most common form of bill-paying procedures.

At the end of the billing period, a **statement** will be sent to the operator from the supplier. It will *list the invoices for the period, the dates and amounts of those invoices, and any credits on the account.* The bookkeeper, accounts payable person, controller, office manager, or owner is responsible for reconciling the statement with the invoices and credit memos on file. It is critical that all invoices and credit memos listed on the statement have a corresponding purchase order and invoice in the accounting office. It is equally important that the accounting office track all credit owed from suppliers. Less than honest suppliers will conveniently "forget" to reflect credits on the billing statements. Figure 7.13 is an example of a monthly statement.

The person responsible for paying the bills should also establish an invoice payment schedule. An **invoice payment schedule** is *a form used to ensure that suppliers are paid in a timely fashion.* This schedule ensures that bills are paid in a time frame that will best take advantage of supplier discounts.

From: MNO Company 12345 Main St. Anywhere, USA 12345	Statement For: Farfalle Arrabbiata 55555 Farfalle Way Anywhere, USA 12345	For Period Ending: 2/29/2XXX	
Date	Invoice No.	Amount of Invoice	Credit Memos
2/2	96321	$435.00	
2/9	78963	$675.00	
2/16	14789		$52.30
2/24	63214	$321.00	
Total Invoices: $1431	Total Credits: $52.30	Please Remit: $1378.70	

FIGURE 7.13   Supplier's Monthly Statement.

Many operators develop an **approved payee list** in conjunction with an invoice payment schedule. This is *a list of vendors approved as legitimate suppliers for the operation.* As a legitimate supplier, any properly signed invoice from that supplier would be paid. Invoices received in the accounting office that are not on the approved payee list would be reviewed automatically. Approved payee lists and approved supplier lists (refer to Chapter 6) are tools in the toolbox to reduce the chance that phony invoices could be sent through the accounting office for payment.

Working with an Invoice Payment Schedule

The simplest way to organize the payment of invoices is to list them on the invoice payment schedule. This is a formal way of documenting all purchases during a given period of time. The invoices are grouped by company and are listed in chronological order. They are then put in alphabetical order and recorded on the invoice payment schedule, as shown in Figure 7.14.

The payment schedule is determined by the terms of agreement initially set forth by each supplier. Their terms may range from requiring payment upon receipt to payment

	Period Ending: 2/14		Page Number: 1 of 4	
	Prepared By: DJF		Invoices Certified Correct By: Marcel	
	Date: 2/16			
Date	**Invoice No.**	**Supplier**	**Amount**	**Total**
		ABC Co.		
2/13	85749		$652.90	
2/14	98765		149.70	
2/15	98886		76.87	
2/16	98945		121.37	$100.84
		DEF Co.		
2/14	7853		188.66	
2/15	7906		310.40	
2/16	8011		112.90	611.96
		LMN Co.		
2/13	4567		60.00	
2/14	8768		267.90	
2/15	5943		345.12	673.02
		Valley Dairy		
2/13	0987		101.40	
2/15	1110		87.35	
2/17	1178		124.52	313.27
		Page Total:		$1669.09

FIGURE 7.14   An invoice payment schedule for Farfalle Arrabbiata.

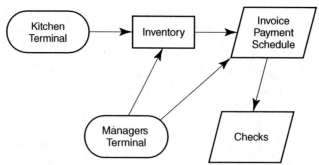

FIGURE 7.15 Flow of information for processing invoices when using computers.

being due within 10 to 30 days from the date of the invoice. Discounts of 2% are occasionally available when payment is made within 10 days. Checks are issued as needed, such as every Friday for the 10-day accounts and on the 15th and 25th of the month for the 30-day accounts.

Invoice payment schedules can be separated by categories (see Figure 7.14). Nonfood categories would be items such as cleaning and maintenance supplies, pest control services, paper supplies, utilities, and so on. This makes cost analysis and percentage calculations an easy task. A quick reference to the invoice payment schedules can determine the total costs in each category for a given period.

The invoice payment schedule in Figure 7.14 is organized according to payment periods. Most payment periods are monthly or semimonthly. The schedule is in chronological order. The invoice numbers are listed in ascending order, with the corresponding invoice amounts. Next, the invoices are alphabetically grouped by supplier. This is done so that only one check per supplier will be issued. This saves time and money.

Electronic Invoice Processing

User-friendly software allows foodservice personnel to enter each item listed on the invoice. Each item is then added to an electronic inventory form. The result is that the manager knows how much inventory is present. As the inventory is used, requisitions and transfers are electronically processed, and an inventory balance is available every day.

As invoices are electronically processed, the program generates invoice payment schedules at the same time. The invoice payment schedules may be organized by type of supplier or by type of inventory item. On the days that checks are to be sent, the computer program can be instructed to total the amounts owed to suppliers, take discounts when applicable, and actually print the checks to the suppliers. In one entry step, all the financial and accounting information needed to track and pay for inventory is processed. Figure 7.15 illustrates the electronic flow of information.

Here are best practices to follow when invoicing:

- Only pay invoices that are stamped and signed off.
- Use approved supplier lists, approved payee lists, and an invoice payment schedule.
- Never pay an invoice addressed to a post office box, unless you know the vendor.
- Pay bills on time to take best advantage of discounts available.
- Cancel invoices and corresponding paperwork after the invoice has been paid.
- Monitor credits to make sure all credit issued is received.

Net **Work**

Explore the following Web sites:

www.costgenie.com—Click on Inventory, Overview.

www.tibersoft.com

www.digitaldining.com—Click Products, Point of Sales Solutions and search the tabs.

Chapter Wrap

The Chapter ✓ at the beginning of the chapter posed several questions. Review the questions and compare your responses with the following answers:

1. What is needed to receive deliveries?

To properly receive deliveries, an operation must have: Adequate receiving space, a trained receiver, copies of all relevant paperwork, standard equipment, and a standard procedure. All these elements are necessary to the integrity of the receiving process.

2. What is invoice receiving?

Invoice receiving is the act of verifying that the quantity of product on the truck is verified against the invoice quantity and the purchase order quantity. In addition, the weight, count, and volume of products is also verified.

3. What are the mechanics of storing product?

Every piece of merchandise must be placed somewhere and kept for a period of time. The orderly placement of merchandise is essential for it to be easily found, retrieved, and issued. In some cases, the storage period may be only for a matter of hours. In other cases, it may be several months.

Once the products are checked in, they must be *quickly* moved to appropriate storage areas to reduce the chances of pilferage, theft, or spoilage. Proper food safety procedures specify that no perishable food item should be left at room temperature for more than 4 hours of cumulative time.

Using carts, dollies, or pallet jacks, the products are moved into storage areas where they become "inventory." The common storage areas for food products are refrigeration units, freezer units, dry storage areas, and chemical storage areas.

Storage areas should be carefully located to eliminate any chance of theft and contamination from garbage, chemicals, or other contaminants. They should be easily accessible to the receiving dock, food preparation areas, and cooking line. All storage areas should be secured with locks. Only authorized staff should have keys to storage areas. Large operations may use video surveillance to assist in monitoring and securing storage areas.

4. What does it mean to process invoices?

The entire paperwork system used to receive product is called *processing invoices*. It includes properly receiving products by verifying quantity, quality, and price; stamping and signing invoices; stamping invoices; tracking credits; tagging product; and completing receiving sheets. The close of the cycle is when invoices are paid.

Key Terminology and Concepts in This Chapter

Approved payee list	Pick-up slip
By the each	Processing invoices
Closed storerooms	Product or Meat Tags
Counting	Quality check
Credit memo	Quantity check
Directs	Receiver's Daily Report
Documenting the receiving process	Receiving
Dry storage	Receiving equipment
Freezer storage	Receiving procedure
Inventory management	Refrigeration
Invoice	Requisitions
Invoice on account	Short
Invoice payment schedule	Statement
Invoice receiving	Storage temperatures
Invoice stamp	Storeroom requisitions
Issuing	Stores
Nonfood items	Volume
Open storerooms	Weight

Discussion Questions and Exercises

1. You are one of the managers at Farfalle Arrabbiata. As such, you receive all deliveries for food and nonfood supplies. This has increasingly demanded more time than you care to commit. You have proposed to the general manager (GM) the idea of training two line cooks to take over this responsibility.

   a. What must you take into consideration when planning for this change?

   b. Create a flow chart of activities and paperwork needed to properly receive and store products.

   c. Develop a training module for verifying quantity, quality, and price.

2. Explain why Marcel (the buyer) is not receiving, storing, issuing, or paying invoices.

3. Larry and Mel were looking at an order of 20 cases of boxed beef (Bistecca). Weight stamps were on the outside of the boxes. What is the best procedure for them to use to check in the order? What is the correct procedure to refuse some or all of the order?

4. Recently, several staff members have noticed evidence of rodents in the dry storage areas. Clearly an unacceptable development, you have been charged with developing a comprehensive plan to take care of this problem. What would your plan look like?

5. Food cost for the past few weeks has been uncharacteristically high. The GM is not happy. All the managers, including you, are on the prowl to figure out what is going on. An investigation has revealed that product is being thrown out due to spoilage and waste. This is unacceptable, given the high degree of standard operating procedures employed at Farfalle Arrabbiata. Prepare a checklist of procedures and paperwork in the areas of ordering, receiving, issuing, and inventory control that need to be reviewed immediately to get to the bottom of this.

6. Marcel is hopping mad. One of the line cooks new to receiving placed all of the delivered meats on the scale, checked the total weight of everything, and signed the invoice. Upon closer inspection, Marcel realized that although 100 pounds of meat came in, the distribution was not exactly as ordered. Here's the distribution of meat received, by type:

PO Order	Amount Actually Received
30 lb. of ground beef	38 lb. of ground beef
60 lb. of rib	55 lb. of rib
10 lb. of sirloin tips	7 lb. of sirloin tips

Note the following:

The AP price of ground beef is $2.10.

The AP price of rib is $6.95.

The AP price of sirloin tips is $7.25.

What is the cost of the PO meat order? The received order? What recourse does Marcel have with the buyer? How does Marcel ensure this never happens again?

7. Determine the procedural and paperwork breakdown for each of the following scenarios. Answers can include procedures and paperwork from Chapters 4 through 6. Discuss the implications of the errors on costs.

- Chef Raoul went to the storeroom to retrieve 3 cases of tomato puree. As he checked the first case, he was not happy to see that it was #303 cans instead of #10 cans.
- Chef Raoul was completely out of olive oil on the hot line. Marcel ordered it earlier in the week, and Chef saw the supplier's truck this morning. Checking the shelf in the storeroom, Chef Raoul is surprised to see there is none. Upon questioning the receiver, Chef was not happy to hear that there was none on the invoice. Because olive oil is used for many dishes, something will have to be done immediately. How will you solve this problem?
- The receivers are in the office complaining that there is no place to store all the produce that has just come in. They want to know what to do with it all.
- Marcel opened the restaurant at 9:30 a.m. His usual routine was to immediately open the storage areas in order to start to assemble orders that would be placed later on. Walking over to the storage areas, he noticed that the locks to both the storeroom and the freezer were missing. In addition to answering the above question, what will he have to do to check whether any product is missing?

8. Determine the receiving principle(s) or standard receiving practice that was used by Larry and Mel in each of the following scenarios:

- Mel opened the loading door to receive an order of fresh fish and shellfish. To his surprise, the usual driver jumped out of a rental van and proceeded to put the fish buckets and other products on the ground. Mel refused the shipment.
- An order of frozen products was waiting to be checked in. A quick inspection by Larry found many of them to be wet. Some of the cases were torn and damaged. Larry also refused this order.
- Larry refused two cases of Romaine lettuce that was substandard to spec. In addition to answering the above question, what actions will he take to document this?

- The driver of the XYZ Foodservice Company was in a hurry to get back on the road. He assured Larry that the order was all set and he could just sign the invoice. Larry refused to do this.

9. The following purchase order was prepared for the order from the JJJ Company. The invoice that follows it accompanied the delivery. Check the PO to the invoice for accuracy.

PURCHASE ORDER FOR ORDER PLACED WITH JJJ COMPANY

Date:	2/16			PO Number: 69421		
Name:	JJJ Company					
Address:	4590 North Street		Terms:			
	Anytown, USA 12345		Freight Charges Amount:			
Telephone:	800-999-5555				☐ Cash	
Delivery Date:	2/17			☐ FOB	☐ Pre-paid	
Telephone:	800-899-3456		Fax: 500-456-7892			
	Contact Name: RM		Special Instructions:			
Stock Number	Quantity	Unit	Item Description		Unit Price	Extension
38697	5	11 lb. cs.	Asparagus		$43.45	$217.25
30827	4	24/cs.	Red leaf lettuce		$23.79	$95.16
76894	3	11/cs.	Eggplant		$22.00	$66.00
45901	1	2 – 5 lb.	Green beans		$13.50	$13.50
56023	2	20 lb.	Red bell pepper		$55.00	$110.00
93014	4	50 lb. bags	Spanish onions		$17.50	$70.00
Ordered By:	Marcel					
Received By:						
Manager OK:						
Office OK:						
					TOTAL	$580.91

JJJ Company
4590 North Street
Any Town, USA 12345

Date	Your Order No.	Our Order No.	Sales Rep.	FOB	Ship Via	Terms	Tax ID
2/17	PO: 8765	10294		NA	Truck	Net 30 days	NA

Stock Number	Quantity	Units	Description	Unit Price	Total	
38697	5	11 lb. cs.	Asparagus	$43.45	$ 217.25	
30827	4	24/cs.	Red leaf lettuce	$23.79	$ 95.16	
76894	3	11/cs.	Eggplant	$25.00	$ 75.00	
45901	1	2–5 lb.	Green beans	$13.50	$ 13.50	
56023	2	20 lb. cs.	Red bell pepper	$65.00	$ 130.00	
				Subtotal	$530.91	
				Balance Due	$530.91	

10. Alice in the office asked you to check this invoice for accuracy. Correct it as needed by manually adjusting the values:

PQR Company
1234 West St
Any Town, USA 12345

Date	Your Order No.	Our Order No.	Sales Rep.	FOB	Ship Via	Terms	Tax ID
2/16	PO: 2580	90876		NA	Truck	Net 30 days	NA

Stock Number	Quantity	Units	Description	Unit Price	Total	
3456	8	50 lb./bags	Flour, all purpose	$14.50	$116.00	
3409	8	50 lb./bags	Flour, pastry	$18.50	$184.00	
5902	1	25 lb./bags	Bread crumbs, Italian	$12.50	$ 12.50	
9832	3	1 - 10 lb.	Oyster cracker	$ 8.50	$ 25.50	
1278	1	20 lb./cs.	White navy beans	$ 9.50	$ 9.50	
				Subtotal	$347.50	
				Balance Due	$347.50	

11. The balsamic vinegar on the invoice in Figure 7.16 was the wrong kind. Larry asked you to fill out the credit memo, because another delivery was coming in. Complete the credit memo, so the driver can be on his way.

XYZABC Co.

567 West Street
Any Town, USA
12345

Phone: 800-555-5555
Fax: 123-555-5555
Email: XYZABC.com

Organization

Invoice

Invoice #: 67890
Invoice Date: 2/14

Bill To:

Farfalle Arrabbiata
12345 Farfalle Way

Ship To:
Same

Date	Your Order No.	Our Order No.	Sales Rep.	FOB	Ship Via	Terms	Tax ID
2/14	12345	98765		NA	NA	2/30 net	NA

Stock Number	Quantity	Units	Description	Unit Price	Total
50976	5	10 lb.	Calamata olives, pitted	$45.00/cs.	$225.00
87654	2	24–1 lb.	LaRizza orzo	13.78/cs.	27.56
36475	4	6/10's	Tomato puree, La Pinta	27.48/cs.	109.92
34890	1	6–1 li.	Sesame oil	94.50/cs.	94.60
83061	2	2–5 li.	Balsamic vinegar	44.00/cs.	88.00
				Subtotal	544.98
				Shipping	NA
				Total	$544.98

FIGURE 7.16   Invoice for XYZABC Company.

	Credit Memo			
Date:			Invoice Number	
Supplier:			Amount of Credit	
Receiver:				
Item	Unit	Quantity	Unit Price	Extension
Comments:				
Signed:				
Signed:			TOTAL	

 12. Complete the receiving report below using the invoices from the JJJ Co., the PQR Co., and the XYZABC Co. Include the WBZ invoice, shown in Figure 7.17. Be sure to check the WBZ invoice for accuracy before proceeding.

WBZ COMPANY
567 EAST STREET
ANY TOWN, USA

Invoice

Invoice #: 789
Invoice Date: 2/15

Bill To: **Ship To:**

Farfalle Arrabbiata
12345 Main Street   Same
Anytown USA

Date	Your Order No.	Our Order No.	Sales Rep.	FOB	Ship Via	Terms	Tax ID
2/15	PO 74561	789	NA	NA	Truck	Net 30 days	NA

Stock	Quantity	Units	Description	Unit Price	Total
4567	10 cs.	6	Palmetto diced tomatoes	$ 37.40	$374.00
4500	3 cs.	24/14 oz.	Artichoke hearts	79.92	239.76
3450	2 cs.	1–3	Chocolate biscotti	19.50	39.00
5671	1 cs.	3–8 lb.	Dark chocolate	168.00	168.00
4501	1 cs.	6/5	Cocoa powder	66.00	66.00
				Subtotal	886.76
				Shipping	NA
				Miscellaneous	$886.76
				Balance Due	

FIGURE 7.17   Invoice for WBZ Company.

RECEIVER'S DAILY REPORT

DATE:	2/14/2XXX		A	B	C					
Invoice Number	Supplier	Item Description	Quantity	Unit Price	Extension	Invoice Total	$$$ Directs	$$$ Stores	$$$ Non-Food	Notes

13. Complete the following invoice payment schedule by adding the invoices from the JJJ Co., the PQR Co., the XYABC Co., and the WBZ Co.

INVOICE PAYMENT SCHEDULE

Period Ending:	2/17		Page Number 1 of 4	
Prepared By:	DJF		**Invoices Certified Correct By:**	
Date:	2/17		Marcel	
Date	**Invoice No.**	**Supplier**	**Amount**	**Total**
2/15	78654	JJJ Company	$357.99	
2/16	79097		$223.76	
2/12	5678	WBZ Company	$459.75	
2/16	5987		$345.63	
2/11	3456	XYABC Company	$345.67	
2/12	3578		$231.65	
2/13	3214		$123.56	
2/11	8762	PQR Company	$456.87	
2/13	8890		$356.43	
2/5	9076		$112.59	
		PAGE TOTAL		

## Chapter Eight

Chapter Objective

To manage and control in-house inventory for use in kitchen production.

Learning Objectives

After reading this chapter and completing the discussion questions and exercises, you should be able to:

1. Differentiate between a perpetual inventory system and a periodic inventory system.
2. Apply standard procedures to inventory product.
3. Extend inventory values using an inventory form.
4. Describe inventory valuation systems.
5. Value inventory using a variety of inventory valuation methods.
6. Complete a Food Spoilage Report.
7. Calculate inventory turnover rate.
8. Use the ABC Inventory System to manage inventory.

About Inventory & Inventory Control

The Menu

Pre-Purchase Functions

STANDARDIZED RECIPES
Standard ingredients, portion size, quality, consistency, quantity, purchasing

COST CARDS
Portion costs, yield factors, sell prices

SPECIFICATIONS
Product descriptions

PAR STOCK
Inventory levels, order building

REQUISITION
Order building, purchasing

SHOPPING LISTS
Call sheets, bid sheets, suppliers, bidding

PURCHASE ORDERS
Security, ship order, price guarantee, contract

GUEST CHECK
Sales history, turnover, average check, cash management, revenue forecasting & budgeting, menu item analysis

GUESTS
Greeting, seating, sales, serving, busing, payment, comment cards

FOH Functions

KITCHEN PRODUCTION
Production schedules, portion tracking, recipe control, serving controls, food safety

PRODUCT ISSUING
Requisitions, transfers, daily & monthly costs, food cost percentage

STORAGE PRACTICES & INVENTORY MANAGEMENT
Best practices, sanitation, security, **inventory methods**

INVOICE MANAGEMENT
Payment, price checking, security

BOH Functions

RECEIVING ACTIVITIES
Best practices, invoices, security, sanitation

Chapter Map

About Inventory Management
- Introduction to Inventory Management
- Types of Inventory Systems

Perpetual Inventory System
- How a Perpetual Inventory System Works

Chapter Map   (Continued)

Periodic Inventory System

- When to Take Inventory
- How to Take a Periodic Inventory
- Using an Inventory Sheet
- Extension

Valuing Inventory

- First In, First Out
- A Note About Valuing Inventory
- Methods of Valuing Inventory
- Comparing Inventory Valuation Methods

Book Inventory Value Versus Actual Inventory Value

- Reasons for Variances

Managing Inventory Using the ABC Inventory System

- What Is the "A" in ABC?
- What Is the "B" in ABC?
- What Is the "C" in ABC?
- Categorizing Products as A, B, or C
- Spoilage Reports

Inventory Turnover

- Optimum Inventory Levels
- Calculating Inventory Turnover Rate
- Evaluating Inventory Turnover Rates
- How to Use Inventory Turnover Information

Chapter ✓

Check the chapter content for the answers to these questions:

1. What is inventory management?
2. What are the two types of inventory systems commonly used in foodservice?
3. How is a physical inventory taken?
4. What methods are used to value inventory?
5. What is the ABC system of inventory management?
6. What does the inventory turnover rate tell management about the inventory?

*A*bout Inventory Management

Inventory is the "cash cow" of an operation—it is what is needed if the business is to generate revenue. Success in managing a foodservice inventory, small or large, is essentially a matter of how well the foodservice manager understands the importance of the dollar investment in the inventory. This investment can range from a few hundred dollars for a small quick-service operation to tens of thousands of dollars for a large foodservice operation.

The financial investment in both food and nonfood items represents the goods that will be processed and sold at a profit. If the goods are wasted, mismanaged, stolen, or allowed to spoil, the profit potential will shrink. If the profit shrinks too much, the foodservice operation's future may be threatened.

Good inventory management is at the top of the To-Do list of techniques to control and manage food cost. This chapter covers standard operating procedures that managers employ to help them with this task.

Introduction to Inventory Management

Inventory management is the process of *keeping enough physical inventory on hand so that customers' needs are met, without spending more than necessary.*

INVENTORY MANAGEMENT INVOLVES

- Controlling the inventory so that everything purchased is available for sale.
- Storing all products properly, in secure locations.

Inventory management starts with taking physical inventory at the close of an **accounting period**. An accounting period can be *one day, one week, one month, three months,* and so on. **Taking inventory** means taking an *actual hands-on count of every item stored in the foodservice operation.* Taking physical inventory can be a fairly easy task to complete. The task, to be accurate, should follow an established procedure. After physical inventory is taken, the dollar value of the inventory must be established. This information is used to calculate inventory cost for an accounting period. These concepts are thoroughly explored in this chapter.

TYPES OF INVENTORY SYSTEMS

Perpetual: *Ongoing (perpetual)* count of inventory

Periodic: Actual physical count done *periodically*

Types of Inventory Systems

Determining physical inventory and calculating its value at the close of an accounting period is referred to as a periodic inventory system. It is different from a perpetual inventory system. The distinction between a perpetual inventory system and a periodic inventory system is as follows:

- A **perpetual inventory system** calculates *the value of inventory each time an item is either used or added to inventory.*
- A **periodic inventory system** calculates *the value of inventory at the end of an accounting period.*

The following is a detailed comparison of the two systems:

PERPETUAL INVENTORY VS. PERIODIC INVENTORY

	Advantages	Disadvantages
Periodic System	• Less costly to use vs. maintaining a perpetual inventory • Easily managed—any operation can implement the system	• Time and training of employees to perform a physical count • Time spent extending and valuing inventory • Inability to know the value of inventory at any time • Decreased internal control
Perpetual System	• Instant access to up-to-date inventory status information • Strong internal control • May help with improving reorder points and inventory turnover	• Time consuming and costly to maintain bin cards • Works best in operations with a separate purchasing department • A periodic physical count is still needed to validate inventory levels on cards

---

Because most operations do not use requisitions, the periodic inventory method is the primary inventory method in use today. The perpetual system gives more control to an operator and is considered more effective in that respect. However, if one understands the fundamental differences between a perpetual system and a periodic system, then the periodic system can be a very effective way to manage inventory.

Perpetual Inventory System

A perpetual inventory system constantly informs the foodservice manager of the current situation of any products kept in inventory. It is a *continuous way of tracking inventory with an on-going physical count.* If the manager wants to know how much crushed tomato product is on hand at any given time, he or she looks at the perpetual inventory chart (Figure 8.1).

A **perpetual inventory bin card** may also be used (Figure 8.2). A **bin card** is *a smaller version of a* **perpetual inventory chart**. The bin card is attached to each product's shelf location. Every time stock is added to the shelf, the storeroom clerk records the date and the number of those units on the bin card. As product is requisitioned

PERPETUAL INVENTORY CHART

Location: Kitchen

Item: Crushed Tomatoes | | | | **Unit:** #10 cans | | |

Date	Beginning	Additions	Deletions	Ending	Unit Price	Extension	Initial
2/14	9	0	2	7	$3.65	$25.55	DJF
2/15	7	0	2	5	3.65	18.25	DJF
2/16	5	0	2	3	3.65	10.95	DJF
2/17	3	0	2	1	3.65	3.65	DJF
2/18	1	12	1	12	3.65	43.80	DJF
2/19	12	0	1	11	3.65	40.15	DJF

FIGURE 8.1   Perpetual inventory chart.

PERPETUAL INVENTORY BIN CARD

Location: Kitchen

Item: Crushed Tomatoes

Date	Beginning	Additions	Deletions	Ending
2/14	9	0	2	7
2/15	7	0	2	5
2/16	5	0	2	3
2/17	3	0	2	1
2/18	1	12	1	12
2/19	12	0	1	11

FIGURE 8.2   Perpetual inventory bin card.

out, the reverse happens. The storeroom clerk records the date and the number of units being taken out. Periodically (think periodic inventory), the clerk has to verify the bin card count to what is actually on the shelf. As you can imagine—this is time-consuming and tedious work, especially given the number of items carried by an operation. Because of this situation, some operators use a perpetual system only for the most expensive items in inventory. In addition, because of the difficulty and cost of managing a perpetual inventory system, its use is somewhat limited to foodservice operations that have installed computer equipment and software to manage the system.

There are two primary purposes for using a perpetual inventory system:

- It ensures that enough inventory is available to prepare menu items at all times.
- It allows the manager to be constantly aware of the status and value of every item in inventory.

Most perpetual inventory systems are really modifications of calculating the book value of inventory. To ensure that the perpetual system is working, an actual physical count of all inventory must be taken. The **physical count** is the only way that the manager can be assured that the perpetual system is accurate because it *verifies that what is on the shelf matches what is on paper.*

How a Perpetual Inventory System Works

Each item in inventory has a perpetual inventory chart. The chart is kept in the accounting office and is, in essence, a "paper" inventory (see Figure 8.1). *Every addition to the existing inventory through* **purchases** *is recorded, and, in turn, every item requisitioned for use is subtracted from the chart.* Although this system represents extreme control and accuracy, it requires dedication and the ability to record and recalculate every time a transaction occurs.

This task is made easier by using scanning devices. Scanning devices look like a pistol that is connected by a cord to a computer-like calculator (as seen in grocery stores). All the operator has to do is point the device at the Uniform Product Code (UPC) symbol on the side of the package and pull the trigger. As the scanner reads the UPC number, the price value and the product identification is recorded. The person using the device then enters on the keypad the number of units on hand. This information is recorded on a tape or disk. The information on the tape or disk is then downloaded onto a computer. The computer compiles the extensions and generates the needed reports. This system is used mainly by large foodservice chains and some large foodservice distributors, but only within product categories to which the system can be applied.

Periodic Inventory System

Under the periodic inventory system, inventory ins and outs are not tracked. Product is stored and used until the end of the month or period, at which time a physical count is taken. Once taken, the inventory is valued and the cost of food consumed is calculated for the month. There are advantages and disadvantages to using this method, as compared to a perpetual inventory system.

When to Take Inventory

Inventory should be taken during a practical time. Many foodservice managers or other trained personnel take inventory when the foodservice operation is closed. This may be either in the late evening or in the early morning. Although that certainly is a good time, it may not be the most practical. Taking inventory after the foodservice operation closes may require paying overtime wages and inconveniencing employees. Many managers prefer to take inventory during slow periods of the business day. Slow periods for foodservice businesses are typically between 9:00 and 11:00 a.m., or between 1:30 and 4:30 p.m.

When inventory is taken during the business day, it is important to remember three critical points:

1. *Establish a consistent day and time that the inventory is to be taken within the accounting period.* For example, inventory is taken every Friday at 10:00 a.m. Doing this will ensure consistent reporting of calculated food cost percentages. The practice creates a standard period of time, so that inventory information can be accurately measured and compared. If a manager decides to take inventory on another day, or perhaps on the same day but at 3:00 p.m. instead of at 10:00 a.m., the inventory amount reported would not be standardized. There would be additional sales and perhaps additional products to consider. Doing this would make the inventory information not exactly comparable with that of the previous week or period, resulting in falsely fluctuating food cost percentages. Consistent information must be used to properly analyze what is going on in the foodservice operation.

2. *Do not schedule or accept deliveries during the time that the inventory is being taken.*

3. *Be sure to inventory the food in actual production.* Food that is in production is called **in-process inventory**—*food that is in the process of getting ready to be sold.* An accurate dollar value must be assigned to the following:
    *   Food that is being prepared in the kitchen
    *   All prepared food held in refrigeration
    *   Food on the steam table
    *   All open stock being used in day-to-day production

Difficult items to count, such as spices, must also be assigned a fixed dollar value. For example, all opened spices may have cost $72.00 unopened. The manager may assume that all of the spice containers will average being half full. Thus, an average of $36.50 will be assigned as the dollar value for all opened spices. This dollar amount will be used until the manager believes that significant price increases have occurred or until the number of spices being used has changed.

How to Take a Periodic Inventory

Before taking inventory, storage areas should be organized according to the type of products to be stored. This means that canned and dry goods are kept in one area; produce, dairy, and other perishables are kept in refrigerated reach-ins or walk-ins; and frozen items are kept in the freezer. In each area, the manager should categorize and alphabetize products as much as possible. If possible, label each shelf under the item so that items cannot be easily misplaced. Every storage area, if more than one is used, should be organized. When multiple revenue centers are operating out of the same storage facility, inventories should be kept separate.

Another important part of managing inventory is **rotating stock**. As items are added to inventory, the items already in stock should be used before the newer items. This process is referred to as **FIFO**, an acronym for **"First In, First Out"** and is the "gold standard" in excellent food storage practices. Proper stock rotation is made easy if products are date-stamped as they are received.

Using an Inventory Sheet

Inventory should be taken by two people. One person conducts the hands-on count and calls out the quantity and product name. The other person *records the quantity*

FIGURE 8.3 Hand-held scanning devices.

numbers on the **inventory sheet** or enters counts into a hand-held computer device designed for inventory management. This procedure maximizes efficiency, speed, convenience, and accuracy. In operations where bar codes and scanners are used, taking inventory is done with a bar code (UPC) reader (Figure 8.3). The information is downloaded onto a computer. Software programs take over and value the inventory (Figure 8.4).

FIGURE 8.4 Back-office computers.

HOW TO TAKE A PHYSICAL INVENTORY

1. Organize all storage areas.
2. Label each shelf.
3. Use two people—one to call out amounts and one to scribe.
4. Record quantities on the preprinted inventory form.
5. Forward completed inventory sheets to the accounting office.

The process of taking inventory follows the format of the Inventory Sheet shown in Figure 8.5. The products on the inventory sheets should be listed as the products appear on the shelves. Each **product category** (Meat, Poultry, Dairy, Fish/Shellfish, Produce, etc.) has a full list of all products carried in inventory. The Quantity column is filled in while taking inventory.

Item Description   The inventory sheet demonstrates how to categorize and alphabetize products. The first column, **Item Description**, *shows the categories of Dairy and*

INVENTORY				
Date: 2/14			**Page Number:** 1 of 10	
Time: 2:00			**Department:** Kitchen	
Taken By: DJF & FTF			**Location:**	
Approved By: LEF			**Priced By:** BLF	
			Extended By: Marcel	
Item Description	**Purchasing Unit**	**Quantity on Hand**	**Unit Price**	**Extension**
Dairy				
Butter	30 lb. case	60 lbs.	$1.65 lb.	$99.00
Cream cheese	12/3 lb. loaf case	3 lbs.	$1.18 lb.	$3.54
Half and Half	12 - ½ gals/case.	10 each	$1.75 ea.	$17.50
TOTAL				$120.04
Produce				
Carrots, baby peeled	2/10 lbs./ case	20 lbs.	$1.25/lb.	$25.00
Carrots, whole	50 lb. bag	50 lbs.	$.41/lb.	$20.50
Celery	24 bn./cs	36 bn.	$1.91/bn.	$68.76
Romaine	24 hd./cs	75 ea.	$1.14 ea.	$85.50
Spanish onions	50 lb. bag	290 lbs.	$.35/lb.	$101.50
TOTAL				$301.26

FIGURE 8.5   A completed periodic inventory sheet.

Produce. Notice that the items are alphabetized within each category. If the same item appears in different unit sizes or at a significantly different price, it should be listed and counted separately. An example in Figure 8.5 is carrots, which is shown in two different **purchasing units**. A few blank lines should be left between product categories to allow adequate space to write in any price or unit size differences as well as new products.

Purchasing Unit   The **Unit** column is used *to list the sizes of the individual items.* The example units are for various product sizes. Units may be in pounds, cans, cases or any other unit of measurement. The units on the inventory sheet correspond with the purchase unit found on the invoice.

Quantity   The **Quantity** column *lists the physical count of items that make up the inventory.* Occasionally, unit size and quantity may be confused. Take flour, for example, it is normally listed by pounds instead of bags. The person counting may say "four," meaning four 25-pound bags of flour, instead of "one hundred," the number of pounds of flour. The inventory would be short by 96 pounds. Proper staff training is the answer to this potential problem.

Price   The **Price** column shows *the individual price of each unit.* To calculate the price per unit, it is essential to know the price of the items according to *how they were purchased.* For example, a 25-pound bag of cake flour may cost $6.90. The unit price could be listed as the cost of one pound of cake flour, or it may be listed as the cost of one 25-pound bag of cake flour. *It is important to list the unit consistently by the pound or by the bag.* If the unit chosen is by the pound, then the cost for one pound of flour is the proper unit price. The method for calculating the **unit price** is as follows:

$$\text{TOTAL EXTENDED PRICE/YIELD} = \text{COST PER POUND}$$
$$\$6.90/25 \text{ pounds} = \$.276 \text{ per pound}$$

This math is the same formula used to calculate unit prices for recipe costing. Revisit recipe costing (Chapter 3) to brush up on this math.

Extension

The **Extension** column amount is calculated by *multiplying the unit price by the quantity on hand.* The unit price is the cost of each unit. The quantity is the physical count. Multiplying these two figures equals the extension dollar amount. This value shows the total amount of money in inventory for that particular item:

$$\text{QUANTITY ON HAND} \times \text{UNIT PRICE} = \text{EXTENSION}$$

This is the same formula used to calculate extensions when costing recipes. After each inventory item extension has been calculated, the extensions should be added. The total is the dollar value of all inventory on hand. This dollar amount is used to calculate food cost and food cost percentages for the operating period. When the inventory is completed, it is important to check for mathematical accuracy. The most common errors occur in calculating extensions.

Once the inventory is complete, the paperwork is brought to the office, where office staff will either manually extend the values or input the information into a computer that will automatically do this work. Operations that use electronic bar-coding systems simply download the information. The software system will compute the values. The value of the inventory is needed to calculate the monthly cost of goods. This topic is covered in Chapter 10.

It is quite likely that there will be partial cases of product in storage areas. Look at the entry on the Inventory Sheet for celery (in Figure 8.5). The quantity is 1½ cases. Recording partial cases is the correct thing to do. Rounding the inventory count up or down will affect the total value of the inventory. Standard policy should be to accurately record all inventory on hand.

*V*aluing Inventory

At this point, it is important to recognize that not all purchases are made at the same price. They are purchased at different times of the month or operating period, and prices change all the time: Prices for certain commodities can fluctuate, even within a given week. Consider this example:

Item	Monday Delivery Price	Wednesday Delivery Price
Ground Beef, NAMP #136	$1.89 per pound 50 pounds ordered	$2.29 per pound 125 pounds ordered

The difference is a $.40-per-pound increase in price, over two days. The $2.29-per-pound price would be listed on the inventory sheet as being the most current cost. If the inventory was taken on Friday and the physical count on hand was 65 pounds, then using $2.29 would provide the accurate price. If for some reason only a small portion of the ground beef was actually used, and the inventory reflected 160 pounds on hand, the ground beef should then be listed twice at the two separate prices, on the inventory sheet, as follows:

160 pounds on hand
− 125 pounds of the most recently purchased ground beef @ $2.29
   35 pounds of the oldest ground beef @ $1.89

First In, First Out

Valuing in this manner is called the **FIFO** method, or *First In, First-out*. Because standard practice in the foodservice industry is to use products purchased first, this is an appropriate way to value stock as it mirrors good stock rotation procedures. Most food service operations value inventory using this method.

The FIFO method provides for complete accuracy in identifying the *actual cost* of products. However, if the price difference between Monday and Wednesday is only three cents, using the higher price would be acceptable. A small degree of accuracy is lost, but this may be fine, as the increase was so minor that total food cost will not be affected.

Extreme caution is emphasized so as not to become too liberal in taking shortcuts in filling out the inventory sheet. Good judgment coupled with inventory-taking experience will allow the process to become automatic.

There are a number of systems other than FIFO in use for valuing inventory. They are:

- LIFO (Last In, First Out)
- Actual Cost
- Weighted Average
- Most Recent Purchase Price

A Note About Valuing Inventory

In most cases, an accountant rather than the chef or manager decides which inventory valuation method to use. It is important to understand the impact of each method on the monthly cost of goods. Why? Because the inventory value is an important component of the monthly cost of goods, and managers make business decisions based on the monthly food cost percentage. Also, be aware that because of IRS rules and other accounting protocols, the inventory valuation method cannot be changed frequently.

Methods of Valuing Inventory

In this section, each method is described, and the impact of each one on the value of the inventory is discussed.

INVENTORY VALUATION METHODS
- FIFO
- LIFO
- Actual Cost
- Weighted Average
- Most Recent Purchase Price

Last In, First Out   Under the **Last In, First Out (LIFO)** system, inventory is valued at its *earliest purchase price* (starting with Beginning Inventory Cost) first. Under certain circumstances, management may choose to use this system; however, this method is not commonly used, as it does not correlate with how inventory is managed and used in a foodservice operation. The LIFO system decreases the value of inventory on hand, which has the effect of increasing the cost of goods for the month. This results in an inflated food cost percentage. Again, there may be reasons to do this, but it is not common business practice.

Actual Cost   As its name indicates, the **Actual Cost** method records the cost under the premise that *the unit price of the item is the invoice cost for that item*. This seems sensible, but to use this system, each item has to be priced as it is received. This means each item would have its invoice unit price manually written onto it. It is quite obvious that this would be very time consuming to execute. On the receiving side, pricing each item would be cumbersome. On the inventory side, each bottle, can, or case of the same item with a different price would have to be recorded on the inventory sheet at the stamped price.

Weighted Average   The **weighted average** system requires the office to determine *the weighted average unit price for every item purchased*. This method is not common in the food service business. Even with a computer, it entails a tremendous amount of work for office staff. It is not feasible to do this manually.

Most Recent Purchase Price   This is a simple system that takes *the most recent purchase price as the unit price to use on the inventory form*. The logic behind this method is that this price will be the replacement price the next time the item is ordered. This system is easy to use and is fairly common.

Comparing Inventory Valuation Methods

The point of **valuing inventory** is to *determine the correct unit price for each item on the inventory list*. The importance of using the correct unit price to value inventory is as follows:

- When all is said and done, the total value of all of the items in inventory is an important part of the formula used to calculate the monthly cost of goods (covered in Chapter 10). The monthly cost of goods is half of the formula used to calculate the actual food cost percentage for the period.

- The ending inventory value does double duty in calculating the monthly cost of goods. It is the Ending Inventory value for the period and it is the Beginning Inventory value for the next period. An error in this figure affects two different accounting periods.

All this matters because:

- The monthly food cost percentage is a significant part of the operating budget.

Once managers or chefs know the actual food cost percentage for the month, they know whether or not they are on budget. If the value of the inventory is wrong because of errors in valuing or counting, then the actual food cost percentage calculation is wrong. In a worse-case scenario, management, because of flawed information, fails to take corrective action when, in fact, they should be, and this jeopardizes profitability.

To illustrate the impact of each method on the value of inventory, we will use the Produce portion of the Inventory Sheet shown in Figure 8.5. Let's work with Spanish onions. Notice that the unit price and extension are missing. The task at hand is to determine which unit price to use to value the onions, and then apply each of the inventory valuation methods, in order to compare them.

Produce	Pur. Unit	Quantity in Inventory	Unit Price	Ext. Price
Carrots, baby peeled	2 – 10 lb.	2 cases	$25.00	$50.00
Carrots, whole	50 lb. bg.	1 bag	$20.50	$20.50
Celery	24/cs.	1½ cs.	$45.90	$68.85
Romaine	24/cs.	2 cs.	$41.28	$82.26
Spanish onions	50 lb. bag	**5 bags**		

To do this, we need a little more information about the purchasing patterns and invoice costs of the onions over the past month. (*Note:* The end of the month inventory for the onions is **5 bags**. A **unit price** is needed to complete the Inventory Sheet in Figure 8.5.) Here is our additional information:

Opening Inventory

Purchases during the month   6 bags of onions valued @ $17.75 per bag

2/1	2 bags	$18.75/bag
2/9	4 bags	$19.50/bag
2/21	5 bags	$19.85/bag
2/29	3 bags	$20.50/bag

Now, we will use this information and the information on the Inventory Sheet in Figure 8.5 to compare the different methods of valuing inventory.

First In, First Out   The **First In, First Out (FIFO)** concept *uses the latest or most recent purchase price* as the unit price to value the onions. However, there are five bags in inventory, and the most recent purchase was for three bags of onions at $20.50 per bag. This means that the unit price for three of the bags of onions in inventory will be

$20.50. The next two bags will use the second unit price—$19.85—because that is the next *most recent purchase price.*

$$FIFO = 5 \text{ bags of onions to be valued}$$
$$3 @ \$20.50 = \$ \ 61.50 \ (2/29 \text{ purchase})$$
$$\underline{2 @ \$19.85 = \$ \ 39.70 \ (2/21 \text{ purchase})}$$

TOTAL VALUE   **$101.20**

Last In, First Out   The **Last In, First Out (LIFO)** concept uses *the oldest cost first as the unit price (start with the Beginning Inventory value).* Looking at the information, we see that there were two bags in the opening inventory, with a price of $17.75 per bag. Because there are five bags to be valued, the calculation will start with the oldest cost and "borrow" the cost from the second-oldest unit price.

$$FIFO = 5 \text{ bags of onions to be valued}$$
$$2 @ \$17.75 = \$ \ 35.50 \ (\text{Beginning Inventory value})$$
$$\underline{3 @ \$18.75 = \$ \ 56.25 \ (2/1 \text{ purchase})}$$

TOTAL VALUE   **$91.75**

Actual Cost   **Actual cost** necessitates us to *stamp the invoice unit price on each item as it is received.* Assume these bags were stamped with one bag at $19.50, one bag at $19.85 and three bags at $20.50.

$$ACTUAL \ COST \ = 1 @ \$19.50 = \$ \ 19.50$$
$$1 @ \$19.85 = \$ \ 19.85$$
$$\underline{3 @ \$20.50 = \$ \ 61.50}$$

TOTAL VALUE   **$101.85**

Weighted Average   If we use the **weighted average** method, we need to *find a weighted average cost per unit and use that figure as the unit price for the inventoried onions.* To find the weighted average, divide the total invoice cost of all the purchased onions by the total number of bags of onions purchased for the month.

Purchases			Invoice Cost	
2/1	2 bags	×	$18.75/bag =	$ 37.50
2/9	4 bags	×	$19.50/bag =	$ 78.00
2/21	5 bags	×	$20.85/bag =	$104.25
2/24	3 bags	×	$20.50/bag =	$ 61.50
2/29	6 bags	×	$17.75/bag =	$106.50
Total	20 bags		Total Cost	$387.75

$387.75/20 = $19.14 (Unit price for the onions)
Weighted Average = 5 bags @ $19.14 per bag = **$95.70 TOTAL VALUE**

Most Recent Purchase Price   If we use the **Most Recent Purchase Price** method, we need to *use the most recent purchase price as the unit price for all the bags of onions.* This is quite simple:

$$MOST \ RECENT \ PURCHASE \ PRICE =$$
$$5 \text{ bags @ } 20.50 \text{ per bag } = \textbf{\$102.50 TOTAL VALUE}$$

To summarize this inventory valuation work:

Method	Value of Onions
FIFO	$101.20
LIFO	$ 91.75
Actual Cost	$100.85
Weighted Average	$ 95.70
Most Recent Cost	$102.50

So which is the best method to use? There is no right answer. This decision is usually left up to the accountant, with management input. Industry wide, FIFO is the method usually used. Right behind that is the Most Recent Cost method. Notice the LIFO value. It is the lowest value. Using this method artificially lowers the inventory cost and is not a good measure of the true cost of goods for the period. Remember, this test is on one item—onions. Overall differences from one method to the next can be significant, given the number of items most operations carry in inventory.

Book Inventory Value Versus Actual Inventory Value

A method for double-checking the value of inventory is to compare the **book inventory value (perpetual inventory value)** of the inventory with the **actual physical count value (periodic count value)**, or **actual inventory value**. The **book inventory value** is the *value of the inventory calculated from invoices minus what was used during the accounting period.* Used product is tracked by requisitions.

Computers have made the calculation of book value fairly easy to do. First, compare the book value and physical count value. The total amounts for both should be close. The **book inventory value** typically is *larger, because the amount on the books usually does not account for some of the small losses attributable to human error or losses that occur during the processing of food products.* Book inventory value is determined as follows:

Opening inventory:	$4,230.00 (Closing inventory for previous accounting period)
+ Purchases	+3,780.00 (Store purchases from Receiving Sheet)
Subtotal	8,010.00
− Requisitions	−4,125.00 (Issues for same period)
= Book Inventory Value	$3,885.00 (Closing inventory for current period)
− Physical inventory value	−3,862.15
= Difference (Variance)	$ 22.85

Reasons for Variances

A wider than acceptable **variance**, *or difference,* between book inventory value and physical inventory value can usually be attributed to one or more of the following factors:

Acceptable Reasons for Variance in Book vs. Actual	Unacceptable Reasons for Variance in Book vs. Actual
• Occasional mathematical mistakes or incorrect counts • Supplier price fluctuations • Using the Most Recent Price vs. the Actual Price for inventory valuation	• Products issued without requisitions • Theft • Poor inventory controls. Spoiled products are tossed out without the dollar amounts being recorded on the Spoilage Report

Managing Inventory Using the ABC Inventory System

It should be apparent by now that a perpetual inventory system represents the tightest control over inventory but is very difficult to use for all items without a dedicated purchasing staff. On the other hand, what the periodic system lacks in control, it makes up for in manageability—any operation can implement it. Because controlling inventory is so important, there must be a means of using both methods in a way that one can have tight control but not expend too much in labor.

And of course, there is. It is called the **ABC Inventory System**. It is a way of identifying *inventory items that require the tightest control measure (and management's undivided attention), those that require moderate controls, and those that require only the simplest inventory control measures.* The driving principal behind the system is that management's time, energy, and dollar investment in inventory management is best focused on those products that consume the most purchasing dollars.

Why would you use this system?

- It can be useful in establishing inventory levels.
- Correct inventory levels minimize the dollars tied up in inventory, thus creating better cash flow.
- It can help control food cost by reducing spoilage and waste.

What Is the "A" in ABC?

Products categorized as "A"—requiring the tightest controls—are those items that consume most of the food cost dollars (as much as 70% to 80%) and thus represent the *maximum investment in inventory.* Interestingly, they may represent only 15% to 20% of all items purchased. These products are typically *highly perishable* and *have a high per-unit cost.* Clearly, as a manager, these are the items that demand the tightest set of controls and oversight, meaning a perpetual inventory system.

What Is the "B" in ABC?

If an "A" item is highly perishable, is very expensive, and devours 70% to 80% of the inventory dollars, then B items must be the next step down. "B" items represent about 10% to 15% of the inventory value and about 25% to 30% of the products in inventory. These items *may be perishable*—such as dairy items or fresh produce—but *are not extremely costly.* Routine controls are usually adequate.

What Is the "C" In ABC?

"C" items are anything that's left! These items represent the least dollar investment (5% to 10% of the inventory value) but 50% to 60% of all items in inventory. These items require only the simplest inventory controls. These items *have a long shelf life, are not highly perishable, and have a low per-unit cost.* In a foodservice operation, they are the staples: flour, sugar, condiments, spices, dry goods, and canned products.

Categorizing Products as "A," "B," or "C"

Here's how to categorize products as an A, B, or C:

- Analyze one month's purchases for each item in inventory. Chart how much was spent to purchase each item. The most costly items will be classified as A—perhaps the top 20%, and so on. (Refer to Figure 8.6 for percentage ranges.)
- Logic can be used to categorize many items without actually creating charts of purchases. Without a doubt, the chef and manager know which items are the most and least costly in terms of unit price and are quite familiar with ordering patterns and quantities. The A and C items are fairly easy to identify. The remaining fall into the B category.

	% of Inventory Value	% of Total Products Purchased	How to Control Each
A Items • Highly perishable • High per-unit cost • Tightest controls	70%–80%	15%–20%	1. Strictly enforce all standard operating procedures for ordering, receiving, storing, and issuing. 2. Label, date, and rotate all stock. 3. Use product tags (Chapter 7). 4. Use perpetual inventory system. 5. Because they are highly perishable, carefully set and monitor ordering levels.
B Items • May be perishable • Moderate to low per-unit cost • Moderate controls	10%–15%	25%–30%	1. Strictly enforce all standard operating procedures for ordering, receiving, storing, and issuing. 2. Label, date, and rotate all stock. 3. Set order levels using a par. 4. Watch for changes in consumption. 5. Use periodic inventory.
C Items • Long shelf life • Not highly perishable • Low per-unit cost • Simple inventory controls	5%–10%	50%–60%	1. Strictly enforce all standard operating procedures for ordering, receiving, storing, and issuing. 2. Label, date, and rotate all stock. 3. Set order levels using a par. 4. Order larger quantities for discounts. 5. Use periodic inventory method.

FIGURE 8.6 ABC Inventory System.

To understand how this system works, look at the ingredients listed in the recipe in Figure 8.7. Which items will require the strictest controls and a lot of our attention? Which will require the least attention? Which are the most valuable? Which are the least valuable? How can you tell?

To practice, let's apply our newly learned principle that says A items are generally highly perishable, with a high cost per unit, and C items are shelf stable, not highly perishable, and have a low per-unit cost. Even though monthly purchases for each of the items listed are not known, product knowledge, along with knowledge of the menu from Farfalle Arrabbiata, can be used to classify each ingredient.

Here is the breakdown of the ingredients:

A ITEMS (highly perishable and high unit cost)
- Mozzarella
- Prosciutto

Note: Both of these items are used in many other menu items.

B ITEMS
- Pomodoro Sauce
- Olive oil
- Balsamic vinegar
- Basil, fresh

Mozzarella in Carrozza Arrabbiata	Yield: 218 servings	
Ingredients	Quantity	A, B, or C?
Mozzarella, fresh	68 lb.	A
Prosciutto, Parma	13 lb.	A
Bread crumbs	10 lb.	C
Pomodoro Sauce	5 gal.	B
Basil, fresh	6 bunches	B
Salt	6 oz.	C
Pepper, black	4 oz.	C
Oil, olive	1 gal.	B
Vinegar, balsamic	½ gal.	B
Red pepper, cracked	6 Tbsp.	C

FIGURE 8.7   Recipe for Mozzarella in Carrozza Arrabiata, with ingredients categorized by value.

(NOTE: Balsamic vinegar and olive oil are classified as B because they are used in many dishes at Farfalle Arrabbiata and are specialty items with a higher per-unit cost than vegetable oils and red wine vinegars.)

C ITEMS

- Bread crumbs
- Salt
- Black pepper
- Red pepper

Spoilage Reports

A **Spoilage Report** should be used to track and account for products that were spoiled and discarded. Spoilage should be a minimum. Good controls ensure that a minimum number of entries appear on this form!

Spoilage Report

Department: Kitchen
Date: 2/14/2XXX

Item	Quantity	Unit Price	Extension
Romaine	½ case	$41.28	$20.64
TOTAL			$20.64

Inventory Turnover

Unlike inventories for other types of industries, the size of inventories that are maintained in foodservice operations relate not only to keeping up the quality of the inventory (avoiding spoilage, ensuring freshness, etc.), but also to the quantities required to be in process to meet the level of usage. Ideally, inventories should be reduced to a controlled minimum, because inventory ties up capital.

Inventory levels must allow for the fact that some time is needed to process goods (cooking, preparation, etc.) and that there will be a period of time between delivery and sale. With highly perishable goods, this period is kept to a minimum. Deliveries of this type of merchandise are more frequent and are often made daily (think Direct Purchases from the Receiving Sheet). In some cases, the size of the storeroom facilities dictates that increased delivery frequency be maintained. In other cases, a larger storeroom combined with the nonperishability of the product permits larger inventories to be stocked.

Optimum Inventory Levels

The **Optimum Inventory Level** should be:

- Large enough to avoid running out of products during peak business times.
- Small enough to be properly rotated.

Average foodservice inventory turns over between 20 and 25 times per year or every 2 to 2½ weeks. This means the entire inventory is replaced or turned about every two weeks. Although these are industry averages, each operation will determine the optimum rate of turn that minimizes waste, spoilage, and inventory dollars and at the same time provides an adequate supply of product.

The appropriate **inventory turnover rate** is directly related to product usage. Some inventory products will be used more and others less. **Rotating the inventory** means that *most items on the shelves should be used within 1 to 28 days*. A well-planned inventory balance is critical in order to avoid frequent small-quantity buying or stockouts. Both **low inventory levels** and **high inventory levels** can have different negative effects.

Low Inventory Levels Can Result In	High Inventory Levels Can Result In
• Higher unit costs for products. • Additional labor and processing expenses. Frustration on the part of staff. • Special trips to a wholesale grocer to pick up stock. Can increase unit costs. • Increased food cost. • Running out of menu items, causing guest dissatisfaction.	• Unnecessary product spoilage or deterioration. • Too much money tied up in inventory, creating potential cash flow problem. • Increased opportunity for theft. • Increased food cost. • Taking up too much space.

Calculating Inventory Turnover Rate

There are two steps to calculating the inventory turnover rate. The first is to calculate the average inventory cost. The second is to use this average in a formula to calculate the inventory turnover rate.

CALCULATING INVENTORY TURNOVER

1. CALCULATE THE **AVERAGE INVENTORY VALUE**

$$\frac{\text{OPENING INVENTORY VALUE} + \text{CLOSING INVENTORY VALUE}}{2} = \frac{\text{AVG. INV.}}{\text{COST}}$$

2. CALCULATE THE **AVERAGE INVENTORY RATE**

$$\frac{\text{COST OF FOOD SOLD}}{\text{AVERAGE INVENTORY COST}} = \frac{\text{INVENTORY}}{\text{TURNOVER RATE}}$$

The Cost of Food Sold is taken from the Food Cost Report (see Chapter 10). Using the **average inventory** helps minimize the impact of low and high inventory counts over the period of time being analyzed.

The following is an example of how to calculate inventory turnover:

- Suppose the Food Cost Report for the first week of May indicates a Closing Inventory of $10,000. This means that the Opening Inventory for the second week of May is also $10,000.
- The Food Cost Report for the end of the one-week period indicates a Closing Inventory of $12,000.
- The actual amount spent on food for the period (Cost of Food Sold) was $23,000.

Step 1: Calculate the Average Inventory Value

$$\frac{\text{OPENING INVENTORY VALUE} + \text{CLOSING INVENTORY VALUE}}{2}$$
$$= \text{AVERAGE INVENTORY COST}$$
$$\frac{\$10,000 + \$12,000}{2} = \$11,000$$

Step 2: Calculate the Inventory Turnover Rate

$$\frac{\text{COST OF FOOD SOLD}}{\text{AVERAGE INVENTORY COST}} = \text{INVENTORY TURNOVER RATE}$$
$$\frac{\$23,000 \text{ (Cost of Food Sold)}}{\$11,000 \text{ (Average Inventory Cost)}} = 2.09 \text{ (Inventory Turnover Rate)}$$

Evaluating Inventory Turnover Rates

What does this ratio (the Inventory Turnover Rate) mean? The number 2.09 means that the entire inventory turned over twice during the accounting period. (Generally, the inventory turnover figure is reported in decimals such as 2.09.) If a figure of 2.09 is calculated, it can be rounded down to 2. If the figure is 1.83, it should be left alone. The degree of rounding depends on the emphasis that the foodservice manager places on decimal reporting.

Recommended Inventory Levels	Quantity
• Bakery products, fresh produce, meat, fish, shellfish, poultry, dairy products	2-day supply
• Frozen products	1-week supply
• Canned or dry goods	1- to 2-week supply
• Other nonperishable low-value items	2- to 4-week supply
• Paper goods	2- to 4-week supply
• Chemicals and cleaning supplies	2- to 4-week supply

How to Use Inventory Turnover Information

A careful foodservice manager wants to keep inventory turnover from being too high or too low (out of those End Zones). To do so, he or she must strike a balance between product **stockouts**—*not enough product on hand for production*—and increased food costs.

The Inventory Turnover Rate Is Too High   If the inventory turnover rate is high and the operation is experiencing frequent shortages, then the amount of food needed for preparation and what is kept in inventory is out of balance. If inventories are too small, several things will happen: Extra time must be spent ordering, stockouts will occur, goods may be improperly processed, and extra labor will be required to ensure that food is processed in a timely fashion. Inventory levels should be examined and increased to a point where shortages or stockouts no longer occur.

The Inventory Rate Is Too Low   If the inventory turnover has slowed and the cost of goods sold has gone up, then the cost of managing inventory has probably gone up. What does this mean? It means there is too much inventory on hand, increased cost is probably attributable to spoilage and waste, and excess money is tied up in capital.

As a general rule, the value of the total food inventory should equal about 1½ times the weekly consumption of food. If an establishment consumes (at cost) $10,000 worth of food per week, the average inventory value should be about $15,000. This allows for safety factors to preclude stockouts and helps to reduce the amount of time spent ordering and processing deliveries.

Large Inventories	Small Inventories
• Loss attributable to spoilage	• Extra time spent ordering
• Excess capital tied up in inventory	• Stockouts
• Waste caused by carelessness	• Goods improperly processed
	• Extra labor

What Does an Acceptable Turnover Rate Mean?   An acceptable turnover rate for inventory means several things:

- The buyer is buying the correct quantity of food for the level of sales.
- Par-stock levels have been calculated and set correctly.
- Safety stock levels are adequate.
- The right amount of money is being invested in products.
- Product is being received correctly, stored correctly, and rotated properly.
- There is a minimum amount of waste and spoilage.
- There is no theft of product.
- There is a balance between how much food needs to be prepared and the amount of food kept in inventory.
- There is maximum return on the investment called inventory.

IT MEANS . . . CONGRATULATIONS ARE IN ORDER!
YOU ARE BUYING THE RIGHT PRODUCT IN THE RIGHT QUANTITY FROM THE RIGHT SUPPLIER AT THE RIGHT PRICE—ALL DELIVERED AT THE RIGHT TIME!

Net Work

Explore the following Web sites:
www.costgenie.com
www.digitaldining.com
www.micros.com
www.advancedhospitality.com
www.accubar.com—Click Demo

Chapter Wrap

The Chapter ✓ at the beginning of the chapter posed several questions. Review the questions and compare your responses with the following answers:

1. **What is inventory management?**

   Inventory management is the process whereby an operation keeps enough physical inventory on hand so that customers' needs are met, but spends no more than necessary. Inventory management starts when an operation takes physical inventory at the close of an accounting period. Then, the dollar value of the inventory can be established. Using a common formula, the cost of goods for the period is computed. With this information, management is able to determine the food cost percentage for the period.

2. **What are the two types of inventory systems commonly used in food-service?**

   Determining physical inventory and calculating its value at the close of an accounting period is referred to as a periodic inventory system. It is different from a perpetual inventory system. The distinction between a periodic inventory system and a perpetual inventory system is that a periodic system calculates the value of inventory at the end of an accounting period and a perpetual system calculates the value of inventory each time an item is either used or added to inventory.

3. **How is a physical inventory taken?**

   Inventory should be taken by two people. One person conducts the hands-on count and calls out the quantity and product name. The other person writes the quantity numbers on the inventory sheet or enters counts into a hand-held electronic device designed for inventory management. This procedure maximizes efficiency, speed, convenience, and accuracy. In operations where bar codes and scanners are used, taking inventory is done with a bar code reader. The information is downloaded onto a computer. Software programs will value the inventory.

4. **What methods are used to value inventory?**

   There are five methods of valuing inventory: FIFO, LIFO, Weighted Average, Actual Cost, and Most Recent Purchase Price. Each business establishes the inventory valuations system to be used.

5. **What is the ABC system of inventory management?**

   It should be apparent by the descriptions here that a perpetual inventory system represents the tightest control over inventory but is very difficult to use for all items without a dedicated purchasing staff. What the periodic system lacks in control, it makes up for in manageability—any operation can implement it. Because controlling inventory is so important, an operation must have a means of using both methods in a way that is not too labor intensive, but at the same time have tighter control. The method used is called the ABC Inventory System. This system is a way of identifying inventory items that require the tightest control measures (and management's undivided attention), those that require moderate controls, and those that require only the simplest inventory control measures. The driving principal behind the system is that management's time, energy, and dollar investment in inventory management is best focused on those products that consume the most purchasing dollars.

6. **What Does the Inventory Turnover Rate Tell Management About the Inventory?**

Careful foodservice managers want to keep inventory turnover from being too high or too low. To do so, they must strike a balance between product stockouts and increased food costs. If the inventory turnover rate is high and the operation is experiencing frequent shortages, then the amount of food needed for preparation and what is kept in inventory is out of balance. If inventories are too small, extra time must be spent ordering, stockouts will occur, goods may be improperly processed, and extra labor will be required to ensure that food is processed in a timely fashion. Inventory levels should be examined and increased to a point where shortages and stockouts no longer occur.

Key Terminology and Concepts in this Chapter

ABC Inventory System
Acceptable inventory turnover rate
Accounting period
Actual inventory value
Average inventory
Average inventory rate
Average inventory value
Bin card
Book inventory value
First In, First Out (FIFO)
High inventory levels
In-process inventory
Inventory management
Inventory sheet
Inventory turnover
Inventory turnover rate
Last In, First Out (LIFO)
Low inventory levels
Most recent purchase price

Optimum Inventory Levels
Periodic count value
Periodic inventory
Periodic inventory sheet
Periodic inventory system
Perpetual inventory bin card
Perpetual inventory chart
Perpetual inventory system
Perpetual inventory value
Physical count
Purchasing units
Rotating stock
Rotating the inventory
Spoilage report
Stockouts
Using spoilage reports
Valuing inventory
Variance
Weighted average

Discussion Questions and Exercises

1. What possible problems might occur in calculating the value of inventory if it is not taken on the same day of the week and at the same time of the accounting period?

2. Marcel is training Mike, the line cook, and Jake, the receiver, to take inventory. You decide that the training would be more effective if a manual were available. After consulting with Marcel, you both agree that this would be a handy tool. You decide to get to it right away. Prepare a detailed training manual covering all aspects of taking inventory.

3. Compare a perpetual inventory system to a periodic inventory system. What are the finer points of each system? How does each control inventory? What are the pros and cons of each?

4. Mike and Jake have finished page 1 of the inventory. Extend the values for the items on the following page.

Inventory					
Date:			Page Number:	1 of 10	
	2 :00		Department:	Kitchen	
Taken By:			Location:		
(and)			Priced By:		
Approved By:			Extended By:		
Item Description	**Pur. Unit**	**Quantity On Hand**	**Price**	**Extension**	
Poultry					
Chicken, breast – 6 ounce	pounds	65 lb.	$3.23/lb.		
Chicken, breast – 8 ounce	pounds	23 lb.	$3.23/lb.		
Chicken, wings	pounds	44 lb.	$1.25/lb.		
Produce					
Romaine	case	4 cs.	$21.23/cs.		
Spinach, whole leaf	10 oz. bag	10 bags	$1.79/bag		
Spinach, baby	3 lb. bag	4½ bags	$7.32/bag		
Strawberries	quarts	9 qt.	$1.44/qt.		
Tomatoes, 6×6	case	1¾ cs.	$29.45/cs.		
TOTAL					

5. Farfalle Arrabbiata has used a periodic inventory system for years. Marcel is interested in instituting a perpetual inventory system. He is trying to convince the folks in the office that it will not be too much work. You decide to help him out with his cause. Draft a memo to the staff explaining the following:

   a. A perpetual inventory system

   b. How the office will manage the system

   c. The benefits of the system

6. To assist with this effort, Marcel wants to show the staff a Perpetual Inventory Chart. He is running late for a meeting and asks for your assistance with the form. Fill out the following chart for Marcel and write a brief explanation of how it will be used in the office.

Perpetual Inventory Chart							
Location: Kitchen							
Item: Oil, Olive, Calvito's				**Unit:** Quarts			
Date	**Beginning**	**Additions**	**Deletions**	**Ending**	**Unit Price**	**Extension**	**Initial**
2/14	12	6	3		$7.45		
2/15		0	4		$7.45		
2/16		0	5		$7.45		
2/17		12	4		$7.85		
2/18		0	6		$8.25		
2/19		12	4		$8.25		

7. After careful consideration, Marcel has decided that the perpetual inventory system will be too much for the office to handle. You have great news for him, though! You have been researching the ABC Inventory System and discover that this may be just the thing for Farfalle Arrabbiata. Describe the system and its benefits. Don't forget to explain to Marcel how the perpetual system is used within the ABC inventory control system.

8. The owners of Farfalle Arrabbiata hired a new accounting company. The firm is trying to convince the owners to change their inventory valuation system. They have turned to you for advice. You dust off your old cost-control book and prepare to give them a lesson in inventory valuation. Using the following information, prepare an example of the FIFO, LIFO, Weighted Average, and Most Recent Price methods of inventory valuation.

[handwritten margin note: Doesn't specify sales or that ending inventory is 5 cases]

Opening Inventory

Purchases this month		5 cases of Calvito's olive oil @ $42.36 per case
2/1	4 cases	$44.70/case
2/9	8 cases	$41.30/case
2/21	10 cases	$45.90/case
2/29	6 cases	$46.25/case

9. Prepare a brief explanation of each method. Recommend a method to use, as well as your reasons for selecting that particular one.

10. Determine the book value difference for the inventory using the following information:

Opening Inventory	$17,964
Purchases	$42,680
Requisitions	$40,503
Actual Inventory Value	$18,362

What does this tell you about the actual inventory versus the book inventory? What would you do about this?

11. Lately, there have been quite a few stockouts, which has been causing some frustration among the cooks. A number of menu items have been running out. You decide to figure the inventory turnover rate, to see if it will shed some light on what is happening. You come up with the following:

Opening Inventory	$17,964
Closing Inventory	$17,879
Cost of Food Sold	$75,629

What does this rate reveal, given what you know about industry average inventory turnover rates? What will you recommend Chef Raoul do about it?

12. Explain why maintaining a high inventory level will cause the inventory turnover rate to be low.

13. If a foodservice operation is not running out of food and the food cost percentage is on target, what is occurring?

## Chapter Nine

Chapter Objective

To effectively manage kitchen production through controls that track sales, kitchen production, portion control, and food cost.

Learning Objectives

After reading this chapter and completing the discussion questions and exercises, you should be able to:

1. Describe two common methods of arranging sales histories.
2. Calculate seat turnover.
3. Use sales history to forecast guest counts.
4. Complete a Food Sales Recap Report.
5. Use popularity percentages and sales forecasts to determine portion production.
6. Complete a Food Production Schedule.
7. Track portion errors on a Food Mishap Report.
8. Use a Portion Control Chart to reconcile kitchen production.

The Menu

Pre-Purchase Functions

GUEST CHECK
Sales history, turnover, average check, cash management revenue forecasting & budgeting, menu item analysis

GUESTS
Greeting, seating, sales, serving, busing, payment, comment cards

FOH Functions

KITCHEN PRODUCTION
Production schedules, portion tracking, recipe control, serving controls, sanitation

PRODUCT ISSUING
Requisitions, transfers, daily & monthly costs, food cost percentage

STORAGE PRACTICES & INVENTORY MANAGEMENT
Best practices, food safety, security, inventory methods

INVOICE MANAGEMENT
Payment, price checking, security

STANDARDIZED RECIPES
Standard ingredients, portion size, quality, consistency, quantity, purchasing

COST CARDS
Portion costs, yield factors, sell prices

SPECIFICATIONS
Product descriptions

PAR STOCK
Inventory levels, order building

REQUISITION
Order building, purchasing

SHOPPING LISTS
Call sheets, bid sheets, suppliers, bidding

PURCHASE ORDERS
Security, ship order, price guarantee, contract

BOH Functions

RECEIVING ACTIVITIES
Best practices, invoices, security, sanitation

Chapter Map

Operating Cycle of Control & Back-of-House Production

- Sales History, Sales Forecasts, and Popularity Percentages: A Review
- How Sales Information Is Tracked

Sales History

- Organizing Sales History Using Dollar Values
- Organizing Sales History Using Guest Counts

Chapter Map   (Continued)

About Food Production Control

- Steps to Controlling Production
- Setting Daily Production Levels
- Standardizing Recipes
- Completing a Food Production Schedule

- Monitoring Sales Levels
- Recording Errors and Waste
- Reconciling Prepared Food Portions to Ordered Food

Chapter ✓

Check the chapter content for the answers to these questions:

1. How can sales history be organized?
2. How is a Food Sales Recap Report used to set portion counts?
3. What is a Food Production Schedule?
4. What is a Food Mishap Report?
5. What is a Portion Control Chart?

Operating Cycle of Control and Back-of-House Production

Observe where we are in the **Operating Cycle of Control**. We are approaching the point at which dining room sales will be generated. Product has been ordered, received, stored, and inventoried. Now, it is up to the manager and chef to control what happens on the preparation side of things. What is needed to do this? Why, more information and more paperwork! Some of the concepts will be familiar because of earlier discussions—sales histories, for instance—and some concepts will introduce more of the basic operating procedures as outlined by the Cycle of Control.

Sales History, Sales Forecasts, and Popularity Percentages: A Review

These three concepts should ring familiar—look back to Chapter 5, where each was described in conjunction with discussions about order quantities. Here is a brief review of each term borrowed from that chapter:

1. **Sales histories** tell what happened in the past and are used to develop sales forecasts. The history can be organized by day, week, month, or year.
2. **Sales forecasts** predict what will occur in the near future and are used to purchase product, plan for menu production, and schedule staff.
3. **Popularity percentages or indexes** (developed from history) track guest's menu preferences. This information is useful when developing order quantities (Chapter 5) and in forecasting portion sales.

The following discussions show how the sales history assists in developing the sales forecast and how that information is used to control kitchen production.

How Sales Information Is Tracked

The primary tool used to capture sales data is the **guest check**. It is here that *guest counts* and *food selections* are recorded and collated into information that is used to determine production quantities. This data is collected either **electronically** through a menu management system or **manually** by completing a variety of forms.

Manual Methods   Operations not using a computerized menu management system manually enter information from each check onto various forms. Typically, the cashier handles this as the check is paid. At the end of the shift or day, the completed forms are sent to the accounting office, where the information is compiled into a number of reports. These reports are known as the **Manager's Report** and are *a summary of the day's business results*. The Manager's Report can be created manually or electronically.

Electronic Methods   Operations that use a computerized menu management system collect this data via a point-of-sale (POS) terminal. Inputting is typically by a touch screen that allows servers to enter customer selections and special requests quickly and efficiently. Once the order is entered, it is electronically sent to a printer in the kitchen, where the expediter will execute the production and final plating of the item. The sales data is then collected and held in the computer's memory. The Manager's Report is run at the end of the shift or day.

What's in the Manager's Report?   The Manager's Report gives a recap of operating statistics for a period. It is run daily, typically at the end of the shift or day. Weekly summaries pull together all the sales data.

Generally, the Manager's Report includes:

- Revenue recap
- Food sales recap
- Guest count recap
- Seat turnover
- Portion sales and popularity
- Cost recap
- Labor recap—front of house and back-of-house
- Shift profitability
- Mishap Report

Foodservice software packages usually include a sales analysis function that produces these reports for management (Figure 9.1). Some operations may have customized reports in addition to these elements.

Sales History

In Chapter 5, **sales history** was described as the "business history" of an operation. A more technical definition is *a record of sales for a predetermined period of time*. It is simply a record of what was sold. This record is kept in two arrangements, or formats:

1. As food and beverage sales that are recorded in **dollar values ($$)**
2. As food and beverage sales that are recorded in **customer counts (☺☺)**

A sales history that is recorded in **dollar values ($$)** is used primarily in *planning and analyzing business activity*. A sales history that is recorded in **customer counts** ☺☺ is used primarily for *operational planning*. Some of the "operational planning" ways to use this information are:

- Setting kitchen production levels
- Determining menu item production
- *S*cheduling employees
- Analyzing sales patterns

Daily Consolidated Revenue Center Menu Item Sales Detail
Subtotal by Family Group
MICROS Systems - Bar & Grille

Monday From: 05/13/2XXX   Monday To: 05/13/2XXX

Bruno The Manager
Printed on May 13, 2XXX - 8:34 PM

			Sales Qty.	% of Total	Rtn Qty.	% of Total	Gross Sales	% of Total	Item Disc.	% of Total	Net Sales	% of Total
1—Restaurant												
101002	Crab Cakes	Reg.	3	50.00%	0	0.00%	20.85	53.12%	0.00	0.00%	20.85	53.12%
101004	Fried Calamari	Reg.	2	33.33%	0	0.00%	11.90	30.32%	0.00	0.00%	11.90	30.32%
101005	Chicken Tenders	Reg.	1	16.67%	0	0.00%	6.50	16.56%	0.00	0.00%	6.50	16.56%
Total Appetizers			6	6.25%	0	0.00%	39.25	10.04%	0.00	0.00%	39.25	10.04%
101103	Onion Soup	Reg.	2	28.57%	0	0.00%	7.00	27.45%	0.00	0.00%	7.00	27.45%
101104	Clam Chowder	Reg.	2	28.57%	0	0.00%	6.50	25.49%	0.00	0.00%	6.50	25.49%
101105	Lobster Bisque	Reg.	3	42.86%	0	0.00%	12.00	47.06%	0.00	0.00%	12.00	47.06%
Total Soups			7	7.29%	0	0.00%	25.50	6.52%	0.00	0.00%	25.50	6.52%
102002	Toasted Salad	Reg.	1	16.67%	0	0.00%	3.75	12.63%	0.00	0.00%	3.75	12.63%
102003	Cobb Salad	Reg.	1	16.67%	0	0.00%	7.95	26.77%	0.00	0.00%	7.95	26.77%
102004	Spinach Salad	Reg.	4	66.67%	0	0.00%	18.00	60.61%	0.00	0.00%	18.00	60.61%
Total Salads			6	6.25%	0	0.00%	29.70	7.60%	0.00	0.00%	29.70	7.60%
103003	Cheeseburger	Reg.	1	100.00%	0	0.00%	7.95	100.00%	0.00	0.00%	7.95	100.00%
Total Burgers			1	1.04%	0	0.00%	7.95	2.03%	0.00	0.00%	7.95	2.03%
105002	Prime Rib	Reg.	2	40.00%	0	0.00%	27.90	50.96%	0.00	0.00%	27.90	50.96%
105005	Roasted Chicken	Reg.	3	60.00%	0	0.00%	26.85	49.04%	0.00	0.00%	26.85	49.04%
Total Entrées			5	5.21%	0	0.00%	54.74	14.01%	0.00	0.00%	54.75	14.01%
198002	Ice Cream	Reg.	1	25.00%	0	0.00%	3.00	20.00%	0.00	0.00%	3.00	20.00%
198004	Creme Brulee	Reg.	1	25.00%	0	0.00%	4.00	26.67%	0.00	0.00%	4.00	26.67%
198005	Tira Misu	Reg.	1	25.00%	0	0.00%	4.00	26.67%	0.00	0.00%	4.00	26.67%
198006	Bread Pudding	Reg.	1	25.00%	0	0.00%	4.00	26.67%	0.00	0.00%	4.00	26.67%
Total Desserts			4	4.17%	0	0.00%	15.00	3.84%	0.00	0.00%	15.00	3.84%
30016	Sprite	Reg	2	100.00%	0	0.00%	2.50	100.00%	0.00	0.00%	2.50	100.00%
Total Soda			2	2.08%	0	0.00%	2.50	0.64%	0.00	0.00%	2.50	0.64%
30007	Grapefruit Juice	Reg	1	50.00%	0	0.00%	1.50	50.00%	0.00	0.00%	1.50	50.00%
30008	Pineapple Juice	Reg	1	50.00%	0	0.00%	1.50	50.00%	0.00	0.00%	1.50	50.00%
Total Juice			2	2.08%	0	0.00%	3.00	0.77%	0.00	0.00%	3.00	0.77%
30002	Coffee/Tea	Reg.	2	14.29%	0	0.00%	2.50	10.00%	0.00	0.00%	2.50	10.00%
30003	Iced Tea	Reg.	3	21.43%	0	0.00%	3.75	15.00%	0.00	0.00%	3.75	15.00%

FIGURE 9.1 Computer-generated Food Sales Recap Report and Menu Analysis. *Courtesy of Micros.*

Organizing Sales History Using Dollar Values

The dollar value of food and beverage products are tracked each day. The information is gathered through manual or electronic means, as described earlier. Managers commonly use this data to set sales goals and evaluate actual business performance to forecast business levels. In addition, these records assist in the preparation of budgets for future time periods. Some of the most common ways to organize this data are by **sales dollars ($$) per operating period** (e.g., *sales per week, month, quarter*), **average sale per server** *(the mean average sale for each server for a specific period of time—also known as server average check.)*, and **average check** *(the mean average amount each guest spends measured for a specific period (week, month, annual).*

SALES HISTORY USING SALES DOLLARS ($$)

- Sales per operating period: annual, semiannual, quarterly, monthly, weekly, daily, per shift.
- Average sale per server.
- Average check.

A complete discussion of these concepts and how they are used is covered in later chapters.

Organizing Sales History Using Guest Counts

The second way to arrange sales history is to use **guest counts (☺☺)**. There are as many ways to organize this data as there are ways to organize sales dollars. Managers in foodservice operations routinely arrange guest counts in the following ways:

- By number of customers or covers for a specific period: annual, semiannual, monthly, weekly, and daily, per meal period, per hour, and even per quarter hour
- By seat turnover
- By popularity percentages

SALES HISTORY USING GUEST COUNTS (☺☺)

- **Number of customers or covers for a specific period:** annual, semiannual, monthly, weekly, and daily, per meal period, per hour, and even per quarter hour
- Seat turnover
- Popularity percentages

Number of Covers by Period   As you can see, there are many possible ways to display guest counts: annually, semiannually, monthly, weekly, and daily, per meal period, per hour, and per quarter hour. The extent of the breakdown is determined by:

- The type of foodservice business (quick service, table service).
- The overall business volume.
- The amount of data necessary to monitor operations.

Quick-service operations may organize guest counts down to quarter-hour increments, whereas full-menu table service operations function quite well with monthly, weekly, daily, and meal period counts. Often, reports combine guest counts in tables using multiple formats. The examples that follow show the guest count history for Farfalle

		Jan. ☺	Feb. ☺	Mar. ☺	Apr. ☺	May ☺	Jun. ☺	Jul. ☺	Aug. ☺	Sept. ☺	Oct. ☺	Nov. ☺	Dec. ☺
A /	**Annual Customer Count:** 167,483 ☺												
B	**Month**	Jan. ☺	Feb. ☺	Mar. ☺	Apr. ☺	May ☺	Jun. ☺	Jul. ☺	Aug. ☺	Sept. ☺	Oct. ☺	Nov. ☺	Dec. ☺
	Meal Period												
B	Lunch ☺	7,671	7,948	7,688	7,692	8,431	5,926	6,133	5,343	10,020	11,040	10,690	11,717
C	Dinner ☺	4,985	5,032	4,996	4,999	5,478	3,851	3,986	3,473	6,512	7,178	6,948	7,614
	TOTALS	14,656	12,980	12,684	12,691	13,909	9,777	10,119	8,816	16,532	18,218	17,638	19,331

FIGURE 9.2   Sales History: Customer counts—annual, monthly, and by meal period.

Arrabbiata organized in a variety of ways. With this information in hand, management aims to:

- Control for two of the three prime costs: food cost and labor cost (beverage cost will not be considered at this time).
- Plan for future time periods.

Figure 9.2 displays **annual** (A), **monthly** (B), **and meal period** (C) guest counts for Farfalle Arrabbiata. Organizing the information in this way allows a more panoramic view of the data.

Skim the monthly sales figures in the figure. The sales pattern by guest count is apparent. Sales for June, July, and August are very slow, whereas the fall and holiday periods appear to be the strongest. January through May show a mixed pattern. Organizing the information in this manner assists management with:

- Forecasting sales levels for future periods.
- Developing sales goals for all periods.
- Researching and implementing appropriate marketing promotions.
- Effectively managing labor and food cost during busy and slow periods.
- Scheduling the correct number of employees for the forecasted sales levels.

An important component of any sales history is the recording of events that have affected sales. These notes are an integral part of the sales history and are usually recorded on a daily basis. The notes include weather events, changes in competition, and external and internal environmental changes. (Refer to Chapter 1 discussions on internal and external environments.)

The next arrangement (Figure 9.3) shows monthly guest counts broken down into weekly counts. The operating period is one quarter. This is an *historical* picture,

	January (2XXX)	February (2XXX)	March (2XXX)
Monthly Totals ☺	14,656 (☺)	12,780 (☺)	12,684 (☺)
Week 1	4,103	2,879	2,793
Week 2	3,957	3,220	3,424
Week 3	3,224	3,112	2,916
Week 4	3,372	3,569	3,551

FIGURE 9.3   Monthly guest counts (previous year).

Day/ Date Feb.	Mon. 2/X	Tues. 2/X	Wed. 2/X	Thurs. 2/X	Fri. 2/X	Sat. 2/X	Sun. 2/X	Meal Totals
Lunch ☺	220	245	255	275	288	290	243	1,816 ☺
Dinner ☺	83	105	123	151	290	304	120	1,176 ☺
Daily Total	**303**	**350**	**378**	**426**	**578**	**594**	**263**	2,879 ☺

FIGURE 9.4   Sales history: Customer counts—daily, weekly, and by meal periods.

so the counts are for January, February, and March (the first quarter) of the *previous year*.

These counts give managers an idea of sales patterns that are more meaningful than just monthly totals. Managers and chefs are concerned with weekly and daily counts, because this is the reality they plan for and work in.

Figure 9.4 displays the sales history for the first week of February *last year* for Farfalle Arrabbiata using three common breakouts—*daily, weekly,* and *by meal periods*. This information is helpful in creating a sales forecast for the first week of February for this year. Remember that a **sales forecast** is defined as *a prediction of business volume for a specific operating period—a day, a week, a month, a year.*

SALES HISTORY USING GUEST COUNTS (☺☺)

- Number of customers or covers for a specific period: annual, semiannual, monthly, weekly, and daily, per meal period, per hour, and even per quarter hour
- Seat turnover
- Popularity percentages

Seat Turnover   **Seat turnover**, or **turns**, represents the number of times a seat in the dining room was "turned" during the course of a meal period. Think of it as *the number of times a server is able to meet and greet the guest, secure the order, deliver all food and beverages, present the check, and reset the table for the next customers in a meal period.*

Proper staffing during service times—and especially peak times—should result in minimum wait times for guests, maximum revenue, and maximum occupancy of seats. Poor staffing increases the amount of time it takes to move a guest through the "turn" process. This will result in decreased revenue for the house and servers alike.

The seat turn enables management to determine the average dining time. This is important information from a revenue and planning perspective. *Decreasing average dining time* (which means increasing the turns) while *maintaining average check* because servers and back-of-house staff are working at peak efficiency will *increase revenue and profits.* Turnover is calculated for meal periods and as an overall ratio. To determine the seat turn, simply divide the number of customers served in the period by the number of seats available:

$$\frac{\text{NUMBER OF CUSTOMERS ☺ SERVED IN A PERIOD}}{\text{NUMBER OF SEATS AVAILABLE}} = \text{TURNOVER RATIO}$$

Using the sales information from Figure 9.4, we can easily calculate the seat turns for Farfalle Arrabbiata for each meal period and the overall turn for the day. The restaurant profile in Chapter 2 lists the number of seats at 130.

To calculate the turns for lunch, divide the lunch guest count by the number of seats available. See the work in the following chart.

Day/ Date Feb.	Mon. 2/X	Tues. 2/X	Wed. 2/X	Thurs. 2/X	Fri. 2/X	Sat. 2/X	Sun. 2/X
Lunch ☺	220/130	245/130	255/130	275/130	288/130	290/130	243/130
Turn-over	1.69	1.88	1.96	2.11	2.21	2.23	1.86

Practice calculating the turns for dinner in the chart below.

Day/ Date Feb.	Mon. 2/X	Tues. 2/X	Wed. 2/X	Thurs. 2/X	Fri. 2/X	Sat. 2/X	Sun. 2/X
Dinner ☺	83/130	105/130	123/130	151/130	290/130	304/130	120/130
Turn-over							

And the answers are:

Day/ Date Feb.	Mon. 2/X	Tues. 2/X	Wed. 2/X	Thurs. 2/X	Fri. 2/X	Sat. 2/X	Sun. 2/X
Dinner ☺	83/130	105/130	123/130	151/130	290/130	304/130	120/130
Turn-over	.64	.81	.95	1.16	2.23	2.34	.92

Figure 9.5 and the following equation show how to find the overall turns for the day (or for any period):

$$\frac{\text{NUMBER OF CUSTOMERS} ☺ \text{SERVED TODAY}}{\text{NUMBER OF SEATS AVAILABLE TODAY}} = \text{TURNOVER RATIO TODAY}$$

Day/ Date Feb.	Mon. 2/X	Tues. 2/X	Wed. 2/X	Thurs. 2/X	Fri. 2/X	Sat. 2/X	Sun. 2/X	Meal Totals
Daily Total	303/130	350/130	378/130	426/130	578/130	594/130	263/130	2,879 ☺
Daily Turn-over	2.33	2.69	2.9	3.28	4.45	4.57	2.02	

FIGURE 9.5   Finding overall turns for the day (or period).

To find the turns for a different period, substitute that period's information (guests and number of seats) into the TODAY part of each part of the equation. For example: Turns for the month can be found by substituting the covers for the month and the seats for the month.

A **weighted average turnover** combines all guests and all available seats for a specific period. Here, we use the weekly information from Figure 9.5 to calculate the weighted average turnover for this week:

$$\frac{\text{TOTAL NUMBER OF GUESTS SERVED IN A PERIOD}}{\text{TOTAL NUMBER OF SEATS AVAILABLE}} = \frac{\text{WEIGHTED AVERAGE}}{\text{TURNOVER}}$$

$$\frac{2,879 \text{ (Guests this week)}}{910 \text{ (Total number of seats available)}} = 3.16 \text{ turns for the week}$$

$$130 \text{ seats} \times 7 \text{ days} = 910 \text{ total seats}$$

All this information is valuable to managers and chefs when analyzing sales. This work will be used in later discussions of revenue forecasting (Chapters 18 and 19).

SALES HISTORY USING GUEST COUNTS (☺☺)
- Number of customers or covers for a specific period: annual, semiannual, monthly, weekly, and daily, per meal period, per hour, and even per quarter hour
- Seat turnover
- **Popularity percentages**

COMMON USES OF POPULARITY INDEXES

1. Track customer preferences
2. Determine order quantities
3. Establish food production quantities

Popularity Percentages   Because this topic was covered thoroughly in previous chapters, our discussion here will serve simply as a quick refresher. The **popularity percentage** or **index** is *the popularity of an item as it competes with all other items to be selected.* The formula is as follows:

$$\frac{\text{NUMBER OF A SPECIFIC ITEM SOLD}}{\text{NUMBER OF ALL ITEMS SOLD}} = \text{POPULARITY \%}$$

In previous chapter discussions, the popularity index was used to

- Track customer preferences
- Determine order quantities

The popularity index can also be used to

- Establish food production quantities

Determining kitchen production quantities is the next common use for this factor. Once customer counts are known, food production can begin. There are two reasons to control food production: (1) *food cost* and (2) *customer satisfaction.* Without a controlled production plan, overages and shortages will abound. **Overproduction** (*producing more food than is needed*) will result in higher than planned food cost. **Underproduction** (*producing less food than is needed*) will cause guest dissatisfaction, frustrate staff, and potentially impact sales.

About Food Production Control

The preparation of food to be sold to customers is a basic manufacturing process. A kitchen is really a production plant. Raw and prepared products are ordered, received, stored, and inventoried, then assembled into products that are resold to customers. Thus, the kitchen is a factory for a foodservice operation.

Controlling exactly how much and what is to be prepared is the responsibility of the manager and chef. This task should never be left to guesswork or hunches. To effectively control production, managers use popularity indexes and sales forecasts to assure that adequate quantities of each menu item are prepared for the expected level of sales. In this way, overproduction and waste are kept to a minimum. Control of kitchen production can be achieved by monitoring for

- Correct portion sizes.
- Plating and cooking errors.
- Kitchen production.
- Actual portion sales.

The purpose of these activities is to validate that food portions prepped for dining room sales were actually sold and generated revenue. If food portions are not sold, then they should still be available at the end of the shift or reported on Mishap (or Void) Reports (covered later in this chapter).

Steps to Controlling Production

This section develops the operational procedures needed to direct food production and reconcile daily production to daily sales. Once production levels are set and food preparation begins, other records *monitor sales* and assist with *reconciling prepared food portions to ordered food portions*. Controlling production is a key management strategy to controlling food cost. It is achieved by following six steps.

STEPS TO CONTROLLING PRODUCTION

1. **Set daily portion counts for every menu item using guest counts, popularity percentages, and the Food Sales Recap Report.**
2. Standardize recipes for every menu item.
3. Complete a Food Production Schedule to set production quantities.
4. Monitor sales levels during shifts.
5. Record errors and waste on a Food Mishap Report.
6. Reconcile prepared food portions to ordered foods using a Portion Control Chart.

Setting Daily Production Levels

The first step in controlling food production is setting daily production levels. This is achieved using guest counts, popularity percentages, and the Food Sales Recap Report. The quantity of food to be prepared should be determined as accurately as possible using portion forecasts derived from popularity indexes and sales forecasts. Remember, if too little is prepared, menu items will run out, leaving customers frustrated and disappointed. If too much is prepared, food costs may increase because of food wasted and not sold. The first step to successful food production is to track portion sales in order to establish menu item counts. Unless a foodservice manager has an understanding of how much food is sold, production quantities must be guessed at and are often inaccurate.

The Food Sales Recap Report By keeping track of the past sales of each menu item per month, week, or day, a foodservice manager can estimate customer orders. Managers track food sales by using a Food Sales Recap Report. The **Food Sales Recap Report** *records the number of menu items sold per day, the total per week, and the current popularity percent.* Notice that the report that follows also includes weather conditions and other external events that might have influenced business (e.g., the Winter Fest that took place that week). A good sales history includes such information and is vital to forecasting correct sales levels. Additional notes should indicate whether external events impacted sales for the week.

Other uses of the Food Sales Recap Report include *determining which items to drop from the menu, which items are the most popular, whether sales promotions are working, as well as tracking the level of business.* All these topics will be visited in a later chapter.

FOOD SALES RECAP REPORT FOR APPETIZERS FOR FARFALLE ARRABBIATA (WEEK OF 2/2 TO 2/8)

Food Sales Recap Report

Department: Kitchen

Page: 1 of 2

Prepared By: Hank

Week Of: Feb. 2–8

Menu Items	Date 2/2 Mon. 303	2/3 Tue. 350	2/4 Wed. 378	2/5 Thur. 426	2/6 Fri. 578	2/7 Sat. 594	2/8 Sun. 263	Total 2992	Pop. %
Mozzarella in Carrozza Arrabbiata	79	89	99	111	150	154	95	778	26%
Aubergine Melanzane	46	53	57	64	88	89	55	452	15%
Totanetti Agli Asparagi e Menta	36	42	46	51	69	72	44	360	12%
Bruschetta con Portobello e Manzo	33	39	42	47	64	65	40	330	11%
Bruschetta con Mozzarella	21	24	27	30	41	42	26	211	7%
Antipasti	61	70	76	85	116	119	73	600	20%
Carpacciao di Manzo	27	32	34	38	52	54	33	270	9%
								2992	100%
Weather	Clear	Cloudy	Rain	Cold & Cloudy	Clear	Clear	Clear		
Other Conditions				←	Winter fest	→			

The Food Production Schedule It's easy to see that the Food Sales Recap Report has multiple applications. One of the most important is to use the information to build a Food Production Schedule. A **Food Production Schedule** *directs the cook's work-day.* It is an effective way to control the amount of food being prepared in the kitchen.

A Food Production Schedule can be very simple or very detailed. It might be just a prep list for the day's production, handwritten by the chef. More detailed schedules could include production quantities or portion amounts, general start times, cook times, and ready-for-service times for all menu items. Even more complex schedules can include all of the above, plus things like notes from the chef regarding production, special instructions, and any other details the chef may wish to include. Production schedules often include a **Pull List**—*a list* of *food items to be removed from storage areas* for use the next day. It can also be used to *schedule appropriate staffing levels in the kitchen.*

The Sales Forecast Let's demonstrate how the Food Sales Recap Report and the Food Production Schedule are used to set production. First, the sales forecast for Farfalle Arrabbiata will be set for the second week of February. Then, this forecast will be used to determine portion counts and production quantities. Watch the flow of the paperwork.

Food Sales Recap Report$\longrightarrow$	**Food Production Schedule**
• Records the number of menu items sold per day and the total per week.	• Provides set production quantities and start and finish times. May include a Pull List.
• Is used to derive popularity percentages for menu items.	• Organizes the cook's day.
• Assists with menu decisions.	• Assists in scheduling the appropriate number of prep personnel for the level of sales forecasted.
• Tracks sales promotions.	
• Tracks the level of business.	
• Is used to develop the Food Production Schedule.	• Controls food production quantities.

A sales forecast is necessary for day-to-day operations. Managers use the counts generated to organize daily production and to schedule the correct level of staffing. To create the sales forecast, managers use:

- Sales history.
- The most recent sales patterns.
- Any internal or external situations that may affect sales.

NEEDED TO CREATE A SALES FORECAST
- **Sales history**
- **The most recent sales pattern**
- Any internal or external situations that may affect sales

Sales History and Sales Patterns First, the sales history for the same period last year must be gathered. Figure 9.6 shows this information. It is the same data included in Figure 9.3, earlier in the chapter. Note that 12,780 guests were served in February of last year. A total of 13,112 are expected this February, a slight increase from last year.

February Sales Forecast ☺	February Sales (Actual)—Last Year 12,780 ☺ (Month Total—Actual)	February Monthly Forecast 13,112 (Monthly Forecast)
Week of		**Count**
2/2–2/8	2,879 ☺	2,992 ☺ (Actual)
2/9–2/15	**3,220 ☺**	**?????**
2/16–2/22	3,112 ☺	?????
2/23–3/1	3,569 ☺	?????

FIGURE 9.6   Sales forecast by week.

This is a raw estimate based on history, current sales patterns, and other information available about this period of time. Next, the *most recent sales pattern* must be reviewed to see how business has actually been running:

- Actual sales for the last week of January were 3,295 guests.
- Actual sales for the first week of February were 2,992 guests.

Note that in both years, Valentine's Day falls during this week. In fact, last year it fell on a Saturday. Management tracks exactly which day of the week this important holiday falls on. Why? This is done for employee scheduling, purchasing, and marketing purposes. Staffing levels will obviously have to be increased and food purchases will have to be adjusted, as business usually picks up on Valentine's Day, especially if the holiday falls on a weekend. The usual par levels will probably not hold for the level of business that could be expected. In addition, managers will have to plan promotions or specials in conjunction with this holiday. The same kind of careful planning is necessary for every holiday or event.

NEEDED TO CREATE A SALES FORECAST
- Sales history
- The most recent sales pattern
- **Any internal or external situations that may affect sales**

Forecasting the Sales Count   Once all known variables and previous sales histories have been taken into consideration, the raw guest count is adjusted to an estimate that reflects the expected impact of these events. Then, internal and external situations that may affect sales are considered and a sales forecast is created. For this example, assume the following:

- Farfalle Arrabbiata's management team has been marketing a special promotion for the entire weekend in conjunction with Valentine's Day.
- Advance reservations indicate that the weekend's business is expected to exceed the previous year's sales.
- The weather is expected to be unseasonably mild.
- One of Farfalle Arrabbiata's biggest competitors closed since this time last year.

Farfalle Arrabbiata's forecasting software has determined that *3,546 is the expected sales level for the week.* This forecast is built strictly from raw numbers and must be refined because of the external variables stated here. Chef Raoul, together with the other managers, decides this forecast is too low. After discussion, they decide to plan for **3,885** ☺ customers for this week. We'll fill this information in on the sales forecast.

SALES FORECAST BY WEEK		
February Sales Forecast	**February Sales (Actual) – Last Year 13,112**	**February Monthly Forecast 13,512** ☺
Week of		**Count**
2/2–2/8	2,879	2,992 ☺ (Actual)
2/9–2/15	3,220	**3,885** ☺
2/16–2/22	3,244	?????
2/23–3/1	3,769	?????

Planning Production Based on the Sales Forecast   What happens next? Planning happens! Chef Raoul prepares for the week by:

- Establishing sales counts for *each day* using historical patterns, advance reservations, and common sense.
- Establishing individual menu item sales using popularity percentages.
- Computing purchase quantities based on the forecasts.
- Finalizing staffing levels for each day's expected level of sales.
- Estimating sales, costs, and profit.

Daily Sales Counts   We can use the same process to derive daily sales counts from weekly sales counts. To do this, we

- Check sales levels for the same periods of the previous year.
- Check sales levels of the most recent week(s).
- Check internal and external events.

Based on this process, guest counts for each day are set. Again, computerized menu management systems create these forecasts based on raw sales data. It is management's responsibility to be aware of and adjust for other internal and external factors.

Figure 9.7 establishes the *daily count for Farfalle Arrabbiata for the second week of February*. To help managers better prepare for the week, the forecast has been broken down into meal periods, based on previous sales levels.

Day/ Date	Mon. 2/9	Tues. 2/10	Wed. 2/11	Thurs. 2/12	Fri. 2/13	Sat. 2/14	Sun. 2/15	Meal Totals
Lunch ☺ ☺	219	230	300	281	412	418	271	2,131 ☺
Dinner ☺ ☺	141	176	211	244	351	421	210	1,754 ☺
Daily Total	360	406	511	525	763	839	481	3,885 ☺

FIGURE 9.7   Daily sales forecast: Week of February 9 to 15.

Weekly Count 3,885 Daily Total	POP. %	Mon. 360	Tue. 406	Wed. 511	Thur. 525	Fri. 763	Sat. 839	Sun. 481	Total
Mozzarella in Carrozza Arrabbiata	26%	95	101	133	137	198	218	125	**1,010**
Aubergine Melanzane	15%	51	62	77	79	114	126	72	**583**
Totanetti Agli Asparagi e Menta	12%	45	50	62	64	92	101	58	**466**
Bruschetta con Portobello e Manzo	11%	40	45	55	58	84	92	53	**427**
Bruschetta con Mozzarella	7%	25	29	36	37	53	58	34	**272**
Antipasti	20%	72	82	102	105	153	168	96	**777**
Carpaccio di Manzo	9%	32	37	46	47	69	76	43	**350**

FIGURE 9.8   Daily portion counts for appetizers.

Setting Portion Counts   Next, portion counts are set for menu items each day, based on current popularity percentages. Figure 9.8 lists the appetizers offered at Farfalle Arrabbiata, their current popularity as determined by the Food Sales Recap Report, and the daily forecast. The popularity percentage multiplied by each day's forecast count establishes just how many servings of each item need to be prepped.

The same process is used for all menu items. Computerized software systems automatically generate these reports. In the case of Farfalle Arrabbiata, Chef Raoul reviews these reports and makes adjustments as needed. Remember, forecasting software is unaware of the Valentine's Day holiday or any other special promotions that might be planned.

Now that the counts have been established for each day and each menu item, the rest of the steps to control production continue naturally.

STEPS TO CONTROLLING PRODUCTION

1. Set daily portion counts for every menu item using guest counts, popularity percentages, and the Food Sales Recap Report.
2. **Standardize recipes for every menu item at the determined prep levels.**
3. Complete a Food Production Schedule to set production quantities.
4. Monitor sales levels during shifts.
5. Record errors and waste on a Food Mishap Report.
6. Reconcile prepared food portions to ordered foods using a Portion Control Chart.

Standarizing Recipes

After forecasting menu item sales, the next logical step to be ready for the week's production is to standardize recipe yields to forecasted levels. This task is easily accomplished with computerized menu management software. Otherwise, each recipe is sized manually. This step is critical to ensure control over the quantity and quality of every menu item. **Standardized recipes** *manage food cost by controlling* *product quality, quantity, purchasing levels, and cost.* Refer to discussions on sizing and standardizing recipes in Chapter 2.

STEPS TO CONTROLLING PRODUCTION

1. Set daily portion counts for every menu item using guest counts, popularity percentages, and the Food Sales Recap Report.
2. Standardize recipes for every menu item at the determined prep levels.
3. **Complete a Food Production Schedule to set production quantities.**
4. Monitor sales levels during shifts.
5. Record errors and waste on a Food Mishap Report.
6. Reconcile prepared food portions to ordered foods using a Portion Control Chart.

Completing a Food Production Schedule

In Chapter 5, the idea of a football field was used to illustrate the goal of ordering levels—order enough product to stay out of the end zones of too much or too little on hand. This same theory applies to food production—produce neither too much nor too little. Overproduction *(producing more than is needed)* increases food cost. Underproduction *(producing less than is needed)* disappoints guests. To stay out of the proverbial "end zones" of over- or underproduction, "inventory levels" or "pars" for food can be determined. Standardized recipes and Food Production Schedules are the tools in the manager's toolbox used to set production quantities.

Using Food Production Schedules to Establish Par   The **Food Production Schedule** controls labor cost and food cost by

- Organizing daily production activities (labor cost).
- Establishing production quantities (food cost).

Once recipes are standardized to production quantities, Food Production Schedules are completed, which, in effect, creates a type of "par" for production, or a **food production par**. These schedules *direct production quantity and timing*. No food service manager should leave production quantities to the discretion of a cook or back-of-house employee.

Food Production Schedules may simply list bulk quantities for menu items. Or, they may break each menu item down into very specific prep amounts, instructions, and time schedules. Generally, the more complex the production, the more complex the Food Production Schedule is likely to be.

A low-volume operation with limited production and staff might employ a very informal system, where the chef simply handwrites a note of what needs to be prepped. Even high-volume operations serving mostly portion-controlled, pre-prepared menu items will not require a Food Production Schedule with the detail of a fine dining operation. *The purpose of the Food Production Schedule is to control food cost and labor cost.* To this end, the schedule is as detailed as necessary to accomplish this goal.

How to Prepare a Kitchen Production Schedule Using a Par System   The Food Production Schedule serves as a guide. This chart and the recipe tell the kitchen staff what and how much to prepare on a daily basis. By using the recipe and the schedule, all food production can be controlled. This reduces the possibility of overproduction, waste, and spoilage. It also ensures that enough products will be on hand and properly rotated.

Food Production Schedules can record production quantities in two ways. They can

1. List total quantities for menu items using a **par system**.
2. Break menu items down into very specific prep amounts, times, and other details.

TYPES OF FOOD PRODUCTION SCHEDULES

- **List total quantities for menu items using a par system.**
- Break menu items down to specific prep amounts, times, and other details.

Figure 9.9 lists the types of items best suited to using an established *food production par—the total amount needed in bulk measures like gallons or pounds.* These items are usually prepared in bulk, are easily produced, and may not even be made every day. For this reason, the food production par system is an appropriate way to manage their production.

The example in Figure 9.10 demonstrates the chart's function. It sets the amounts of salad dressings and soups to be prepared for the week in bulk quantities. Like an inventory par, the par amounts have been established by Chef Raoul on the basis of anticipated sales. Keep in mind that the par is adjusted as sales increase or decrease just like an inventory par. This ensures that enough product is on hand and maintains product freshness. Similar to using an inventory par, the chef or any cook can determine the amount to produce by checking leftovers to see the quantity needed to bring the amount of product up to the par for the day. In the example, two gallons of olive oil, balsamic vinegar, and garlic dressing are needed for Saturday. Chef Raoul or any of the cooks can check the amount on hand and determine the amount needed for the day. These production quantities are monitored and adjusted as needed. Seasons, weather, and special events all impact actual production quantities.

Notice that the dressings are only prepped every other day, except on the weekend. The production quantity on the production day should be sufficient to carry both days' anticipated sales. Because salad dressings are easily prepared, running short is not a production catastrophe. Soups, on the other hand, could pose a little more of a problem. Food pars for soup and other items with a more complex production method need to be carefully calculated to avoid running out. Otherwise, they can be included in the next version of a Food Production Schedule.

- Soups, stews, chili, and other similar items produced in bulk
- Salad dressings and marinades
- Condiments—chili sauce, cocktail sauce, herbed olive oil
- Stuffing and similar items
- Stocks and sauces produced in bulk
- Garnishes
- Dough for assorted baked goods—pizza, rolls, breads
- Salads used for sandwiches—tuna, chicken, and so on
- Herbed butters and like condiments

FIGURE 9.9   Menu items suited to a food production par.

Department: Kitchen

Prepared By: Larry

Week Of: 2/8–2/15

Item Description	Recipe Number	Monday Par	Monday Prep	Tuesday Par	Tuesday Prep	Wednesday Par	Wednesday Prep	Thursday Par	Thursday Prep	Friday Par	Friday Prep	Saturday Par	Saturday Prep	Sunday Par	Sunday Prep
Salad Dressings															
Olive Oil, Balsamic Vinegar & Garlic Dressing	D – 1	1 gal.	½ gal.			1 gal.	½ gal.			3 gal.	2 gal.	2 gal.	2 gal.	0	
Olive Oil, Balsamic Vinegar & Sundried Tomatoes	D – 2	½ gal.	½ gal.			½ gal.	½ gal.			1½ gal.	1 gal	1 gal.	1 gal.	0	
House Anchovy Dressing	D – 3	½ gal.	½ gal.			½ gal.	½ gal.			1½ gal.	1 gal.	1 gal.	1 gal.	0	
Soups															
Pasta e Fagioli	S – 1	2 gal.	2 gal.	2½ gal.	1 gal.	2½ gal.	1 gal.	2½	2 gal.	3 gal.	2½ gal.	3½ gal.	3 gal.	2 gal.	1 gal.
Minestrone	S – 2	2 gal.	2 gal.	1½ gal.	0	2 gal.	½ gal.	2½ gal.	½ gal.	2½ gal.	½ gal.	3 gal.	1 gal.	1½ gal.	½ gal.
Chicken Noodle	S – 3	4 gal.	4 gal.	4 gal.	2 gal.	4½ gal.	4½ gal.	4½ gal.	4½ gal.	4½ gal.	4½ gal.	5 gal.	5 gal.	3 gal.	3 gal.

FIGURE 9.10 A Food Production Schedule.

Examine the food production par and prep amounts for the Minestrone Soup.

	Monday		Tuesday		Wednesday		Thursday		Friday		Saturday		Sunday	
Item	Par	Prep	Par	Prep	Par	Prep	Par	Prep	Par	Prep	Par	Prep	Par	Prep
Minestrone Soup	2 gal.	2 gal.	1½ gal.	0	2 gal.	½ gal.	2½ gal.	½ gal.	2½ gal.	½ gal.	3 gal.	1 gal.	1½ gal.	½ gal.

It is clear to see by examining **par and prep amounts** that the food par for Minestrone soup is too high. Actual production amounts for the soup are quite low, meaning that it is not moving. This has quality and cost implications—if the previous days' production is carried to the next day because it did not sell, the quality may be compromised. If the soup is discarded because it is not up to standard, food cost could be affected. The par level must be adjusted down to an amount that is more representative of consumption. Next, the overall history for this item should be reviewed. If this item is normally more popular than this production level is showing, then the cause needs to be investigated. There are a number of possibilities for this problem, including inconsistent taste or competition from a new menu item. Seasonality will, of course, affect par levels for items like soups and salads. These are known variables for which management naturally adjusts.

	Monday		Tuesday		Wednesday		Thursday		Friday		Saturday		Sunday	
Item	Par	Prep	Par	Prep	Par	Prep	Par	Prep	Par	Prep	Par	Prep	Par	Prep
Chicken Noodle Soup	4 gal.	4 gal.	4 gal.	2 gal.	4½ gal.	4½ gal.	4½ gal.	4½ gal.	4½ gal.	4½ gal.	5 gal.	5 gal.	3 gal.	3 gal.

Look at the **production levels** in the Food Production Schedule for the Chicken Noodle Soup. Remember that this is *the* signature soup for Farfalle Arrabbiata. The production levels are extremely close to consumption levels. Too close, really. Because this item is so popular, the risk of running out is quite high. Producing the soup is not as easy as producing salad dressing. It requires a long cooking time, so running out means the item would be sold out for the day. This could affect customer satisfaction. The par for this item should be adjusted up.

TYPES OF FOOD PRODUCTION SCHEDULES
- List total quantities for menu items using a par system.
- **Break menu items down to specific prep amounts, times, and other details.**

Food Production Schedules for Menu Items Not Produced in Bulk   Next, production quantities have to be set for menu items *not produced in bulk*. Several of the appetizer selections for Farfalle Arrabbiata for February 14 will be used to demonstrate this process. The sales forecast and popularity percentages in Figure 9.11 set the portion counts for all the appetizers. Then, standardized recipes are sized for the production level.

Now, using the standardized recipe as a guide, each menu item is broken down into prep amounts and production steps. Mozzarella in Carrozza Arrabbiata and Antipasti will

Forecast: Saturday, Feb. 14	**839**	
Appetizers	**Pop. %**	**No. of Portions to Prep**
Mozzarella in Carrozza Arrabbiata	26%	218
Aubergine Melanzane	15	126
Totanetti Agli Asparagi e Menta	12	101
Bruschetta con Portobello e Manzo	11	92
Bruschetta con Mozzarella	7	58
Antipasti	20	168
Carpaccio di Manzo	9	76
TOTAL	**100%**	**839**

FIGURE 9.11 One-day sales forecast for appetizers.

be used to demonstrate this concept. The following table lists the ingredients and their quantities needed to prep for the forecasted number of servings—218.

MOZZARELLA IN CARROZZA ARRABBIATA	Yield: 218 servings	ANTIPASTI	Yield: 168 servings
Ingredients	**Quantity**	**Ingredients**	**Quantity**
Mozzarella	68 lb.	Fresh mozzarella	16 lb.
Prosciutto	13 lb.	Roma tomatoes	21 lb.
Bread crumbs	10 lb.	Black and green olives	5 qt. each
Pomodoro Sauce	5 gal.	Fresh Parmesan	11 lb.
Basil	6 bunches	Salami	6 lb.
		Roasted peppers	32 lb.
		Sauteed eggplant	21 lb.
		Provolone	10 lb.
		Grilled polenta	7 hotel pans

The Food Production Schedule used in this way records *ingredients for each menu item that needs special attention or instruction.* This detail controls the back-of-the-house production, ensuring that menu items will be ready on time. It is also an easy and efficient way for chefs to communicate special instructions or information to staff, especially if the chef is not present (Figure 9.12). In addition, all start times, ready times, and other service instructions should be included on the form. Every menu item not included on a food par sheet should be on the production schedule, even if there are no special instructions. Why? Because we have to control food portions and production. Again, the decision as to how much detail to include on the Food Production Schedule is entirely up to the discretion of the management.

Key to Columns on Sample Production Schedule   Refer to the following list for an explanation of labels used in Figure 9.12:

Menu item: Each menu item is listed. Items should be categorized by menu category.

	A	B	C	D	E	F				
Date: 2/14 Menu Item	Forecast	Portion on Hand	Safety Portion	Portion to Prep	Portion Over(-)/ Under(+)	No. Sold	Chef's Instructions	Service	Start By	Ready By
Mozz. in Carrozza Prosciutto Pomodoro Sauce Mozzarella	218	15	10	213			1. Slice Prosciutto on slicer setting No. 5. Layer slices on parchment paper on sheet pan. Store in reach-in 'til ready to use. 2. Retrieve 5 gallons of Pomodoro Sauce from a.m. prep cook; place 2 gallons on hot line. Label & store 3 gallons in reach in. Check reach-in for leftover sauce—use first. Do not mix with fresh sauce. 3. Place breaded mozzarella on lined sheet pans and place in reach-in for service. Be sure to cover with parchment paper before placing in walk-in. Label before storing.	Place prepped items in cold station by 11:00; dinner plate chilled by 10:00.	10:00 A.M.	11:00 A.M.
Antipasti Black/ green olives Parmesan cheese Salami Provolone Grilled polenta	168	0	10	178			1. Make sure black & green olives are stored in separate containers on the cold line. 2. Parmesan cheese has to be grated today. 3. Slice salami on slicer setting No. 2. Slice Provolone on No. 1.5. 4. Cut provolone slices into quarters. Wrap in plastic wrap before storing on cold line to prevent drying out. 5. Cut hotel pans of polenta 6×4. Store in hot box. Turn bread hot box on at 9:30.	Place prepped items in cold station by 11:00; oval serving platter chilled by 10:30.	9:30 A.M.	11:00 A.M.

A – B + C = D ± E = F

FIGURE 9.12 A sample Food Production Schedule for complex menu items and special instructions.

Forecast:	Number of covers forecast for that day.
Portions on hand:	Overproduction still in servable condition from previous shift or day.
Safety portions:	Number of extra servings to be produced. This amount is at the discretion of the chef. Erratic and fast-moving items should have something added. Slow-moving items would have no extra production.
Portions to prep:	Total number of portions to prep.
Over- and underproduction:	At the end of the shift, inventory is taken of all portions of food. Over- and underproduction is recorded. Overproduction (−) is *subtracted* from prepped portions, because they were not sold and are available for the next shift or day. Underproduction (+) is *added* to prepped portions, because these portions were prepared in addition to the forecast amount. Ultimately, these figures will be reconciled with dining room sales.
Number Sold:	This is the amount to reconcile to dining room sales. It represents all portions of food that have to be accounted for.
Start by:	Start time to prep the item for service.
Ready by:	Time the item needs to be on the service line.
Chef's instructions:	Chef's notes about production. The recipe should not be rewritten onto this form. The Food Production Schedule assists with production; it is not the whole recipe rewritten.
Service:	Any special instructions or communication from the chef.

A more simplified version of a Food Production Schedule is displayed in Figure 9.13 which shows appetizer and soup selections for Farfalle Arrabbiata. This example simply lists all menu items. It includes no instructions other than the "Ready By" time. Notice that the beginning columns mirror the example used earlier. Although the production details may be limited, control is still maintained with these figures. This format is appropriate in an operation with an experienced workforce.

With a map for each day's production in hand, cooks are more efficient (saving labor cost) and production is standardized (saving food cost). Production schedules reduce questions from staff and can be used to train new employees.

STEPS TO CONTROLLING PRODUCTION

1. Set daily portion counts for every menu item using guest counts, popularity percentages, and the Food Sales Recap Report.
2. Standardize recipes for every menu item at the determined prep levels.
3. Complete a Food Production Schedule to set production quantities.
4. **Monitor sales levels during shifts.**
5. Record errors and waste on a Food Mishap Report.
6. Reconcile prepared food portions to ordered foods using a Portion Control Chart.

Monitoring Sales Levels

The next step is monitoring sales levels for accuracy during shifts. Once the doors are open, guests will come in to dine. Whether or not they selected what was predicted is

	A	B	C	D	E	F	
Food Production Schedule **Date: Sat. 2/14**	**Forecast**	**839**					
Appetizers	**Forecast**	**Portion on Hand**	**Safety Portions**	**Portions to Prep**	**Over(-)/ Under(+) Prod.**	**No. Sold**	**Ready By**
Mozzarella in Carrozza Arrabbiata	218	15	10	213			11:00 A.M.
Aubergine Melanzane	126	10	5	121			11:00 A.M.
Totanetti Agli Asparagi e Menta	101	0	5	106			11:00 A.M.
Bruschetta con Portobello e Manzo	92	0	0	92			11:00 A.M.
Bruschetta con Mozzarella	58	0	0	58			11:00 A.M.
Antipasti	168	0	10	178			11:00 A.M.
Carpaccio di Manzo	76	5	5	76			11:00 A.M.
Soups							
Pasta e Fagioli	112	0	10	122			10:30 A.M.
Minestrone Soup	78	0	0	78			10:30 A.M.
Chicken Noodle Soup	215	20	10	205			10:30 A.M.

A − **B** + **C** = **D** ± **E** = **F**

FIGURE 9.13 A simplified Food Production Schedule (with no special instructions).

a guess. Because of this, sales and production during a shift are closely watched. Most production "blips" (shortages) can be eliminated by close monitoring. Any extra production is recorded in the Under-Production column on the Food Production Schedule.

STEPS TO CONTROLLING PRODUCTION

1. Use guest counts, popularity percentages, and the Food Sales Recap Report to set daily portion counts for every menu item.
2. Standardize recipes for every menu item at the determined prep levels.
3. Complete a Food Production Schedule to set production quantities.
4. Monitor sales levels during shifts.
5. **Record errors and waste on a Food Mishap Report.**
6. Reconcile prepared food portions to ordered foods using a Portion Control Chart.

Recording Errors and Waste

At the end of each shift or each day, all portions produced should be accounted for. Three forms can be used to document food portions:

1. The Food Production Schedule
2. The guest check
3. The Food Mishap (or Void) Report

Using the Food Production Schedule and Guest Checks to Track Errors The Food Production Schedule indicates how many portions were "sold." See column F in Figures 9.12 and 9.13. This amount is a product of the number of portions prepped, any on-hand inventory, and any over- or underproduction adjustments. The number sold according to the schedule may not balance with the number of portions validated by the guest checks. If that is the case, what could have happened?

An end-of-shift inventory records either how many portions are available for the next shift (Portion Over) or how many additional portions were prepped (Portion Under); see Figure 9.12. Completing the math on the form will reveal the total number of portions "sold" according to kitchen records. This amount should match guest check records. Discrepancies between the production schedule count (No. Sold) and the guest check count should be found on the Food Mishap Report—the next form we will talk about. Portions not accounted for in these ways must be tracked down. The goal for all foodservice operations is that *all menu items prepared for dining room consumption generate dining room sales.*

Using the Food Mishap Report to Account for Waste Mistakes and errors are part of doing business and are part of the food production process. Honest mistakes and errors are often made as a result of clumsiness or lack of attention to the work at hand. As much as perfection is the goal, it is quite likely that a plate will be sent back from the dining room or a mistake will be made on the line, making an item unservable. Whatever the circumstances, wasted products need to be accounted for. Any food portions ready for service that did not generate dining room sales are contributing to food cost. One way to track these items is to use a **Food Mishap (or Void) Report** (Figure 9.14). These forms *track portions of food that did not generate dining room sales.*

The **Food Mishap Report** serves two significant functions:

1. When balanced with the Food Portion Reconciliation Chart, it accounts for wasted food portions. (This is Step 6 in controlling production and will be discussed in more detail in the next section.)

Day	Date	Shift	Item Description	Mishap	Name
Mon.	2/9	Lunch	Chicken Noodle Soup	Spilled 2 cups	Juan
Mon.	2/9	Lunch	Carpaccio	Ordering error	Juan
Mon.	2/9	Lunch	Antipasti	Too much dressing	Larry
Mon.	2/9	Lunch	Bruschetta—Portobello	Slow pickup; soggy	Juan
Mon.	2/9	Dinner	Bistecca	Overcooked	Mikel
Mon.	2/9	Dinner	Rack of Lamb	Overcooked	Mikel

FIGURE 9.14 A Food Mishap Report.

2. It identifies responsibility and accountability for errors within the production and service staff.

There are many reasons why a food portion may be wasted. Here are the top four:

1. Cooking error
2. Ordering error
3. Customer dissatisfaction with some aspect of the item.
4. The item has been dropped, spilled, spoiled, or is otherwise compromised and cannot be sold.

THE TOP REASONS AN ITEM IS REPORTED ON A FOOD MISHAP REPORT
- Cooking error
- Ordering error
- Customer dissatisfaction with some aspect of the item
- The item has been dropped, spilled, spoiled, or is otherwise compromised and cannot be sold.

When an item is prepped but not sold, the reason(s) should be investigated. Management can use the Food Mishap Report to

1. Identify production problems.
2. Evaluate employee performance—especially new employees.
3. Single out employees in need of retraining.
4. Develop standards or goals for mistakes for both front-of-house and back-of-house employees.

A word of caution is in order regarding employee performance and mistakes, however: Perfection is desired, but in the food business, there are many variables. To help, management strives to do the following:

- Staff (front and back of house) appropriately for the sales level
- Train employees so they have the appropriate skills
- Purchase the correct supplies for sales levels
- Provide an adequate physical plant: tools, equipment, equipment capacity, and so on

If this goal is achieved, then a Food Mishap Report should contain a minimal number of entries.

A Food Waste Scenario   In the example in Figure 9.14, Juan has made three "mistakes" during his shift. What questions should the manager ask before speaking to Juan about the problem?

1. Was the dining room properly staffed?
2. How many guests did Juan serve?
3. Is Juan a new employee? If so, was his training adequate? Is this his first shift on his own?
4. Did Juan arrive ready to work? Was he ill? Was he tired from working double shifts in the days before?

Review the rest of the report (see Figure 9.14). What questions should be asked of the back of the house?

STEPS TO CONTROLLING PRODUCTION

1. Use guest counts, popularity percentages, and the Food Sales Recap Reports to set daily portion counts for every menu item.
2. Standardize recipes for every menu item at the determined prep levels.
3. Complete a Food Production Schedule to set production quantities.
4. Monitor sales levels during shifts.
5. Record errors and waste on a Food Mishap Report.
6. **Reconcile prepared food portions to ordered foods using a Portion Control Chart.**

Reconciling Prepared Food Portions to Ordered Food

Finally, at the end of the day, prepped food portions are reconciled to served food portions. A **Portion Control Chart** is used for this task. This report shows discrepancies, overages, and shorts in production. It collates information from the Food Production Schedule, the Food Mishap Report, and guest checks. We will use Figure 9.16 to demonstrate using this form, and we'll use information from the Food Production Schedule (Figure 9.15) and the Food Mishap Report (Figure 9.14), created earlier.

In the Portion Control Chart shown in Figure 9.16, the Total Sold from Checks (C) and the kitchen's Number Sold (D and G) should be in balance. Any discrepancies should be investigated and the reason recorded on the form.

The top half of the form is designed to collate data from the Food Production Schedule. It is completed at the end of a shift, usually by the line staff. The last column

Date: 2/14 **Day:** Saturday				**Forecast:** 839			
Appetizers	**Forecast**	**Portions on Hand**	**Safety Portions**	**Portions to Prep**	**Over (–)/ Under(+) Prod.**	**No. Sold**	**Ready By**
Mozzarella in Carrozza Arrabbiata	218	15	10	213	+20	233	11:00 A.M.
Aubergine Melanzane	126	10	5	121	–5	116	11:00 A.M.
Totanetti Agli Asparagi e Menta	101	0	5	106	–7	99	11:00 A.M.
Bruschetta con Portobello e Manzo	92	0	0	92	–3	89	11:00 A.M.
Bruschetta con Mozzarella	58	0	0	58	+2	60	11:00 A.M.
Antipasti	168	0	10	178	+5	183	11:00 A.M.
Carpaccio di Manzo	76	5	5	76	–10	66	11:00 A.M.
Soups							
Pasta e Fagioli	112	0	10	122	0	122	10:30 A.M.
Minestrone Soup	78	0	0	78	0	78	10:30 A.M.
Chicken Noodle Soup	215	20	10	205	15	220	10:30 A.M.

FIGURE 9.15 Food Production Schedule.

Date: 2/14

Kitchen Reconciliation:

	A	B	C	D	E	F	G
Appetizers	Forecast	On Hand (−)	Safety (+)	Under-Production (+)	Total Available =	Over-Production (−)	No. Sold (Kit.)
Mozzarella in Carrozza Arrabbiata	218	15	10	20	233	0	233
Aubergine Melanzane	126	10	5	0	121	5	116
Totanetti Agli Asparagi e Menta	101	0	5	0	106	7	99
Bruschetta con Portobello e Manzo	92	0	0	0	92	3	89
Bruschetta con Mozzarella	58	0	0	2	58	0	58
Antipasti	168	0	10	5	183	0	178
Carpacciao di Manzo	76	5	5	0	76	10	66
	A	**B**	**C**	**D**	**E**	**F**	**G**
Dining Room Reconciliation	No. Sold/ Checks	Por./ Mishap	Total Sold	No. Sold − Kit. Production	Difference	Reason	
Mozzarella in Carrozza Arrabbiata	232	0	232	233	1	Missing check—Juan	
Aubergine Melanzane	116	0	116	116			
Totanetti Agli Asparagi e Menta	98	0	98	99	1	Forgot to record on Mishap Report	
Bruschetta con Portobello e Manzo	88	1	89	89			
Bruschetta con Mozzarella	58	0	58	58			
Antipasti	177	1	178	178			
Carpaccio di Manzo	65	1	66	66			

A − B = C D

FIGURE 9.16 A Portion Control Chart.

(No. Sold—Kitchen) reports the number of portions sold according to the kitchen's records.

The bottom half of the form collates the guest check sales, the Mishap Report, and the kitchen production records. It reconciles *all portions that were available for sale with actual sales data*. The Total No. Sold (C) should be in balance with the Total Number Sold as per the kitchen's production records (D).

Consistent discrepancies are cause for investigation by management. Problems in reconciliation can be a reason for high food cost in an operation.

*N*et Work

Explore the following Web sites:
www.micros.com
www.positouch.com
www.visualonesystems.com—Click Products, Point-of-Sale
www.cbord.com—Click around the Products page
www.fooduniversity.com—Sign up for a free week to explore this site
www.guestbridge.com—Guest reservation system and guest tracking

Chapter Wrap

The Chapter ✓ at the beginning of the chapter posed several questions. Review the questions and compare your responses to the following answers.

1. How can sales history be organized?

Sales histories can be organized into two formats: as food and beverage sales that are recorded in dollar values and as food and beverage sales that are recorded in customer counts. A sales history recorded in dollar values is used primarily in planning and analyzing business activity. A sales history that is recorded in customer counts is used primarily for operational planning.

2. How is a Food Sales Recap Report used to set portion counts?

By keeping track of the past sales of each menu item per year, month, or week, a foodservice manager can estimate customer orders. Managers keep track of food sales by using a Food Sales Recap Report. The Food Sales Recap Report records the number of menu items sold per day, the total per week, and the current popularity percentage. The report also includes weather conditions and other external events that might have influenced business. These reports are saved for periods of time and become the sales records for the business. Other uses of the Food Sales Recap Report include determining which items to drop from the menu, which items are the most popular, and whether sales promotions are working, as well as tracking the level of business.

3. What is a Food Production Schedule?

The Food Production Schedule serves as a guide. This chart and the recipe tell the kitchen staff what and how much to prepare on a daily basis. By using the recipe and the schedule, all food production can be controlled. This reduces the possibility of overproduction or waste.

4. What is a Food Mishap Report?

Mistakes and errors are part of doing business and are part of the food production process. Honest mistakes and errors are often made as a result of clumsiness or inattention to the work at hand. As much as perfection is the goal, it is quite likely that a plate will be sent back from the dining room or a mistake will be made on the line, making an item unservable. Whatever the circumstances, the wasted products need to be accounted for. Any food portions ready for service that did not generate dining room sales are contributing to food cost. One way to track these items is to use a Food Mishap (or Void) Report. These forms track portions of food that did not generate dining room sales.

The Food Mishap Report serves two significant functions:

a. It accounts for wasted food portions when balancing with the Food Portion Reconciliation Chart.

b. It identifies responsibility for errors among the production and service staff.

5. What is a Portion Control Chart?

At the end of the day, the number of prepped food portions is reconciled to the number of served food portions. A Portion Control Chart shows discrepancies, overages, and shorts in the production. It collates information from the Food Production Schedule, the Food Mishap Report, and guest checks.

Key Terminology and Concepts in This Chapter

Average check	Portion Control Chart
Average sale per server	Pull List
Food Mishap (or Void) Report	Safety portions
Food Portion Reconciliation Chart	Sales forecast
Food production par	Sales history
Food Production Schedule	Sales dollars per operating period
Food Sales Recap Report	Seat turnover
Forecasting	Standardized recipes
Guest check	Turns
Manager's Report	Underproduction
Overproduction	Weighted average turnover
Par system	
Popularity percentage (index)	

Discussion Questions and Exercises

1. Explain the following statement: "At the heart of earning a profit in a foodservice operation is the ability of the manager to control food cost."

2. What factors play a role in determining an appropriate food cost percentage for a restaurant?

3. What is the key difference between sales history reported in dollars and sales history reported in guest counts?

 4. Chef Raoul is reviewing the sales reports from the past week. He would like to know the turn for each day and for the week as a whole. You begin to figure it out (using the information in the following boxes).

This Week's Results:								
Day/ Date Feb.	Mon. 2/X	Tues. 2/X	Wed. 2/X	Thurs. 2/X	Fri. 2/X	Sat. 2/X	Sun. 2/X	Meal Totals
Lunch ☺	250	241	271	262	270	301	220	
Turn-over								
Dinner ☺	101	110	98	160	270	281	102	
Turn-over								
Daily Total								
Daily Turn								

OVERALL WEEKLY TURN

The Previous Weeks Results							
Day/Date Feb.	Mon. 2/X	Tues. 2/X	Wed. 2/X	Thurs. 2/X	Fri. 2/X	Sat. 2/X	Sun. 2/X
Turn-over Lunch	1.69	1.88	1.96	2.11	2.21	2.23	1.86
Turn-over Dinner	.64	.81	.95	1.16	2.23	2.34	.92

5. How does this past week's results compare with the results from the previous week? Should Chef Raoul and the other managers be concerned? Why or why not?

 6. The following are the monthly guest counts for Farfalle Arrabbiata. Compute the popularity percentage of each month. How could a monthly guest count popularity percentage be used in planning?

Annual Customer Count: 167,483 ☺												
Month	Jan. ☺	Feb. ☺	Mar. ☺	Apr. ☺	May ☺	Jun. ☺	Jul. ☺	Aug. ☺	Sept. ☺	Oct. ☺	Nov. ☺	Dec. ☺
Monthly Totals	14,656	13,112	12,684	12,691	13,909	9,777	10,119	8,816	16,532	18,218	17,638	19,331
Popularity %												

7. What is the value of preparing and using a Food Sales Recap Report? How can it be used in planning?

 8. The following is a Food Sales Recap Report for the entrée selections at Farfalle Arrabbiata. Compute the popularity percentage for each menu item.

Food Sales Recap Report										
Department: Kitchen				Page 1 of 2						
Prepared By: Hank				**Week Of:** Feb. 2–8						
	Date 2/2	**2/3**	**2/4**	**2/5**	**2/6**	**2/7**	**2/8**			
Menu Items	**Mon.**	**Tues.**	**Wed.**	**Thur.**	**Fri.**	**Sat.**	**Sun.**	**Total**	**Pop. %**	
Cioppino	89	84	109	106	160	148	105			
Scallopine di Vitello	56	48	67	59	98	84	65			
Salmon a la Griglia	46	37	56	45	79	67	54			
Bistecca	43	34	52	42	74	60	35			
Filetto di Maiale	31	19	37	25	51	37	36			
Costatine D'Agnello	71	65	86	80	126	100	83			
Pollo con Carciofini e Limone	37	27	44	33	62	49	43			
Weather										
Other Conditions										

 9. The sales forecast for next week is 3,112 guests. Help Chef Raoul by figuring out the number to prep for each of the following entrées.

Menu Item	Popularity %	No. to Prep
Cioppino		
Scallopine di Vitello		
Salmon a la Griglia		
Bistecca		
Filetto di Maiale		
Costatine D'Agnello		
Pollo con Carciofini		

10. What research should Marcel, Chef Raoul, and the other managers do before starting to plan for next week's sales? Next month's sales?

 11. Of the 3,112 guests expected this week, 763 are expected on Friday. Determine how many orders of each entrée will be needed using the popularity percentage from Exercise 9. Complete the production schedule on the next page and determine the number sold.

Food Production Schedule							
Date: 2/14 **Day:** Friday		**Forecast:** 763					
Entrées:	**Pop. %**	**Forecast**	**Portions on Hand**	**Safety Portions**	**Portions to Prep**	**Over (−)/ Under (+) Prod.**	**No. Sold**
Cioppino			8	0		+ 0	
Scallopine di Vitello			5	10		+ 10	
Salmon a la Griglia			3	10		− 6	
Bistecca			4	6		0	
Filetto di Maiale			6	4		− 5	
Costatine D'Agnello			0	0		+ 10	
Pollo con Carcofini			2	5		+ 6	

12. At the end of the shift, the Food Mishap Report recorded the following:

Food Mishap Report					
Day	**Date**	**Shift**	**Item Description**	**Mishap**	**Name**
Fri.	2/9	Dinner	Cioppino	Spilled 1 order	Ricky
Fri.	2/9	Dinner	Bistecca	Ordering error	Juan
Fri.	2/9	Dinner	Bistecca	Overcooked	Larry
Fri.	2/9	Dinner	Costatine	Slow pick-up; cold	Juan
Fri.	2/9	Dinner	Pollo	Overcooked; too dry	Mike
Fri.	2/9	Dinner	Salmon	Complaint: smell	Larry
Fri.	2/9	Dinner	Salmon	Complaint: smell	Larry
Fri.	2/9	Dinner	Salmon	Complaint: smell	Larry

Chef Raoul was none too happy when he saw this. Neither are you. What obvious things went wrong? What not so obvious things went wrong? Consider all of the steps in the Operating Cycle of Control.

 13. The Portion Control Chart on page 293 is for Friday night. Reconcile the kitchen production to the dining room sales by completing the chart. Do you see any problems? What does it tell you about Friday night's sales? Transfer your figures from Exercise 11 to the chart. Be sure to include the items on the Food Mishap Report.

14. Review the menu for Farfalle Arrabbiata. Which items, in addition to soup and salad dressings, would lend themselves to a food par versus a full food production schedule?

15. In spite of his efforts to control production, Chef Raoul is still having problems controlling soup and salad production. There are consistent overages and shortages with both items. He's asked for your help to solve this mystery. What could be going wrong? Use the Operating Cycle of Control to focus your comments.

Portion Control Chart							
Date: 2/14							
Kitchen Reconciliation							
Item Appetizers	**Fore-Cast**	**On Hand (−)**	**Safety (+)**	**Under-Production (+)**	**Total Available =**	**Over-Production (−)**	**No. Sold (Kit.)**
Cioppino							
Scallopine di Vitello							
Salmon a la Griglia							
Bistecca							
Filetto di Maiale							
Costatine D'Agnello							
Pollo con Carciofini							

Dining Room Reconciliation	**No. Sold/ Checks**	**Por./ Mishap**	**Total Sold**	**No. Sold-Kit. Production**	**Difference**	**Reason**	
Cioppino	225						
Scallopine di Vitello	93						
Salmon a la Griglia	61						
Bistecca	54						
Filetto di Maiale	61						
Costatine D'Agnello	187						
Pollo con Carciofini	94						

16. What actions can a foodservice manager possibly take when product costs unexpectedly and rapidly increase? Use the Operating Cycle of Control to frame your answer.

17. How does the Food Sales Recap Report, the Food Production Schedule, the Food Mishap Report, and the Portion Control Chart help control product usage, food production, and food cost?

18. Why is it important to document errors on a Food Mishap Report? How can this tool be used to improve employee performance?

## Chapter Ten

About Food Cost & Food Cost Percentage

Chapter Objective

To compute and interpret the effect of food cost percentage on a foodservice operation's profitability.

Learning Objectives

After reading this chapter and completing the discussion questions and exercises, you should be able to:

1. Describe how a standard for food cost is determined.
2. Use the Triangle of Enlightenment to calculate food cost percentage.
3. Compute daily food cost percentage.
4. Compute monthly food cost percentage.
5. Determine whether cost results are acceptable.
6. Identify causes of unacceptable variances.
7. Strategize corrective actions for unacceptable variances.

The Menu

Pre-Purchase Functions

GUEST CHECK
Sales history, turnover, average check, cash management, revenue forecasting & **budgeting**, menu item analysis

GUESTS
Greeting, seating, sales, serving, busing, payment, comment cards

FOH Functions

KITCHEN PRODUCTION
Production schedules, portion tracking, recipe control, serving controls, food safety

PRODUCT ISSUING
Requisitions, **transfers, daily & monthly costs, food cost percentage**

STORAGE PRACTICES & INVENTORY MANAGEMENT
Best practices, sanitation, security, inventory methods

INVOICE MANAGEMENT
Payment, price checking, security

STANDARDIZED RECIPES
Standard ingredients, portion size, quality, consistency, quantity, purchasing

COST CARDS
Portion costs, yield factors, sell prices

SPECIFICATIONS
Product descriptions

PAR STOCK
Inventory levels, order building

REQUISITION
Order building, purchasing

SHOPPING LISTS
Call sheets, bid sheets, suppliers, bidding

PURCHASE ORDERS
Security, ship order, price guarantee, contract

BOH Functions

RECEIVING ACTIVITIES
Best practices, invoices, security, sanitation

Chapter Map

About Food Cost

- Introduction to Food Cost
- Let's Count the Ways to Understand Food Cost

Chapter Map   (Continued)

Food Cost & Types of Foodservice Operations

- Type of Operation
- Type of Food Served, Theme, & Service Style

Food Cost as a Part of the Income Statement

- The Income Statement
- Costs vs. Sales
- Cost Percentages

Food Cost as a Piece of a "Pie"

- The Plan for Expenses
- Costs Over Budget
- Costs Under Budget

Food Cost as a Daily Percentage

- Components of the Daily Food Cost Percentage
- Cost of Food Today & To Date
- Finding the Daily Food Cost Percentage Without Requisitions

- Compiling a Daily Food Cost Worksheet Using Requisitions & Other Adjustments
- Differences Among Types of Food Cost Worksheets
- Other Shortcomings of the Daily Food Cost Percentage
- Purchasing Patterns
- Sales Patterns

Food Cost as a Monthly Percentage

- The Monthly Food Cost Report
- Finding the Actual Monthly Food Cost Percentage
- Departmental Food Cost Reports

Variances in Food Cost

Managing Unfavorable Variances

- Management Control Procedure
- Variances Within the Control of Management
- Variances Outside the Direct Control of Management

Chapter ✓

Check the chapter content for the answers to these questions:

1. What is food cost and food cost percentage?
2. What are all the ways to understand food cost and food cost percentage?
3. What is a variance?
4. How are unfavorable variances managed?

About Food Cost

The successful foodservice manager must fully understand all the areas within the foodservice operation that can increase or decrease food cost. Hopefully, by now, you realize that all these "areas" are the steps in the Operating Cycle of Control, featured at the beginning of each chapter.

Simply stated, **food cost** is *the actual cost of purchasing the raw food products and related ingredients that are used to generate dining room sales.* Food cost is measured for specific periods (daily, weekly, monthly, annually) and is always expressed in terms of a percentage, which is referred to as the **food cost percentage**. This percentage is an important indicator to an owner, a manager, and the chef. What does it indicate? It indicates whether or not management is doing its job! This chapter explains how the foodservice manager calculates a food cost percentage for a variety of periods and uses the information to determine how the kitchen is performing financially.

The task of calculating food cost percentage is not at all difficult. The formula was covered in Chapter 1—the Triangle of Enlightenment. The math is the easy part. It is simply:

FOOD COST/FOOD SALES = FOOD COST %

The more difficult part of the equation is the first part—FOOD COST. This chapter covers how food cost is determined, so the dollars on that side of the equation truly represent all the money spent on food to generate the reported food sales.

Once the dollar amounts are gathered from the various types of food cost reports, the foodservice manager is able to calculate the food cost percentage. More advanced foodservice operations use a computer to complete this task. Today, most food service managers are not bogged down with the actual calculations—they are reading and interpreting reports that a software program has organized. The foodservice manager must still *comprehend* the information fed into the computer; thus, he or she needs to understand the factors influencing food cost. As the foodservice manager becomes skilled at managing food cost, this task becomes part of the daily routine of managing a foodservice operation.

A foodservice manager may be asked the question, "What should the food cost be for this or that type of foodservice operation?" The question will be easy to answer if the foodservice manager has a basic understanding of food cost, then acquires a few years of successful management experience.

Introduction to Food Cost

When foodservice managers talk about food cost, they are usually referring to the cost as a percentage. For instance, a manager may state, "Food cost was 32% last month." Understanding food cost goes beyond calculating a simple percentage. A foodservice manager who effectively manages food cost

- Understands that the Operating Cycle of Control represents all the internal control areas in a foodservice operation.
- Understands the effect of food cost percentage on the budget.
- Understands the effect of all other costs on the budget.
- Understands how all expenses affect profit.
- Understands the effect of variances (favorable and unfavorable) on profit.
- Understands the concept of controllable and noncontrollable expenses.
- Understands where to look in an operation when unacceptable variances are reported.
- Understands how business volume affects profit.

This is a tall order of "Understandings," which cannot all be mastered in this one chapter. In fact, the next few chapters (Chapters 11 and 12, then 18 and 19) work with all of these concepts.

Let's Count the Ways to Understand Food Cost

There are a number of ways to understand food cost. Foodservice managers look at the food cost percentage they wish to have as an operating goal. They attempt to reach that goal by

- Setting quality standards for menu items.
- Setting standard portion sizes.
- Setting standard operating procedures.

The food cost percentage should be controlled with only a small degree of fluctuation. Food cost is managed through the effective use of information and control reports prepared on a regular and scheduled basis.

For most students of foodservice management, two of the most difficult concepts to grasp are food cost and food cost percentage. Understanding these two concepts, however, is critical to the success of a foodservice operation. Some of the "misunderstandings" concerning food cost and food cost percentage have their roots in the following questions:

- Where does the food cost percentage come from?
- Who makes it up?
- How do you know it's right?
- How often does it need to be checked?
- Is it a reliable measure?
- What does it mean if it's too high?
- What does it mean if it's too low?
- What do managers do with the information once they have it?

These questions are at the heart of understanding food cost. Grasping the answers to all of these questions will help you understand the same issues as they apply to all of the operational costs in a foodservice operation. The next seven sections explain food cost and food cost percentage in an effort to address these common "misunderstandings," but with the greater goal of understanding *all costs* in a foodservice operation.

LET'S COUNT THE WAYS TO UNDERSTAND FOOD COST

1. **Food cost and types of foodservice operations**
2. Food cost as a part of the income statement
3. Food cost as a piece of a "pie"
4. Food cost as a daily percentage
5. Food cost as a monthly percentage
6. Variances in food cost
7. Managing unfavorable variances

$\mathcal{F}$ood Cost and Types of Foodservice Operations

FACTORS THAT SHAPE FOOD COST PERCENTAGE

- Type of foodservice establishment.
- Type, quality, and theme of food served.
- Style of service.

Many philosophies exist as to what a normal food cost or food cost percentage should be for the typical foodservice operation. Generally, three factors shape the food cost percentage: (1) type of foodservice establishment; (2) type, quality, and theme of food served; and (3) style of service.

Type of Operation

The first consideration is the *type of foodservice operation.* We are all familiar with different types of foodservice operations. Scan the following list—are there any at which you have NOT yet had a meal? Foodservice operations generally fall into one of the following business segments:

- Family or casual dining
- Fine dining
- Quick service or fast casual
- Cafeteria
- Buffet

Type of Food Served, Theme, and Service Style

Within each of these categories, different types of foods are served (regional foods, ethnic foods, steak dinners, and so on). Each may have a different theme (western BBQ, French bistro, or American diner). Also, service styles range from formal fine dining to a walk-up snack bar. *Each business segment or category has a food cost percentage range that is normal for that particular type of operation.* Typical food cost percentages by category are listed in Figure 10.1.

	Low (%)	Median (%)	High (%)
Family/casual dining	27	32	36
Fine dining	25	27	38
Fast food/fast casual	28	31	39
Cafeteria	33	36	37
Buffet	35	40	46

FIGURE 10.1   Typical food cost percentages.

Variable Profile of Foodservice Operations

It is important to understand that each type of foodservice operation listed in the figure has a specific business "recipe" that spells profitability. Like the recipe for a menu item, the "business recipe" is made up of a common set of "ingredients," or **variables**, that *distinguishes one segment from the next* and is a basis for understanding how each makes a profit in the competitive world of foodservice management. These variables are

- Sales volume
- Food and beverage cost percentage
- Guest check average
- Labor cost

Fine Dining vs. Fast Food   Each variable has a norm that is described as either high or low for each business segment. Consider the differences between fine dining and quick service operations. It is the specific combination of highs and lows among the four variables that makes each business segment run profitably.

As a general guideline, if a foodservice operation runs a high food cost percentage (cost to sales ratio), the labor cost percentage should be lower. Such is the case with fast-food restaurants. These operations hire people with limited skills at minimal pay to prepare menu items, often with frozen, ready-to-serve products that are inexpensively priced but have a high per-unit cost. In the front of the house, guest energy is used to place orders, pick up food, and clear tables after eating. Generally, this type of operation experiences high-volume sales. So the right combination of

- high volume,
- high portion cost in relation to selling price,
- low guest check, and
- low labor cost

is the formula needed to be profitable in the quick service/fast casual business segment. Any time these business profile descriptors are anything other than what is "normal" for that business segment, then the operation is likely to be unprofitable or, at the least, not at targeted profit levels.

BUSINESS PROFILE DESCRIPTORS FOR QUICK SERVICE COMPARED TO FINE DINING

Quick Service/Fast Casual Profile	Fine Dining Profile
• High volume sales	• Low sales volume
• High food cost percentage	• Low-to-moderate food cost percentage
• Low guest check	• High guest check
• Low labor cost	• High labor cost

An opposite situation is that of a **fine dining** restaurant. These operations employ highly skilled chefs and professional servers serving higher-priced food. The menu items are typically prepared from scratch; they are not purchased prepared or frozen and assembled quickly. As a result, the food cost percentage (cost-to-sales ratio) is lower and the labor cost higher in a full-service operation than in a limited-service operation. Sales volume on a per-person basis is much lower compared to that of a fast-food operation. The combination of

- lower volume,
- low-to-moderate food cost percentage,
- high guest check, and
- high labor cost

is the formula needed to be profitable in the fine dining business segment. The point is this: Each category, *fine dining to fast food, maintains a cost-to-sales ratio and business segment profile that is typical for its own function.* All things being equal, operating a business within these norms should produce profit given adequate levels of volume.

LET'S COUNT THE WAYS TO UNDERSTAND FOOD COST

1. Food cost and types of foodservice operations
2. Food cost as a part of the income statement
3. Food cost as a piece of a "pie"
4. Food cost as a daily percentage
5. Food cost as a monthly percentage
6. Variances in food cost
7. Managing unfavorable variances

Food Cost as a Part of the Income Statement

The next way to look at food cost percentage is in its role on an income statement. Although income statements are covered in depth in Chapters 18 and 19, it is appropriate to begin to familiarize yourself with income statement basics now.

The Income Statement

What's an **income statement**, anyway? Simply, it is a report of *all income, expenses, and profit for a defined period of time.* It reports the financial standing of an operation. Income statements are also referred to as a **budget** or a **Profit and Loss Statement (P&L)**.

What kind of information is on an income statement? **Income**, of course. Income is reported as **sales** or **revenue**—all three terms are interchangeable. Expenses are reported in categories: **Cost of Sales, Controllable Expenses,** and **Occupation Costs**. The last line reports **Profit or Loss**. Income statements are produced for a specific period of time (daily, weekly, monthly, etc.).

Who uses an income statement? Managers and chefs rely on the income statement to report the financial status of the operation. Here are some ways they are used:

- To report sales and expense *history.*
- To report sales and expense *forecasts.*
- To report sales and expense *actual results.*
- To report sales and expenses for a *future period.*

These descriptors should sound familiar. They are the same breakouts used in Chapter 9, in our discussion of sales history. All of these uses will be covered in a later chapter.

Costs vs. Sales

Figure 10.2 is an example of an income statement. It reports sales and expenses for Farfalle Arrabbiata for the month of February. The format is typical of income statements for commercial foodservice operations. Notice that categories or sections of the income statement have been highlighted (in bold face type). Notice, too, that **Food**

Sales	February	
Food	$140,743	80.00%
Beverage	35,186	20.00
Total Sales	175,929	100.00
Cost of Sales		
Food Cost	47,290	33.6
Beverage Cost	9,011	25.61
Total Cost of Goods	56,301	32.00
Gross Profit	119,628	68.00
Controllable Expenses		
Payroll	52,075	29.60
Employee Benefits	7,917	4.50
Direct Operating Expenses	5,982	3.40
Music & Entertainment	880	0.50
Advertising & Promotion	4,398	2.50
Utilities	6,509	3.70
Administration & General	4,222	2.40
Repair & Maintenance	2,463	1.40
Total Controllable Expenses	84,446	48.00
Income B4 Occupation Costs	35,182	20.00
Occupation Costs		
Rent	10,556	6.00
Property Tax	3,167	1.80
Other Taxes	1,500	0.85
Property Insurance	1,833	1.04
Interest	2,750	1.56
Depreciation	4,825	2.74
Total Occupational Costs	24,631	14.00
Restaurant Profit B4 Taxes	10,556	6.00

Sales

Cost of Sales

Controllable Expenses

Occupation Costs

Profit

FIGURE 10.2 Income statement for Farfalle Arrabbiata.

Cost is located under **Cost of Sales**. This is because this cost is *incurred in order to generate sales*—it's an operating cost. All **operating costs** are *incurred in order to generate sales*. Basically, it is needed to operate. Anyone in the food business has to buy food in order to generate sales. No food equals no sales!

The next category, **Controllable Expenses**, is also an operating cost. Look at some of the expenses in this category: Payroll, Direct Operating Expenses, Utilities. Can any business operate without funds in these expense categories? Of course not. That's why **Controllable Expenses** are considered operating costs.

The third category is **Occupation Costs**. These costs are not "operating costs" per se. In fact, they are called **nonoperating costs**—unlike food cost or labor cost, you don't really need them to serve guests! The restaurant's doors can still open for customers even if the rent bill hasn't been paid (probably not for very long, though). Even though insurance is required by law, guests can still dine without an insurance certificate in the office. All of these costs are **fixed costs**, meaning *they have to be paid whether the business is open or closed, busy or slow.*

Last is **Profit or Loss**. When all is said and done (all expenses are paid from the income), this is what remains. This is the fruit of all the labor! Profit, however, is not a left-over and should not be viewed in that way. That idea will be discussed in more detail later.

Cost Percentages

Notice the asterisks (*) next to **Food Cost** and **Total Cost of Goods**. Notice also that **Beverage Cost** is included in this category. When alcohol beverages are sold, Beverage Cost appears as a separate line item in the Cost of Goods section. Why? Because beverage costs are incurred in order to generate **beverage sales.** The food cost percentage shown (33.6%) is derived by dividing Food Cost by Food Sales and multiplying by 100%. This percent, 33.6%, is the **budgeted or target food cost percentage** for the operation. Beverage Cost divided by Beverage Sales will yield the **Beverage Cost Percentage**. The overall cost percentage for both food and beverage is 32%; this is found by dividing Total Cost of Goods by Total Sales.

COST OF GOODS COST PERCENTAGE FORMULAS

Food Cost/Food Sales × 100 = Food Cost %

Beverage Cost/Beverage Sales × 100 = Beverage Cost %

Total Cost of Goods (COG)/Total Sales × 100 = Total COG %

What does the Food Cost % (Percentage), Beverage Cost % and the Total Cost of Goods % mean? These percentages represent the portion of a sales dollar that each consumes. For every one dollar in food sales, an average of 33.6 cents should be spent on raw food cost. When food and beverage sales are combined—for every one dollar in food and beverage sales, 32 cents is required for product cost alone. This is where it is critical to know portion costs and to control portion sizes for all menu items, including beverages. Remember recipe costing and portion sizes? Recipe costing and portion control are two of the most important cost control tools in a manager's cost control toolbox.

Let's simplify the income statement in Figure 10.2 and look closely at how the average sales dollar is spent at Farfalle Arrabbiata.

Sales	100%	$1.00
Total Cost of Goods	32%	.32
Total Controllable Expenses	48%	.48
Total Occupation Costs	14%	.14
Profit or Loss	6%	.06

This figure shows the **composition of costs** for Farfalle Arrabbiata. First, recognize that sales are always 100% on an income statement. All expenses are paid from this sum. The Total Cost of Goods percentage reports that it takes close to 1/3 of these sales dollars to cover just the food and beverage products needed to generate the sales. Another large chunk of the dollar (48%) goes to Controllable Expenses—this is almost half of all dollars taken in! These two categories of expenses, Total Cost of Goods and Controllable Expenses, consume 80% (32% + 48%) of all monies generated. The remaining category (Occupation Costs) is at 14%—a much smaller piece of the dollar. Last, Profit is 6%, or 6 cents of every dollar.

LET'S COUNT THE WAYS TO UNDERSTAND FOOD COST

1. Food cost and types of foodservice operations
2. Food cost as a part of the income statement
3. **Food cost as a piece of a "pie"**
4. Food cost as a daily percentage
5. Food cost as a monthly percentage
6. Variances in food cost
7. Managing unfavorable variances

$\mathcal{F}$ood Cost as a Piece of a "Pie"

Imagine that the income statement is like an apple pie. Think of the slices in the pie as representing the cost categories on the income statement. These costs can be thought of as "guests" invited for dessert. Some of the guests (costs) have sizeable appetites and will consume large slices of pie. Some of the guests (costs) will only want a small piece of the pie. And there is usually one little piece left over (profit), which is the slice of pie reserved for the host or hostess (owner). Anytime any cost "consumes" a little more of the pie than it is supposed to, the leftover piece (profit) gets squeezed and becomes smaller. The reverse is also true—any time a cost consumes a little less than it is supposed to, a little more pie will remain for the host or hostess in the form of more profit.

CATEGORIES ON AN INCOME STATEMENT

Sales: The whole pie ⟶ $$$$

Costs:
Food and Beverage Costs ⟶ Expense slices
Controllable Costs
Occupation Costs

Profit: What remains ⟶ The extra slice!

Figure 10.3 shows what the "cost pie" for Farfalle Arrabbiata looks like. Notice the size of each pie wedge. Visually, it is easy to see which expense categories are consuming most of the pie—Cost of Goods and Controllable Expenses.

What should be clear to you is that an awful lot of the pie is required to feed these two expense categories. If either were to "wiggle" just a little—in other words, consume more than their fair share of the sales dollars or "pie"—then Profit will be squeezed in order to pay expenses. Why is that? Remember that these two groups of expenses are **operating costs** and are *necessary for day-to-day operations*. Operating costs include supplier invoices for product, time cards for employees,

FIGURE 10.3 Cost "pie" for Farfalle Arrabbiata.

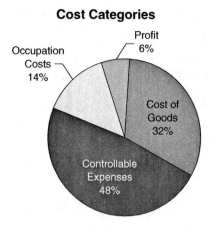

and the electric and gas bills—these bills have to be paid and kept current or the business cannot operate. Guests cannot be served without these expenses being incurred.

The Plan for Expenses

What does this picture show? What this pie chart shows is a picture of the profit that *should be available* if all expense categories behave as planned and actually come in at the levels identified by the cost percentages. This is *management's **plan** for expenses.* It is the *target that actual results are measured against and with which future budgets are planned.* Keep this sentence in mind as you read on.

Costs Over Budget

Watch what happens when the Cost of Goods section of the pie suddenly uses up more dollars (and thus more percentage) than budgeted for—say, 34% instead of 32%. What do you notice about the pie slices? What's going on with the Profit slice? With the Cost of Goods slice?

Check Figure 10.4. As the Cost of Goods piece expands, the profit piece shrinks. Because the profit slice is not very large to start with, any shrinking is cause for alarm. What's a manager to do? Rather, the question is: "Who's been eating too much of the pie." Or, *why is this cost out of line?*

FIGURE 10.4 New cost "pie" for Farfalle Arrabbiata.

Cost Categories

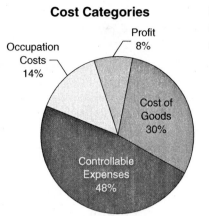

FIGURE 10.5   Another new cost "pie" for Farfalle Arrabbiata.

Costs Under Budget

Let's try applying the concept of changing pie slices the opposite way. Let's say that Cost of Goods is 30% rather than 32%. Figure 10.5 shows how the pie chart looks now.

Things are certainly looking better now. With Cost of Goods at 30% instead of 32%, profit rises to 8%. There's more "pie," or money in profit for the owners, and they certainly like that result! In spite of the fact that this might seem like a terrific outcome, a manager still questions why Cost of Goods is less than budget. Read on for a discussion of this topic.

The point of using pie charts and varying the Cost of Goods percentage is to show how important it is to control food cost. When an operation is **operating to budget**, *as long as all expense categories are within acceptable ranges of the standard and sales have hit their forecasted levels, the forecasted profit should be achieved.* Being **"on budget"** occurs *when sales and expenses behave as expected.* When "unexpected" cost behavior occurs, it is management's job to find the root cause and fix the problem. Watch for more on this topic in later chapters.

Laying all three pie charts side by side (Figure 10.6) makes it easy to see the effect that changes in Cost of Goods has on Profit. As the Cost of Goods slice wiggles up, Profit wiggles down. As Cost of Goods wiggles down, Profit wiggles up. This is an important concept to master. You will see more of this work in Chapter 18.

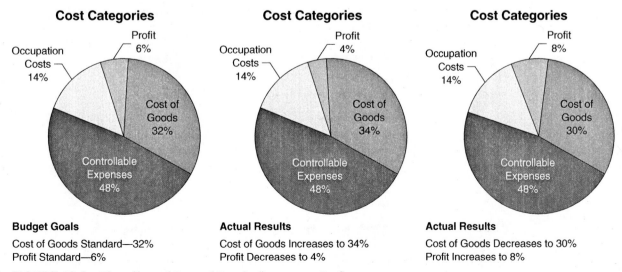

Budget Goals

Cost of Goods Standard—32%
Profit Standard—6%

Actual Results

Cost of Goods Increases to 34%
Profit Decreases to 4%

Actual Results

Cost of Goods Decreases to 30%
Profit Increases to 8%

FIGURE 10.6   The effect of Cost of Goods changes on Profit.

Food Cost as a Daily Percentage

The income statement is an important barometer of a foodservice operation's financial health. It is the tool that managers and chefs use to evaluate sales, expenses, and profit. Because these statements cover a specific time period, the information is not usually available until that period of time is over and the figures have been gathered. It is important that managers and chefs have more immediate (daily) knowledge of their food cost percentages than just at the close of an operating period. To facilitate this, a **Daily Food Cost Worksheet** can be prepared that *reports food cost percentage on a daily basis.* The Daily Food Cost Worksheet is easily completed in just a few minutes using basic cost and sales information readily available from paperwork that is commonly used. This report is useful because it indicates how food costs are running on a daily basis, which can than be compared to budget to get a sense of how the operation is performing financially. Because the worksheet *accumulates the cost, sales, and food cost percentage over a specific operating period*, it is essentially a **weighted average food cost percentage**.

Components of the Daily Food Cost Percentage

The components of a **daily food cost percentage** are simply *costs for the day* and *sales for the day,* which is the basic formula to calculate food cost percentage. The trick is in determining daily food cost dollars.

The formula for determining **daily food cost dollars** is simply Direct Purchases + Storeroom Requisitions + Transfers In (adjustments that increase cost) − Transfers Out (adjustments that decrease cost) = Cost of Food Today. We can get these values from a number of sources.

DETERMINING DAILY FOOD COST DOLLARS

DIRECT PURCHASES
+ STOREROOM REQUISITIONS
+ TRANSFERS IN (adjustments that increase cost)
− TRANSFERS OUT (adjustments that decrease cost)
= **COST OF FOOD TODAY**

Direct Purchases   The term *Direct Purchases* should sound familiar. In Chapter 7, **Direct Purchases** were defined as *"purchases that go directly into production."* It makes sense, then, to use this figure as a part of daily cost of goods. Recall that this figure was a part of the Receiving Report, so it is readily available.

Storeroom Requisitions   Requisitions are prepared, filled, and extended for specific dates, so this information is also readily available. Each day's requisitions are totaled for this entry. Meat or product tags (Chapter 7), if they are used, are included in this figure. Recall that requisitions were also covered in Chapter 7.

Transfers In (+)   Any cost estimate has to include transfers. Transfers are used to *document the movement of food from one department to the next.* The difference between a requisition and a transfer is that a **requisition** *is used to document and obtain products from storage areas,* whereas transfers keep track of products that have already been accounted for by a requisition or invoice. Because the formula we are using determines the daily cost of food, transfers here will be products requested from other departments that are needed to generate dining room sales.

A transfer provides a record that accurately tracks costs. For example, an initial cost occurs when the department (kitchen or bar) purchases products. After product is received by each respective department, it may be moved to a different department on an as-needed basis. In a foodservice operation, it is common practice for the kitchen and bar to swap regularly purchased products with one another: The kitchen may use wine or other alcohol-based products for menu items, and the bar commonly uses fruit and other items for drink garnishes and bar snacks. Generally, neither department purchases these items independently. Because each department has what the other needs, it makes sense to simply "swap" or transfer the needed items. The key here is to track the cost of the products that move between departments. Why? Each department has already been charged with these items (through invoices), but they were *not used to generate dining room sales for that department.* Instead, they were used to generate sales for another department. Each department adjusts its costs (increases and decreases) accordingly. Transfers are also used to track product between units or stores within the same geographic area. In this case, the same principle holds: Items purchased on invoice at one store but needed at another must be tracked and charged appropriately. Remember, any transfers into a department *increase costs* for that department, because *the products were used to generate dining room sales.*

Transfers Out (−)   A **transfer out** means that *another department has asked the kitchen for items needed for that departments' production.* A **transfer out** *allows the cost of these items to be subtracted from the cost for the day of the originating department.* Remember, any **transfer out** of a department *decreases costs* for that department, because *the products were not used to generate dining room sales.*

IMPACT OF TRANSFERS ON DEPARTMENTAL COST

- **Transfers In:** increase costs to the importing department and decrease costs for the exporting department.
- **Transfers Out:** decrease costs to the exporting department and increase costs for the importing department.

Figure 10.7 shows a **transfer form**, which looks mysteriously like a requisition. It *lists the departments involved in the switch and the items, quantity, unit price, and extensions for those items.* These forms make it easy to track information for the food cost worksheet.

Cost of Food Today and To Date

Do the math and the result is the **Food Cost Today**, in dollars. This is the *approximate amount of money that was spent to generate food sales today.* With this information, it

Dept.: (From) Kitchen				Charge To: Bar	
Date: 2/14/2XXX				Transfer Number: 1234	
Time: 10:00 A.M.				Priced By: Marcel	
Prepared By: DJF				Extended By: DJF	
Delivered By: Zach				Approved By: LEF	
Received By: Stacey					
	Rec.				
Item	✓	**Unit**	**Quantity**	**Price**	**Extension**
Mangoes	✓	each	25	$1.00 each	$25.00
Pineapples	✓	each	4	2.00 each	8.00
Peaches	✓	each	25	1.00 each	25.00
Lemons	✓	each	15	0.65 each	9.75
Total					**$67.75**

FIGURE 10.7   A transfer form.

is easy to calculate today's food cost percentage. Simply divide this cost by today's food sales (readily available from sales reports):

$$\frac{\text{COST OF FOOD TODAY}}{\text{FOOD SALES TODAY}} = \text{TODAY'S FOOD COST \%}$$

Look at Figure 10.8. It is an example of a Daily Food Cost Worksheet for an operation using storeroom requisitions. Notice the **Today** columns and **To Date** columns on the worksheet. For a Daily Food Cost Worksheet to be valuable to a manager, the information must be accumulated. These columns *accumulate the information over a period*

Date	A Dir. Pur.	B Store Reqs.	C (+) Trans. In	D (−) Trans. Out	E Food Cost Today	Food Cost to Date	Sales Today	Sales to Date	Food Cost % Today	Food Cost % to Date
2/2	$714	$1,965	$65	$42	$2,702 →	$2,702	$4,107	$4,107	65.79%	65.79%
2/3	757	1,210	0	8	1,959	4,661	4,118	8,225	47.57	56.66
2/4	406	1,906	0	15	2,297	6,958	5,370	13,595	42.27	51.18
2/5	462	1,738	0	0	2,200	9,158	5,015	18,610	43.86	49.21
2/6	616	1,970	33	19	2,600	11,758	7,198	25,808	36.12	45.55
2/7	115	1,059	0	36	1,138	12,896	7,496	33,304	15.18	38.72
2/8	0	0	25	0	25	12,921	4,855	38,159	.51	33.86

A + B + C − D = E

FIGURE 10.8   A Daily Food Cost Worksheet.

Food Cost Today	Sales Today	Food Cost % Today
$2,702	$4,107	65.79%
1,959	4,118	47.57
2,297	5,370	42.27
2,200	5,015	43.86
2,600	7,198	36.12
1,138	7,496	15.18
25	4,855	.51

FIGURE 10.9   A summary of daily food cost percentages 2/2 to 2/8.

of time. Figure 10.9 is the record of costs and sales for the first week of February at Farfalle Arrabbiata. Each week of the operating cycle (typically, the month) is entered. The second week's records would appear directly under the first week.

What the Daily Food Cost Worksheet Shows   It's easy to figure out Column D—just follow the letter formula A + B + C − D = E at the bottom of the chart. What Column E tells is the cost of the food *used today*. The **Food Cost to Date** is simply *an accumulation of the costs of one day added to the costs of the previous day.* Because Monday is the start of the cycle, Monday's costs are both the Today and To Date costs. To get Tuesday's accumulated cost, add Monday's cost to Tuesday's costs. By zig-zagging down the column, one can learn the total food cost dollars for the whole week. Note that the same zig-zagging method is used to accumulate the sales dollars.

Food Cost Percentage Today   To find the Food Cost Percentage Today, simply divide today's cost of food by today's sales. Do this for each day of the period:

$$\frac{\text{COST OF FOOD TODAY}}{\text{FOOD SALES TODAY}} = \text{FOOD COST \% TODAY}$$

Figure 10.9 summarizes the daily food cost percentage from the worksheet in Figure 10.8.

Food Cost Percentage To Date   To find **Food Cost Percentage To Date**, simply divide each day's *accumulated food cost by the accumulated food sales* (this is a **weighted average food cost percent**).

$$\frac{\text{COST OF FOOD TO DATE}}{\text{FOOD SALES TO DATE}} = \text{FOOD COST \% TO DATE}$$

Figure 10.10 summarizes the food cost percentage **to date**. The accumulated cost and sales information presented as a percentage tells an important part of the budget story for an operation. It is here that management looks to monitor the back-of-the-house for any cost "hot spots."

Notice how the food cost percentage changes as the food cost and food sales accumulate over the course of the week. Earlier in the chapter, the income statement identified the standard cost percentage for Farfalle Arrabbiata as 33.6%. This worksheet shows that when all costs and all sales for the week are added together, Farfalle Arrabbiata has, in fact, made budget. The difference between the budget (33.6%) and the actual result (33.86%) is not significant. We will talk about interpreting variances later in the chapter.

Food Cost to Date	Sales to Date	Food Cost % to Date
$2,702	$4,107	65.79%
4,661	8,225	34.28
6,958	13,595	51.18
9,158	18,610	49.21
11,758	25,808	45.55
12,896	33,304	38.72
12,921	38,159	33.86

FIGURE 10.10   Summary of to-date food cost percentages.

At the end of the month, all four weeks are reported on the same worksheet, so daily and to-date numbers provide an interesting snapshot of the fluctuations of the food cost percentage prior to the end-of-the-month reporting. Using a form such as this gives management an early "head's up" on food cost. When end-of-month reports are available, there should be no surprises about the food cost percentage. In fact, early information should lead to early intervention by management to correct any unacceptable food cost variances. The mantra of management should be "No surprises!"

Finding the Daily Food Cost Percentage Without Requisitions

Many operations do not use requisitions but still want to know their daily food cost percentage. In that case, all purchases for the day would be entered on the worksheet. The Receiver's Daily Report (Chapter 7) Sheet is the source of this information. All the day's purchases are entered under the Direct Purchases column. There would be no need for a Storeroom Requisition column, because this adjustment to the cost is not a part of the internal control system. The formula without requisitions would simply be Daily Purchases + Transfers In (adjustments that increase cost) – Transfers Out (adjustments that decrease cost) = Cost of Food Today.

DETERMINING DAILY FOOD COST DOLLARS

DAILY PURCHASES
+ STOREROOM REQUISITIONS
+ TRANSFERS IN (adjustments that increase cost)
– TRANSFERS OUT (adjustments that decrease cost)
= COST OF FOOD TODAY

Compiling a Daily Food Cost Worksheet Without Storeroom Requisitions
Figure 10.11 shows a **Daily Food Cost Worksheet** for *an operation that does not use storeroom requisitions*. Keep in mind the formula to calculate daily food cost dollars.

The same process used in the first example of a worksheet is used here to find the **Food Cost Percentage** Today. Simply divide the today cost by the today sales. The **Food Cost to Date** columns are also calculated exactly as in the previous example. Like with the previous example, all four weeks would be reported on the same worksheet.

Date	A Pur. Today	B (+) Trans. In	C (−) Trans. Out	D Food Cost Today	E Food Cost to Date	F Sales Today	G Sales to Date	D/F Food Cost % Today	E/G Food Cost % to Date
2/2	$2,679	$65	$42	$2,702 →	$2,702	$4,107	$4,107	65.79%	65.79%
2/3	1,967	0	8	1,959 →	4,661	4,118	8,225	47.57	56.66
2/4	2,312	0	15	2,297 →	6,958	5,370	13,595	42.27	51.18
2/5	2,200	0	0	2,200 →	9,158	5,015	18,610	43.86	49.21
2/6	2,586	33	19	2,600 →	11,758	7,198	25,808	36.12	45.55
2/7	1,174	0	36	1,138 →	12,896	7,496	33,304	15.18	38.72
2/8	0	25	0	25 →	12,921	4,855	38,159	.51	33.86
	A	+ B	− C	= D	E	F	G	D/F	E/G

FIGURE 10.11 Food Cost Worksheet (no requisitions used).

Compiling a Daily Food Cost Worksheet Using Requisitions and Other Adjustments

It is possible to sort daily food costs even further for closer monitoring by management. In Figure 10.12, a more detailed version of the Daily Food Cost Worksheet shows how to do this. Direct Purchases can be sorted into Produce, Dairy, and Baked purchases. If desired, Produce could be further subdivided into Fruits and Vegetables. Storeroom Requisitions can be subdivided into a number of common purchasing categories, such as meat, poultry, fish and shellfish, and groceries. Meats can be further broken down to beef, veal, lamb, pork, and so on, if that degree of detail is needed.

In operations with large inventories and high volume, this information can be useful for a variety of reasons. Remember the ABC system of inventory analysis in Chapter 8? A Daily Food Cost Worksheet organized in this way easily identifies where most of the purchasing dollars are spent. These categories are a good place to begin to analyze purchasing quantities, patterns, and management techniques for tight control. Let's review the Daily Food Cost dollars formula, from earlier in this chapter:

DETERMINING DAILY FOOD COST DOLLARS

　　　DIRECT PURCHASES

　　+ STOREROOM REQUISITIONS

　　+ TRANSFERS IN (adjustments that increase cost)

　　− TRANSFERS OUT (adjustments that decrease cost)

　= COST OF FOOD TODAY

Watch how Direct Purchases and Storeroom Requisitions are detailed out by product type in Figure 10.12. What is this all about? It's all about detailing costs. The form, although it appears complicated, is nothing more than the original worksheet with a few extra columns of added detail. The process to find **Total Direct Purchases** (Column D) and **Total Storeroom Requisitions** (Column J) is laid out at the bottom of the chart. Finding the **Cost of Food Today** (Column M) is a matter of adding **Total Direct Purchases** (Column D) and **Total Storeroom Requisitions** (Column J) and adjusting this amount for any **transfers** (Columns K and L). The To Date columns for both Food

Date	A Direct Pur. Produce	B Dairy	C Baked	D Total Dir. Pur.	E Storeroom Req. Meat	F Poultry	G Fish/Shell.	H Groc.	I Other	J Total Storeroom Req.	K Trans In. (+)	L Trans Out. (−)	M Cost of Food Today	N Cost of Food to Date	O Food Sales Today	P Food Sales to Date	M/O Food Cost % Today	N/P Food Cost % to Date
2/2	$382	$150	$182	$714	$964	$466	$267	$208	$60	$1965	$65	$42	$2,702	$2,702	$4,107	$4,107	65.79%	65.79%
2/3	289	322	146	757	456	128	354	166	106	1210	0	8	1,959	4,661	4,118	8,225	47.57	56.66
2/4	166	186	54	406	469	328	578	377	154	1906	0	15	2,297	6,958	5,370	13,595	42.27	51.18
2/5	179	197	86	462	636	402	488	112	100	1738	0	0	2,200	9,158	5,015	18,610	43.86	49.21
2/6	375	147	94	616	301	487	558	369	255	1970	33	19	2,600	11,758	7,198	25,808	36.12	45.55
2/7	58	0	57	115	246	357	267	189	0	1059	0	36	1,138	12,896	7,496	33,304	15.18	38.72
2/8	0	0	0	0	0	0	0	0	0	0	25	0	25	12,921	4,855	38,159	.51	33.86
	A +	B +	C =	D	E +	F +	G +	H +	I =	J	+ K −	L =	M	N	O	P	M/O	N/P

FIGURE 10.12 Daily Food Cost Worksheet with food categories, requisitions, and transfer adjustments.

Cost (Column N) and Food Sales (Column P) are found exactly as explained earlier (the zig-zag method). The food cost percentage (both Today and To Date) is also calculated exactly as in Figure 10.11.

Note that **Direct Purchases** information is readily available through the Receiver's Daily Report, as these are the *purchases today that are going directly into production*. Storeroom Requisitions are available for the information for the remaining columns. Sales information is easily ascertained from the POS system.

Differences Among Types of Food Cost Worksheets

Any version of the Daily Food Cost Worksheet will give valuable clues to management about how food cost is running. The primary difference among all three versions is the detail of the components within food cost. The first version uses *Daily Purchases and Storeroom Requisitions* to determine daily food cost. The second version uses *all purchases for a given day* to compute daily food cost. The third worksheet breaks down *direct purchases and storeroom requisitions into specific product categories to track all food used for a day*. Because all purchases today will obviously not all be used today, it seems like the first version of the Daily Food Cost Worksheet would not deliver very reliable information. Remember that good inventory management practices suggest that inventories "turn" approximately every 2 weeks (Chapter 8). By accumulating the data week to week for an operating period (month), this weakness is removed. Read on to learn more.

Other Shortcomings of the Daily Food Cost Percentage

What could be "wrong" with the Daily Food Cost Percentage, other than the composition of the actual food cost dollars used in the two versions of the worksheet? To answer this question, we need to examine the elements of daily food cost more closely:

- Look at the column headings and think about how a foodservice operation purchases products.
- Consider the typical sales pattern for a restaurant.

Put these two "ingredients" together, and it is clear to see that there are some potential shortcomings with the daily food cost percentage.

Purchasing Patterns

Most operations do not purchase every product every day. In fact, certain days of the week tend to be heavy receiving days and on others, no deliveries at all are received. Generally, purchases are high at the beginning of the week because inventory has been depleted over the busy weekend period. Purchases taper or are nonexistent at the end of the week because inventories have been built up in anticipation of week-end sales. Because of this **purchasing pattern**, the Direct Purchases entry on the worksheet will

- Be highest earlier in the week, when inventories are low and have to be replenished.
- Be lowest at the end of the week, when inventories have been replenished and purchases are low.
- Have a noticeable effect on the daily food cost percentage.

Sales Patterns

The same thing that happens with purchases happens with sales, except in reverse. The typical restaurant **sales pattern** is that the beginning of the week is slow, whereas the end of the week is very busy. Mix this pattern in with the purchasing pattern (heavy purchases at the beginning of the week and light or no purchases on weekends), and it is easy to see that there will be a tremendous fluctuation in food cost percentage on a daily basis. For this reason, a To Date column is used on all versions of the Daily Food Cost Worksheet.

The accumulating **To Date** column *flushes out the daily inconsistencies of the purchasing pattern and the sales pattern*. By the end of the first week of the operating period, the food cost percentage will start to smooth out because of the blending of the high cost/low sales and low cost/high sales phenomenon. After two weeks, the skews of the purchase and sales pattern have less of an impact on the accumulated food cost percentage. After three and four weeks, which is the end of the normal operating period, the daily cost should be very accurate. The To Date column is, in effect, a weighted average food cost percentage (all costs divided by all sales), which is the most accurate way to report food cost.

EFFECT OF SALES AND PURCHASING PATTERN ON FOOD COST PERCENTAGE

High Purchases + Low Sales = High Food Cost Percentage

Low Purchases + High Sales = Low Food Cost Percentage

One more thing: Management must also remember that the cost of employee meals is not reflected in the daily food cost percentage. It is possible to add this column into the Daily Food Cost Worksheet. Generally, though, adjusting for employee meals is done only at the end of the month. The next section will deal with this adjustment.

As long as management understands the implication of the typical purchase and sales patterns in a foodservice operation, the Daily Food Cost Worksheet is safe and reliable to use to track daily food cost percentage.

LET'S COUNT THE WAYS TO UNDERSTAND FOOD COST

1. Food cost and types of foodservice operations
2. Food cost as a part of the income statement
3. Food cost as a piece of a "pie"
4. Food cost as a daily percentage
5. Food cost as a monthly percentage
6. Variances in food cost
7. Managing unfavorable variances

Food Cost as a Monthly Percentage

The Monthly Food Cost Report

The only way to accurately identify the cost of food sold and the **actual food cost percentage** for the identified operating period is to prepare a Monthly Food Cost Report. The Monthly Food Cost Report indicates the *actual cost percentage of food used for all food sales for an identified period of time— usually a 4-week period or a month.* Opinions differ on how often a Food Cost Report should be prepared. Some managers believe that tabulating once a month is adequate. Others feel that once every two weeks is sufficient. Still others insist that any longer than a week is far too risky.

Preparing a Food Cost Report on a weekly basis provides for tight control of costs. This frequency allows comfortable control and leaves less room for any big surprises at the end of the operating period. Doing a weekly report allows management adequate time to react intelligently to fluctuating food costs. The problem with computing food cost percentages using the formula for the Food Cost Report, however, is the time needed to inventory and value product. Because this figure is an important part of the formula, a physical inventory has to be taken, then valued every week. In many instances, the staffing needed to take and value inventory weekly is not readily available. A Daily Food Cost Worksheet, together with a bi-weekly or monthly Food Cost Report, should provide adequate information to manage most foodservice operations.

The **Monthly Food Cost Report** is a tool used to *track food costs incurred to generate food sales for the month*. It can help determine why food costs fluctuate. The formula demonstrates the basic method of identifying the **Cost of Food Sold,** as well as the **food cost percentage** for the month or operating period.

Here is the formula to find the cost of food sold in a given month:

Adjustments that Increase Food Cost

$$
\left. \begin{array}{l} \text{Opening Inventory} \\ + \text{ Total Food Purchases for the Month} \\ + \text{ Transfers In} \end{array} \right\} \text{Debits}
$$

Cost of Food Available for Sale

Adjustments that Decrease Food Cost

$$
\left. \begin{array}{l} - \text{ Transfers Out} \\ - \text{ Steward Sales} \\ - \text{ Promotional/Complimentary Meals} \\ - \text{ Employee Meals} \\ - \text{ Closing Inventory} \end{array} \right\} \text{Credits}
$$

= Cost of the Food Used this Month to Generate
Dining Room Sales this Month

What's a Debit to the Cost of Food Available for Sale?   The three components on the plus side of the formula are adjustments that are considered debits. A **debit** is an accounting term used to *indicate an inflow into an account*. In this example, Opening Inventory, Total Food Purchases, and Transfers In are *inflows into the food cost this month*. The sum of these three elements—the **Cost of Food Available for Sale**—represents *all of the dollars spent on food this month*. The thing is, all of these "spent" dollars did not necessarily *generate dining room sales*. If we are to fairly evaluate the financial performance of an operation, the cost of food available for sale will have to be adjusted or credited for products purchased but not used to generate dining room sales.

As it stands right now, this figure represents *all dollars spent on food this month,* but not *all dollars spent to generate dining room sales this month.* There is a big difference between the two.

What's a Credit to the Cost of Food Available for Sale?   A **credit** is *an outflow from the food cost account.* In other words, a credit is *an adjustment to the cost of food available for sale for products purchased on invoice but not used to generate dining room sales.* These items came in through the receiving door. The invoices were paid for via normal invoice processing procedures, but the products were used for something other than dining room sales.

Here's the underlying question:

"How Much Money Was Spent to Generate Dining Room Sales This Month?"

Credit adjustments clean up the Cost of Food Available for Sale by crediting the food cost account. These adjustments *decrease the cost of food available for sale,* allowing management to determine just how much money was really spent to generate dining room sales. Once this is known, then the *adjusted cost can be divided by food sales for the month or operating period*. The result is the *food cost percentage for the month*.

Let's Review Debits or Adjustments That Increase Food Cost   The three debit adjustments are: Opening Inventory, Total Food Purchases, and Transfers In.

Opening Inventory   The Monthly Food Cost Report begins with the Opening Inventory, which is the value of the previous month's Closing Inventory. Every Closing Inventory becomes the Opening Inventory for the following period, because this product is still on the shelves and in the refrigerators the first day of the new operating period. (It was not used before the new month began.) It's easy to see how important it is to be sure the inventory figure is accurate. Remember Chapter 8 discussions about taking inventory? Look at where this figure is used:

- It is used first as the Opening Inventory. This is the value of the product that was not used from the previous month.
- A second inventory figure pops up as a credit. The Ending Inventory figure is the value of the inventory taken at the end of the current operating period.

So the inventory values—albeit different values for different times of the operating period—are used twice in this formula. This is the primary reason to train employees to take an accurate inventory and to be sure all product, open or otherwise, is accurately counted (see Chapter 8).

Total Food Purchases   **Total Food Purchases** represents *all of the food items purchased this month*. Purchases are easily tracked using the Invoice Payment Schedule or the Receiver's Daily Report, if one is used. (See Chapter 7 for a review of these forms.) This amount is added to the opening inventory, because it was available for sale during the month. Careful attention must be given to the Invoice Payment Schedule because only the value of the products that have been used in production and counted as inventory should be included. The schedule should be scrutinized to be sure products to be used in the next operating period are not charged to this month's cost. Products that have not been used or counted as inventory will be listed on the following period's payment schedule. Their value will count toward the next month's food cost.

Remember those **transfers** from earlier in the chapter—specifically the **Transfers In**? It makes sense to include the value of all the Transfers In for the month, as this product was used to generate dining room sales. Transfers can be interdepartmental or from store to store. Remember, a **transfer in** always *increases cost*. There may be other adjustments in this category that are specific to operations. The most important thing to remember is that all costs incurred to generate dining room sales must be accounted for in this debit section.

Let's Review Credits or Adjustments that Decrease Food Cost, Because They Did Not Generate Dining Room Sales   Essentially, any entries listed here are costs incurred to the business that did not generate dining room sales. These items were paid for on an invoice during the normal purchasing activities for the month, but they were not used to generate dining room sales. The goal of these adjustments is to refine the Cost of Food Available for Sale to a figure that is truly representative of the actual costs to generate dining room sales.

The primary items most commonly used as credits in the formula are Transfers Out, Steward Sales, Promotional/Complimentary Meals, Employee Meals, and Closing Inventory. Some operations may have additional adjustments specific to that business.

Transfers Out Because this product (and subsequent cost) never made it to a diner's plate, the value of it had best be removed from the Food Available for Sale. This is product sent to another department or store via a Transfer slip. These items have been received on invoices currently included in the Purchases charges.

Steward Sales **Steward sales** represent food *sold to an employee, manager, or owner at cost.* This practice is not standard in the industry and is a function of institutional policy. Like items in the Transfer category, these products were purchased on invoices processed through the accounting office and are currently included in the Purchases charges. Because these items never made it to a diner's plate, their value must be removed from the Food Available for Sale.

Promotional/Complimentary Meals **Promotional (promo)/complimentary (comp) meals** *are those meals given away by the owner/manager for various reasons:*

- For the entertainment of friends or professional associates
- To accommodate a dissatisfied customer
- As a promotional gift certificate

Because the dining room will receive no sales value for these items, their cost must also be removed from the food cost for the month. Remember that when all is said and done, food cost is divided by food sales. No food sale? Then remove the cost!

Employee Meals An employee meal credit is the amount charged for employee meals. It is usually taken from the payroll register, which identifies the days of the week and number of hours worked by each employee, together with the amount charged per day for each employee meal. This food, too, was received on invoice and is included in the Purchases section of the Debits. The food was never served in the dining room, though, so remove it from food cost. The value of these meals is accumulated for the operating period. The total is used in the Cost of Goods formula under Employee Meals.

NO. OF EMPLOYEE MEALS SERVED × AMOUNT PER DAY = EMPLOYEE MEAL
CREDIT

Some operations may allow staff to order a limited selection of meals from the dining room menu. A guest check is used to record the sales value. At the end of the period, the sales value for all the employee meal "purchases" is multiplied by the standard food cost percentage, to get the meal credit.

SALES VALUE OF EMPLOYEE MEALS × FOOD COST % = EMPLOYEE MEAL CREDIT

Facilities large enough to feed employees via an employee cafeteria track the cost of food with separate requisitions or invoices.

Closing Inventory The **closing inventory** is *the dollar value of the inventory taken the last day of the operating period.* All standard operating procedures concerning taking and valuing inventory discussed in Chapter 8 should be in place. Errors in the inventory count or valuing translates into an error in the cost of food sold this month, which then translates to an inaccurate food cost percentage.

Cost of Food Used this Month to Generate Dining Room Sales this Month The **cost of food sold** this month is calculated by *subtracting the credit total from the debit total.* The result is, hopefully, the *true cost of the food used to generate dining room sales for this operating period.* This adjusted figure is used to compute monthly food cost percentages and analyze financial performance.

Finding the Actual Monthly Food Cost Percentage

The Triangle of Enlightenment taught us that finding a cost percentage for any expense is simply cost divided by sales. With this in mind, the computation for the monthly food cost percentage is monthly food cost divided by monthly food sales. The food cost is determined using the formula found on page 315. The food sales records are found on the Daily Sales Report (see Chapter 11). Both components—food cost and food sales—are used to calculate the monthly food cost percentage: Total Cost of Food this Month/Total Food Sales this Month = Actual Food Cost % this Month.

TO CALCULATE MONTHLY FOOD COST PERCENTAGE

$$\frac{\text{Total Cost of Food this Month}}{\text{Total Food Sales this Month}} = \text{Actual Food Cost \% this Month}$$

Departmental Food Cost Reports

The **Departmental Food Cost Report** functions in the same way as the Monthly Food Cost Report. The only difference is that it *focuses on a specific department within a foodservice operation that has more than one revenue center.* The goal is to arrive at an accurate Cost of Food Sold and food cost percentage for the department. The importance of departmentalizing is to be able to determine the actual costs for each department. This allows the manager maximum financial control for each department. It removes the possibility of a problem going undetected in a department.

The formula for a Departmental Food Cost Report looks like this:

Adjustments that Increase Food Cost

    Opening Inventory
+ Total Food Requisitions for the Month
+ Kitchen In-Process Production   } Debits
+ Transfers In

Cost of Food Available for Sale

Adjustments that Decrease Food Cost

− Transfers Out
− Steward Sales
− Promotional/Comp Meals } Credits
− Employee Meals
− Closing Inventory

= Cost of the Food Used this Month to Generate Dining Room Sales this Month

What's different? Notice that **requisitions** replace purchases in the debit column. Operations with multiple revenue centers most likely use a centralized purchasing program, so requisitions are the standard tool used by departments to procure goods. In the event a department did some invoice purchasing along with requisitions, Purchases would be included in the adjustments.

What else is different? **In-process inventory** is *the value of the product in process on the last day of the operating period.* It is important to capture the value of this food and include it in the monthly cost of goods.

The remaining adjustments—credits—are exactly as described earlier. Any adjustment not in use at the departmental level would logically be eliminated. Then, the departmental food cost percentage is calculated by dividing departmental food cost for the month by departmental food sales for the month.

When food cost percentages are calculated with the aid of an integrated computer system, the program will often allow for a detailed breakout of specific food cost percentages by different departments. In an integrated computer system, the software and hardware are combined so that an accounting program will include traditional account reports, point-of-sale information, and various types of managerial accounting reports using one or more computer terminals.

TO CALCULATE MONTHLY FOOD COST PERCENTAGE BY DEPARTMENT

$$\frac{\text{Total Departmental Cost of Food this Month}}{\text{Total Departmental Sales this Month}} = \text{Dept. Food Cost \% this Month}$$

LET'S COUNT THE WAYS TO UNDERSTAND FOOD COST

1. Food cost and types of foodservice operations
2. Food cost as a part of the income statement
3. Food cost as a piece of a "pie"
4. Food cost as a daily percentage
5. Food cost as a monthly percentage
6. **Variances in food cost**
7. Managing unfavorable variances

$\mathcal{V}$ariances in Food Cost

What happens after the food cost percentage is calculated? Is it time for coffee after all that work? Hardly! This percentage is then compared to budgeted food cost percentage. *The difference between the budgeted percentage and the actual percentage* is called a variance. Think of a **variance** as *a deviation from a standard.* It is the responsibility of management to

- Determine whether variances between the budgeted food cost percentage and the actual food cost percentage are acceptable or unacceptable.
- Track down reasons for unacceptable variances. Find out WHY!
- Fix the problem. Then go have coffee!

Acceptable variances *indicate that the difference between budget and actual is insignificant*—it's not enough to worry about. Each operation sets the amount of variance that is considered acceptable. The amount is in percentage points. *Variances exceeding this standard—* **unacceptable variances**—call for immediate analysis and action.

When unacceptable variances are identified, management is charged with pinpointing the problem area and "fixing" it. The next section—Managing Unfavorable Variances—covers strategies for correcting unacceptable variances.

The following table is part of the income statement we reviewed earlier in the chapter.

February 2XXX	Budget		February Actual	
Sales	$$	%	$$	%
Food	$140,743	80.00%	$147,614	82.54%
Beverage	35,186	20.00	31,234	17.46
Total Revenue	175,929	100.00	178,848	100.00
Cost of Sales				
Food Cost	47,290	33.60	49,997	33.87
Beverage Cost	9,011	25.61	8,223	26.32
Total Cost of Goods	56,301	32.00	58,220	32.55

The first set of values is February's budget figures for Farfalle Arrabbiata. The second set is the actual figures, as per the Monthly Food Cost Report in Figure 10.13. The standard amount of acceptable variance for controllable expenses at Farfalle Arrabbiata is .5 %. What does this mean? It means that Chef Raoul can be +/− .5% on the food, beverage, and total cost of goods percentages. It is his margin of error. Take a look at the **actual food cost percentage**. Compare it to the **budgeted food cost percentage**. How did the food cost percentage turn out? Do the same for the beverage cost percentage. What do you see? And Total Cost of Goods? Are the variances favorable or unfavorable, or are the results mixed?

Armed with this information, Chef Raoul and the other managers will be getting together pretty quickly to discuss what happened. This method of comparing budgeted to actual will be continued in Chapter 18. Read on to learn what to do next.

Monthly Food Cost Report for Farfalle Arrabbiata		
Period Ending: February 2XXX		
Debits		
Opening Inventory	$17,964	
+ Purchases	54,018	
+ Transfers In	411	
Cost of Food Available for Sale		**$72,393**
Credits		
Transfers Out	$ 697	
Steward Sales	86	
Promo/Comp Meals	374	
Employee Meals	3,360	
Closing Inventory	17,879	
Cost of Adjustments		**−$22,396**
Cost of Food Sold this Month		**$ 49,997**
Total Food Sales		**$147,614**
Actual Food Cost %		**33.87%**
Prepared By:_____	**Date:**_____	

FIGURE 10.13   A Monthly Food Cost Report.

LET'S COUNT THE WAYS TO UNDERSTAND FOOD COST

1. Food cost and types of foodservice operations
2. Food cost as a part of the income statement
3. Food cost as a piece of a "pie"
4. Food cost as a daily percentage
5. Food cost as a monthly percentage
6. Variances in food cost
7. **Managing unfavorable variances**

Managing Unfavorable Variances

The "fun" part of managing a foodservice operation comes with interpreting information from reports and strategizing how to "fix" problems. Go back to Chapter 1. Let's use the control procedure as a model to assist with the "fixing" part of every manager's job. As a refresher, the control model is replicated in Figure 10.14.

Management Control Procedures

1. Set standards.
2. Measure performance.
3. Determine whether standards have been met.
4. Take corrective action.
5. Recycle through the process.

FIGURE 10.14   Management control procedure.

This looks familiar. In fact, all the steps in the box "Let's Count the Ways to Understand Food Cost" follow this procedural outline.

Management Control Procedure

Let's follow the Ways to Understand Food Cost and see how those steps correlate with the management control procedure we just discussed.

1. Set Standards   The first three Ways to Understand Food Cost address common standards for types of foodservice businesses and standard costs. They are:

- Food cost and types of foodservice operations
- Food cost as a part of the income statement
- Food cost as a piece of a "pie"

2. Measure Performance   Ways 4 and 5 address this point:

- Food cost as a daily percentage
- Food cost as a monthly percentage

Finding daily and monthly food cost percentages are tools used by managers to track business performance.

3. Determine Whether Standards Have Been Met   Ways to Understand Food Costs 2, 3, and 6 all address this concept:

- Food cost as a part of the income statement
- Food cost as a piece of a "pie"
- Variances in food cost

Comparing budget figures to actual results is at the heart of a manager's job. Timely accurate data is critical to moving to the next step—corrective action.

4. Take Corrective Action**   **YOU ARE HERE! You are about to learn *how to take corrective action to manage unfavorable variances.* Here is the Way to Understand Food Cost Point 7 that you will be considering:

- Managing unfavorable variances

5. Recycle Through the Process   As each operating period comes to a close, the process automatically continues. Reports are completed. Managers review and analyze the information. They determine corrective action and strategies as needed. Recycling is just a natural part of the cycle.

There is one *important question* that must be answered so a manager knows where to direct his or her attention and subsequent actions:

*Is this Variance the Result of Something **Within** the Manager's Direct Control or **Outside** the Manager's Direct Control?*

Variances Within the Control of Management

Variances identified as within a manager's control means that *there is a (are) problem(s) within the four walls of the operation.* To find it, look at the elements in the steps of the Cycle of Control. One or more of these steps is *out of control.*

A problem within management's control is "fixable" by either:

- Enforcing an existing standard or standard operating procedure that has been overlooked.
- Creating a new standard or standard operating procedure to address the problem. Something is missing within the existing system.

The most common causes of increasing or fluctuating food costs can usually be attributed to one or more of the following circumstances:

1. *Staff is not using standardized recipes.* Nothing more needs to be said here. See Chapter 3.
2. *Staff is not serving identified standard portion size.* Need more be said here? See Chapter 3.
3. *Employees lack training in standard operating procedures.* Poorly trained employees may make costly errors in just about every area of an operation. This can easily wreak havoc on food cost.
4. *Staff practice poor receiving, issuing, and storing procedures.* Control of product once in-house is a critical part of the Operating Cycle of Control.
5. *Products or cash from sales is stolen.* Foodservice operations are always vulnerable to theft by employees, unscrupulous delivery people, and sometimes even customers.
6. *Product spoils or is wasted.* If any food items spoil or are not fresh because of improper handling or incorrect product rotation, they cannot be served to the customer. Some food items are only partially used, then thrown away. All of these things add to the cost of food.
7. *Owner or manager is on vacation or on sick leave.* The owner/manager usually is the person supervising the operation to ensure that people are trained, that theft does not occur, and that portions are what they should be, and so on. If the owner or manager is not present in the operation, this function goes unattended, which means that costs could increase.

8. *Mathematical mistakes or incorrect counts on inventory are made.* Arithmetic errors may dramatically increase or decrease the reported cost.

9. *Products are issued without requisitions or transfers.* This means that items are taken from inventory or the kitchen without being recorded as being taken. The Food Cost Report would then indicate that there is more in inventory than really exists.

10. *Invoices are not recorded on the Invoice Payment Schedule.* This means that there is less food recorded as being purchased than was actually purchased.

11. *Employee meal credits, promotional or other free meals, or steward sales are not being properly recorded.* All these items cost money. If they are not recorded, the Food Cost Report will not indicate all the food costs of the operation.

12. *Menu mix is out of balance.* The menu mix is the number of each menu item sold in relationship to the other items sold. If recipes are followed and suppliers' prices are constant, each menu item has a fixed cost for its ingredients. Some menu items cost more than other items. If more of the expensive menu items are sold, the food cost would increase more than was expected.

Positive Variances (One or More Expenses Came in Under Budget)   Popular thought would say that a good manager is one who can produce actual food cost percentages that are less than the budgeted food cost percentages. In fact, how could this situation not be great? To answer this, think about what a standard food cost percentage means:

- It means that this dedicated percentage of sales is needed to buy a very specific level of quality and quantity of food to produce menu items meeting organizational standards and customer expectations.

Standard food cost percentage is a standard—a measure of excellence. It was not picked out of a hat. It is not something made of some whim or fancy. It has been carefully chosen as *the correct proportion of sales needed to meet standards for quality identified by management.* With this in mind, there are good reasons and bad reasons for being under budget. So, even positive expense variances must be looked at from a budget standpoint.

Positive Reasons for Positive Variances	Negative Reasons for Positive Variances
• Improvements in overall adherence to standard operating procedures • Better AP pricing through product research • Better AP pricing through supplier research • Purchasing alternative products at lower AP prices that decrease portion costs • Reviewing recipes for ingredient changes that decrease cost but do not negatively affect taste and appearance • Implementing new standard operating procedures that decrease costs • Improved control in purchasing, receiving, storing, issuing, and kitchen production that decrease overall operating costs	• Purchasing products of lower quality • Decreasing portion size • Buying from suppliers who cannot meet standards • Substituting inferior products in recipes • Manipulating recipes to reduce food cost. The change negatively affects product taste and appearance • Removing standard operating procedures or controls

These are just a few good and bad reasons an operation might see a positive variance in food cost.

- If the reasons for the variance are good ones, then the standard itself—the budgeted food cost percentage—should be permanently changed. It then becomes the new operating goal for the operation.
- If the reasons for the variance are negative, then negative outcomes may ultimately overtake the initially positive result. These kinds of short-sighted strategies ultimately affect guest satisfaction. Over time, sales will most likely be affected and food cost will eventually rise. Alienating customers for these poor reasons is never a sign of good management.

What's a manager to do? Avoid the easy way out. Anyone can improve their immediate cost picture by purchasing products of lower quality and decreasing portions sizes. Avoid this quick-fix mentality. Instead, make permanent improvements to cost percentages by implementing better operating controls. The effect on the bottom line will then be permanent.

Variances Outside the Direct Control of Management

If the variance is deemed outside of management's direct control, a different tactic is needed. Operational procedures are working properly, but something external to the four walls of the operation is causing the cost overrun. As a professional sleuth, it is management's job to be aware of external environmental changes that could impact business. Look at Chapter 1 for a discussion of these external environments.

A problem outside of management's control should be dealt with in several ways:

- By analyzing the problem as to impact, duration of impact, and permanence of the impact.
- By formulating strategies—in the long and short term—to deal with the problem.
- Continuous monitoring of the situation.

The following are four of the most common external situations that can affect food cost:

1. **Product cost increases.** Suppliers may increase prices because of shifts in market conditions. This means that total costs of food preparation will also increase. Although these changes are outside a manager's control, he or she should not be blindsided by a sharp change in product cost. Research of product cost and market conditions is a part of a manager's job.
2. **Changes in government regulations.** Federal, state, and local governments require compliance with certain laws that govern the foodservice industry. Staying current with changes and their potential impact on expenses and profit is critical.
3. **Changes in local market conditions.** This includes business and competitor's openings, closings or expansions, demographics, tourism efforts or lack of them, competitors' marketing strategies, and construction projects.
4. **National, regional, and local economic conditions.** Labor strikes, energy costs, weather events, and so on—all these have the potential to affect supply and distribution systems and thus product cost.

Identifying unfavorable variances and taking the proper corrective action to "right the ship" is a critical part of a manager's job. Expertise can be gained through

- Experience in the industry.
- Strategic career changes.
- Involvement in professional associations.

- Interactions with other industry professionals.
- Attention to professional development.

These are all strategies that build the knowledge and confidence to successfully manage both internal and external business challenges.

_Net Work

Explore the following Web sites:

www.restaurant.org

www.restaurantowner.com

Chapter Wrap

The Chapter ✓ at the beginning of the chapter posed several questions. Review the questions and compare your responses with the following answers:

1. **What is food cost and food cost percentage?**

   Simply stated, food cost is the actual cost of purchasing the raw food products and related ingredients that were used to generate dining room sales. Food cost is measured for specific periods (daily, weekly, monthly, annually) and it is always expressed in terms of a percentage, which is referred to as the food cost percentage. This percentage is an important indicator to an owner, a manager, and the chef.

2. **What are all the ways to understand food cost and food cost percentage?**

   For most students, two of the most difficult concepts to grasp are food cost and food cost percentage. However, understanding these two concepts is critical to the success of a foodservice operation. Some of the "misunderstandings" concerning food cost and food cost percentage have their roots in the following questions:

   1. Where does the food cost percentage come from?
   2. Who makes it up?
   3. How do you know it's right?
   4. How often do you need to check it?
   5. Is it a reliable measure?
   6. What does it mean if it's too high?
   7. What does it mean if it's too low?
   8. What do managers do with the information once they have it?

   All these questions are at the heart of understanding food cost. These questions can easily be answered by understanding food cost and food cost percentage as a function of the type of foodservice operation, as a piece of a pie, as a daily and monthly cost percentage, and through variances identified by income statements.

3. **What is a variance?**

   The difference between the budgeted percentage and the actual percentage is called a variance. A variance is a deviation from a standard. Management determines what the acceptable degree of variance is for an operation.

4. How are unfavorable variances managed?

When variances are acceptable, it means that the difference between budget and actual is insignificant—it's not enough to worry about. Each operation sets the amount of variance that is considered acceptable. The amount is in percentage points. Variances exceeding this standard call for immediate analysis and action.

When unacceptable variances are identified, management is charged with pinpointing the problem area and "fixing" it. Strategies for correcting unacceptable variances begin with identifying whether the variance can be attributed to operational issues or to external factors.

*K*ey Terminology and Concepts in This Chapter

Acceptable variances
Actual food cost percentage
Beverage Cost Percentage
Beverage sales
Budget
Budgeted food cost percentage
Closing inventory
Controllable Expenses
Cost of Food Available for Sale
Cost of Food Sold
Cost of Sales
Credit
Credit adjustments
Daily food cost dollars
Daily food cost percentage
Daily Food Cost Worksheet
Debit
Departmental Food Cost Report
Direct Purchases
Fixed costs
Food cost
Food cost percentage
Food Cost to Date
Food Cost Today

Food sales
Income
Income statement
In-process inventory
Nonoperating costs
Occupation Costs
Operating costs
Profit and Loss Statement (P&L)
Promotional (promo)/complimentary
   (comp) meals
Purchasing pattern
Quick service or fast casual
Requisition
Revenue
Sales
Sales pattern
Steward sales
Target food cost percentage
Total Food Purchases
Transfers
Variables
Variance
Weighted average food cost percentage

*D*iscussion Questions and Exercises

1. Thinking about the business variables of food and beverage cost, labor cost, guest check average, and sales volume, what would happen to the financial picture of a quick-service operation if sales volume drops? Using the variables, describe how you could solve the problem.

2. What would happen to a fine dining operation if sales volume increases? How is it possible that this increase could result in a decrease in profit? Answer using the business variables from Question 1.

3. Find the cost composition for the month of March for Farfalle Arrabbiata by filling in the cost percentages for each dollar value in the following table. Do not round cost percentages. Leave two places after the decimal.

	March		February	
Sales	$$	%	$$	%
Food	$129,457	80%	$140,743	80%
Beverage	32,364	20	35,186	20
Total Revenue	161,821	100	175,929	100
Cost of Goods				
Food Cost	43,782	33.82	47,290	33.6
Beverage Cost	8,156	25.20	9,011	25.61
Total Cost of Goods	51,938	32.10	56,301	32
Controllable Expenses	77,026	47.60	84,446	48
Occupation Costs	24,631	15.22	24,631	14
Profit/Loss	8226	5.08	10,551	6

4. Create a pie chart of the cost composition for February and March from the table shown in Question 3. How does March's picture compare to the picture of February's sales and expenses?

5. Compare February and March's cost and profit percentages. Assume that February's percentages represent the financial targets for Farfalle Arrabbiata. What has to happen to the pie wedges to get back in line?

6. Using the Operating Cycle of Control at the front of the chapter, prepare a checklist of immediate areas to monitor for compliance with standards and standard operating procedures. Your checklist should include pre- and post-purchasing functions and all back-of-house procedures.

7. Complete the Daily Food Cost Worksheet on the next page (Figure 10.15) for the week of 2/9 through 2/15 for Farfalle Arrabbiata.

8. Top management (the owners!) of Farfalle Arrabbiata are reviewing cost and sales information contained in last week's Food Cost Report and the one completed in Question 7. They are confused as to what the report really means. In fact, they sent you a frenzied email late last night. Remember that the targeted food cost % is 33.6%.

    a. Write a memo explaining how the reports work, their strengths and weaknesses, and the impact of cost and sales patterns on the results for the first two weeks of February.

    b. In your memo, explain why you, as manager, are worried or not worried (depending on your interpretation) about the picture presented for February.

    c. If you are worried, be sure to include strategies you plan to take to monitor the situation.

Date	Dir. Pur.	Store Reqs.	(+) Trans. In	(−) Trans. Out.	Food Cost Today	Food Cost to Date	Sales Today	Sales to Date	Food Cost % Today	Food Cost % to Date
2/2	$714	$1,965	$65	$42	$2,702 —	→$2,702	$4,107	$4,107	65.79%	65.79%
2/3	757	1,210	0	8	1,959	→ 4,661	4,118	8,225	47.57	56.66
2/4	406	1,906	0	15	2,297	→ 6,958	5,370	13,595	42.27	51.18
2/5	462	1,738	0	0	2,200	→ 9,158	5,015	18,610	43.86	49.21
2/6	616	1,970	33	19	2,600	→11,758	7,198	25,808	36.12	45.55
2/7	115	1,059	0	36	1,138	→12,896	7,496	33,304	15.18	38.72
2/8	0	0	25	0	25	→12,921	4,855	38,159	.51	33.86

Date	Dir. Pur.	Store Reqs.	(+) Trans. In	(−) Trans. Out	Food Cost Today	Food Cost to Date	Sales Today	Sales to Date	Food Cost % Today	Food Cost % to Date
2/9	$850	$2,100	$95	$40			$4,823			
2/10	865	1,350	0	22			4,470			
2/11	450	2,050	50	20			5,760			
2/12	475	1,721	40	30			5,576			
2/13	650	1,985	49	10			7,325			
2/14	100	1,192	0	36			7,996			
2/15	0	0	19	0			4,992			

FIGURE 10.15   Daily Food Cost Worksheet for Farfalle Arrabbiata, 2/2 through 2/15.

9. Complete the Monthly Food Cost Report shown here.

Monthly Food Cost Report for Farfalle Arrabbiata

Period Ending: February 2XXX

Debits

Opening Inventory	$17,964
+ Purchases	$65,136
+ Transfers In	695

Cost of Food Available for Sale

Credits

Transfers Out	$625
Steward Sales	110
Promo/Comp Meals	294
Employee Meals	3,127
Closing Inventory	19,471

Cost of Adjustments

Cost of Food Sold this Month
Total Food Sales $175,929
Actual Food Cost %

Prepared By:_____   Date:_____

The standard food cost percent for Farfalle Arrabbiata is 33.6%. The actual food cost percentage is _____ (fill in). At Farfalle Arrabbiata, +/− .5% is considered the acceptable degree of variance from standard. How did the restaurant fare this month?

10. How should Marcel, Chef Raoul, and the other managers use the paperwork system to avoid finding out about food cost problems after the fact? Explain how this paperwork system should be used by Marcel, Chef Raoul and other managers to routinely monitor food costs during the month.

11. The owners are anxious to fix the food cost problem. They suggest purchasing all meats, seafood, and poultry items from the Fly by Night Foodservice Company (in business for 6 months). The Fly by Night Company has quoted some pretty nice prices for these products. You know how it is with new start-up businesses—their pricing is always great. The owners have also been doing a little brainstorming and came up with the idea of decreasing portion sizes and substituting some lower-quality ingredients into some menu items. Mr. Fly by Night is suggesting food cost could go down by as much as 3% to 4%.

    a. Explain why these ideas are bad ones.

    b. Explain how this strategy could backfire.

    c. Using the Operating Cycle of Control, bullet all the potential problems from the start of the cycle to kitchen production.

12. Against your recommendation, the owners decide to go with the Fly by Night Foodservice Company and implement the ideas they had brainstormed about last week. At the end of the next week, the food cost percentage is down to 30.4%, a positive variance. And there they are, celebrating at the bar for being such great managers! Convince them with sound cost control reasons and explanations that this is probably a short-lived result. It is your job to convince them that there are better ways to fix the problem. Use specific examples in your arguments.

## Chapter Eleven

About Monitoring Sales

Learning Objectives

After reading this chapter and completing the discussion questions and exercises you should be able to:

1. Employ standard operating procedures to document cash and credit sales.
2. Complete a Cash Turn-In Report.
3. Reconcile guest check information by completing a Daily Sales Report.
4. Evaluate a Daily Sales Report.
5. Properly complete a guest check.
6. Apply standard guest check control procedures by using a Guest Check Daily Record.

The Menu

Pre-Purchase Functions

STANDARDIZED RECIPES
Standard ingredients, portion size, quality, consistency, quantity, purchasing

GUEST CHECK
Sales history, turnover, average check, **cash management**, revenue forecasting & budgeting, menu item analysis

COST CARDS
Portion costs, yield factors, sell prices

GUESTS
Greeting, seating, **sales**, serving, busing, **payment**, comment cards

SPECIFICATIONS
Product descriptions

FOH Functions

PAR STOCK
Inventory levels, order building

KITCHEN PRODUCTION
Production schedules, portion tracking, recipe control, serving controls, food safety

REQUISITION
Order building, purchasing

PRODUCT ISSUING
Requisitions, transfers, daily & monthly costs, food cost percentage

SHOPPING LISTS
Call sheets, bid sheets, suppliers, bidding

STORAGE PRACTICES & INVENTORY MANAGEMENT
Best practices, sanitation, security, inventory methods

PURCHASE ORDERS
Security, ship order, price guarantee, contract

INVOICE MANAGEMENT
Payment, price checking, security

BOH Functions

RECEIVING ACTIVITIES
Best practices, invoices, security, sanitation

Chapter Map

About Monitoring the Sales Process

Introduction to Sales, Cash, & Credit Card Control

- Cashier Control
- Completing the Cash Turn-In Report
- Completing the Cashier's Report

Chapter Map   (Continued)

- Accepting Cash
- Accepting Checks
- Accepting Traveler's Checks
- Accepting Credit & Debit Cards

Daily Sales Control

Introduction to Guest Service Accounting
- Guest Checks
- Guest Service Accounting Cycle

Taking the Guest's Order
- Completing a Guest Check
- Placing an Order with the Kitchen

Controlling Customer Guest Checks
- Guest Check Daily Record
- Guest Check Control System
- Balancing and the Cycle of Guest Service Accounting

Special Controls for Beverage Service

Chapter ✓

Check the chapter content for the answers to these questions:

1. How is cash controlled in a foodservice operation?
2. What reports do managers use to control cash?
3. What is guest service accounting?
4. What procedures are used to control guest checks?

About Monitoring the Sales Process

The foodservice business is like every other business when it comes to recording sales, correctly handling cash, recording credit and debit card transactions, and maintaining control of the process that documents customer orders (guest checks).

"Selling" in today's business climate covers everything from food and beverage items to packaged signature restaurant products to retail items, such as coffee mugs, T-shirts, and other memorabilia. Recording the sales and ensuring that all the money goes to the right place are separate functions. These tasks can all be accomplished through a few quick and easy steps that should be performed as a simple business routine. An established procedure provides a comfort level of accountability for the employees handling all the different payment transactions. Once employees are trained to the level of management's expectations, they can perform their tasks correctly and with confidence.

Foodservice operations range in size from small beverage carts to multiunit operations. Whatever the size of the establishment, cash, credit, and debit handling should not be left to chance. Procedures and accountability eliminate errors and temptation that may lead to theft.

Introduction to Sales, Cash, and Credit Card Control

Sales are *the dollar amount of food and beverage items sold in a given period of time.* Cash and credit card transactions must be tightly controlled and documented through the use of appropriate control procedures. A **Cashier's Report** is used to

- Control cash and credit card charges.
- Balance the total of the guest checks with the cash register reading and the actual cash and credit card charges taken in.

The **Daily Sales Report** *recaps the entire day's sales activity by each department and shift, with the accompanying totals.*

Thorough training for cashiers is essential. Cashiers should be trained in proper cash, check, and credit- and debit-card handling procedures. They should be trained to be accurate, but they should also learn the importance of being personable and congenial, for the cashier is often the last person to make contact with the customer. The cashier is in a position to foster goodwill and become aware of any customer dissatisfaction.

Cashier Control

At the end of each shift, before completing a Cashier's Report, the cashier should complete a Cash Turn-In Report (Figure 11.1). A **Cash Turn-In Report** is a form used to

Date: 2/2/2XXX Day: Saturday Shift: Lunch	Department: Dining Room	Cashier: Stacey Checked By: Mary
(A) Beginning Bank		$250.00
(B) Item	(C) Number	(D) Amount
(E) Currency		
$100	3	$300.00
50	12	600.00
20	35	700.00
10	36	360.00
5	38	190.00
2	0	0
1	16	16.00
(F) Currency Sub Total		$2,166.00
(G) Coin		
.50	0	0
.25	18	$4.50
.10	63	6.30
.05	22	1.10
.01	50	.50
(H) Coin Subtotal		$12.40
(I) Total Currency & Coin		$2,178.40
(J) Checks		+$212.74
(K) Subtotal		$2,391.14
(L) Less Bank		$250.00
(M) Total Turn-In		$2,141.14

FIGURE 11.1   Cash Turn-In Report.

account for cash collected during a specific period of time, such as a shift. Typically, this report is printed on the side of a cash deposit envelope. The *purpose of the form is to assist the cashier in counting the cash drawer at the end of a shift.* It is very similar to preparing a deposit slip for a bank deposit. The total Cash Turn-In Report is then used to complete the Cashier's Report (Figure 11.2).

Cash Turn-In Report: A form used to *account for cash collected during a specific period of time,* such as a shift. It assists the cashier in counting the cash drawer at the end of a shift. It is prepared prior to completing the Cashier's Report.

Cashier's Report: A form used to *account for the total revenue collected during a specific period of time,* such as a shift. It is prepared at the end of every shift and for each register in operation.

A **Cashier's Report** is a form *used to account for the total revenue collected during a specific period of time, such as a shift.* It is prepared at the end of every shift. If more than one cash register is used during a shift, a Cashier's Report is completed for each cash register. The following sections detail the procedures that should be followed for operations using a traditional cash register system. The procedure may vary according to the type of computerized point-of-sale (POS) terminal in use.

Completing the Cash Turn-In Report

To complete the Cash Turn-In Report, the cashier counts the cash in the drawer and records the amounts on the form. Note how this is done in Figure 11.1.

- The **Beginning Bank (A)** records the *cash in the drawer at the start of the shift.* It is the cash needed on hand to make change during the shift.
- The **Item (B)** column records *the denomination: currency and coin.*
- The **Number (C)** column is the *number of coins and bills in the drawer.* It is *the actual physical count of the number of coins and bills present.*
- The **Amount (D)** column results from *multiplying the denomination by the number of items recorded in the Number column:*

ITEM × NUMBER PRESENT = AMOUNT OF $$ IN DRAWER

- The **Total Currency and Coin (I)** is the *sum of the amount column and includes all currency and coin:*

ALL CURRENCY + ALL COIN = TOTAL CURRENCY & COIN

- **Checks (J)** are recorded under Total Currency & Coin.
- The **Subtotal (K)** results from *adding the currency and coin totals with the check total:*

ALL CURRENCY (F) + ALL COIN (H) + ALL CHECKS (J) = SUBTOTAL

- The **Bank (L)** is the total *cash in the drawer at the start of the shift.*
- **Total Turn-In (M)** results from subtracting the bank from the subtotal:

SUBTOTAL − BANK = TOTAL TURN-IN

The information here is used to complete the Cashier's Report. Because the Cashier's Report totals the cash and checks received during the shift, these figures can be quickly transferred to the Cashier's Report. The following is the Cash Turn-In Report for February 2, for the lunch shift, at Farfalle Arrabbiata.

```
Date: 2/2/2XXX                          Department: Dining Room
Day: Saturday                           Cashier: Stacey
Shift: Lunch                            Prepared By: Mary

(1)   Total Cash Guest Checks                $  2,141.19
(2)   Total Charged Guest Checks             +    231.75
(3)      Total Receipts                      =  2,372.94
(4)   Total Cash—Guest Checks                   2,141.19
(5)   Total Cash Turned In                    − 2,141.14
(6)      Difference                          = $   (−.05)   (plus/minus)
(7)      Reason for Difference: Error in Making Change

                         Register Reading
(8)   Ending Reading                             002224718
(9)   Beginning Reading                        − 001987424
(10)  Difference                               = $2,372.94

         (Register Reading To Be Taken By Department Manager Only.)

(11)  Register Reading                           $2,372.94
(12)  Total Receipts                             $2,372.94
(13)  Difference                                      −0−   (plus/minus)
(14)  Reason for Difference
```

FIGURE 11.2   Cashier's Report.

The cash turn-in according to the register draw is $2,141.14. This amount has to be reconciled with actual guest check records. The Cashier's Report will do just that.

Completing the Cashier's Report

The **Cashier's Report** is used to *reconcile cash collected on the Cash Turn-In Report with what the cash register or POS system is reporting.*

First, the cashier separates the receipts into two categories:

- *Guest checks that were paid by cash or check.* This information is found on the Cash Turn-In Report (see Figure 11.1).
- *Guest checks that were paid by* **credit** *or* **debit card**. This information is from the register or POS system. In some cases, credit- and debit-card slips will be tallied manually at the register. This practice is less and less common, though, because of the widespread use of technology and POS systems.

After each group is totaled, the amounts are written in lines 1 and 2 on the Cashier's Report (Figure 11.2). Then, both categories are added together on line 3 to ascertain **total receipts for the shift**. Lines 4 and 5 (Total Cash − Guest Checks and Total Cash Turned In) *compare the total of the guest checks paid by cash or check to the total of the cash and checks turned in*. If there is a difference it must be adequately explained (see lines 6 and 7). Management policy should establish an internal policy regarding discrepancies in the cash drawer.

The second part of the process is to compare the cash collected with what the cash register or POS computer terminal reports say should be present. To do this, beginning and ending register readings must be recorded on the form. At the end of every shift, the **ending register reading** is taken by a manager. It is recorded on line 8. The register tape is then removed from the cash register and used to complete the Cashier's Report.

Next, the **register reading** must be determined. To calculate the register reading, the manager first takes the **beginning reading**, which was the previous shift's ending reading, and records it on line 9. This amount is subtracted from the current ending reading. The **difference** is the difference between the beginning and ending register readings, as shown on line 10. The register reading (line 11) is then compared to the total receipts (line 12). Any difference (line 13) is explained on line 14.

The Cashier's Report checks the accuracy of the cashier. It not only analyzes shift receipts, but also detects mistakes made by the cashier. The difference amounts should be small and always followed by an acceptable reason. If the reason is not acceptable, management should take immediate corrective action.

COMMON GUEST CHECK PAYMENT METHODS
- **Cash**
- Checks
- Traveler's checks
- Credit/debit cards

Accepting Cash

Standard cash-handling procedures are needed for every type of foodservice operation. Those businesses utilizing a cashier (cafeterias, kiosks, food carts, quick-service, casual dining) may have a different procedure than would operations where servers handle the check-paying procedure. Regardless, strict control and standards must be in place in every operation.

The following cash-handling procedure is a recommended standard for every cashier. It can be easily modified for those operations where the server handles the check payment function:

1. Take the guest check from the customer. Staff should be trained on the art of querying the guest as to the quality of the food and service.
2. Look at the guest check and verbalize the amount to the customer. For example, a guest check with a balance of $13.95 should be verbalized as "Thirteen dollars and ninety-five cents."
3. Repeat the amount that the customer tenders. If the customer gives the cashier a $20.00 bill, the cashier should state, "Thirteen ninety-five out of twenty dollars."
4. Place the amount tendered on the cash register ledge. (Putting it in the drawer may cause confusion later, as the cashier could forget the denomination.)
5. If using a traditional cash register system, ring the sale by first entering the amounts of each food and beverage item. A POS system may require only pushing a single button for a menu item to be recorded.
6. Make change by counting upward from the total of the check. The cashier would say, "Thirteen ninety-five, fourteen, fifteen, twenty." As the cashier states these amounts, he or she hands back a nickel, a one-dollar bill, and a five-dollar bill.
7. After the cashier gives the guest the change, he or she puts the amount given (the $20.00 bill) into the cash register drawer, remembering to always keep the cash register drawer closed between customers. Large bills—$50 or $100 denominations—should be placed underneath the cash drawer.

When a customer believes that the correct change was not given, either the manager or cashier must assess the need to correctly collect what is owed to the foodservice operation against risking the loss of a valuable customer. Often, if the discrepancy is five dollars or less, the policy is to take the customer's word for it and give the person the change he or she requested, considering any losses as good public relations. If the amount in dispute is larger, the cashier should take the customer's name, complete address, and telephone number. Then the cashier should explain to the customer that the office will check the cash balances and cash register readings at the end of the day and will be in contact shortly. If the dispute is substantial, it may be necessary to count the drawer and check the register readings immediately.

During any rush time, human error is apt to occur: **Over-rings** or **under-rings** on the cash register happen. An **over-ring** is anytime *a cashier rings a higher amount than the sale on a cash register or POS terminal.* An **under-ring** is when *a cashier rings a lower amount than the sale on a cash register or POS system.* Should this occur, the recommended procedure is to correctly re-ring the guest check. The error will be reported through the POS system. Operations that do not have this capability through the POS system track errors manually. An Over/Under Ring Form lists the error and the guest check number and shows the signatures of the cashier and manager:

Over/Under-Ring Form				
Over/Under-Ring Form		Date: 2/2/2XXX	Shift: Lunch	
Check Number:	**Amount of Over-Ring**	**Amount of Under-Ring**	**Cashier**	**Manager**
#5693	.22		Hank	ABC
Totals	.22			

COMMON GUEST CHECK PAYMENT METHODS
- Cash
- **Checks**
- Traveler's Checks
- Credit/Debit Cards

Accepting Checks

In some locales, it is common to accept checks as a form of payment. As such, every foodservice operation that accepts checks as a form of payment should establish a check-cashing policy that protects the business but is also friendly to the customer. Customer relations are important, and nothing is more humiliating and irritating to a customer than to have his or her check improperly rejected. See Figure 11.3 for features of an acceptable check.

Foodservice operations handle guest check payment in a variety of ways. Historically, cash was the only form of payment. Then, checks came into use as another acceptable form of payment of a guest check. Today, debit and credit cards are slowly replacing these two methods of payment. In any case, each operation must decide which forms of payment will be accepted, then devise standard policies to ensure that all checks accepted result in cash in the register.

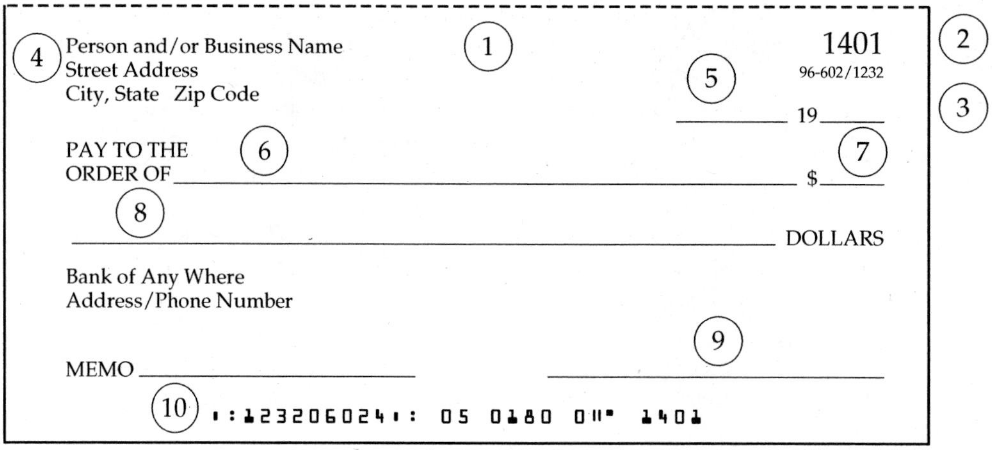

FIGURE 11.3   Features of an acceptable check.

Compare these points to the check sample in Figure 11.3:

1. All checks should have at least one perforated edge.
2. All checks should be individually numbered.
3. Bank routing numbers should correspond with the bank identification number located on the bottom left hand corner.
4. The name of the person or business should be printed on the check. Preferably, a street address and phone number should be present. Only local checks should be accepted.
5. The date of purchase should be written on the check; postdated checks should not be accepted.
6. Checks should be made out to the foodservice operation. Do not accept checks made out to someone else or to another company. Two-party checks should not be accepted.
7. Checks should be made out only for the amount of purchase, plus tip.
8. The amount, written in words, should be the same as the amount written in numbers.
9. Checks should be signed, and the signature should be compared to another source of identification. This is a protection for both the person who is writing the check and the foodservice operation.
10. The ink used to print the band numbers at the bottom of the check is typically dull.

COMMON GUEST CHECK PAYMENT METHODS

- Cash
- Checks
- **Traveler's Checks**
- Credit/Debit Cards

Accepting Traveler's Checks

Traveler's checks represent another form of payment. You can expect to see these used in busy tourist areas. These special checks, commonly purchased through banks and travel institutions, protect the purchaser's money by insuring it against loss or theft. Using traveler's checks is a protection for those who buy them. The check is first signed when purchased by the purchaser. Then, when the check is redeemed or used, the check is countersigned. The **double signature** is *a control or protection that the check is original and that the person cashing it is the owner.* In addition to the signature check, some operations also require a photo ID.

The cashier should check the signatures and make certain they are the same. The traveler's check must be signed in the presence of the cashier or other qualified staff. If the check is already signed, the cashier should ask the guest to sign a piece of paper and then compare all of the signatures to verify that they are the same. In addition, the cashier should ask for some other form of identification.

COMMON GUEST CHECK PAYMENT METHODS

- Cash
- Checks
- Traveler's Checks
- **Credit/Debit Cards**

Accepting Credit and Debit Cards

Credit cards are the predominant method of payment in many foodservice operations (Figure 11.4). The decision to accept credit cards involves knowing the costs associated with accepting them and understanding the procedures needed to process them. Financial institutions that support the use of credit cards earn their money by charging foodservice operations a fee. The *amount of the fee*, called a **discount**, depends on the negotiated arrangement that the foodservice operation has with the bank or company

(A)

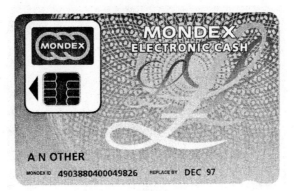

(B)

FIGURE 11.4   (A) Debit card. (B) Credit card.

that issues the credit card. This fee is paid by the foodservice operation to the financial institutions for the task of processing credit and debit card transactions. State restaurant associations often offer negotiated discount fees to their members, although most independent foodservice operations are subject to the standard fee schedule being offered at any given time.

𝒩et Work

Explore the following Web sites:

www.visa.com

www.mastercard.com

www.discovercard.com

www.americanexpress.com

In today's high-tech world, credit-card authorization terminals (also known as merchant machines) are used by nearly all foodservice operations (see Figure 11.5). These terminals offer the opportunity to complete the credit transaction electronically. These machines

- Check the credit card to ensure that it is not stolen.
- Verify that the credit card holder is authorized to charge the amount being tendered.
- Electronically deposit the amount of the transaction, less the discount fee, into the merchant's checking account.

The machine shown in Figure 11.5 is the Express 3200. It is a versatile terminal for restaurants, retailers, travel agencies, and cruise lines. It provides quick authorization and submission of charges made on all major credit cards. An easy-to-read, two-line, lighted display provides helpful prompts that guide personnel through the entire transaction process.

Typically, the transaction occurs as follows: The cashier takes the guest's credit card and passes it through a card reader. The magnetic code on the card identifies the credit card number. The cashier enters the amount of the guest check onto the keypad.

FIGURE 11.5   Credit card authorization terminal.

The terminal identifies the merchant's account number. Once the transaction is approved, the terminal is automatically signaled to print the charge receipt. The customer simply signs the receipt, which also doubles as a voucher. The receipt/voucher is placed in the cash drawer and is treated with the same security precautions as cash. The customer will also be given a copy of the receipt. Standard procedures must also be in place for transactions that are not approved.

Credit or debit cards that are not approved can be a touchy situation with guests. Standard procedures may include running the card through the card reader again, calling to verify the refusal and, finally, asking for a second form of payment. In any event, the guest should not be made to feel embarrassed about the situation.

STANDARD CREDIT CARD TRANSACTION PROCEDURES

- Slide the credit card through the card reader.
- The card reader identifies the credit card number.
- Enter the guest check amount on the keypad.
- The terminal identifies the merchant's account number.
- The transaction is either approved or not approved.
- Approved transactions will automatically print a receipt.
- The customer signs and receives a copy of the charge receipt.
- The signature is checked against the card. Some businesses may require additional forms of identification.
- The expiration date is validated.
- The receipt is placed in the cash drawer.

Employees should be taught that **credit card vouchers** (also known as **tickets**) are as important as cash. A **credit** or **debit card voucher** is a *paper receipt that is used to record a sales made to a customer using a credit or debit card.* It is the only *record of the transaction,* and there is always the possibility that the financial institution may not credit the foodservice operation's account properly, so they must be kept for reconciliation of statements. Most important, the vouchers are counted along with the checks and cash to compare against the totals report on the cash register or POS terminal.

Debit cards are treated in the same way as credit cards. A **debit card** looks exactly like a credit card, but *charges made using one are subtracted from the cardholder's checking account at the end of the day's business.* A debit card *allows the guest to pay for the meal as if writing a check.* Processing debit cards is the same as processing credit cards, however. Foodservice operators are charged a fee for accepting debit cards just as they are when they accept credit cards.

To avoid problems with accepting stolen cards, the cashier could ask guests to write their phone number on the voucher and check the signature on the voucher against another form of identification. If there is a dispute or problem later, the number allows a manager to contact the guest quickly and resolve the problem.

As with checks, cashiers should ask to see another form of identification that shows a signature. Compare the signature on the identification with that on the credit voucher and on the back of the credit card, and always check to see whether the credit card has expired. (The expiration date is printed on the face of the card.)

Credit card fraud is a serious problem. To ensure that the foodservice operation is not victimized, cashiers should be trained to check credit cards that are tendered for the following symptoms:

- Blurred holograms
- Glue on the edges

- Numbers changed, such as 3 to 8 or 5 to 6.
- Misaligned numbers

All of these are indications of bogus credit cards or possible credit card tampering.

The Cost of Credit Cards Foodservice operations are charged a discount fee for every credit card transaction processed. The fee for some cards may be fixed, such as a flat 3% of the total amount of every voucher processed. Thus, a foodservice operation with a 3% discount would pay a $.60 fee to the credit card company for each $20.00 transaction ($20.00 × .03 = $.60). Others have a sliding scale based on the dollar amount of an individual transaction.

Some financial institutions charge a fee based on the average dollar amount per foodservice transaction. Thus, if the average transaction is $50.00, a rate of 3% might be charged; if the average is $30.00, a rate of 4% might be charged, and so on. Discounts typically do not go below 1.65%.

Not all banks and credit card companies charge the same fees. Rates and costs should always be compared. Foodservice operators may find the best deal available through a professional association, such as a state restaurant association that contracts with a bank for a large volume of business.

Daily Sales Control

The Daily Sales Report is a *daily sales record used for review and analysis*. It also can be used as a permanent accounting record. For larger foodservice operations, which have more than one unit within the operation, the Daily Sales Report begins with the department name. This is followed by the shift description and cash register readings. The register readings are taken from the Cashier's Report and the total receipts, including cash and charges. The over and short amounts are also listed. Finally, the sales breakdown includes the total sales, food sales, and bar sales (where liquor is served). The totals are taken for each department, as well as the final totals for the entire foodservice operation. It is important to recognize that many cash registers/POS systems include computerized functions that can generate a very extensive detailed analysis of sales.

The Daily Sales Report in Figure 11.6 reports the activity for the dining room at Farfalle Arrabbiata for two shifts (lunch and dinner) for February 2. Once the day's business has ended, the Daily Sales Report is completed and the manager is assured that cash, charges, and accountability for overs or shorts have been finalized.

Notice the columns on the report shown in Figure 11.6. They should look familiar. The information for this report is retrieved from the Cashier's Report. Column A (Department) is used to list all revenue centers. In the case of Farfalle Arrabbiata, it is simply the dining room. Because the report is a summary of sales for the day, any other revenue-generating departments, such as a bar or coffee shop, would also be listed. The Shift column (B) represents meal periods. Register Readings (C, D, and E) are taken from the Cashier's Report. Total Receipts (F, G, and H) and Overs/Shorts (I) information is also from the Cashier's Report. The Sales Breakdown (J, K, and L) would be found in the POS system report. The report column totals at the bottom of the form summarize the day's sales activity and also serve as a check and balance to the rest of the work on the form.

Figure 11.7 is an example of a computer-generated sales report. Notice the details included on this type of report. The ease with which this information is generated (a simple key-stroke) makes using a menu management software package a worthwhile investment. This degree of detail provides invaluable information to management.

Date:		Day:						Page:			
Weather:					Prepared By:			Approved By:			

Department	Shift	Register Readings			Total Receipts			Over/Short	Total Sales	Sales Breakdown	
		Ending Reading	Beginning Reading	Difference	Cash	Charge	Total			Food Sales	Bar Sales
Dining Room	Lunch	2224718	1987424	$2,372.94	$2,141.19	$231.75	$2,372.94	0	$2,372.94	$1,898.35	$474.59
	Dinner	2421318	2224718	1,966.00	1,672.80	293.20	1,966.00	0	1,966.00	1,572.80	393.20
Totals				4,338.94	3,813.99	524.95	4,338.94	0	4,388.94	3,471.15	867.79
				E	F	G	H	E – H	J	K	L

A   B   C   –   D   =   E   F   +   G   =   H   I   J   =   K   +   L

(E – H)

FIGURE 11.6   Daily Sales Report

Daily System Sales Detail
Mike Rose Cafe - Beltsville, MD

Friday 09/27/1996

Net Sales	18,895.07	Returns	0	0.00	
+Service Charge	1,705.03	Voids	84	-296.01	
+Tax Collected	947.22	Credit Total		-23.10	
=Total Revenue	21,547.32	Change Grand Ttl		22,180.51	
		Rounding Total		0.00	
Item Discount	0.00	Grand Total		22,180.51	
+Subtotal Discount	-314.08	Training Total		0.00	
=Total Discounts	-314.08	Mgr Voids	0	0.00	
		Error Corrects	285	1,018.85	
		Cancel	134	289.26	

Gross Receipts	19,168.82
Charged Receipts	3,038.20
Service Charges	935.46
+Charged Tips	762.27
+Tips Declared	0.00
=Total Tips 8.86%	1,697.73
Tips Paid	1,697.73
Tips Due	0.00

Order Type	Net Sales	% of Ttl	Guests	% of Ttl	Avg/Guest			Checks	% of Ttl	Avg/Chk	Tables	% of Ttl	Avg/Tbl	Turn Time
1 - Dine In	18,588.52	98.38%	1,217	97.67%	15.27	Carried Over	0 0.00	1,094	97.94%	16.99	46	93.88%	404.10	0.62
2 - To Go	306.55	1.62%	29	2.33%	10.57	+Checks Begun	1,117 21,547.32	23	2.06%	13.33	3	6.12%	102.18	1.64
Total	18,895.07		1,246		15.16	-Checks Paid	1,116 21,475.93	1,117		16.92	49		385.61	
						=Outstanding	1 71.39							

1 - System Tracking

Food	4,220	12,066.90	Beverage Tax	0	335.33	Dead Liquor	11	-50.95
Less To Go	0	306.55		0	0.00	20% Teacher	0	0.00
Total Food	0	0.00	Charged Tip	95	762.27	Barter	0	0.00
Liquor	1,640	4,809.88	15% Gratutity	124	942.76	House 10	0	0.00
Beer	458	1,197.62	Non Rev Svc Chg	0	0.00	House 11	0	0.00
Wine	188	725.48		0	0.00	House 12	0	0.00
Soft Beverage	595	409.27	Less Discounts	54	-314.08	House 13	0	0.00
Total Liquor	0	0.00	100% Discount	0	0.00	House 14	0	0.00
Gift Certificates	0	0.00	60% Employee Meal	7	-57.35	House 15	0	0.00
Novelties	0	0.00	40% Employee Meal	12	-45.78	House 16	0	0.00
Liquor Issue	0	0.00	40% Employee Comp	1	-2.46	House 17	0	0.00
+ To Go	0	306.55	20% Coupon	0	0.00	Cash	995	15,404.93
	0	0.00	Dead Food	0	0.00	Less Tips	218	1,697.73
Food Tax	0	611.89		23	-157.54	Cash Due	0	0.00
Subtotal	7,101	20,434.14	Subtotal	316	1,463.15	Subtotal	1,224	17,051.71

FIGURE 11.7 Computer-generated daily sales POS printout.

Introduction to Guest Service Accounting

The cycle of guest service accounting begins when the guest places an order and ends when the manager or bookkeeper reconciles the cash register amounts with the guest checks. This procedure is standard to all foodservice operations—commercial and non-commercial, alike. One of the distinguishing differences between commercial foodservice operations (restaurants) and noncommercial foodservice operations (institutional foodservice operations) is the timing and method of ordering meals and paying for those meals. Restaurants normally collect payment for food and service at the time they are rendered. Institutional foodservice operations (schools, healthcare facilities, and so on) commonly collect for food and service after they are rendered or during a specific billing period. Institutional foodservice operations typically do not collect for food and service at the time of the meal.

Guest Checks

Guest checks are used in restaurants *to record information about what the guests order.* It is a form used to

- Record guest food orders and prices.
- Record total sales to guest.
- Request food from the kitchen.

In most institutional foodservice operations, there are no guest checks, because food selections are usually based on a limited offering of food items. Given the differences between commercial and noncommercial foodservice operations, the focus here will be on commercial accounting of guest checks.

Guest Service Accounting Cycle

The cycle of guest accounting in full-menu table service restaurants is illustrated in Figure 11.8. The cycle usually involves the following steps:

1. If a manual system is used, the server is issued numbered guest checks. With an electronic system, servers are granted access to the menu ordering system via a PIN number. All food is ordered through the POS terminal.

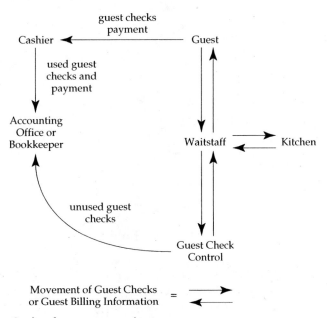

FIGURE 11.8   *Cycle of guest accounting.*

2. The order is taken from the customer.
3. The order is delivered to the kitchen, either manually or electronically.
4. The order is produced and served to the guest.
5. The check is delivered to the guest; with electronic systems, it is in the form of a printout.
6. The guest pays the total amount on the guest check.

The cycle will vary depending on the restaurant concept. As an example, the quick-service guest accounting cycle looks something like this:

1. The guest makes a selection using a menu board.
2. The cashier inputs the order into a computer terminal (POS terminal).
3. The kitchen either receives a printout of the order or the order is displayed on a monitor as soon as the cashier presses the Enter button.
4. The guest pays for the order at the time the order is placed.
5. The order is then assembled.
6. The order is delivered to the guest by counter staff.
7. Guests find their own seats and bus their own tables.

Each restaurant concept has its own unique system of order processing. Regardless, all foodservice operations employ a standard ordering system to expedite the service of food to guests and to monitor and track sales. The accounting cycle will be explained in more detail in the following sections.

Taking the Guest's Order

Servers or counterpersons are the frontline sales force of any restaurant. These employees are face to face with guests nearly every minute of their shift. They can make or break a guest's experience. As such, all servers or counterpersons must be trained in standard guest (customer service skills). These skills are needed as soon as they take the order. The Service System Chart in Chapter 17 is a good example of a standard front-of-the-house training procedure. Servers and counterpersons should also be trained to up-sell. Sales techniques such as suggestive selling are some of the easiest to train employees to use. These techniques, if carried out correctly, enhance the guest's experience, increase sales, and increase server tips.

The server records sales on the customer guest check, which represents the customer's order and bill. The order must be taken accurately and communicated clearly to the kitchen staff. It is the responsibility of the servers to communicate special requests, allergies, substitutions, and special cooking instructions to the cooks and expediter. The **expediter** *is responsible for firing out orders and checking that plates match checks (and special requests) as they leave the kitchen.* At pickup, however, the server is the last line of defense against plating errors—he or she must check the plate for accuracy.

Guest checks can take many different forms. Traditionally, they may look similar to the ones in Figure 11.9. Another type of format is a form with a preprinted menu on it. Yet another method is a point-of-sale terminal with a keyboard coded with the menu or a hand-held computer terminal.

Completing a Guest Check

Even though the manual use of customer guest checks is on the decline, reviewing a manual system makes the process of billing the guest for menu items easier to understand. The customer **guest check** is also *the itemized food and beverage bill* that is presented to the customer for payment. Therefore, it must be presented in a clear, concise, and correct manner.

Guest Check		Farfalle Arrabbiata		Date: 2/2 Time: 6:32 P.M.	
Table Number: 21	**Server Number:** 864	**Number of Guests:** 2	**Change Amount:** $40.00	**Check Number:** 37201	
Amount Ordered: (A)	**Item**		**Menu Price: (B)**	**Extension: (C)**	
2	Chicken Noodle Soup		$1.75	$3.50	
1	Farfalle Arrabbiata		15.97	15.97	
1	Pizza Pomodoro Caprese		9.95	9.95	
2	Coffee		1.25	2.50	
			Total:	31.92	
			Tax: (7%)	2.24	
			Total Amount:	$34.16	
Table Number: 21	**Server Number:** 864	**Number of Guests:** 2	**Total Amount:** $34.16	**Check Number:** 37201	

A   ×   B   =   C

FIGURE 11.9   Manual Guest Check.

STANDARD GUEST CHECK INFORMATION (Manual System)

- Date/time
- Table number
- Server number
- Number of guests
- Change amount
- Check number
- Quantity, item description, price, and extension
- Check stub

The guest check, manual or electronic, is typically divided into sections that include the following (revisit Figure 11.9):

1. The **table number** helps the server associate the order with the given restaurant tables. Some food delivery systems require that the first available server pick up the order and deliver it to the guest. The only way the server would know to what table to deliver the food is if a table number is indicated on the guest check.

2. The **server number** identifies the server who wrote the information on the guest check. This helps to track sales by individual server. It also allows the manager to measure performance.

3. The **number of guests** helps the server take the customer orders. It helps the manager keep track of *total customer counts* (often referred to as covers). This data is essential for determining productivity of both the kitchen staff and the servers. The information is also used for tracking promotional efforts and as a general barometer of how well the restaurant is doing.

4. Recording the **change amount** helps to reduce the risk of making incorrect change. The customer in Figure 11.9 paid the check with two $20 bills; that amount is written in the change amount box. When the amount tendered is recorded, the customer is less likely to receive incorrect change. Restaurants can easily lose money if cashiers and servers are not careful in how they make change. The type of guest check depicted is especially useful to foodservice operations where servers carry a bank and act as their own cashier.

5. The **check number** is used to *control the issuance of guest checks*. Each guest check is sequentially numbered. Each server is responsible for every assigned check. At the end of every shift, the checks are put into sequential order and accounted for individually.

6. The middle section of the guest check is for recording the **quantity, item description, and price**. How the order is written helps the server deliver the food in the proper manner, to ensure that guests receive what they ordered. Trained and experienced servers write the order in such a manner that they can easily identify each guest's specific order. If every server in the restaurant uses the same system, it doesn't matter which server picks up the order and serves the guest.

7. The *bottom part of the guest check,* **the stub**, will usually be torn along the perforated edge and given as the guest's copy of the check. Most of the information that appears on the heading of the check is also recorded on the customers' receipt.

The procedures to use and control customer guest checks will vary according to the policies of management, but the following should be standard operating procedure:

- All guest checks should be tightly controlled.
- All checks should be accounted for and kept in a secured and locked area.
- The only people who should have access to guest checks are the manager, head server, and cashier. These individuals have full responsibility for issuing guest checks to the servers.

ORDER-PLACING SYSTEMS

- Dupe pads
- Two-copy guest checks
- Computer-generated guest checks

Servers should be instructed to write in ink, which will make any erasure difficult. Should a mistake occur in writing the customer's order, a single line should be drawn through the mistake. The manager or head server should initial the error.

Placing an Order with the Kitchen

Several systems can be used in placing the orders with the kitchen. One of the most common manual methods is a dupe (duplicate) pad. A second method is two-copy guest checks. The third and most convenient is the computer-generated guest check. The widespread use of technology has made the first two methods almost obsolete.

A **dupe pad** is *a pad of order checks that are sequentially numbered and issued to the server*. The server writes the initial order on the dupe pad, submits it to the kitchen for preparation, and recopies it onto the guest check for the customer.

Both the dupe check and the guest check are compared for accuracy at the end of every shift. This system is typically used in large restaurants, when there is more than one cook's station. Suppose a customer has ordered Antipasti as an appetizer and the 12-ounce Bistecca for dinner.

- One dupe check goes to the appetizer/salad prep cook.

USING DUPES

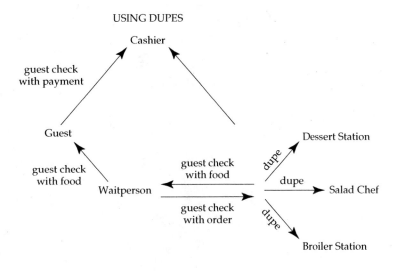

NOT USING DUPES

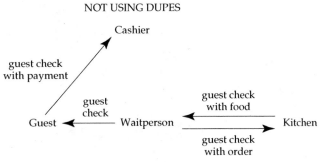

FIGURE 11.10 The two-guest-check system.

Then, as the customer is served the appetizer,

- A second dupe check goes to the hot-line cook, allowing smooth and timely service (see Figure 11.10).

Another method would be the use of a **two-copy order**, with *the original going to the customer and the copy remaining with the cook.* The traditional one-copy method is most often used, however, with the form serving both the kitchen (for the food order) and the customer (for the bill).

Finally, many excellent computer-generated ordering and guest-check-writing systems are available for all types of foodservice operations. These systems are most effective. Figure 11.11 shows an example of one type of POS terminal system. One of the key differences between a manual system and a computerized system is that in the computerized system, the computer application software generates guest check numbers only when an order is input using a keyboard or touch screen. With this system, the need for tracking guest check numbers is eliminated. At the end of the shift, the software prints a computer-generated Guest Check Daily Record.

Controlling Customer Guest Checks

Guest Check Daily Record

The **Guest Check Daily Record**, as shown in Figure 11.12, *serves to control the issue and use of customer guest checks.* The server names are recorded, together with an assigned server number. The use of the number system allows speed in writing for the server and ease in identifying a server with a customer guest check.

FIGURE 11.11   Point-of-Sale System Terminal. *Courtesy of Micros.*

The beginning check number is the very *first number in the book of guest checks,* which will be either a new book or one that has been used previously but still contains blank checks. The beginning check number is *the number of the last check returned by the server at the end of the preceding scheduled shift.* The number of checks used is found by *subtracting the beginning check number from the ending check number.*

The number by actual count *is then compared to the number of checks, to identify any missing checks,* as in the case of the customer walk-out shown in Figure 11.12.

Finally, the server signature *indicates that he or she has taken the responsibility for the guest checks issued.* The Guest Check Daily Record is usually kept by the manager, the head server, or a cashier who is responsible for guest check control.

Department: Dining Room			Page 1 of 1				
Day: Monday			**Prepared By:**				
Date: 2/2/2XXX							
Server Name	**Server Number**	**Beginning Check Number**	**Ending Check Number**	**Number of Checks Used**	**Number by Actual Count**	**Number of Missing Checks**	**Server Signature**
Bud	864	37201	37218	17	17	0	Bud
Laura	786	37219	37241	22	22	0	Laura
Gisele	421	37242	37269	27	26	1 walk-out	Gisele
Beth	458	37270	37293	23	23	0	Beth
Lynn	654	37294	37309	15	15	0	Lynn
Martine	469	37210	37234	24	24	0	Martine

FIGURE 11.12   Guest Check Daily Record.

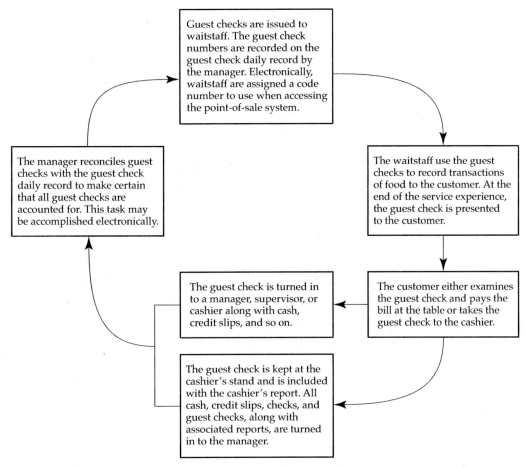

FIGURE 11.13   Guest check control system.

Guest Check Control System

Figure 11.13 illustrates the process of guest check control. This entire process becomes unnecessary when a foodservice operation uses computers. The application software in the computer tracks guest checks by using a guest check or transaction number. What is known as a guest check number may also become a transaction number in a computer. Security is provided through proper access to the computer. Only those with passwords or PIN numbers are allowed access to the POS terminal. An example of a computer-generated Guest Check Daily Record is shown in Figure 11.14.

The information on a computer-generated Guest Check Daily Record is similar to that included on a manual Guest Check Daily Record. Servers access the system with a PIN number and open a check to input an order. The check is closed *when the check is paid*. The form displays:

- The number of guests.
- Table/group number information.
- The time the check was opened.
- The amount of the check.
- Payment information.

Balancing and the Cycle of Guest Service Accounting

Manual or electronic guest check control offers three major benefits:

1. It assists in the balancing of food ordered by the guest and the food produced by the kitchen.

Employee Open Guest Checks
MICROS Systems—Bar & Grille

Bruno the Manager
Printed on May 13, 2XXX—8:23 PM

Check	Table/Group	Guests	Check ID	Open Date & Time	Subtotal	Tax Total	Svc Total	Payment Total
1 Phoebe								
975	1/1	4		05/13—8:20 P.M.	$ 8.75	$ 0.44	$0.00	$0.00
976	4/1	4		05/13—8:20 P.M.	192.85	9.16	0.00	0.00
977	1/2	4		05/13—8:21 P.M.	35.40	1.77	0.00	0.00
	Employee Total	12	3		237.00	11.37	0.00	0.00
2 Chandler								
978	1/3	4		05/13—8:22 P.M.	40.25	0.20	0.00	0.00
	Employee Total	4	1		40.25	0.20	0.00	0.00
3 Rachel								
979	78/1	4		05/13—8:22 P.M.	6.25	0.31	0.00	0.00
	Employee Total	4	1		6.25	0.31	0.00	0.00
5 Ross								
980	47/1	4		05/13—8:22 P.M.	26.85	1.34	0.00	0.00
	Employee Total	4	1		26.85	1.34	0.00	0.00
6 Monica								
981	44/1	4		05/13—8:22 P.M.	91.05	4.56	0.00	0.00
	Employee Total	4	1		91.05	4.56	0.00	0.00
11 Joey								
314		0		05/13—1:32 P.M.	0.00	0.00	0.00	0.00
	Employee Total	0	1		0.00	0.00	0.00	0.00
	Grand Total	28	8		$401.40	$17.78	$0.00	$0.00

FIGURE 11.14 Computer-generated Guest Check Daily Record.

2. It prevents theft of food by guests and employees.

3. It helps track the flow of all food and beverages.

BENEFITS OF GUEST CHECK CONTROL

1. It assists in the balancing of food ordered by the guest and food produced by the kitchen (see Chapter 10—Portion Control Chart).
2. It prevents theft of food by guests and employees.
3. It helps track the flow of all food and beverages.

First, guest check control assists in the balancing of food ordered by the guest and food produced by the kitchen. It assists in the necessary accounting for every bit of food produced by the kitchen. The food ordered by the servers should be the food delivered to the guest. Sometimes, servers and kitchen staff want to give away food to guests or friends. The amount of food given away needs to be accounted for, regardless of whether it is for guests or friends. The process of using guest checks helps to prevent food from being given away.

Second, effective guest check control systems prevent theft by guests and employees. Without guest checks, orders would be called in and delivered to a guest without accountability. Lack of accountability enables the server to serve food to a guest and keep the money paid by the guest. The server would be able to give away food as an inducement for a larger tip. Also, without the use of guest checks, employees would be able to eat whatever they wanted and not have to account for it.

Third, an effective guest check control system helps to track the flow of all food and beverages. The guest check is a **source document** in the accounting process; it is *used to track total sales, individual sales, and productivity.* The guest check also is used to help track inventory and waste. As a source document, it is essential for keeping a set of accounts.

Special Controls for Beverage Service

There are many ways to lose control of a beverage operation. Controlling how the beverage order is processed is essential for lounges and bars, if they are to be successful.

At a minimum, guest checks should be used for beverage service, and all beverages prepared by a bartender should have a guest check. All beverages should be paid for when they are served; a **tab**, *a bill that accumulates and is paid at the end,* should be granted only if a guest has a credit card imprinted or pays in advance. See Chapters 13 through 15 for more on beverage management techniques.

$\mathcal{N}$et Work

Explore the following Web sites:

www.mastercard.com

www.visa.com Click Visa Corporate

www.digitaldining.com Check Point of Sale Software, Products, Back Office

www.cbord.com

www.csrsi.com

www.discovercard.com

www.americanexpress.com

www.smartconnect.net

Chapter Wrap

The Chapter ✓ at the beginning of the chapter posed several questions. Review the questions and compare your responses with the following answers:

1. How is cash controlled in a foodservice operation?

Cash is controlled in a foodservice operation by developing strict standard operating procedures for all cashiers, completing all paperwork correctly and accurately, and establishing procedures for checks, traveler's checks, credit cards, and debit cards.

2. What reports do managers use to control cash?

Managers use a number of standard reports to control cash. The Cashier's Report, completed by the cashier, is used to control cash and credit card charges. The Daily Sales Report recaps the entire day's sales activity by department and shift. The Cash Turn-In Report accounts for cash collected during a specific period of time.

3. What is guest service accounting?

The cycle of guest service accounting begins when the guest places an order and ends when the manager or bookkeeper reconciles the cash register amounts with the guest checks. It is a system of order processing. Each restaurant concept has its own unique system of order processing that expedites the service of food to guests and monitors and tracks sales. This procedure is standard to all foodservice operations.

4. What procedures are used to control guest checks?

All guest checks are tightly controlled. They should be accounted for and kept in a secured and locked area, with access limited to the manager, head server, or cashier. Checks should be issued to servers for each shift. They are tracked on a Guest Check Daily Record.

*K*ey Terminology and Concepts in This Chapter

Cashier's Report	Guest Check Daily Record
Cash Turn-In Report	Menu
Covers	Over-ring
Credit card voucher	Overs/shorts
Daily Sales Report	Sales
Debit card	Source document
Debit card voucher	Stub
Discount	Tab
Double signature	Traveler's checks
Dupe pad	Two-copy order
Expediter	Under-ring
Guest check	

*D*iscussion Questions and Exercises

1. What is the purpose of a Cash Turn-In Report? A Cashier's Report? A Daily Sales Report? Explain how each of these forms is used to control sales and cash in an operation.

2. List some of the probable causes of overages and shortages in the cash drawer.

3. Desmond, the dining room manager, has observed an increase in the number of incidents with overs and shorts in the cash drawer. He has asked for your thoughts on the situation. Discuss some of the causes of overs and shorts in the cash drawer. How should Desmond go about solving this problem?

4. In addition to the overs and shorts problem, there have been a number of recent incidents where guests have complained that they have not received the correct change. After observing a few of the servers in action, Desmond decides that a training session is needed to formalize cash handling procedures and making change. Desmond has asked for your help with the training. Design a standard operating procedure for making change and handling cash. You may want to do further research on cash handling procedures before completing your training component.

5. There have also been an increasing number of problems with checks and credit cards. Go ahead and set up standard operating procedures for checks and credit cards.

6. Laura, a new server, is quite flustered. A customer has just handed her a traveler's check. She has no idea what it is or what to do with it. Explain what a traveler's check is and how it is handled.

 7. Desmond was looking over the day's paperwork when he noticed that some of the reports for the lunch shift were not completed. Finish the Cash Turn-In Report, Cashier's Report, and Daily Sales Report for May 31 for Desmond, and brief him on the results.

Cash Turn-In-Report		
Date:	**Department:** Dining Room	**Cashier:**
Day: Thursday		
Shift: Lunch		**Checked By:**
(A) Beginning Bank		$250.00
(B) Item	**(C) Number**	**(D) Amount**
(E) Currency		
$100	3	
50	13	
20	41	
10	41	
5	42	
2	0	
1	31	
(F) Currency Sub-Total		
(G) Coin		
.50	0	
.25	20	
.10	20	
.05	6	
.01	10	
(H) Coin Subtotal		
(I) Total Currency & Coin		
(J) Checks	$462.74	
(K) Subtotal		
(L) Less Bank		
(M) Total Turn-In		

Cashier's Report

Date:	**Department:** Dining Room
Day: Saturday	**Cashier:**
Shift: Lunch	**Prepared By:**

(1) Total Cash Guest Checks $2,641.14

(2) Total Charged Guest Checks   462.74

(3) Total Receipts   _____

(4) Total Cash—Guest Checks   2,641.14

(5) Total Cash Turned In   _____

(6) Difference   _____ (Plus/Minus)

(7) Reason for Difference:

Register Reading

(8) Ending Reading   002229998

(9) Beginning Reading   001919610

(10) Difference   _____

(Register Reading To Be Taken By Department Manager Only.)

(11) Register Reading   _____

(12) Total Receipts   _____

(13) Difference   _____ (plus/minus)

(14) Reason for Difference:

Daily Sales Report

Date:			Day:					Page:			
Weather:			Prepared By:					Approved By:			

Dept.	Shift	Register Readings			Total Receipts			Over/ Short	Sales Breakdown		
		Ending Reading	Beg. Reading	Diff.	Cash	Charge	Total		Total Sales	Food Sales	Bar Sales
Dining Room	Lunch									$2,638.30	$465.58
	Dinner	2586970	2229998		$2,496.80	$1,070.92	$3,567.72			2,855.80	713.92
		Totals									

8. How would you train a server to complete a guest check?

9. How does an operation control the issuance and use of guest checks?

## Chapter Twelve

About Menus, Menu Pricing, Sales Forecasts, & Sales Analysis

Chapter Objective

Use the Five Rights of Menu Selection to develop a marketable, producible, and profitable menu selection; create a menu bank; price menus; forecast sales; and analyze menu mix.

Learning Objectives

After reading this chapter and completing the discussion questions and exercises, you should be able to:

1. Develop a marketable, producible, and profitable menu selection.
2. Set menu prices using a variety of menu pricing methods.
3. Use standard sales forecasts, menu prices, and portion costs to forecast sales and food cost.
4. Complete a menu analysis.
5. Analyze results of a menu analysis.

The Menu

Pre-Purchase Functions

STANDARDIZED RECIPES
Standard ingredients, portion size, quality, consistency, quantity, purchasing

GUEST CHECK
Sales history, turnover, **average check,** cash management, revenue forecasting & budgeting, **menu item analysis**

COST CARDS
Portion costs, yield factors, **sell prices**

GUESTS
Greeting, seating, **sales,** serving, busing, payment, comment cards

SPECIFICATIONS
Product descriptions

FOH Functions

PAR STOCK
Inventory levels, order building

KITCHEN PRODUCTION
Production schedules, portion tracking, recipe control, serving controls, food safety

REQUISITION
Order building, purchasing

PRODUCT ISSUING
Requisitions, transfers, daily & monthly costs, food cost percentage

SHOPPING LISTS
Call sheets, bid sheets, suppliers, bidding

STORAGE PRACTICES & INVENTORY MANAGEMENT
Best practices, sanitation, security, inventory methods

PURCHASE ORDERS
Security, ship order, price guarantee, contract

INVOICE MANAGEMENT
Payment, price checking, security

BOH Functions

RECEIVING ACTIVITIES
Best practices, invoices, security, sanitation

Chapter Map

About Menu Selection, Menu Pricing, & Sales Analysis

The Right Menu Selection

- Customer Fit
- Operational Fit
- Profitability
- Shaping a Winning Menu Selection Using Customer, Operational, and Profitability Criteria
- Standard Control Documents: The Menu Bank
- Competition
- Competitive Analysis

Calculating the Right Portion Cost & Selling Price

- Determining the True Cost per Dish
- Selecting a Menu Pricing Method
- Considering Other Differentiating Factors

- Setting the Actual Selling Price
- Menu Pricing Methods
- Special Pricing Situations

Sales & Food Cost Forecasts

- The Sales Forecast
- The Food Cost Forecast

Menu Profitability

- Analyzing Sales Using a Food Sales Recap Report
- Analyzing for Popularity & Profitability
- What's Next? Analyze & Strategize!
- Strategies for Popularity Problems
- Strategies for Profitability Problems
- Menu Analysis at Farfalle Arrabbiata

Chapter ✔

Check the chapter content for the answers to these questions:

1. In what ways must a menu selection fit an operation?

2. How are menu prices determined?

3. What role do sales and food cost forecasts play in menu selections and menu analysis?

4. How is menu analysis used to make menu decisions?

---

*A*bout Menu Selection, Menu Pricing, and Sales Analysis

We are now at a critical juncture in the Operating Cycle of Control. The first step in the cycle is titled ***The Menu***. It is the start of all the processes covered in Chapters 1 through 11. Yet here we are at the end of the cycle talking about menu selection. Why is that? One of the ways decisions are made about menu offerings is through sales analysis, and sales analysis can't begin until guests actually purchase menu items—the data is only gathered after guests have left. Of course there is more to creating a great menu selection than just sales analysis: There are marketplace trends to review, industry research to study, and external environments to watch. And, of course, there is one's own sales history. Once all this "homework" is complete, then the menu selection should be one that is marketable to the customer, "producible" by the staff, and profitable for an operation.

Selling the "right items" is not simply making a list of all the favorites of the restaurant staff and tossing in a few things a competitor has on their menu. It is the result of research, analysis, hard work, and a bit of luck. In fact, this process can be described using a spin on the Five Rights that described the purchasing functions in

THE FIVE *RIGHTS* TO MENU SELECTION

1. SELL THE *RIGHT MENU ITEMS*
2. AT THE *RIGHT PORTION COST*
3. AT THE *RIGHT SELLING PRICE*
4. AT THE *RIGHT SALES VOLUME*
5. TO PRODUCE THE *RIGHT PROFIT*

FIGURE 12.1   The Five Rights to Menu Selection.

Chapter 4. Think of the work of this chapter as the "Five Rights to Menu Selection" (Figure 12.1).

Here's What to Do		Here's How to Do It
1. Sell the right menu items	→	Offer the right menu selection.
2. At the right portion cost	→	Determine standard portion costs.
3. At the right selling price	→	Choose a standard menu pricing method.
4. At the right sales volume	→	Forecast sales and food cost.
5. To produces the right profit	→	Use Menu Analysis to analyze the sales mix for maximum profitability.

Some of the "rights," such as standardized recipes, standard portion costs, and the Minimum Menu Pricing formula are familiar turf—all were covered earlier in the text. Building off this foundation, this chapter focuses on developing a menu selection, determining a menu price, converting covers forecasted into sales, forecasting costs, and analyzing menu selections.

THE FIVE RIGHTS TO MENU SELECTION

1. **Sell the right menu items.**
2. At the right portion cost.
3. At the right selling price.
4. At the right sales volume.
5. To produce the right profit.

The Right Menu Selection

The first step in the Five Rights to Menu Selection says that a successful foodservice operation has to sell the right menu items. Selling the "right menu items" is not about making a list of all the favorites of the restaurant staff and tossing in a few things a competitor has on its menu. This process involves researching customer fit, operational fit, and profitability.

Researching Menu Selection

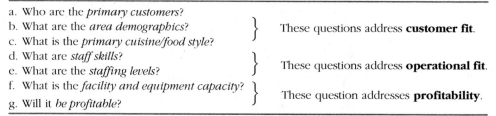

a. Who are the *primary customers?*
b. What are the *area demographics?*
c. What is the *primary cuisine/food style?*

These questions address **customer fit**.

d. What are *staff skills?*
e. What are the *staffing levels?*

These questions address **operational fit**.

f. What is the *facility and equipment capacity?*
g. Will it *be profitable?*

These question addresses **profitability**.

Customer Fit

First, let's address **customer fit**.

Who Are the Primary Customers?   Foodservice establishments typically appeal to certain types of customers—their primary customers. It is reasonable to say that fast-food restaurants generally appeal to young families and those interested in a quick meal at an affordable price; buffets and cafeterias tend to attract senior citizens; a small ethnic restaurant may appeal to the residents of a certain neighborhood; and a deli in an office building focuses on the needs of those who occupy the building. Designing an appropriate menu selection for the multiple markets in the typical customer base is critical.

Foodservice managers must know their customers. Getting answers to the following questions will help managers identify menu items that fit the customer base.

- What do the customers "do" prior to coming in for a meal? Are they tourists, employees, travelers, or athletes?
- How much time do customers have to eat? The longer the time available to dine, the more cook-to-order food can be offered to customers who are willing to pay a higher price.
- How price sensitive are customers? Every location has a **price threshold**—*a range of acceptable prices*—for meals.
- What is the reason for the diner's presence in your dining room? A special occasion? To experience the cuisine? Or is it just a matter of convenience?
- What is the customer's food expertise and consequent expectation? What is the sophistication of the palate of the customer base?

By answering these questions, foodservice managers can develop a business instinct for recognizing menu items that are most desired by the customer.

What Are the Area's Demographics?   Good menu planning strategy is not complete without a periodic review of the **demographics** of an area—*information about an area and the people who live there.* The demographic information for any town, city, or state is easily accessible via the Internet. Visit www.census.gov for a wealth of free information published by the U.S. government. The following is a list of some of the common categories of census information, or demographics, of interest to foodservice operators:

- Socioeconomic groups
- Competitors
- Education
- Occupation
- Income

- Ethnic groups
- Housing information
- Autos
- Trade
- Average commute time

- Dietary needs
- Customer preferences
- Businesses
- Number of restaurants
- Minority and women owned businesses
- Government
- Foreign

Customer comment cards, informal personal conversations with guests, and knowledge of customer preference patterns are additional ways to gather information. Today, software is available to create a guest preference database that includes demographic as well as psychographic customer data. **Psychographic market segmenting** involves gathering *information about customers' lifestyle, attitudes, beliefs, values, buying motives, and so on.* As management gets to "know" customers, information is entered into their guest profile, creating the opportunity to carefully craft customized marketing programs to increase customer retention, satisfaction, and sales.

What Is the Food Style or Theme of the Target Group?   Menu selections and restaurant themes go hand in hand. Savvy operators tailor their menus to offer options for all diners—and that can be a very diverse crowd. Consider that traditional steak houses now commonly offer seafood, pasta, and chicken dishes.

The **food style** or **theme** indicates foods that are based on

- A region (the Southwest, New England, the South).
- A style or flavor (Cajun, Tex-Mex, BBQ).
- A nation or ethnic group (Italian, Mexican, Asian, Indian).
- A cooking method or technique (fusion, grilled, broiled, sautéed, poached).
- A food trend (low-fat, vegetarian).
- A specific food item (beef, specialty items, seafood).

Generally, successful and interesting menu selections incorporate a variety of food styles, cooking methods, tastes, and even service. An adventurous customer base expects a selection that challenges their palate.

In addition, menu items have to have a "plate fit," in terms of

- ***Taste:*** Every item on a plate should have a distinctive taste or flavor. The tastes and flavors should complement each other. Expert menu planners pair complementary flavors on each plate.
- ***Texture or Shape:*** An attractive presentation requires variety in the texture, shape, and height of food items as they are arranged on the plate.
- ***Color:*** People eat with their eyes! A well-designed plate is not by chance. Even the simplest item can be tastefully presented. Interesting plate presentations are one way to increase menu prices.
- ***Cooking method:*** A menu should include a variety of cooking methods. This is an easy way to introduce unique menu items and unusual flavors and to distribute cooking loads in the back-of-the-house.
- ***Cross-utilization of product:*** Every menu should cross-utilize as many products as possible, to appeal to customer food preferences, reduce the number of items in inventory, minimize the need for storage space, and reduce inventory costs.

What Is the Service Style?   Most restaurants move food from the kitchen to the guests via servers. This process describes the typical **American service style**. American service is effective and efficient, and it makes for faster table turns. Varying the service style, however, is an interesting way to differentiate a foodservice operation, enhance food offerings, and build the average guest check.

COMMON SERVICE STYLES
- **Self-Serve Buffet or Food Bar:** Guests plate and serve themselves.
- **Family Style:** Platters or bowls of food are placed on the table; guests serve themselves.
- **American Service:** Food is plated in the kitchen and delivered to guests via servers.
- **French Service:** Food is prepped in the kitchen. The service staff finishes and plates the food tableside.
- **Russian (Banquet Service):** Food is fully prepared in the kitchen, where it is decoratively displayed on trays. Servers then run trays to the dining room and serve guests directly from the trays.

Staff skills, labor cost, food cost, equipment, facility capacity, and flow are all variables that must be carefully evaluated when entertaining a change in service.

Operational Fit

Next, let's talk about operational fit.

What Are the Staff's Skills   The skills and quality of the existing staff and the labor pool from which you draw will affect the type and quality of menu selections. A young labor force with little experience in the food industry and work in general will not be able to produce intricate menu items. Menu selections may be constrained to preprepared items that are easy to produce—basically, heat it and eat it!

Knowing the abilities of your current staff is key to planning menu items that are producible. Take an "inventory" of staff skills. Where and what kind of training is most needed? How will developing your staff affect menu selection? Selling prices? Customer satisfaction?

Recruiting employees from beyond the normal search area or through professional hospitality organizations or college or university programs, together with investing in in-house training and development programs, are all ways to develop and retain a professional staff.

What Are the Staffing Levels?   On the heels of staff ability come staffing levels. The designated ratio of employees to guests is not a chance happening. Managers use guest service standards to determine these ratios and to describe the level of service that employees are expected to deliver. Staffing tables are the management tool used to control both labor cost and guest service. See Chapter 16 for a more in-depth discussion of this topic.

What Is the Facility and Equipment Capacity?   One of the often forgotten ways to analyze a menu selection is in regards to the facility and equipment.

- Proposing a salad bar? How will it affect seating? Traffic flow? Is the space close to the kitchen for ease in refilling?
- Considering a new fried item? Check the capacity of the equipment and analyze the effect on the workstation. An overloaded workstation affects the timely serving of food. This, in turn, could affect guest satisfaction, seat turns, average check, and server tips.
- New menu items may require the operation to purchase additional food product that may affect storage space and inventory costs.

Introducing new items or a new menu without analyzing beforehand the effect on staff and equipment capacity is a recipe for disaster.

Profitability

Next in our research into menu selection, let's ask this question: Will it be profitable?

Foodservice operations are in business to make a profit by selling food and beverage items. The best menu price is one that covers the cost of producing the item (True Cost per Dish, or TCPD, from Chapter 3) and contributes to all other operating costs, fixed costs, and profit. Beyond these factors, sufficient overall sales volume is necessary for operational success. A complete discussion of cost per portion, menu pricing, menu analysis, and profitability is included later in this chapter.

Shaping a Winning Menu Selection Using Customer, Operational, and Profitability Criteria ☺

The questions we just asked about menu selection can be used within an evaluation tool to help determine the best menu items to offer. They help take the guesswork and politics out of menu decisions. If a menu fits ☺ within each criteria, it is safe to say it deserves a place on the menu or at least in the menu bank file. A scorecard approach, such as the one that follows, can be used to evaluate potential menu items:

Menu Selection Scorecard			
Question	☺	☹	**Strategy**
Who are the primary customers?	✓		
What are the area demographics?	✓		
What is the primary cuisine or food style?	✓		
What are the staff skills?	✓		
What are the staffing levels?	✓		
What is the facility and equipment capacity?	✓		
Will it be profitable?	✓		

A ✓ in the ☺ column indicates an item has been thoroughly evaluated on that question and does not pose a problem. A check in one or more of the ☹ boxes identifies trouble spots in relation to the three key areas of customer, operational, and profitability fit. These issues must be resolved before this item can be adopted.

An Item Doesn't "Fit" In Some Way ☹—Now What?   If an item doesn't fit in some way, what do you do? It depends. This system identifies the "fit" issue(s). It is up to management to decide on a course of action. Management can decide to

- Scrap the item.
- Address the areas of concern, or in other words, fix it.
- Put it away and look at it again at some other time.

The decision often lies in customer demand. If there is strong consensus that this item is desired, hot, and you've just "gotta have it" on the menu, then any ☹ issues(s) have to be resolved before this item is rolled out. In some instances, the case for the item may be so strong that one ☹ check is reason enough to eliminate the item.

Standard Control Documents: The Menu Bank

Once menu items are decided on, control documents have to be prepared. One way to organize these documents is through the creation of a **menu bank**. A **menu bank** is *a file of **all** menu items that are profitable ☺ for the operation*. The file contains current menu items, weekly specials, holiday specials, seasonal items, new items to be used at a later time, and works in progress.

Operating documents in each menu item's file include

- The standardized recipe.
- The standard plate card.
- The standardized cost card.
- Purchasing research.
- Menu price.

It is not uncommon to have 2 to 4 times more items in the file than are currently served on the menu. The beauty of developing a menu bank file system is that all items in the bank are identified as winners ☺. As a "winner," menu items fit the operation in terms of marketability, producibility, and profitability. Any item in the bank has passed muster and is ready to be brought immediately into production—it is ready to sell, because

- The recipe has been standardized.
- The standard portion cost is in line.
- The raw products to produce the item have been researched and are available.
- The kitchen and dining room can manage the production and service.
- The menu price is in line with other items.
- The item is profitable.
- And most important, the item is marketable—the customer desires the item.

By doing all the preliminary field work and research, new items can be instantly offered with confidence that they "fit" and there will be no confusion when the new item or menu is rolled out.

Competition

A successful foodservice manager closely examines what the competition is doing. To better understand the competition, the foodservice operator should conduct a competitive analysis. A **competitive analysis** is *the process of determining the number of competitors and analyzing their strengths and weaknesses to discover opportunities.* A competitive analysis is the tool in the manager's toolbox to use to answer the rest of the questions about the competition.

No foodservice manager should ever copy a competitor's menu. Part of the job, however, is to study the competition. A foodservice manager must research the answers to a number of questions about the competition in order to be sure the menu selection is competitive.

COMPETITIVE ANALYSIS QUESTIONS

1. What is the total demand for eating out in the competitive geographic area?

2. How many competitors exist?

3. What are the competition's customer counts?

4. What do competitors charge for similar items?

5. What are the competitors' signature menu items?

What Is the Total Demand for Eating Out in the Competitive Geographic Area? The **competitive geographic area** or **trading area** is *the area defined as that from which most customers originate.* In small communities, this question is fairly easy to answer. In larger communities, it becomes more difficult and requires an investment in research. A relatively easy way to find out is to ask customers directly where they live or work when they pay the guest check. The information gathered is then categorized. Software packages that track customer data are becoming more common as operators seek to build repeat customers through customer service programs. The kinds of information stored may include: the customer's name, address, telephone and fax numbers, birth date, anniversary date, e-mail, food likes and dislikes, favorite table, favorite server, personal likes and dislikes, and so on. In some cases, the information may be gathered via forms the customer is encouraged to fill out with some incentive to receive a reward.

How Many Competitors Exist?   Once the trading area is determined, travel the area and identify the competitors. Most foodservice managers know who the competition is just by driving to work and consciously taking note of establishments they pass along the way.

What Are the Competition's Customer Counts?   The only way to determine this information is to actually count the number of guests in a competitor's establishment. A reasonably accurate guess is acceptable. This can be accomplished by

- Counting tables and booths and determining seating capacity.
- Actually eating at the competition and taking a physical customer count during peak periods.
- Noting the number of cars in the parking lot.

What Do Competitors Charge for Similar Items?   This is probably the easiest information to obtain. All the foodservice manager needs to do is obtain a copy of a competitor's menu and compare prices by visiting the competitor as a customer and taking notes. This information may also be readily available on the competitor's Web site.

What Are Competitors' Signature Menu Items?   **Signature items** are *menu items that distinguish competitors from each other.* A McDonald's Big Mac is an example. At Farfalle Arrabbiata, it is the dish Farfalle Arrabbiata, as well as the Chicken Noodle Soup. Some foodservice establishments have desserts that distinguish their operation, some have appetizers, and still others may have a drink or service style. These items establish the uniqueness of a foodservice operation.

Competitive Analysis

A Competitive Analysis Form is a tool that foodservice managers use to *overview their competitor's menus.* It is a way of collecting menu information in order to compare menu prices and study menu selections. Look at Figure 12.2 before you continue reading.

Using a Competitive Analysis Form   Assume that Farfalle Arrabbiata's customers have requested Fettuccini Alfredo similar to that offered at Tuscany Hill and Pastino's. All Chef Raoul has to do is create a similar dish and offer it at a competitive price between $10.95 and $9.50.

If Chef Raoul wants to compete strictly on price to bring in more customers, he could offer the Fettuccini at less than $9.95. If he decides to make a signature dish out of it, so that customers rave and go out of their way to eat at Farfalle Arrabbiata, the selling price could be set at $11.95. People will pay a premium for an item if they feel that they have received a good value in return for their money.

If a new restaurant were to open in the same area as Farfalle Arrabbiata, Tuscany Hill, and Pastino's, the management of the new restaurant should recognize that

	Competitors		
Prepared By:			
Date:			
Menu Items	**Farfalle Arrabbiata**	**Tuscany Hill**	**Pastino's**
Fettucini Alfredo	???	$10.95	$ 9.95
Pizzas	$ 8.95–$9.95	9.95–Average	8.95–Average
Steak/Bistecca	17.95	15.95	16.95
Cioppino	19.95	18.95	19.95
Spaghetti Bolognese	8.50	7.95	8.95
Risotto	13.95	12.95	11.95

FIGURE 12.2 Competitive Analysis Form.

Fettuccine Alfredo priced at $11.95 is probably not going to sell unless the restaurant is unique in design, location, or service. Watching competitors' menus provides the information necessary to competitively price a menu. If prices are in line with the amount of food being offered, customers generally will believe they are receiving a good value.

Good value is generally viewed as a relationship between the amount and quality of food and the price charged. Presenting a menu that will be perceived as having good value is subjective in nature. Management should constantly monitor customer responses to the price and value perception by calculating the sales activity for each menu item.

THE FIVE RIGHTS TO MENU SELECTION

1. Sell the right menu items.
2. **At the right portion cost.**
3. **At the right selling price.**
4. At the right sales volume.
5. To produce the right profit.

Calculating the Right Portion Cost and Selling Price

Some of the toughest decisions a foodservice manager must make are made when **setting a menu price**. The term refers to *the act of setting prices for items to be listed on a menu or changing the prices that are currently listed on the menu.* Setting a menu price has four steps:

1. Determining the TCPD (True Cost per Dish)
2. Selecting a menu pricing method to calculate the **mathematical** Minimum Menu Price (MMP)
3. Considering other differentiating factors
4. Setting the actual selling price

TO SET A MENU PRICE

1. Determine the TCPD (True Cost per Dish).
2. Select a menu pricing method to calculate the **mathematical** Minimum Menu Price (MMP).
3. Consider other differentiating factors.
4. Set the actual selling price.

Determining the True Cost per Dish

Because **True Cost per Dish (TCPD)** was covered extensively in Chapter 3, there is no need to repeat that information. Suffice it to say that calculating TCPD is an integral part of any foodservice operations' standard operating procedures. Regardless of the pricing method used, the TCPD drives the selling price. Why? Because the TCPD comes from the standard cost card and the standard recipe—two of the primary control documents. As a quick refresher, the Minimum Menu Price formula is reproduced here for your convenience. Refer to Chapter 3 for a review of this topic.

MINIMUM MENU PRICE FORMULA

Extended Price/Recipe Yield = Cost per Portion
Cost per Portion + Q Factor = Cost per Dish (CPD)
Cost per Dish $\times$ 1.SF % = True Cost per Dish (TCPD)
True Cost per Dish/Standard Food Cost % = Minimum Menu Price (MMP)

Selecting a Menu Pricing Method

Next, Select a Menu Pricing Method, so you can calculate the Minimum Menu Price (MMP). The menu price often determines how profitable a foodservice operation has the potential of becoming. In earlier times (very early!), competition among foodservice operations was limited or nonexistent and cost control systems were largely undeveloped. Thus, menu pricing was often the result of guessing, pricing according to what the market would bear, or copying a competitor. Because of the lack of competition, many operations were very successful and, amazingly, quite profitable, given the lack of cost control systems. In fact, it was the era of Prohibition and the Great Depression that ushered in the development of cost control systems. Today, competition is fierce (there are more than 950,000 restaurants in the United States) and the cost structure of each operation and business segment is so unique that guessing, pricing strictly on what the market will bear, or copying a competitor's menu prices is a serious mistake.

Considering Other Differentiating Factors

Consider Other Differentiating Factors Before Setting the Actual Selling Price. Did you notice No. 2 in the **To Set a Menu Price** box? Specifically, did you wonder why the word "**mathematical**" is bolded? It is in bold to make the point that any time a menu pricing method is used to calculate a minimum menu price, the result is not necessarily the **ACTUAL** selling price that will be printed on the menu.

Why? Because it is simply a function of the TCPD and a formula. Put into an equation, the formula for the **actual selling price** might look like this:

$$\begin{array}{l} \text{Mathematical Selling Price (MMP)} \\ \underline{+ \text{ Other Differentiating Factors}} \\ = \text{Actual Menu Price} \end{array}$$

The first part of the equation—the mathematical menu price—is easy. Now it's on to the second part, which is equally as important. Remember that there are more than 950,000 restaurants in the United States? This means there are a lot of dining options out there. What makes a guest opt for one restaurant over another? It's hard to say with certainty, but the answer lies in how an operation differentiates itself from competitors.

Operators must discover just what their customer will pay extra for, then set menu prices accordingly. Every detail of a customer's experience should be directed and planned. The uniqueness of each operation means that creating differentiation is restaurant specific. The following punch list provides a number of ideas to help create the attention to detail that turns the ordinary dining experience into an extraordinary experience that guests will *willingly pay you extra for*

CUSTOMIZING THE GUEST'S DINING EXPERIENCE
- Menu design and layout
- Wine list
- Plate presentation—garnish, color coordination, ingredient coordination
- Tableware—size, shape, quality, color, and pattern
- Table top decor
- Glassware—size, shape, quality, color, and pattern
- Flatware—pattern, quality
- Table linens—quality, color
- Waiting areas/all other public areas—décor, space, lighting
- Tables, booths, chairs—color, cleanliness, style, comfort, table lighting
- Bar design/décor/ambiance, lighting, and restroom ambiance—cleanliness, décor, lighting, types of equipment
- Dining room/guest service areas—décor/ambiance, cleanliness, lighting, flow, space, sounds, aromas, music
- Staff attire
- Reputation of owner or chef
- Location of restaurant
- Community relations
- Service staff—attire, training, quality and style of service, guest-to-server ratio, level of staffing
- Other services—valet service, take-away service, Web site, retail sales, music, entertainment
- Customization of each guest's experience: food, service, or any other detail

---

Setting the Actual Selling Price

The following are options for setting actual menu prices:

- Set the menu price *at* the mathematical MMP.
- Set the menu price *higher* than the mathematical MMP.
- Set the menu price *lower* than the mathematical MMP.

Whether menu prices are set *at, higher,* or *lower* than the mathematical MMP is a function of

- ***The effort to successfully differentiate from the competition.*** You have to *earn the right to set menu prices higher than those of your competitors.*
- ***Low portion costs.*** Some menu items—like Chicken Noodle Soup or pizzas—are, in and of themselves, inexpensive to produce. In most of these cases, the actual menu price can easily be set higher than the mathematical minimum menu price with no resistance from customers. Items sold at a menu price higher than the minimum help balance items that are sold at a price less than the minimum.
- ***High portion costs.*** Other items will, in and of themselves, be expensive to produce. Setting the price at the mathematical minimum menu price may be the only choice.
- ***Selling price less than MMP.*** In some cases, the actual selling price may be set at *less* than the minimum. How can this be? This is where sales mix comes into play. Look for further discussion on this topic later in the chapter.
- ***What the market will bear.*** Without a doubt, what the market will bear is the ultimate decision-making factor when setting actual menu prices. The theoretical selling price can only be achieved when the customer perceives the price-value relationship to be in harmony. Inasmuch as the operator exceeds the customer's perceived value in some way, the actual selling price can be set higher than the mathematical minimum. The reverse also holds true—a price-value perceived as poor means the minimum price may not be possible.
- ***Overall demand.*** It's a hot new dish. Your restaurant is a leader in the marketplace. You've got it on the menu. People have to have it. You do the math!
- ***Competition.*** Although it is never a good idea to copy a competitor's prices, managers should know the going rate of similar menu items offered by competitors.

Menu Pricing Methods

The following menu pricing methods are commonly used by foodservice operators to determine mathematical menu prices.

- Food Cost Percentage Method
- Contribution Margin
- Ratio Method
- Prime Cost Method

MENU PRICING METHODS
- **Food Cost Percentage Method**
- Contribution Margin Method
- Ratio Method
- Prime Cost Method

Food Cost Percentage Method   The **Food Cost Percentage Method** is based on the presumption that *costs should be maintained as a fixed percentage of sales.* The work in Chapter 10 set the foundation for this concept. Simply stated:

- The relationship between the amount of money spent on purchasing raw products and the sales revenues generated by converting raw products into final menu products should always be the same.

In Chapter 10, the standard food cost percentage for Farfalle Arrabbiata was determined to be 33.6%. Assume that management subscribes to the theory we discussed earlier—*that food cost is a percentage of sales.* Then, if food cost has been determined to be 33.6% and sales are expected to be $400, the food cost should be $134.40 ($400 × 33.6% = $134.40). If sales are forecasted to be $1,600, the expected food cost would be $537.60 ($1,600 × 33.6% = $537.60). Subscribing to the theory that food cost is a percentage of sales means three things:

1. In the first cost-to-sales example, $134.40 should be sufficient to purchase the raw products in the *quality and quantity* needed to generate the $400.00 in sales.

2. Regardless of the amount of sales, overall food costs should *always* be 33.6% at Farfalle Arrabbiata, because that is the identified operational standard.

3. The standard food cost percentage can be used along with the TCPD to determine the minimum menu price for an item. Here is the formula:

TRUE COST PER DISH/STANDARD FOOD COST % = MINIMUM MENU PRICE (MMP)

If you accept the premise that **food cost is a percentage of sales**, then the Food Cost Percentage Method is an acceptable way to determine a mathematical menu price. Generally, it is best used in operations that have average profits or low prices and consistently steady business. There is one qualifying note to make, however: The Food Cost Percentage Method is an acceptable way to determine a selling price inasmuch as the business *operates at or very close to its desired standard food cost percentage.* Any operation that lacks control of food cost and, as such, food cost percentage, cannot be certain that the sales price calculated in this way is adequate to cover all expenses and profit.

Use the Food Cost Percentage method to practice calculating the mathematical selling price for these sample menu items from Farfalle Arrabbiata. The math should be familiar to you.

	A /	B =	C
Menu Item	**TCPD**	**Food Cost %**	**Mathematical Selling Price**
Chicken Noodle Soup	$0.44	33.6%	
Pizza Picante	1.89	33.6	
Farfalle Arrabbiata	3.10	33.6	
Cioppino	7.24	33.6	

And the answers are as follows:

Menu Item	**TCPD**	**Food Cost %**	**Mathematical Selling Price**
Chicken Noodle Soup	$0.44	33.6%	$1.31
Pizza Picante	1.89	33.6	5.63
Farfalle Arrabbiata	3.10	33.6	9.23
Cioppino	7.24	33.6	21.54

Contribution Margin Method   The term **Contribution Margin (CM)** refers to *the contribution that the **sale** of each menu item makes toward covering raw food cost*

(TCPD), all other operating costs, fixed costs, and profit. The **Contribution Margin Pricing Method** is valuable for those who believe that:

- *Profit should be treated as an expense to be covered by sales and not as the money left over after expenses.*

MENU PRICING METHODS
- Food Cost Percentage Method
- **Contribution Margin Method**
- Ratio Method
- Prime Cost Method

Basically, *the foodservice manager calculates the average amount each menu item should contribute to a predetermined profitability level.* This amount is then *added* to each item's TCPD to arrive at the selling price. It is a communistic approach to menu pricing in that this method *assumes that all items compete equally, so all should contribute equally.* In this way, the same Contribution Margin amount is added to all menu items.

Here is the Contribution Margin Formula:

TCPD + AVERAGE CONTRIBUTION MARGIN = MINIMUM MENU PRICE

We know where TCPD comes from—the standard cost card. What about this **Average Contribution Margin**? Go back to the definition. It says it is *the amount of money needed to cover:*

- *Other operating costs*
- *Fixed costs*
- *Profit*

Sound familiar to you? It should. These are the expense categories found on an income statement. That is probably a good place to start to determine the Average Contribution Margin per guest. Because the Contribution Margin is the per-person average of all other costs and profit, it makes sense to use the income statement.

To find the Average Contribution Margin, first find *the sum of the Controllable Costs, Fixed Costs,* and *Profit.* Next, divide this by the *number of customers for the year.* This information would be found in sales history records. The number of guests for the year was 167,483: (Figure 12.3 is the source document for these figures.)

Tot. Controllable Exp.	$1,002,929
Tot. Occupancy Costs	292,429
Restaurant Profit B4 Taxes	+ 125,417
Total	= $1,420,775

ALL OTHER COSTS + PROFIT/NUMBER OF GUESTS = AVG. CONTRIBUTION MARGIN

$1,420,775/167,483 ☺ = $8.48

What does $8.48 mean? It means that on average, in 2005 every person who came to dine at Farfalle Arrabbiata gave the restaurant:

- The cost of preparing the food item (TCPD)

plus

- An average of $8.48 toward all other operating expenses and profit.

Remember that this is strictly an average. Some guests paid *more* than $8.48 and some paid *less than* $8.48. The Contribution Margin Method is a very logical approach to menu pricing. If the Average Contribution Margin is known, then that sum can be added to the TCPD of any menu item, and the menu price needed to be able to pay all the bills and make a profit can be determined. By dividing up the expenses and profit into an amount that each person is "charged," profit is all but guaranteed, as long as *guest counts hit forecasts*. As with the Food Cost Percentage Method, this is true inasmuch as the operation has *tight control over the budget*. Complete the following chart to calculate the minimum menu price for the four menu items:

Menu Item	TCPD	Avg. CM	Contribution Margin Selling Price
Chicken Noodle Soup	$0.44	$8.48	
Pizza	1.89	8.48	
Farfalle Arrabbiata	3.10	8.48	
Cioppino	7.24	8.48	
	A +	B =	C

Problems with this Pricing Method   There are two inherent problems with the Contribution Margin method.

The first and biggest problem with Contribution Margin (CM) Pricing Method has to do with the average itself. The current average CM for Farfalle Arrabbiata is $8.48. It is the average of *all expenses and profit for all guests purchasing from all menu categories during all meal periods*. Adding this amount to every single menu item produces some very interesting results. Observe what happens when applying the strategy of adding $8.48 to every menu item. Can we sell Chicken Noodle Soup for $8.92? Of course not. How do these selling prices compare to the selling prices computed using the Food Cost Percentage Method? The only one that is remotely close is Farfalle Arrabbiata, and it isn't even all that close.

What we are seeing is the communistic approach of this method in action—that is, every item for sale must contribute the same amount to cover expenses and profit. CM pricing works best when the *TCPD costs of all the items are close*. The greater the disparity in the TCPDs, the greater the disparity in final menu prices. There are two ways to solve this problem:

1. ***Assign different Average Contribution Margins for different menu items.***
   It is not fair to add $8.48 to the Chicken Noodle Soup simply because that is the calculated average. It's just a little cup of soup—customers would balk at paying that price. The solution is to use a CM for soup that is different from that used for entrees, pizza, and pasta dishes. How do you do this? Some part of $8.48 is appropriate to add to the TCPD for the Chicken Noodle Soup. Look at the sales records for the soup category—how popular are soups, overall? What percentage of sales do they represent? It makes sense to use this proportion as a guide to determine how much of the $8.48 should be allocated to the soups. The same logic can be used for each menu category. Determine the relative popularity of a menu group and distribute the Average Contribution Margin accordingly.

2. ***Use a different menu pricing method for some menu items or menu categories.*** It may be more sensible to price soups (and any other menu items/categories management chooses) using the Food Cost Percentage Method. Look at the selling price for the soup using Food Cost Percentage—$1.31. No customer would complain about this price. It is well within normal selling prices for soup. The Average CM is now distributed over select menu categories or items.

The second problem with the Contribution Margin Method is that the average is determined by using customer counts. This works just fine if customer counts stay to forecast. Any time business slows down and *customer counts are fewer than forecast,* however, the average CM will be *less* than is needed to cover all expenses and profit. If guest counts do not improve, it is likely the operation will start to lose money. Managers should be aware of the effect of erratic or falling customer counts on profit.

Any time the reverse happens—*guest counts increase more than the forecast*—then the average CM used to calculate the selling prices will actually be greater than the true average. This means menu prices are higher than they mathematically need to be and if the trend continues, profits will be higher. Operations with stable or rising customer counts can feel confident using this method to adopt menu prices.

Another Way of Looking at Contribution Margin   Once menu prices are assigned, an item's *actual* Contribution Margin can easily be determined. It is a simple process of subtracting each item's TCPD from its actual selling price.

ACTUAL MENU PRICE − TCPD = MENU ITEM CONTRIBUTION MARGIN

Practice with the rest of the items below. Find the Menu Item or Plate Contribution Margin, given these actual menu prices.

Menu Item	Mathematical Selling Price	TCPD	Menu (Plate) Contribution
Chicken Noodle Soup	$ 1.75	$0.44	
Pizza	8.50	1.89	
Farfalle Arrabbiata	11.95	3.10	
Cioppino	19.95	7.24	
	A	− B	= C

And the answers are:

Menu Item	Mathematical Selling Price	TCPD	Menu (Plate) Contribution
Chicken Noodle Soup	$ 1.75	$0.44	$ 1.31
Pizza	8.50	1.89	6.61
Farfalle Arrabbiata	11.95	3.10	8.85
Cioppino	19.95	7.24	12.71

What Does Menu/Plate Contribution Mean?   Every time an order of Chicken Noodle Soup is paid for, $.44 is collected to cover the cost of producing the item (TCPD), which leaves $1.31 toward a part of all the other costs and profit. It doesn't tell us much about whether it is enough or not enough. Right now it is simply the amount of money left over after paying for the raw food product. Watch how the Plate CM is used in a later section on menu analysis.

The Contribution Margin method is best used in less price-sensitive operations that have medium to high prices or are seasonal. If this method is used to price every menu item, it may discourage customers from buying less expensive items because of a poor perceived value. CM works best when the TCPD of the menu items are very close to each other.

MENU PRICING METHODS
- Food Cost Percentage Method
- Contribution Margin Method
- **Ratio Method**
- Prime Cost Method

Ratio Method   The Ratio Method creates a relationship between Total Food Cost and all other costs (Controllable Expenses, Occupation Costs, and Profit = Gross Profit). This is then used to find a selling price. The income statement is the source of this information. There are three steps to this method:

1. Find the ratio of Cost of Goods to all other costs.
2. Multiply the ratio times the TCPD for the item.
3. Add this amount to the TCPD for each item.

Using the income statement data in Figure 12.3, the calculation would look like this:

All Other Costs + Profit/Total Food Cost = Ratio
$1,420,775/$561,641 = 2.53

Ratio × TCPD = Total Noningredient
Costs For The Item
2.53 × $.44 (Chicken Noodle Soup) = $1.11

TCPD + Noningredient Cost = Minimum Menu Price
$.44 + $1.11 = $1.55

Complete the minimum menu price for the rest of the examples below:

Menu Item	TCPD	Ratio	Noningredient Costs	Minimum Menu Price
Chicken Noodle Soup	$0.44	2.53	$1.11	$1.55
Pizza	1.89	2.53		
Farfalle Arrabbiata	3.10	2.53		
Cioppino	7.24	2.53		

Your answers should look like this:

Menu Item	TCPD	Ratio	Noningredient Costs	Minimum Menu Price
Chicken Noodle Soup	$0.44	2.53	$ 1.11	$ 1.55
Pizza	1.89	2.53	4.78	6.67
Farfalle Arrabbiata	3.10	2.53	7.84	10.94
Cioppino	7.24	2.53	18.32	25.56

Sales		
Food	$1,671,550	80.00%
Beverage	417,887	20.00
Total Revenue	2,089,437	100.00
Cost of Sales		
Food	561,641	**33.60%**
Beverage	107,021	25.61
Total Cost of Goods	668,662	32.00
Gross Profit	**$1,420,775**	**68.00%**
Controllable Expenses		
Payroll	$618,473	29.60%
Benefits	94,025	4.50
Direct Operating Expenses	71,041	3.40
Music And Entertainment	10,447	0.50
Advertising & Promo	52,236	2.50
Utilities	77,309	3.70
Administration & General	50,146	2.40
Repair & Maintenance	29,252	1.40
***Total Controllable Expenses**	**$1,002,929**	**48.00%**
Income B4 Occupancy Costs	**$417,846**	20.00%
Occupation Costs		
Rent	123,529	5.91
Property Taxes	38,004	1.82
Other Taxes	18,000	0.86
Property Insurance	21,996	1.05
Interest	33,000	1.58
Depreciation	57,900	2.77
***Total Occupancy Costs**	**$292,429**	**14.00%**
***Restaurant Profit B4 Taxes**	**$125,417**	**6.00%**

FIGURE 12.3   Income statement for Farfalle Arrabbiata

MENU PRICING METHODS

- Food Cost Percentage Method
- Contribution Margin Method
- Ratio Method
- **Prime Cost Method**

Prime Cost Method   The name **Prime Cost Pricing Method** should sound familiar. It is a method that factors food cost and labor cost (including benefits) into the menu pricing equation. The income statement in Figure 12.3, on page 375, is the source document for the figures. There are five steps to this method:

1. Determine the TCPD for each menu item.
2. Find the Labor Cost per Guest (including benefits).
3. Determine the Prime Cost per Guest.
4. Determine the Prime Cost Percentage.
5. Determine the Minimum Menu Price.

You will need the following equations:

Labor Cost per Guest

PAYROLL + BENEFITS/TOTAL NUMBER OF GUESTS = LABOR COST PER GUEST
$618,473 + $94,025/167,483 = $4.25

Prime Cost Per Guest for Farfalle Arrabbiata

TCPD + LABOR COST PER GUEST = PRIME COST PER GUEST
$3.10 + $4.25 = $7.35

Prime Cost Percentage

FOOD COST % + LABOR & BENEFIT COST % = PRIME COST PERCENTAGE
33.6% + 29.6% + 4.5% = 67.7%

Now we can calculate the **Minimum Menu Price**

PRIME COST PER GUEST/PRIME COST % = MINIMUM MENU PRICE
$7.35/67.7% = $10.86

Menu Item	TCPD	Labor Cost/ Guest	Prime Cost per Guest	Prime Cost %	Minimum Menu Price
Chicken Noodle Soup	$0.44	$4.25		67.7%	
Pizza	1.89	4.25		67.7%	
Farfalle Arrabbiata	3.10	4.25	$7.35	67.7%	$10.86
Cioppino	7.24	4.25		67.7%	
	A +	B =	C /	E =	F

Your answers should look like this:

Menu Item	TCPD	Labor Cost/ Guest	Prime Cost per Guest	Prime Cost %	Minimum Menu Price
Chicken Noodle Soup	$0.44	$4.25	$ 4.69	67.7%	$ 6.93
Pizza	1.89	4.25	6.14	67.7%	9.07
Farfalle Arrabbiata	3.10	4.25	7.35	67.7%	10.86
Cioppino	7.24	4.25	11.49	67.7%	16.97

Like the Contribution Margin method, this method works best when the TCPDs for menu items are similar. As you can see from the chart, items with low TCPDs end up with a disproportionately high selling price. The first two methods studied—Food Cost Percentage and Contribution Margin—are more widely used than the Ratio and Prime Cost methods. The menu pricing method of choice should be the method that generates the highest profit for each specific foodservice operation. Compare the four methods, as they appear below.

Summary of Formulas for Menu Pricing Methods

Method	Formula
FOOD COST %	TCPD/STANDARD FOOD COST % = MMP
CONTRIBUTION MARGIN	ALL NONFOOD COSTS + PROFIT/NO. OF GUESTS = AVG. CM TCPD + AVG. CM = MMP
RATIO METHOD	ALL NON-FOOD COSTS + PROFIT/FOOD COST = RATIO RATIO × TCPD = NONINGREDIENT COST TCPD + NONINGREDIENT COST = MMP
PRIME COST METHOD	PAYROLL + BENEFITS/NO. OF GUESTS = LABOR COST PER GUEST LABOR COST PER GUEST + TCPD = PRIME COST PER GUEST FOOD COST % + PAYROLL & BENEFITS COST % = PRIME COST % PRIME COST PER GUEST/PRIME COST % = MMP

Special Pricing Situations

In determining menu pricing, a special situation should be considered: food bars, or buffets. Food bars are unique. They appeal to customers who are value conscious—who seek a large amount of food for a relatively small amount of money. The challenge is to price the food so that a reasonable profit can be made.

Calculating portion costs for salad bars is not as difficult as it may seem. It is important to inventory and track all products put on the salad bar over a given period. The manager then calculates the total cost of the items consumed during the period and divides the total cost by the number of people who ate from the salad bar. The guest checks and sales history will indicate the guest count. The result is the cost per person for the food bar or buffet.

TOTAL COST OF ALL FOOD CONSUMED/NO. OF PEOPLE (☺) = COST OF FOOD BAR PER PERSON

Any of the menu pricing methods can be used to determine a selling price for a food bar or buffet, once the cost per person is known. The most challenging part of managing food bars or buffets is tracking the customer count—that is, the number of people who purchase a salad bar or food bar as a part of their menu choice. Using POS systems to track sales information ensures an accurate guest count. Also, it is important to realize that the price of produce fluctuates with seasonal changes. It probably would be wise to price this item using the highest expected prices to be paid for the ingredients. Figure 12.4 shows a sample salad bar cost sheet.

Rules for Price Rounding

A common **price rounding** rule is that all prices should be just under half and whole dollars. Research has shown that people generally do not perceive much of a difference in the price between $4.25 and $4.45. The price difference is not enough to cause buyer resistance. The final price will depend on competition and the nature of the operation.

Date:	Shift:		
Item	**Quantity**	**Unit Price**	**Extension**
Romaine	5 heads	$1.22/head	$6.10
Iceberg lettuce	5 heads	1.07/head	5.35
Tomatoes	4 lb.	1.19/lb.	4.76
Cucumbers	4 each	.35 each	1.40
Eggs	12 each	.09 each	1.08
Onions	1 lb.	.50/lb.	.50
Peppers	2 lb.	1.35/lb.	2.70
Carrots	1 lb.	.69/lb.	.69
Bacon bits	½ lb.	2.26/lb.	1.13
Potato Salad	5 lb.	1.25/lb.	6.25
Pasta Salad	5 lb.	1.25/lb.	6.25
Ranch Dressing	1 qt.	3.50/qt.	3.50
Blue Cheese Dressing	1 pt.	3.25/pt.	3.25
Raspberry Viniagrette	1 pt.	2.50/pt.	2.50
Caesar	1 qt.	3.10/qt.	3.10
Total Cost of Salad Bar: **Number of Guests:** **Cost per Person:**			**$48.56** 40 **$1.22**

FIGURE 12.4   Salad Bar Cost Sheet.

THE FIVE RIGHTS TO MENU SELECTION

1. Sell the right menu items.
2. At the right portion cost.
3. At the right selling price.
4. At the right sales volume.
5. To produce the right profit.

Sales and Food Cost Forecasts

The Sales Forecast

The **sales forecast** is directly related to pricing. It can be compared to The Five Rights—at the Right Volume. It is *an estimate of the foodservice operation's sales based on the number of expected customers and the average amount each customer will spend.* A forecast depends on three factors:

1. The count or number of people purchasing items prepared by the foodservice operation.
2. The menu price of the items sold.
3. The **average check** for the menu items sold.

A sales forecast is determined by *multiplying the forecasted guest count (☺) by the average check per person:*

NO. OF GUESTS FORECAST × AVERAGE CHECK = SALES $$

Returning to the sales forecast in Chapter 10 for the week of 2/9 to 2/15 (see p. 274), we can prepare the sales and food cost budget for the week. The forecast predicts 3,885 customers, at an overall average check for lunch and dinner of $12.55.

NO. OF GUESTS FORECASTED × AVERAGE CHECK = SALES $$
3,885 (☺) × $12.55 = $48,795

Simply put, Farfalle Arrabbiata is expecting sales of $48,795 this week, generated by 3,885 customers, who will each spend an average of $12.55.

The Food Cost Forecast

Using the standard budgeted food cost percentage of 33.6%, it is also possible to determine the budget for food. In this example, the food cost budget for the week would be $16,395.

FORECAST FOOD SALES × STANDARD COST % = FOOD COST DOLLARS
$48,795 × 33.6% = $16,395

A sales forecast by menu item would be similar to a Food Sales Recap Report or a Menu Analysis (to be discussed later). The difference is that the **Food Sales Recap Report** and the **Menu Analysis** *are based on an actual sales history*, whereas a **Menu Item Sales Forecast** is *an estimate of what is expected to happen.* It gives managers *a baseline for sales and costs.* A Menu Analysis, completed for the same period after sales are actually recorded, gives a basis for comparison. Figure 12.5 shows an example of a Menu Item Sales Forecast for 2/14. After the period, a comparison will be made between the forecast sales and actual sales. A Menu Item Sales Forecast is the best method for projecting sales and food costs if the Contribution Margin Method is used for pricing.

A sales forecast is necessary to see the outcome of actual menu prices. A sales forecast sets an estimate or a sales goal. At the end of an accounting period (week, month), a menu analysis will show what actually occurred. At that point, management will learn if they estimated correctly. If they didn't, hopefully they will gain an understanding of why the forecast was not met. Read on for a discussion of menu analysis.

Department: Dining Room					Page: 1 of 4	
Prepared By: Frank					Day: 2/14/2XXX Saturday	
Category: Appetizers					Forecast: 839	
Item	Forecast	Pop. %	Menu Price	TCPD	Plate Contrib. Margin	Total Sales	Total Food Cost
Mozzarella in Carrozza Arrabbiata	218	26%	$9.95	$4.62	$5.33	$2,169.10	$1,007.16
Aubergine Melanzane	126	15	7.95	2.46	5.49	1001.70	309.96
Totanetti Agli As paragi e Menta	101	12	12.95	5.12	7.83	1,307.95	517.12
Bruschetta con Portobella e Manzo	92	11	9.95	3.51	6.44	915.40	322.92
Brushetta con Mozzarella	58	7	8.25	2.04	6.21	478.50	118.32
Antipasti	168	20	11.95	5.32	6.63	2,007.60	893.76
Carpacciao di Manzo	76	9	12.95	5.63	7.32	984.20	427.88
Totals						$8,864.45	$3,597.12
	A	B	C – D = E			F	G
						A × C	A × D

FIGURE 12.5   Menu Item Sales Forecast.

THE FIVE RIGHTS TO MENU SELECTION

1. Sell the right menu items.
2. At the right portion cost.
3. At the right selling price.
4. At the right sales volume.
5. **To produce the right profit.**

---

*M*enu Profitability

The final topic to consider in the Five Rights of Menu Selection is menu profitability. Managing a foodservice operation is much like managing any retail store that sells general merchandise along with certain specialty items. The success of the operation depends to a large extent on management's ability to:

- Consistently provide the products that customers want at the quality and price that they expect
- Satisfy their needs and desires for new products.

To accomplish this goal, management must constantly review sales information. This data is collected from customer guest checks as each item from the menu is totaled according to the amount sold. Therefore, foodservice managers need to identify items that are strong sellers along with items that do not sell as well. Popular items should be among the more profitable for the foodservice operation. Less popular items may need to be kept on the menu if they remain profitable *and* generate some loyal patronage from a select group of customers, or they may need to be replaced with new items. Read on for a look at how to make menu decisions.

Week: 2/9/2XXX		2/9	2/10	2/11	2/12	2/13	2/14	2/15	
Weekly Count: 3,885 Daily Total:	☺ Popularity %	Mon. 360	Tues. 406	Wed. 511	Thurs. 525	Fri. 763	Sat. 839	Sun. 481	Total
Mozzarella in Carrozza Arrabbiata	26%	95	101	133	137	198	218	125	1,010
Aubergine Melanzane	17	61	72	87	89	124	140	82	655
Totanetti Agli Asparagi e Menta	13	55	60	72	64	84	102	63	500
Bruschetta con Portobello e Manzo	8	30	35	45	48	54	67	43	322
Bruschetta con Mozzarella	7	25	29	36	37	53	58	33	271
Antipasti	20	72	82	102	105	153	168	96	777
Carpacciao di Manzo	9	32	37	46	47	69	76	43	350

FIGURE 12.6   Food Sales Recap Report.

SALES MIX

A mix of menu items that reflects varying degrees of popularity and profitability.

Analyzing Sales Using a Food Sales Recap Report

One of the easiest ways to analyze a **sales mix** is by looking at the Food Sales Recap Report (Chapter 9). After all, it reports the number of each item sold. It is here that it is obvious which items are selling well (popular) and which items are not selling well (unpopular). Menu decisions are pretty easy to make with this picture: Stop offering items that are not popular!

With this in mind, look at Figure 12.6. According to this report, Bruschetta con Mozzarella and Bruschetta con Portobello e Manzo are the least popular items in this sales mix. As long as this report was typical of other weeks, it would be reasonable for management to draw the conclusion that these two items need to go. Mozzarella in Carrozza Arrabbiata and Antipasti are clearly the top sellers—these should be left alone. The remaining items are somewhere in the middle.

The Food Sales Recap Report makes it very easy to see the items that are the most popular and the items that are least popular. This is strictly *a one-dimensional view of sales,* however. What makes it one-dimensional is the fact that menu items are considered successful simply because they sell. Basing menu decisions on just menu item popularity alone is a mistake. Why? Read on for a look at the next way to analyze a sales mix.

A **Menu Analysis** is the next tool to use to analyze sales. The difference between this tool and the Food Sales Recap Report is that this analysis uses *two variables:*

- Menu item popularity ☺ (Popular ☺/Not Popular ☹, as in the Food Sales Recap Report)
- Menu item profitability $ (Profitable ☺/Not Profitable ☹)

This method helps foodservice managers better identify items that may not be a good fit because they are not popular or profitable. Two variables give a *two-dimensional view* of the sales mix by using sales and cost (TCPD) data rather than just sales data. With two variables, there now become four categories into which to sort menu items. The four categories are:

1. Menu items that are popular and profitable.
2. Menu items that are popular but unprofitable.

3. Menu items that are unpopular but profitable.

4. Menu items that are both unpopular and unprofitable.

Menu Popularity and Profitability
What's a 1, 2, 3, & 4?

No. 1 Items—Popular ☺ & Profitable ☺: These items are frequently selected by customers and are profitable, meaning they contribute strongly to profit.

• Management likes to sell these!

No. 2 Items—Popular ☺ & Unprofitable ☹: These items are frequently selected but, unfortunately, they do not contribute much to profit.

• Management wishes people would not order these items!

No. 3 Items—Unpopular ☹ & Profitable ☺: These items are not very popular with customers, but they contribute strongly to profit.

• Management wishes customers would order these items more frequently!

No. 4 Items—Unpopular ☹ & Unprofitable ☹—It's a good thing these items are not selected very frequently because they do not contribute to profit!

• Management is glad customers do not order these items very frequently.

Analyzing for Popularity and Profitability

The first step in this form of analysis is to record and analyze the sales activity. Columns A and B in Figure 12.7 are used for this purpose. This information is drawn from the Food Sales Recap Report. Column C is the popularity analysis column. The task is to determine whether or not each item is popular or not popular against some standard or benchmark. Unless there is something to compare each item's current number sold to, there is no real way to say an item is popular or not popular. Yes, those items on the extreme ends (the most and least popular) can easily be identified through simple observation—but what about the ones in the middle? These are important to classify. Right now, these "middle items" represent 38% of this sales mix—not a small piece of the action!

How to Find a Popularity Benchmark   The first task is to find *a standard with which to compare each item's current number sold*—a **popularity benchmark**. Look at Figure 12.6. To find the popularity benchmark, first calculate the *average number of items sold* in this mix.

TOTAL NUMBER OF ITEMS SOLD/NUMBER OF SELECTIONS IN THIS MENU
CATEGORY = AVERAGE NUMBER SOLD
3,885/7 (Number of Appetizers in this Category) = 555

The **Menu Analysis Theory** next states that *any item that can sell 70% of the **average number sold** will be considered "popular."* Where did the 70% come from? It came about as a result of studying the sales records of many commercial table-service restaurants. The results of the research showed that a straight average as the means of comparison was too high—too many items would be considered unpopular. Further review of the data revealed that any item that could sell 70% of the average number sold would be considered "popular." So **popular** is defined as *any item that sells 70% of the average number sold*. Try this out to determine the popularity benchmark for this mix.

AVERAGE NUMBER SOLD × 70% = POPULARITY BENCHMARK
555 × 70% = 389

MENU ANALYSIS I

Item	(Avg. Popularity: 389) Number Sold:	Pop. %	Pop. ☺ Not Pop. ☹	Menu Sales Price	TCPD	(Avg. CM: $6.27) Plate CM	Prof. ☺ Not Prof. ☹	Total Menu Sales	Total Menu Cost	Total Menu CM	Menu Food Cost %
Mozzarella in Carrozza Arrabbiata	1,010	26%	☺	$9.95	$4.62	$5.33	☹	$10,049.50	$4,666.20	$5,383.30	46.4%
Aubergine Melanzane	658	17	☺	7.95	2.46	5.49	☹	5,231.10	1,618.66	3,612.42	30.9
Totanetti Agli Asparagi e Menta	491	13	☺	12.95	5.12	7.83	☺	6,358.45	2,513.92	3,844.53	39.54
Bruschetta con Portobello e Manzo	327	8	☹	9.95	3.51	6.44	☺	3,253.65	1,147.77	2,105.88	33.6
Bruschetta con Mozzarella	272	7	☹	8.25	2.04	6.21	☹	2,244.00	554.88	1,689.12	24.0
Antipasti	777	20	☺	11.95	5.32	6.63	☺	9,285.15	4,133.64	5,151.51	44.5
Carpacciao di Manzo	350	9	☹	12.95	5.63	7.32	☺	4,532.50	4,532.50	2,562.00	43.47
Totals	**3,885**	**100%**						**$40,954.35**	**$16,605.59**	**$24,348.76**	**$40.54%**
	A	B	C	D	E	F	G	H	I	J	K
					D–E			A × D	A × E	A × F	E/D

FIGURE 12.7 Popularity Benchmark I.

Popularity Benchmark	Profitability Benchmark
3,385/7 = 555 555 × 70% = **389**	$24,348.76/3,885 = **$6.27**
Weighted Average Food Cost % (Sum of I/Sum of H) = $16,605.59/$40,954.35 = **40.54%**	

FIGURE 12.8 Popularity Benchmark II.

Now we have a benchmark! What does this mean?

- Any item that sold *more* than 389 items is considered **POPULAR**. ☺
- Any item that sold *less* than 389 items is considered **UNPOPULAR**. ☹

Using this benchmark, it is easy to classify the popularity of each appetizer in the menu mix. Column C on the Menu Analysis form identifies the popular and unpopular menu items. Before the next benchmark—the profitability benchmark—is computed, it is best to complete the remaining columns on the form. Review Figure 12.7.

POPULARITY FORMULA

Total Number of Items Sold/Number of Selections in This Menu Category
= Average Number Sold

Average Number Sold × 70% = Popularity Benchmark

How to Complete the Menu Analysis Columns The following statements refer to Figure 12.7. They explain how to complete the menu analysis columns:

Menu Sales Price (Column D): This is the current menu price. Simply transfer the current menu price to the chart.

True Cost per Dish (TCPD, Column E): This is retrieved from the standard cost card. TCPD is used because it includes the Q factor (if applicable) and the Spice Factor. See Chapter 3 for a refresher.

Plate Contribution Margin (CM, Column F): This is found by *subtracting TCPD (E) from the current menu price (D).*

Total Menu Sales (Column H): This is found by *multiplying each item's Number Sold (A) by each item's Menu Price (D).*

Total Menu Cost (Column I): Find Total Menu Cost by *multiplying each item's Number Sold (A) by each item's TCPD (E).*

Total Menu Contribution Margin (CM; Column J): Total Menu Contribution Margin is found *by multiplying each item's Number Sold (A) by each item's Plate CM (F).*

Menu Food Cost Percentage (Column K): Menu Food Cost Percentage is found by dividing *each item's TCPD (E) by its menu price (D).*

Weighted Average Food Cost Percentage: It is always important to compute the Weighted Average Food Cost Percentage for any menu mix. This average *shows the effect of customer selection and high and low food cost menu items on the food cost and is a more accurate picture of food cost percentage.* It is calculated by dividing the sum of the Total Menu Cost (I) column by the sum of the Total Menu Sales (H) column. Since this is a food cost percentage, do not round. Leave two places after the decimal.

Finally, Columns H, I, and J are summed. These figures are important for determining

- Weighted Average Food Cost Percentage
- Weighted Average Plate Contribution Margin
- Total Menu Contribution Margin

How to Find the Profitability Benchmark The next step is to calculate a **profitability benchmark**. *In order to determine whether or not an item is "profitable," it, too, must be compared to something—a standard or a benchmark.* The Menu Analysis Theory identifies the **Weighted Average Plate Contribution** as the proper measure of profitability. It is found by *dividing the sum of the Total Menu Contribution Margin column by the Number of Covers (A).* This average *shows the effect of customer selection on the average amount each plate "contributes" to all other operating expenses, fixed costs, and profit.*

To find the Total Menu Contribution Margin (Column J):

1. Calculate each item's Plate Contribution Margin by subtracting each item's TCPD (Column E) from each item's Menu Price (Column D).

2. Multiply each item's Number Sold (Column A) by each item's Plate Contribution Margin (Column F).

3. Sum the Plate Contribution Margin column (Column F).

Then, you can find the Weighted Average Plate Contribution Margin, or profitability benchmark:

TOTAL MENU CONTRIBUTION MARGIN/NUMBER OF COVERS =
WEIGHTED AVERAGE PLATE CM

$24,348.76/3,885 = $6.27

The Weighted Average Plate Contribution Margin is then compared to each item's Plate CM (Column F):

- Any item with a Plate CM that is *greater* than the Weighted Average Plate CM is considered **PROFITABLE** ☺.
- Any item with a Plate CM that is *less* than the Weighted Average Plate CM is considered **NOT PROFITABLE** ☹.

Results of this comparison are recorded in Column G:

Classification	Description		Symbols
#1 Items	Popular and Profitable	(P, P)	☺ ☺
#2 Items	Popular and Unprofitable	(P, UP)	☺ ☹
#3 Items	Unpopular and Profitable	(UP, P)	☹ ☺
#4 Items	Unpopular and Unprofitable	(UP, UP)	☹ ☹

PROFITABILITY FORMULA

Total Menu Contribution Margin/Number of Covers
= Weighted Average Plate Contribution Margin
(Profitability Benchmark)

What's Next? Analyze and Strategize!

Now that the Menu Analysis chart is complete, it's time to interpret what it reveals. The outcome of menu analysis is to develop a menu selection of items that are popular with guests and profitable for the operation. By categorizing items as a 1, 2, 3, or 4, management is able to exactly identify the problem—popularity, profitability, or both—and decide on a course of action. If an item is unpopular, the question is always WHY? If an item is unprofitable, the question, again, is WHY?

Strategies for Popularity Problems

Three easy fixes for popularity problems are as follows:

- Eliminate the item(s).
- Replace the item(s) with more popular item(s).
- Leave the unpopular item(s) alone, but encourage guests to select them.

Beyond these three strategies, the following points can be used to solve popularity problems.

✓ **Check that standard recipes and cost cards are consistently used.** Unpopular items should not be unpopular because of back-of-house inconsistencies.

✓ **Check the item for taste, plate appearance, and overall quality.** Adjust the recipe if needed. Redo the plate appearance. Check the match with accompanying items.

✓ **Check an item's placement on the menu itself.** An item can be buried in an exhaustive list, or otherwise be hard to find. Its lack of popularity may not be attributable to lack of customer interest—maybe the item just can't be found.

✓ **Check specials.** Competition from specials will affect the popularity of individual items. If the forecast number of guests holds true, then any specials will affect the menu mix and item popularity of all items.

✓ **Check who orders the item.** An unpopular item is not necessarily a candidate for deletion. There may be a group of core customers that frequent the operation specifically for that item. Removing it would be a mistake. These slow-moving items may help sell more profitable, higher-selling items.

✓ **Check the desirability of the menu selection.** Ultimately, Menu Analysis can show when it is, in fact, time to retire a menu item or update the overall menu selection. Researching menu selections that satisfy the existing customer base and attract new customers is a challenge.

Strategies for Profitability Problems

There are a number of strategies for dealing with unprofitable items, and they include improving Plate Contribution Margins. An unprofitable item is easy to fix—make it profitable! There are really only four things to do:

1. **Check the portion cost.** Inspect the recipe for ways to reduce portion cost.

2. **Change the quality of ingredients.** Substitute lower quality ingredients. This can only be done with extreme caution. Any attempt to lower the quality of a popular item by substituting inferior products can backfire, causing lower overall sales when customers become disenfranchised with the dish and operation. See discussions in Chapter 3 on reducing overall product cost.

3. **Change the portion size.** The same cautions listed here hold for changing the portion size. A signature dish cannot be easily changed in portion size or quality without customer resistance.

4. **Check the selling price.** Menu Analysis can indicate when it is time to reprice a menu or an item(s). Product costs increase over time; this is a fact of life. Repricing the entire menu or specific items are strategies to improve a Plate Contribution Margin. Sometimes price changes have to be done incrementally over time to bring Plate Contribution Margins more in line with benchmarks.

It may not be possible to raise a selling price enough to move a Plate Contribution Margin into a positive position without inciting customer displeasure. In this case, management has two options:

• Raise selling prices slowly over a period of time.
• Evaluate the overall popularity and profitability of the menu mix. One item with a Contribution Margin lower that the standard is not necessarily a cause for alarm if all other items are selling at higher-than-standard Contribution Margins. In the end, the menu mix is profitable overall.

Menu Analysis at Farfalle Arrabbiata

Look at the results of the Menu Analysis chart for the Appetizer selections for Farfalle Arrabbiata:

Item	Pop. ☺ Not Pop. ☹	Prof. ☺ Not Prof. ☹	Is It a 1, 2, 3, or 4?	Strategy
Mozzarella in Carrozza Arrabbiata	☺	☹	# 2	
Aubergine Melanzane	☺	☹	# 2	
Totanetti Agli Asparagi e Menta	☺	☺	# 1	
Bruschetta con Portobello e Manzo	☹	☺	# 3	
Bruschetta con Mozzarella	☹	☹	# 4	
Antipasti	☺	☺	# 1	
Carpacciao di Manzo	☹	☺	# 3	

Review the classifications in the chart and strategies for popular and unpopular classifications listed earlier. Can you suggest a number of strategies to improve the Total Menu Contribution Margin? Develop a new menu analysis chart showing the results of your ideas. Is the total Contribution Margin improved? What has happened to the popularity and profitability benchmarks? If you decide to remove an item, redistribute the covers to other items. Menu Analysis is a great way to test "what if" strategies. The menu analysis chart can easily be set up on a spreadsheet program to allow for easy manipulation of data.

What Could Be Wrong with this Method of Menu Analysis?   The goal of this model is to develop a menu mix with the highest *Total Menu Contribution* possible. The focus is on Contribution Margin, or the amount of money left after product cost is deducted. As such, there are a few inherent problems with the system. If management understands these shortcomings, this system can be used to develop a menu selection that delivers maximum menu profitability. The following are some shortcomings of focusing on the Contribution Margin alone:

- ***Using popularity and profitability as measures of a successful menu.*** This approach is inherently simplistic. Labor cost and other variable costs are not taken into consideration. This fact does not discount this system of menu analysis but should be kept in the back of the manager's mind.
- ***The reliance on Average Menu Contribution Margin versus Food Cost Percentage as the measure of profitability.*** Items with a high Contribution Margin tend to have high food cost percentages. This system rejects food cost percentage as a measure of profitability.
- ***The "problem" of unpopular and/or unprofitable items.*** There will always be items categorized as unpopular and/or unprofitable. No mix will ever be all no. 1's. Every time an "un" is fixed and thus eliminated, another item shifts into the "un" spot. The goal is to reduce the number of "un's" (unpopular, unprofitable) in the mix. It is possible to run a mix with no 4's. This will occur when the popularity of items is very close. The mix of 2's and 3's would be tackled next.

- ***The effect of menu mix changes.*** Every time the menu mix changes, the popularity and profitability benchmarks also change, possibly creating a whole new set of "un's."

Regardless of its shortcomings, Menu Analysis can assist with developing a menu selection that is popular and profitable. The ease with which it can be created from existing sales and cost data makes it a valuable tool.

Net Work

Explore the following Web sites:

www.restaurant.org—Research food trends on this site.
www.usfoodservice.com
www.softcafe.com—Check out the MenuPro 8 menu design software
www.cbord.com
www.movingtargets.com—Check this unique way to build sales
www.venturafoods.com
www.boxerbrand.com—Review this site for menu design ideas
www.uhl-systems.com—Review this site for menu design ideas
www.costgenie.com—Check Menu
www.guestbridge.com
www.capitalrestaurants.com
www.pfchangs.com

Chapter Wrap

The Chapter ✓ at the beginning of the chapter posed several questions. Review the questions and compare your responses with the following answers:

1. **In what ways must a menu selection fit an operation?**

   A menu must fit an operation in terms of the customer, the competition, the operation, and the desired profit level. A competitive analysis is used to study the competition. Management must be aware of staff skills and abilities, the facility, and equipment capacity when making menu decisions. Last, management must offer menu selections that enable the operation to generate the level of profit desired by management.

2. **How are menu prices determined?**

   The menu price often determines how profitable a foodservice operation has the potential of becoming. In earlier times (very early!), competition among foodservice operations was very limited or nonexistent and cost control systems were largely undeveloped. Thus, menu pricing was often the result of guessing, pricing according to what the market would bear, or copying a competitor. Today, operations set menu prices by first determining a plate cost and then applying a menu pricing method to find a minimum menu price. The actual menu price is set from that point.

3. **What role do sales and food cost forecasts play in menu selections and menu analysis?**

   The sales forecast is directly related to pricing because it is an estimate of the foodservice operation's sales based on the number of expected customers and the average amount each customer will spend. A forecast depends on three factors:

1. The count or number of people purchasing items prepared by the food-service operation.
2. The menu price of the items sold.
3. The average check for the menu items sold.

A sales forecast is determined by multiplying the forecasted guest count (☺) by the average check per person. This, in turn, helps in setting budgets.

4. **How is menu analysis used by managers to make menu decisions?**
One of the easiest ways to analyze a sales mix is by reviewing the Food Sales Recap Report because it reports the number of each item sold. It is here that it is obvious to see which items are selling well (popular) and which items are not selling well (unpopular). This is strictly a one-dimensional view of sales, however. Menu decisions are pretty easy to make with this picture—stop offering items that are not selling well! A Menu Analysis is the next tool to use to analyze sales. The difference between this tool and the Food Sales Recap Report is that this analysis uses two variables—menu item popularity together with menu item profitability. This method helps foodservice managers better identify items that may not be a good fit because they are not popular or profitable.

Key Terminology and Concepts in This Chapter

Actual selling price
Average check
Average Contribution Margin
Average number sold
Competitive analysis
Competitive geographic area
Contribution Margin (CM)
Contribution Margin Pricing Method
Cross-utilization of product
Demographics
Food Cost Percentage Method
Food Sales Recap Report
Labor Cost per Guest
Menu Analysis
Menu bank
Menu Food Cost Percentage
Menu Item Sales Forecast
Minimum Menu Price (MMP)
Operational fit

Plate Contribution Margin
Popularity benchmark
Price rounding
Price threshold
Prime Cost Percentage
Prime Cost Pricing Method
Profitability benchmark
Psychographic market segmenting
Ratio Method
Sales forecast
Sales mix
Service style
Total menu contribution
Total Menu Cost
Total Menu Sales
Trading area
True Cost per Dish (TCPD)
Weighted Average Food Cost Percentage
Weighted Average Plate Contribution

Discussion Questions and Exercises

1. Why is it necessary to consider all constituencies when developing menu selections?
2. Assume Farfalle Arrabbiata is located in your city or town. Research the demographic data for your area using www.census.gov, the local Convention and Visitors Bureau or similar agency, and any other resources at your disposal. Write

a memo to management summarizing the relevant information. Explain how it can be used to plan menu changes.

3. Using the blank Competitive Analysis form that follows, visit two or three restaurants in your area that are similar to Farfalle Arrabbiata. Check their menu selections and look for similar items to those listed on the form. Compare their pricing to the prices listed below. Revisit the property description for Farfalle Arrabbiata in Appendix A. In addition to completing the form, note the complete menu offerings, other services, menu design, décor, cleanliness, seating, customer base, service style, quality of service, and any other property details that differentiate these properties from Farfalle Arrabbiata. Note shortcomings as well. How much of a competitor do you think each of these operations would be to Farfalle Arrabbiata if they were, in fact, close competitors?

Prepared By:			
Date:			
Menu Items:	Competitor		
	Farfalle Arrabbiata		
Fettucini Alfredo	$11.95		
Pizzas	$8.95–$9.95		
Steak/Bistecca	$17.95		
Cioppino	$19.95		
Spaghetti Bolognese	$8.50		
Risotto	$13.95		
Insalata Cesare	$6.95		
Calzone Spinachhia (Spinach)	$6.95		
Penne Con Pollo—Pasta with Chicken	$9.95		
Spaghetti alle Vongole (Spaghetti with Clam Sauce)	$10.95		
Tira Misu	$5.95		
Gellato	$4.95		

4. Research menu trends using the National Restaurant Association's Web site www.restaurant.org. Create a punch list of the top trends and government action expected to affect the restaurant industry in the coming year. Note those that would seem to especially concern Farfalle Arrabbiata.

5. Review the menu selection for Farfalle Arrabbiata. (See Appendix A for the complete selection.) Given what you have found through your research of questions 2, 3, and 4, what menu-related changes, additions, deletions, or other action would you recommend to top management with regard to menu planning for the next

year? Where should Farfalle Arrabbiata go with its menu choices? Are there any new services or amenities that Farfalle Arrabbiata should consider adding to its current repertoire?

6. Maxine, your long-time hostess, has just returned from an exotic vacation to a secluded tropical island. She brought back a menu from a fabulous restaurant she had dinner at on her last night. She has been ranting and raving about a particular dish—Flaming Tahitian Beef Brochette. She insists this will be a hit for Farfalle Arrabbiata and it should be added to the menu immediately. In fact, she is hinting that Chef Raoul should try it as a special next week. You are keeping an open mind about this item. What steps would you take to determine whether or not this item is a good fit for Farfalle Arrabbiata? Explain why or why not you think this item will or won't fit. (Continue to assume that Farfalle Arrabbiata is located in your town or city.)

7. Read over the description of Farfalle Arrabbiata in Chapter 1 and Appendix A. What differentiating factors do you think Farfalle Arrabbiata has as compared to each of the restaurants you visited?

8. Use each of the menu pricing methods to find the minimum menu price for each entrée selection below. Use the income statement (Figure 12.3) found earlier in the chapter for the figures you need to complete the work for each formula. The number of customers for the period is 174,619.

Item	TCPD	Food Cost % Method	Contribution Method	Ratio Method	Prime Cost Method
Cioppino	$7.24				
Scallopine di Vitello	4.75				
Salmon a la Griglia	4.72				
Bistecca	6.10				
Filletto di Maiale	5.16				
Costantine d'Agnello	6.17				
Pollo con Carciofino	3.21				

9. Based on your research of competitors, recommend *actual* selling prices for these entrees. (Assume Farfalle Arrabbiata uses the Food Cost Percentage method of pricing.)

10. Using the following menu analysis form (or the one on the component CD), complete a menu analysis for February 21. Compute the popularity and profitability benchmarks. Classify items as 1, 2, 3, or 4. Include the weighted average food cost percentage. If this picture were typical for Farfalle Arrabbiata, what strategies would you suggest to improve Total Contribution Margin? Write a memo to management summarizing your analysis. Suggest a course of action where needed. Produce a "what if" picture—what if the sales mix changed to the direction you are suggesting? Show how total Contribution Margin would improve.

Item	Avg. Popularity ——— Number Sold	Pop. %	Pop. ☺ Not Pop. ☹	Menu Sales Price	TCPD	Avg. CM ——— Plate CM	Prof. ☺ Not Prof. ☹	Total Menu Sales	Total Menu Cost (TCPD)	Total Menu CM	Menu Food Cost %
Mozzarella in Carrozza Arrabbiata		27%		$9.95	$4.62						
Aubergine Melanzane		22		7.95	2.46						
Totanetti Agli Asparagi e Menta		10		12.95	5.12						
Bruschetta con Portobello e Manzo		12		9.95	3.51						
Bruschetta con Mozzarella		6		8.25	3.04						
Antipasti		9		11.95	6.32						
Carpaccio di Manzo		14		12.95	5.63						
Totals	**4,885**	**100%**									

 11. Using the menu analysis form that follows (or the one on the component CD), complete a menu analysis form for the entrees using your suggested selling prices from Question 9.

Item	Avg. Populariy ——— Number Sold	Pop. %	Pop. ☺ Not Pop. ☹	Menu Sales Price	TCPD	Avg. CM ——— Plate CM	Prof. ☺ Not Prof. ☹	Total Menu Sales	Total Menu Cost (TCPD)	Total Menu CM	Menu Food Cost %
Cioppino	684	14%			$7.24						
Scallopine di Vitello	439	9			4.75						
Salmon a la Griglia	293	6			4.72						
Bistecca	586	12			6.10						
Filletto di Maiale	489	10			5.16						
Costantine d'Agnello	1,075	22			6.17						
Pollo con Carciofino	1,319	27			3.21						
Totals	**4,885**	**100%**									

## Chapter Thirteen

About Beverage Production Control & Service

Chapter Objective

To control beverage operations and beverage costs by using standardized recipes and pour costs, monitoring employee activities, and developing house policies for responsible beverage service.

Learning Objectives

After reading this chapter and completing the discussion questions and exercises, you should be able to:

1. Use standardized recipes for all alcohol drinks.
2. Standardize pour methods to control alcohol production.
3. Calculate the pour cost for each alcohol beverage on the menu.
4. Calculate beverage menu prices.
5. Reconcile sales by comparing register sales to guest check sales.
6. Identify ways management and nonmanagement employees can steal from bar operations.
7. Develop house policies for responsible beverage service.
8. Use an Incident Report Log Sheet as a protection against lawsuits.
9. Identify certification programs in responsible beverage service.

Chapter Map

About Beverage Production Control, & Service

Introduction to Beverage Service
- Beverage Production Control
- Types of Alcohol Drinks

Pour Cost
- Drink Costing Using a Standard Cost Card
- Calculating the Menu Price

Reconciling Sales
- Writing Guest Checks
- Issuing Receipts with Drinks
- Reconciling Sales

Avoiding Theft by Management & Bookkeeping Staff
- Unauthorized Consumption
- Kickbacks
- Bookkeeping Theft
- Inventory Theft

Avoiding Theft by Nonmanagement Employees
- Methods of Theft
- Protecting Against Theft

State Liquor Laws & Service
- The Seven Most Important Things About Having a Liquor License
- Responsibly Providing Alcohol Beverages

About Beverage Production Control, and Service

Beverage production and inventory control are very similar to food production control. The primary difference is that beverages are always in standard-sized bottles and containers. Standard recipes for each drink must be established and uniformly followed in the same manner in which food recipes are followed, however. If the beverage operation does not have standardized recipes, bartenders will prepare drinks according to their own preferences or the way they were previously trained.

Management's responsibility is to create a system that promotes honesty and accuracy in accounting for sales dollars and correct product usage, always keeping in mind the temptations associated with preparing alcohol beverages.

The final responsibility of management is to promote responsible alcohol beverage service. Increasingly, law enforcement agencies are holding beverage operations responsible for ensuring that the customer does not drink too much. The financial consequences of serving too many alcohol beverages to a customer may be devastating to the beverage operator, server, and customer.

Introduction to Beverage Service

ALCOHOL SERVICE SETTINGS

1. Front bar
2. Service bar
3. Special-function bar
4. Lounge or bar

Beverage service can take place in a number of locations in a foodservice operation. In fact, there are four different places or settings from which alcohol beverages can be served.

The first area from which alcohol beverages are served is the **front bar**. The front bar is *located in a public area of the restaurant, in full view of the dining room area*. The second is a **service bar**. A service bar *is often in or next to the kitchen; it is used by servers to pick up beverages to go with meals*. It is not in a public area of the restaurant. The third is a **special-function bar**, which *is a bar set up for functions. It is portable and is used for private parties, catered events, and group functions*. The fourth is a lounge or bar. The **lounge** or **bar** is *part of the foodservice operation and is located in a separate room that is expressly designed for serving alcohol beverages*. It may also serve as a service bar for a nearby dining room. Each type of bar has its own par amount and is subject to the inventory management procedures described in Chapter 15.

Beverage Production Control

Controlling the production of alcohol beverages is done primarily by consistently pouring the correct amount of alcohol into a glass. Bartenders who believe they should be able to customize drinks according to customer taste are not consistently pouring the

Controlling the production of alcohol beverages is primarily done by consistently pouring the correct amount of alcohol into a glass.

same amount of alcohol beverage for the same type of drink. When bartenders do this, it becomes difficult to price drinks and to control costs.

The primary way of controlling pour costs (or the cost of one serving of a drink) is to ensure that the bartender is using a **standardized recipe**. As with food items, every drink sold should have a standardized recipe. A standardized drink recipe identifies the following:

- Name and file code
- Recipe yield and **standard portion size**
- Glassware
- Equipment
- Standard drink ingredients and quantity to be used
- Garnish
- Ice
- Method of prep
- Service instruction

METHODS TO CONTROL POUR COSTS

1. Free pouring
2. Measured pouring
3. Bottle control systems
4. Pour guns

Figure 13.1 shows an example of a standardized drink recipe.

Wine and tap beers also have standard portion sizes and glassware. A "recipe" for these types of drinks is still required, because it identifies the portion size necessary to determine the cost of one serving and, subsequently, the menu price. After deciding what recipes to use, the bar manager should use one of four pour methods to ensure that drink ingredients are dispensed properly. These methods are free pouring, measured pouring, bottle control systems, and pour guns. Each method is designed to control the production of alcohol beverages.

Free Pouring   **Free pouring** occurs *when a bartender pours the alcohol beverage straight from the bottle, estimating how much liquid has left the bottle.* The bartender

---

Name: Bloody Mary   **File:** Juice – 8
Yield: 1 serving
Glassware: 10 oz. glass; highball glass
Equipment: Jigger, ice scoop, bar spoon, stir stick
Ingredients/Quantity:
Vodka (well): 1 oz. Tomato juice: 3 oz. Lemon juice: Juice of ½ lemon Worcestershire Sauce: 2–3 dashes Tabasco: 2–3 drops Lemon wedge: 1 wedge Salt and pepper Ice

Method of Prep:
  1. Fill glass half way with ice.
  2. Add 1 ounce of vodka and 3 ounces of tomato juice.
  3. Add lemon juice, Worcestershire Sauce, and Tabasco.
  4. Stir lightly with bar spoon.

Serve:
  1. Stir stick
  2. Salt and pepper
  3. Lemon wedge at 12 o'clock
  4. Cocktail napkin

FIGURE 13.1   A standardized drink recipe.

estimates how much beverage is coming out of the bottle as he or she prepares drinks to customer orders. Obviously, there are some control issues associated with this system. With a free-pouring system, bartenders will **overpour** or **underpour** drinks. A professionally experienced bartender will pour with a high degree of accuracy, on average. Underpouring cheats the customer and overpouring cheats the beverage operation. Also, there will be some spillage. As a general rule, with this method, plan for 3 to 4 drinks out of 100 to be spilled by a bartender or server.

Measured Pouring   **Measured pouring** occurs *when the bartender uses a marked measuring glass. Most alcohol beverages are measured by ⅞ ounce, 1 ounce, or 1⅛ ounce.* The bartender pours the alcohol beverage into the measuring glass (called a **jigger** or **shot glass**), then pours the alcohol into the serving glass. These measuring glasses are marked so the bartender pours to the line that represents a certain amount of liquor. They are commonly used in Europe.

Bottle Control Systems   **Bottle control systems** involve *using devices to control the amount of beverage poured from a bottle.* With this system, servers place a special type of pouring cap in the bottle top; this cap releases a set measurement when poured (see Chapter 15). Use of the pouring cap has the feel of free pouring, although the pour is controlled.

Pour Guns   **Pour guns** are *hand-held devices servers use to control pouring alcohol and nonalcohol drinks.* The nonalcohol type of pour gun is used for club soda, seltzer, ginger ale, cola, and so on. The bartender estimates the amount actually poured. A variety of commercial systems are also available for controlling how much alcohol is poured (see Chapter 15). The pour gun has a series of buttons on the back of the handle; each button indicates the type of alcoholic beverage to be dispensed. For example, if the bartender presses the appropriate button for gin, a prescribed amount of gin comes out. As we mention in Chapter 14, automated pouring devices have been developed to such a level of complexity that all a bartender needs to do is to press the button, and out comes the mixed drink!

The size of the serving glass is another method by which a server can control the portion size of an alcohol beverage. A six-ounce wine glass can be used to serve four ounces of wine. A small stein controls how much beer can be poured into it. A large glass for large drinks and a small glass for small drinks is the general rule. Standard glassware for each drink is indicated on the recipe.

Historically, the free pour method is the preferred pour method by both the bartender and the customer. Some customers believe they actually get more alcohol beverage when a free pour is used, as the bartender displays the personal touch of pouring and mixing the drink. It represents a nostalgic way of preparing alcohol drinks. Customer attitudes are changing, however, as the demand for drinks served consistently every time becomes more prevalent.

Types of Alcohol Drinks

The following are types of alcohol drinks commonly served in beverage operations. Each type is followed by a definition and a description of the the way in which it is prepared.

- **Mixed drinks** *use a combination of an alcohol beverage and water or some other nonalcohol ingredient, such as club soda, ginger ale, and so on.*
- **Cocktails** *use a combination of two or more alcohol beverages; sometimes referred to as a blended drink.*
- **Neat drinks** *are alcohol beverages poured from the bottle into a glass and consumed—no ice, water, or anything else is added.*
- **Aperitifs, liqueurs,** and **cordials** *are types of liquors, served from the bottle or used in recipes of multiple alcohol beverages.*

**TYPES OF
ALCOHOL
DRINKS**

- Mixed drinks
- Cocktails
- Neat drinks
- Aperitifs and
  cordials
- Beers and ales
- Wines
- Tap products

- **Beers** and **ales** are *served by the bottle* or *drawn from a keg and served by the glass or pitcher.*
- **Wines** are *served by the glass* from a bottle or carafe.
- **Tap products** are *those alcohol beverages poured from a tap, usually beers and ales.*

In addition to common drink ingredients, most alcohol drinks are served in specific, **standard glassware**. The standardized recipe specifies ingredients, as well as the type of glass used. Figure 13.2 and 13.3 show examples of glassware commonly used to serve alcohol beverages.

SHOT GLASS: Lined or unlined; 1- to 2-ounce capacity with $\frac{3}{4}$ - to $1\frac{1}{2}$ -ounce line.

OLD-FASHIONED: 6 to 9 ounces; average size is 8 ounces. Used for "on the rocks."

ROLY POLY: Adaptable for many drinks; ranges from 5 ounces to 15 ounces in size. May be used for "on the rocks."

STANDARD HIGHBALL OR TUMBLER: 8- to 12-ounce capacity; straight-sided shell or sham.

COOLER: Tall, slim glass for summer beverages (Zombie, Collins, etc.), varied capacity; 14 to 16 ounces are popular. Often frosted.

STEMMED COCKTAIL GLASS: (Martini, Manhattan, etc.) Ranges in capacity from 3 to $4\frac{1}{2}$ ounces.

WHISKEY SOUR: $3\frac{1}{2}$ to $4\frac{1}{2}$ ounces.

CORDIAL: Sometimes called a Pony; 1-ounce capacity is normal.

TULIP CHAMPAGNE: 6- to 8-ounce capacity; sometimes hollow-stemmed.

SAUCER CHAMPAGNE: Ranges from $4\frac{1}{2}$ to $7\frac{1}{2}$ ounces.

ALL-PURPOSE WINE: 4 to 8 ounces; stemmed glass.

STANDARD WINE: 3 to 4 ounces; stemmed glass.

SHERRY: 2-ounce capacity is normal.

BRANDY SNIFTER: Designed to enhance aroma; 6- to 12-ounce capacity.

TAPERED CONE PILSNER: 8- to 12-ounce capacity.

SHAM PILSNER: 8- to 12-ounce capacity.

PILSNER: 8 to 12 ounces; 10-ounce size is most popular.

STEM PILSNER: 8- to 12-ounce capacity.

GOBLET: 6- to 10-ounce capacity.

STEIN OR BEER MUG: 8- to 12-ounce capacity.

FIGURE 13.2   Types and sizes of glassware.

Sommeliers
Handmade, mouthblown, 24% lead crystal

Bordeaux Grand Cru

Burgundy Grand Cru

Hermitage

Chianti Classico, Zinfandel, Riesling

Beaujolais Nouveau

Rosé

Bordeaux red & white, Burgundy white

Burgundy Montrachet

Rheingau

Alsace

Sauternes

Water

Vintage Port

Tawny Port

Sherry

Aperitif

Champagne

Vintage champagne

Moscato

Sparkling wine

Cognac V.S.O.P.

Cognac XO

Single Malt Whisky

Martini

Underberg

Vinum
Machine-made, 24% lead crystal

Bordeaux

Burgundy

Syrah

Brunello di Montalcino

Chianti Classico, Zinfandel, Riesling

Chardonnay

Rheingau

Sauvignon blanc

Water

Gourmet

Beer

Moscato

Prestige Cuveé

Champagne

Grappa

Port

Spirits

Single Malt Whisky

Cognac

Dessert

Illustration courtesy of RIEDEL Crystal

FIGURE 13.3   Types and sizes of wine glasses.

*P*our Cost

As with food, each drink must have a *standard cost per portion*. In the beverage world, this is referred to as the **pour cost**. It is *the total cost of all the ingredients used in a drink as served to the guest*. Drink costs are figured the same way as food costs in several ways:

- The pour cost is tied directly to the standardized recipe used.
- Each individual ingredient has a cost.
- A cost card is used to determine the pour cost for all drinks.

Drink Costing Using a Standard Cost Card

Figure 13.4 shows an example of a standard cost card for a Bloody Mary. The procedure for costing alcohol beverages is exactly the same as costing for food recipes.

The ingredient quantity is multiplied by the unit price to determine the extension. In the case of beverage costing, however,

- Recipes are typically for one serving.
- The unit price is typically in cost per ounce, or in the standard liquor unit for that drink.

To determine the standard liquor portion cost, determine the number of standard liquor portions in one bottle. Divide the cost of the bottle by this amount. The vodka commonly used in the Bloody Mary is purchased in half-gallon purchasing units. The cost for one bottle is $20.48. To determine the cost for one ounce, the familiar costing formula from Chapter 3 is used:

$$\text{EXTENDED PRICE/YIELD} = \text{COST PER OUNCE}$$

$$\$20.48/64 \text{ OUNCES} = .32 \text{ PER OUNCE}$$

Because drink recipes are for one serving only, cost cards typically show unit prices in cost per ounce units versus bottle or case prices. Assume the tomato juice is purchased in #5 cans. There are approximately 46 servable ounces in one can. The cost for one ounce would be determined as follows:

$$\text{EXTENDED PRICE/YIELD} = \text{COST PER OUNCE}$$

$$\$3.36/46 = .073 \text{ PER OUNCE}$$

Three ounces are needed for the drink, so the final extension would be determined using the same costing formula covered in Chapter 4:

$$\text{QUANTITY} \times \text{UNIT PRICE} = \text{EXTENDED PRICE}$$

$$3 \text{ OUNCES} \times .073 \text{ PER OUNCE} = .22$$

The concepts of evaporation and spillage are unique to beverage costing. The following are common percentages of loss for different alcohol beverages:

- Liquors: 5%
- Tap products: 8% to 20%
- Wine: 5%
- Distilled spirits: 5%

This percentage is added to the cost of the alcohol product only. Figure 13.4 shows this amount as a separate line item after the cost of the vodka. Pour costs should reflect the difference in **evaporation loss** and **spillage loss** percentages for the alcohol product used in the recipe. Because the delivery system for keg beer is sealed, loss of product is more often than not from overpouring and spillage, rather than from evaporation. Experience has shown that about 8% to 20% of tap products are lost. Each beverage operation should calculate its actual loss. As a guideline, it should be adequate to allow a 12% loss.

Next, we calculate cost for the remaining ingredients. The process is the same as that used for costing food recipes. In cases where the amount is difficult to compute, figure the minimum amount needed to cover the ingredient. Notice how this is done with the extensions for Worcestershire Sauce and Tabasco in the Bloody Mary example.

Calculating the Menu Price

As with food pricing, one of the most common methods of computing a selling price, or **Menu Price**, is to *divide the Cost per Portion by the standard Beverage Cost Percentage*. The Beverage Cost Percentage standard for Farfalle Arrabbiata is 25%. The Minimum Menu Price would be calculated as follows:

$$\text{COST PER PORTION/BEVERAGE COST \%} = \text{MINIMUM MENU PRICE}$$

$$.78/.25 = \$3.12$$

Name: Bloody Mary	File: Juice – 8		
Glassware: 10 oz. glass; Highball glass			
Ingredients	**Quantity**	**Unit Price**	**Extension**
Vodka	1 ounce	.32/oz.	.32
Evaporation loss 5%			.02
Tomato juice	3 ounces	$3.36/#5 can (46 oz.)	.22
Lemon juice	½ lemon	.22 each	.11
Worcestershire Sauce	2–3 dashes	.01	.01
Tabasco	2–3 drops	.01	.01
Lemon wedge	1 wedge (1/8th)	.05	.05
Salt and pepper	To taste	.01	.01
Ice	½ glass	.03 per glass	.03
		Cost per Portion: **Beverage Cost %:** 25% .78/.25 = $3.12 **Minimum Menu Price:**	.78 $3.12

FIGURE 13.4   A standard drink cost card.

Actual drink menu prices are set using the same guidelines as used in food menu pricing. For discussion of this issue, refer to Chapter 12.

Reconciling Sales

When **reconciling sales**, the manager *compares what the cash register indicates was sold to what inventory indicates was sold.* For a manager to do a sales reconciliation, however, a system must be in place. The system chosen must include several activities: Checks must be written for every drink ordered and a receipt issued for and served with each drink. Guest check totals and register totals are then compared, to see if they agree.

STEPS TO RECONCILE SALES

1. Checks must be written for every drink ordered.
2. Every drink is issued a receipt.
3. Receipts are served with each drink.
4. Guest check total, and register totals are reconciled.

Writing Guest Checks

Probably the simplest system to use is similar to the one suggested for a foodservice operation. Thus, no drinks are prepared unless a guest check has been written and handed to the bartender. Even the bartender must prepare a guest check if he or she serves drinks at the bar. Electronic or computer systems do this automatically.

Issuing Receipts with Drinks

Every drink is also issued a cash register receipt. The receipt is placed on the table or bar with the drink. This allows a simple visual check. Usually, by issuing receipts, the manager may be able to quickly look over the room or at a table and know that a customer has paid.

Reconciling Sales

If guest checks and receipts are issued for drinks, the totals on the guest checks can be compared to the cash register totals. The totals on the guest checks should be the same as those on the cash register. This system protects against most cash shortage problems.

Probably the best protection for the operation and the customer is an attentive manager and an appropriate electronic cash register or point-of-sale liquor control system. An attentive manager watches to ensure that systems are being used and policies are being followed. In addition, an attentive manager will be able to see if a server and bartender are colluding to steal from the operation (see the section "Avoiding Theft by Nonmanagement Employees" later in this chapter). Finally, effective inventory controls and watching the pour cost and overall beverage costs will ensure a properly operated beverage service.

Avoiding Theft by Management and Bookkeeping Staff

Any foodservice operation that serves alcohol beverages risks theft. Also, practically any control mechanism that is put into place to prevent theft is vulnerable to being breached. An operation should protect itself to the maximum against theft, however, and make efforts to steal easier to detect. Some of the more common methods of theft used by management or bookkeepers are discussed here.

COMMON METHODS OF THEFT

1. Unauthorized consumption: Consuming alcohol beverages at work
2. Kickbacks: Suppliers bribing buyers or managers
3. Bookkeeping: Loss of revenue through poor record-keeping procedures
4. Inventory: Loss of inventory through poor operating procedures

---

Unauthorized Consumption

The downfall of many managers has been a cavalier attitude about drinking on the job or just before or after work. Some states prohibit managers, including owners, from consuming alcohol beverages while at work. A recommended rule is that *all employees, including managers,* may not drink on the job. Occasionally customers will want managers to drink with them. This is not a good idea. In fact, it is not a good idea to give any drinks away even as a promotion. Giving out free alcohol beverages is suggestive of irresponsible beverage service. The establishment may be open to lawsuits if free drinks are given to customers.

Kickbacks

Suppliers may offer money to managers personally to sell their products, rather than offering legitimate discounts for volume purchases. This is called a **kickback**. A manager may also be offered a bribe to carry a line of products. Although the bribe is not necessarily stealing from the operation, the practice usually leads to overpricing and other costs to cover the bribe. Besides, this type of collusion (secret agreement) is against the law.

Bookkeeping Theft

Bookkeepers may steal by not making deposits or by reporting cash shortages. Also, they may pay fictitious bills to themselves.

Inventory Theft

Some employees may deliberately under-report items in inventory, then steal the item. Proper attention by management, correct completion of inventory, and constant vigilance of the operation should minimize opportunities for managers and bookkeepers to steal. Nearly all thefts will eventually be discovered if a proper inventory system, cash system, and other controls are being used.

Avoiding Theft by Nonmanagement Employees

Some employees are tempted to cheat the bar operation or customers when serving alcohol beverages. This section covers a few of the more common methods of employee dishonesty.

Methods of Theft

COMMON METHODS OF EMPLOYEE DISHONESTY

1. Playing with the cash register
2. Phony walkout
3. Phantom bottles
4. Short pour
5. Overcharging customers
6. Diluting bottles
7. Outright theft

Playing with the Cash Register   The following are ways that employees may tamper with the sales process:

- The employee doesn't ring up the sale and keeps the cash, or **under-rings** the sale (*rings up too little*) and keeps the difference.
- Bartenders serve and collect for sales during shift changes.
- Servers reuse guest checks and register receipts to order drinks that have not really been ordered, pocketing the cash from the sale of these "second" drinks.
- An employee performs an incorrect **over-ring** (*rings up too much*) or void and keeps the money.

Phony Walkouts   A server claims a phony customer walkout after the customer has paid and keeps the money. If an operation allows a customer to "run up a tab" (or buy on account), the amount taken by the server or bartender could be sizable.

Phantom Bottle   A bartender brings in his or her own bottle of liquor (a **phantom bottle**) onto the shift and pockets the cash from its sale. A way to guard against this is to have a policy that prohibits employees from bringing in any large purses, jackets, or bags to the bar. Also, the manager should frequently review and analyze the sales figures on the Beverage Cost Report (see Chapter 14.). If sales appear to fluctuate during a bartender's days off (in other words, if more sales occur in those days), the potential for a phantom bottle problem exits. A change in the bartender's shift schedule may reflect further sales fluctuations. Therefore, identifying sales trends is important.

The Short Pour   In a **short pour** situation, drinks are prepared with less than the recipe amount of alcohol beverages. The difference between the amount that should have been sold and the amount that was sold is kept by the bartender. This method can also be used when a bartender and server collude (have a secret agreement) in selling the amount of the difference and equally pocketing the cash.

Overcharging Customers   The customer is deliberately charged more than the menu price. The difference between the menu price and the amount collected is kept by the employee. Another way to do this is to have a customer sign a credit card voucher in advance, then overcharge for drinks or charge for drinks not served.

Diluting Bottles   When an employee **dilutes bottles**, he or she substitutes water for liquor, then uses the "liquor" to mix drinks. The liquor poured off is also sold, and the employee keeps the money for the drinks.

Outright Theft   Sometimes, employees decide to practice outright theft, wherein they physically take bottles of liquor, beer, or wine from storage areas.

Protecting Against Theft

Every operation needs to institute controls to protect against these practices. All these practices are difficult to trace. A sound beverage service system will help to prevent theft from the operation and from the customer.

Discouraging and preventing theft can be accomplished by

- Controlling pouring techniques
- Creating an order system that documents drink orders
- Maintaining tight controls over inventory

Although free pouring may be the most impressive and desirable method of making drinks according to many bartenders, pouring a consistently sized shot requires much practice. Using a shot glass helps to limit overpours; however, it still is easy to abuse. Automatic drink dispensers give management the greatest control. Although automated dispensing systems represent a significant investment, they typically pay for themselves in a short period of time.

A variety of systems are available to help track drink orders and their preparation. The basic principle behind these systems is to separate the ordering and preparation of drinks, so that a double-check system is in place. All orders should be submitted on guest checks or front-of-the-house electronic systems that report orders of drinks to the bartender. This creates evidence of an order and helps management to track problems that may occur. Drinks ordered by customers at the bar directly from the bartender are the most difficult to track.

State Liquor Laws and Service

Alcohol service is highly controlled; every state has laws regulating the sale, service, and consumption of alcohol beverages. Matters regulated by some or all states include **legal drinking age** (21 in all states), **open container laws**, **hours of operation**, required **alcohol service training, third-party liability, license requirements**, and in some cases, **suggested pace of service**. Many other areas of alcohol service are regulated, depending on the political culture of the state.

COMMON AREAS OF REGULATION BY STATE LIQUOR LAWS

Open Container Laws: State laws that restrict the transfer of open alcohol beverages in an automobile.

Alcohol Service Training: Certain states require those who serve alcohol beverages to complete an approved training program.

Third-Party Liability: State laws that make those who serve alcohol beverages liable for serving people who are considered legally drunk.

License Requirements: State laws that require foodservice and beverage operations to acquire a license to serve alcohol beverages.

Prudent Person Rule: A legal standard that compares what a prudent person would do in a situation to the behavior that actually occurred.

Currently, many states require servers to take alcohol service training programs. Some states have also mandated courses designed to train servers how to

- Pace service
- Identify an intoxicated customer
- Deal with an abusive drunk
- Watch for fake personal identification (ID)

Social mores are changing. The general public is demanding responsible alcohol beverage service. Legally, those who serve alcohol beverages are increasingly being held to the **Prudent Person Rule**, which basically asks, "What would a prudent person do in this or a similar situation?" The basic answer to the question is that a prudent or responsible person would not serve alcohol to someone who is intoxicated. Nor would a prudent person allow someone who is visibly intoxicated to drive himself or herself anywhere. In some states, the law is quite specific: Do not serve visibly intoxicated customers.

The Seven Most Important Things About Having a Liquor License

It is a privilege to hold a liquor license. With this privilege comes responsibility. It is in every operator's best interest to be vigilant in protecting this license. As such, stringent standard operating procedures are necessary to prevent the loss of the license and to protect against lawsuits that could financially devastate the business.

THE SEVEN MOST IMPORTANT THINGS ABOUT HAVING A LIQUOR LICENSE

1. Selling liquor is serious business.
2. Know license requirements.
3. Know license privileges.
4. Check IDs as part of standard operating procedures.
5. Train employees to never serve a guest if they are not sure of his or her age.
6. Know whether food must be offered.
7. Work cooperatively with state agencies responsible for licensing.

The Seriousness of Selling Alcohol Beverages   Selling liquor is serious business. Alcohol is a leading cause of traffic accidents and is deemed to be a major social problem. One out of every 10 people has the propensity to become an alcoholic. Of those involved in accidents who have been drinking, between 40% and 60% became drunk in a public drinking establishment (depending on the geographic area).

License Requirements   Know license requirements. Each state has different classes of licenses. Managers should know which type of license best suits their particular needs.

License Privileges   Know license privileges. Each state has specific regulations. It behooves the manager to know what hours of operation, seating capacity, written reports, beverage container laws, and so on apply to those who serve alcoholic beverages. The state grants the privilege to do business. Managers must prove that they are worthy of the privilege. In some states, the liquor license is considered a property right. By complying with state regulations, the manager will be able to conduct business successfully.

Checking IDs   Check the ID of anyone who looks younger than 26. The minimum drinking age in the United States is 21. Age appearances can be deceiving. Underage people may look older than 21. As a general rule, post a sign that says, "All persons 26 and younger will be carded." The sign informs the public and makes the server or bartender's job easier.

Being Sure   "If you are not sure, don't serve." The general operating rule is that if you are uncertain of the age of a person, don't serve that person.

Offering Food   In some states, if liquor is served, food must be offered. It is a proven fact that certain foods help to absorb some of the alcohol. Therefore, some states require that food such as chicken, pizza, or sandwiches be offered.

Working with State Agencies   Work cooperatively with the state agency responsible for licensing. Some states conduct inspections by visitors from the agency responsible for monitoring and enforcing alcohol service laws. The manager should accompany any inspectors doing inspections.

Responsibly Providing Alcohol Beverages

Management proves that it is a responsible provider of alcohol beverages in several ways. One sign of responsibility is to have and enforce a house policy that states the house rules concerning visibly intoxicated persons. Other signs are posted rules, incident reports, server training, and recorded portion control liquor systems. These systems provide reports of items sold, specific quantities, dates, and times.

TO RESPONSIBLY PROVIDE ALCOHOL BEVERAGES

- Have and enforce a house policy toward visibly intoxicated persons.
- Post house rules for drinking.
- Keep detailed incident reports.
- Train and certify servers in responsible beverage service.
- Review reports from recorded portion control liquor systems.

House Policy   A **house policy** is the summation of the philosophy and attitude of management. It is *a written policy indicating how employees are to behave in given situations of alcohol beverage service.* Figure 13.5 is an example of a house policy on serving visibly intoxicated persons. It is important that the house policy be written and posted in a conspicuous place. Everyone must have access to reading the house policy. This way, if the operation is ever sued, part of the defense would be that the

---

To: ALL EMPLOYEES

From: OWNER/MANAGER

Re: HOUSE RULES CONCERNING VISIBLY INTOXICATED PERSONS
           DRINKING AND DRIVING ARE BAD MIXERS

Although we derive our livelihood from the sale of alcohol beverages, we are concerned about the abuse of these products; patrons who drive while intoxicated are detrimental to our livelihood.

Do not serve a visibly intoxicated guest. To ensure that a guest does not leave the establishment visibly intoxicated, make a good-faith effort to remove the drink and substitute with coffee or other beverages.

The bottom line is that it is our responsibility to carefully consider our actions and judge each and every patron as to whether or not they are intoxicated. We must make this judgment whether the patron is drinking or not. Excuses such as "I am taking a cab" (whether true or not) do not relieve our responsibility.

It is my policy and the policy of this establishment to make every effort to curb service to visibly intoxicated persons. This includes regular patrons.

If you feel that someone is intoxicated and wish to stop the sale of alcohol beverages, notify the manager on duty. You will be supported in this decision. I will never overrule decisions made by the staff.

Bartenders and floor-service personnel must be aware of the customer. They must also communicate with each other regarding possible problems or when a patron has been refused service. Chronic problems will be dealt with by permanently refusing admittance.

It is the policy of this establishment that patrons are here at our hospitality. This means that patrons shall respect the establishment and patrons shall respect all other people, including staff. We will not lose business because of a loud, unpleasant, obnoxious person! Patrons shall be cut off and asked to leave if they violate these policies.

We will not encourage excessive drinking, offer "two-fers" or other bargain rates, or permit alcohol consumption contests on our premises. When appropriate, encourage the service of a "spacer" (coffee, soft drink, or other nonalcohol beverage, or food).

At closing time, announce that it is closing time and that you will have to pick up the drinks in 30 minutes. Do not announce "last call." Put a limit of one drink per customer on any orders taken in the last 30 minutes of service.

If someone appears visibly intoxicated, try to arrange safe transportation home through his or her friends (friends don't let friends drive intoxicated!) or call a taxi.

Any incident that is alcohol related or involves excessive alcohol consumption shall be recorded in our Daily Incident Log, including a brief description and the witnesses and employees involved or present. Each employee will initial the log at the end of his or her shift, regardless of whether an incident occurred.

Remember, we must recognize that taking good care of our customers and protecting them against the effects of alcohol abuse not only constitutes good business and is our legal obligation, but is also a moral imperative.

FIGURE 13.5   House policy.

operation made a reasonable effort to inform its employees regarding the policy of the house. A public statement also helps management to be consistent in enforcing policy.

Daily Incident Log   Possibly the best defense, as part of a third-party liability claim, if ever sued, is to keep an accurate **Daily Incident Log**. This is *a form used to record incidents that occurred in serving or denying service to customers.* Many liability cases that go to court end up with witnesses providing conflicting testimony. Often, the case comes down to just one person's word against another. A written record clearly documents and dates what took place and can be submitted in a court of law. A Daily Incident Log can provide that written record.

The Daily Incident Log is used to record a description of any episodes that occur. It also provides a place for a witness to make comments. Finally, it provides a space for all those concerned to sign. The personal signatures validate the testimony that has been offered. Figure 13.6 shows a Daily Incident Log. The log effectively documents irresponsible behavior and helps an establishment avoid a lawsuit.

Day: Friday	**Date:** 1/18/XX		**Shift:** 5:00 P.M.–2:00 A.M.
Who Prepared Log: Bartender	**Manager on Duty:** Manager		

Incident (Describe, Patron's Name, Address, Phone No.)	Time It Occurred	Name/Phone No. of Employee Involved	Witness Names/ Phone Numbers
Drink order refused to James J. Drunk who was acting belligerent and appeared visibly intoxicated. James J. Drunk left. Cocktail server tried to get cab, but person refused help and wouldn't give address or phone number.	10:30 p.m.	Cocktail Server 333-3333 Signed:	Bartender and Fred Witness 444-4444 Signed:

To the best of my knowledge, the above incidents occurred as described.

Shift Servers: Witnesses:

Anna Server   Fred Witness
_____   _____

George Server
_____   _____

_____   _____

FIGURE 13.6   Daily Incident Log.

Server Name: Ann Server

Date Employed: 1/7/XX

Evaluated By: Owner

Outcome	Date Demonstrated	Needs Improvement
1. Can describe visible signs of intoxication.	1/13/XX	
2. Knows the general drink limits.	1/17/XX	
3. Demonstrates how to track the number of drinks customers have consumed.	1/17/XX	
4. Knows not to serve more than one drink per person at a time.		1/13/XX
5. Knows the house policies on serving drinks.		1/17/XX
6. Knows how to slow service if a customer is nearing intoxication.		1/17/XX
7. Knows how to cut off service.	1/13/XX	
8. Knows the procedures for dealing with difficult customers.		1/17/XX
9. Knows to encourage customers to order food and nonalcohol drinks.	1/13/XX	

FIGURE 13.7   Alcohol service training page.

Server Education   Several states require **server education**, or *a training program for alcohol beverage servers*. Although most foodservice operations offer some type of server education, the mood of the nation is that operations should take more responsibility in serving alcohol. Both the National Restaurant Association Educational Foundation and the National Licensed Beverage Association has developed server education programs.

As a help to operators, the checklist in Figure 13.7 provides an example of a method of ensuring and documenting that employees have been trained properly. The table indicates the skill areas that employees should have mastered.

Net Work

Explore the following Web sites:

www.softcafe.com

www.barmedia.com—Click American Mixologist; Products

www.webtender.com

www.santemagazine.com

www.smartwine.com

Chapter Wrap

The Chapter ✓ at the beginning of the chapter posed several questions. Review the questions and compare your responses with the following answers:

1. **What information is included on a standardized beverage recipe?**

   A standard beverage recipe includes the following information:

   1. Name and file code
   2. Recipe yield and standard portion size
   3. Glassware
   4. Equipment
   5. Standard drink ingredients and quantity to be used
   6. Garnish
   7. Ice
   8. Method of prep
   9. Service instructions

2. **What types of pour systems are commonly used in beverage service?**

   Free pouring, measured pouring, bottle control systems, and pour guns are the four most common systems in use to control beverage production.

3. **What is a pour cost?**

   As with food, each drink must have a standard cost per portion. In the beverage world, this is referred to as the pour cost. It is the total cost of all the ingredients used in a drink, as served to the guest.

4. **What is meant by reconciling sales?**

   Reconciling sales is comparing what the cash register indicates was sold to what inventory indicates was actually sold. A sales reconciliation system must be in place. Guest checks, receipts, and register totals are used to reconcile sales.

5. **What areas are commonly regulated by state liquor laws?**

   Open container laws, alcohol service training, third-party liability, license requirements, and the Prudent Person Rule are common areas of regulation by state liquor boards.

6. **What standard procedures should be in place to protect a liquor license?**

   Having and enforcing a house policy toward visibly intoxicated persons, having and enforcing house rules for drinking, keeping comprehensive Incident Reports, training and certifying servers in responsible beverage service, and reviewing reports are all standard procedures necessary to protect a liquor license.

Key Terminology and Concepts in This Chapter

Alcohol service training
Ales
Aperitifs
Bar
Beers
Bottle control systems
Cocktails
Cordials
Daily Incident Log
Diluting bottles
Evaporation loss
Free pouring
Front bar
Hours of operation
House policy
Jigger
Kickback
Legal drinking age
License requirements
Lounge
Measured pouring
Mixed drinks

Neat drinks
Open container laws
Overpour
Over-ring
Phantom bottle
Pour cost
Pour guns
Prudent Person Rule
Service bar
Short pour
Shot glass
Special-function bar
Spillage loss
Standard glassware
Standard portion size
Standardized recipe
Tap products
Third-party liability
Underpour
Under-ring
Wines

Discussion Questions and Exercises

1. What challenges are inherent in any beverage production operation?

2. Fran is looking to develop a file of unique drinks to offer to increase beverage sales. Research five drinks that you think would work at Farfalle Arrabbiata. Standardize a recipe for their production. How will you differentiate these drinks to customers? Write a catchy menu description for each that could be used to market these drinks.

3. Determine the portion cost for each of these drinks. Use the standard guidelines for evaporation loss listed in the chapter.

4. Determine a selling price for each drink, using Farfalle Arrabiata's beverage cost percent. Given your ideas to differentiate these drinks in Exercise 2, what would you actually sell these drinks for? Why? Validate your rationale.

5. What are the problems inherent in a free pour system? A measured pour system? Pour guns?

6. Farfalle Arrabbiata currently uses a free pour system for their beverage service. Research measured pour systems. Write a memo to Fran: Describe how a measured pour system works, highlight advantages and disadvantages to the system, research two systems, and compare them. Which system would you recommend to Fran? Why?

7. Describe what it means to reconcile sales.

8. Discuss ways a beverage manager can control the cost of serving wine and keg beer.

9. Management has decided to train and certify all servers and bartenders at Farfalle Arrabbiata in responsible beverage service. Research the different certification

programs available. Write a memo summarizing the content of the programs. Compare the programs and recommend one to Fran.

 10. Complete the cost card for Long Island Iced Tea. Calculate the Minimum Menu Price.

Name: Long Island Iced Tea File: Mixer – 11			
Classware: 10 oz. glass; Highball glass			
Ingredients	**Quantity**	**Unit Price**	**Extension**
Gin (well)	½ oz.	.352/oz.	
Vodka (well)	½ oz.	.242/oz.	
Light rum (well)	½ oz.	.47/oz.	
Tequila (well)	½ oz.	.62/oz.	
Triple Sec (well)	½ oz.	.234/oz.	
Evaporation loss: 5%			
Sweet & Sour Mix	2 oz.	.211/oz.	
Cola	~~1 wedge~~ 2 oz.	.01/oz.	
Lemon wedge	1 wedge (1/8th)	.08 ea	
Ice	½ glass	.03 per glass	
		Cost per Portion:	
		Beverage Cost %: 25%	
		Minimum Menu Price:	

[handwritten note in left margin: 8 wedges per lemon]

11. Contact the agency in your home state that deals with licensing issues and laws regarding alcohol beverage service, and get answers to the following questions:

    a. Is there an open container law in your state?

    b. What is the blood alcohol level at which a person is considered legally drunk?

    c. What are the different types of licenses for a person who wants to serve liquor as part of a foodservice operation?

    d. Are servers required to complete some type of alcohol beverage service training in your state?

    e. Does your state have a third-party liability law?

12. It is the week after Christmas; the time is about 5:00 p.m. Four people walk into the lounge at Farfalle Arrabbiata. They are boisterous and talking loudly. They seat themselves in a six-person booth. One of them waves his hand with a broad gesture, signaling the server to walk over to the table. As the server walks over, she hears various members of the party exclaim what fun they had cross-country skiing and it was too bad that they ran out of booze. The server introduces herself to the group. Everyone in the group acknowledges the server's presence. Two members of the group are slurring their words. The server approaches you for advice on how to handle this situation.

    a. How would you handle this situation?

    b. Would you serve this group? Why? Why not?

    c. What standard operating procedures should be in place in a situation like this?

13. How would you prevent managers and hourly employees from stealing from a bar or lounge operation? What standard operating procedures should be in place to prevent this type of activity?

## Chapter Fourteen

About Beverage Cost & Beverage Cost Percentage

Chapter Objective

To apply standard operating procedures to purchasing, cost management, and sales analysis for beverage operations.

Learning Objectives

After reading this chapter and completing the discussion questions and exercises, you should be able to:

1. Recognize the similarities between foodservice and beverage-service cost control procedures.
2. Compare purchasing methods for beverage products to purchasing methods for foodservice.
3. Identify nonalcohol ingredients used in drink production.
4. Determine pour costs and beverage costs.
5. Identify reasons for higher-than-normal pour costs.
6. Use bar requisitions and bar transfers to track bar costs.
7. Calculate beverage cost percentage using a Beverage Cost Report.
8. Analyze sales using a Beverage Cost Report.

Chapter Map

Chapter ✓

Check the chapter content for the answers to these questions:

1. What similarities exist between the food cost control process and the beverage cost control process?
2. How is beverage purchasing different from food purchasing?
3. How is beverage cost controlled?
4. How is beverage cost percentage used to analyze operations?

*I*ntroduction to the Beverage Cost Control Process

Chapter 12 concluded the Operating Cycle of Control process for the food side of operations. Many restaurants also generate revenue through the sale of alcohol beverages, however. This chapter and the chapters before and after it (Chapters 13, 14, and 15) cover common beverage management principles. Because standard operating procedures used for food products are easily applied to beverage operations, discussion in these chapters concentrate specifically on the terminology, operating procedures, and principles that are unique to controlling beverage operations.

The Menu

Just like in a restaurant, beverage management has to start with the menu. An alcohol beverage menu is the first step in the beverage cost control process. In the case of beverage operations, the "menu" consists of:

- The wine list
- General drink selections—alcohol-based and non–alcohol-based
- Specialty drinks
- Tap selections

Each operation must determine its own beverage menu based on research of customer preferences. An example of a beverage menu is shown in Figure 14.1. The breadth and depth of the offerings in each category will vary greatly from operation to operation. Without exception, the same degree of care and control exercised over food operations must be exercised over beverage operations if profit is to be realized.

Standardized Beverage Recipes

Once the beverage menu is developed, proper drink "recipes" must be followed to maintain a consistent beverage presentation. The recipes will not be nearly as complex as a food recipe, but their importance as a control piece cannot be underestimated. Most mixed drinks already have a universally recognized recipe (a Bloody Mary is a Bloody Mary), so beverage recipes are used to standardize the quantity and quality of the ingredients, ice, method of preparation, glassware, garnish, and service. A beverage recipe may specify one ounce of Jack Daniels with ice and four ounces of club soda to make a Jack Daniels bourbon and soda. The exact amount of alcohol beverage used in drinks will vary according to the specifications set forth by management. Beverage

TRADITIONAL

If you thought no one could improve on these time-honored traditions, think again. Order one and discover how history has been rewritten the Friday's way.

FRIDAY'S MARGARITAS
Frozen or on-the-rocks, blended to perfection.

Gold—Made exclusively with Jose Cuervo Gold Tequila and triple sec.

Top Shelf—A Friday's classic featuring Jose Cuervo 1800, Cointreau and Grand Marnier.

BLOODY MARY
Vodka with Friday's special vegetable juice blend.

TEQUILA MARIA
Tequila and Friday's special vegetable juice blend.

MADRAS
Vodka with cranberry and orange juices.

SCREWDRIVER
Vodka and orange juice.

WHISKEY SOUR
Bourbon and sweet & sour.

MARTINI
Gin or vodka with dry vermouth. Chilled, straight up or on-the-rocks, served with an olive or a twist.

MANHATTAN
Bourbon and vermouth with Angostura Bitters over ice.

GIMLET
Vodka or gin and Rose's Lime Juice, garnished with a lime squeeze.

GIBSON
Vodka or gin, dry vermouth and cocktail onions.

BLACK RUSSIAN
Vodka and Kahlúa on-the-rocks.

RUSTY NAIL
Scotch and Drambuie on-the-rocks.

SEA BREEZE
Vodka, cranberry and grapefruit juices.

OLD FASHIONED
Bourbon with sweetened orange and cherry juices and a dash of Angostura Bitters.

WHITE RUSSIAN
Vodka, Kahlúa and half & half on-the-rocks.

ROB ROY
Scotch with vermouth and just a touch of orange bitters.

PLANTER'S PUNCH
Myer's Original Dark Rum, grenadine, lime and orange juices.

VODKA COLLINS
Vodka and sweet & sour topped with soda.

FIGURE 14.1 Beverage menu. (T.G.I. Friday's is a registered trademark of T.G.I. Friday's of Minnesota, Inc.)

recipes are standardized for the same reasons that food recipes are standardized—to control quality, quantity, and cost.

A closer look at beverage recipes and pour costs can be found in Chapter 13.

STANDARDIZED BEVERAGE RECIPES

Beverage recipes are used to standardize
- The quantity and quality of the ingredients
- Ice
- Method of preparation
- Glassware
- Garnish
- Service

Standardized Pour Costs

Continuing with the control process, the standardized recipe determines the standard **pour cost** or *cost per portion* for all beverages. The pour cost covers

- Liquor
- Wine
- Beer
- Mixers
- All other ingredients used to prepare drinks
- Garnishes
- Ice
- Evaporation and spillage loss

In some operations, the list of other ingredients can be extensive.

Selling prices are commonly calculated in the exact same way that food sales prices are calculated: The cost per portion is divided by the standard beverage cost percentage:

Cost Per Portion/Standard Beverage Cost % = Minimum Menu Price

Purchasing Procedures

From recipes and pour costs come the standard purchasing functions—purchasing, receiving, storing, and inventory control. Standard receiving practices and procedures are similar to those for receiving food products. Because of the cost involved and the accountability required, though, the bar manager, general manager, or owner should receive most of the alcohol beverages.

The function of the beverage manager (like that of the food manager) is to purchase the best-quality product at the lowest price for a specific purpose. To this end, the purchase of alcohol beverages should be based on **specifications** developed by management for liquor, wine, beer, and all other drink ingredients. In food purchasing, specifications were used to identify the right product to purchase. The sheer number of food purchasing options made the use of specifications a must. Purchasing beverages is much less complex. All alcohol beverages are purchased primarily *by brand name, unit size, and price.* Because of this, specifications written for **liquor** are developed along only these parameters, making them far less complicated to write than food specs.

Bartenders who need to obtain beverages and supplies to stock the bar need to prepare a requisition. Any alcohol used in the kitchen (wine for cooking and so on) should be tracked via a **transfer** to account for these items, which are taken from the bar. A **requisition** is used to obtain any products from the liquor storeroom. Alcohol beverage storage facilities should be locked and controlled by management at all times.

Operations commonly identify *a particular brand* to act as their **well stock**. These liquors are also sometimes referred to as **house brands**. Well liquors are less expensive than **call brands** or liquors. Management may specify specific brands for its well stock or may identify several acceptable brands within common liquor categories—bourbon, vodka, gin, and so on. The brand with the best price in each category would become the call brand. Because well-stock selections are based solely on price, it is quite possible that the specific brand in use will change. Figure 14.2 shows the placement of well stock in a typical bar.

Call brands are *other brand name liquors carried on the bar that customers may ask be used in their drink.* Call brands automatically command a higher drink price. These liquors are more expensive than well stock. Sales records, customer requests, and beverage trends help determine the variety and quality of items stocked as call brands.

WELL STOCK VERSUS CALL BRANDS

Well Stock, or House Brands: Less expensive liquors used by bartenders to mix drinks whenever a customer does not specify a brand name

Call Brands: Other brand-name liquors carried on the bar that customers may ask be used in their drinks.

Beverage Purchasing

The beverage purchasing process is unique. It involves specific pricing and discounts, supplier product lines, well-stock products, size of inventory and breadth of product lines, and methods of payment.

FIGURE 14.2   Well stock is the liquor that is conveniently located for quick service (at the speed rail), as it is the most-used liquor in any given bar.

UNIQUE ASPECTS OF BEVERAGE PURCHASING

1. Pricing and discounts
2. Supplier product lines
3. Well-stock products
4. Size of inventory and breadth of product lines
5. Methods of payment

Pricing and Discounts

In many states, the wholesale prices of alcohol beverages are controlled, as liquor must be purchased through state-owned stores. If prices are not controlled, as in some states that have independent liquor **suppliers**, a common procedure is to have the suppliers submit a list of prices for each brand item. In some beverage operations, which are either large volume or limited in the brands being offered to customers, special arrangements may be made to purchase a complete line of one brand of liquor at a certain percentage below the listed monthly price. Also, variations in price may occur because a particular brand may be listed as a special for a given period of time. In addition, **volume discounts** may become available, should the buyer wish to purchase that product. For example, a particular brand of scotch may normally sell for $96 per case, but if it is purchased in 5-case lots, a 1% discount is available, and if it is purchased in 10-case lots, a 3% discount may be allowed. The alert buyer may be able to lower beverage costs simply by taking advantage of sale-priced brands or purchasing in liter or 1.75-liter bottles.

Supplier Product Lines

Many brands are assigned to only a few suppliers. In some areas of the country, only one supplier may carry a particular brand or product line. In this case, it becomes impossible for the beverage buyer to shop around to get the lowest price. Even if more than one supplier distributes the merchandise, the price is often fixed by the distiller or importer. Obviously, when buyers purchase brand names, they have no trouble obtaining quality, because all liquor of a particular brand will be of the same quality. There is normally no deterioration of quality while the liquor is in transit or storage.

Quality of Well-Stock Products

Well-stock products such as bourbon, vodka, gin, Canadian whiskey, scotch, rum, vodka, blended American liquor (sometimes called rye), and so on—can vary considerably in quality. Management should select four or five brands within each category that are deemed acceptable. The buyer can then shop around to purchase any of the selections from the supplier with the lowest price.

Size of Inventory and Breadth of Product Line

Determining how large an inventory to stock and how large a selection of brands to carry are primary responsibilities of management. Decisions are based on:

- Clientele
- Type of establishment
- Sales volume of the operation

For example, a small bar that has a volume of $1,500 per week would certainly not be able to stock as many brands as one that has a volume of $15,000 per week, nor would the clientele expect the variety. A large bar operation would certainly be expected to stock all the major call brands (that have an asked-for name) and would perhaps have a larger selection of wines, beers, and liquors, as well as specialty drinks.

Methods of Payment

In many states, the method of payment made by the bar operation to the supplier is governed by state law. These payments must be made within a specified period of time. Penalties are imposed should an establishment fail to pay within a specific time period. Usually, as a penalty, the supplier is required by the state to have the establishment pay for all future sales at the time of delivery. In some states, regulations require that all deliveries be on a **COD** (or *cash on delivery*) basis.

Beverage Production

In producing mixed drinks, several issues need to be considered per the needs of the operation. These include drink ingredients, purchasing units, and means of dispensing soda.

Standard Nonalcohol Drink Ingredients

Not only does a bar supply alcohol beverages, but it must also have on hand all the ingredients necessary to make various mixed drinks. The items used depend on the system used by the bar operation. The variety depends on the size and volume of the operation.

COMMON DRINK INGREDIENTS AND PURCHASING UNITS
- Sodas: 12 oz. cans, bottles; 1- or 2-liter, pre-mix systems, post-mix systems
- Bar juices: gallons, ½ gallons, #5 cans, quarts, 5 oz. individual cans
- Other mixer: bottles, cans, ½ gallons
- Fresh fruits and vegetables
- Seasonings, flavorings, spices, herbs
- Garnishes

Sodas such as ginger ale and colas are used as a mix with alcohol beverages. **Mixers** are *items such as fruit, Bloody Mary mix, Collins mix, and so on, that are used to prepare or flavor alcohol beverages.* Because the cost of mixers is usually low compared to the cost of alcohol beverages, operators should attempt to use only high-quality mixers. A comparison can be made to the chef who makes excellent sauces but still utilizes the poorest quality meat—the end product still is not very tasty.

Dispensing Soda

Management can use one of the following ways of dispensing soda in order to mix drinks:

- Cans
- Bottles
- A pre-mix nonalcohol beverage system
- A post-mix nonalcohol beverage system

In a **pre-mix system**, *flavored soda that is ready to serve (pre-mixed with water) is packaged in stainless steel tanks.* The carbonated water and syrup are delivered to the establishment already mixed. In a **post-mix system**, *the mixer flavor comes in large syrup containers, usually packaged as a bag-in-a-box; the syrup is then mixed in a carbonator with water to produce a carbonated beverage.* This system is ideal for high-volume operations, as it comes at the most economical cost.

One of the problems with a post-mix system is that the taste of the end product is affected by the quality of the local water supply. Special filtration systems may be needed to avoid undesirable flavors. In some areas, poor water quality may preclude the use of a post-mix system. Management may decide to purchase individual bottles, cans, or tanks of premixed soda, even though the unit cost is higher, because style of service, quality, and presentation may be of greater importance.

Purchasing Nonalcohol Drink Ingredients

Juices for the bar normally are purchased in gallons, half-gallons, 46-ounce cans (#5 cans), or 5-ounce individual serving cans. The larger units are less expensive, but they may be more difficult to handle. In addition, once they are opened, they need to be used quickly to reduce spoilage. It is common practice to pour juices into bottles to maintain quality, reduce spoilage, and, in the case of large units, make the containers easier to handle by bar staff.

Bar juices (*fruit juices used in mixed drinks*), fruits, and other production ingredients may be purchased by the bar department or the food department. If the food department is purchasing for the bar, a requisition or transfer is used to account for the cost of the product. The food department then issues them to the bar. Issues may be in bulk or as needed, depending on the procedure of the operation. As with food, tracking the cost of these products is necessary in order to compute the cost of beverages sold for the day, week, or month.

Some operations, particularly those that have a limited food selection, may deal with a supplier specializing in nonalcohol bar supplies. Others may buy fruit from a produce supplier, prepared products such as cherries and olives from a wholesale grocer, and soft drinks from a local bottling company. Each operation will base its decisions on its particular needs, volume of sales, and internal control methods.

Beverage Cost

Beverage cost is the *cost of goods sold in the preparation of alcohol beverages.* Costs include:

- The cost of the alcohol ingredients
- Any mixers used in beverage production
- Any condiments used in beverage production or as requested by guests
- Any other items used in the preparation of drinks (e.g., ice)
- Any items used as garnishes for drinks
- Waste or spillage

Pour Cost and Beverage Cost

The terms *pour cost* and *bar cost* are often used interchangeably with the term *beverage cost.* Pour cost refers to *the cost of preparing a single drink,* whereas beverage cost refers to *the total cost of goods sold for a specific accounting period.* Like food cost, beverage cost is used to report *the total dollar amount spent to generate sales for the period.* Also, like the food cost percentage, the **beverage cost percentage** is the beverage cost reported as a percentage. For instance, a manager may state, "Bar cost is 18%."

POUR COST, BAR COST, AND BEVERAGE COST
- **Pour Cost, or Bar Cost:** The cost of preparing a single drink. This cost includes the cost of the alcohol, mixers, condiments, ice, and other ingredients, including ice, garnishes, waste, and spillage.
- **Beverage Cost:** The total cost of goods sold for a specific accounting period.

Beverage cost percentages may differ from one operation to the next, depending on the location, clientele, type of operation, competition, and laws affecting service of alcohol beverage. Like with food, goals are established by management for target beverage cost percentages. It is management's responsibility to monitor operations through standard operating procedures to ensure this goal is met.

High Pour Costs

Like with high food costs, there are a number of reasons for high pour costs. It is important to control pour costs and, consequently, overall beverage costs. The most common reasons for (and effects of) high pour costs are the following:

- Serving larger than standard drinks → Portion costs are higher than standard
- Setting minimum menu prices too low → Cost-to-sales ratio is too high

- High inventory turnover → Lack of control of inventory, resulting in theft, pilferage, or waste
- Ineffective cash and sales controls → Loss of revenue, attributable to lack of standard operating procedures for employees handling cash

Controlling Beverage Costs

To solve these problems, management has simply to review the steps in the Cycle of Control. To control beverage (bar) costs, a manager should know how to

- Manage beverage inventory.
- Receive alcohol beverages.
- Control bar requisitions.
- Use bar transfers.
- Maintain pour systems.

As with food requisitions and transfers, **bar requisitions** and **bar transfers** are *forms used to monitor beverage inventory*. They have the same appearance as food requisitions and transfers. **Pour systems** are used to *control the quantity of alcohol beverages used in drinks*.

Lack of control in any of these key areas will most likely result in higher product cost to sales ratios than planned. As with food, if this situation is not identified and rectified quickly, sales prices will not be adequate to cover product cost and all other operating costs. Most likely, profit will be needed to cover operating costs.

Beverage Cost Percentage Goals

In controlling the costs of a beverage service operation, it is important that an owner or manager establish clear beverage cost goals. This is achieved with a close review of the operation's beverage cost percentage and through use of the Beverage Cost Report.

Beverage Cost Percentage

Beverage managers choose the beverage cost percentage they wish to have as an operating goal. This decision usually depends on how the manager or owner wants the operation to be perceived by customers, which is determined by location, clientele, competition, and so on.

The beverage cost percentage can be maintained through the use of information and control reports prepared on a regular basis. (Many of the reports discussed in this chapter are generated by application software, referred to hereafter as automated systems. Automated beverage systems will be discussed in Chapter 15.)

Beverage Cost Report

All the techniques and paperwork (think daily, weekly, and monthly cost reports) used for food production and control are easily adapted for beverage operations. The primary tool for tracking beverage cost is the **Beverage Cost Report** (Figure 14.3). By tracking the beverage cost percentage and the fluctuations that occur between accounting periods, the manager is alerted to operational corrections that need to be made.

Bar Location: <u>Lounge</u>   **Period Ending:** <u>1/17/XX</u>

Date		Day		Sales
January	11	Sunday	(1st shift)	$ 157.50
			(2nd shift)	278.90
	12	Monday	(1st shift)	151.85
			(2nd shift)	465.75
	13	Tuesday	(1st shift)	219.55
			(2nd shift)	603.75
	14	Wednesday	(1st shift)	208.25
			(2nd shift)	542.50
	15	Thursday	(1st shift)	294.30
			(2nd shift)	777.50
	16	Friday	(1st shift)	574.15
			(2nd shift)	1,631.65
	17	Saturday	(1st shift)	511.10
			(2nd shift)	1,525.50
			Total	$7,942.25

$$\frac{\text{Cost of Goods Sold (\$1,481.90)}}{\text{Total Beverage Sales (\$7,942.25)}} = \text{Beverage Cost Percentage } (0.186 \times 100 = 18.6\%)$$

Prepared By: <u>Clerical</u>

Date: <u>1/20/XX</u>

FIGURE 14.3   Beverage Cost Report.

Calculating Beverage Cost Percentage

·Calculating a beverage cost percentage is an activity similar to calculating a food cost percentage: Divide the beverage cost by the beverage sales.

BEVERAGE COST/BEVERAGE SALES × 100 = BEVERAGE COST %

In Figure 14.4, the **Cost of Goods Sold** (beverage cost) is $1,481.90 for the period. (The cost is calculated in the same way cost of goods for food was determined.) This amount is divided by the Total Beverage Sales of $7,942.25. The result, 0.186, is converted to a percentage of 18.6%.

BEVERAGE COST/BEVERAGE SALES × 100 = BEVERAGE COST %

$1,481.90 / $7,942.25 × 100 = 18.6%

The Total Cost of Goods Sold is the total cost of the liquor, wine, beer, and all other complements used. These figures are taken directly from the **Bar and Inventory Control Report (Discussed in Chapter 15)**, which *provides a comprehensive method for tracking beverage inventory.*

Calculating Beverage Cost Percentage Using a Beverage Cost Report

The Beverage Cost Report is prepared at the end of the accounting period. We already looked at one example of a Beverage Cost Report in Figure 14.4. Whereas Figure 14.3 is a simple chart that shows total figures by shift and period, Figure 14.4 goes into more detail: It provides a cost breakdown and sales analysis.

Commonly, *the accounting period for a bar is one week.* If the operation is computerized, the Beverage Cost Report can be run daily, by shift, and even hourly, depending on the system. Experience will help management determine the type of operation checks needed. The accounting period, however, should reflect the beverage cost and beverage cost percentage for that period, or **sales per period**, as well as the **sales per day** and **sales per shift**. Any fluctuations in the beverage cost percentage will immediately indicate that a problem may exist.

Notice that the beverage cost is broken down according to product type sold: liquor, wine, and beer (as shown in Figure 14.4). It indicates the individual cost percentages for each. A **cash comparison**, which *indicates the dollar amount that should be in the cash register,* is calculated by *comparing sales to retail value versus quantity of liquor dispensed per shift.* Calculating the **sales dollars per shot** is critical. Various methods exist to assist in this process and will be discussed in Chapter 15. Finally, the Bar and Inventory Control Report, along with the Liquor Storeroom Inventory Report (which will be discussed in Chapter 15), will accurately account for every item of merchandise. This report *tracks the inventory of each beverage item.*

Completing a Beverage Cost Report

The purpose of a Beverage Cost Report is to *indicate the actual cost percentage of liquor, wine, beer, and complements.* It shows the bar location and cost of goods sold. Further, it shows the total amount of beverage sales for any given period of time (see Figure 14.4).

ELEMENTS OF A BEVERAGE COST REPORT

- Bar location
- Sales by shift, day, and period
- Cost of goods sold
- Beverage cost percentage
- Beverage cost breakdown

Bar Location: Lounge				Period Ending: 1/17/XX			
Item	Sunday 1/11	Monday 1/12	Tuesday 1/13	Wednesday 1/14	Thursday 1/15	Friday 1/16	Saturday 1/17	Week Total

1st Shift Sales								
Liquor	$110.50	$105.00	$169.85	$158.45	$248.15	$515.70	$457.35	$1,765.00
Wine	21.20	23.55	26.10	28.20	25.75	30.30	27.70	182.80
Beer	25.80	23.30	23.60	21.60	20.40	28.15	26.05	168.90
Shift Total	$157.50	$151.85	$219.55	$208.25	$294.30	$574.15	$511.10	$2,116.70

2nd Shift Sales								
Liquor	$168.85	$257.20	$332.95	$284.00	$441.65	$1,059.95	$852.70	$3,397.30
Wine	16.70	18.90	22.50	22.10	25.95	49.15	59.25	214.55
Beer	93.35	189.65	248.30	236.40	309.90	522.55	613.55	2,213.70
Shift Total	$278.90	$465.75	$603.75	$542.50	$777.50	$1,631.65	$1,525.50	$5,825.55
DAILY TOTAL	$436.40	$617.60	$823.30	$750.75	$1,071.80	$2,205.80	$2,036.60	$7,942.25

Period Beverage Cost Breakdown   **Sales Management Analysis**

Item	Cost of Goods Sold	Sales (Shift Totals)		Beverage Cost %		Sales	Retail Value	Over (Short)
Liquor	$ 945.30	$5,162.30		18.3%		$5,162.30	$5,213.00	($50.70)
Wine	101.45	397.35		25.5		397.35	398.75	(1.40)
Beer	435.15	2,382.60		18.3		2,382.60	2,409.40	(26.80)
Total	$1,481.90	$7,942.25		18.6%		$7,942.25	$8,021.15	($78.90)

Prepared by: Clerical   **Date:** 1/20/XX

FIGURE 14.4   Beverage Cost Report with cost breakdown and sales analysis.

Bar Location   The bar location is important because a separate report must be prepared for each bar, in each separate location. Hotels and resorts may have several different bars. Also, some restaurant operations may have more than one bar location (such as a lounge and a service bar).

Sales by Shift, Day, and Period   Sales by shift, and by date and day, as well as the total sales for the period, are listed. These numbers can be used to determine trends. It is extremely important to continually analyze the sales figures. If there is an unaccountable fluctuation in the trends, a thorough investigation should be made. Even if it is determined that the controls are in good order, there is still the possibility of theft by employees.

Cost of Goods Sold   The cost of goods sold is the total cost of the liquor, beer, wine, and other complements used. These figures are taken directly from the Bar and Inventory Control Report (which will be discussed in Chapter 15).

Beverage Cost Percentage   As mentioned earlier, the beverage cost percentage is calculated by dividing the Cost of Goods Sold by the Total Beverage Sales and multiplying by 100.

Beverage Cost Breakdown   A beverage cost breakdown, as shown in the bottom left section of Figure 14.4, separates the liquor, wine, and beer, and determines a cost percentage for each.

BEVERAGE COST BREAKDOWN

- Total liquor cost
- Liquor cost percentages by product and shift
- Wine
- Beer
- Sales management analysis: sales, cost of goods, beverage cost percentages, total retail value, over/shorts

---

Total Liquor Cost and Percentages   **Total liquor sales** comprises all distilled alcohol beverages. Sales can be tracked electronically by a cash register, a point-of-sale device, or a computer. The sales may also be tracked manually by guest checks, individual servers, or bartenders. To calculate the total liquor percentage, divide the Total Liquor Cost (total Cost of Goods Sold) by Total Liquor Sales.

LIQUOR COST OF GOODS SOLD/TOTAL LIQUOR SALES = LIQUOR COST %

In Figure 14.4, Liquor Cost of Goods Sold is $945.30 (Total Liquor Cost) divided by Total Liquor Sales of $5,162.30, which equals 18.3%, the Liquor Cost Percentage:

LIQUOR COST OF GOODS SOLD/TOTAL LIQUOR SALES

$945.30/$5,162.30 = 18.3%

Wine and Beer   The same procedure is followed for **wine** and **beer**. Each product's cost is divided by each product's sales, which gives the cost percentage for each product. Once the desired cost percentages are achieved, they should be continually maintained. The beverage cost breakdown on the report keeps these percentages in check, quickly reflecting any fluctuations by individual staff and shifts.

WINE COST OF GOODS SOLD/TOTAL WINE SALES = WINE COST %

$101.45/$397.35 = 25.5%

BEER COST OF GOODS SOLD/TOTAL BEER SALES = BEER COST %

$435.15/$2,382.60 = 18.3%

CALCULATING LIQUOR COST PERCENTAGES

Liquor Cost of Goods Sold / Total Liquor Sales = Liquor Cost %

Wine Cost of Goods Sold / Total Wine Sales = Wine Cost %

Beer Cost of Goods Sold / Total Beer Sales = Beer Cost %

Total Liquor Cost of Goods Sold / Total Beverage Sales = Beverage Cost %

Sales Management Analysis

For a dollar comparison, the actual sales according to liquor, wine, and beer, as well as the total sales, are listed for the period in the bottom right section of this report. The individual sales may be recorded through the use of different cash register or computer keys; for example, all liquor sales could be rung on the A key, the wine on the B key, and the beer on the C key. At the end of each shift, a register reading is taken totaling the sales for each category as well as the total sales. The majority of cash registers automatically have this separation function, with point-of-sale systems offering very detailed information on individual product sales, inventory status, and so on.

The total retail value is taken from the Bar and Inventory Control Report (which will be discussed in Chapter 15). The total retail value is compared to the total sales reports to determine the actual dollar amount and whether it is over or short. In Figure 14.4, liquor sales are $5,162.30. This amount is taken from the sales register. The retail sales value is taken from the Bar and Inventory Control Report. In Figure 14.4, the amount is $5,213.00. The difference is $50.70. This means that less cash was received than product sold. Possible causes for this could be overpours, spills, improper change given, and pricing done incorrectly.

Using a Beverage Cost Report

The Beverage Cost Report determines *the cost of goods sold over a specific accounting period*. The report will identify what has occurred during the accounting period. Even with the use of excellent controls, there always exists the element of human error. Careless or dishonest bartenders, servers, shift managers, and bookkeepers may dramatically affect the financial health of the beverage operation.

The Beverage Cost Report is an information tool that informs management of operational efficiencies. If planned costs are to be 18.5%, and in reality, they are 18.6%, operations are going as planned. If costs are planned to be 18.5% and in reality they are 22%, it is quite obvious operations are not going according to plan.

If operations are not going according to plan, management needs to identify the problem. The obvious first area to search is theft by employees. If theft does not seem feasible, other operational areas must be reviewed. These areas may involve a review to determine whether:

- Beverage recipes are being followed.
- Accurate portioning is occurring.
- Prices are in line with costs.
- Suppliers have raised their prices.

Beverage costs need to be checked frequently, because they are crucial in judging how well the operation is doing. If employees are aware that management maintains tight control, they will be motivated to perform at their best. This does not mean that management is looking over the employees' shoulders all the time, but it does mean that employees know that management is concerned about their performance.

Net Work

Explore the following Web sites:

www.berg-controls.com

www.barmedia.com—Click Recipes; Resources

www.beveragenet.net

www.beertown.org

www.discus.org

www.smartwine.com

Chapter Wrap

The Chapter ✓ at the beginning of the chapter posed several questions. Review the questions and compare your responses with the following answers:

1. **What similarities exist between the food cost control process and the beverage cost control process?**

   Just as in a restaurant, beverage management needs to begin with the menu. An alcohol beverage menu is the first step in the beverage cost control process. Each operation must create its own beverage menu based on its research of customer preferences. The breadth and depth of the offerings in each category will vary greatly from operation to operation.

   Once the beverage menu is developed, proper drink recipes must be followed to maintain a consistent beverage presentation. The recipes will not be nearly as complex as food recipes, but their importance as a control piece cannot be underestimated. Beverage recipes are standardized for the same reasons that food recipes are standardized—to control quality, quantity, and cost.

2. **How is beverage purchasing different from food purchasing?**

   From recipes and pour costs come standard purchasing functions—purchasing, receiving, storing, and inventory control. Standard receiving practices and procedures are similar to those for receiving food products. Because of the cost involved and the accountability required, however, the bar manager, general manager, or owner should receive most of the alcohol beverages.

   In many ways, beverage purchasing is less complex than food purchasing. Because of state regulations, however, beverage purchasing is unique. Anyone can purchase food products, but not just anyone can purchase or distribute alcohol beverages.

3. **How is beverage cost controlled?**

   Beverage cost percentages may differ from one operation to the next, depending on the location, clientele, type of operation, competition, and state laws affecting the service of alcohol beverage. Beverage cost percentage is a different story. As with food, standards are established regarding beverage cost percentages. It is management's responsibility to monitor operations through standard operating procedures to ensure this goal is met. To control beverage costs, a manager must control the beverage inventory, receive alcohol beverages, control bar requisitions, use bar transfers, and maintain standard pour systems.

4. How is beverage cost percentage used to analyze operations?

The beverage cost percentage can be maintained through the use of information and control reports prepared on a regular basis. All of the techniques and paperwork (think daily, weekly, and monthly cost reports) used for food production and control are easily adapted for beverage operations. The primary tool for tracking beverage cost, however, is the Beverage Cost Report. By tracking the beverage cost percentage and the fluctuations that occur between accounting periods, the manager is alerted to the need for operational corrections.

Key Terminology and Concepts in This Chapter

Bar and Inventory Control Report	Post-mix system
Bar cost	Pour cost
Bar juices	Pour systems
Bar requisitions	Pre-mix system
Bar transfers	Requisition
Beer	Sales dollars per shot
Beverage cost	Sales per day
Beverage cost percentage	Sales per period
Beverage Cost Report	Sales per shift
Call brands	Specifications
Cash comparison	Total liquor sales
COD (Cash on Delivery)	Transfer
Cost of Goods Sold	Volume discounts
House brands	Well stock
Liquor	Wine
Mixers	

Discussion Questions and Exercises

1. Define beverage cost.

2. How is a beverage cost percentage calculated? A liquor cost percentage? A wine cost percentage? A beer cost percentage?

3. In your opinion, why is purchasing for beverage service operations easier than purchasing for foodservice operations?

4. Name some unique aspects of purchasing alcohol products for restaurant distribution. Research liquor purchasing and serving laws in your home state. Prepare a summary of your findings.

5. Two of the bartenders at Farfalle Arrabbiata are being trained as assistant managers. Fran, the bar manager, would like you to explain to the new assistant managers the standard paperwork that Farfalle Arrabbiata uses in the bar operation. Specifically, she has asked that you explain the workings of the Beverage Cost Report. Prepare a lesson for these new recruits.

6. What is the value of a beverage cost breakdown analysis?

7. What effect will a supplier price increase have on the beverage cost percentage?

8. You and Fran are reviewing the Beverage Cost Reports for the past five accounting periods (each period is one week). In each of these periods, the percentage has increased about 1%. The employees have worked at Farfalle Arrabbiata for more than 5 years and are considered to be very honest. Besides theft, what else could be causing the increases? Where would you start looking for problems? Consider all areas of control.

 9. The computer is down at Farfalle Arrabbiata, and Fran needs the Beverage Cost Report ASAP. She's not sure how to complete the report. You jump in to help her out. Complete the report with the following information and summarize the results. Use the blank Beverage Cost Report form included on the accompanying CD.

First Shift Sales	Second Shift Sales
Sunday, January 11: $195	Sunday: $495
Moday, January 12: $125	Monday: $250
Tuesday, January 13: $155	Tuesday: $310
Wednesday, January 14: $190	Wednesday: $380
Thursday, January 15: $225	Thursday: $525
Friday, January 16: $423	Friday: $1,023
Saturday, January 17: $567	Saturday: $1,567

Invoices showed the following costs
Liquor: $118
Wine: $848
Beer: $828

## Chapter Fifteen

About
Bar & Inventory
Control

Chapter Objective

To control bar inventory through automated beverage control systems, Bar and Inventory Control Reports, and Liquor Storeroom Inventory Reports.

Learning Objectives

After reading this chapter and completing the discussion questions and exercises, you should be able to:

1. Apply standard procedures to bar inventory control.
2. Identify systems used to control inventory.
3. Determine inventory size for a bar operation.
4. Explain the different types of automated beverage control systems.
5. Track bar inventory using a Bar and Inventory Control Report and a Liquor Storeroom Inventory Report.
6. Use requisitions to track product costs.
7. Calculate cost of goods using perpetual and periodic inventory methods.
8. Calculate beverage cost percentage for a period.

Chapter Map

About Bar & Inventory Control

- Beverage Control Systems
- Ounce or Drink Control
- Automated Beverage Control Systems
- Advantages & Disadvantages of Automated Beverage Control Systems
- Bottle Exchange System

Beverage Inventory

- Bar Inventory Control
- Bar & Inventory Control Report
- Liquor Storeroom Inventory Report
- Bin Card System

Nonalcohol Items

Chapter ✓

Check the chapter content for the answers to these questions:

1. What types of control systems are used to manage beverage inventories?
2. How is bar inventory size determined?
3. What are automated beverage control systems?
4. Which reports are used to track bar inventory?
5. How is a perpetual inventory system used to control beverage products?

About Bar and Inventory Control

Typically, the greatest concentration of dollars invested in a food and beverage inventory is associated with alcohol beverages (beer, wine, and liquor). A single bottle of wine may cost several hundred dollars. Most of the time, the cost of a bottle of liquor or wine will range from $5.00 to $45.00.

Like food products, all alcohol beverages must be

- Accounted for when used.
- Inventoried.
- Constantly monitored.

Beverage Control Systems

Controlling alcohol beverages involves monitoring not only the inventory but the flow of inventory through an operation. For an overview of how alcohol beverages flow within a foodservice operation or bar, see Figure 15.1.

Adequate alcohol beverage inventory systems may employ several types of controls to determine dispensing costs, record sales, and account for merchandise. Systems may be used independently or in combination, depending on the needs of the operation.

Basically, there are three types of systems used to manage alcohol beverage inventories:

1. Ounce or drink control
2. Automated system (beverages are automatically counted as they are sold)
3. Bottle exchange system (a bottle is emptied and exchanged for a full bottle)

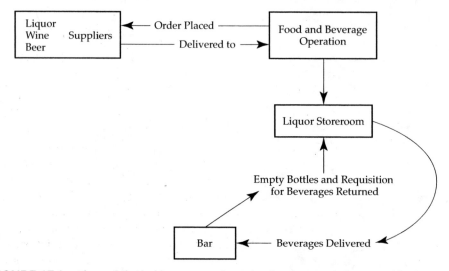

FIGURE 15.1   Flow of alcohol beverages through a beverage service operation.

Comparison of Metric and English Measure	
English	**Metric**
½ gallon → 64 ounces	1.75 liter → 59.2 ounces
1 quart → 32 ounces	1.0 liter → 33.8 ounces
1 fifth → 25.6 ounces	750 milliliter → 25.4 ounces

FIGURE 15.2 Comparison of metric and English measure of alcohol beverages.

For the vast majority of bars, the bartender is responsible for dispensing liquor, collecting payment for the liquor, and possibly even collecting payment for food sales at the bar. For this reason, when discussing beverage service and the types of inventory controls used, the methods of service and cash collection should be considered concurrently.

Ounce or Drink Control

Although the measurement of bottle containers is in the metric system, practically every American bar and recipe book still gives measurements for individual drinks in ounces. Figure 15.2 compares the two systems of measurement.

In the United States, drinks are typically measured in ounces; the average drink will hold from ⅞ ounce to 1½ ounces of liquor. There are no laws requiring beverage operators to have a standard measure. In Europe, the amount poured by management is generally standardized and a notice of the amount may have to be posted. Individual **drink control** helps with general beverage control.

Automated Beverage Control Systems

Automated beverage control systems can take various shapes:

- Reserve (gun-type) systems, similar to a soda system
- Individual bottle systems
- A combination of both (e.g., the gun system for house brands and an individual bottle system for call brands)

In an automated system, each time a drink is poured, the electronic system automatically counts what has been sold. Equally important is the fact that automated systems are designed to pour exact measured amounts. This type of system has several advantages:

- Cash accountability is maintained.
- The customer always gets the same drink.
- There is no waste from spillage.
- Underpouring or overpouring can be reduced or eliminated.

Simple control systems like a pourer attached to each bottle to control the amount poured can be used (Figure 15.3). Advanced electronic systems allow for separate pumps for each liquor, the recording of sales on guest checks, and the pouring of several liquors simultaneously. Sometimes, the system can actually mix the drinks and make cocktails. If the system is even more advanced, it will tie into a computer that provides further information for management. Some systems also control and integrate draft beer sales with liquor (Figure 15.4). Fully integrated electronic bar systems are available from a number of manufacturers. A bar system of this type measures the drinks, controls the inventory, registers the amount of sales, notes who made the sales and when, and can even record them on the accounts of guests registered in a hotel.

Systems can be custom designed and tailored for the user. The dispensing system will interface with most computer and cash-control systems. Figures 15.5 through 15.8 show examples of sophisticated beverage control systems. Figure 15.6 illustrates how the components of an automated system are related. The point-of-sale hardware (upper right corner) records sales and can interface with a remote printer or PC for a full range of detailed reports, such as hourly sales reports, price level changes, price or portion reports,

DRINKS PER BOTTLE			
Shot Size	**750 ML** *replaces fifth*	**1 LITER** *replaces quart*	**1.75 LITER** *replaces half gallon*
⅝ oz.	40	54	94
¾ oz.	34	45	79
⅞ oz.	29	38	67
1 oz.	25	34	59
1⅛ oz.	22	30	52
1¼ oz.	20	27	47
1½ oz.	17	22	39

STANDARD MIXING RATIOS	
Glass Size	**Recommended Shot Sizes**
6 ounce	⅝, ¾, ⅞ ounce
7 ounce	¾, ⅞, 1 ounce
8 ounce	⅞, 1, 1⅛ ounce
9 ounce	1, 1⅛, 1¼ ounce
10 ounce	1⅛, 1¼, 1½ ounce
12 ounce	1¼, 1½, 2 ounce
14 ounce	1½, 2, 2½ ounce

Shot size can vary depending on taste & volume of ice used.

FIGURE 15.3   Liquor control pourer. *Courtesy of Precision Pours, Inc.*

and a variety of summary data. The system interfaces with electronic cash registers (ECRs) that have pouring systems to tally sales automatically as they occur (Figure 15.7). Figure 15.8 illustrates the use of pouring dispensers. Fast pouring allows the bartender to provide faster, more consistent service to customers. Other benefits include cutting drink preparation time, minimizing the loss of liquor, and better inventory control.

Advantages and Disadvantages of Automated Beverage Control Systems

Completely automated systems have certain disadvantages. A major goal of management is to please the guests' tastes. This may be difficult to do with some automated systems, particularly gun-type systems that are visible to patrons. Unless the right presentation is made through careful selection of the system and its installation, customer satisfaction may be adversely affected. Atmosphere and personal service may be difficult to create when customers know that their drinks are served from an electronically controlled system.

ADVANTAGES OF AN AUTOMATED BEVERAGE SYSTEM

1. Measured pours
2. Consistently prepared drinks
3. 1.75-liter bottles
4. Automatic count
5. Automatic accounting and record keeping
6. Usually faster than manual
7. No moving of inventory
8. More space behind bar/no clutter

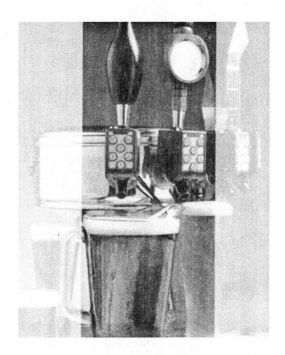

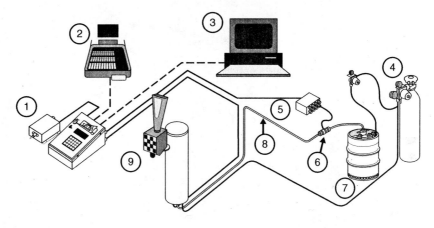

1. Power supply	6. Flow meter
2. Remote console	7. Draft supply room
3. POS Terminal	8. Beer lines
4. Compressed air or CO_2 to Tap head	9. Tap head
5. Flow meter junction box	

The picture shows a type of automated draft beer control system.
This particular system offers the following features:
- Optional interface to automated dispensing system and point-of-sale systems
- Designed for ease of cleaning
- Empty-keg indicator and optional shut-off
- Compact size
- Remote console
- Four portion sizes plus cancel and repeat functions
- Continual system operation
- Full range of management reports
- Dispenses wine or margaritas without modification
- Measures and dispenses by volume or time.

FIGURE 15.4   Draft beer control. *Courtesy of Berg Company LLC.*

FIGURE 15.5   Automated beverage system. *Courtesy of Berg Company LLC.*

The companies marketing these systems and beverage operators who have installed them are almost unanimous in praising them, however. For one thing, most agree that the systems reduce liquor cost percentages. These systems are also much more accurate in pouring exact amounts of liquor. Finally, part of the savings is

FIGURE 15.6   Features of an automated beverage system. The picture illustrates how the components of an automated system are related. The point-of-sale hardware, in the upper right corner, records sales and can interface with a remote printer or PC for a full range of detailed reports such as hourly sales reports, price level changes, price/portion reports, and a variety of summary data. The system interfaces with electronic cash registers (ECR's) with pouring systems to tally sales as they occur, automatically. *Courtesy of Berg Company LLC.*

① Infinity System Overview

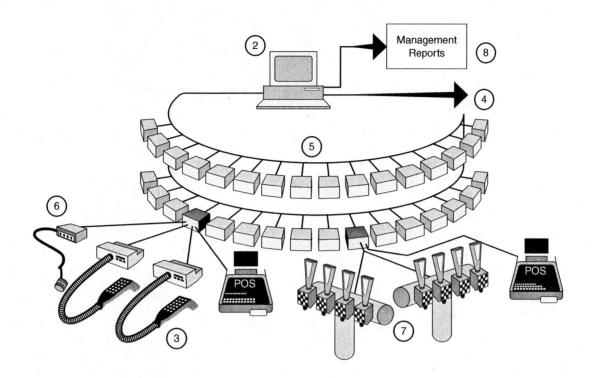

2. PC running Infinity Software
3. Laser Liquor system with Infinity
4. Data sharing with other PCs.
5. Up to 32 Electronic Control Units (ECU's) can be connected to a single network—local or remote. Multiple networks can be used.
6. Up to 2 laser units and/or 1 all-bottle unit can be controlled by a single liquor ECU.
7. Up to 8 TAP1 faucets can be controlled by a single TAP1 ECU
8. Reports that can be generated are:
 Most recent activity report—display of current daily sales
 X1 system summary—display of total drinks and sales of entire system
 X2 station sales summary—report of total drinks and sales by price level and code brand
 X3 station detail—display of total drinks and sales by size, price, and code (brand) per station
 X4 hourly sales—display of hourly total drinks and sales recorded for each station in the
  last 48 hours
 Week ending summary—total drinks and sales by price level and code (brand) at each
  station over the last seven days
 Month ending summary—usage (by volume) for each code (brand) and total sales for the
  past 30 days
 Annual summary—usage (by volume) for each code (brand) and total sales for past year
 Revenue yield—monetary return by volume (oz or mL) for each code (brand)

FIGURE 15.7 Overview of an automated beverage system. *Courtesy of Berg Company LLC.*

attributable to the reduction in theft. The advantages of the system, therefore, far outweigh the disadvantages, as the following summary shows:

1. Automated systems provide measured pouring, which eliminates problems of overpouring, underpouring, and spillage.
2. Customers are assured of receiving the amount they pay for and enjoying a consistently prepared drink.

FIGURE 15.8   A pouring dispenser. *Courtesy of Berg Company LLC*

3. Many systems are designed to use 1.75-liter bottles, which saves the beverage operation an additional 5% to 10% in beverage (because of the economy of the larger than normal bottle size) costs.

4. Beverages cannot be dispensed without automatically being counted.

5. Most, though not all, systems incorporate accounting and record keeping, so that these tasks are greatly simplified.

6. In some cases, the systems are significantly faster than manually operated ones, particularly in the making of mixed drinks or when various well liquors are poured consecutively.

7. Because all the liquor in the system is controlled by the storeroom manager, no merchandise needs to be moved. The labor cost incurred in the physical moving of the merchandise and recording the issues is eliminated.

8. Space behind the bar can be freed up, and the clutter of empty bottles is all but eliminated.

Bottle Exchange System

A **bottle exchange system** is very simple and easy to use: When a bottle is emptied, it is exchanged for a full bottle. The system usually works in the following manner:

1. As the bottles are emptied by the bartender, they are stored in a convenient location within the bar.

2. At the end of the shift, or the next morning, the empty bottles are taken to the bar manager.

3. The bar manager takes the empty bottles into the beverage storeroom and replaces them with full bottles.

4. The empty bottles are discarded or broken with a bottle crusher, unless such an act is unlawful. (Each state has its own specific law regarding the disposal of empty liquor bottles.)

Beverage Inventory

As a general rule, the size of the inventory should be equal to the cost of goods used during a period (typically one week). For example, if an operation had $10,000 in sales and the cost of sales was $3,000, the inventory should be about $3,000. At the same time, in each period, the purchases should be approximately $3,000. In effect, period purchases are equal to inventory, which, in turn, is equal to the cost of goods sold.

Note that these are estimates. In fact, the kinds of alcohol beverages (liquor, wine, beer) purchased and the time required for delivery also affect the size of inventory. With fine wines, it may be necessary to purchase a sufficient amount to ensure that the item can be kept on the wine list for a year or two. With liquor and beer, however, enough for about 10 days of consumption is normally an adequate supply. For convenience and because of some state government regulations that control payments to vendors, often only a 2-week supply may be purchased at a given time.

Management must decide what brands should be carried. This decision will be influenced to a large part by the requests and tastes of guests. A club that caters to a small number of members certainly should stock the brands that the members prefer, bearing in mind how often a particular brand is requested. It would be unwise to stock a specific brand requested by only one member, who orders that drink brand once a year, on her birthday. At that rate, it could take 24 years to empty one bottle! Furthermore, the selection of a particular stock to be carried will be influenced by the time of year—for example, lighter spirits, such as rum, are typically consumed more frequently during the summer months. Also, any scheduled special events, such as a fish or seafood dinner, that may call for a white wine should be taken into account. Customer preferences and space limitations should also be considered when purchasing stock.

Bar Inventory Control

Bar Inventory Control can be divided into two steps.

1. Calculating the value of the storeroom inventory.
2. Determining if the inventory has been used properly.

With a liquor control system in place, it is a simple matter to have complete inventory control over the liquor. The control system

1. Accounts for all liquor usage.
2. Reconciles receipts against bottles used.
3. Automatically reorders liquors.

The **Bar and Inventory Control Report** and the **Liquor Storeroom Inventory Report** are the tools in the manager's toolbox that complete these two steps. These reports provide a complete system for managing alcohol beverage inventory.

The Bar and Inventory Control Report

The **Bar and Inventory Control Report** (Figure 15.9) is one of the best ways to control alcohol beverage inventory. It is *a comprehensive method of tracking beverage inventory.* This report is completed for each bar (if more than one bar exists within a given foodservice operation). The person completing the Bar and Inventory Control Report and Liquor Storeroom Inventory Report forms will obtain the information from requisitions. The requisition form can also be used for those who use bottle exchange systems, or Inventory Card, or Bin Card, systems. The Bar and Inventory Control Report keeps track of:

- Beginning and ending inventories.
- Use of product by day in the period, and for the entire period.
- The number of drinks that should have been sold.
- The retail value of those drinks.
- Liquor cost percentages by type of beverage.

This information will help the bar manager to determine variances. Like with food, **variances** are *the differences between what was actually used and what should have been used.* If 108 bottles of Jack Daniels should have been used but actually 107 were used, then there is a one-bottle variance. In this case (as shown in Figure 15.10),

Date: 1/18/XX

Time: 9:00 A.M.

Taken By: Bar Manager and Assistant

Bar Location: Cedar Room

Page: 1 of 7

Prepared By: Clerical

Approved By: Owner/Manager

Item No. 1 Item Description	2 Unit	3 Opening Inventory	4 Requisitions by Day of Period — Month: January 11	12	13	14	15	16	17	5 Total (3 + 4)	6 Closing Inventory	7 Amount Sold (5 − 6)	8 Price	9 Cost of Goods Sold (7 × 8)	10 No. Drinks Sold	11 Sales Price	12 Total Retail Value (10 × 11)	13 Liquor Cost % (9 ÷ 12)
Bourbon																		
Early Times	750 mL	6.8	1				1		2	10.8	5.9	4.9	$12.95	$ 63.46	122	$3.35	$408.70	15.53%
I.W. Harper	750 mL	7.2			2	1		2		12.2	7.7	4.5	16.25	73.13	112	3.50	392.00	18.66
Jack Daniels	750 mL	9.4	3	1	1		1	1	4	20.4	8.8	11.6	21.45	248.82	290	4.15	1,230.50	20.22
Subtotal														$385.41			$2,031.20	18.97%
Beer																		
Heineken	btl	97	72			24		24	48	265	88	177	0.95	$168.15	177	$2.50	$442.50	38.00%
Miller	½ keg	1.5	1		1		1	1	1	5.5	1.3	4.2	89.20	374.64	1,848	1.65	3,049.20	12.29
Budweiser	½ keg	1.5	1		1			1	1	5.5	1.3	4.2	89.20	374.64	1,848	1.65	3,049.20	12.29
Subtotal														$917.43			$6,540.90	14.03%
Wine																		
Gallo Vin Rose	liter	3.1	1				1		2	7.1	3.9	3.2	4.60	$14.72	19	$2.75	$52.25	28.17%
Subtotal														$14.72			$52.25	28.17%
Total														$1,317.56			$8,624.35	15.28%

FIGURE 15.9 Bar and Inventory Control Report.

Date: 1/18/XX Time: 8:00 A.M.

Period Ending: January 17, XXXX Taken By: Bar Manager and Assistant

Prepared By: Clerical Approved By: Owner/Manager

Item Description	Unit	Opening Inventory	Purchases	Totals (A)	Requisitions by Day of Period Month: January							Totals (B)	Balance A Less B	Closing Inventory	+ or –	Price	Extension
					11	12	13	14	15	16	17						
Bourbon																	
Early Times	750 mL	87	48	135	11	4	5	7	9	8	10	54	81	81	0	$12.95	$1,048.95
I.W. Harper	750 mL	63	24	87	3			2	4	2	6	17	70	70	0	16.25	1,137.50
Jack Daniels	750 mL	91	48	139	8	2	2	7		3	9	31	108	107	–1 (broken)	21.45	2,295.15
Jim Beam	750 mL	103	72	175	14	6	5	1	4	8	12	50	125	125	0	13.25	1,656.25
Old Crow	750 mL	48		48	2				1		4	7	41	41	0	11.95	489.95
Old Grand-Dad	750 mL	51		51		2				6	1	9	42	42	0	18.45	774.90
Canadian																	
Canadian Club	750 mL	49	24	73	7	1	1	1	2	8	6	26	47	47	0	18.00	846.00
Seagram's VO	750 mL	57	24	81	5	3	1	2	1	1	6	19	62	62	0	18.25	1,131.50
Seagrams CR	750 mL	15		15		1						1	14	14	0	37.95	531.30
																Total	$9,911.50

FIGURE 15.10 Liquor Storeroom Inventory Report.

the bottle was broken and noted on the Liquor Storeroom Inventory Report. Bar managers would want to know why there is a variance. The most common reason for variances are

- Error
- Breakage
- Theft

Figure 15.9 displays a Bar and Inventory Report. The report is organized by column. Refer to Figure 15.9 as the following column descriptions are explained:

Column 1: Item Description   Each type of beverage is listed according to beverage category (such as bourbon, beer, or wine).

Column 2: Unit   This is the *size of the purchasing unit* described in Column 1 (such as 750-mL bottle, liter, or ½ keg).

Column 3: Opening Inventory   Like with food product, at the end of each **accounting period**, *a physical inventory, or hand count, is taken and valued.* This is called the closing inventory. The previous accounting period's closing inventory is the current accounting period's **opening inventory**.

Column 4: Requisitions   A **requisition** from the bar to the liquor storeroom should be prepared daily. This enables the bartender to maintain a **par amount** at the bar. As requisitions are filled and completed, they are transferred to the Bar and Inventory Control Report. In this way, every item taken is accounted for. If Inventory Cards, or Bin Cards (or a similar system) are used, then the use figures would be taken directly from the bin cards. Inventory or bin cards are kept with the physical inventory; when a bottle is removed from or added to the inventory, it is noted on the card.

Column 5: Total   The total includes the opening inventory plus the requisitions by day of period (Column 3 + Column 4 = Column 5).

Column 6: Closing Inventory   The **closing inventory** is the *actual physical count of all items on hand.* This is usually taken the morning after the last day of the ending period, before the bar opens. If the last day of the accounting period is a Saturday, the inventory would be taken Sunday morning, before opening. Bottles that are in use are weighed and inventoried in tenth amounts. For example, a half-full bottle would be .5.

Column 7: Amount   Column 7 indicates *the number of bottles or parts of bottles sold.* The **amount sold** is determined by *subtracting the closing inventory from the total* (Column 5 − Column 6 = Column 7).

Column 8: Price   Price is the *actual cost paid for the merchandise.* The price is taken from the invoices provided by the suppliers.

Column 9: Cost of Goods Sold   The **cost of goods sold** extension represents *the invoice price multiplied by the number sold* (Column 7 × Column 8 = Column 9).

Column 10: Number of Drinks Sold   The **number of drinks sold** is determined by *multiplying the amount sold (Column 7) by 25.* The number 25 would represent 25 one-ounce drinks per 750-mL bottle of liquor. Typically a one-ounce drink is poured, but house policy may specify another size, such as ⅞ ounce or 1⅛ ounces. The main point to remember is that the total possible number of drinks per bottle or unit must be established. This total number of drinks possible assumes that all conditions are perfect and bartenders make drinks in compliance with house policy on portion amounts. Obviously, some of the portions may vary if used in cocktails. (Most automated systems will account for the actual portion used.) On average, even allowing for cocktails, a basic number of drinks will be poured from a standard unit, such as a 750-mL bottle.

Column 11: Sales Price   The **sales price** is *the menu price,* the price the customer pays. This price should be used even if the beverage is used to make a cocktail.

Column 12: Total Retail Value   The **total retail value** is *determined by multiplying the number of drinks sold by the sales price* (Column 10 × Column 11 = Column 12).

Column 13: Liquor Cost Percentage   The idea of calculating a percentage is to figure out the **liquor cost**, or the **pour cost**, in relationship to the amount of revenue taken in by liquor sales. The **liquor cost percentage**, also known as the **pour cost percentage**, is obtained by dividing the Cost of Goods Sold by the Total Retail Value and multiplying by 100.

$$\text{COST OF GOODS SOLD/TOTAL RETAIL VALUE} = \text{POUR COST \%}$$
$$\$1,317.56/\$8,624.35 = 15.28\%$$

The liquor cost percentage will fluctuate with an increase or decrease in the cost of the merchandise. The Cost of Goods Sold and Total Retail Value columns are separately totaled by category (liquor, beer, and wine) in order to provide this information for the bar cost breakdown.

The benefit of maintaining the information provided by the Bar and Inventory Control Report is that it can be used *to compare what should have happened against what did happen.* For example, in Figure 15.9, Column 12, if the value of all drinks sold is reported as $8,624.35, and the amount reported by the cash registers is $8,622.35, there is a $2.00 difference. Usually, the variances are not very large. It is up to management to determine the acceptability of the variance amounts. In this example, a drink may not have been rung up. Similarly, the liquor cost percentage should compare to the one established when pricing drinks. If the liquor cost percentage is 3 or more percent higher than what it should be, there probably is a problem. Revisit Chapter 13 for a discussion of pricing to attain a certain liquor cost percentage and possible reasons for large variances.

Liquor Storeroom Inventory Report

With the **Liquor Storeroom Inventory Report** (Figure 15.10), the manager *always knows how much inventory is available, and its value.* The report begins with the Item Description column, which lists the liquors and wines by category and in alphabetical order. For speed and convenience, the bottles should also appear in the same order on the storage shelves.

The **Unit Size** is listed next, followed by the Opening Inventory, which was the Closing Inventory of the previous accounting period. For Early Times bourbon, the unit size is a 750-milliliter bottle. The Opening Inventory is 87 – 750 milliliter bottles. The 750-milliliter bottle is one of the most popular sizes because of its ease in handling when pouring.

Next, all Purchases during the period are listed (remember that purchases are taken from invoices provided by suppliers). These are added to the Opening Inventory, to make up the totals in the Totals (A) column. Forty-eight 750-milliliter bottles of Early Times bourbon were purchased during the accounting period.

The columns that follow under Requisitions by Day of Period list the dates of the period and the number of items used per day as recorded from requisitions. For Early Times bourbon, 11 bottles were requisitioned January 11; 4 bottles were requisitioned on January 12; 5 bottles were requisitioned on January 13; 7 bottles were requisitioned on January 14; 9 bottles were requisitioned on January 15; 8 bottles were requisitioned on January 16; and 10 bottles were requisitioned on January 17.

The second totals column, Totals (B), is the total number of items that have been requisitioned daily (during the accounting period), added together. Fifty-four bottles of Early Times bourbon were requisitioned during the week of January 11 through the 17. The Balance A Less B column represents the difference between the Totals (A) column and the Totals (B) column. The Totals (A) entry for Early Times bourbon was 135 bottles and the Totals (B) entry was 54 bottles; the difference is 81 bottles (135 − 54 = 81).

The Closing Inventory column should be identical to the Balance A Less B column. (A plus or minus may show up, however, because of error, breakage, or theft.) The Balance A Less B column for Early Times bourbon was 81 bottles, and the closing inventory was 81 bottles. Therefore, there is a zero in the + or − column.

Next, the price (the unit cost of the merchandise, taken from invoices) multiplied by the closing inventory will determine the extension. The closing inventory for Early Times bourbon was 81 bottles. This amount is multiplied by its invoice price of $12.95 per bottle, which equals $1,048.95, the extension.

$$\text{QUANTITY} \times \text{UNIT PRICE} = \text{EXTENSION}$$
$$81 \text{ BOTTLES} \times \$12.95 = \$1,048.95$$

The accounting period is indicated at the top of the form. For Figure 15.10, the accounting period was for the period ending January 17, 2XXX.

If an exchange system or card system is used, the manager would, instead of filling out a requisition, record the beverage use information directly on the Bar and Inventory Control Report.

Bar managers who use a Liquor Storeroom Inventory Report have the ability to be constantly aware of the quantity and value of the inventory. The dollar amount invested in inventory is typically determined by frequency and availability. The financial investment in inventory can be held to a minimum if beverage items are conveniently available and weekly purchases and deliveries are possible. Tracking the ordering, receiving, and inventory is only the beginning of managing inventory control. Proper use of the Bar and Inventory Control report will help the bar manager to analyze whether the inventory is being managed properly.

Bin Card System

An **Inventory Card or Bin Card system** provides a manual alternative to inventory control. For each type of alcohol beverage ordered or used, an Inventory or Bin Card is created. Every time an item is added to or removed from inventory, the change is recorded on the card. Figure 15.11 is a typical example of an Inventory or Bin Card.

As with food items, Inventory or Bin Cards are kept with the physical inventory; when a bottle is removed from or added to inventory, it is noted on the card. A card is

Product Description: Christian Bros. Chardonnay, 1 gallon							

Date: 1/07/XXXX				Card Number: 271			
Prepared By: Bar Manager				Extended By: Clerical			
Cost per Case/Unit: $76.80				Cost per Bottle: $19.20			

Beginning Inventory	Amount Used/Bought	Date Used	Balance	Price		Extension	
15	−1	1/15	14	$19	20	$268	80
14	−1	1/16	13	19	20	249	60
13	−3	1/17	10	19	20	192	00
10	+8	1/17	18	19	20	345	60

FIGURE 15.11   Inventory, or Bin Card.

kept for each type of beverage. For example, separate cards should be kept for Early Times Bourbon, I.W. Harper Bourbon, and so on. Historically, wine was put into bins and bin cards affixed next to the wine; thus the term "Bin Card" evolved. Today, Bin Cards may not even be in the storage room, but instead they may be kept in a file box or on a computer disk or hard drive, as part of application software. The major benefit of using a card system is that the current value of inventory is always known. This type of system is a **perpetual inventory system**.

Nonalcohol Items

All nonalcohol items should be accounted for along with alcohol beverages. Check the list below for nonalcohol items that are typically part of the bar inventory.

Common Nonalcohol Bar Inventory Items	
Item Description	**Purchasing Unit**
Cherries	Gallons
Olives	Gallons
Onions	Quarts
Lemons	Pounds, each, or cases
Limes	Pounds, each, or cases
Oranges	Pounds, each, or cases
Tomato Juice	46 oz.
Grapefruit Juice	46 oz.
Pineapple Juice	46 oz.
Orange Juice	Gallons
Bitters	12 oz.
Tabasco	12 oz.
Sugar	Pounds
Sour Mix	Gallons
Tonic	Quart
7 UP	Tank/box
Coke	Tank/box
Ginger Ale	Tank/box

Net Work

Explore the following Web sites:

www.berg-controls.com
www.alcoholcontrols.com
www.beveragenet.net
www.accubar.com—Click Demo
www.wunderbar.com—View Pour Systems

Chapter Wrap

The Chapter ✓ at the beginning of the chapter posed several questions. Review the questions and compare your responses with the following answers:

1. **What types of control systems are used to manage beverage inventories?**

   Adequate alcohol beverage inventory systems may employ several types of controls to determine dispensing costs, record sales, and account for merchandise. Systems may be used independently or in combination, depending on the needs of the operation. Basically, there are four types of systems used to manage alcohol beverage inventories:

1. Ounce or drink control.
2. Automated system—beverages are automatically counted as they are sold.
3. Bottle exchange system—a bottle is emptied and exchanged for a full bottle.

2. How is bar inventory size determined?

As a general rule, the size of the inventory should be equal to the Cost of Goods used during a period (typically one week). For example, if an operation had $10,000 in sales, and the cost of sales was $3,000, the inventory should be about $3,000. At the same time, the purchases should be approximately $3,000 in each period. In effect, period purchases are equal to inventory, which in turn is equal to the Cost of Goods Sold. Note that these are estimates, and in fact, the kinds of alcohol beverages (liquor, wine, beer) purchased and the time required for delivery also affects the size of inventory.

3. What are automated beverage control systems?

With an automated beverage control system, each time a drink is poured, the electronic system automatically counts what has been sold. Automated systems are designed to pour exact measured amounts. Automated systems are based on gun-type systems similar to a soda system or individual bottle systems. Many operations use a combination of both. Advanced electronic systems allow for separate pumps for each liquor and records on guest checks, pours several liquors simultaneously, and actually mixes the drinks and makes cocktails. If the system is even more advanced, it will tie into a computer that provides further information for management. Some systems also control and integrate draft beer sales with liquor. Fully integrated electronic bar systems are available from a number of manufacturers.

4. Which reports are used to track bar inventory?

A Liquor Storeroom Inventory Report and a Bar and Inventory Control Report are the tools in the manager's toolbox that track bar inventory. These reports provide a complete system for managing alcohol beverage inventory. The Bar and Inventory Control Report is one of the best ways to control alcohol beverage inventory. It is a comprehensive method of tracking beverage inventory. The Liquor Storeroom Inventory Report allows the bar manager to be constantly aware of the quantity and value of the inventory.

5. How is a perpetual inventory system used to control beverage product?

A perpetual inventory system is a manual alternative to inventory control. This system is based on an inventory card or bin card arrangement. For each type of alcohol beverage ordered or used, an Inventory or Bin Card is created. Every time an item is added to or removed from inventory, the change is recorded on the card.

𝒦ey Terminology and Concepts in This Chapter

Accounting period	Bottle exchange system
Amount sold	Closing inventory
Automated beverage control systems	Cost of goods sold
Bar and Inventory Control Report	Drink control

Inventory Card or Bin Card system
Liquor cost
Liquor cost percentage
Liquor Storeroom Inventory Report
Number of drinks sold
Opening inventory
Par amount
Perpetual inventory system
Physical inventory

Pour cost
Pour cost percentage
Price
Requisition
Sales price
Total retail value
Unit Size
Variances

Discussion Questions and Exercises

1. What types of external circumstances can affect the size of an operation's inventory?
2. Identify and describe the different types of automated control systems.
3. Explain the advantages and disadvantages of automated control systems.

4. Complete the following bin card for Absolut Vodka:

Product Description: Absolut Vodka

Date: 2/07   **Card Number:** 376

Prepared By: Fran   **Extended By:** Clerical

Cost per Case/Unit: $87.00/6—1.75 liter   **Cost per Unit:** $14.50

Beginning Inventory	Amount Used/Bought	Date Used	Balance	Unit Price	Extension
9	+6	2/15		$14.50	
	−3	2/16		$14.50	
	−4	2/17		$14.50	
	+6	2/17		$14.50	
	−4	2/18		$14.50	

5. Explain how a bottle exchange system works.
6. Explain how the Liquor Storeroom Inventory Report and the Bar and Inventory Control Report control bar operations.

7. The following are the Liquor Storeroom Inventory Report and the Bar and Inventory Control Report for Farfalle Arrabbiata for January. Complete the reports and summarize the information for Fran.

The physical (closing) inventory taken on 1/18/XXXX was as follows:

Early Times	35 units
IW Harper	70 units
Jack Daniels	98 units
Jim Beam	117 units
Old Crow	51 units
Old Grand-Dad	32 units
Canadian Club	47 units
Seagram's VO	73 units
Seagram's CR	23 units

Date: 1/18/XX **Time:** 8:00 A.M.

Period Ending: January 17, 2XXX **Taken By:** Bar Manager and Assistant

Prepared By: Clerical **Approved By:** Owner/Manager

Item Description	Unit	Opening Inventory	Purchases	Totals (A)	Requisitions by Day of Period Month: January 11	12	13	14	15	16	17	Totals (B)	Balance A Less B	Closing Inventory	+ or −	Price	Extension
Bourbon																	
Early Times	750 mL	67	48		11	4	10	15	10	10	20					$12.95	
I.W. Harper	750 mL	73	24		3			2	4	2	6					16.25	
Jack Daniels	750 mL	81	48		8	2	2	7		3	9					21.45	
Jim Beam	750 mL	95	72		14	6	5	1	4	8	12					13.25	
Old Crow	750 mL	58			2				1		4					11.95	
Old Grand-Dad	750 mL	41				2				6	1					18.45	
Canadian																	
Canadian Club	750 mL	49	24		7	1	1	1	2	8	6					18.00	
Seagram's VO	750 mL	67	24		5	3	1	2	1	1	6					18.25	
Seagram's CR	750 mL	25				1											37.95	
Total																	

FIGURE 15.12 Liquor Storeroom Inventory Report.

Date: 1/18/XX
Time: 9:00 A.M.
Taken By: Bar Manager and Assistant

Bar Location: Cedar Room
Page: 1 of 7
Prepared By: Clerical
Approved By: Owner/Manager

Item No. 1	2	3	4 Requisitions by Day of Period — Month: January							5	6	7	8	9	10	11	12	13
Item Description	Unit	Opening Inventory	11	12	13	14	15	16	17	Total (3 + 4)	Closing Inventory	Amount Sold (5 − 6)	Price	Cost of Goods Sold (7 × 8)	No. of Drinks Sold	Sales Price	Total Retail Value (10 × 11)	Liquor Cost % (9 ÷ 12)
Bourbon																		
Early Times	750 mL	13.6	2				2		4		11.8		$12.95		224	$3.35		
I.W. Harper	750 mL	14.4			4	2		4			15.4		16.25		224	3.50		
Jack Daniels	750 mL	18.8	6	2	2		2	2	8		17.6		21.45		580	4.15		
Beer																		
Heineken	btl	194	144			48		48	96		176		0.95		354	$2.25		
Miller	½ keg	3.0	2		2			2	2		2.6		89.20		3,696	1.65		
Budweiser	½ keg	3.0	2		2			2	2		2.6		89.20		3,696	1.65		
Wine																		
Gallo Vin Rose	liter	6.2	2				2		4		7.8		4.60		38	$2.75		
Total																		

FIGURE 15.13 Bar and Inventory Control Report.

## Chapter Sixteen

About Controlling Payroll Costs & Employee Turnover

Chapter Map   (Continued)

Hiring & Managing Employees

- Management Quality & Employee Turnover
- Cost of Employee Turnover
- Calculating Employee Turnover Rate & Cost

Steps to Controlling Payroll Cost

- Hiring the Right People
- Hiring to the Job Description
- Training
- Setting Employee Performance Standards

Chapter ✓

Check the chapter content for the answers to these questions:

1. What is payroll cost control?
2. What is payroll cost?
3. What is a payroll budget?
4. How is a work schedule prepared?
5. What are standard time card practices?
6. What is employee turnover?
7. How can payroll costs be controlled?

About Payroll Costs and Employee Turnover

The cost of labor continues to go up; minimum wage increases at the state level and, occasionally, at the federal level; and working conditions throughout the entire economy continue to improve. Labor concerns have a dominating influence on the development of foodservice systems and the products used throughout the foodservice industry. The method or system under which the lowest combined food and labor costs can be achieved, without lowering quality, often drives operating policy.

A continuing trend in controlling payroll costs, one that is forecast to be used increasingly, is to lessen the size of an operation's work staff. Using frozen, refrigerated, and preprepared foods, while at the same time maintaining food quality standards, reflects the industry's response to this problem.

Another solution is to employ the improvements in food technology and advancements in labor-saving kitchen equipment that are frequently introduced to the market. In real dollars, the productivity of the foodservice worker has declined in some foodservice operations that have not begun using newer methods of purchasing and preparation.

Labor costs generally vary from about 18% to 38% of sales, depending on the type of foodservice operation. Consequently, the importance of controlling payroll costs and employee turnover cannot be overemphasized. This chapter specifically details methods and procedures that have proven to be effective in controlling payroll costs and the cost of employee turnover.

Introduction to Payroll Cost Control

Payroll cost is *the total cost of employee labor*. Payroll costs are usually calculated once per accounting period. An accounting period can be monthly, biweekly, weekly, or even daily, if using computer software. Payroll cost indicates *the number of dollars spent in* *achieving the total amount of gross sales and profits for any given accounting.* The payroll cost budget is usually prepared at the same time as the food cost budget. **Food cost** is *the total dollar amount spent on food prepared in a foodservice operation*, as discussed in Chapter 10. Managing payroll cost is as important to an operation as managing food cost.

Payroll Cost
- The total cost of employee labor; it indicates the number of dollars spent in achieving the total amount of gross sales and profits for any given period of time.

Payroll Cost Control
- The process of meeting a cost target by establishing a payroll budget, properly organizing the workplace, hiring correctly, reducing employee turnover, scheduling properly, and comparing actual costs to projected costs, with the intent of reducing variances.

The Payroll Cost Control Process

Payroll cost control is *the process of meeting cost targets by establishing a payroll budget, properly organizing the workplace, hiring correctly, reducing employee turnover, scheduling properly, and comparing actual costs to projected costs, with the intent of reducing variances.* Payroll cost control takes place in two stages—planning and doing.

The first stage, **planning**, involves

- Establishing a payroll budget.
- Properly organizing the workplace.
- Hiring correctly.
- Reducing employee turnover.

The second stage, **doing**, involves

- Scheduling properly.
- Incurring costs.
- Comparing what happened to what was planned to happen.
- Correcting for unacceptable variances.

Payroll Cost Control—Two Stages

Planning	Doing
• Establishing a payroll budget.	• Scheduling properly.
• Organizing the workplace.	• Actually incurring payroll costs.
• Hiring correctly.	• Comparing actual costs to planned costs.
• Reducing employee turnover.	• Correcting unacceptable variances.

The **payroll cost control process** is basically *the efficient use of physical facilities, employee labor, and other resources associated with payroll to maximize productivity.*

Payroll Cost Budgets

As with food and beverage cost, **payroll cost budgets** are *a planned estimate of expenses, expressed in dollar amounts or as a percentage of sales. They are an estimate of* *the cost of labor needed to manage an estimated level of sales.* Payroll cost budgets are *established by examining payroll costs in relationship to sales by an operating area or department.*

For example, the payroll cost of operating a French bistro that is part of a large resort would be calculated and compared to the total sales of only the French bistro. This cost would *not* typically be calculated and compared to *all* the foodservice units that might exist at the resort. Budgets are established based on the goals of management. These goals establish the quality and level of service necessary to serve customers according to established standards.

PAYROLL COST BUDGETS

• A planned estimate of expenses, expressed in *dollar amounts* or *as a percentage of sales.*
• An estimate of the cost of labor needed to manage an estimated level of sales.

Work Schedules

Work schedules are developed to *ensure that the proper number of employees are working in order to meet the needs of customers.* To best use employees to accomplish the objectives of the foodservice operation, a **work schedule form**, or template, *is used to list the employees and the hours they work.* After the work schedule is developed, the estimated payroll from the schedule is compared to the payroll cost budget. If the estimate is the same or less, the schedule remains unchanged. If the estimate is higher than the budget, the schedule should be changed to meet the budget.

Components of Payroll Costs

The line item **payroll cost** on the income statement (see discussion of income statements, later in the chapter) has two components:

• *Salaries: Compensation for employees, calculated weekly, semimonthly, monthly, or annually.*
• *Wages: Compensation for employees based on hours worked.*

Controllable Expenses

Salaries vary somewhat according to sales, but they are not as flexible as wages. For the most part, *salaries are considered to be fixed.* This means that they do not change with sales. The second component of costs is **wages**. These costs do vary according to sales. Why? Because wages are paid to hourly employees, who are scheduled according to forecasted sales levels and standard staffing tables. Both salaries and wages are generally considered to be **controllable expenses**. Controllable expenses are *a type of variable expense that management has the direct ability, and responsibility, to control.*

The Income Statement

Controllable expenses are listed as part of an income statement. Figure 16.1 is the monthly income statement for Farfalle Arrabbiata used in Chapter 10. As covered in Chapter 10, an **income statement** is the tool that *lists the sources of revenue and the*

Sales	$	%
Food	140,743	80.00
Beverage	35,186	20.00
Total Revenue	**175,929**	**100.00**
Cost of Sales		
Food Cost	47,290	33.60
Beverage Cost	9,011	25.61
Total Cost of Goods	**56,301**	**32.00**
Gross Profit	119,628	68.00
Controllable Expenses		
Payroll	52,075	29.60
Benefits	7,917	4.50
Direct Operating Expenses	5,982	3.40
Music & Entertainment	880	0.50
Advertising & Promo	4,398	2.50
Utilities	6,509	3.70
Administration & General	4,222	2.40
Repair & Maintenance	2,463	1.40
Total Controllable Expenses	**84,446**	**48.00**
Income B4 Occupancy Costs	35,182	20.00
Occupation Costs		
Rent	10,556	6.00
Property Taxes	3,167	1.80
Other Taxes	1,500	0.85
Property Insurance	1,833	1.04
Interest	2,750	1.56
Depreciation	4,825	2.74
Total Occupancy Costs	**24,631**	**14.00**
Restaurant Profit B4 Taxes	**10,556**	**6.00**

Labels alongside the table: SALES · COST OF SALES · CONTROLLABLE EXPENSES · OCCUPATION COSTS · PROFIT

FIGURE 16.1   Sample monthly income statement for Farfalle Arrabbiata.

expenses incurred to obtain the sales. To review, the parts of an income statement are as follows:

- **Sales:** Food sales and beverage sales
- **Cost of sales:** *Costs associated with producing the food and beverages served*
- **Controllable expenses:** *Controllable because these costs tend to vary according to sales.* Management has some degree of control over these costs.
- **Profit** or **loss:** The result of sales minus expenses

Because payroll costs are controllable expenses, the percentage of salaries and wages in relation to sales will generally stay the same. Recall that costs such as rent, depreciation, and interest expenses generally are not considered controllable costs. These are **fixed costs** that do not vary according to sales. In its simplest form, the income statement formula is:

$$\text{Sales} - \text{Expenses} = \text{Profit}$$

$\mathcal{R}$elationship Between Costs and Sales

The far right column of the income statement in Figure 16.1 shows the percentage of either sales or expenses for every item on the income statement. For **sales**, *the percentages are the ratio of the sources of sales to the total sales.* In the example, 80%, or $8 of every $10 in sales, came from food sales. Twenty percent, or $2 of every $10, came from the sale of beverage items. Total sales is equal to 100%. Costs other than food cost and beverage cost are calculated in relation to total sales. For example, the food cost percentage is calculated as follows:

$$\text{FOOD COST/FOOD SALES} \times 100 = \text{FOOD COST \%}$$
$$\$47,290/140,743 \times 100 = 33.60\%$$

and beverage cost percentage is calculated in this way:

$$\text{BEVERAGE COST/BEVERAGE SALES} \times 100 = \text{BEVERAGE COST \%}$$
$$\$9,011/\$35,186 \times 100 = 25.61\%$$

The rest of the percentages in the right column of the income statement are calculated using total revenue. For example the cost of goods percentage is calculated by:

$$\text{TOTAL COST OF GOODS/TOTAL REVENUE} \times 100 = \text{COST OF GOODS \%}$$
$$\$56,301/\$175,929 \times 100 = 32.00\%$$

This means that $32 of every $100 of revenue is spent on goods resold to the customer. Each relationship shown in the right column of Figure 16.1 is used to measure operating performance of the foodservice establishment.

Payroll Cost Percentage

Profit is directly related to the total costs and the sales volume. Recall from Chapter 10 that costs are expressed in dollars, but for purposes of controlling them, they are also expressed in percentage form. Thus, just as the food cost percentage shows the relationship between food cost and food sales, the **payroll cost percentage** *shows the relationship between payroll costs and total sales.* The same relationship is true for all expenses on the income statement. Here is the basic formula for showing the relationship between sales, costs, and profit:

$$\text{COST/SALES} \times 100 = \text{COST \%}$$

The payroll cost percentage would be calculated as follows:

$$\text{COST/SALES} \times 100 = \text{COST \%}$$
$$\$52,075/\$175,929 = .2960\%$$
$$.2960 \times 100 = 29.60\%$$

The same procedure is used with all expense line items on the income statement. The cost percentage calculations for the major expense categories are shown on the next page:

Sales	$175,929	100%	
Cost of Goods	$56,301	32.00%	$56,301/$175,929 = 32%
Controllable Expenses	$84,446	48.00%	$84,446/$175,929 = 48%
Occupation Costs	$24,631	14.00%	$24,631/$175,929 = 14%
Profit	$10,556	6.00%	$10,556/$175,929 = 6%

In Chapter 1, prime costs were identified as

- Food costs.
- Beverage costs.
- Payroll costs.

These three expenses alone often account for as much as 60% of every foodservice operation's sales. Check this fact against Figure 16.1. From the income statement shown there, prime costs are as follows:

Total Cost of Goods: 32%
Payroll Cost: 29.6%
Benefits: 4.5%
Total Prime Cost: 66.1%

As such, in order to remain profitable, both payroll cost and food cost must be controlled according to the sales volume. The amount of profit will vary from operation to operation.

Payroll Budgets

To control the cost of payroll, it is necessary to set a payroll budget. Setting the proper payroll budget is related to

- How a menu is priced.
- The type of service system used.
- The level of service offered to customers.

Using the Payroll Cost Percentage

Payroll cost percentages vary according to the type of foodservice operation and volume of business.

Typical Payroll Cost Percentages for Foodservice Operations			
	Low (%)	Medium (%)	High (%)
Family Restaurant	25	31	35
Fine Dining	23	33	38
Quick Service	18	32	37
Cafeteria	26	30	35
Buffet	20	22	26

The income statement in Figure 16.1 shows the payroll cost percentage at 29.6%. If this example is for a family restaurant operation, then the payroll cost is in the low to medium area. As a general rule, the payroll cost percentage tends to become lower as the sales volume becomes higher, as long as the increase in sales volume can be handled by the same number of employees while still maintaining standard levels of service.

Foodservice managers exercise control over an operation by limiting expenses so that costs do not exceed a predetermined level. The level of cost is usually expressed as a percentage. If payroll costs have been predetermined to be 29.6% and in reality are 34.6%, then there is a 5% variance. The variance needs to be analyzed and the cost needs to be reduced. This amount of variance will have a negative effect on profit.

CONTROLLING PAYROLL MEANS

The manager must spend the correct amount of money on payroll in relation to the sales generated by those who were paid.

Using Payroll Budgets

A **payroll budget** is *a planned estimate of payroll expenses*. Usually, budgets are established based on expected sales. Management has total control over payroll budgets. A manager's success is often strongly related to his or her ability to control payroll budgets. This means that the manager must spend the correct amount of money on payroll in relationship to the sales generated by those who were paid.

A **payroll estimate** is *a plan developed by using a work schedule* (Figure 16.2) and a **payroll budget estimate** (Figure 16.3). A **work schedule** is *a form or template used to list the employees and the hours they work to best use employees to accomplish the objectives of the foodservice operation*. A **payroll cost estimate** is *calculated by position and person from the work schedule*. A payroll budget estimate is prepared in advance for an entire week (Figure 16.3). It is *a planned estimate of expenses, expressed in dollar amounts or as a percentage of sales*. It is an estimate of the cost of labor needed to manage an estimated level of sales. The budget is usually processed at the same time the work schedule is decided.

Budgets for payroll usually range from 18% to 38% of sales, depending on the type of foodservice operation. It is the responsibility of the foodservice manager to set the budgets. This is done by:

- Pricing meals.
- Estimating the number of meals to be sold during specific periods of time.
- Calculating what the income should be for a specific period of time.

Allocating Payroll Costs   Once a budget is established, it may be subdivided by employee category. A payroll budget may be designated toward several groups of employees:

- Kitchen staff
- Service staff
- Salaried employees

Although the entire payroll budget may be 29.6% of total sales, each employee category represents a separate part of the cost percentage. Assume that payroll budget for the kitchen staff is 61.5% of the total payroll cost percentage, payroll for service staff represents 23.5% of the payroll cost percentage, and payroll for salaried personnel equals 15% of the total payroll cost percentage. The proportion of the total cost percentage that each group represents would be determined as follows:

Total Payroll Cost Percentage: 29.6%
Kitchen: $29.6\% \times 61.5\% = 18.2\%$ of the total payroll cost percentage
Service Staff: $29.6\% \times 23.5\% = 6.96\%$ of the total payroll cost percentage
Salaries: $29.6\% \times 15.0\% = \underline{4.44\%}$ of the total payroll cost percentage
Total: 29.6%

Week of: January 13, XXXX

Date Prepared: 1/6/XX

Department: Kitchen

Prepared By: Kitchen Manager

Position	Name	Monday	Tuesday	Wednesday	Thursday	Friday	Saturday	Sunday
Production Cook	Joe Sample	Off	6 A.M.–2 P.M.	6 A.M.–2 P.M.	6 A.M.–2 P.M.	6 A.M.–2 P.M.	6 A.M.–2 P.M.	Off
	(Scheduled Lunch Break)→		10 A.M.	10 A.M.	10 A.M.	10 A.M.	10 A.M.	
Production Cook	Jane Sample	6 A.M.–2 P.M.	8 A.M.–4 P.M.	8 A.M.–4 P.M.	Off	Off	8 A.M.–4 P.M.	6 A.M.–2 P.M.
	(Scheduled Lunch Break)→	10 A.M.	1:30 P.M.	1:30 P.M.			1:30 P.M.	10 A.M.
Production Cook	Eric Sample	8 A.M.–4 P.M.	Off	(Salad Pantry) 6 A.M.–2 P.M.	8 A.M.–4 P.M.	8 A.M.–4 P.M.	(Salad Pantry) 6 A.M.–2 P.M.	Off
	(Scheduled Lunch Break)→	1:30 P.M.		10:30 A.M.	1:30 P.M.	1:30 P.M.	10:30 A.M.	
Salad Pantry	Emily Sample	6 A.M.–2 P.M.	6 A.M.–2 P.M.	Off	6 A.M.–2 P.M.	6 A.M.–2 P.M.	Off	6 A.M.–2 P.M.
	(Scheduled Lunch Break)→	10:30 A.M.	10:30 A.M.		10:30 A.M.	10:30 A.M.		10:30 A.M.
Dishwasher	Don Sample	8 A.M.–noon	8 A.M.–noon	Off	Off	8 A.M.–noon	8 A.M.–4 P.M.	8 A.M.–4 P.M.
	(Scheduled Lunch Break)→						10:30 A.M.	10:30 A.M.
Dishwasher	Lesli Sample	noon–4 P.M.	noon–4 P.M.	8 A.M.–4 P.M.	8 A.M.–4 P.M.	noon–4 P.M.	Off	Off
	(Scheduled Lunch Break)→			10:30 A.M.	10:30 A.M.	10:30 A.M.		
	(Scheduled Lunch Break)→							
	(Scheduled Lunch Break)→							
	(Scheduled Lunch Break)→							

FIGURE 16.2 Sample work schedule.

Week of: January 13, XXXX Date Prepared: 1/6/XX				Department: Kitchen Prepared By: Kitchen Manager	
Name	**Position**	**Rate of Pay**	**Scheduled Hours**	**Scheduled Overtime**	**Total Earned**
Hourly Employees					
Joe Sample	Cook	$9.50	37.5		$ 356.25
Jane Sample	Cook	8.50	37.5		318.75
Eric Sample	Cook	7.50	22.5		168.75
Eric Sample	Sal Pantry	5.50	14.5		79.75
Emily Sample	Sal Pantry	5.15	37.5		193.13
Don Sample	Dishwasher	5.15	27		139.05
Leslie Sample	Dishwasher	5.15	27		139.05
Total			203.5		**$1,394.73**
Allowance for Social Security, Medicare, Federal & State Unemployment Taxes: Total Hourly Wages $1,394.73 × Rate 1.12 =					$1,562.10
Employee Meals (*Note: Could be added to or subtracted from the payroll according to management's policy.*)					
			Estimated Number of Meals	**Cost**	
		Total	24	$3.00	$ 72.00
Total (Wages & Meals)					$1,634.10
Estimated Sales for Week					$9,000.00
Estimated Payroll Cost Percentage for Week					18.16%
Payroll Cost Percentage Goal					18.00%

FIGURE 16.3 Payroll budget estimate.

To determine the payroll budget in dollars for each wage category, multiply the budget dollars times each category's budget percentage.

$$\text{Kitchen: } \$52{,}075 \times 61.5\% = \$32{,}026.13$$
$$\text{Service: } \$52{,}075 \times 23.5\% = \$12{,}237.63$$
$$\text{Salary: } \$52{,}075 \times 15.0\% = \underline{\$ \ 7{,}811.25}$$
$$\text{Total: } \qquad\qquad\qquad \$52{,}075.01$$

The practice of splitting payroll cost into labor categories is fairly common in large foodservice operations. Operations with fewer than 15 employees generally do not categorize their budgets.

Developing a Work Schedule

The work schedule should represent the best effort of the foodservice manager to schedule employees in anticipation of sales. Managers should follow several rules when creating work schedules:

- Review sales history records and comments before making scheduling decisions.
- Prepare schedules weekly.
- Post schedules at least one week in advance.
- Minimize scheduling changes to avoid frustrating employees.
- Schedule employee breaks.

WORK SCHEDULE PRINCIPLES

- First, review sales history records and comments.
- Prepare schedules weekly.
- Post schedules at least one week in advance.
- Minimize scheduling changes.
- Schedule employee breaks.

Using a Sales History

When they prepare work schedules, managers must take many things into consideration, including the following:

- Peak business periods
- Holidays
- Weather conditions
- Special community events
- Employee vacations

A well-kept sales history can serve as a tremendous aid in making scheduling decisions, especially for peak sales days, such as Mother's Day. The previous year's sales for that day can serve as an indication of expected sales for the current year. If sales were high, a decision to schedule additional staff would be consistent with meeting the operational requirements of those sales.

Maintaining Consistency

A work schedule should be prepared weekly and posted at least a week in advance, preferably the same day each week. This allows employees who do not have regular schedules to *plan* to find out their schedules, to actually find out their schedules in a timely manner, and to make arrangements to be at work the following week. The schedule should be posted next to the time clock or in the most convenient place for all employees to read.

Although scheduling should meet the needs of business, it is also important to remember to maintain some degree of consistency. Radical or frequent changes in the schedule can be frustrating and upsetting and can result in the loss of good employees.

It may also result in "no-shows" on a shift, as some employees may not check the schedule more than once.

∕Vet Work

Explore the following Web sites:

www.softcafe.com—Click Schedule Writer and examine product features
www.digitaldining.com—Click Back Office, Products, Back Office Solutions

---

Lunch breaks should be scheduled along with the work hours for each day. The lunch break schedule must be flexible enough to accommodate business. If the foodservice operation is too busy, a break should be postponed until a more convenient time. If breaks need to be postponed frequently, additional scheduling adjustments should be made (for example, extra staff should be assigned to a shift) or a portion of the work such as prep is done at a different time so as not to further frustrate employees.

One main reason employees often give for quitting a good job is frequent work schedule changes and not being able to take scheduled breaks. A well-planned work schedule will not eliminate job stress, but it can certainly reduce job frustration.

The Work Schedule Form

The main tool for planning the use of labor resources is the work schedule form. Refer back to Figure 16.2; it is an example of such a form.

- The manager prepares the work schedule, taking into consideration the principles listed earlier.
- After the work schedule is prepared, a payroll budget estimate should also be determined (refer back to Figure 16.3).

The schedule ensures that enough people will be present to do the work, whereas the budget ensures that those scheduled to work can be afforded or justified.

Figures 16.2 and 16.3 show that the work is covered and within budget. Estimated sales are $9,000 for the week, and the kitchen staff payroll budget is 18% of sales. The work schedule will cost the operation $1,634.10 for the week, including indirect costs; the payroll budget estimate is 18.16%. This amount is just within the budget.

In this case, management would use the budget. As the week progresses, management will need to watch for any necessary changes to the schedule to ensure that the budget is not exceeded. If sales do not materialize as estimated, management may need to change the schedule. As previously stated, this should not be done in a casual manner, or employees may become frustrated and seek other employment. Maintaining payroll budgets can be difficult because foodservice industry sales are often cyclical and unpredictable.

ℂalculating Payroll Costs

Payroll cost is computed in two steps:

1. The actual cost is established using time cards or an electronic timekeeping system.
2. The payroll cost percentage is determined using a Payroll Cost Report.

Although there are a variety of ways to calculate payroll cost, most methods may be classified into one of two categories: manual methods or electronic methods.

Methods of Calculating Payroll Cost

In the manual method of tracking payroll cost, foodservice managers may calculate their own payroll costs, employ a bookkeeper or accountant, or use a combination of these two systems. If a manager chooses to track payroll costs, he or she may use a simple form such as a payroll cost sheet (Figure 16.4). A **payroll cost sheet** is *a form*

Prepared By: Manager		**Day:** Monday		**Date:** 1/13/XX	
Name	**Position**	**Rate of Pay**	**Hours Worked**	**Overtime Worked**	**Total Earned**
Hourly Employees					
John Cook	Cook	$9.50	8		$ 76.00
Fred Cook	Cook	8.50	8		68.00
Al Cook	Cook	7.50	6		45.00
Wonda Dishwasher	Dishwasher	5.15	4		20.60
Don Dishwasher	Dishwasher	5.15	4		20.60
Leslie Waitperson	Waitress	5.15	4		20.60
Mary Waitperson	Waitress	5.15	4		20.60
Judy Waitperson	Waitress	5.15	4		20.60
Lisa Waitperson	Waitress	5.15	4		20.60
Jack Waitperson	Waiter	5.15	4		20.60
Nick Waitperson	Waiter	5.15	4		20.60
Total			**54**		**$353.80**
Allowance for Social Security, Medicare, Federal & State Unemployment Taxes: Total Hourly Wages $353.80 × Rate 1.12 =					$396.26
Salaried Employees					
Joe Manager	Manager				$155.00
Lynn Shift	Shift Mgr.				112.00
Dan Shift	Shift Mgr.				106.00
Total					**$373.00**
Allowance for Social Security, Medicare, Federal & State Unemployment Taxes: Total Salaries $373.00 × Rate 1.12 =					$417.76
Total (Hourly + Salaried)					$814.02

FIGURE 16.4   Payroll cost sheet.

used to calculate payroll cost percentage and sales production per hour. If a manager uses a bookkeeper or accountant, she or he will typically use a type of mechanical time card system. **Time cards** are *a method for tracking employee time worked.* The time cards are given to the bookkeeper or accountant to calculate payroll costs.

Electronic methods for calculating payroll costs include the following:

- Electronic time clocks
- Computer software
- A time and attendance feature included in a point-of-sale system that may connect to payroll software

A vast array of hardware and software products on the market can be used to track employee work hours and calculate the payroll.

The Manual Method of Calculating Payroll Costs

Manual methods use a payroll cost sheet or a time clock, and sometimes both. Figure 16.4 shows a payroll cost sheet that can be used by foodservice operations with a limited number of employees. The **payroll cost sheet** *lists all the employees' names, positions, rates of pay, hours worked, overtime worked, total earned, and the total amount spent that particular day for labor.*

Calculating Indirect Payroll Costs

Indirect payroll costs include *social security, Medicare, federal and state unemployment taxes, and workers' compensation.* These are added to the payroll. They are calculated as a percentage of the payroll and are dictated by law. Workers' compensation taxes vary according to the accident history of the business. These costs should be included as part of payroll costs because they are directly related to the payroll. Other benefit-associated costs are often included as part of the payroll. As shown in Figure 16.4, these costs are listed on a separate expense line.

An easy way to calculate indirect costs of payroll is *to add 1 to the indirect cost rate percentage.* This becomes a multiplier that is multiplied by the total direct costs. For an example, see Figure 16.4. The amount of wages (direct cost of wages) for hourly employees shown is $353.80. The indirect rate is 12% of wages:

$$\text{INDIRECT RATE} + 1 = \text{MULTIPLIER}$$
$$12\% \text{ or } .12 + 1 = 1.12$$

Add the rate of 12%, which is equal to .12, to 1. The total is 1.12. Multiply $353.80 by 1.12 to arrive at a total of $396.26. This amount represents the total payroll cost of hourly employees:

$$\text{TOTAL DIRECT COSTS} \times \text{MULTIPLIER} = \text{PAYROLL COST OF HOURLY EMPLOYEES}$$
$$\$353.80 \times 1.12 = \$396.26$$

Calculating Direct Payroll Costs

Payroll costs are calculated manually by multiplying the rate of pay that an employee earns by the number of hours worked. This simple task is repeated for each employee (see Figure 16.4.) and the total represents the **direct costs** of payroll. After all wages are determined, they are added together. Then, indirect costs are calculated and added to the gross wages to determine the total payroll for the operation. The equations look like this:

$$\text{RATE OF PAY} \times \text{NUMBER OF HOURS WORKED} = \text{GROSS WAGES}$$

$$\text{INDIRECT PAYROLL COSTS} + \text{GROSS WAGES} = \text{TOTAL PAYROLL}$$

Calculating Daily Payroll Cost of Salaried Employees

The same process is used for salaried employees. The major difference with salaried employees, however, is that instead of an hourly cost, a *daily cost* must be established. If a person is making $32,000 a year as a salaried employee, this equals about $16.00 per hour. You can find this hourly rate by dividing the annual salary of $32,000 by 2,000 hours, which is the number of hours a typical employee works during a year: $32,000/2,000 = $16.00. The total amount the employee earns per day is determined by multiplying the hourly rate by 8 hours: $16.00 × 8 = $128.00 per day:

ANNUAL SALARY/NO. OF HOURS WORKED ANNUALLY = HOURLY RATE OF PAY
$32,000/2,000 = $16.00 per hour

HOURLY RATE OF PAY × NO. OF HOURS PER DAY = PAY PER DAY
$16.00 × 8 Hours per Day = $128.00

It is recognized that most salaried people work more than 40 hours per week. Even if actual hours were used to calculate daily costs, the salaried amount would be calculated by determining the total number of hours a person works per year, then multiplying by the average number of hours worked per day. The total would still be close to $128.00 per day.

Calculating the Total Cost of Payroll

The daily salaried amounts are totaled and multiplied by the indirect cost rate. In Figure 16.4, the salary total amount is $373.00 and the indirect rate is 12%. The total is $373.00 multiplied by 1.12, which equals $417.76. Thus, adding in the total payroll for hourly employees calculated earlier ($396.26), the total payroll for Monday was $814.02.

DAILY SALARIED AMOUNTS × MULTIPLIER = PAYROLL COST OF
SALARIED EMPLOYEES
$373.00 × 1.12 = $417.76

Using Time Cards

The working times listed on the payroll cost sheet are typically entered by management. Time cards are used for verification of actual times worked. Much of the information listed on the payroll cost sheet is also listed on the time cards (Figure 16.5). In some very small foodservice operations, time cards are not used and an honor system may be in place. An honor system dictates that employees work the hours assigned without a time card, or they sign in and sign out on a form that is assumed to be accurate. Obviously, the trust level must be high for an honor system to be used.

Time Card System

In a **time card system**, *the employee's actual hours worked are recorded on the time card.* The hours recorded on the card should correspond to the work schedule. If an electronic time clock is used, there may not be a traditional time card, but a time card will exist in the computer. The information is processed and a hard copy is printed, which accompanies employee paychecks. Summary information is also provided such as shown in the Management Report in Figure 16.6. This figure shows by department how many hours were worked, tips reported, standard (ST) and overtime (OT) hours, and payroll cost. This information helps managers to determine variances between the payroll budget and actual payroll costs.

MULTIPLE TIMECARD REPORT *CUSTOM* TIME PERIOD FROM: 10/28/XX TO 11/01/XX										

2-Sayre, Grace

Date	Time In	Time Out	Lunch	Dept	Dept Hrs	Tips	Std	Ot	Labor	Flags
10/28/__	Mon 6:30a	Mon 1:30p		SERVERS	7.00	12.50	7.00	0.00	34.65	
10/29/__	Tue 7:00p	Tue 11:02p		HOSTESS ①	4.00		4.00	0.00	30.00	
10/30/__	Wed 6:29a	Wed 1:35p		SERVERS	7.00	15.00	7.00	0.00	34.65	
10/31/__	Thu 6:27a	Thu 1:33p		SERVERS	7.00	10.00	7.00	0.00	34.65	
11/01/__	Fri 6:25a	Fri 1:35p		SERVERS	7.00	20.00	7.00	0.00	34.65	
Employee Totals: (5 Days Worked)					32.00	57.50 ②	32.00	0.00	168.60 ③	

Signature: _____

1. Worked as a hostess at a different hourly wage rate.
2. Reported tips earned.
3. Gross wage.

FIGURE 16.5   Electronic time card.

One major advantage of using an electronic time and attendance system is that employees cannot log in until their programmed time to start work. This prevents people from clocking in 10 or 15 minutes early. It also prevents employees from working at times other than those that are programmed. Some large foodservice operations have reported saving tens of thousands of dollars by using an automated timekeeping system. If an unusual situation occurs, a manager is always able to manually override the system to properly credit the employee with time worked.

Occasionally, employees are requested to work longer than they were scheduled. In these cases, the manager should

1. Initial the employee's time card.
2. Enter the code in the time clock (or other computer) authorizing approval.
3. Write a brief note on the back of the time card explaining why the employee had to work longer.

Standard Time Card Practices

As with any procedure in an operation, **time card practices** should be standardized to minimize employee confusion and reduce costs.

CUSTOM DATE RANGE DEPARTMENT SUMMARY REPORT FOR TIME PERIOD FROM: 10/28/XX TO 11/01/XX					
Department	**Dept Hrs**	**Tips**	**St**	**Ot**	**Labor**
BUSPERSONS	38.75	0.00	38.75	0.00	191.81
CLEANUP	10.50	0.00	10.50	0.00	51.98
COOKS	61.00	0.00	61.00	0.00	655.00
HOSTESS	4.00	0.00	4.00	0.00	30.00
SERVERS	33.00	67.50	33.00	0.00	163.35
Grand Totals:	147.25	67.50	147.25	0.00	1,092.14

FIGURE 16.6   Management Report.

STANDARD TIME CARD PRACTICES
- Start and finish times for each shift should be recorded on each card.
- Start and finish times for each scheduled lunch break should be recorded.
- Start and finish times for each scheduled break should be recorded.
- Actual time worked is recorded and totaled for each day.
- Regular and overtime hours are recorded.
- Employees sign time cards and verify hours.

The current time should be entered on the time card at the start and finish of every employee's shift. In addition, it should also be entered at the beginning and end of the scheduled lunch break, keeping in mind that the scheduled lunch break and the actual lunch break may be different. Requiring employees to clock in and out for fifteen-minute breaks during the shift further controls and documents the employee's time. The actual time worked is computed and totaled for each day. The regular and over-time hours are recorded, together with wage rates and totals for the period. Finally, on receiving a paycheck, the employee should double-check the days, hours, and positions worked (if more than one), and sign the bottom of the time card, acknowledging receipt of pay and verifying the time recorded as being correct.

Overtime

Overtime occurs when employees covered by the Fair Labor Standards Act work more than 40 hours per week *and an employer is required to pay the employees more than the normal wage.* Usually, in cases of overtime, employees are paid in increments of 1.5, 2.0, 2.5, or 3.0 times their normal hourly rate of pay. A mimimum overtime pay of 1.5 is mandated by law. Employees who work more than 40 hours during one week must be paid overtime, with limited exceptions. Overtime can usually be averted with sufficient planning.

Avoiding overtime helps to keep payroll costs down. The primary causes of over-time include:

- Poor scheduling, so that employees are required to work longer hours to meet customer needs.
- Unexpected increases in the number of customers.
- Circumstances caused by sudden changes in the weather.
- Medical or other emergencies that require an employee to leave work early and other employees to work longer hours than originally scheduled.

*P*ayroll Cost Report

The **Payroll Cost Report** is used *to determine payroll percentage and sales per person-hour.*

PAYROLL COST REPORT DETERMINES
1. **Payroll cost percentage**
2. Sales per person-hour

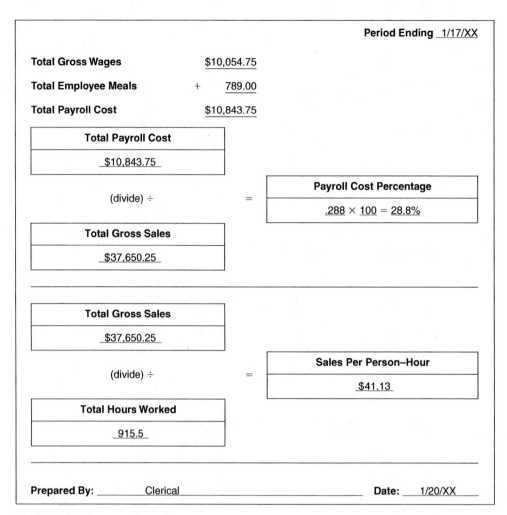

FIGURE 16.7   Payroll cost report.

Payroll Cost Percentage

The Payroll Cost Report in Figure 16.7 begins with the total gross wages. **Total gross wages** are *all wages, including indirect costs*. This amount is taken from the payroll cost sheet (Figure 16.4) or Payroll Journal (Figure 16.8) and prepared by the foodservice operation's application software, accountant, bookkeeper, or payroll service. Some operations include both salaries and hourly wages in calculating controllable payroll expenses, whereas others use only hourly wages.

In addition to wages, the cost of employee meals, if provided, should be added. **Employee meals** are *a form of compensation and are therefore a part of the payroll costs*. In most cases, the meal credit is assigned a **value per given shift**. Perhaps $3.00 per 8-hour shift is the dollar amount representing the actual cost of the food, not the retail selling price. This dollar amount at cost could represent as much as $8.00 for the retail menu price, thus allowing the employee to eat up to that amount. The cost of employee meals may be deducted from the employee's pay. If an employee decides not to eat the meal, obviously there is no deduction.

TOTAL PAYROLL COST/TOTAL GROSS SALES × 100 = PAYROLL COST %

The total payroll cost is divided by the total gross sales and multiplied by 100 to generate the payroll cost percentage. The total gross sales figure is obtained by adding the daily sales totals for the period.

PAYROLLS BY PAYCHEX — PAYROLL JOURNAL

40004 (R-8) 0090-1461 JOES SAMPLE CAFE PAGE 1

EMP NBR	EMPLOYEE NAME	TYPE	RATE	REG	OT	REGULAR	OT	1 OE I / 2 OE II	WAGES	SOC SEC MED	FEDERAL	STATE	LOCAL DBL/SUI	WORK COMP	WORK HOURS INFO	TIPS COMP	MEALS	DRAWS	NET PAY	CHK NBR
**** 000100 KITCHEN																				
0001	JOHNSON, TIM A		6000	4000	250	24000	2250		26250	1674 / 392	2550	1620 OR			47	4250	750	1075		18892	7
0002	TURNER, GARY		6000	4000		10000			10000	6200 / 1450	12031	7250 OR			44	4000			25000	46025	8
**** 000101 WAIT STAFF																				
0005	DYER, LINDA		4850	4000	225	19400	1637		21037	1619 / 379	3154	1659 OR			46	4225	5083	600		13580	9
0003	FRANKLIN, SHERRY		5500	4000		22000			22000	1834 / 429	2937	1817 OR			44	4000	7580	750		14189	10
0006	PILOTTE, JOYCE		4750	3200		15200			15200	1203 / 281	1203	627 OR			35	3200	4200	500		13054	11
0004	WENTZEL, DEBBY		4750	4000	450	19000	3207		22207	1935 / 453	2085	1563 OR			49	4450	9000	500		15622	12

TOTALS

PAY TYPE	HOURS	EARNINGS
REGULAR	23200	199600
OVERTIME	925	7094
VACATION	00	00
HOLIDAY	00	00
QUAL SICK	00	00
NONQUAL SICK	00	00
MISCELLANEOUS		

WAGES	FICA	FEDERAL	STATE	LOCAL DBL/SUI	WORK COMP	WORK HOURS	TIPS	MEALS	DRAWS	NBR ENTRIES
206694	SOC SEC 14469 / MEDICARE 3384	22757	14536		265	24125	26613	2925	25000	6

TOTAL WAGES
NET PAY   206694
VOUCHER NET   123362
TOTAL NET   123362

FIGURE 16.8 Payroll Journal.

469

THE PAYROLL COST REPORT DETERMINES

1. Payroll cost percentage
2. Sales per person-hour

Sales per Person-Hour

The **sales per person-hour**, which *measures productivity, is obtained by dividing the total gross sales by the total hours worked.* The total hours worked are taken from a payroll cost sheet (Figure 16.4) or Payroll Journal (Figure 16.8):

TOTAL GROSS SALES/TOTAL HOURS WORKED = SALES PER PERSON-HOUR

Payroll cost, like food cost, will vary by the type of operation, so it is difficult to compare the payroll cost of a fine-dining restaurant to that of a fast-food restaurant. In hotels, resorts, schools, healthcare facilities, and large foodservice operations, payroll may be determined by department. In a hospital, there may be a cafeteria, coffee shop, dining room, and executive dining room. Each of these dining facilities may have its own kitchen and its own cooks and servers. That being the case, each would have its own sales and cost centers, and each would determine its own payroll cost percentage (see Figure 16.9).

Hiring and Managing Employees

Management Quality and Employee Turnover

One measure of management quality is directly tied to payroll cost control. Payroll cost control results from competent management, which involves

- Selecting and using the correct equipment.
- Efficiently utilizing space and work flow.
- Exercising good hiring and training practices.
- Properly training employees.
- Reducing employee turnover.

Ineffective management can result in costly errors, high employee turnover, and a poor work environment. History has repeatedly shown that effective management improves both profit and work conditions.

Among the most challenging tasks of management is to hire and manage a quality workforce. If a foodservice manager hires competent and skilled individuals but fails to train them properly, the outcome will be poor work quality. The vital ingredient of any foodservice operation is the quality of the workforce and how well that workforce is managed and motivated. High employee turnover is a sign of ineffective management or a poor working environment created by the owners or managers.

Cost of Employee Turnover

Employee turnover is expensive. **Employee turnover** is *the number of times the total number of positions are filled with employees during an accounting period.* **Turnover** is often expressed as a percentage of the average number of employees needed to operate a foodservice operation. Direct costs of employee turnover include:

- ***Recruiting costs:*** Newspaper classified ads, employment agencies, and so on.
- ***Training costs:*** Cost of time to train and orient to the job function.

DEPARTMENT SUMMARY

40005 (R-8) PAYROLLS BY PAYCHEX

0090-1461 JOES SAMPLE CAFE PAGE 1

HOURS AND WAGES SUMMARY

CHECK DATE	REG HRS	REG WAGES	OT HRS	OT WAGES	VAC HRS	VAC WAGES	HOL HRS	HOL WAGES	SICK HRS	SICK WAGES	MISC HOUR	MISC PAY	OTHER EARN1	OTHER EARN2	CASH WAGES
****** 000100 KITCHEN															
01/03	80.00	1240.00	2.50	22.50											1262.50
MTD	80.00	1240.00	2.50	22.50											1262.50
****** 000101 WAIT STAFF															
01/03	152.00	756.00	6.75	48.44											804.44
MTD	152.00	756.00	6.75	48.44											804.44
****** ALL DEPARTMENTS															
01/03	232.00	1996.00	9.25	70.94											2066.94
MTD	232.00	1996.00	9.25	70.94											2066.94

EMPLOYEE WITHHOLDING TAXES SUMMARY

CHECK DATE	SOC SEC W/H	MED W/H	FED W/H	STATE NAME	STATE W/H	LOCAL NAME	LOCAL W/H	LOCAL NAME	LOCAL W/H	LOCAL NAME	LOCAL W/H	OTHER NAME	OTHER W/H	OTHER NAME	OTHER W/H	TOTAL W/H TAX
01/03	144.65	33.84	227.57	OR	145.36											551.42
MTD	144.65	33.84	227.57	OR	145.36											551.42
QTD 1	144.65	33.84	227.57	STATE	145.36											551.42
YTD	144.65	33.84	227.57	STATE	145.36											551.42

EMPLOYEE VOLUNTARY DEDUCTIONS AND ADJUSTMENTS SUMMARY

CHECK DATE	WORK COMP 1	WORK HOURS 2	TIPS 3	MEALS 4	DRAWS 5	NET PAY
01/03	2.65	241.25	266.13	29.25	250.00	1233.62
MTD	2.65	241.25	266.13	29.25	250.00	1233.62
QTD 1	2.65	241.25	266.13	29.25	250.00	1233.62
YTD	2.65	241.25	266.13	29.25	250.00	1233.62

EMPLOYER TAX EXPENSES SUMMARY

CHECK DATE	SOC SEC EXP	MED EXP	FUTA EXP	STATE NAME	SUI EXP	SUI PERCENT	OTHER NAME	OTHER EXP	OTHER NAME	OTHER EXP	EMPLOYER TAX EXP
01/03	144.65	33.84	18.67	ORSUI	56.00	2.4000					253.16
MTD	144.65	33.84	18.67	ORSUI	56.00						253.16
QTD 1	144.65	33.84	18.67		56.00						253.16
YTD	144.65	33.84	18.67		56.00						253.16

MISCELLANEOUS INFORMATION

CHECK DATE	FED TAX LIABILITY	TOTAL COMPENSATION
01/03	584.55	2333.07
MTD	584.55	2333.07
QTD 1	584.55	2333.07
YTD	584.55	2333.07

FIGURE 16.9 Department summary page.

> **Employee turnover** is *the number of times that the total number of positions are filled with employees during an accounting period.*
>
> **Turnover** is often *expressed as a percentage of the average number of employees needed to operate a foodservice operation.*

Some hidden costs of turnover are often overlooked because it is difficult to assign them a direct value. Hidden costs include

- New employee training time
- New employee learning curve
- Management time used to interview potential employees
- Customer loss as a result of mistakes or poor service by new employee
- Accounting and reporting costs (payroll expenses related to employee turnover)
- Loss of productivity by departing employees prior to leaving the job

Determining the actual cost of employee turnover is extremely difficult, although foodservice managers should be aware of and track these costs as much as possible. At the end of the year, the total amount should be calculated and the information used to identify employee turnover costs.

Calculating Employee Turnover Rate and Cost

Figure 16.10 shows employee turnover for a fine-dining restaurant that employs 65 people on average. The accountant prepared 212 W-2s at the end of the year, to be sent out to current and past employees. In the example, there are 65 current employees; thus there are 147 past employees (212 W-2 forms − 65 = 147 past employees). The 147 past employees divided by the 65 average number of employees equals 2.26. This number converted to a percentage (2.26 × 100) equals a turnover rate of 226%.

			Period Ending 12/31/XX
	Employee Turnover Rate		
Number of W-2s Completed	Current Number of Employees		Number of Past Employees
1. 212 −	65	=	147
Number of Past Employees	Average Number of Employees Employed		Employee Turnover Rate
2. 147 ÷	65	=	2.26 × 100 = 226%
	Cost of Employee Turnover		
Number of Past Employees	Cost to Hire Each		Cost of Employee Turnover
3. 147 ×	$ 50.00	=	$7,350.00

FIGURE 16.10   Employee turnover rate and cost chart.

Segment	Salaried Employees (%)	Hourly Employees (%)	Combined (%)
Family Restaurant	20	107	100
Fine Dining	15	102	95
Quick Service	25	122	120
Cafeteria	15	107	98
Buffet	15	107	98

FIGURE 16.11 Typical yearly foodservice employee turnover rates.

TO CALCULATE EMPLOYEE TURNOVER RATE

No. of W-2s at End of Year − No. of Current Employees = No. of Past Employees

No. of Past Employees/Average Number of Employees = Turnover Rate

---

The actual cost of employee turnover is difficult to calculate. As shown in Figure 16.10, during the year, the restaurant spent $7,350 to advertise for and train new employees, with additionally scheduled work hours. This cost still does not reflect some of the hidden costs that cannot be specifically identified. This amount divided by 147 (the number of past employees) equals $50 in turnover costs per past employee.

Compare the employee turnover rate in Figure 16.10 with the typical fine-dining turnover rate in Figure 16.11. The employee turnover rate in the example is 226%. The typical average for this type of restaurant is 95%. The employee turnover rate in the example is more than twice the typical average. What is the cost of this difference? The cost of employee turnover in the example is $7,350. The cost of employee turnover using the typical employee turnover rate should be about $2,850. The difference is $4,500. The conclusion is that the foodservice operation in the example spent about $4,500 more than it should have. This amount of money could have gone directly into profits if management had quickly recognized and reduced the high turnover rate.

Some foodservice operations claim as much as a 300% to 400% annual employee turnover rate. This means that if the foodservice operation needs 100 employees to operate, 400 employees were hired during the year. The direct and hidden costs associated with such a high employee turnover are tremendous. Remember from a discussion earlier in this chapter that the primary reason former foodservice employees give for leaving a job is poor management supervision. Competent management is the best resource for reducing employee turnover.

Steps to Controlling Payroll Cost

The goal of every successful foodservice manager should be to recruit, motivate, guide, direct, and lead employees in achieving optimal performance, which results in high overall efficiency. To further support this goal, a productive and conducive workplace needs to exist—one that includes the following:

1. Labor-saving equipment, such as a power chopper, instead of relying on hand chopping when several recipes require chopped food products.
2. Well-arranged floor plans in order to save time and steps. When the work flow is smooth, employees feel that they are able to accomplish more with less stress. This improves productivity and increases profits.
3. Improved efficiency of employees through a strong ongoing training program.

4. Use of prepared foods where applicable (e.g., prepared vegetables and salads, and refrigerated and frozen soups, entrées, and desserts), instead of relying on employees preparing these items from scratch.

5. Lower employee turnover through competent supervision, competitive wages and benefits, good working conditions, and a positive work environment to which employees can remain loyal.

Remember that good management needs to do the following: hire the right people, train them to do the job, provide the necessary resources to do the job, and then get out of their way and let them do their job (while monitoring results and being available when needed).

STEPS TO CONTROLLING PAYROLL COSTS

1. Hiring the right people
2. Training
3. Setting employee performance standards

THE JOB DESCRIPTION

Describes the job objectives, the work to be performed, job responsibilities, skills needed, working conditions, and the relationship of the job to other jobs.

Hiring the Right People

Hiring the right people is the first step to controlling payroll costs. To do so, prospective employees need to know what is required to do the job. The chain of events begins with a newspaper or online advertisement of an open position (Figure 16.12). When prospective employees answer the ad and apply for the job, the job description is critical for operational success. A **job description** is *a document that describes the job objectives, the work to be performed, job responsibilities, skills needed, working conditions and the relationship of the job to other jobs.* At the minimum, the job description should clearly define job qualifications, responsibilities, and functions.

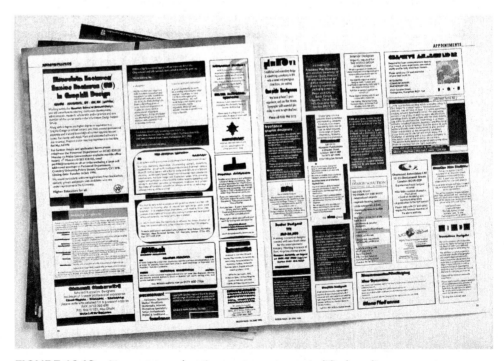

FIGURE 16.12   Newspaper advertisement to attract qualified applicants.

The job description should include the following components:

1. Required knowledge, skills, and abilities (KSAs).
2. A complete explanation of the work to be performed and the schedule of days and shifts to be worked. The explanation should also include a description of working conditions.
3. A concise list of specific duties, tasks, responsibilities, and performance standards.
4. The position of the person's immediate supervisor.
5. Prerequisites needed by a person interested in applying for the job.
6. (Optional) Wage range and review dates.
7. (Optional) Name and telephone number of immediate supervisor.

Keeping these seven components in mind, examine the job description example in Figure 16.13. This job description was adapted from Model Position Descriptions for the Hospitality and Tourism Industry, which was compiled by the International Council on Hotel, Restaurant, and Institutional Education. These descriptions were developed with a grant from the U.S. Department of Labor.

Compare how closely the example in Figure 16.13 meets the five required and two optional components of a job description:

Hiring to the Job Description

After establishing a clear job description, management can evaluate possible candidates for the job, to see if they possess the qualities needed to do the job. Without the job description, the hiring process is hit or miss. There is no way to compare the attributes of possible employees, and the process of selection becomes less focused on the actual labor to be performed.

The process of hiring involves

- Selecting a group of people to be interviewed.
- Conducting interviews.
- Hiring the most qualified person.

There are a variety of theories on how to accomplish this. Basically, the process comes down to comparing the possible candidates according to needed competencies and prerequisites. The best way to do this is to use a prospective employee **selection sheet**, as illustrated in Figure 16.14. A **selection sheet** is used to *compare the prerequisites and competencies of employment applicants.*

It is permissible to use **preemployment tests**, if they are related to the job. Such tests are used to prove that the person is capable of performing job tasks. In this example, the person should be able to multiply decimals and whole numbers, do simple accounting that would be related to completing cash register deposits, and write simple reports about what occurs during the day. The potential employee should also be able to complete a work schedule that meets payroll goals.

The interview process begins with selecting the applicants that come closest to meeting the requirements. All applicants should be asked the same questions, and the job description should have been given to all the applicants prior to their completion of the application. The interview questions should be based on job-related issues and the job description. Therefore, the job description should be the primary document used to select employees.

STEPS TO CONTROLLING PAYROLL COSTS

1. Hiring the right people
2. Training
3. Setting employee performance standards

	POSITION DESCRIPTION
Position Title:	Counter Supervisor
Reports To:	Manager
Position Summary:	The Counter Supervisor directly supervises the daily operation of a specified unit and ensures that daily activity schedules and established quality standards are maintained. This includes the coordination of individual and collective efforts of assigned staff.

Tasks

1. Demonstrates complete understanding of departmental requirements and interprets their intent accurately to staff members.
2. Monitors daily performance of staff and ensures compliance with established timetables.
3. Monitors quality of products and services produced by staff and ensures compliance with established timetables.
4. Monitors food safety and food-handling practices of assigned unit and ensures staff compliance with established standards.
5. Routinely inspects areas of assigned responsibility and reports all substandard safety, security, or equipment conditions to manager.
6. Consistently monitors standards and makes recommendations for change as observed by manager.
7. Supervises staff in a consistently fair and firm manner. Maintains steady productivity through close observation. Provides direction when necessary.
8. Schedules staff to assigned unit within daily F.T.E. allocation and projected workload.
9. Adjusts daily schedule and shifts personnel to complete essential duties when the need arises.
10. Coordinates work of staff to promote efficiency of operations.
11. Consistently recommends actions necessary for staff discipline, terminations, promotions, and so on.
12. Trains staff, as assigned, and assists with orientation of new employees in a timely and efficient manner.
13. Schedules employee time off so as not to interfere with heavy workload periods.
14. Monitors employee attendance and notices all absence patterns and brings to the attention of management all relevant findings.
15. Monitors customer traffic and makes appropriate adjustments to decrease waiting time.
16. Monitors customer buying trends and makes relevant recommendations for product additions and deletions.
17. Accurately inventories supplies daily and requisitions items needed to meet par levels.
18. Ensures that supplies are utilized properly and cost-effectively as per standards.
19. Reports changes in menus or item substitutions to managers.
20. Ensures that all food and supplies are stored and/or maintained under proper conditions as per standards.
21. Monitors food and supply quality and makes relevant recommendations for product utilization.
22. Inspects all unit storage facilities each day so that proper temperatures and conditions are maintained and food is covered, labeled, and dated.
23. Completes counter supervisor reports in an accurate and timely manner.
24. Completes employee appraisals in a timely fashion.
25. Keeps immediate supervisor informed of all relevant information and encourages suggestions for service and/or quality improvements.
26. Meets routinely with assigned staff to relate relevant information and encourages suggestions for service and/or quality improvements.
27. Works effectively and efficiently with other department supervisors and consistently demonstrates the ability to solve problems at this level.
28. Analyzes relevant data to make informed decisions compatible with department philosophy.
29. Treats staff with courtesy, respect, and empathy and displays good listening skills.
30. Displays team-building skills and always handles all assignments with a positive and enthusiastic attitude.
31. Maintains professional appearance as per standards.

Prerequisites

Education:	High school diploma or equivalent.
Experience:	A minimum of two years as a counter server or equivalent position.
Physical:	Position requires walking and giving direction most of the working day.
	May be required to push heavy food carts. May be required to lift trays of food or food items weighing up to 30 pounds.

FIGURE 16.13 Job description. (Adapted from *Model Position Descriptions for the Hospitality and Tourism Industry*, compiled by the International Council on Hotel, Restaurant, and Institutional Education and developed with a grant from the U.S. Department of Labor.)

Attributes	John	Mary	Dan	Sue	Les	Nancy
Prerequisites						
High school diploma	Yes	No	GED	Yes	Yes	Yes
Two years as counter server or equivalent position	No exp.	5 yrs.	2 yrs.	1 yr.	3 yrs.	No exp.
Can lift 30-lb. trays	Yes	Yes	Yes	Yes	Yes	Yes
Can push heavy food carts	Yes	Yes	Yes	Yes	Yes	No
Critical Competencies						
Passed math test	No	Yes	Yes	Yes	No	No
Passed written test	Yes	Yes	No	Yes	Yes	Yes
Passed payroll cost test	No	No	No	Yes	Yes	No
Passed work schedule test	No	No	Yes	Yes	Yes	No

FIGURE 16.14   Prospective employee selection sheet.

Training

Once the employee is selected, it is the manager's responsibility to ensure that the employee be trained to perform the tasks listed in the job description. Again, the job description is used as the primary source document to train employees to perform so that they meet the expectations of management. How the training should take place is beyond the scope of this book. However, the training must take place, especially if performance standards are based on the job description. Finally, using control procedures to hire employees is just as critical as using a Payroll Cost Report to ensure the success of the foodservice operation.

STEPS TO CONTROLLING PAYROLL COSTS

1. Hiring the right people
2. Training
3. Setting employee performance standards

Setting Employee Performance Standards

Performance standards are *statements of a job task, in terms of activity requirements needed to complete the task.* Performance standards are generally based on the tasks listed in the job description. The actual transformation of a task written in the job description into a performance standard is unique to the requirements of each foodservice operation. For example, Task 2 in Figure 16.13 states, "Monitors daily performance of staff and ensures compliance with established timetables." This task may be transformed into a standard in the following ways:

- "Preparation for meal periods is completed no less than 15 minutes before a meal period."
- "95% of all banquets are served on time, according to the event planner of the banquet."

Task 13 states: "Schedules employee time off so as not to interfere with heavy workload periods." The standard could be:

- "An adequate number of employees are present to do the work required for the shift."

Another example could be Task 17:

- "Accurately inventories supplies daily and requisitions items needed to meet par levels."

The standard is established by the supervisor to ensure that there are no **outs**. Outs *occur when a menu item cannot be provided to a customer because there are not enough raw ingredients to prepare the item*. This means that all the products needed to prepare the meal period items are present. To do this, par amounts need to be maintained.

Figure 16.15 shows a partial conversion of the job description in Figure 16.13 to a list of performance standards to be used to evaluate a person's job performance.

Performance standards should be known by all those who work in the foodservice establishment. Good management means that both managers and employees have a mutually clear understanding of the job tasks and performance standards. All employees know what they need to do and against what standards their performance will be measured. In this type of work environment, employees have the freedom to improve and employee turnover will decrease as job frustration is eliminated or reduced to a minimum.

POSITION DESCRIPTION	
Position Title:	Counter Supervisor
Reports To:	Manager
Position Summary:	The Counter Supervisor directly supervises the daily operation of a specified unit and ensures that daily activity schedules and established quality standards are maintained. This includes the coordination of individual and collective efforts of assigned staff.

Tasks	**Standards**
1. Demonstrates complete understanding of departmental requirements and interprets their intent accurately to staff members.	When asked the department requirements, is able to list them with 90% accuracy.
2. Monitors daily performance of staff and ensures compliance with established timetables.	Prep for food periods is completed 15 minutes before the food period.
3. Monitors quality of products and services produced by staff and ensures compliance with established standards.	Randomly checks three entrée items during the meal period to ensure that they are prepared according to specifications.
4. Monitors food safety and food-handling practices of assigned unit and ensures staff compliance with established standards.	Follows food safety procedure manual.
5. Routinely inspects areas of assigned responsibility and reports all substandard safety, security, or equipment conditions to manager.	Completes safety check every day and uses maintenance request form to inform management of needed changes or improvements.

FIGURE 16.15   Partial list of performance standards.

Net Work

Explore the following Web sites:

www.softcafe.com—Click Schedule Writer and Sample Schedules
www.positouch.com
www.chefdesk.com—Click Management Guides
www.restaurantowner.com

Chapter Wrap

The Chapter ✓ at the beginning of the chapter posed several questions. Review the questions and compare your responses with the following answers:

1. **What is payroll cost control?**

   Payroll cost control is the process of meeting cost targets by establishing a payroll budget, properly organizing the workplace, hiring correctly, reducing employee turnover, scheduling properly and comparing actual costs to projected costs with the intent of reducing variances.

2. **What is payroll cost?**

   Payroll cost is the cost of employee labor; it indicates the number of dollars spent in achieving the total amount of gross sales and profits for any given period of time.

3. **What is a payroll cost budget?**

   Payroll cost budgets are a planned estimate of expenses, expressed in dollar amounts or as a percentage of sales. It is an estimate of the cost of labor needed to manage an estimated level of sales. Payroll cost budgets are established by examining payroll costs in relation to sales by an operating area or department.

4. **How is a work schedule prepared?**

   The work schedule should represent the best effort of the foodservice manager to schedule employees in anticipation of sales. When preparing a work schedule, the manager must take many things into consideration. These include:
   a. Peak business periods
   b. Holidays
   c. Weather conditions
   d. Special community events
   e. Employee vacation times

   A well-kept sales history can serve as a tremendous aid in making scheduling decisions. A work schedule should be prepared weekly and posted at least a week in advance. This allows time for employees to check their schedules. It should be posted next to the time clock or in the place most convenient for all employees to read.

5. **What are standard time card practices?**
   a. Start and finish times for each shift should be recorded on each card.
   b. Start and finish times for each scheduled lunch break should be recorded.
   c. Start and finish times for each scheduled break should be recorded.
   d. Actual time worked is recorded and totaled for each day.
   e. Regular and overtime hours are recorded.
   f. Employees sign time cards and verify hours.

> **6. What is employee turnover?**
>
> Employee turnover is the number of times that the total number of positions are filled with employees during an accounting period.
>
> **7. How can payroll costs be controlled?**
>
> Hiring the right people, developing training programs, and setting employee performance standards are all ways to control payroll costs.

*K*ey Terminology and Concepts in This Chapter

Controllable expenses	Payroll Cost Report
Cost of sales	Payroll cost sheet
Direct costs	Payroll estimate
Direct payroll costs	Performance standards
Doing (stage)	Planning (stage)
Employee meals	Preemployment tests
Employee turnover	Profit
Fixed cost	Salaries
Food cost	Sales
Income statement	Sales history
Indirect payroll costs	Sales per person-hour
Job description	Selection sheet
Loss	Time cards
Outs	Time card practices
Overtime	Time card systems
Payroll budget	Total gross wages
Payroll budget estimate	Training
Payroll cost	Turnover
Payroll cost budgets	Value per given shift
Payroll cost control	Wages
Payroll cost control process	Work schedule
Payroll cost estimate	Work schedule form
Payroll cost percentage	

*D*iscussion Questions and Exercises

1. Define the following terms: payroll cost, payroll cost control, controllable expenses, income statement, indirect payroll costs, social security tax, Medicare tax, payroll cost budget, work schedule.

2. How often should payroll cost be determined?

3. Explain the purpose of using a Payroll Cost Report.

4. Assume that you have just completed a payroll cost sheet. The payroll cost for hourly and salaried employees is $600 for the day. The indirect cost rate is 12%. What is the total payroll cost for the day?

5. Why is it important to include the indirect costs when calculating payroll cost for the day?

6. Why is it important to use time cards? Explain what justification there might be for not using time cards.

7. Using a blank Payroll Cost Report from the accompanying CD, calculate the payroll cost percentage and sales per person-hour. Use the following information: total sales, $150,000; total employee meals, $900; total gross wages, $42,800; and total hours worked, 1,800.

8. What are payroll budgets and what are they used for?

9. What considerations must be taken into account when developing a work schedule?

10. Explain how a work schedule and a payroll budget estimate help control payroll costs.

11. Given the following information, determine if Farfalle Arrabbiata will meet its weekly target payroll budget of 22%: expected sales for week, $15,000; food preparation staff hours scheduled, 145; server hours scheduled, 290; average wage for food preparation staff, $8.00; average wage for server, $5.50; and indirect payroll costs (social security tax, Medicare, state and federal unemployment tax, workers' compensation, and other benefits, 20%).

12. Why is it important to calculate the employee turnover rate?

13. Given the following information, calculate the employee turnover rate for a fast-food restaurant and the turnover cost for the past year: number of W-2s used during the year, 242; normal number of employees, 100; current number of employees, 121; and estimated cost of turnover per employee, $60. Is the employee turnover rate higher or lower than the typical average?

14. List at least five ways of reducing payroll costs.

15. What are generally considered to be the direct costs of employee turnover?

16. What are the hidden costs of employee turnover?

17. What is a job description?

18. How can job descriptions be used to hire new employees?

19. Describe using a job description to hire a new employee.

20. Why do job descriptions help to reduce employee turnover?

21. Describe the five required and two optional components of a job description. Why is it important to include all these components in a job description?

22. Make up a job description for a dishwasher that includes the five required components of a job description.

23. What is a performance standard?

24. Write three performance standards based on the job description you developed for a dishwasher.

## Chapter Seventeen

About Measuring Staff Performance & Productivity

Learning Objectives

After reading this chapter and completing the discussion questions and exercises, you should be able to:

1. Create a process for gathering information on sales per hour, covers per hour, and number of production people employed per hour.
2. Use a Shift Productivity Chart to measure current levels of productivity.
3. Use a Monthly Productivity Chart and an Annual Productivity Chart to measure long-term productivity.
4. Set goals to improve productivity and use tools to measure productivity.
5. Use a Server Productivity Chart for evaluating sales and volume of work accomplished by servers.
6. Describe the relationship between the foodservice system, job descriptions, and performance evaluations of service personnel.
7. Develop a Service System Chart.

Chapter Map

About Measuring Staff Performance & Productivity

Productivity

Measuring Kitchen Staff Performance & Productivity
- The Shift Productivity Chart: An Introduction
- Finding Shift Averages
- The Shift Productivity Chart: Doing the Math
- Monthly & Annual Productivity Reports
- Using Productivity Information

Measuring Server Performance & Productivity
- The Server Production Chart: An Introduction
- The Server Production Chart: Preparation

Service Standards and the Service System
- Service System Chart
- Applications for the Service System Chart

Chapter ✓

Check the chapter content for the answers to these questions:

1. How are staff performance and productivity measured?
2. How is food production measured?
3. How is service production measured?
4. What is a Shift Production Chart?
5. What is a Server Productivity Chart?
6. What is a Service System Chart?

*A*bout Measuring Staff Performance and Productivity

Performance and **productivity measurements** indicate *the amount of work produced in a given period of time.* Common production measurements in the foodservice industry include

- Sales per server per hour.
- The speed with which an order is produced and served.

Many others will be discussed. Performance and productivity can be measured by several different methods and compared to various standards that are either common to the foodservice industry or unique to a certain foodservice operation.

Effective management strives to maintain a desired level of performance and productivity within the foodservice operation. Management continually seeks production methods and procedures that can improve on existing employee performance. This may be accomplished in the kitchen through the use of new and improved food products that can be purchased either completely or partially prepared. Also, through advanced technology, new cooking systems speed up and simplify cooking procedures.

Management continues to focus its attention on kitchen and server performance and productivity, as demand for fast and efficient customer service increases. Technology with new and improved computer applications has become common, facilitating communication between server and kitchen staff. This results in faster, more efficient service. Consequently, many foodservice operations are improving their food production and service systems in order to remain competitive.

A key factor in creating a highly efficient foodservice operation with high standards is the proper recruiting, training, and evaluating of a professional staff.

*P*roductivity

Productivity is *a term used to describe how well hourly employees* (also known as *variable cost employees) are performing their work.*

- **High productivity** indicates that employees *are meeting or exceeding performance standards* (expected employee performance).
- **Low productivity** reflects that they *are not producing at established performance standards.*

The factors considered to be part of a **performance standard** are:

1. *Quantity*—How much work is performed in a measurable period of time.
2. *Efficiency*—How much work is completed in relation to costs or sales generated.
3. *Quality*—How many mishaps are avoided.
4. *Dependability and Responsibility*—How much supervision management must provide for the employee to accomplish his or her work.

Measuring Kitchen Staff Productivity and Performance

This section deals with measuring the productivity of those who produce the meals and beverages served to customers—the back-of-house (BOH) personnel. The principles of measuring productivity between front-of-house (FOH; customer service) and BOH personnel are not very different.

Basically, management is interested in knowing if value is being obtained from employees. Some typical questions that management may ask are as follows:

1. Was the employee performing his or her duties the entire time he or she was at work?
2. Did the employee perform according to established standards and the standards required by the needs of the day's business?
3. Was the employee self-directed in accomplishing the work?

The manner in which these questions will be answered is unique to each foodservice operational situation. As a way to understand at least one method of answering these questions, productivity can be analyzed on a shift, monthly, and annual basis. A manual or electronic system may be employed.

There are three primary tools that can be used to analyze productivity on a shift, monthly, and annual basis. These are:

1. The Shift Productivity Chart
2. The Monthly Productivity Report
3. The Annual Productivity Report

The Monthly Productivity Report is built from the Shift Productivity Chart; it summarizes shift data. The Annual Productivity Report is built from the Monthly Productivity Report; it summarizes the monthly data.

PRODUCTIVITY REPORTS
1. **Shift Productivity Chart**
2. Monthly Productivity Report
3. Annual Productivity Report

The Shift Productivity Chart: An Introduction

The **Shift Productivity Chart** *examines productivity per shift*. It is a form that *measures the productivity of food preparation personnel*. The chart, or a similar tool, is used to collect information and organize it into a meaningful manner for use by management. Inputs of information must be gathered and organized by using a Shift Productivity Chart. **Inputs** are *data put into a system or process to accomplish a designated purpose*.

The inputs of productivity are distinctive to each foodservice operation. Inputs generally include

- Type of equipment
- Facility layout
- Physical structure
- Customers
- Employee availability
- Culture
- Location of the facility
- Financial strength of the foodservice operation
- Training and the technical expertise of the employees
- Volume of business

Generally, the *major inputs used to measure food production productivity are*

- The amount of labor time required, in relation to sales.
- The number of people that may be served for a specific period of time.

The problem is that sales and the number of people served are usually unknown until the moment the food is served. By tracking sales, a foodservice manager can estimate fairly accurately what is going to happen. Over time, the unexpected is averaged out. Shift performance is compared to similar shifts; that is a breakfast shift is compared to other breakfast shifts and a lunch shift is compared to other lunch shifts, and so on. The foodservice manager then can make decisions based on long-term averages. Take a look at Figure 17.1 and read the following explanation to better understand how to prepare a Shift Productivity Chart. Since all shifts use the same kinds of data, only the breakfast shift will be shown.

Preparing the Shift Productivity Chart   The first column shows Hours of Operation. In every foodservice establishment, certain hours of operation comprise the shift or shifts. Consider the breakfast shift, from 6:00 a.m. to 10:00 a.m., in Figure 17.1. Hours of operation are established to attract customers and fulfill their foodservice needs. The hours should remain the same if the productivity figures are to be used to compare what occurred from one period to another.

Most foodservice operations that have computer application software or point-of-sale computer systems are able to collect hourly information. Even if a computer is not used, the cashier can easily be trained to obtain the important data necessary to complete the form.

Three pieces of information are required:

1. The amount of sales that occurred during an hour of operation (easily taken from the point-of-sale terminal or cash register).
2. The number of people working in food preparation for each hour (from the time cards or work schedule).
3. The number of people consuming and paying for food and beverages during each hour (from the guest checks).

From these three inputs, productivity data can be calculated.

- **Sales per Hour** (Column 1) *is the amount of sales that occurred during an hour of operation.*
- **Covers per Hour** (Column 2) *is the number of people eating and paying for meals during the hour.*
- **Person-Hours** (Column 3) *are the total of all the hours worked by all persons who worked.* So if one person works, one person-hour has occurred. If three people worked, then three person-hours have occurred. Obviously, the more people working, the more person-hours have taken place.

Department:	Bagel Shop Kitchen Staff		Page:	1 of 1		
Shift:	Breakfast		Prepared By:	Bagel Shop Manager		
Date:	January 17, XXXX					

Hours of Operation	(1) Sales per Hour	(2) Covers per Hour	(3) Person-Hours	(4) Sales per Person-Hour (1 ÷ 3)	(5) Covers per Person-Hour (2 ÷ 3)	(6) Mishaps per Hour	(7) Mishap Percentage (6 ÷ 2)
6:00–7:00 A.M.	$ 75.00	13	1	$ 75.00	13.00	1	7.7%
7:00–8:00 A.M.	335.00	59	3	111.67	19.67	5	8.5
8:00–9:00 A.M.	380.00	63	4	95.00	15.75	6	9.5
9:00–10:00 A.M.	175.00	29	4	43.75	7.25	1	3.4
Shift Average	$241.25	41	3	$80.41	13.67	3.25	7.93%

FIGURE 17.1   Shift Productivity Chart.

Sales per Person-Hour The **Sales per Person-Hour** (Column 4 in Figure 17.1) *measures efficiency.* It informs management of *the amount of sales generated per preparation person.* The idea is that each person produces a certain amount of product per hour. The higher the sales per hour, the greater the productivity of the producer. Preparation personnel who constantly try to improve their productivity are worth more to the foodservice operation.

Covers per Person-Hour The **Covers per Person-Hour** (Column 5) *measures quantity and, to some degree, capacity. The higher the number, the greater the output per input.* **Capacity** is *the maximum number of people for whom a preparation staff* *can prepare.* Because food preparation personnel work in teams most of the time, **covers per person-hour** is *an average of how many covers are prepared by each member of the team.*

Mishaps per Hour   The **Mishaps per Hour** (Column 6) is *a measurement of quality.* This number is *how many mistakes (such as food items overcooked, undercooked, or dropped on the floor; and food returned to the kitchen for a variety of reasons) occur on average per hour.* Whether the food was served at its peak of flavor, hot food hot and cold food cold, will be considered later. The focus of giving attention to mishaps per hour is to keep track of the ability of the preparation staff to prepare food without making too many mistakes. See Chapter 9 for further discussion of this issue.

Mishap Percentage   The **Mishap Percentage** (Column 7) is also part of measuring quality. It is *the ratio of mishaps to total covers served* and is calculated by dividing Mishaps per Hour (Column 6) by Covers per Hour (Column 2), the result being a decimal multiplied by 100 to obtain the **mishap percentage**.

MISHAPS PER HOUR/COVERS PER HOUR × 100 = MISHAP %

Finding Shift Averages

At the bottom of the Shift Productivity Chart, the **Shift Average** figures are calculated. In Figure 17.1, the Sales per Hour is $241.25. This is *determined by adding the sales per hour for each hour, then dividing by the number of hours in the shift* ($75.00 + $335.00 + $380.00 + $175.00 = $965.00 ÷ 4 hours = $241.25). This process is performed for each of the columns:

SALES PER HOUR FOR SHIFT/NO. OF HOURS IN SHIFT = SHIFT AVERAGE SALES
PER HOUR

$965.00/4 Hours = $241.25

The Shift Productivity Chart: Doing the Math

Sales per Person-Hour   **Sales per person-hour** is determined by *dividing the sales per hour by the person-hours.* In Figure 17.1, the sales from 7:00 a.m. to 8:00 a.m. were $335.00. Dividing $335.00 by 3 person-hours gives $111.67. This dollar amount represents the sales per person-hour ($335.00/3 = $111.67).

SALES PER HOUR/PERSON-HOURS = SALES PER PERSON-HOUR
$335.00/3 = $111.67

Covers per Person-Hour   **Covers per person-hour** are similar to sales per person-hour. The **covers per person-hour** are determined by *dividing the covers per hour by the number of person-hours.* The covers from 7:00 a.m. to 8:00 a.m. total 59; therefore, 59 covers per hour divided by 3 person-hours gives 19.67 covers per person-hour (59 ÷ 3 = 19.67).

COVERS PER HOUR/NUMBER OF PERSON-HOURS = COVERS PER-PERSON HOURS
59 Covers/3 Person-Hours = $19.67

Mishaps per Hour & Mishap Percent   **Mishaps per Hour** is *the number of mishaps that occur during an hour.* The only mishaps counted are those directly attributed to the food preparation staff. The total number of mishaps per hour from 7:00 a.m.

to 8:00 a.m. was 5. This number divided by the covers per hour equals the mishap percentage of 8.47% (5 ÷ 59 = .08474100 × 100 = 8.47%).

TOTAL NO. OF MISHAPS PER HOUR/COVERS PER HOUR × 100 = MISHAP %
5 Mishaps/59 Covers = 8.47%

Whether this percentage is too high will depend on management's interpretation of allowable mistakes. In general, a foodservice operation should not experience a mishap-per-hour rate higher than 1% of total transactions. That is, if 100 entrees are served, no more than one should be wasted through mishaps.

SHIFT PRODUCTIVITY CHART ANALYSIS DATA

Sales per Hour For Shift/No. of Hours in Shift = Shift Average Sales per Hour
Sales per Hour/Person-Hours = Sales per Person-Hour
Covers per Hour/Number of Person-Hours = Covers per Person-Hours
Total No. of Mishaps per Hour/Covers per Hour × 100 = Mishap %

PRODUCTIVITY REPORTS

1. Shift Productivity Chart
2. Monthly Productivity Report
3. Annual Productivity Report

Monthly and Annual Productivity Reports

The next step is to measure productivity over the long term. This is accomplished by completing the **Monthly Productivity Report** and the **Annual Productivity Report**. Each of these reports builds on the other. To visualize how these reports work together, refer to Figure 17.2.

LONG-TERM PRODUCTIVITY MEASURES

Monthly Productivity Chart: Summarizes monthly averages from the Shift Productivity Chart

Annual Productivity Report: Summarizes the averages reported on the Monthly Productivity Chart

---

The **Monthly Productivity Report** (Figure 17.3) *lists the shift averages by each day of the month.* For example, the breakfast shift Average Sales per Hour (Column 1) are listed as they were calculated on the Shift Productivity Chart (in Figure 17.1). Then the column for Average Sales per Hour is totaled. The total is divided by the number of days in the month. The final number is the Monthly Average Sales per Hour.

This same process is used to calculate the Monthly Average Covers per Hour (Column 2), the Average Person-Hours (Column 3), and the Average Number of Mishaps per Hour (Column 6). These monthly averages are then used to calculate the Average Sales per Person-Hour (4), Average Covers Per Person-Hour (5), and Average

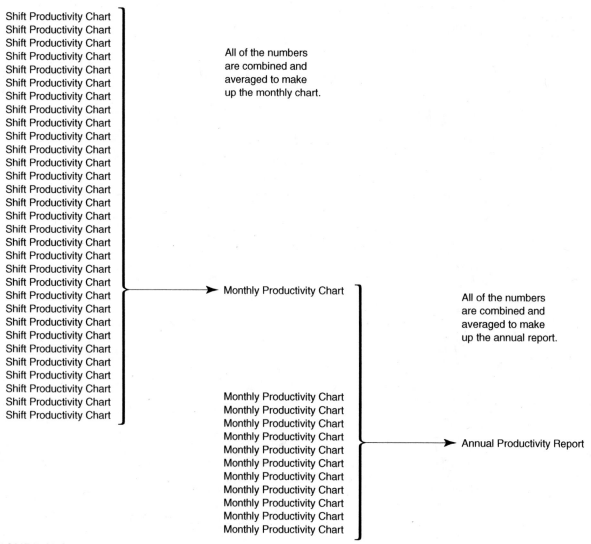

FIGURE 17.2 Integration of Productivity Charts.

Mishap Percentage (7). The process is repeated for the Annual Productivity Report (Figure 17.4), using the Monthly Productivity Charts as sources.

MONTHLY PRODUCTIVITY AVERAGES

Total Average Sales per Hour/No. of Days in Month = Monthly Average Sales per Hour

Total Covers per Hour/No. of Days in Month = Monthly Average Covers/Hour

Total Avgerage Person-Hours/No. of Days in Month = Monthly Average Person-Hours

Total Average No. of Mishaps per Hour/No. of Days in Month × 100 = Monthly Average Mishap %

Using Productivity Information

Productivity measures do not dramatically change over time. The information collected reflects the productivity of a foodservice operation over the long run. Shift reports may be compared to data from a previous day, a previous month, or a previous year. By

Department: Kitchen Staff

Month: January

Year: XXXX

Page: 1 of 1

Prepared By: Chef Raoul

Date/Day	Shift	(1) Average Sales per Hour	(2) Average Covers per Hour	(3) Average Person-Hours	(4) Average Sales per Person-Hour (1 ÷ 3)	(5) Average Covers per Person-Hour (2 ÷ 3)	(6) Average Number of Mishaps per Hour	(7) Average Mishap Percentage (6 ÷ 2)
1/10/XX	Breakfast	$240.92	44	3	$ 80.31	14.67	1.00	2.27%
Friday	Lunch	380.63	59	4	95.16	14.75	6.00	10.20
	Dinner	165.68	21	3	55.23	7.00	.31	1.15
1/11/XX	Breakfast	190.13	32	3	63.38	10.67	1.17	3.65
Saturday	Lunch	165.22	25	2	82.61	12.50	.29	1.18
	Dinner	320.19	36	4	80.05	9.00	.63	1.75
1/12/XX	Breakfast	290.19	48	3	96.73	16.00	.60	1.25
Sunday	Lunch	310.65	34	4	77.66	8.50	1.39	4.1
	Dinner	125.41	16	2	62.71	8.00	.44	2.75
1/13/XX	Breakfast	241.75	41	3	80.58	13.67	.53	1.3
Monday	Lunch	300.03	46	3	100.01	15.34	1.56	3.4
	Dinner	125.11	16	2	62.56	8.00	.42	2.63
.								
.								
.								
1/31/XX	Breakfast	241.25	41	3	80.41	13.67	3.25	7.93%
Friday								

FIGURE 17.3   Monthly Productivity Report.

correctly utilizing this information, the foodservice manager can set goals to improve on previous productivity records.

For example, if the Monthly Productivity Report indicates that the dinner shift average sales per person-hour for the month is $45, and the Annual Productivity Report indicates that the average sales per person-hour is $65, the manager knows that corrective action needs to be taken. If the lunch covers per person-hour ratio is 14.22 and the Annual Productivity Report indicates 12.12, the manager might want to know why things are going so well. Covers per person-hour is a fundamental tool for trying to improve the quantity of production.

The **mishap percentage** is *a method for measuring efficiency and quality.* The percentage, like the other tools, should be used to help set goals and monitor how well employees are performing their jobs.

Department: Kitchen							
Prepared By: Chef Raoul				Year: XXXX			Page: 1 of 1

Month/Year	Shift	(1) Average Sales per Hour	(2) Average Covers per Hour	(3) Average Person-Hours	(4) Average Sales per Person-Hour (1 ÷ 3)	(5) Average Covers per Person-Hour (2 ÷ 3)	(6) Average Number of Mishaps Per Hour	(7) Average Mishap Percentage (6 ÷ 2)
January XXXX	Breakfast	$220.45	37	3	$ 73.48	12.33	2.13	5.76%
	Lunch	343.27	51	4	85.82	12.75	1.79	3.5
	Dinner	180.61	21	3	60.20	7.00	.35	1.67
February	Breakfast	225.50	40	3	75.17	13.33	2.00	5.00
	Lunch	375.20	55	4	93.80	13.75	1.95	3.55
	Dinner	204.30	27	3	68.10	9.00	.35	1.30
March	Breakfast	230.75	45	3	76.92	15.00	2.10	4.67
	Lunch	400.22	62	4	100.06	15.50	2.00	3.23
	Dinner	200.15	25	3	66.72	8.33	.35	1.40
...								
...								
...								
December	Breakfast	210.10	33	3	70.03	11.00	1.60	4.85
	Lunch	315.65	47	4	78.91	11.75	1.20	2.55
	Dinner	321.02	38	4	80.35	9.50	.40	1.05

FIGURE 17.4   Annual Productivity Report.

ℳeasuring Server Performance and Productivity

Servers comprise the sales force of the foodservice operation. By definition, **servers** are *people who take orders from customers, deliver the orders to the kitchen, and serve the food to the customers.* How this is done constitutes the quality of service to the guest. Three parts of the server's job are tracked:

- Sales
- Number of people served
- Quality of work performed

Department: Dining Room						Page: 1 of 1			
Day: Friday		Date: 1/17/XX				Prepared By: Desmond			
Shift: 11:00 A.M. – 7:00 P.M.						Approved By: Owner/ Manager			

(1) Server Name	(2) Station Number	(3) Number of Hours Worked	(4) Total Sales	(5) Sales per Person-Hour (4 ÷ 3)	(6) Total Number of Customers	(7) Average Customer Sale (4 ÷ 6)	(8) Sales		
							Salads *10%	Soups 25%	Granitas 2%
Ann Server	1	7	$576.25	$82.32	96	$6.00	*8 (−2)	16 (−8)	4 (+2)
Mary Server	3	6	538.65	89.78	81	6.65	9 (+1)	26 (+6)	11 (+9)
Jack Server	4	7	651.90	93.13	121	5.39	6 (−6)	16 (−14)	13 (+11)
Sue Server	2	7	547.60	78.23	107	5.18	11 (0)	8 (−19)	1 (−1)
							*Note: The numbers are calculated by multiplying column 6 by the sales goal percentage in each category. The number in parentheses will be plus or minus from the sales goal.		

FIGURE 17.5   Server productivity chart.

The Server Production Chart: An Introduction

A Server Production Chart (Figure 17.5) is the primary tool for measuring server production. The chart measures sales, sales per person-hour, number of customers served, average customer sales, and other sales objectives. The chart should be prepared at least once per week, or more often if management deems it necessary.

THE SERVER PRODUCTION CHART

- Server Name
- Station Number
- Number of Hours Worked
- Total Sales
- Sales per Person-Hour
- Total Number of Customers
- Average Customer Sale
- Sales (by food category)

The Server Production Chart: Preparation

The Server Production Chart (Figure 17.5) *measures the productivity of each server*. The chart has eight components: (1) server name, (2) station number, (3) number of hours worked, (4) total sales, (5) sales per person-hour, (6) total number of customers, (7), average customer sale, and (8) sales (by food category).

Server Name   The name of each server on a given day, date, and scheduled shift is listed.

Station Number   The **station number** indicates *a designated work area*. It should be recognized that certain stations may be more active than others. A station that includes counter service or is close to the entrance of the restaurant may be busier than other stations in the restaurant.

Number of Hours Worked   The *total number of hours worked on the floor* is given here. Lunch and shift breaks are not included.

Total Sales   The *total sales for the server listed for that shift is noted here.*

Sales per Person-Hour   The sales per person per hour is calculated by dividing the total sales for each server by the number of hours worked. For Ann Server, sales per person-hour is calculated by dividing her total sales of $576.25 by the number of hours she worked on the floor, which is 7. Her sales per person-hour is $82.32 ($576.25/7 hours worked = $82.32 in sales per person-hour).

TOTAL SALES PER SERVER/NUMBER OF HOURS WORKED = SALES PER PERSON-
HOUR

Total Number of Customers   The Total Number of Customers is taken directly from the customer guest checks. The server should write how many people were served on each guest check, or the information should be entered into a computer terminal at the time the order is placed.

Average Customer Sale   The average customer sale is obtained by dividing total sales by the total number of customers. For Ann Server, the average customer sale is calculated by dividing $576.25 in total sales by 96, which is the total number of customers. Her average sale is $6.00 ($576.25 ÷ 96 = $6.00). This term is also known as **average check**.

TOTAL SALES/TOTAL NUMBER OF CUSTOMERS = AVERAGE CUSTOMER SALE

Sales   This is a special section of the Server Productivity Chart. It deals with sales of items that management wants to track. In this case, the sales of salads, soups, and granitas are totaled from the guest checks or from data provided by computer application software.

The Server Productivity Chart shows sales goal percentages beneath the type of sales goal. For example, the sales goal for salads is 10%. The sales goal for soups is 25%. The sales goal for granitas is 2%. The percentages are taken from the total number of customers.

If the sales goal for 96 customers is 10%, then 10 customers should buy the item. Ann Server should have sold 10 salads out of a potential of 96 salad sales that she could have made. The chart is used to record the actual number of salads sold; for Ann, this was 8 salads. Next to the listed number of items sold, in parentheses, is the number that represents the difference between the goal and the actual number sold. Note the following when reviewing these sales goal percentages:

- If the number sold is greater than the goal, a plus is written.
- If the number sold is less than the goal, a minus is written.

For Ann Server, the goal was 10 and the actual number sold was 8. Thus, −2 (minus two) is written in parentheses. She sold two salads short of the goal.

Sales goals are set by management. Instead of salads, soups, and granitas, the sales goals may have been for appetizers, specialty coffees, and **add-ons** (*items ordered in addition to the standard item,* such as shrimp added to a lunch salad). Any item that management believes would increase sales may appear in the Sales columns. One additional advantage for the server in seeking to reach sales goals is the potential for a larger tip. Overall, the Server Productivity Chart allows management to analyze the performance of every server, recognizing that the server is the sales force for the food-service operation.

Service Standards and the Service System

The concept of a standardized method can be used in serving the customer. Every foodservice operation should carefully consider how customers will be served, from the time they come in until they leave the foodservice environment. Each detail of service must be carefully examined. The details are the service standards (see Figure 17.6 service system chart). **Service standards** are *the individual actions taken by service personnel that collectively create the service experience provided to the customer as defined by management.* The sample of service standards shown in Figure 17.6 is only one possibility among many as to the best way a service standard should be developed. Each foodservice operation should develop its own standards.

Service System Chart

The standardized method for providing service is better understood by examining a **Service System Chart** (also known as a Cycle of Service or Service Cycle; Figure 17.6). It is *a form that lists the service tasks, service standards, and person responsible for accomplishing each service task.* The Service System Chart

- Lists the tasks, service standards, and person responsible for accomplishing each task.
- Formalizes the way the foodservice manager believes the customer should be served.
- Can be used for training, evaluation, and marketing.

Applications for the Service System Chart

Using the Service System Chart to Train Staff   The Service System Chart can be used as a way to transfer information from the service standard to the job description, which is then used as a guide for training the employee. The following list shows how the transfer of information should occur:

1. The service standard in the Service System Chart states that the waitperson should clear the dishes from the table or counter after each course is served.
2. The job description should state that the waitperson should clear the dishes after each course is served.
3. The newly hired waitperson should be trained to clear the dishes after each course is served.

If the foodservice manager trains according to the Service System Chart, all employees who serve customers will know what they need to do. The Service System Chart can also be used as a source document for training because it lists the service

	Manager: General Manager	Page: 1 of 2
Task	**Service Standard**	**Person Responsible**
Answer Phone	Within 3 rings.	Host/Hostess
Take Reservations	100% accuracy: name, phone number, number in party, time, special requests, table assignment.	Host/Hostess
Greeting the Customer	Within 1 minute of entering restaurant, use an approved greeting format, check for customer reservation.	Host/Hostess
Seating the Customer	Personally escort customers to preassigned table, seat women first, distribute menus, mention the evening special and the name of the person who will be their server.	Host/Hostess
Water Service	Ask if the customers want water.	Busperson
Waitstaff Greeting the Customer	Stand at a table corner if a four-top, or at the center end of the table if a booth, and introduce yourself. Mention the evening special; request any orders from the bar and ask if they want appetizers. If the customers order, take the orders. If they don't, invite the customers to look at the menu.	Waitstaff
Taking Meal Order	Return to table within 3 minutes. Ask for dinner order. Ask customers for add-ons (shrimp in salad, etc.).	Waitstaff
Processing Meal Order	Take meal order to waitstaff station and input into computer. Order-in should be completed in 2 minutes.	Waitstaff
Order Preparation	From printout, prepare menu item using standardized recipes. All the meals for a specific table should be prepared within 15 minutes.	Cook Staff
Salad Service or Appetizers	After order-in has taken place, take a basket of rolls and butter to the table. If any of the orders require salads or appetizers, prepare in the waitstaff station and take to the table. Deliver any beverages ordered.	Waitstaff
Water Service	While customers are waiting, check to see if they need water glasses refilled.	Busperson
Dinner Ready	When dinners are ready for the table, notify the waitperson using the silent pager.	Cook
Deliver Dinner	Order is picked up within 1 minute of notification and delivered to table. Ask for beverage orders or refills.	Waitstaff
Check Backs	After the order is placed before the customer, check back within 2 minutes and see if the customers are enjoying the meal. Ask for additional beverage orders or refills.	Waitstaff
Clearing the Table	When the customers have finished each course, ask for permission to take plates. Using clearing procedure, clear table.	Waitstaff
Dessert Order	When the last customer has finished eating and the table is cleared, take the dessert tray out to the customers and ask if they would like to select a dessert item.	Waitstaff
Final Coffee/ Beverage	Offer coffee or other beverages. This should be done whether the customers order dessert or not. If they order dessert, bring the beverage with the dessert.	Waitstaff
Bill Preparation	Go to waitstation and print out the bill.	Waitstaff
Bill Delivery	While customers are eating dessert and/or drinking coffee, present them with the bill, thank them, and instruct customers to pay the bill at the cashier's station.	Waitstaff
Final Payment	When the customers reach the cashier's station, ask if they enjoyed their dinner and invite them to return. If a customer is not happy, follow unhappy customer procedure. Thank customers for coming.	Host/Hostess

FIGURE 17.6 Service System Chart.

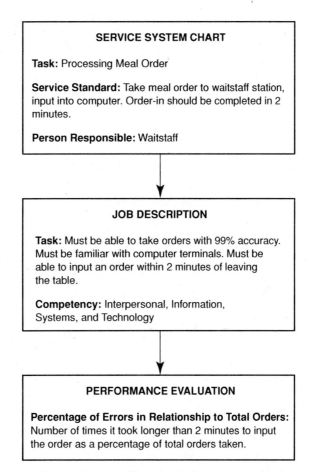

FIGURE 17.7   From Service System Chart to performance evaluation.

standards that employees should be trained to do. Training is focused on doing the operational processes required to serve the customer correctly. The outcome should be that all employees recognize that they are members of a team and that each person's work depends on how well others do their work.

Using the Service System Chart to Evaluate Staff   The tasks and standards in the Service System Chart can be used to evaluate staff performance. An employee either does or does not perform the task according to the standard described. The Service System Chart may be used by management and employees to develop a job-based personal performance review (Figure 17.7). Probably the greatest strength of a Service System Chart is that all the employees know the standards. When everyone knows the standards, there is the possibility that the employees will encourage each other to perform according to the performance standards and therefore reinforce them. If this happens, the manager can concentrate on increasing business rather than on getting employees to do their jobs.

Using the Service System Chart as a Marketing Tool   The foodservice operation may use the Service System Chart as a marketing document in two or more ways. One way is to use the service standards in the Service System Chart as part of an advertising claim (Figure 17.8). For example, if a service standard is speed in processing the meal order, the advertising claim could be "The quicker the kitchen gets your order, the quicker you get your food" (see Figure 17.8). Another way is to use the service standard as part in the development of customer comment cards. It forms the basis for having customers evaluate how well the entire foodservice operation is performing.

```
SERVICE SYSTEM CHART

Task: Processing Meal Order

Service Standard: Take meal order to waitstaff station,
input into computer. Order-in should be completed in 2
minutes.

Person Responsible: Waitstaff
```

```
NEWSPAPER ADVERTISEMENT
The Quicker the Kitchen Gets Your Order,
The Quicker You Get Your Food

At Hilsands
we just started using
the latest point-of-sale system available.
Your order travels to the kitchen faster so
you'll be able to enjoy our ribs, steaks, and tortes
just a few minutes faster.
Waiting for a taste of heaven
just got shorter at Hilsands.

HILSANDS
20889 S.E. VIRGINIA STREET
BALTIMORE, MD 10021
880-8080
```

FIGURE 17.8 From Service System Chart to newspaper advertisement.

For example, if a foodservice operation has a standard that the customer is to be greeted within one minute of entering the restaurant, the customer comment card should ask if they were greeted within one minute.

```
APPLICATIONS OF A SERVICE SYSTEM CHART
• Provides service standards for the operation
• Acts as a source document for training
• Standardizes service procedures
• Evaluates staff performance
• Aids job-based personal performance reviews
• Creates a basis for evaluating individual employees
• Creates marketing documents
• Develops input for customer comment cards.
```

The four measurement and control tools presented in this chapter are designed to improve production, efficiency, and quality:

1. The Shift Productivity Chart
2. The Monthly Productivity Report
3. The Annual Productivity Report
4. The Server Productivity Chart

The primary tool, the Service System Chart, can be used to set the standards for service, show how the job description can be put into action, and be employed as a tool for training. Carefully used, these tools will help reduce employee turnover and enhance the foodservice manager's ability to deliver service promises communicated to customers.

Net Work

Explore the following Web sites:

www.theelliotgroup.com

www.hcareers.com

www.micros.com—Check Select Industry, Restaurants, Tableservice, Kitchen
  Display System, Case Studies

www.chefjobsnetwork.com

www.yum.com—Check Careers

Chapter Wrap

The Chapter ✓ at the beginning of the chapter posed several questions. Review the questions and compare your responses with the following answers:

1. **How are staff performance and productivity measured?**

   Performance and productivity measurements indicate the amount of work produced in a given period of time. Some of the more common production measurements in the foodservice industry are sales per server per hour and the speed at which an order is produced and served.

2. **How is food production measured?**

   Food production can be measured by examining what occurs during a specific time period of operation, revenues per time period, number of people working during the time period, and the number of mishaps per time period. From this information, productivity data can be generated. Food productivity data are sales per hour, covers per hour, person-hours, sales per person-hour, covers per person-hour, mishaps per hour, and mishap percentage. These data may be compiled by using a shift productivity chart.

3. **How is service production measured?**

   Service production may be examined in two ways. First, data can be analyzed for each worker according to total sales, sales per hour, number of customers served, average sales per customer, and whether sales goals have been achieved. Second, performance may be measured to ensure that service standards are being met.

4. **What is a shift productivity chart?**

   The Shift Productivity Chart examines productivity per shift. It is a form that measures the productivity of food preparation personnel. The chart, or a similar tool, is used to collect information and organize it into a meaningful manner for use by management. Information must be gathered and organized using a Shift Productivity Chart. Inputs are data put into a system or process to accomplish a designated purpose.

5. What is a server production chart?

A Server Production Chart is the primary tool for measuring server production. The chart measures sales, the number of people served, sales per customer, and other sales objectives. The chart should be prepared at least once per week or more often if management deems it necessary.

6. What is a Service System Chart?

It is a form that lists the service tasks, service standards, and person responsible for accomplishing each service task.

Key Terminology and Concepts in This Chapter

Add-ons	Personal performance review
Annual Productivity Report	Person-hours
Average check	Productivity
Capacity	Productivity measurements
Covers per hour	Sales per hour
Covers per person-hour	Sales per person-hour
High productivity	Servers
Inputs	Server Productivity Chart
Low productivity	Service standards
Mishap percentage	Service System Chart
Mishaps per hour	Shift average
Monthly Productivity Report	Shift Productivity Chart
Performance measurements	Station number
Performance standard	

Discussion Questions and Exercises

1. Teach the principles of measuring kitchen staff performance and productivity to someone else.
2. How should kitchen staff performance and productivity be evaluated?
3. How do you prepare a Shift Productivity Chart for food production?
4. Why should productivity information be compiled monthly and annually?
5. How should productivity information be used?
6. What does the Monthly Productivity Report tell management about the operation?
7. How can management use this information to improve productivity?
8. Describe a service standard and how it can be used as a control device for better operating a foodservice operation.
9. Write a service standard for washing your hands.
10. Describe how a service standard may be used to develop a job description.
11. Describe how a service standard may be used to do a performance evaluation or personal performance review.
12. Describe the purpose of developing a Service System Chart. What kinds of information would be on a Service System Chart?
13. Go to a local restaurant, dine there, and then write up a Service System Chart for that business.
14. Discuss how a manager can effectively measure server performance.

15. Why should managers set sales goals for items or categories of items on the menu?

 16. Figure 17.9 shows a Server Productivity Chart prepared by Desmond, one of the managers at Farfalle Arrabbiata. Finish the chart, given the information already presented. Evaluate the performance of the servers. Should any of the servers be retrained or reassigned?

Department: Dining Room   **Page:** 1 of 1

Day: Friday   **Date** 1/17/XX   **Prepared By:** Desmond

Shift: 11:00 A.M. – 7:00 P.M.   **Approved By:** Owner/ Manager

(1) Waitstaff Name	(2) Station Number	(3) Number of Hours Worked	(4) Total Sales	(5) Sales per Person- Hour (4 ÷ 3)	(6) Total Number of Customers	(7) Average Customer Sale (4 ÷ 6)	(8) Sales Soups 5%	Desserts 15%	Add-Ons 20%
Ann Server	1	5	$576.35		89		5 ( )	5 ( )	16 (−2)
Mary Server	4	6	568.45		80		9 ( )	17 ( )	10 (−6)
Jack Server	3	7	657.90		109		2 ( )	2 ( )	5 (−17)
Sue Server	2	7	707.60		115		1 ( )	5 ( )	5 (−18)

FIGURE 17.9 Service productivity chart for Farfalle Arrabbiata.

Chapter Eighteen

About Operating Statements

Chapter Objective

To use standard operating statements to monitor the financial position of a foodservice operation and explain operating results.

Learning Objectives

After reading this chapter and completing the discussion questions and exercises, you should be able to:

1. Describe the three basic operating statements commonly used in foodservice operations.
2. Describe the types of income statements used in foodservice operations.
3. Identify the parts of an income statement.
4. Define variable, fixed, and mixed costs.
5. Classify expenses into variable, mixed, and fixed categories.
6. Complete an income statement.
7. Complete a Declining Balance Budget.
8. Explain the effect of changes in sales on cost behavior.
9. Analyze income statements using Common Size and Comparative Analysis.

The Menu

Pre-Purchase Functions

GUEST CHECK
Sales history, turnover, **average check,** cash management, revenue forecasting & budgeting, **menu item analysis**

GUESTS
Greeting, seating, **sales,** serving, busing, payment, comment cards

FOH Functions

KITCHEN PRODUCTION
Production schedules, portion tracking, recipe control, serving controls, food safety

PRODUCT ISSUING
Requisitions, transfers, daily & monthly costs, food cost percentage

STORAGE PRACTICES & INVENTORY MANAGEMENT
Best practices, sanitation, security, inventory methods

INVOICE MANAGEMENT
Payment, price checking, security

STANDARDIZED RECIPES
Standard ingredients, portion size, quality, consistency, quantity, purchasing

COST CARDS
Portion costs, yield factors, **sell prices**

SPECIFICATIONS
Product descriptions

PAR STOCK
Inventory levels, order building

REQUISITION
Order building, purchasing

SHOPPING LISTS
Call sheets, bid sheets, suppliers, bidding

PURCHASE ORDERS
Security, ship order, price guarantee, contract

BOH Functions

RECEIVING ACTIVITIES
Best practices, invoices, security, sanitation

Chapter Map

About Operating Statements

Basic Operating Statements
- Income Statement
- Balance Sheet
- Cash Flow Statement

Chapter Map   (Continued)

About Sales History & Operating Periods

Income Statements & Operating Periods
- Budgets
- Expenses
- Common Size Income Statement
- Cost of Goods
- Cost Percentages
- Controllable Expenses
- Occupation Costs
- What Lines Did We Miss?
- Profit or Loss

Cost Behavior
- What Is An Operating Cost, & Why Is It Controllable & Variable?

- Controllable & Noncontrollable Costs
- What Is a Nonoperating Cost, & Why Is It a Fixed Cost?
- Cost Behavior When Sales Change
- Applying Cost Behavior To a Sales Forecast

Working Budgets
- Declining Balance Budget
- Actual Results

Analyzing An Income Statement
- Completing a Common Size Analysis
- Completing a Comparative Analysis

Chapter ✓

Check the chapter content for the answers to these questions:

1. Which basic operating statements measure performance?
2. What are the components of an income statement?
3. What is a variable cost? A fixed cost? A mixed cost?
4. What is a variance?
5. What is a common size analysis?
6. What is a comparative analysis?

*A*bout Operating Statements

Up to this point, chapter discussions have been about control systems for day-to-day operations. The other half of life as a foodservice manager is spent doing work that is more globally focused—that of monitoring the financial health of an operation, identifying and correcting trouble spots, and planning for future operating periods. Chapter 10 laid the groundwork for the basic concept of an Income Statement, Food Cost Percentage, Cost Behavior, and Food Cost Variance. This chapter expands the discussion, covering the analysis of revenue, all expenses, and profit. The focus of the content is on measuring actual results against planned results, interpreting the information, and developing action plans. Chapter 19 takes the next step: budgeting for a future period.

*B*asic Operating Statements

All businesses use three basic financial statements to understand the financial position of a business. These tools are

- The income statement
- The balance sheet
- The cash flow statement

Income Statement

The **income statement** was defined in Chapter 10 as *a report of all income, expenses, and profit or loss for a defined period of time*. It is the key financial statement used by managers to track income, expenses, and profit. Income statements measure the performance of a company for various periods of time.

Balance Sheet

The **balance sheet** *reports the financial position of a company*. It is a record of the assets, liabilities, and equity of an operation for a specific period of time. The balance sheet is not used in day-to-day operations. It is a tool used by executives, investors, or creditors to assist them with business decisions about an operation.

Cash Flow Statement

The **cash flow statement** is the third operating document used to measure the financial health of an operation. It *reports cash receipts and disbursements*. It is prepared for the same period of time as the income statement. Because managing cash flow is the responsibility of higher management, this statement is another one that is not used for day-to-day management.

Of these three financial statements, the income statement is the "go to" report a manager uses when asking the question "How are we performing?" The income statement is not peculiar to the hospitality business. Every business, organization, club, or group wants to know "How are we performing?" Although all of these reports can answer the question, it is the income statement that can answer it quickly and with the detail a manager needs.

*A*bout Sales History and Operating Periods

Chapters 5 and 9 worked with sales history concepts in guest counts and popularity percentages. Recall from that work that sales history is kept in both guest counts and sales dollars for a variety of time frames. A sales history recorded in dollar values is used primarily for operational planning, whereas a sales history recorded in guest counts is used primarily for day-to-day operations. A set of interesting activities is at the heart of any operation's attempt to collect data useful for operational planning and analysis. The steps flow like this:

1. Historical Information
   - Historical information is organized into a variety of formats for ease in creating budgets and analyzing performance.
   - Expense and profit history is tracked, monitored, and analyzed.

2. Budget Development
   - Sales, expenses, and profit are forecast for operating periods.
   - Budgets are prepared for these operating periods.

3. Actual Budget
   - Actual sales, expenses, and profit are compared to forecast business levels.
   - Variances are analyzed.
   - Corrective action is taken where needed.

4. Future Budget
   - From this information and these activities, budgets are prepared for future time periods.

The first three steps are the focus of this chapter. The last step, budgeting for future operating periods, is covered in Chapter 19. These activities are quite different from the Operating Cycle of Control: Most notably, employees are not dependent on this information to serve guests—the data does not drive production. Recall how the sales history in guest counts was necessary to complete kitchen production schedules, determine popularity percentages, compute menu portions, order product, and schedule labor—all part of the nitty-gritty daily operations in a foodservice business. In fact, day-to-day production happens quite nicely without anyone but the manager worrying about the average check or next month's budget.

Like guest count history, sales data is commonly organized as follows:

- Sales per operating period: annual, semiannual, quarterly, monthly, weekly, daily, per shift, per hour
- Average check
- Average sales per seat

Income Statements and Operating Periods

As covered in previous chapters, income statements are prepared for a variety of time periods. Large businesses and even the government produce income statements for 5 or more years out. These long-range plans are very general and, of course, very flexible.

Budgets

On a day-to-day basis, most businesses work with *budgets for a more immediate time frame*. These budgets are called **working budgets**. The time periods are:

- Annual
- Semiannual
- Quarterly
- Monthly
- Weekly
- Daily
- Per shift
- Per hour

The most useful breakdown of an annual budget is into monthly, weekly, and daily sales and cost estimates. These budgets are prepared as an operating plan for management—one that they can ultimately use to assess "How are we performing?" A budget for any of these time periods may look a little different from the budget sample used in Chapter 10. Often, the detail for the Cost of Goods section is broken out into common product purchasing categories for both food and beverage costs. Some budgets may show detail for other operating costs. We will talk more about this later in the chapter.

Operations with multiple departments or revenue centers have **departmental budgets**, as well as *a budget for the entire operation:* a **master budget**. A master budget includes all departmental budgets, as well as all other administrative costs. A departmental budget reports *income, expenses, and profit or loss for a single department.* Department managers may be responsible for departmental budgets. Small operations may rely on an accountant to assemble the budget. More than likely, it is the owner.

Expenses

When looking at an income statement, understand that the figures you are studying are lump sum figures—they represent the total amount of money spent on that specific expense. Inside each of these figures are details that tell specifically what all that money was used for—*all the individual expenses that make up a specific line item*. This information is known as the **expense detail**. Figure 18.1 outlines some of the most common expenses covered by each expense line item.

Each operation has an expense detail that is tailored to the actual expenses incurred to generate the sales. It is important to capture every single cost associated with operating the business—if servers sing *Happy Birthday* to guests using kazoos, then kazoos must be listed in the expense detail of Direct Operating Costs!

Expense	What It Covers
Cost of Goods	
Food Cost	The cost of all food and nonalcohol beverages served to guests, delivery charges, trade discounts
Beverage Cost	Beer, wine, liquor, mixers, all other ingredients involved in serving alcohol drinks
Controllable Expenses	
Payroll & Benefits	Salaries & wages, all employee taxes, employee meals, workers comp insurance, all employee benefit plans, housing, employee parties, tuition reimbursement
Direct Operating Costs	China, glass, silver, uniforms, kitchen smallwares, cleaning & paper supplies, menus, contract cleaners, laundry & dry cleaning, licenses, flowers, guest supplies, bar supplies, any other operating costs
Music & Entertainment	Entertainers, licenses, royalties & agent fees, courtesy meals, equipment rentals, programs, other costs
Advertising & Marketing	Complimentary food & beverage, direct mail, all forms of advertising, point-of-sale merchandise, advertising agency fees, postage, dues, subscriptions, commissions, franchise fees
Utilities	Electricity, gas, water, oil, waste removal, other fuel
Administrative & General	Office postage and general office supplies, data processing costs, postage, telephone, Internet access, insurance, cash overs or shorts, bank fees, doubtful accounts, credit and debit card fees, charitable donations, professional fees, and recruiting, relocating and training fees
Repair & Maintenance	Building supplies, furniture, fixtures & equipment, grounds maintenance, refrigeration, hvac [CE1], parking lots, maintenance contracts, building improvements
Occupation Costs	
Rent	Rental fees, rentals of computers, telecommunications equipment, other equipment
Insurance	Property insurance, general insurance
Interest Expense	All interest expenses associated with mortgages, notes, and debt
Other Taxes	Property taxes, real estate taxes, other taxes
Depreciation	Buildings, furniture, fixtures, equipment, amortization of leasehold improvements, preopening expenses & goodwill

FIGURE 18.1   Expense detail for food and beverage operations.

Sales—Reports income earned from all revenue centers. The terms *revenue* and *sales* are interchangeable.

– **Cost of Goods**—Reports all product costs incurred by each revenue center. Each revenue center has a separate Cost of Goods entry.

– **Controllable Expenses**—Reports all other operating costs directly related to generating sales.

– **Occupation Costs**—Reports all nonoperating costs. These are expenses indirectly related to generating sales.

= **Profit or Loss**—Reports income that is left for the reporting period (either Profit or Loss)

FIGURE 18.2   Ingredients of an income statement.

Common Size Income Statement

How does the common size income statement work? Notice that the sections of the income statement have been labeled for ease in identifying each part. The ingredients for an income statement are shown in Figure 18.2.

Figure 18.3 is an example of a common size income statement for Farfalle Arrabbiata. This income statement was first seen in Chapter 10, but it has been modified to demonstrate the concepts in this chapter. Notice the Cost of Goods section in the monthly statement shows costs by common purchasing categories. Other than this difference, the format is the same as used in Chapter 10.

Sales

Sales reports *income earned from all revenue centers*. **Revenue** and **sales** are interchangeable terms.

Sales		
Food	$140,743	80.00%
Beverage	35,186	20.00
Total Sales	**$175,929**	**100.00%**

The **sales mix** is *the ratio of each revenue source to total sales*. It is found with the following formula:

$$\text{DEPARTMENTAL SALES}/\text{TOTAL SALES} = \text{SALES MIX \%}$$
$$\text{(Food Sales) } \$140,743/\$175,929 = 80\%$$
$$\text{(Beverage Sales) } \$35,186/\$175,929 = 20\%$$

Eighty percent of the sales is derived from selling food products. Twenty percent is from beverage sales. The sales mix is important from a cost perspective. Beverage products are much less expensive (in both product and labor cost) to produce than food items, and they enjoy a much higher markup. The ratio of food and beverage sales to total sales is monitored. Any shifts in the sales pattern can affect overall profit.

Cost of Goods

Cost of Goods reports *all product costs incurred by each revenue center*. In the case of Farfalle Arrabbiata, sales are a result of selling food products and alcohol beverages. As such, there are two revenue sources, so there are two components of Cost of

Sales			
Food	$140,743	80.00%	
Beverage	35,186	20.00	SALES
Total Sales	**175,929**	**100.00**	
Cost of Goods			
Food Cost			
Meat	11,541	8.20	
Poultry	7,319	5.20	
Fish & Shellfish	6,193	4.40	
Produce	7,037	5.00	
Dairy	4,363	3.10	
Baked	1,689	1.20	
Grocery	5,489	3.90	
Other	3,659	2.60	**COST OF SALES**
Total Cost of Food	**47,290**	**33.60**	• Operating Cost • Variable Cost • Identified by %
Beverage Cost			
Beer	1,970	5.60	
Wine	3,272	9.30	
Spirits	2,287	6.50	
Other	1,481	4.21	
Total Cost of Beverage	**9,011**	**25.61**	
Total Cost of Goods	**56,301**	**32.00**	
Gross Profit	**119,628**	**68.00**	
Controllable Expenses			
Payroll	52,075	29.60	
Employee Benefits	7,917	4.50	
Direct Operating Expenses	5,982	3.40	
Music & Entertainment	880	0.50	**CONTROLLABLE EXPENSES**
Advertising & Promotion	4,398	2.50	• Operating Cost • Mixed Cost • Identified by %
Utilities	6,509	3.70	
Administration & General	4,222	2.40	
Repair & Maintenance	2,463	1.40	
Total Controllable Expenses	**84,446**	**48.00**	
Income B4 Occupation Costs	**35,182**	**20.00**	
Occupation Costs			
Rent	10,556	6.00	
Property Tax	3,167	1.80	**OCCUPATION COSTS**
Other Taxes	1,500	0.85	• Nonoperating Cost • Fixed Cost • Identified by $$
Property Insurance	1,833	1.04	
Interest	2,750	1.56	
Depreciation	4,825	2.74	
Total Occupation Costs	**24,631**	**14.00**	
Restaurant Profit B4 Taxes	**$10,551**	**6.00%**	→ PROFIT

FIGURE 18.3 Common size income statement for Farfalle Arrabbiata.

Sales		
Food	$140,743	80.00%
Beverage	35,186	20.00
Total Sales	**175,929**	**100.00**
Cost of Sales		
Food Cost		
(A) Meat	11,541	8.20
(B) Poultry	7,319	5.20
(C) Fish & Shellfish	6,193	4.40
(D) Produce	7,037	5.00
(E) Dairy	4,363	3.10
(F) Baked	1,689	1.20
(G) Grocery	5,489	3.90
(H) Other	3,659	2.60
(I) Total Cost of Food	**47,290**	**33.60**
Beverage Cost		
(J) Beer	1,970	5.60
(K) Wine	3,272	9.30
(L) Spirits	2,287	6.50
(M) Other	1,481	4.21
(N) Total Cost of Beverage	**9,011**	**25.61**
(O) Total Cost of Goods	**$56,301**	**32.00%**

FIGURE 18.4   Total cost of goods.

Goods—**Food Cost** and **Beverage Cost**. Figure 18.4 shows the two cost categories extracted from the budget. Each has been expanded to show the costs for the major purchasing categories. This detail allows management to easily identify trouble spots when analyzing food and beverage costs on the income statement.

   Total Food Cost is *the sum of the costs of all food product cost categories* (A through H). **Total Beverage Cost** is *the sum of all beverage product cost categories* (J through M). **Total Cost of Goods** is the result of *totaling all food and beverage product costs* (I + N = O).

TOTAL COST OF FOOD + TOTAL COST OF BEVERAGE = TOTAL COST OF GOODS
$$\$47,290 + \$9,011 = \$56,301$$

Cost Percentages

How about those cost percentages? Recall from Chapter 10 that **food and beverage cost percentages** are *a result of dividing departmental costs by departmental sales, versus dividing by total sales*. Figure 18.5 shows the computations for these line items. **Food Sales and Beverage Sales** are the *total amount patrons have paid for those items*.

| FOOD COST/FOOD SALES = FOOD COST % |
| BEVERAGE COST/BEVERAGE SALES = BEVERAGE COST % |
| TOTAL COST OF GOODS/TOTAL SALES = TOTAL COST OF GOODS % |

FIGURE 18.5 Cost of goods cost percentage formulas.

Notice how the *divisor changes* in the Cost of Goods section. Sales for each revenue center is the divisor in each equation. One very common error is to use Total Sales to determine departmental cost of goods percentages. This is a serious mistake.

Now let's look at Figure 18.6. There are two important points to remember about this part of the income statement:

1. This is the only place on the income statement where *the departmental cost is divided by departmental sales versus total sales.* To illustrate this point, try dividing the meat cost by Total Sales ($11,541/$175,929 = 6.5%). Compare this percentage

Sales	
Food	$140,743
Beverage	35,186
Total Sales	**$175,929**

Total Cost of Goods

	A	/	B	=	C
Cost of Sales	**Food Cost**		**Food Sales**		**Food Cost %**
Food Cost					
Meat	$11,541		$140,743		8.2%
Poultry	7,319		140,743		5.2
Fish & Shellfish	6,193		140,743		4.4
Produce	7,037		140,743		5.0
Dairy	4,363		140,743		3.1
Baked	1,689		140,743		1.2
Grocery	5,489		140,743		3.9
Other	3,659		140,743		2.6
Total Cost of Food	**$47,290**		**$140,743**		**33.6%**
Beverage Cost	**Bev. Cost**		**Bev. Sales**		**Bev. Cost %**
Beer	$ 1,970		$35,186		5.6%
Wine	3,272		35,186		9.3
Spirits	2,287		35,186		6.5
Other	1,481		35,186		4.21
Total Cost of Beverage	**9,011**		**35,186**		**25.61**
Total Cost of Goods	**$56,301**		**$175,929**		**32.00%**

FIGURE 18.6 Income statement.

to the cost percentage for meat on the Cost of Goods section. Is it very different? Try the same exercise with the Total Cost of Food. What percentage did you get? How different is it from the correct percentage? How serious is this error?

2. All other expenses after the Cost of Goods section are divided by Total Sales.

Controllable Expenses

Controllable Expenses are easy. They comprise *Payroll, Employee Benefits, Direct Operating Expenses, Music and Entertainment, Advertising and Promotion, Utilities, Administration and General Expenses, and Repair and Maintenance.* Look at Figure 18.7: Each expense is divided by Total Sales to get the Cost Percentage. Total Controllable Expenses is simply the sum of the expense column. The Total Controllable Cost Percentage can be found by:

1. Dividing the Total Cost by Total Sales (A / B = C).
2. Summing the Cost Percentages in Column C.

Controllable Expenses	A / Cost	B Sales	= C Cost %
Payroll	$52,075	$175,929	29.60%
Employee Benefits	7,917	175,929	4.50
Direct Operating Expenses	5,982	175,929	3.40
Music & Entertainment	880	175,929	0.50
Advertising & Promotion	4,398	175,929	2.50
Utilities	6,509	175,929	3.70
Administration & General	4,222	175,929	2.40
Repair & Maintenance	2,463	175,929	1.40
Total Controllable Expenses	**$84,446**	**$175,929**	**48.00%**

FIGURE 18.7   Total Controllable Cost Percentage.

Occupation Costs

Last are the **Occupation Costs**. Now let's look at Figure 18.8. Each *cost is divided by total sales to get the cost percentage.*

Occupation Costs	A / Cost	B Sales	= C Cost %
Rent	$10,556	$175,929	6.00%
Property Tax	3,167	175,929	1.80
Other Taxes	1,500	175,929	0.85
Property Insurance	1,833	175,929	1.04
Interest	2,750	175,929	1.56
Depreciation	4,825	175,929	2.74
Total Occupation Costs	**$24,631**	**$175,929**	**14.00%**

FIGURE 18.8   Occupancy Costs.

What Lines Did We Miss?

In addition to these "parts" (Cost of Goods, Controllable Expenses and Occupation Costs) the income statement includes two subtotal lines:

- Gross Profit
- Income Before Occupancy Costs

These two lines can be used to quickly ascertain what the financial position is prior to paying the next set of expenses. Look at **Gross Profit** (Figure 18.9). What does it report? It simply reports *the amount of revenue left after the cost of goods expenses are paid off.*

$$\text{SALES} - \text{COST OF GOODS} = \text{GROSS PROFIT}$$

Total Sales	$175,929	100.00%
− Total Cost of Goods	56,301	32.00
= Gross Profit	**$119,628**	**68.00%**

FIGURE 18.9   Gross Profit.

Now look at Income Before Occupancy Costs (Figure 18.10). This line reports how much revenue is left after the controllable expenses are taken care of.

$$\text{GROSS PROFIT} - \text{CONTROLLABLE EXPENSES} = \text{INCOME BEFORE}$$
$$\text{OCCUPANCY COSTS}$$

Total Sales	$175,929	100.00%
− Total Cost of Goods	56,301	32.00
= Gross Profit	119,628	68.00
− Total Controllable Expenses	84,446	48.00
= Income B4 Occupancy Costs	**$35,182**	**20.00%**

FIGURE 18.10   Income before Occupancy Costs.

Profit or Loss

Last, look at **Profit or Loss** (Figure 18.11). *This is the amount left after the occupancy costs are paid:*

$$\text{INCOME BEFORE OCCUPANCY COSTS} - \text{OCCUPANCY COSTS} = \text{PROFIT}$$

Notice that the income statement works by continuously subtracting Cost Dollars from Total Sales. At no time should Profit ever be greater than Sales. The boss might like this, but it is not possible. When this occurs, the usual error is that expenses have been treated as income. An income statement is simply subtracting expenses (bills) from income. This is an important concept to understand.

Total Sales	$175,929	100.00%
− Total Cost of Goods	56,301	32.00
= Gross Profit	119,628	68.00
− Total Controllable Expenses	84,446	48.00
= Income B4 Occupancy Costs	24,631	14.00
− Occupancy Costs	24,631	14.00
= **Profit**	**$10,556**	**6.00%**

FIGURE 18.11   Profit or Loss.

Cost Behavior

The work we just did illustrates the mechanics of income statements. The math part is not too difficult—some adding, subtracting, and dividing are all it really takes. The next important concept to understand is cost behavior. Each category of costs has unique characteristics and behaviors. As such, it is of critical importance to understand how each is

- Described.
- Classified.
- Represented—Is it a %, $, or both?

Why? There are two reasons:

1. The first reason to understand cost characteristics and behaviors is because when sales change (and they do), each can do some strange things to profit! Take a quick visit to the pie charts in Chapter 10 for an example.
2. The second reason is that in order to analyze an income statement—to assess how the organization is performing—you have to know what to look at. Figure 18.12 is a summary of cost characteristics and their behavior.

What Is An Operating Cost, and Why Is It Controllable and Variable?

Controllable and Noncontrollable Costs

An **operating cost** is *an expense incurred to generate sales.* As such, it is considered variable in relationship to sales because as sales increase or decrease, more or fewer dollars have to be spent to generate the new level of sales. *Spending more or fewer dollars to generate that increase or decrease in sales is acceptable.* That is the controllable aspect of the cost. This concept is true for all variable costs.

Cost Category	Description	Classification	Is It a % or $$?
Cost of Goods	Operating Cost & Controllable ⟶	Variable Cost	%
Controllable Expenses	Operating Cost Controllable ⟶ Noncontrollable ⟶	Variable Cost Fixed Cost	% $
Occupation Costs	Nonoperating Cost & Noncontrollable ⟶	Fixed Cost	$

FIGURE 18.12   Cost characteristics and their behavior.

Controllable costs are *costs that managers can manage—they are within a manager's control*. These are *operating costs that are incurred as a part of day-to-day operations within the four walls of the business*. Standard operating procedures are in place to control each cost. Interestingly, income statements are arranged so that the most controllable costs are at the top, including Cost of Goods and Controllable Expenses. Those costs *over which management has little or no control*, or **noncontrollable costs**, are reported at the bottom (e.g., Occupation Costs).

Variable costs are variable because *the amount of money allocated to that line item has to fluctuate or change with sales*. Why? Consider food cost. It is a variable cost. It is the amount of money spent to purchase the food needed to generate food sales. The amount to purchase is determined through par sheets (Chapter 5) that are computed using standardized recipes, standardized portion sizes, and guest count forecasts. As such, the amount of food purchased for a forecast count of 5,000 guests will not be the amount of food needed if sales are actually running closer to 5,500 guests, especially if you plan on serving the standard portion size. *You are going to have to buy more food!* So the dollar value of the food cost on the income statement will be more (or less, depending on the sales direction) than budgeted. It has to be. *A variable cost that does not change in dollar value (+/−) when sales change is going to cause a problem.*

The most important point to understand about variable costs is that *even though the dollars might be changing because of sales increases or decreases, the percent-to-sales ratio must not change*. Why? Remember our earlier discussions about food cost in Chapter 10? The food cost percentage was established because it bought the right quality and quantity of product needed to serve menu items to operational standards. This same principle is true for all variable costs. Consider payroll. Payroll cost, another highly variable cost, is budgeted to provide the right amount of money and labor hours to staff at levels that deliver the quality of service defined by operational standards.

What about Controllable Expenses? They seem to be all mixed up (we will discuss this idea later in the chapter), but they are still considered to be controllable. This section of the income statement records all other operating costs needed to run the operation. Take a look at the types of expenses under the heading. They are also *described* as **operating costs** but a number of them are actually classified as a **mixed cost**—that is, *there are elements of variable and fixed qualities in each one*. The degree of variable and fixed dollars in each depends on the cost itself. Generally, those at the top of the list are more variable than fixed. Those at the bottom tend to be more fixed than variable. Those at the top of the list also tend to consume the greater proportion of sales dollars than those at the bottom of the list. For this reason, controllable costs are generally recognized as more variable than fixed and, as such, are treated as a mostly variable cost. A close evaluation of each expense's detail will determine how true this is for each operation.

Payroll is a good example of a **mixed controllable cost**. The variable portion of this cost is the number of hourly workers scheduled; according to sales forecasts, more employees are put on the schedule at busy times and fewer are scheduled at slower times. The fixed component of payroll has two elements: the cost of hourly staff needed to open the business, and salaries. Why are these portions of payroll considered fixed? Because they are unresponsive to sales. Every business should know the proportion of variable and fixed costs within their controllable expenses before analyzing business performance.

What Is a Nonoperating Cost, and Why Is It a Fixed Cost?

A **nonoperating cost** is *an expense incurred that is not used to generate sales*. As such, it is *not* variable with sales fluctuations. Regardless of what is happening with sales (increases or decreases), the expense stays the same. Because of this characteristic, these costs are **fixed costs**—*they stay the same for a period of time*.

Cost Category	Classification	Is It a % or $$?	What Happens When Sales Change? (+/−)	
Cost of Goods (Controllable)	Variable	%	$$ Change	% to Sales = Same
Controllable Expenses (Controllable)	Variable Fixed	% $	$$ Change $$ Same	% to Sales ≈ Same
Occupation Costs (Noncontrollable)	Fixed Cost	$	$$ = Same	% to Sales = Change

FIGURE 18.13 Cost behavior when sales change.

Fixed Costs

The nature of a fixed cost is that it's always the same for a period of time. Look at the expenses under Occupation Costs (review Figure 18.3). Rent is a fixed cost because, generally, rent is a set amount each and every month. (In some cases, it may be based on a percentage of sales or a combination of a set amount and a percentage of sales.) Rent is due each month, regardless of what has happened—good or bad. If sales are up from forecast, the rent is still the same amount. If sales are down from forecast, ditto. Fixed dollars have no reaction to sales increases or decreases. Businesses with a high proportion of fixed costs to variable costs run into trouble more quickly when sales are less than expected than does a business with a low proportion of fixed to variable costs. The funny thing about fixed costs, though, is that although they have no reaction to sales from a dollar perspective, the cost percentage behavior is an entirely different story. Read on for more about this.

Cost Behavior When Sales Change

Let's pull all this together. Figure 18.13 shows all of these factors together. It will be very useful in our discussion over the next few pages.

Applying Cost Behavior to a Sales Forecast

Use the Cost Behavior Chart shown in Figure 18.14 to help with this exercise. Chef Raoul has just received the sales forecast for next month (March). Total revenue is forecast to be $169,576. Apply the concepts of cost behavior and determine the budget for the month. Use Figure 18.15 (Income Statement for Farfalle Arrabbiata for March). Remember that the standards were established by the budget in Figure 18.3. Use the Triangle of Enlightenment (Chapter 3) to compute either dollars or percentages. The cost percentages and dollars that should remain the same have been transferred to make the job a little easier.

Check your work against the budget shown in Figure 18.16. Your figures for March for Farfalle Arrabbiata should look similar.

What is the point of this exercise? You have now produced a financial plan for the month of March, and Chef Raoul and the other managers now know the sales and cost

Cost	Sales	Cost $$	Cost %
Variable & Mixed (%)	Up Down	Increase Decrease	Stays the same Stays the same
Fixed ($)	Up Down	Stays the same Stays the same	Decreases Increases

FIGURE 18.14 Cost Behavior Chart.

Sales	February		March	
Food	$140,743	80.00%		80.00%
Beverage	35,186	20.00		20.00
Total Sales	**175,929**	**100.00**	**$169,576**	**100.00**
Cost of Sales				
Food Cost				
Meat	11,541	8.20		8.20
Poultry	7,319	5.20		5.20
Fish & Shellfish	6,193	4.40		4.40
Produce	7,037	5.00		5.00
Dairy	4,363	3.10		3.10
Baked	1,689	1.20		1.20
Grocery	5,489	3.90		3.90
Other	3,659	2.60		2.60
Total Cost of Food	**47,290**	**33.60**		
Beverage Cost				
Beer	1,970	5.60		5.60
Wine	3,272	9.30		9.30
Spirits	2,287	6.50		6.50
Other	1,481	4.21		4.21
Total Cost of Beverage	**9,011**	**25.61**		
Total Cost of Goods	**56,301**	**32.00**		
Gross Profit	**119,628**	**68.00**		
Controllable Expenses				
Payroll	52,075	29.60		29.60
Employee Benefits	7,917	4.50		4.50
Direct Operating Expenses	5,982	3.40		3.40
Music & Entertainment	880	0.50		0.50
Advertising & Promotion	4,398	2.50		2.50
Utilities	6,509	3.70		3.70
Administration & General	4,222	2.40		2.40
Repair & Maintenance	2,463	1.40		1.40
Total Controllable Expenses	**84,446**	**48.00**		
Income B4 Occupation Costs	**35,182**	**20.00**		
Occupation Costs				
Rent	10,556	6.00	$10,556	
Property Tax	3,167	1.80	3,167	
Other Taxes	1,500	0.85	1,500	
Property Insurance	1,833	1.04	1,833	
Interest	2,750	1.56	2,750	
Depreciation	4,825	2.74	4,825	
Total Occupation Costs	**24,631**	**14.00**		
Restaurant Profit B4 Taxes	**$ 10,556**	**6.00%**		

FIGURE 18.15 Income Statement for Farfalle Arrabbiata (March).

Sales		
Food	$135,661	80.00%
Beverage	33,915	20.00
Total Sales	**169,576**	**100.00**
Cost of Sales		
Food Cost		
Meat	11,124	8.20
Poultry	7,054	5.20
Fish & Shellfish	5,969	4.40
Produce	6,783	5.00
Dairy	4,205	3.10
Baked	1,628	1.20
Grocery	5,291	3.90
Other	3,527	2.60
Total Cost of Food	**45,582**	**33.60**
Beverage Cost		
Beer	1,899	5.60
Wine	3,154	9.30
Spirits	2,204	6.50
Other	1,428	4.21
Total Cost of Beverage	**8,686**	**25.61**
Total Cost of Goods	**54,268**	**32.00**
Gross Profit	**115,308**	**68.00**
Controllable Expenses		
Payroll	50,194	29.60
Employee Benefits	7,631	4.50
Direct Operating Expenses	5,766	3.40
Music & Entertainment	848	0.50
Advertising & Promotion	4,239	2.50
Utilities	6,274	3.70
Administration & General	4,070	2.40
Repair & Maintenance	2,374	1.40
Total Controllable Expenses	**81,396**	**48.00**
Income B4 Occupation Costs	**33,912**	**20.00**
Occupation Costs		
Rent	10,556	6.22
Property Tax	3,167	1.87
Other Taxes	1,500	0.88
Property Insurance	1,833	1.08
Interest	2,750	1.62
Depreciation	4,825	2.85
Total Occupation Costs	**24,631**	**14.53**
Restaurant Profit B4 Taxes	**$ 9,281**	**5.47%**

FIGURE 18.16   Budget for Farfalle Arrabbiata (March).

goals for the period. Using all the tools described in Chapter 9 (sales history, external and internal environments, etc.), this monthly picture will be further broken down into weekly, then daily, sales and cost budgets that become the operating plans for each week and day. Daily budgets deal primarily with sales, food cost, beverage cost, and labor cost versus all the expenses on the income statement. Because these are the **prime costs** that are controllable and consume most of the sales dollars (60% +/−), this makes sense. Note that this work is easily done with any spreadsheet program.

Figure 18.17 shows the March budget, broken down into weekly sales and cost budgets. Notice that the Occupation Costs have been allocated for each week. Because this is a working budget, the cost percentages for each week are not included on this spreadsheet.

$\mathcal{W}$orking Budgets

The sales forecast, together with the target food cost percentage, establishes the working food budget for the week. This is the dollar amount Chef Raoul should spend if he is spending to budget. Now, actual purchases can be subtracted from the allocated food cost dollars every day, allowing management to monitor food cost and not overspend the budget. The same procedure can be used with beverage cost and labor cost.

Declining Balance Budget

The process of *starting with a budgeted figure and drawing down (drawing off of) the budget over the course of the operating period* is called a **declining balance budget**—the balance declines over time. This is a common way of working with a food budget.

Let's look at Figure 18.18. Chef Raoul's food budget for the first week of March is $11,901:

$$\text{FOOD SALES FORECAST} \times \text{TARGET FOOD COST \%} = \text{FOOD COST BUDGET}$$
$$\$35,421 \times 33.6\% = \$11,901$$

The figure shows a declining balance budget for food cost for this particular week. Notice that food purchases are distributed by food category and according to a percentage. This *proportion of the food cost percentage that each product category consumes is,* essentially, a **food category popularity percentage**—a similar concept to menu item popularity. The percentage identifies *the proportion of the food sales necessary to but the quality and quantity of food for the forecasted level of sales.*

On this form, food cost is broken down to the major purchasing categories, making it easy to see where over- or underspending is occurring. Notice those categories that are over budget—poultry and dairy. Notice those that are under budget. The underspent categories compensate for the two categories that are overspent. By breaking out the spending categories, Chef Raoul is able to pinpoint trouble spots. Now he can focus his attention on these specific product categories and determine why they are out of line.

Labor cost and beverage cost can be set up in a similar way. A daily budget is established and actual costs are subtracted over the course of the week. Data for labor cost is taken from time cards or electronic scheduling software programs. Information for beverage cost is tracked the same way as food cost.

Actual Results

Once business actually occurs, a new picture of income, expenses, and profit or loss is compiled. This is the **actual budget**. It shows *actual sales, actual costs, and profit or loss as each accrued over the course of the period.* The actual figures are recorded next to budget figures, where they can be easily compared with the budget plan. Variances are calculated and analyzed for trouble spots. This is the heart of a manager's job. He

Sales	March Budget		Week 1	Week 2	Week 3	Week 4
Food	$135,661	80.00%	$35,421	$30,748	$34,294	$35,198
Beverage	33,915	20.00	8,855	7,687	8,573	8,800
Total Sales	**169,576**	**100.00**	**44,276**	**38,435**	**42,867**	**43,998**
Cost of Sales						
Food Cost						
Meat	11,124	8.20	2,905	2,521	2,812	2,886
Poultry	7,054	5.20	1,842	1,599	1,783	1,830
Fish & Shellfish	5,969	4.40	1,559	1,353	1,509	1,549
Produce	6,783	5.00	1,771	1,537	1,715	1,760
Dairy	4,205	3.10	1,098	953	1,063	1,091
Baked	1,628	1.20	425	369	412	422
Grocery	5,291	3.90	1,381	1,199	1,337	1,373
Other	3,527	2.60	921	799	892	915
Total Cost of Food	**45,582**	**33.60**	**11,901**	**10,331**	**11,523**	**11,827**
Beverage Cost						
Beer	1,899	5.60	496	430	480	493
Wine	3,154	9.30	824	715	797	818
Spirits	2,204	6.50	576	500	557	572
Other	1,428	4.21	373	324	361	370
Total Cost of Beverage	**8,686**	**25.61**	**2,268**	**1,969**	**2,196**	**2,254**
Total Cost of Goods	**54,268**	**32.00**	**14,169**	**12,300**	**13,718**	**14,080**
Gross Profit	**115,308**	**68.00**	**30,107**	**26,135**	**29,149**	**29,918**
Controllable Expenses						
Payroll	50,194	29.60	13,106	11,377	12,689	13,023
Employee Benefits	7,631	4.50	1,992	1,730	1,929	1,980
Direct Operating Expenses	5,766	3.40	1,505	1,307	1,457	1,496
Music & Entertainment	848	0.50	221	192	214	220
Advertising & Promotion	4,239	2.50	1,107	961	1,072	1,100
Utilities	6,274	3.70	1,638	1,422	1,586	1,628
Administration & General	4,070	2.40	1,063	922	1,029	1,056
Repair & Maintenance	2,374	1.40	620	538	600	616
Total Controllable Expenses	**81,396**	**48.00**	**21,252**	**18,449**	**20,576**	**21,119**
Income B4 Occupation Costs	**33,912**	**20.00**	**8,854**	**7,686**	**8,573**	**8,799**
Occupation Costs						
Rent	10,556	6.22	2,639	2,639	2,639	2,639
Property Tax	3,167	1.87	792	792	792	792
Other Taxes	1,500	0.88	375	375	375	375
Property Insurance	1,833	1.08	458	458	458	458
Interest	2,750	1.62	688	688	688	688
Depreciation	4,825	2.85	1,206	1,206	1,206	1,206
Total Occupation Costs	**24,631**	**14.53**	**6,158**	**6,158**	**6,158**	**6,158**
Restaurant Profit B4 Taxes	**$ 9,280**	**5.47**	**2,696**	**$ 1,528**	**$ 2,415**	**$ 2,641**

FIGURE 18.17   Week-to-Week Budget for Farfalle Arrabbiata (March).

Weekly Food Sales: $35,421			Weekly Food Budget: (33.6%) $11,901							
Food Category	% of Food Cost	Ideal Cost $$ Budget	3/1 Mon.	3/2 Tue.	3/3 Wed.	3/4 Thurs.	3/5 Fri.	3/6 Sat.	3/7 Sun.	
Meats Used: $$ Left	8.2%	$2,904	$915 $1,989	0 $1,989	$825 $1,164	0 $1,164	$882 $342	$243 $99	0 $99	IDEAL: $2,904 Spent: $2,805
Poultry Used: $$ Left	5.2%	$1,842	$638 $1,204	0 $1,204	$732 $472	0 $472	$512 ($40)	$102 ($142)	0 ($142)	IDEAL: $1,842 Spent: **$1,984**
Seafood Used: $$ Left	4.4%	$1,559	$385 $1,174	0 $1,174	$392 $782	0 $782	$423 $359	$318 $41	0 $41	IDEAL: $1,559 Spent: $1,518
Produce Used: $$ Left	5.0%	$1,771	$362 $1,409	$316 $1,093	$241 $993	$120 $873	$375 $498	$219 $279	0 $279	IDEAL: $1,771 Spent: $1,663
Dairy Used: $$ Left	3.1%	$1,098	$159 $939	$169 $770	$177 $593	$185 $408	$182 $226	$236 ($10)	0 ($10)	IDEAL: $1,098 Spent: **$1,108**
Baked Used: $$ Left	1.2%	$426	$61 $365	$42 $323	$66 $257	$53 $204	$74 $130	$72 $58	0 $58	IDEAL: $426 Spent: $368
Grocery Used: $$ Left	3.9%	$1,301	$876 $425	0 $425	0 $425	0 $425	$385 $40	0 $40	0 $40	IDEAL: $1,301 Spent: $1,261
Other Used: $$ Left	2.6%	$921	$154 $767	0 $767	$460 $307	0 $307	$271 $36	0 $36	0 $36	IDEAL: $921 Spent: $885
Total Tot. $$ Spent: Tot. $$ Left:	33.6%	$11,901	$3,550 $12,463	$557 $11,071	$2,893 $7,517	$358 $5,475	$3,044 $2,039	$1,190 $349	0 $349	IDEAL: **$11,901** Spent: **$11,592**

FIGURE 18.18   Declining Balance Budget.

Farfalle Arrabbiata	Week 1		Week 1	
Week of 3/1–3/7 2XXX	Budget		Actual	
Sales				
Food	$35,421	80.00%	$33,245	82.33%
Beverage	8,855	20.00	7,135	17.67
Total Sales	**44,276**	**100.00**	**40,380**	**100.00**
Cost of Sales				
Food Cost				
Meat	2,905	8.20	2,630	7.91
Poultry	1,842	5.20	1,872	5.63
Fish & Shellfish	1,559	4.40	1,423	4.28
Produce	1,771	5.00	1,559	4.69
Dairy	1,098	3.10	1,041	3.13
Baked	425	1.20	332	1.00
Grocery	1,381	3.90	1,184	3.56
Other	921	2.60	831	2.50
Total Cost of Food	**11,901**	**33.60**	**10,871**	**32.70**
Beverage Cost				
Beer	496	5.60	449	6.29
Wine	824	9.30	649	9.10
Spirits	576	6.50	490	6.87
Other	373	4.21	313	4.39
Total Cost of Beverage	**2,268**	**25.61**	**1,901**	**26.65**
Total Cost of Goods	**14,169**	**32.00**	**12,773**	**31.63**
Gross Profit	**30,107**	**68.00**	**27,607**	**68.37**
Controllable Expenses				
Payroll	13,106	29.60	11,654	28.86
Employee Benefits	1,992	4.50	1,817	4.50
Direct Operating Expenses	1,505	3.40	1,664	4.12
Music & Entertainment	221	0.50	202	0.50
Advertising & Promotion	1,107	2.50	800	1.98
Utilities	1,638	3.70	1,692	4.19
Administration & General	1,063	2.40	1,119	2.77
Repair & Maintenance	620	1.40	565	1.40
Total Controllable Expenses	**21,252**	**48.00**	**19,512**	**48.32**
Income B4 Occupation Costs	**8,854**	**20.00**	**8,096**	**20.05**
Occupation Costs				
Rent	2,639	5.96	2,639	6.54
Property Tax	792	1.79	792	1.96
Other Taxes	375	0.85	375	0.93
Property Insurance	458	1.03	458	1.13
Interest	688	1.55	688	1.70
Depreciation	1,206	2.72	1,206	2.99
Total Occupation Costs	**6,158**	**13.91**	**6,158**	**15.25**
Restaurant Profit B4 Taxes	**2,696**	**6.09%**	**1,938**	**4.80%**

FIGURE 18.19   Actual Results for Farfalle Arrabbiata (First Week of March).

or she must be able to interpret the information on the income statement and determine whether these results are acceptable or not acceptable.

This process of creating a budget plan, collecting actual data, comparing the budget to actual results, and analyzing variances should sound familiar—it is the control procedure first introduced in Chapter 1 and used in Chapter 10 to analyze food cost. The difference here is that the analysis now is not just for food cost. It's for *all income sources, all expenses, and profit or loss.*

Figure 18.19 shows the actual results for the first week of March. These results are placed next to the budget figures.

Before attempting an analysis of budget and actual income statements, a quick review of the pie wedge story from Chapter 10 is in order. The Week 1 budget in Figure 18.19 is the financial "plan" for Farfalle Arrabbiata. Assume variable cost percentages and fixed dollars associated with that budget are the operational standards for Farfalle Arrabbiata. The pie chart in Figure 18.20 depicts this cost structure.

Next, look at the pie chart of the actual results (Figure 18.21). What do you notice? There has been some shifting among all the pieces. In Chapter 10, we made the pie charts change because of shifts in food cost alone. Here, all the pieces (all costs and profit) are in play. In fact, even sales changed! The overall effect of all the wiggling is shown in the profit piece of Figure 18.21. Unfortunately, the net effect of all the changes (sales and costs) has negatively affected profit.

What do you notice? In Figure 18.21, Cost of Goods is *slightly lower* than plan, but the Controllable Expenses and Occupation Costs are *higher* than plan. Even though one category, Cost of Goods, was a little under, it is not enough to offset the difference in Controllable Expenses and Occupation Costs. Why is this? The primary problem is attributable to the fact that *fixed cost dollars are unresponsive to changes in sales*—they

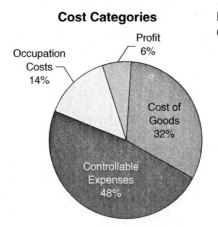

Cost Categories

Profit 6%
Occupation Costs 14%
Cost of Goods 32%
Controllable Expenses 48%

FIGURE 18.20   Budgeted Cost Categories.

Cost Categories

Profit 4.21%
Occupation Costs 15.25%
Cost of Goods 31.63%
Controllable Expenses 48.32%

FIGURE 18.21   Actual Cost Categories.

are fixed no matter what happens. Try this same exercise using $50,000 as the monthly sales. Watch what happens now. This is an example of the impact of fixed costs on profit when sales are less than plan. The next task is to analyze the results of the actual income statement. Read on about how to do this.

Analyzing An Income Statement

There are two methods of analyzing an income statement. One is a common size analysis. The second is a comparative analysis using variance. Both methods are commonly used by all businesses to analyze income statements. The first method, **common size analysis**, *analyzes the variance in the percentages between budget and actual results*. A common size analysis is commonly used to analyze operating results for current operating periods. The second method, **comparative analysis**, *computes the dollar difference between budget and actual results for each line item, converts this difference into a percentage, and analyzes the variance*. A comparative analysis is commonly used to compare current operating results against previous accounting periods (last month, quarter, year).

METHODS OF ANALYZING AN INCOME STATEMENT

Common Size Analysis: A common size analysis involves *analyzing the variance between budget and actual results.* The percentage column on the income statement is the source of this information. This analysis is commonly used to analyze operating results for current operating periods. Variances are termed acceptable or unacceptable.

Comparative Analysis: A comparative analysis involves *calculating the variance dollars between budget and actual, and converting this difference into a percentage.* These variances are termed favorable or unfavorable and are the subject of analysis. A comparative analysis can be performed for a budget period (month, quarter) or to compare results between years.

Completing a Common Size Analysis

There are five steps to a common size analysis. These steps start with an overall assessment of "How are we performing?" by taking a look at profit. Next, we review each broad income statement category. Then, a line item analysis is performed. Finally, we ask "Why?" What are the reasons for the results we see? A comparative analysis is a test of your understanding of variable and fixed costs, how they are represented, and what to look at when analyzing an income statement. The steps to a common size analysis are shown in Figure 18.22.

To do a common size analysis, budget, actual figures, and percentages are arranged on one statement, as in Figure 18.19. Next, management defines the **acceptable degree of variance**. Recall from Chapter 10 that a **variance** is *a deviation from a standard.* When variances are **acceptable**, it means that *the difference between*

STEPS TO A COMMON SIZE ANALYSIS

1. Check overall profitability. Did the operation produce profit? Was it at desired levels?
2. Assess the overall performance of income statement categories: Sales, Cost of Sales, Controllable Expenses, Occupation Costs, and Profit or Loss.
3. Assess the performance of each line item. Sales, all costs, and profit or loss are examined line by line for variance from standards. Management sets the acceptable degree of variance in a percentage.
4. Determine the reason for unacceptable variances. Ask WHY?
5. Take corrective action—fix the problem.

FIGURE 18.22   How to do a Common Size Analysis.

budget and actual is insignificant—it is not enough to worry about, and no action is required. Each operation sets the percentage of variance considered acceptable. Variances exceeding this standard are labeled **unacceptable** *and call for immediate analysis and action*. When unacceptable variances are identified, management is charged with pinpointing the problem and fixing it.

The acceptable variance for Farfalle Arrabbiata is 0.5%. This means that any **variable cost** can have an **actual cost percentage** of +/−0.5%. Any variance outside of this range is considered **unacceptable** and must be addressed.

Step 1. Check Overall Profitability
Check the Profit/Loss line of the budget in Figure 18.23.

Farfalle Arrabbiata	Week 1		Week 1	
Week of 3/1–3/7, 2XXX	Budget		Actual	
Restaurant Profit Before Taxes	$ 2,696	6.09%	$ 1,938	4.80%

FIGURE 18.23   Profit/Loss Line.

A profit standard can be in the form of dollars or percentage of sales. Assume that the standard for Farfalle Arrabbiata is 6%. Clearly, this week is not up to standard. Note that this step is simply to look at overall profit. Analysis in the next steps should uncover why the profit was lower than budgeted.

Step 2. Assess the Performance of Income Statement Categories
In this step, the charge is to analyze the overall performance of income, expenses, and profit as a *category* or *group*. We will consider Total Sales, Total Cost of Food, Total Cost of Beverage, Total Controllable Expenses, and Total Occupation Costs.

Total Sales   Figure 18.24 shows the sales results.

Week of 3/1–3/7 2XXX	Budget		Actual	
Sales				
Food	$35,421	80.00%	$33,245	82.33%
Beverage	8,855	20.00	7,135	17.67
Total Sales	$44,276	100.00%	$40,380	100.00%

FIGURE 18.24   Budgeted and Actual Total Sales.

Sales this week are not at forecast levels. Notes for the week should explain any unforeseen events that have contributed to this result—weather, cancellations, road construction, and so on. These notes alone may explain the difference. In addition to the overall sales level, the sales mix—food and beverage sales—must also be assessed. This week, it appears that the sales composition has shifted slightly. Is this of concern to management? Why or why not?

Week of 3/1–3/7 2XXX	Budget		Actual	
Total Cost of Food	$11,901	33.60%	$10,871	32.70%
Total Cost of Beverage	2,268	25.61	1,901	26.65
Total Cost of Goods	$14,169	32.00%	$12,773	31.63%

FIGURE 18.25   Cost of Food, Beverage, and Total Cost of Goods Variance.

Before these items (Figure 18.25) can be analyzed, the following question must be answered: What kind of cost is this? The kind of cost (variable or fixed) dictates exactly what it is (% or $) that you must look at in order to determine whether or not Chef Raoul had a "good" cost week. The cost behavior information in Figure 18.26 will assist with answering this question.

Cost Category	Classification	Is It a % or $$?	Sales	Cost $$	Cost %
Cost of Goods (Controllable)	Variable	%	Up Down	Increase Decrease	Same Same
Controllable Expenses (Controllable)	Variable	%	Up Down	Increase Decrease	Same Same
Occupation Costs (Noncontrollable)	Fixed Cost	$$	Up Down	Same Same	Decreases Increases

FIGURE 18.26   Cost Behavior.

Analysis of Food Cost Variance   As you can see by Figure 18.26 Cost of Goods (Food and Beverage Cost) is a variable cost, so *we must assess the food cost percentage and not the actual dollars spent.*

Food Cost Variance				
Week of 3/1–3/7 2XXX	**Budget**		**Actual**	
Total Cost of Food	$11,901	**33.60%**	$10,871	**32.70%**

Here is a summary of the analysis:

- The **standard** food cost percentage is 33.6%.
- The **actual** food cost percentage is at 32.7%
- The standard degree of variance is +/− 0.5%.
- The degree of variance is −0.9% (33.6% − 32.7%).

How did Chef Raoul do this week? This week, he is under budget on food by 0.9%. Some would say this was a "GOOD" cost week. Chef Raoul actually spent *less* than his plan. Is this a good thing or a bad thing? Why should the Chef be questioned about this? What are some of the ways he may have been able to save money on food this week? Read the discussion on food cost in Chapter 10.

Analysis of Beverage Cost Variance   The Beverage Cost category shows some serious issues. Here are the details:

Beverage Cost Variance				
Week of 3/1–3/7 2XXX	**Budget**		**Actual**	
Total Cost of Beverage	$2,268	**25.61%**	$1,901	**26.65%**

- The **standard** cost percentage is 25.61%.
- The **actual** cost percentage is 26.65%.
- The standard degree of variance is +/− 0.5%.
- The degree of variance is +1.04% (26.65% − 25.61%).

As a manager, red flags should be flying everywhere. There is a major cost problem that must be fixed. How is this cost problem combined with the sales mix shift contributing to the profit problem? See Chapter 13 for ideas on controlling beverage cost.

Analysis of Total Cost of Goods Variance   As a whole, Total Cost of Goods is performing better than expected (Figure 18.27):

Week of 3/1–3/7 2XXX	Budget		Actual	
Total Cost of Goods	$14,169	32.00%	$12,773	31.63%

FIGURE 18.27   Total Cost of Goods Variance.

- The **standard** cost percentage is 32.00%.
- The **actual** cost percentage is 31.63%.
- The standard degree of variance is +/− 0.5%.
- The degree of variance is −0.37% (32.00% − 31.63%).

Because the degree of variance is less than 0.5%, Chef Raoul would be satisfied that *as a group*, the Cost of Goods part of the income statement is in line with the budget.

Controllable Expenses   For this example, Controllable Expenses will be evaluated as though they were a completely variable cost (Figure 18.28). This means that the cost percentage is the criteria with which to evaluate. This week's results show the following:

Week of 3/1–3/7 2XXX	Budget		Actual	
Total Controllable Expenses	$21,252	48.00%	$19,512	48.32%

FIGURE 18.28   Controllable Expenses Variance.

- The **standard cost percentage** is 48%.
- The **actual cost percentage** is 48.32%
- The standard degree of variance is +/− 0.5%.
- The degree of variance is +0.32% (48.32% − 48%).

According to the standard for Farfalle Arrabbiata, this is not a concern. This category is within the 0.5% acceptable degree of tolerance for a variance.

Occupation Costs   What kind of cost is this? Occupation costs are **fixed costs**. Use Figure 18.29 to determine what to look at to make an assessment.

Week of 3/1–3/7 2XXX	Budget		Actual	
Occupation Costs	$ 6,158	13.91%	$ 6,158	15.25%

FIGURE 18.29   Occupation Costs Variance.

The evaluative criteria are the dollars actually spent. In this case, the budgeted dollars and the actual dollars are the same. What has happened to the cost percentage? It has behaved as a fixed cost percentage behaves—it has increased. Why? The result seen here is directly attributable to the poor sales for the week versus a lack of control over the expense. Because fixed costs are noncontrollable from a cost perspective, there is nothing management can do about this result.

Step 3 Assess the Performance of Line Items   The next step is to look directly at individual line items using the same process as described in Steps 2 and 3. To assist with this, the Income Statement has been reproduced in Figure 18.30, and several columns have been added:

- A column identifying what to check
- A column for recording the amount of difference
- A column to record the result. An "A" notation means the difference is acceptable. A "U" notation means the difference is unacceptable.

Complete the chart. The Sales and Cost of Goods section are complete as an example of how to record the results. Notice that the Controllable Expenses have both a percentage and a dollar symbol as the analysis factor. This is to recognize the fact that these expenses are **mixed costs**—*they are made up of both variable and fixed costs.* Management knows the ratio of fixed dollars to variable dollars in each line item. Any cost with a greater amount of fixed to variable dollars would have to be assessed differently. Management will know if changes in a line item are attributable to a fixed portion of the cost and if this change is causing the result. For the purposes of this exercise, assume the percentage is the evaluative criteria.

Line by line, it is easy to pick out which expenses are causing the problem. The next step is to find out why. The answer to WHY must be framed in the context of internal and external environments.

Step 4 and 5 Determine the Reason(s) for the Results and Take Corrective Action
Chapter 10 addressed the concept of identifying whether a result was caused by something within management's control or something external to it. In that chapter, internal causes were identified as "fixable." To fix the problem, management had to refer to the Operating Cycle of Control and do one of the following:

- Enforce an existing standard or standard operating procedure that has been overlooked

or,

- Create a new standard or standard operating procedure to address the problem (something is missing within the existing system)

When results are caused by something external to the operation, fixing the problem is more complex. Only management knows whether a storm or a business closure has hurt sales, the cost of certain food products are unusually high because of bad weather conditions or some external problem, fuel prices have spiked, or any number of other factors could have affected sales. It is management's responsibility to monitor external environments to reduce the impact of these kinds of incidents. The manager's mantra should be "No surprises!"

Identifying the Trouble Spots on This Statement   First, each problem has to be categorized as an internal or external issue. Internal issues are "fixable"; external issues have to be managed differently if the cause is deemed long term or permanent. The following is a summary of the trouble spots identified by the Common Size Analysis:

1. Sales are under budget.
2. Food Cost is under budget.
3. Beverage Cost is over budget.
4. Controllable Expenses as a whole are slightly over budget. There are troublesome line items that need to be addressed.
5. The Occupation Cost Percentage is out of line, but the dollars are in line. The problem is attributable primarily to lower than expected sales.
6. Line items: Make a list of any line item(s) that are troublesome.

Farfalle Arrabbiata	Week 1		Week 1		Is It a % or $$?	Change	Acceptable (A) or (U) Unacceptable
Week of 3/1–3/7 2XXX	Budget		Actual				
Sales							
Food	$35,421	80.00%	$33,245	82.33%	%,$	2.33%	U
Beverage	8,855	20.00	7,135	17.67	%,$	2.33	U
Total Sales	44,276	100.00	40,380	100.00		($3,896)	U
Cost of sales							
Food Cost							
Meat	2,905	8.20	2,630	7.91	%	.29	A
Poultry	1,842	5.20	1,872	5.63	%	.43	A
Fish & Shellfish	1,559	4.40	1,423	4.28	%	.12	A
Produce	1,771	5.00	1,559	4.69	%	.31	A
Dairy	1,098	3.10	1,041	3.13	%	.03	A
Baked	425	1.20	332	1.00	%	.2	A
Grocery	1,381	3.90	1,184	3.56	%	.34	A
Other	921	2.60	831	2.50	%	.1	A
Total Cost of Food	11,901		10,871	32.70	%	.9	U
Beverage Cost							
Beer	496	5.60	449	6.29	%	.69	U
Wine	824	9.30	649	9.10	%	.2	U
Spirits	576	6.50	490	6.87	%	.37	A
Other	373	4.21	313	4.39	%	.18	A
Total Cost of Beverage	2,268	25.61	1,901	26.65	%	1.04	U
Total Cost of Goods	14,169	32.00	12,773	31.63	%	.37	A
Gross Profit	30,107	68.00	27,607	68.37	%	.37	A
Controllable Expenses							
Payroll	13,106	29.60	11,654	28.86	$,%		
Employee Benefits	1,992	4.50	1,817	4.50	$,%		
Direct Operating Expenses	1,505	3.40	1,664	4.12	$,%		
Music & Entertainment	221	0.50	202	0.50	$,%		
Advertising & Promotion	1,107	2.50	800	1.98	$,%		
Utilities	1,638	3.70	1,692	4.19	$,%		
Administration & General	1,063	2.40	1,119	2.77	$,%		
Repair & Maintenance	620	1.40	565	1.40	$,%		
Total Controllable Expenses	21,252	48.00	19,512	48.32	$,%		
Income B4 Occupation Costs	8,854	20.00	8,096	20.05	%		
Occupation Costs							
Rent	2,639	5.96	2,639	6.54	$		
Property Tax	792	1.79	792	1.96	$		
Other Taxes	375	0.85	375	0.93	$		
Property Insurance	458	1.03	458	1.13	$		
Interest	688	1.55	688	1.70	$		
Depreciation	1,206	2.72	1,206	2.99	$		
Total Occupation Costs	6,158	13.91	6,158	15.25	$		
Restaurant Profit B4 Taxes	$2,696	6.09%	$1,938	4.80%	$,%		

FIGURE 18.30 Income Statement with Difference and Analysis.

The fun part of analyzing is realizing that the income statement really tells a story about what happened. Although line items may appear unrelated, they are not. Look closely at the findings. Are there any results in the analysis of the line items in the cost categories that could have contributed to the sales problem? What do you notice about Payroll? Advertising? Could there be any connection?

Problem Area	How to Fix the Problem
Sales	Increase the number of guests.
	Increase the overall sales.
	Increase average check.
	Increase menu prices.
Expenses	Increase sales.
	Increase average check.
	Increase menu prices.
	Decrease expenses.
Profit	Increase sales.
	Decrease expenses.
	Increase sales while decreasing expenses.
	Increase average check.

Congratulations! You have just completed a Common Size Analysis of the sales and expenses for this week.

Completing a Comparative Analysis

A comparative analysis is a different form of analysis. It compares the figures on one financial statement with the same figures on a statement from a base period. It is a helpful tool to detect trends in income, expenses, profit, and line items over time. By showing changes in percentages from year to year, it is easy to see how the numbers are affecting the business. This form of analysis is commonly used with income statements and with balance sheets.

To do a comparative analysis, the information from the base period is listed next to the period under consideration, for comparison. The variance dollars are recorded, and the percentage of change is calculated. The March income statement for Farfalle Arrabbiata will again be used to demonstrate this process.

To calculate the budget variance percentage for sales, actual results are subtracted from budgeted dollars. This difference is divided by the budgeted dollars. To calculate the budget variance percentage for expenses, the budgeted dollars are subtracted from the actual results. The difference is divided by the budgeted dollars. In this form of analysis, each line item is treated separately.

Budget $$ − Actual $$ = Variance $$ (+/−)			
Farfalle Arrabbiata	**Week 1**	**Week 1**	**Variance Dollars**
Week of 3/1–3/7 2XXX	Budget	Actual	$$
Sales			
Food	$35,421	$33,245	($2,176)
Beverage	$ 8,855	$ 7,135	($1,720)
Total Sales	$44,276	$40,380	($3,896)
	A	− B	= C

To calculate the **variance percentage**, divide the variance dollars by the *budget* dollars. Unlike in a common size analysis, the percentages of one line item are not related to the percentages of any other line item because a common divisor is not used to compute these percentages.

$$\text{VARIANCE DOLLARS/BUDGET DOLLARS} = \text{VARIANCE \%}$$
$$(\$2,176)/\$35,421 = (6.14\%)$$

Farfalle Arrabbiata	Variance Dollars	Week 1 Budget	Variance Percentage
Week of 3/1–3/7 2XXX	$$		%%
Sales			
Food	($2,176)	$35,421	(6.14%)
Beverage	($1,720)	$ 8,855	(19.42%)
Total Sales	($3,896)	$44,276	(8.80%)
	A	/ B =	C

TO CALCULATE VARIANCE PERCENTAGE

Expense Variance

$$\text{Budgeted Dollars} - \text{Actual Dollars} = \text{Variance \$\$}$$
$$\text{Variance \$\$/Budget Dollars} = \text{Variance \%}$$

Sales Variance

$$\text{Actual Dollars} - \text{Budget Dollars} = \text{Variance \$\$}$$
$$\text{Variance \$\$/Budget \$\$} = \text{Variance \%}$$

Figure 18.31 shows a complete comparative analysis of the March budget for Farfalle Arrabbiata.

A **favorable variance** *is when actual sales exceed budgeted sales, when actual expenses are less than budget to the degree of variance that is acceptable, and when profit exceeds budget.* An **unfavorable variance** *is when actual sales are less than budget, when actual expenses exceed budget, and profit is less than expected.* As we have learned, from a cost-savings point of view, extreme variances from budget are not necessarily "good." They are only "good" if the results seen were achieved through excellence in operations and not as an attempt to cheat the customer or the operation.

What Does the Analysis Reveal About This Week? Use the definitions in Figure 18.32 to analyze the results:

1. ***Sales:* Unfavorable Variance** Food sales are down 6.14%. Beverage sales are down 19.42%. Overall, sales for the week are off by 8.8%.
2. ***Cost of Goods:* Favorable Variance** Overall, food cost was well below budget. Common size analysis told us this was not good. Comparative analysis tells us it is good. So which is it? From a cost perspective, it is a good thing. From a standards perspective, it could signal a problem. As stated previously, *as long as costs are down for good reasons, such as tight operating controls or better purchasing prices, then this is an indication that management is doing its job.* It may mean, however, that the standard should be adjusted to better reflect the proportion of the budget it really takes to fund the expense.

Farfalle Arrabbiata	Week 1		Week 1		Over (Under) Budget	Over (Under) Budget	Favorable (F) or (U) Unfavorable
Week of 3/1–3/7 2XXX	Budget		Actual		$$	%	
Sales							
Food	$35,421	80.00%	$33,245	82.33%	($2,176)	(6.14%)	U
Beverage	8,855	20.00	7,135	17.67	($1,720)	(19.42%)	U
Total Sales	44,276	100.00	40,380	100.00	(3,896)	(8.80%)	U
Cost of Sales							
Food Cost							
Meat	2,905	8.20	2,630	7.91	($275)	(9.47%)	F
Poultry	1,842	5.20	1,872	5.63	$30	1.63%	U
Fish/Shellfish	1,559	4.40	1,423	4.28	($136)	(8.72%)	F
Produce	1,771	5.00	1,559	4.69	($212)	(11.97%)	F
Dairy	1,098	3.10	1,041	3.13	($58)	(5.28%)	F
Baked	425	1.20	332	1.00	($93)	(21.88%)	F
Grocery	1,381	3.90	1,184	3.56	($197)	(14.27%)	F
Other	921	2.60	831	2.50	($90)	(9.77%)	F
Total Cost of Food	11,901	33.60	10,871	32.70	($1,031)	(8.66%)	F
Beverage Cost							
Beer	496	5.60	449	6.29	($47)	(9.48%)	F
Wine	824	9.30	649	9.10	($175)	(21.24%)	F
Spirits	576	6.50	490	6.87	($86)	(14.93%)	F
Other	373	4.21	313	4.39	($60)	(16.09%)	F
Total Cost of Beverage	2,268	25.61	1,901	26.65	($367)	(16.18%)	F
Total Cost of Goods	14,169	32.00	12,773	31.63	($1,397)	(9.86%)	F
Gross Profit	30,107	68.00	27,607	68.37	($2,499)	(8.30%)	F
Controllable Expenses							
Payroll	13,106	29.60	11,654	28.86	($1,452)	(11.08%)	F
Employee Benefits	1,992	4.50	1,817	4.50	($175)	(8.79%)	F
Direct Operating Expenses	1,505	3.40	1,664	4.12	$159	10.56%	U
Music & Entertainment	221	0.50	202	0.50	($19)	(8.60%)	F
Advertising & Promotion	1,107	2.50	800	1.98	($307)	(27.73%)	F
Utilities	1,638	3.70	1,692	4.19	$54	3.30%	U
Administration & General	1,063	2.40	1,119	2.77	$56	5.27%	U
Repair & Maintenance	620	1.40	565	1.40	($55)	(8.87%)	F
Total Controllable Expenses	21,252	48.00	19,512	48.32	($1,740)	(8.19%)	F
Income B4 Occupation Costs	8,854	20.00	8,096	20.05	($758)	(8.56%)	F
Occupation Costs							
Rent	2,639	5.96	2,639	6.54	$0	0.00%	F
Property Tax	792	1.79	792	1.96	$0	0.00%	F
Other Taxes	375	0.85	375	0.93	$0	0.00%	F
Property Insurance	458	1.03	458	1.13	$0	0.00%	F
Interest	688	1.55	688	1.70	$0	0.00%	F
Depreciation	1,206	2.72	1,206	2.99	$0	0.00%	F
Total Occupation Costs	6,158	13.91	6,158	15.25	$0	0.00%	F
Restaurant Profit B4 Taxes	$ 2,696	6.09%	$ 1,938	4.80%	($758)	(28.12%)	U

FIGURE 18.31 Comparative Analysis of the March Budget for Farfalle Arrabbiata.

Variance Analysis		
Favorable Variances	=	Actual sales exceed budget sales.
		Actual expenses are lower than budget (with caution). Profit is more than expected.
Unfavorable Variances	=	Actual sales are less than budget sales. Actual expenses are higher than budget. Profit is less than expected.

FIGURE 18.32   Analysis of Variance.

3. **Controllable Expenses: Favorable Variance**   There are three expenses with unfavorable variances—Utilities, Administrative & General, and Direct Operating Costs. To pinpoint the exact problem within these expenses, management would examine the **expense detail** to see, specifically, which components of the account are out of line. An expense detail is *a list of the cost of all the individual items covered under an expense.* All expenses have such a list.

   Because the remaining line items all show a favorable variance, the category, as a whole, is not a problem. Being under budget with Controllable Expenses is good, but with the same cautions as for Cost of Goods.

4. **Occupation Costs: Favorable Variance**   There is no change here. The budget and actual results are as expected.

5. **Profit: Unfavorable Variance**   This week, profit is not at expected levels. This is a result of a combination of events, as seen by the information on the Income Statement. Because this budget is for one week, management has time to analyze causes, isolate problems, and correct deficiencies before there is further erosion of the business.

Comparative and common size analysis can be done on a weekly, monthly, quarterly, and annual basis. The key to sales, cost, and profit analysis is timely information. Without it, businesses are at a loss to quickly zero in on specific problem area(s) and take timely corrective action. Managers are "blind" to exactly where the problems lie.

Net Work

Explore the following Web sites:

www.restaurant.org
www.restaurantowner.com
www.digitaldining.com
www.micros.com
www.yum.com

Chapter Wrap

The Chapter ✓ at the beginning of the chapter posed several questions. Review the questions and compare your responses with the following answers:

1. **Which basic operating statements measure performance?**

   The income statement, the balance sheet, and the cash flow statement are the three operating statements that measure performance. The income statement is a report of all income, expenses, and profit or loss for a defined period of time. It is the key financial statement used by managers to track income, expenses, and profit. Income statements measure the performance of a company for periods of time. The balance sheet reports the financial position of a company. It is a record of the assets, liabilities, and equity of an operation for a specific period of time. The balance sheet is not used in day-to-day operations. It is a tool used by executives, investors, or creditors to assist with business decisions about an operation. The cash flow statement is the third operating document used to measure the financial health of an operation. It reports cash receipts and disbursements. It is prepared for the same period of time as the income statement. Of these three financial statements, the income statement is the report a manager immediately goes to when asking the question "How are we performing?"

2. **What are the components of an income statement?**

Sales, Cost of Goods, Controllable Expenses, Occupation Costs, and Profit or Loss are the components of an income statement. Sales reports income earned from all revenue centers. Cost of Goods reports all product costs incurred by each revenue center. Controllable Expenses are all other operating costs directly related to generating sales. Occupation Costs are all other non-operating costs. Profit or Loss reports income left for the reporting period.

3. **What is a variable cost? A fixed cost? A mixed cost?**

A variable cost is a cost that fluctuates or changes with sales. A fixed cost is fixed for a period of time. It is a cost that has no linear relationship to sales. A mixed cost is a cost that has characteristics of both variable and fixed costs: Some proportion of the cost is linked to sales behavior; the other part is not.

4. **What is a variance?**

A variance is a deviation from a standard. When variances are labeled *acceptable*, it means that the difference between budget and actual is insignificant—it is not enough to worry about, and no action is required. Each operation sets the percentage of variance that is considered acceptable. Variances exceeding this standard are labeled *unacceptable* and call for immediate analysis and action. When unacceptable variances are identified, management is charged with pinpointing the problem and fixing it.

5. **What is a common size analysis?**

A common size analysis involves analyzing the variance between budget and actual results. The percentage column on the income statement is the source of this information. Variances are termed *acceptable* or *unacceptable*.

6. **What is a comparative analysis?**

A comparative analysis involves calculating the variance dollars between budget and actual and converting this difference into a percentage. These variances are termed *favorable* or *unfavorable* and are the subject of analysis.

Key Terminology and Concepts in This Chapter

Acceptable variance	Cost percentage
Actual budget	Declining balance budget
Actual cost percentage	Departmental budget
Balance sheet	Expense detail
Beverage cost	Expenses
Beverage cost percentage	Favorable variances
Beverage sales	Fixed cost
Cash flow statement	Food category popularity percentage
Common size analysis	Food cost
Comparative analysis	Gross profit
Controllable Expenses (costs)	Income statement
Cost of goods	Labor cost percentage

Master budget

Mixed controllable cost

Mixed cost

Noncontrollable costs

Nonoperating costs

Occupation costs

Operating costs

Payroll

Prime costs

Revenue

Sales

Sales mix

Sales per operating period

Standard cost percentage

Unacceptable variances

Unfavorable variances

Variable costs

Variance

Variance percentage

Working budgets

$\mathcal{D}$iscussion Questions and Exercises

1. After studying this chapter, what is it about the Income Statement that makes it more useful to a manager or chef than a Balance Sheet or Cash Flow Statement?

2. Which budget operating period(s) is(are) most useful to a manager for day-to-day operations?

3. Define each type of cost. Explain the characteristics of each. Use terminology and definitions included in the chapter.

4. Why is it important to understand the difference between fixed, mixed, and variable costs? Design an example to explain your answer.

5. Explain how changes in the sales mix can positively or negatively affect profit. Provide an example to explain your answer.

6. If sales are greater than forecast, what should happen to the food cost dollars? Explain this phenomenon. As long as all other budget items remain on target, what would happen to profit if sales increased?

7. If sales are less than forecast, what should happen to the occupation costs? Explain why. If all other budget items remain on target, what would happen to profit if sales decreased? Why?

8. Create an income statement of your finances using the concepts of variable, mixed, and fixed costs using the following form. Categorize your expenses as best you can into one of the three categories shown, based on the descriptions in the chapter. Determine your profit or loss. Determine your cost percentages.

Income Sources

Work: _____

Mom & Dad: _____

Other Sources: _____   **Cost %:**

Variable Expenses:

Controllable Expenses:

Fixed Expenses:

Profit or Loss:

9. Create a pie chart of your expense categories and profit or loss.

10. You have just struck it rich—your income is going to double as of next month. Determine the new cost percentages. Create a new pie chart of your expense categories and profit.

11. Oh no! You have just lost your job or some significant portion of your income—your income will be cut in half. Recreate your expense and profit picture now. What do your cost percentages look like?

 12. Perform a comparative analysis for the results of this period. Summarize your findings in a report to the general manager (GM).

Farfalle Arrabbiata Week of 4/1			Over (Under) Budget	Over (Under) Budget	Favorable (F) or Unfavorable (U)
Sales	Budget	Actual	$$	%%	
Food	$36,718	$ 37,267			
Beverage	9,180	7,525			
Total Sales	45,898	44,792			
Cost of Sales					
Food Cost					
Meat	3,011	3,253			
Poultry	1,909	1,908			
Fish & Shellfish	1,616	1,569			
Produce	1,836	2,001			
Dairy	1,138	1,077			
Baked	441	544			
Grocery	1,432	1,532			
Other	955	839			
Total Cost of Food	12,337	12,723			
Beverage Cost					
Beer	514	401			
Wine	854	695			
Spirits	597	535			
Other	386	336			
Total Cost of Beverage	2,351	1,967			
Total Cost of Goods	14,688	14,690			
Gross Profit	31,210	30,102			
Controllable Expenses					
Payroll	13,586	12,636			
Employee Benefits	2,065	2,137			
Direct Operating Expenses	1,561	1,711			
Music & Entertainment	229	148			
Advertising & Promotion	1,147	1,205			
Utilities	1,698	1,492			
Administration & General	1,102	1,133			
Repair & Maintenance	643	735			
Total Controllable Expenses	22,031	21,196			
Income B4 Occupation Costs	9,179	8,906			
Occupation Costs					
Rent	2,639	2,639			
Property Tax	792	792			
Other Taxes	375	375			
Property Insurance	458	458			
Interest	688	688			
Depreciation	1,206	1,206			
Total Occupational Costs	6,158	6,158			
Restaurant Profit B4 Taxes	$ 3,021	$ 2,748			

13. Using the following form, calculate the cost percentages for the actual results, and perform a common size analysis for this period. Summarize your findings in a report to the GM.

Common Size Analysis Week of 4/1 Sales	Budget		Actual	Cost %	Is It a % or $$	Amount of Change	Acceptable (A) Unacceptable (U)
Food	$36,718	80.00%	$37,267		%,$		
Beverage	9,180	20.00	7,525		%,$		
Total Sales	45,898	100.00	44,792				
Cost of Sales							
Food Cost							
Meat	3,011	8.20	3,253		%		
Poultry	1,909	5.20	1,908		%		
Fish & Shellfish	1,616	4.40	1,569		%		
Produce	1,836	5.00	2,001		%		
Dairy	1,138	3.10	1,077		%		
Baked	441	1.20	544		%		
Grocery	1,432	3.90	1,532		%		
Other	955	2.60	839		%		
Total Cost of Food	**12,337**	**33.60**	**12,723**		%		
Beverage Cost							
Beer	514	5.60	401		%		
Wine	854	9.30	695		%		
Spirits	597	6.50	535		%		
Other	386	4.21	336		%		
Total Beverage Cost	**2,351**	**25.61**	**1,967**		%		
Total Cost of Goods	**14,688**	**32.00**	**14,690**		%		
Gross Profit	**31,210**	**68.00**	**30,102**		%		
Controllable Expenses							
Payroll	13,586	29.60	12,636		$,%		
Employee Benefits	2,065	4.50	2,137		$,%		
Direct Operating Expenses	1,561	3.40	1,711		$,%		
Music & Entertainment	229	0.50	148		$,%		
Advertising & Promotion	1,147	2.50	1,205		$,%		
Utilities	1,698	3.70	1,492		$,%		
Administration & General	1,102	2.40	1,133		$,%		
Repair & Maintenance	643	1.40	735		$,%		
Total Controllable Expenses	**22,031**	**48.00**	**21,196**		$,%		
Income Before Occupation Costs	**9,179**	**20.00**	**8,906**				
Occupation Costs							
Rent	2,639	5.75	2,639		$		
Property Tax	792	1.73	792		$		
Other Taxes	375	0.82	375		$		
Property Insurance	458	1.00	458		$		
Interest	688	1.50	688		$		
Depreciation	1,206	2.63	1,206		$		
Total Occupational Costs	**6,158**	**13.42**	**6,158**		$		
Restaurant Profit Before Taxes	**$ 3,021**	**6.58**	**2,748**		$,%		

Chapter Nineteen

About Preparing Income Statements

Chapter Objective

To prepare income statements for future operating periods by studying a business's history, current results, and internal and external environments.

Learning Objectives

After reading this chapter and completing the discussion questions and exercises, you should be able to:

1. Organize sales history into meaningful formats.
2. Evaluate information from sales history, current operating results, and research.
3. Formulate assumptions for future budget periods.
4. Use assumptions to prepare a budget for a future operating period.
5. Develop an income statement for a new operation.

The Menu

Pre-Purchase Functions

GUEST CHECK
Sales history, turnover, **average check,** cash management, revenue forecasting & budgeting, **menu item analysis**

STANDARDIZED RECIPES
Standard ingredients, portion size, quality, consistency, quantity, purchasing

COST CARDS
Portion costs, yield factors, **sell prices**

SPECIFICATIONS
Product descriptions

GUESTS
Greeting, seating, **sales,** serving, busing, payment, comment cards

PAR STOCK
Inventory levels, order building

FOH Functions

KITCHEN PRODUCTION
Production schedules, portion tracking, recipe control, serving controls, food safety

REQUISITION
Order building, purchasing

PRODUCT ISSUING
Requisitions, transfers, daily & monthly costs, food cost percentage

SHOPPING LISTS
Call sheets, bid sheets, suppliers, bidding

STORAGE PRACTICES & INVENTORY MANAGEMENT
Best practices, sanitation, security, inventory methods

PURCHASE ORDERS
Security, ship order, price guarantee, contract

INVOICE MANAGEMENT
Payment, price checking, security

BOH Functions

RECEIVING ACTIVITIES
Best practices, invoices, security, sanitation

Chapter Map

About Preparing Income Statements

- Future Budgets & the Crystal Ball
- Using the Crystal Ball

539

Chapter Map   (Continued)

Studying & Analyzing Current Sales, Expense & Profit History

- Sales per Operating Period:
- Expense and Profit History
- Prime Costs
- Average Check

Studying & Analyzing Current Sales, Expense, & Profit Patterns

- Sales per Operating Period:
- Current Expense & Profit
- Prime Costs

Researching Internal & External Variables for the Next Budget Period

- Studying Financial Notes About the Current Operating Period

- Researching Internal & External Environments for the Next Operating Period
- The Effect of Changes in Internal & External Environments

Developing Assumptions About Sales, Expenses, & Profit, or, Let's Take Out the Crystal Ball

- Converting Assumptions Into Budget Figures

Using Assumptions to Create a Budget Plan

- Sales
- Cost of Goods & Controllable Expenses
- Occupation Costs
- Proposed Solutions

Calculating Revenue Using Other Operating Information

Chapter ✓

Check the chapter content for the answers to these questions:

1. What steps are needed to prepare budgets for future periods?
2. How are sales, expense, and profit history used to prepare budgets for future periods?
3. What are assumptions?
4. How are assumptions used to develop budgets for future operating periods?

About Preparing Income Statements

It's quite likely that at some time in your career you will be called on to prepare a budget for your department or business. Chapter 10 and 18 covered basic income statement concepts and the process of organizing and analyzing income, expense, and profit data. This chapter will refer frequently to that work, as it is applied to developing budgets for future operating periods.

Future Budgets and the Crystal Ball

Gathering and making sense of all the information needed to prepare a financial plan for a future operating period is an ominous task. It's like peering into a crystal ball to see what the future holds. Sometimes, the picture inside the ball is fuzzy and distorted;

the message is difficult to understand. At other times, the picture is crystal clear and easy to interpret.

Using the Crystal Ball

Just imagine that you are the newly hired general manager (GM) at a very high profile restaurant. You have been charged with preparing the budget for the next operating period. This financial plan will chart the financial course for the operation for the next year. Although you have little or no experience with this particular restaurant, you do have experience in the foodservice business. The crystal ball is at your disposal to aid you with this task. There is one catch, however: You can only ask three questions of the crystal ball. What will they be? How about:

- What has happened to sales, expenses, and profit in the past?
- What is happening to sales, expenses, and profit right now?
- How will internal and external factors affect this business?

Now there is a very strong chance that you will not be able to rely on a crystal ball to plot the future course of a business. More than likely, you will rely on many of the tools already covered in this text. Let's put the process into more "professional" language and answer those crystal ball questions.

Crystal Ball Question	Crystal Ball Answer
What has happened to sales, expenses, and profit in the past?	• Study and analyze sales, expense, and profit history.
What is happening right now to sales, expenses, and profit?	• Study and analyze current sales, expense, and profit patterns.
What internal and external factors will affect this business?	• Research internal and external environments.
	• Develop assumptions about sales, expenses, and profit.
	• Create a budget plan.

Hopefully, this does not sound all that new to you. Review Chapter 10 and 18, and you will see a similar process. The difference here, though, is in the scope. Earlier work was one-dimensional; it focused mainly on day-to-day life in a foodservice operation. The work of this chapter is of a higher order—it has a broader perspective. Here we study the global picture—history, internal, and external environments—to get a sense of what the next period might hold.

The following material presents the financial results (income, expenses, and profit) for Farfalle Arrabbiata. You will be prompted to record notes and questions about the data. Next, you will be called on to research internal and external conditions that could affect the business. By the end of this chapter, Farfalle Arrabbiata will have a financial plan for the following year.

STEPS TO USE TO PREPARE BUDGETS FOR FUTURE PERIODS
1. **Study and analyze sales, expense, and profit histories.**
2. Study and analyze current sales, expense, and profit patterns.
3. Research internal and external variables for the next budget period.
4. Develop assumptions about sales, expenses, and profit.
5. Use assumptions to create a budget plan.

Studying and Analyzing Sales, Expense, and Profit History

Studying and analyzing financial history is not a new concept. In order to prepare budgets, however, the work needs to be expanded to include not only sales history, but expense and profit history as well. Here, the discussion will start with sales history. Because there are many ways to collect and arrange this data, you will see a variety of methods displayed. Some of these arrangements are used more frequently in daily planning (monthly, weekly, daily, shift), whereas others lend themselves more to long-range budget planning (annual, semiannual, quarterly, monthly). For this reason, the figures in this section will present examples of sales history for annual, semiannual, quarterly, and monthly operating periods only. The next section, Studying and Analyzing Current Sales, Expense, and Profit Patterns, will demonstrate examples of monthly, weekly, and daily history. As a foodservice manager, all of these arrangements are important in order to understand the answer to the question "How are we performing?"

The most common ways to collect and study current and historical sales, expense, and profit data are by

- Sales, expenses, and profit per operating period: annual, biannual, quarterly, monthly.
- Average check.
- Average sales per seat.

ORGANIZING HISTORIC SALES, EXPENSE, AND PROFIT DATA

- **Sales, expenses, and profit per operating period: annual, semiannual, quarterly, monthly**
- **Average check**
- **Average sales per seat**

Sales per Operating Period: Annual Statements (Historical Picture)

Tracking multiple years of sales data reveals an even clearer picture of sales, expense, and profit patterns than does just looking at the current year. Businesses with a long history have the benefit of multiple years of data to use in their planning. Figure 19.1 shows annual sales, expense, and profit figures for three consecutive years. Both the budgeted and the actual figures for the third year are included. In addition to the figures, side notes were kept during these years; they tell the story or reasons—good and bad—behind the **actual results**.

Chapter 18 covered both common size analysis and comparative analysis. Week to week and month to month, the management team would have performed these analyses and recorded notes about that period's results and the corrective actions taken in response to problem areas identified through the analysis. These records should also include whether the action worked. Managers working on next year's budget have access to this information or know first hand the month-to-month picture and accumulated picture. He or she should also perform either or both analyses on these annual statements.

Sales per Operating Period: Annual, Semiannual, Quarterly, and Monthly

The first organization of sales data is simply **annual sales**. This is the *total sales for one year* for as many years as is desired or is available. This figure is commonly broken down into **semiannual** (*twice yearly*) and **quarterly figures (sales)** (*every three months*). **Monthly sales** are the next logical unit or breakdown. Figure 19.2 displays

	Year 1 (Actual)		Year 2 (Actual)		Year 3 (Actual)		Year 3 (Budget)	
Sales								
Food	$1,603,138	82.00%	$1,671,550	80.00%	$1,688,919	80.00%	$1,654,496	78.00%
Beverage	351,909	18.00	417,887	20.00	422,230	20.00	466,653	22.00
Total Sales	**1,955,047**	**100.00**	**2,089,437**	**100.00**	**2,111,149**	**100.00**	**2,121,149**	**100.00**
Cost of Sales								
Food	525,829	32.80	561,641	33.60	570,855	33.80	555,911	33.60
Beverage	87,977	25.00	107,021	25.61	108,133	25.61	116,663	25.00
Total Cost of Sales	**613,807**	**31.40**	**668,662**	**32.00**	**678,988**	**32.16**	**672,574**	**31.71**
Gross Profit	**1,341,240**	**68.60**	**1,420,775**	**68.00**	**1,432,161**	**67.84**	**1,448,575**	**68.29**
Controllable Expenses								
Payroll	566,964	29.00	610,116	29.20	624,900	29.60	627,860	29.60
Employee Benefits	56,696	2.90	81,488	3.90	95,002	4.50	91,209	4.30
Direct Operating Expenses	87,977	4.50	71,041	3.40	71,779	3.40	72,119	3.40
Music & Entertainment	17,204	0.88	15,671	0.75	10,556	0.50	10,606	0.50
Advertising & Promotion	48,876	2.50	56,415	2.70	52,779	2.50	53,029	2.50
Utilities	58,651	3.00	76,264	3.65	78,113	3.70	78,483	3.70
Administration & General	41,056	2.10	52,236	2.50	50,668	2.40	50,908	2.40
Repair & Maintenance	29,326	1.50	39,699	1.90	29,556	1.40	29,696	1.40
Total Controllable Expenses	**906,751**	**46.38**	**1,002,930**	**48.00**	**1,013,352**	**48.00**	**1,013,909**	**47.80**
Income B4 Occupation Costs	**434,490**	**22.22**	**417,846**	**20.00**	**418,810**	**19.84**	**434,666**	**20.49**
Occupation Costs								
Rent	123,529	6.32	123,529	5.91	123,529	5.85	123,529	5.82
Property Tax	35,678	1.82	38,004	1.82	38,004	1.80	38,004	1.79
Other Taxes	17,654	0.90	17,869	0.86	18,000	0.85	18,000	0.85
Property Insurance	17,890	0.92	19,876	0.95	21,996	1.04	21,996	1.04
Interest	33,000	1.69	33,000	1.58	33,000	1.56	33,000	1.56
Depreciation	62,300	3.19	59,300	2.84	56,900	2.70	56,900	2.68
Total Occupation Costs	**290,051**	**14.84**	**291,578**	**13.95**	**291,429**	**13.80**	**291,429**	**13.74**
Restaurant Profit B4 Taxes	**$144,439**	**7.39%**	**$126,268**	**6.04%**	**$127,381**	**6.03%**	**$143,237**	**6.75%**

FIGURE 19.1   Annual sales, expense, and profit figures for three consecutive years.

Annual Sales for Farfalle Arrabbiata	Year 1 (Actual)	Year 2 (Actual)	Year 3 (Actual)	Year 3 (Budget)
Total Sales	$1,955,047	$2,089,437	$2,111,149	$2,121,149
Month	$$ Sales	$$ Sales	$$ Sales	$$ Sales
January	$142,327	$157,584	153,690	154,420
February	154,840	164,632	167,272	167,995
March	156,404	164,503	169,576	169,692
Quarter	453,571	486,719	490,538	492,107
April	149,952	163,930	161,904	178,177
May	164,224	172,932	177,439	159,061
June	115,543	126,892	124,729	129,602
Quarter	429,719	463,754	464,072	466,840
Jan.–June Total (6 Months)	$883,290	$950,473	$954,610	$958,947
July	119,453	125,402	129,087	128,991
August	104,204	115,760	112,470	113,057
September	195,505	212,609	210,900	212,115
Quarter	419,162	453,771	452,457	454,163
October	215,837	231,872	232,459	234,175
November	208,408	222,834	225,012	226,114
December	228,349	230,487	246,611	247,750
Quarter	652,594	685,193	704,082	708,039
July–Dec. Total (6 Months)	$1,071,756	$1,138,964	$1,156,539	$1,162,202

FIGURE 19.2 Three years of annual sales for Farfalle Arrabbiata by month, quarter, and half year.

each of these units through this progression, starting with Total Annual Sales. Because this is a historical picture, the data begins three years previous.

The outcome of this chapter is *to develop a budget for next year for Farfalle Arrabbiata*. Keep this in mind as you look at total sales, 6-month totals, and quarterly figures. Look for **business patterns**—the *periods that are busiest, slowest, and mixed*. It is important to identify each of these periods in the life of an organization as they factor into the budget plan. Some businesses may have relatively level business year round. Others may be seasonal, with extremely busy periods for a short period of time. Each operation has its own business pattern. Because this is the **historical** side of the sales picture, there is no need, at this time, to break sales down any further. Step 2 in preparing budgets for future periods covers that work.

Use the space that follows to develop some notes about your observations and knowledge of the sales history and sales pattern of Farfalle Arrabbiata.

SALES NOTES AND QUESTIONS

Expense & Profit History

Figure 19.3 shows the expense history for Farfalle Arrabbiata. As with sales, common size analysis and comparative analysis identify specific trouble spots, and written notes detail any unusual occurrences.

Sales	Year 1 (Actual)		Year 2 (Actual)		Year 3 (Actual)		Year 3 (Budget)	
Cost of Sales								
Food	$525,829	32.80%	$561,641	33.60%	$570,855	33.80%	$555,911	33.60%
Beverage	87,977	25.00	107,021	25.61	108,133	25.61	116,663	25.00
Total Cost of Sales	**$613,807**	**31.40%**	**$668,662**	**32.00%**	**$678,988**	**32.16%**	**$672,574**	**31.71%**
Controllable Expenses								
Payroll	$566,964	29.00%	$610,116	29.20%	$624,900	29.60%	$627,860	29.60%
Employee Benefits	56,696	2.90	81,488	3.90	95,002	4.50	91,209	4.30
Direct Operating Expenses	87,977	4.50	71,041	3.40	71,779	3.40	72,119	3.40
Music & Entertainment	17,204	0.88	15,671	0.75	10,556	0.50	10,606	0.50
Advertising & Promotion	48,876	2.50	56,415	2.70	52,779	2.50	53,029	2.50
Utilities	58,651	3.00	76,264	3.65	78,113	3.70	78,483	3.70
Administration & General	41,056	2.10	52,236	2.50	50,668	2.40	50,908	2.40
Repair & Maintenance	29,326	1.50	39,699	1.90	29,556	1.40	29,696	1.40
Total Controllable Expenses	**$906,751**	**46.38%**	**$1,002,930**	**48.00%**	**$1,013,352**	**48.00%**	**$1,013,909**	**47.80%**
Occupation Costs								
Rent	$123,529	6.32%	$123,529	5.91%	$123,529	5.85%	$123,529	5.82%
Property Tax	35,678	1.82	38,004	1.82	38,004	1.80	38,004	1.79
Other Taxes	17,654	0.90	17,869	0.86	18,000	0.85	18,000	0.85
Property Insurance	17,890	0.92	19,876	0.95	21,996	1.04	21,996	1.04
Interest	33,000	1.69	33,000	1.58	33,000	1.56	33,000	1.56
Depreciation	62,300	3.19	59,300	2.84	56,900	2.70	56,900	2.68
Total Occupation Costs	**$290,051**	**14.84%**	**$291,578**	**13.95%**	**$291,429**	**13.80%**	**$291,429**	**13.74%**
Restaurant Profit B4 Taxes	**$144,439**	**7.39%**	**$126,268**	**6.04%**	**$127,381**	**6.03%**	**$143,237**	**6.75%**

FIGURE 19.3 Expense History for Farfalle Arrabbiata.

Take notes about your observations of the cost patterns for each category and line item. Develop this information into a history. Use the common size analysis format to help with this job. (See Chapter 18.) Be sure to review cost behavior and classification information before starting your work. The key places to look are in the areas of operational control. Reference the Cycle of Control if you need to.

In Figure 19.4, pie charts of the expense categories shed a visual light on the **cost structure** for Farfalle Arrabbiata. Note the changes over the course of the three-year period. Although the changes are not dramatic, the slight shifting of the pie wedges results in a squeeze on the profit piece, as seen in the Year 3 Actual chart.

Prime Costs

In Chapter 1, **prime costs** were defined as *food cost, beverage cost, and labor cost (including benefits)*. One look at this list and we know that these are, in fact, the "Big Three"—the costs a foodservice operation spends most of its sales dollars on. If one applied the ABC inventory concept to costs, these costs, without a doubt, would be in

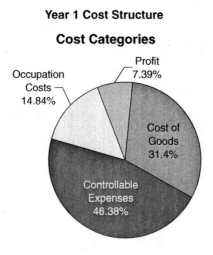

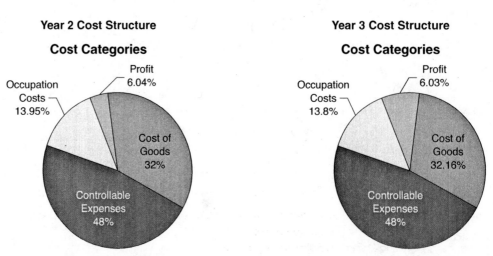

FIGURE 19.4   Cost structures for Year 1, Year 2, and Year 3.

	Year 1 (Actual)	Year 2 (Actual)	Year 3 (Actual)	Year 3 (Budget)
Total Cost of Sales	31.40%	32%	32.16%	31.71%
Payroll	29.00	29.20	29.60	29.60
Benefits	2.90	3.90	4.50	4.30
Totals	**63.3%**	**65.1%**	**66.2%**	**65.61%**

FIGURE 19.5   Prime costs for three years at Farfalle Arrabbiata.

the A category. In fact, most foodservice operations spend about 60% of their sales on these three expenses alone. This is a scary fact. As such, they, too, deserve a little bit of our attention from a budget perspective. Figure 19.5 shows three years of cost percentages for the prime costs for Farfalle Arrabbiata.

Historically, Prime Costs have been on the move—there has been a steady progression upward over the past three years. Consequently, the actual percentage for Year 3 is well off the budget—66.2% versus 65.61%. Review the information about costs, and record your own notes or questions about the results.

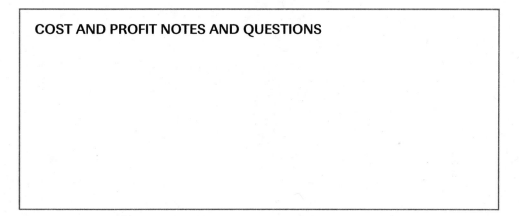

COST AND PROFIT NOTES AND QUESTIONS

The budget clearly shows that management's plan was to *reduce* operating costs (Controllable Expenses) and Cost of Goods slightly in Year 3, while increasing sales. However, the trend via the history shows a slow but steady climb of operating expenses and Cost of Goods. A close look at the expense detail for operating costs will reveal exactly which accounts caused the problems. Remember that operating costs are the invoices received every day for goods and services used to generate sales. These bills have to be paid. Suppliers will not keep sending product to businesses that don't pay their bills. The net result is seen in the decline in the profit percentage over the years. The plan for the Year 3 budget was to generate 6.75% profit. In order to achieve this goal, a combination of sales increases and cost decreases were needed. Although sales did increase from Year 1, the increase was not to the level expected. At the same time, expenses did not come in at budgeted levels. The result was 6.03% in profit—about the same profit percentage as in Year 2.

ORGANIZING HISTORIC SALES, EXPENSE, AND PROFIT DATA

- Sales, expenses, and profit per operating period: annual, semiannual, quarterly, monthly
- **Average check**
- Average sales per seat

Average Check	Calculation
Average Check—Defined Period	$\dfrac{\text{Total \$\$ Sales for Period}}{\text{Total No. of Guests} \odot \text{ for Period}}$ = Average Check for Period
Average Check per Server	$\dfrac{\text{Server's \$\$ Sales per Shift}}{\text{No. of Guests} \odot \text{ Served per Shift}}$ = Average Sales per Server
Average Check—Food	$\dfrac{\text{Total Food Sales \$\$}}{\text{Total No. of Guests} \odot}$ = Food Average Check
Average Check—Beverage	$\dfrac{\text{Total Beverage Sales \$\$}}{\text{Total No. of Guests} \odot}$ = Beverage Average Check
Average Check—Food & Beverage	$\dfrac{\text{Total Food \& Beverage Sales}}{\text{Total No. of Guests} \odot}$ = Average Check

FIGURE 19.6 Methods of calculating an average check.

Average Check

Average check can be a misleading term. There are many possible averages that can be calculated. Some of these are

- Average check for a defined period (annual, month, week, day, shift)
- Server's average check
- Average check for food
- Average check for beverage
- Food and beverage average check

and just about any other way management may decide to compute an average sale. The guest check and the POS system are the tools that capture the guest counts and sales figures needed to do all these calculations. Figure 19.6 summarizes the calculations for each method of figuring average check.

Let's calculate the **average check history** for Farfalle Arrabbiata to get a picture of what has happened over time. To do this, guest counts for previous years have been retrieved from the archives.

Look at Figure 19.7. It appears that the average check at Farfalle Arrabbiata has eroded slightly over time. The goal was to increase the average check to $13.00 for Year 3. The actual results show a slip to below Year 2 levels. Even though revenue and guest counts rose from Year 2 and Year 3, the average check has not kept pace. Management might have congratulated itself on a great job increasing sales and guest counts, but these increases have not correlated with a better average check. The actual

	Year 1 (Actual)	Year 2 (Actual)	Year 3 (Actual)	Year 3 (Budget)
Total Revenue	$1,955,047	$2,089,437	$2,111,149	$2,121,149
Guest Count ☺	151,789	163,877	167,483	163,165
Average Check	$12.88	$12.75	$12.61	$13.00

FIGURE 19.7 Average check history for Farfalle Arrabbiata.

	Year 1 (Actual)	Year 2 (Actual)	Year 3 (Actual)	Year 3 (Budget)
Total Revenue	$1,955,047	$2,089,437	$2,111,149	$2,121,149
Number of Seats	130	130	130	130
Sales per Seat	$15,038	$16,073	$16,240	$16,317

FIGURE 19.8   History of annual sales per seat for Farfalle Arrabbiata.

results for Year 3 were lower than budget. The cause of this budget shortfall needs explanation.

ORGANIZING HISTORICAL SALES, EXPENSE, AND PROFIT DATA
- Sales, expenses, and profit per operating period: annual, semiannual, quarterly, monthly
- Average check
- **Average sales per seat**

The **average sales per seat** measures *the annual revenue each seat produces for an operation*. Operators compare this figure to the annual seat revenue of other similar operations. It is another way of asking the question "How are we performing?" In this case, however, the "How are we performing?" is in comparison to other operations versus the budget. Figure 19.8 shows a history of the annual sales per seat for Farfalle Arrabbiata.

The National Restaurant Association's annual report on restaurant statistics lists average sales per seat for a variety of restaurant concepts and service styles. This information is useful to operators who want to compare their average to the average of other restaurants with similar descriptors. The full report is available through their Web site, www.restaurant.org. Because revenue has increased each year and the number of seats has stayed the same, the average revenue per seat has increased in each of these reporting years.

STEPS TO USE TO PREPARE BUDGETS FOR FUTURE PERIODS
1. Study and analyze sales, expense, and profit histories.
2. **Study and analyze current sales, expense, and profit patterns.**
3. Research internal and external variables for the next budget period.
4. Develop assumptions about sales, expenses, and profit.
5. Use assumptions to create a budget plan.

Studying and Analyzing Current Sales, Expense, and Profit Patterns

What's the difference between the material we will discuss here and the material we discussed in Section 1? This section will paint a picture of sales, expenses, and profit for the *current* operating period (one year). Here we will review the difference between the budget and the actual results. This "current" data was included in the previous section as part of a panoramic review of Farfalle Arrabbiata's financial history.

Remember—the Year 3 Budget was the master **financial plan** for Farfalle Arrabbiata. The Year 3 Actual is what really did happen. The **actual budget** is the result of *the effects of internal and external events on income, expenses, and profit.* Some of these events were predicted in research during previous years. Some are the result of "nature taking its course"—or unanticipated events. Some are operational issues—the restaurant not operating to standards. History gives the baseline; actual performance is the reality check.

It should be pretty clear to you by now that there are many ways to arrange sales data. Bear in mind that many of the arrangements in this next section are more likely used in *daily planning* (monthly, weekly, daily, shift) than in *budget planning* (annual, semiannual, quarterly, monthly). To a foodservice manager, however, all these arrangements count when trying to understand "How are we performing?"

ORGANIZING CURRENT SALES, EXPENSE, AND PROFIT DATA
- Current sales per operating period: annual, monthly, weekly, daily, per meal period, per hour
- Current expenses
- Current profit

Sales per Operating Period: Annual (Current Figures for Year 1)

Figure 19.9 displays the budget and actual figures for Year 3. These are the **current sales**, **expenses**, and **profit** per operating period figures for Farfalle Arrabbiata. Right now, a closer look at Year 3 is needed. History is very helpful in budgeting, but most decision making will be based on current information. Notice the differences between budget and actual. Take notes about what you observe. Keep in mind the concepts of variable and fixed costs when reviewing the information. Use the space provided in the following box for your notes and questions.

OPERATING PERIOD NOTES AND QUESTIONS

Sales per Operating Period: Monthly

Figure 19.10 displays monthly sales for Farfalle Arrabbiata for Year 3. Included is a percentage-to-sales column (Each Month's Sales/Total Sales). Notice the fluctuations for this particular operation. It is not realistic to think that sales levels will be the same

Current Sales, Expense & Profit History	Year 3 (Actual)		Year 3 (Budget)	
Sales				
Food	$1,688,919	80.00%	$1,654,496	78.00%
Beverage	422,230	20.00	466,653	22.00
Total Sales	**2,111,149**	**100.00**	**2,121,149**	**100.00**
Cost of Sales				
Food	570,855	33.80	555,911	33.60
Beverage	108,133	25.61	116,663	25.00
Total Cost of Sales	**678,988**	**32.16**	**672,574**	**31.71**
Gross Profit	**1,432,161**	**67.84**	**1,448,575**	**68.29**
Controllable Expenses				
Payroll	624,900	29.60	627,860	29.60
Employee Benefits	95,002	4.50	91,209	4.30
Direct Operating Expenses	71,779	3.40	72,119	3.40
Music & Entertainment	10,556	0.50	10,606	0.50
Advertising & Promotion	52,779	2.50	53,029	2.50
Utilities	78,113	3.70	78,483	3.70
Administration & General	50,668	2.40	50,908	2.40
Repair & Maintenance	29,556	1.40	29,696	1.40
Total Controllable Expenses	**1,013,352**	**48.00**	**1,013,909**	**47.80**
Income B4 Occupation Costs	**418,810**	**19.84**	**434,666**	**20.49**
Occupation Costs				
Rent	123,529	5.85	123,529	5.82
Property Tax	38,004	1.80	38,004	1.79
Other Taxes	18,000	0.85	18,000	0.85
Property Insurance	21,996	1.04	21,996	1.04
Interest	33,000	1.56	33,000	1.56
Depreciation	6,900	2.70	56,900	2.68
Total Occupation Costs	**91,429**	**13.80**	**291,429**	**13.74**
Restaurant Profit B4 Taxes	**$127,381**	**6.03%**	**$143,237**	**6.75%**

FIGURE 19.9   Budget and actual figures for Year 3 at Farfalle Arrabbiata.

each and every month. All businesses have busy, slow, and shoulder periods. **Shoulder periods** are something in *between very busy and very slow and are ripe for marketing and development.* By studying sales records, the business pattern for each operation becomes apparent. Knowing the business pattern helps when forecasting and planning for future operating periods.

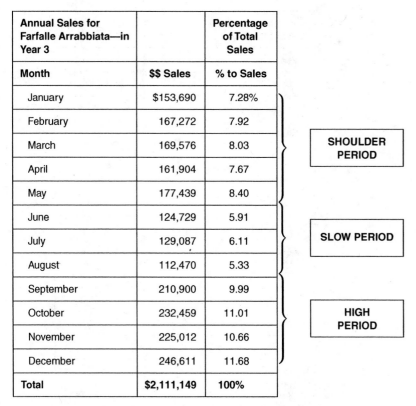

Annual Sales for Farfalle Arrabbiata—in Year 3		Percentage of Total Sales	
Month	$$ Sales	% to Sales	
January	$153,690	7.28%	
February	167,272	7.92	SHOULDER PERIOD
March	169,576	8.03	
April	161,904	7.67	
May	177,439	8.40	
June	124,729	5.91	
July	129,087	6.11	SLOW PERIOD
August	112,470	5.33	
September	210,900	9.99	
October	232,459	11.01	HIGH PERIOD
November	225,012	10.66	
December	246,611	11.68	
Total	$2,111,149	100%	

FIGURE 19.10   Slow, busy, and shoulder periods in Year 3 at Farfalle Arrabbiata.

Sales per Operating Period: Weekly, Monthly, and Quarterly Combination

Now lets's take a look at Figure 19.11. It shows **weekly sales** for each month of a quarter in Year 3. The Year 2 data would be available in the same format. In this way, managers can compare the sales per week and month for Year 3 with sales for the same periods a year earlier. The Year 2 sales data would have been used to develop the Year 3 figures. Likewise, the Year 3 figures will be used to develop the Year 4 forecast budget.

	January of Year 3		February of Year 3		March of Year 3
Week	Sales	Week	Sales	Week	Sales
Jan. 4	$36,250	Feb. 2	$38,159	Mar. 7	$44,276
Jan. 11	42,320	Feb. 9	47,305	Mar. 14	38,435
Jan. 18	39,370	Feb. 16	40,574	Mar. 21	42,867
Jan. 25	35,370	Feb. 23	41,234	Mar. 28	43,998
Total	$153,690	Total	$167,272	Total	$169,576

FIGURE 19.11   Weekly food sales for Farfalle Arrabbiata accumulated month to month for one quarter of Year 3.

Sales for Week of February 2		This Week's Sales: $38,159			
Day	Date	Daily Sales	% of Weekly Sales	Lunch Sales	Dinner Sales
Monday	Feb. 2	$4,107	10.76%	$2,141	$1,966
Tuesday	Feb. 3	4,118	10.79	2,271	1,847
Wednesday	Feb. 4	5,370	14.07	2,939	2,431
Thursday	Feb. 5	5,015	13.14	2,357	2,658
Friday	Feb. 6	7,198	18.86	2,448	4,750
Saturday	Feb. 7	7,496	19.64	2,558	4,938
Sunday	Feb. 8	4,855	12.72	3,174	1,681
Totals		$38,159	100%	$17,888	$20,271

FIGURE 19.12   Daily sales as a percentage of weekly sales and as sales per meal period at Farfalle Arrabbiata.

Sales per Operating Period: Meal Periods

Remember, too, that each **week's sales record (weekly sales)** is made up of each **day's sales (daily sales)**. In addition, each day's sales are made up of **meal period sales**. These figures can even be broken down to **hourly sales**, if management finds it useful. **Hourly sales** are common in the quick service segment and noncommercial foodservice businesses, such as foodservices for healthcare operations, schools, stadiums and arenas, colleges and universities, and so on, but they are used less in table service businesses. To demonstrate meal period sales, let's work with sales for the week of February 2. Figure 19.12 displays weekly sales broken down by day of week and by meal period, which is an example of incorporating multiple formats into one report.

Notice the column % of **Weekly Sales (Daily Sales Percentage).** This column shows *each day's sales as a percentage of total sales.* What does this reveal? It shows, by percentage, which days are the highest revenue generators and which are the lowest. If these percentages remain relatively accurate, this information can be used to calculate daily sales dollars when the weekly sales forecast is known:

WEEKLY SALES FORECAST × DAILY SALES PERCENTAGE = SALES FORECAST FOR THE DAY

$$\$42,867 \times 10.76\% = \$4,612$$
(Monday's Sales Forecast)

Using the percentage in this manner is the same principle as using a **popularity percentage** to determine menu item sales, as discussed in previous chapters. Think of this percentage as the "**popularity percentage for the day**."

How is the percentage calculated?

$$\frac{\text{EACH DAY'S SALES \$\$}}{\text{SALES \$\$ FOR THE WEEK}} = \%$$

Sales per Operating Period: By Day of the Week

In this next scenario (Figure 19.13), sales are recorded for all Mondays, all Tuesdays, and so on, for a one-month operating period. Arranging sales in this manner allows

Month: Feb. Year 3													
Monday		Tuesday		Wednesday		Thursday		Friday		Saturday		Sunday	
Date	Sales	Date	Sales	Date	Sales	Date	Sales	Date	Sales	Date	Sales	Date	Sales
												2/1	$6,000
2/2	$4,107	2/3	$4,118	2/4	$5,370	2/5	$5,015	2/6	$7,198	2/7	$7,496	2/8	$4,855
2/9	$5,641	2/10	$5,575	2/11	$5,855	2/12	$6,415	2/13	$7,598	2/14	$8,966	2/15	$7,255
2/16	$4,874	2/17	$4,680	2/18	$5,425	2/19	$5,950	2/20	$6,670	2/21	$7,650	2/22	$5,325
2/23	$4,724	2/24	$5,078	2/25	$5,630	2/26	$5,522	2/27	$6,313	2/28	$7,711	2/29	$6,256

FIGURE 19.13   Sales history recorded as sales by day of the week.

managers to see revenue patterns for specific days. This arrangement is especially helpful when scheduling labor.

As one can see, there are many possible ways to organize sales dollars. All of these manipulations are different ways of understanding the business pattern and are just a few of the most common ways that managers organize sales data to prepare budgets and forecast sales for future periods. A review of all of the records in every form gives managers a sense of how business flows in an operation.

CURRENT SALES, EXPENSE, AND PROFIT DATA

- Current sales per operating period: annual, monthly, weekly, daily, per meal period, per hour
- **Current expenses**
- **Current profit**

Current Expenses and Profit

It's easiest to look at expenses and profit together. Figure 19.14 shows the information for expenses and profit for Farfalle Arrabbiata for Year 3. Total Sales are included as a point of reference.

The expense picture shows some troubling results. Another reminder about costs is in order: Be aware of the type of cost (**variable, fixed**), as that dictates the information you need to check to do your analysis. Cost of Sales as a whole is up slightly. Total Controllable Expenses are down slightly. Occupancy Costs are as expected. (The percentage change is because sales are not at forecasted levels). This combination—sales lower than expected and expenses slightly higher than expected have combined to produce a profit percentage that is less than planned.

The Cost of Sales problem should have been documented throughout the course of the year. The final result reported here should not come as much of a surprise to management. If it is, then management has not been doing its job. Remember that the task here is not to analyze, but to compile a picture of the old and the current, so a realistic future budget can be prepared. All or most of the answers as to the who, what, when, where, why, and how questions should already be known.

Current Sales, Expense & Profit History	Year 3 (Actual)		Year 3 (Budget)	
Total Sales	**$2,111,149**	**100.00%**	**$2,121,149**	**100.00%**
Cost of Sales				
Food	570,855	33.80	555,911	33.60
Beverage	108,133	25.61	116,663	25.00
Total Cost of Sales	678,988	32.16	672,574	31.71
Controllable Expenses				
Payroll	624,900	29.60	627,860	29.60
Employee Benefits	95,002	4.50	91,209	4.30
Direct Operating Expenses	71,779	3.40	72,119	3.40
Music & Entertainment	10,556	0.50	10,606	0.50
Advertising & Promotion	52,779	2.50	53,029	2.50
Utilities	78,113	3.70	78,483	3.70
Administration & General	50,668	2.40	50,908	2.40
Repair & Maintenance	29,556	1.40	29,696	1.40
Total Controllable Expenses	**1,013,352**	**48.00**	**1,013,909**	**47.80**
Occupation Costs				
Rent	123,529	5.85	123,529	5.82
Property Tax	38,004	1.80	38,004	1.79
Other Taxes	18,000	0.85	18,000	0.85
Property Insurance	21,996	1.04	21,996	1.04
Interest	33,000	1.56	33,000	1.56
Depreciation	6,900	2.70	56,900	2.68
Total Occupation Costs	**91,429**	**13.80**	**291,429**	**13.74**
Restaurant Profit B4 Taxes	**$ 127,381**	**6.03%**	**$ 143,237**	**6.75%**

FIGURE 19.14   Current Expenses and Profit for Year 3.

Prime Costs

Prime costs for Year 3 can also shed some light on what is happening at Farfalle Arrabbiata. Once again, actual costs did not come in as expected. Review the following chart. Add to your list any questions or comments you may have.

Prime Costs for Year 3				
Cost of Sales	**Year 3 (Actual)**		**Year 3 (Budget)**	
Total Cost of Sales— Food & Beverage	$668,662	32.00%	$672,574	31.71%
Payroll	618,473	29.60	627,860	29.60
Benefits	94,025	4.50	91,209	4.30
Total	**$1,381,160**	**66.1%**	**$1,391,693**	**65.91%**

STEPS TO USE TO PREPARE BUDGETS FOR FUTURE PERIODS

1. Study and analyze sales, expense, and profit histories.
2. Study and analyze current sales, expense, and profit patterns.
3. **Research internal and external variables for the next budget period.**
4. Develop assumptions about sales, expenses, and profit.
5. Use assumptions to create a budget plan.

$\mathcal{R}$esearching Internal and External Variables for the Next Budget Period

There are two steps to researching internal and external variables for the next budget period:

1. Study financial notes about the current operating period.
2. Research internal and external variables for the next budget period.

Studying Financial Notes About the Current Operating Period

Good record keeping includes *sales, expense, and profit figures,* as well as *notes.* Notes detail the reasons behind actual results. These notes prove invaluable to managers when analyzing information to plan for future periods. They help to explain whether differences between budget and actual results were caused by events or conditions that are *within* the control of management or events or conditions that were *beyond* the control of management.

In preparing for a future period, all notes must be carefully reviewed for clues and guidance. They will assist in creating reasonable assumptions for the budget period.

Researching Internal and External Environments for the Next Operating Period

Internal Environments   In this step, management researches internal environments—what, if anything, needs "fixing." Changes in an **internal environment** *are produced in-house*; they are not the result of a new federal or state law (that's an external environment). The management team develops a prioritized "wish list" of ideas or plans to increase sales and decrease or control expenses. In some cases, an idea may actually increase a cost. Some of these ideas stem from analysis of income statements. Some are the result of brainstorming and planning for the future—they are the operating goals for the business for the next period. The internal variables were described in Chapter 1 as follows:

Front-of-House	Back-of-House
Seating	Menu planning
Sales	Purchasing
Serving	Receiving, storing, inventory management
Bussing	Food production
Payment	Dishroom operations

Notice that these 10 functions correlate to the Operating Cycle of Control. Management needs only to look at the cycle and their budget analysis to identify the trouble spots in operations—places where food, labor, and other dollars are frittered away. Trouble spots cause **I**nefficiency, **F**raud, **E**rror, and **W**aste (Remember IFEW from Chapter 1?)—the prime culprits of budget mishaps. Internal environments are **controllable;** management can solve internal operating problems by:

- Tight control systems in all front- and back-of-house procedures.
- Enforcement of existing standard operating procedures.
- Introduction of new standard operating procedures.

What does this have to do with budgeting? Instituting tight controls where none existed or were lacking will reduce operating costs. Any permanent savings in these areas increases profit and creates a new standard for the budget.

Any intentional changes to internal environments must have a corresponding effect on costs, sales, or both. If there are no expected returns in the form of reduced costs or increased sales, management must look seriously at the purpose of expending company resources in that particular area.

Let's consider this example: Suppose management has purchased a new dishwasher to replace an old, inefficient model. The new model will use fewer chemicals, less water, less electricity, and fewer labor hours. Utility Expense, Direct Operating Expenses, and Payroll will be affected. Initially, the savings to the budget are estimated via manufacturer's data and other estimates. When the budget is prepared, it will reflect these expected changes. Once the equipment is up and running, exact cost savings will be measured and reported on the actual budget. Budget notes alert management to monitor these accounts for actual savings. From there, management assesses whether or not the cost savings met expectations. The assessment part of the process is very important because the savings realized should result in a permanent change in the budgeted cost percentages for the affected expenses.

External Environments The **external environment** or variables described in Chapter 1 are as follows:

- Government regulations
- Local market conditions
- Labor force demographics
- National, regional, and local economic conditions
- Supplier relations
- New technology
- Media

These variables are much harder to manage because they are *not* activities happening every day within the four walls of the operation—things managers can keep an eye on or read about in a shift report. They are external to day-to-day operations. In fact, day-to-day work goes on with few employees except managers giving them much thought. Remember, a change in one or more of these external variables can positively or negatively affect income, expenses, and profit. Take a look at the list again. Think about the income statement—which line items or categories are potentially affected by changes, good or bad?

- ***Government regulations*** → Sales, Cost of Goods, Payroll, Benefits, Direct Operating Costs, Administration & General, Taxes
- ***Local market conditions*** → Sales, Cost of Goods
- ***Labor force demographics*** → Payroll, Benefits, Human Resources, Administration & General
- ***National, regional, and local economic conditions*** → Sales, Cost of Goods, Payroll, Benefits, Administration & General, Utilities, Interest, Taxes
- ***Supplier relations*** → Cost of Goods, Furniture, Fixture, Equipment
- ***New technology*** → Sales, Cost of Goods, Payroll, Benefits, Direct Operating Costs, Administration & General, Utilities, Repair and Maintenance
- ***Media*** → Sales, Cost of Goods, Advertising and Marketing

Notice that most of the expenses affected by these variables are the controllable costs. Many are tied directly to Cost of Goods, Payroll, and Benefits. These are the prime costs with which every foodservice business grapples. Any changes (+/−) in these environments will certainly have a direct effect on profit. What's a manager to do? As a future professional in the foodservice business, you are responsible to keep a close eye on each of these areas. How do you do this?

- Read local and national newspapers regularly.
- Join and become active in the local Chamber of Commerce or Convention and Visitors Bureau.
- Monitor area demographics.
- Monitor economic forecasts and reports for the area and region of your business's location.
- Monitor economic forecasts and reports about the foodservice business.
- Participate in local government meetings. Become knowledgeable about how to oppose changes that are not in your personal or business's best interest. Become knowledgeable about how to champion/lobby for positive changes.
- Become an **active** member in professional associations. Network with members and member organizations.
- Become an **active** member of local community organizations.
- Network with peers.
- Use suppliers as resources for information.
- Faithfully read respected trade journals.
- Use the Internet.

You are probably thinking: "What? Don't I have enough to do just to deal with customers and employees and sales and costs and income statements and paperwork?" That's only half the job! If these items are not on your radar screen, you will be out of the loop. There is a strong possibility the business will fail and you will be out of a job.

Changes to external environments can affect sales, costs, or both. Understand, too, that it is unlikely that only one force is at play. It is more than likely that many of the items on the income statement are wiggling around. So the name of the game is to figure out which things are changing (income or expenses) and which way they are changing (increasing or decreasing) or if they are staying the same and how profit makes out in the end. Are the changes expected to be

☺ Good news for the operation?

or

☹ Bad news for the operation?

or

■ Neither—it will have no effect on either sales or costs

Sales	Costs
The change is neutral; there is no expected effect on sales.	The change is neutral; there is no expected effect on costs.
The change is positive; sales are expected to increase. (☺ **Good News Change**)	The change is positive; costs are expected to decrease. (☺ **Good News Change**)
The change is negative; sales are expected to decrease. (☹ **Bad News Change**)	The change is negative; costs are expected to increase. (☹ **Bad News Change**)

Here is an example of a "good news" change: "Great news! Our insurance carrier has just informed us that our health insurance premium is decreasing by 20% next year."

Here is an example of a "bad news" change: "Oh no! The price of beef is forecast to increase by 11% next year. Beef items are our top sellers."

When all is said and done, managers take all the good news and bad news and compute the total impact on profit. If they don't like what they see at the bottom of the statement, they will be forced to make decisions about income, expenses, and operations in order to hit target profit goals.

The Effect of Changes in Internal and External Environments

How do you know what the net effect of change(s) in all environments will do to profit? The algebraic formula $A/B = C$ can help to understand the overall effect of any changes $(+/-)$ in expenses or sales on profit levels. Check out all the possible combinations in Figure 19.15.

$$\left.\begin{array}{l} A = \text{Expenses} \\ B = \text{Sales} \\ C = \text{Profit} \end{array}\right\} A/B = C$$

Watch how changes to (or lack of changes to) A and B affect profit:

STEPS TO USE TO PREPARE BUDGETS FOR FUTURE PERIODS
1. Study and analyze sales, expense, and profit histories.
2. Study and analyze current sales, expense, and profit patterns.
3. Research internal and external variables for the next budget period.
4. **Develop assumptions about sales, expenses, and profit.**
5. Use assumptions to create a budget plan.

Situation	Can You Say that in a Way that is Easier to Understand?
A = the same; B = the same; C = the same	If costs stay the same and sales stay the same, profit stays the same.
A = increases; B = the same; C = decreases	If costs increase and sales stay the same, profit decreases.
A = decreases; B = the same; C = increases	If costs decrease and sales stay the same, profit increases.
A = the same; B = increases; C = increases	If costs stay the same and sales increase, profit increases.
A = increases; B = increases; C = the same	If costs increase in the same proportion as sales increase, profit will be the same.
A = decreases; B = increases; C = increases	If costs decrease and sales increase, profit increases.
A = the same; B = decreases; C = decreases	If costs stay the same and sales decrease, profit decreases.
A = increases; B = decreases; C = decreases	If costs increase and sales decrease, profit decreases.
A = decreases; B = decreases; C = decreases	If costs decrease and sales decrease, profit decreases.

FIGURE 19.15   How changes in expenses and sales affect profit.

$\mathcal{D}$eveloping Assumptions About Sales, Expenses, and Profit, or, Let's Take Out the Crystal Ball

Steps 1 through 3 of preparing budgets for future periods are all about gathering information—information about sales and expense histories (Step 1), information about plans and goals for the business (Step 2), and information about the larger world in which we reside (Step 3). Although it may seem that a lot of time has been spent to get to this point, all of this work is ongoing—it is part of what a manager does every day.

Step 4 is about developing assumptions. Developing assumptions is like seeing the future with the help of a crystal ball. Steps 1 through 3 create the backdrop inside the crystal ball—they give context to the picture. In Step 4, the meaning of the information is clear—it is possible to figure out what to do. **Assumptions** in budgeting are financial directives for a new operating period. They represent *management's best estimate as to the economic effect of a change* (+/−) *in an internal or external environment*. The estimate can be in the form of dollars or a percentage. These changes are incorporated into the new financial plan. This is like using a crystal ball to see into the future!

TWO TYPES OF ASSUMPTIONS

Historical Information + Actual Information + Research = Assumptions

Operating Goals = Assumptions

Assumptions are developed for all three areas of the income statement: sales, all expenses, and profit. They are the result of historical information, actual information, and research into internal and external environments.

There are really two types of assumptions:

1. Assumptions developed in response to history, actual information, and research.
2. Assumptions developed as operating goals for the next period—things management would like to see happen.

Regardless of which category an assumption fits into, budgeting for a new operating period cannot begin until all the data is on the table. Once the data is compiled, assumptions can be formulated. Assumptions have to come with plans. Increasing sales is a reasonable assumption or goal for a new operating period. This doesn't just "happen," though, simply because it is written on a piece of paper. There has to be a reason *why* sales are expected to increase. How is management planning to make this happen? Every assumption has to come with a *rationale, a plan* to make it happen, and a way to *monitor results*. As an example: Suppose management plans to give employees a raise during the next fiscal year—this is the rationale part. This is a nice idea, and the employees are sure to go for it, but the raise has to be funded. There has to be a way to pay for this change—this is the "plan" part of assumptions. Unless sales increase, expenses decrease, or a combination of both occurs, profit will be the only way to fund this assumption (review Figure 19.15).

Research provides some of the back-up for assumptions. History and current operating information provide the rest. Figure 19.16 is an example of organizing information for the purpose of developing assumptions. Each income source and expense detail must be reviewed to accurately forecast the resources needed to produce desired levels of profit for the coming period. Figure 19.16 is not meant to be an exhaustive analysis of income and expenses. The final assumptions for the Year 4 budget for Farfalle Arrabbiata will follow.

The list in Figure 19.16 represents a sample of events that are expected to affect Farfalle Arrabbiata in the Year 4 budget. The next task is to correlate the data into assumptions that are used to prepare the budget. This budget is really a test, because it is unknown until all the numbers are crunched whether or not 6.2% profit is achieved. If 6.2% is achieved on the first run, that's great. If not, changes have to be made to either revenue or expenses or both. It may be that some plans cannot go forward this year because management is unable to fund the cause. Let's see what happens. The next figure takes some artistic license by converting the information in Figure 19.16 into concrete assumptions. Figure 19.17 reports the **Master List of Assumptions** for the Year 4 budget.

Converting Assumptions Into Budget Figures

The Percentage Method of Budgeting works by increasing or decreasing income and variable expenses by a predetermined percentage. The percentage is derived by calculating the dollar cost of something—say the pay raise—and calculating the percentage of change. It is then added to the *existing cost percentage*, to produce a new standard cost percent. Assume the percentage of increases in the Controllable Expenses section have been computed in this way.

A caution about using the Percentage Method of Budgeting, however:

- This method is widely used. It is effective as long as *the existing cost dollars allocated in the line item fairly represent what it takes to fund the expense*. The expense detail for each line item *must be checked and monitored for accuracy*. Increasing cost percentages by adding the percentage of change onto the existing cost percentage without verifying that all the dollars allocated are, in fact, necessary means line items may be artificially inflated. You will not have a true budget.

	Sales	Expenses
From History	1. Year 1–Year 2 = 6.8% increase. Expanded dining room seating this year. 2. Year 2–Year 3 = 1.03% increase. 3. Slight shift in sales mix.	1. Year 2–Year 3 = 1.03% increase. Budget = 1.5% increase. 2. Sales increases in years prior to Year 1/Year 2 averaged 3%–4% per year. 3. Key to beverage storage area was lost. Locks have been re-keyed in kitchen and storage areas. Key control in place.
From Budget & Actual	1. Year 2–Year 3 = 1.03% increase. 2. Budget plan was for 1.5% sales increase. 3. Sales increases in years prior to Year 1–Year 2 averaged 3%–4% per year.	1. Food = .2% increase. Acceptable. Dairy prices spiked. 2. Beverage = Cost up 0.61. Key to beverage storage area was lost. Locks have been re-keyed in kitchen and storage areas. Key control in place. 3. Tot. COG up because of beverage cost problem. 4. Benefits up because of healthcare costs.
From Internal Environments	1. No planned changes in seating capacity. 2. Menu prices for food will be increased by 2%. 3. A take-away service will roll out in April of Year 2. Statistics show food sales impact of 3% in first year. 4. Upgrade of POS system complete. 5. Pour system installed at bar.	1. Food & beverage—Locks re-keyed in kitchen and all storage areas. Key control in place. 2. Payroll— Oncrease from April of Year 2 for take-away service. 3. Dir. Op [CE1] —Increases for new menus, POS system and take away service. 4. Advertising & Promo—Increase for take-away service. 5. Occupation costs on target.
From External Environments	1. Restaurant industry stats forecast 4.6% sales increases for full-service restaurants. 2. Tourism reports for local area forecast 2% increase for Year 4. 3. Economic indicators show growth in region. 4. Unemployment rate is down. 5. Convention bookings are down 3%.	1. Payroll—3% increase across the board. 2. Benefits—4% increase in healthcare costs for Year 4. (1.2% budget increase). 3. Dir. Op.—Increase 1.25% because of take-away service, reprint of menus, linen cost increases, general supply increases. 4. Advertising & Promo—Increase 0.25% for take-away service. 5. Utilities–Increase 0.6% because of industry forecast for gas & electricity. 6. Admin. & Gen.—Increase 0.25%; general increases. 7. Repair & Maint.—Increase .2%; trash removal increase. 8. Property taxes—Rate hike – $1,000 increase. 9. Insurance—Rate decrease – $3,000. 10. Depreciation—Decrease $3,000.
From Management Goals	1. No history with expanded seating. 2. A new office building scheduled to open in February of Year 3 was delayed 'til February of Year 4. Sales forecast in Year 1 anticipated an on-schedule opening. 3. Take-away service will be operational by February of Year 4. 4. One office suite was empty from May to October. 5. 2% increase in food & beverage selling prices for Year 4.	1. Operate at 33.6% food cost and 25% beverage cost. Install pour system on bar. 2. Profit goal = 6.2%.

FIGURE 19.16 Building rationale and assumptions for Year 2 Budget Period (Farfalle Arrabbita)
—Summary of Data.

Fixed expenses are computed by adding the dollars of change to the existing expense line item to compute the adjusted expense total. This new amount becomes the expense line item on the existing budget. A new cost percentage has to be calculated.

In the example shown in Figure 19.17, the new sales dollars have to be computed. Cost of Goods and Controllable Expenses have changes listed in percentage values. These values are computed by researching expense details to determine

Sales	Food: 4.5% increase (new business & menu price increases) Beverage: 80%/20% sales mix
Cost of Goods	Food: 33.6% Beverage: 25%
Controllable Expenses	Payroll: 2% increase Benefits: 1.2% increase Direct Operating: 1.25% increase Music & Entertainment: No change Advertising & Promotions: 0.25% increase Utilities: 0.6% increase Administrative & General: .25% increase Repair & Maintenance: 0.2% increase
Occupation Costs	Rent: No change Property Taxes: Rate increase +$1,000 Property Insurance: Rate decrease −$3,000 Interest: Refinanced debt, −8,000 Depreciation: Decrease $3,000
Profit	6.2%

FIGURE 19.17   Assumptions for the Year 4 Budget.

which items are increasing or decreasing and therefore computing the change. The assumption is that the original cost dollars were adequate for the old level of sales. This amount plus or minus the change will be needed for the coming period.

Sales are forecast to increase by 4.5. Management reached this conclusion by studying the information gathered about history, actual data, internal events, and external influences. Here is their rationale:

- It appears that a 2.5% sales increase can be expected because of general business increases. This is reasonable, given the short history with the seating expansion. Industry statistics for take-away service shows 3% sales increase is average. Take away is not scheduled to start until April. The plan is for 2% increase for this change. (This change could also be estimated by a guest count and average check.) Although economic forecasts are favorable, tourism is not a significant part of the customer base.

This sales forecast is a modest one. As the period unfolds, the forecast and budget can be modified up or down, depending on actual results. Taking everything into consideration, management feels this is reasonable. Look at the chart, review your own notes about the history and current budgets, and see if you agree with this conclusion. If not, what would you predict? Why? What is your rationale?

STEPS TO USE TO PREPARE BUDGETS FOR FUTURE PERIODS

1. Study and analyze sales, expense, and profit histories.
2. Study and analyze current sales, expense, and profit patterns.
3. Research internal and external variables for the next budget period.
4. Develop assumptions about sales, expenses, and profit.
5. **Use assumptions to create a budget plan.**

$\mathcal{U}$sing Assumptions to Create a Budget Plan

Now that the assumptions have been fine tuned, they can be incorporated into an income statement. First, the income statement will be produced with the assumptions as is. Next, profit will be checked to see whether it is at 6.2%. If it is not at goal, the income and expense plan has to be adjusted. To start, the sales for Year 4 have to be determined.

Sales

To find the food and beverage sales for Year 4, follow these calculations:

YEAR 3 ACTUAL TOTAL SALES $$ $\times$ % CHANGE = NEW SALES DOLLARS
$2,111,149 $\times$ 4.5% = $95,002

ACTUAL TOTAL SALES + NEW SALES DOLLARS = SALES FOR NEW OPERATING
PERIOD
$2,111,149 + $95,002 = $2,206,151

	Old Sales	+/− $ Change	New Sales
Total Sales	$2,111,149	+$95,002	$2,206,151

Management would like an 80/20 food-to-beverage sales mix. To find food sales and beverage sales:

TOTAL REVENUE $\times$ FOOD SALES MIX % = TOTAL FOOD SALES
$2,206,151 $\times$ 80% = $1,764,921

TOTAL REVENUE $\times$ BEVERAGE SALES MIX % = TOTAL BEVERAGE SALES
$2,206,151 $\times$ 20% = $441,230

Total Sales	Sales Mix % Food	New Sales Dollars
$2,206,151	80%	$1,764,921
	Sales Mix % Beverage	**New Sales Dollars**
$2,206,151	20%	$441,230

Cost of Goods & Controllable Expenses

To find the new cost percentages for **Cost of Goods** and **Controllable Expenses**:

OLD COST PERCENTAGE +/− % CHANGE = NEW COST %

Expenses	Existing Cost Percentage	+/− Change	New Cost Percentage
Cost of Goods			
Food			33.6%
Beverage			25.0
Controllable Expenses			
Payroll	29.2%	+2.0%	31.2
Benefits	4.5	+1.2	5.7
Direct Operating Costs	3.4	+1.25	4.65
Music & Entertainment	0.5		0.5
Advertising & Promotions	2.5	+.25	2.75
Utilities	3.7	+.6	4.3
Administrative & General	2.4	+.25	2.65
Repair & Maintenance	1.4	+.2	1.6
Total Controllable Expenses	**48.0%**	**6.75%**	**53.35%**

Occupation Costs

To find the new Fixed Cost dollars:

$$\text{OLD COST \$\$} +/- \text{\$\$ CHANGE} = \text{NEW FIXED COST DOLLARS}$$
$$\$38,004 + \$1,000 = \$39,004$$
$$(\text{New Property Tax Cost})$$

Expenses	Old Cost Dollars	+/− Change	New Cost Dollars
Occupation Costs			
Rent	$123,529	0	$123,529
Property Taxes	38,004	+$1,000	39,004
Other Taxes	18,000	0	18,000
Property Insurance	21,996	−3,000	18,996
Interest	33,000	−8,000	25,000
Depreciation	56,900	−3,000	53,900
Total Occupancy Costs	**$291,429**	**−$13,000**	**$278,429**

Figure 19.18 shows the new budget, unedited, for Farfalle Arrabbiata for Year 4. It is simply a function of all the ups and downs from the assumptions. Take a look and see how things shake out.

Proposed Solutions

On a first run, this budget (Figure 19.18) is not at goal—profit is only **2.15**%. Now, management must study the assumptions and make some changes in order to come in with a budget that is at planned profit levels. Let's say that after study, the following solutions have been proposed to solve the problem.

Sales   Management believes this is an appropriate sales level, given the external and internal changes for the next year.

Sales		
Food	$1,764,921	80.00%
Beverage	441,230	20.00
Total Sales	**2,206,151**	**100.00**
Cost of Sales		
Food	593,013	33.60
Beverage	110,308	25.00
Total Cost of Sales	**703,321**	**31.88**
Gross Profit	**1,502,830**	**68.12**
Controllable Expenses		
Payroll	688,319	31.20
Employee Benefits	125,751	5.70
Direct Operating Expenses	102,586	4.65
Music and Entertainment	11,031	0.50
Advertising and Promotion	60,669	2.75
Utilities	94,864	4.30
Administration & General	58,463	2.65
Repair & Maintenance	35,298	1.60
Total Controllable Expenses	**1,176,982**	**53.35**
Income Before Occupation Costs	**325,848**	**14.77**
Occupation Costs		
Rent	123,529	5.60
Property Tax	39,004	1.77
Other Taxes	18,000	0.82
Property Insurance	18,996	0.86
Interest	25,000	1.13
Depreciation	53,900	2.44
Total Occupation Costs	**278,429**	**12.62**
Restaurant Profit Before Taxes	**$47,419**	**2.15%**

FIGURE 19.18   Year 4 Budget (unedited).

Expense Changes

- Healthcare cost increases will be split with employees. Farfalle Arrabbiata will not absorb the entire increase. Budget increase was 1.2%. Savings = 0.6%.
- Payroll was budgeted for 3% across-the-board increases. Because of past performance, management will not be given an increase. After 6 months of performance in the new fiscal period, increases will be revisited, if actual performance in sales and expenses is better than plan. Currently, fixed payroll is 35% of total payroll. This amounts to a savings of 0.2%.
- Advertising and Promotions—cut 0.5% from all areas. Ad campaign for take-away service will go as planned.

- Music and Entertainment—cut 0.25%.
- Direct Operating Costs—cut 0.75% by reducing linen usage and flower costs. Tables will not be double draped. Fewer flowers in centerpieces.
- Administration and General—0.5% cut overall. Management will manage this cut.
- Food cost will be budgeted at 33% instead of 33.6%. Chef Raoul will have to manage this cut.
- Beverage cost will be budgeted at 24% instead of 25%. Again, managers will have to manage this cut.
- Labor hours will be cut—all departments will manage the cut. Payroll will be at 30.4%.

The adjusted budget is as follows. Currently it is in balance. The challenge is put to managers in all departments to work at the proposed funding levels. Expense details for Direct Operating Costs, Administrative and General, and Music and Entertainment will be scrutinized for the best way to spend allocated dollars. As the new fiscal period unfolds, management may revise the budget based on actual results. Sales may exceed expectations. Actual costs may be different from budget. It's all a part of the great mystery of the crystal ball!

After preparing the budget, management might want to compare the cost structure of Farfalle Arrabbiata to other similar restaurants. If you are a member of the National Restaurant Association, you can easily do this through their Web site (www.restaurant.org). If you are not a member, check the information under the Industry Research Tab as well as the Restaurant Performance Index. What can be learned from this? It is a chance to see how your business stacks up from a cost and sales perspective with other like operations. Figure 19.19 shows the Year 4 budget plan for Farfalle Arrabbiata.

Congratulations! You have just completed the budget forecast for Farfalle Arrabbiata for the next operating period. This is the kind of analysis and planning that trained food-service professionals do in addition to managing the daily operations of the Cycle of Control. In fact, it is this work that is the challenge of managing a foodservice business or any business. Anyone can master daily operations (all the paperwork in the boxes around the Cycle of Control), but it takes training, experience, vision, and a bit of luck to use information captured by the paperwork in the boxes to be successful in the food business.

Calculating Revenue Using Other Operating Information

In the previous example, revenue for Year 4 was calculated using the **Percentage Method**—*estimates of changes in sales were prepared and converted to a percentage.* This percentage was used to mark up the base level of sales. Another way to determine sales is to use other operating data. The formula to calculate sales in this way is as follows:

$$\text{SEATS} \times \text{TURNOVER} \times \text{AVERAGE CHECK} \times \text{DAYS OPEN} = \text{FOOD SALES}$$

Seats are, of course, the number of seats available. Turnover and average check are calculated from restaurant records. **Days Open** is the *number of days the operation is open to the public.* Meal periods can be calculated independently—lunch and dinner, in the case of Farfalle Arrabbiata.

Meal Period	Seats	Turn-over	Average Check	Days Open	Food Sales
Lunch	130	2.3	$8.43	352	$887,241
Dinner	130	1.3	$14.75	352	$877,448
Total Food Sales					$1,764,689
	A ×	B ×	C ×	D =	F

Sales			Industry Statistics
Food	$1,764,921	80.00%	
Beverage	441,230	20.00	
Total Sales	**2,206,151**	**100.00**	
Cost of Sales			
Food	582,424	33.00	
Beverage	105,895	24.00	
Total Cost of Sales	**688,319**	**31.20**	
Gross Profit	**1,517,832**	**68.80**	
Controllable Expenses			
Payroll	670,670	30.40	
Employee Benefits	112,514	5.10	
Direct Operating Expenses	86,040	3.90	
Music & Entertainment	5,515	0.25	
Advertising & Promotion	49,638	2.25	
Utilities	94,864	4.30	
Administration & General	48,094	2.18	
Repair & Maintenance	35,298	1.60	
Total Controllable Expenses	**1,102,634**	**49.98**	
Income Before Occupation Costs	**415,198**	**18.82**	
Occupation Costs			
Rent	123,529	5.60	
Property Tax	39,004	1.77	
Other Taxes	18,000	0.82	
Property Insurance	18,996	0.86	
Interest	25,000	1.13	
Depreciation	53,900	2.44	
Total Occupation Costs	**278,429**	**12.62**	
Restaurant Profit Before Taxes	**$136,769**	**6.20%**	

FIGURE 19.19   Year 4 Adjusted Budget for Farfalle Arrabbiata.

Beverage sales can be calculated using a "popularity percentage" for beverage. Selling food will generate beverage sales. Generally, beverage percentages for lunch sales are between 10% and 15%. Dinner percentages are 15% to 25%. These are only guidelines. Exact percentages will be restaurant specific—some may be more, some less. To use a beverage percentage:

FOOD SALES × BEVERAGE % = BEVERAGE SALES

Beverage Sales	Food Sales	Beverage Percentage	Beverage Sales
Lunch	$887,241	18%	$159,703
Dinner	877,448	32	280,783
Total Beverage Sales			**$440,487**
	A	× B	= C

TOTAL REVENUE = TOTAL FOOD REVENUE + TOTAL BEVERAGE REVENUE

$2,285,176 = $1,764,689 + $440,487

The rest of the budget would be compiled using the same methods as in the earlier example. Congratulations again! You now have the skills necessary to create a budget for a foodservice operation.

Net Work

Explore the following Web sites:

www.restaurant.org
www.acfchefs.org
www.ahla.com
www.restaurantowner.com
www.nrn.com
www.hospnews.com
www.hospitalitynet.org
www.ontherail.com
www.qsrmagazine.com
www.rimag.com
www.yum.com—Check Investors; Financial Information

Chapter Wrap

The Chapter ✓ at the beginning of the chapter posed several questions. Review the questions and compare your responses to the following answers:

1. **What steps are needed to prepare budgets for future periods?**
   - Study and analyze sales, expense, and profit history.
   - Study and analyze current sales, expense, and profit patterns.
   - Research internal and external environments for the next budget period.
   - Develop assumptions about sales, expenses, and profit.
   - Use assumptions to create a budget plan.

2. **How are sales, expense, and profit history used to prepare budgets for future periods?**
   Studying and analyzing financial history is not a new concept. In order to prepare budgets, the studying and analyzing is expanded to include sales history, expense history, and profit. Annual, semiannual, quarterly, and monthly income, as well as expense and profit history are studied. Average check and average sales per seat are additional pieces of data studied for budget purposes.

3. **What are assumptions?**
   Assumptions in budgeting are financial directives for a new operating period. They represent management's best estimate as to the economic effect of a

change in an internal or external environment. Assumptions are developed for all three areas of an income statement.

4. How are assumptions used to develop budgets for future operating periods?

Each assumption is used to create a rationale or plan around the change. These directives are then monitored for results. Research provides backup for assumptions. History and current operating information are also used to develop and monitor assumptions.

Key Terminology and Concepts in this Chapter

Actual budget	Current sales
Actual results	Daily sales percentage
Annual sales	External environment
Assumptions	Fixed costs
Average check	Internal environment
Average check per server	Master budget
Average sales per seat	Percentage method of budgeting
Controllable expenses	Popularity percentage
Cost of goods	Prime costs
Cost structure	Sales per operating period
Current expenses	Shoulder periods
Current profit	Variable costs

Discussion Questions and Exercises

1. After studying Chapters 18 and 19, explain why the income statement is the key operating document managers and chefs go to when they need an answer to the question "How are we performing?"

2. Explain which historical operating periods are appropriate to use for budgeting for future periods. Which are appropriate to use for day-to-day operations?

3. Draw a pie chart of expenses for both the unedited and adjusted 2007 budgets. Explain the challenges this budget poses for the managers and Chef Raoul.

4. Perform a Comparative Analysis of the Year 3 Actual (Figure 19.3) and Year 4 (adjusted) (Figure 19.18) budgets for Farfalle Arrabbiata. Write a memo to the other managers explaining how the cost structure of the Year 4 adjusted budget differs from the Year 3 actual budget. Explain what all this will mean to the people responsible for the day-to-day management of Farfalle Arrabbiata. Draw on all your knowledge of operations at Farfalle Arrabbiata. Refer to the Cycle of Control.

5. Create an income and expense history for yourself based on the personal budget you prepared in Chapter 18. Record any notes that explain unusual increases and decreases in your income and expenses for the last year or two. Think about the coming year. What are you expecting for that period? Are you graduating? Will you still be in school? How will your income, expenses, and "profit" picture change from your current financial picture? Create a master list of assumptions for your income, expenses, and savings. With all this data in hand, complete a budget for yourself for the next year. Is it in balance? If not, how will you manage to close the gap? Will you have a surplus? What will you do with it?

6. Do you agree with the adjusted budget for Farfalle Arrabbiata for the coming year? Why or why not? Explain your response in detail.

7. Assume Farfalle Arrabbiata is located in the area in which you currently reside. You are responsible to gather the data needed to develop assumptions for sales and expenses for the next budget period. Research as much information about the following external environments that could (positively or negatively) affect the restaurant's income and expenses in the coming year. Your research may cover the following topics:

   • Government regulations
   • Local market conditions
   • Labor force demographics
   • National, regional, and local economic conditions
   • Supplier relations
   • New technology
   • Media

8. Develop a set of master assumptions for Farfalle Arrabbiata. Based on your research of your current location and surrounding area, what do you think business is going to be like in the coming year? How will Farfalle Arrabbiata be affected by the information you have compiled?

 9. Develop next year's budget for Farfalle Arrabbiata using the assumptions you have developed in the previous questions. Prepare a memo explaining your rationale for the figures you have developed.

Sales	This Year (Actual)		Next Year (Budget)
Food	$1,688,919	80.00%	
Beverage	422,230	20.00	
Total Sales	**2,111,149**	**100.00**	
Cost of Sales			
Food	570,855	33.80	
Beverage	108,133	25.61	
Total Cost of Sales	**678,988**	**32.16**	
Gross Profit	**1,432,161**	**67.84**	
Controllable Expenses			
Payroll	624,900	29.60	
Employee Benefits	95,002	4.50	
Direct Operating Expenses	71,779	3.40	
Music & Entertainment	10,556	0.50	
Advertising & Promotion	52,779	2.50	
Utilities	78,113	3.70	
Administration & General	50,668	2.40	
Repair & Maintenance	29,556	1.40	
Total Controllable Expenses	**1,013,352**	**48.00**	
Income B4 Occupation Costs	**418,810**	**19.84**	
Occupation Costs			
Rent	123,502	5.85	
Property Tax	38,004	1.80	
Other Taxes	17,945	0.85	
Property Insurance	21,956	1.04	
Interest	32,934	1.56	
Depreciation	57,001	2.70	
Total Occupational Costs	**291,339**	**13.80**	
Restaurant Profit B4 Taxes	**$ 127,469**	**6.04%**	

What Is Farfalle Arrabbiata?

*C*hapter 1 covers the concept of the control process, as applied to foodservice operations. Chapter 2 presents to you the Operating Cycle of Control (OCC). Chapters 3 through 12 tease out the details of the OCC by applying all the steps and paperwork to a conceptual restaurant. A restaurant profile has been developed, as discussed in this appendix, and is used to illustrate the paperwork system in action. The profile thoroughly describes everything from the corporate philosophy to, of course, the food! End-of-chapter problems, as well as chapter discussions, used this operation as the model, providing continuity between the paperwork system and its actual application and use in a restaurant.

Restaurant Profile

The restaurant created for this text is named **Farfalle Arrabbiata**, which means "**the angry bow tie**." A southern Italian theme has been selected for the operation. Southern Italy is well known for its spectacular scenery, favorable climate (hot and dry), abundant wheat fields, and rich cuisine. Olive groves and vineyards grace the hillsides, providing the area with the finest olive oils and wineries that produce exceptional vintages. The coastal Mediterranean location means fresh seafood is abundant and a natural part of the local cuisine. Pastas of all shapes are still made by hand from family recipes handed down through generations. These timeless dishes are typically served with rich vegetable sauces. Calzone, pizza, and bruschetta are classic luncheon selections and are often served with fresh seafood and vegetables. Traditional dinner dishes naturally feature pasta, seafood, and vegetables.

Farfalle Arrabbiata is a full-menu table-service restaurant serving authentic southern Italian food. Menu selections have been developed through meticulous research of the area and its cuisine. Professional relationships have been developed with some of the oldest continuously operating restaurants in the area.

Traditional preparation methods have been adapted to the modern kitchen facilities at Farfalle Arrabbiata. Pastas are produced by hand, in-house, using time-honored methods. Menu items are prepared fresh from the best ingredients available. Specialty suppliers are used to procure authentic ingredients. There is minimal use of convenience items.

A professional restaurant design firm was employed to develop the store design concept. The original design around the bow tie theme has been very successful, and there have been no major modifications to this overall plan, other than to update and fine tune the kitchen 4 years ago. The dining room was refurbished just a year ago.

Farfalle Arrabbiata is located in a mid-size city, in a remodeled factory building with an existing tenant mix of 75% business firms and 25% boutique retail stores. There are about 250 people employed by these businesses. Other foodservice operations in the building include the following:

- 1 small sandwich shop with 5 tables and counter seating for 10. This shop deals primarily in carry-out.
- 1 specialty coffee cart serving coffee, muffins, and limited breakfast selections

The restaurant occupies a corner storefront in the mill; it has excellent street visibility. The exterior of the building features brick walls with windows that run nearly from ceiling to floor. Exterior window boxes display floral arrangements year round. The 12'-by-5'-wide windows introduce plenty of natural light to the restaurant interior. The original wood trim on the soffets, face boards, and ridge boards accentuate the fine exterior workmanship of the building. Ample parking is available.

Outside, two specially designed neon signs feature the trademark bow tie and the restaurant's name. These are mounted on both exterior walls, creating easy identification of the restaurant from the street. There is one arched entranceway at the corner. Two sets of double doors with brass pulls provide access to the restaurant. Wide pine board floors have been tastefully stenciled with the signature bow tie, then sealed.

The restaurant has been in operation for 10 years and is independently owned. Since opening, Farfalle Arrabbiata has developed a significant reputation in the area for exceptional food and fine service.

*R*estaurant Description

The view of the restaurant floor as one enters from the street reveals a dining room sectioned into three distinct areas. The first is the bar and bar seating, which is about 25% of the space. To the left of the bar space is an open dining section. This is about 50% of the space. The last dining section is to the left of the open area and is the remaining 25% of the dining room floor. There are 175 seats between the two primary dining areas. Eight-foot walls serve as dividers, creating unique "dining spaces," which are an integral part of the décor. Flower boxes top these partitions, where cascading plants are used to create atmosphere. The dividers are light colored, with bow ties stenciled on a fine stucco finish. This finish is also used on the walls.

The middle dining section consists of four tops that are easily moved to accommodate larger parties. The smaller dining section also has table seating, but it becomes somewhat private, as it is behind the second partition. This is especially useful for parties holding meetings or otherwise desiring privacy. Half-round booths rim the perimeter of the floor.

The 12-foot windows are dressed with specially designed window treatments that include a bow tie as a tie-back. The drapery fabric is a small floral print. Decorative medallions featuring bow ties hang three quarters of the way down the windows on heavy cording. Artwork in the form of paintings and wall hangings finish the walls.

The top of the walls feature 8-inch oak moldings. Stenciling beneath the moldings adds a touch of color and design to the dining room. This stenciling matches the stenciling used on the floor. Tiffany-style chandeliers with ceiling fans hang across the dining room, providing light and air movement.

Tables are topped with off-white linen and top-dressed with floral cloths that match the draperies. Off-white linen napkins in a bow tie fold are pre-set. Flatware is silver plate. Fresh flowers, lighted candles, and salt and pepper shakers complete the tabletop.

Kitchen Description

The open kitchen concept is featured at Farfalle Arrabbiata. A large tiled counter stenciled with bow ties separates the diners from the chefs and provides visual and entertainment opportunities. Freshly baked rolls and breads are artistically displayed on either end of the line.

Chefs and line cooks work behind the counter preparing and sautéing guests' meals. The counter top provides the hot line, cold line, plating station, and pickup area. A wood-fired oven, sauté stations, range space, and other preparation equipment are located against the back wall. Backsplashes on rear and side walls are of highly polished copper, and hanging racks above cook stations are used to display copper pots, pans, and utensils as part of the décor. Server stations for bread—antique tables—are positioned on the dining room floor opposite the line.

Bar Description

The bar area showcases an antique bar removed from an old hotel before its demolition. It is solid cherry and is a striking piece. It has been modified to accommodate modern bar needs and is extremely functional. The bar occupies half of the exterior wall. The remaining space is filled with an impressive display of wine bottles set in a specially designed wall wine rack. Bar seating can accommodate 15 guests. There are six 4-tops in the bar area. Patrons can order full menu items at the bar or at these tables.

Mission Statement for Farfalle Arrabbiata

Our mission is to cultivate a loyal repeat customer base by hiring the right employees, who expertly serve every guest the right (best) food and beverage products right on time, every time.

The following are the "Five Rights" at Farfalle Arrabbiata, or, how we will fulfill our mission:

1. By hiring the **right people** with the right attitude and the right job skills for the right job.
2. By supporting the right people with the **right training** and development.
3. By delivering the **right (best) food and beverage** items to meet guest expectations and management goals.
4. By doing the **"right thing"** for our guests and our staff.
5. By doing the **right thing in our community**.

Core Philosophies at Farfalle Arrabbiata

Guest Philosophy

Each time a guest chooses to dine at Farfalle Arrabbiata, a unique opportunity presents itself to staff to deliver a dining experience unlike any other. As such, management recognizes that:

1. Customers are the reason we exist.
2. Each guest deserves
   - Courteous professional treatment at all times from all staff members.
   - Excellence in every food and beverage product delivered.
   - Expert service all the time.

Staff Philosophy

Each staff member is a stakeholder in the success of Farfalle Arrabbiata. Without a dedicated staff committed to guest satisfaction, Farfalle Arrabbiata will be just another restaurant among many. As such, management at Farfalle Arrabbiata pledges to support each crew member by

- Hiring the most qualified employees.
- Treating each staff member as part of the team.
- Empowering all staff members to "make it right" with each guest.
- Provide employees with opportunities to grow through in-house training, financial support for professional training, and opportunities to progress within the operation.

Farfalle Arrabbiata—Menu Selections

The following is the current menu selection for Farfalle Arrabbiata. The restaurant is open for lunch and dinner, 7 days a week. Restaurant hours are 11:00 a.m. until 10:00 p.m. The bar is open until 1:00 a.m., with desserts only served after 10:00 p.m.

Appetizers

- ***Mozzarella in Carrozza Arrabbiata (house specialty)***—Fresh, homemade mozzarella stuffed with Prosciutto di Parma and fresh basil. Breaded and pan-fried. Served with a side of house specialty Pomodoro Sauce
- ***Aubergine Melanzane***—Baby eggplant grilled in olive oil, balsamic vinegar, parsley, capers, and pecorino cheese
- ***Totanetti Agli Asparagi e Menta***—Fresh squid rings and asparagus sautéed in extra virgin olive oil, dry white wine, cracked black pepper, and mint
- ***Bruschetta con Portobello e Manzo***—grilled Tuscan bread topped with a seared portobello mushroom and pan-seared tenderloin tips in a Madeira wine and fresh thyme cream sauce
- ***Bruschetta con Mozzarella***—Foccacia bread topped with marinated Roma tomatoes, fresh green peppers, onions, and Calamata olives
- ***Antipasti***—Mixed selection of fresh mozzarella, Roma tomatoes, black and green olives, fresh Parmesan, sliced Parma Prosciutto, salami, roasted peppers, sautéed eggplant, Auricchio provolone, and grilled polenta
- ***Carpaccio di Manzo***—Paper-thin raw beef tenderloin, arugula, and çapers. Finished with lemon juice, extra virgin olive oil, and shaved Parmigiano-Reggiano cheese

Soups

- ***Pasta e Fagioli***—A classic, straight from the shores of Italy. Bean soup prepared from fresh chicken stock, pancetta, tomatoes, garlic, and fresh herbs.
- ***Minestrone***—Another of the Tuscan classics, with a medley of vegetables, fresh chicken, Prosciutto, and herbs.
- ***Chicken Noodle***—Mama's own special family recipe. A house favorite

Salads (Lunch and Dinner)

- ***Insalata Cesare***—Classic Romaine, Grana Parmesan, fresh black pepper, croutons, and special house anchovy dressing
- ***Insalata Mista***—Traditional mix of radicchio, endive, frisee Romaine, red onion, and tomatoes. Seasoned with extra virgin olive oil, aged balsamic vinegar, and garlic

- ***Portobello, Prosciutto, and Vegetables***—Grilled marinated portobello mushrooms Parma prosciutto, red peppers, and onions served over Mista mixed with arugula. Drizzled with extra virgin olive oil, crushed black pepper, and shaved Parmigiano-Reggiano cheese
- ***Insalata Gorgonzola***—Mista mix topped with Gorgonzola cheese. Dressed with extra virgin olive oil, aged balsamic vinegar, and sun-dried tomatoes

Panino—Sandwiches (Lunch Only)

- ***Calzone Melanzane Arrabbiata (house specialty)***—Classic Eggplant Parmesan with a twist. Pomodoro sauce, breaded eggplant, and Parmesan cheese
- ***Calzone Spinacchio (spinach calzone)***—Pizza dough with marinated spinach, sliced Roma tomatoes, Calamata olives, fresh mozzarella cheese
- ***Calzone Luna***—Pizza dough, tomato sauce, Proscuitto, Capicola, bruschetta, tomatoes, and arugula
- ***Panini al Salmone***—Salmon fillet marinated in olive oil, white wine, garlic, and fresh thyme
- ***Panini Pollo Balsamico***—Grilled boneless chicken breast marinated in balsamic vinegar and extra virgin olive oil
- ***Panino Polpetta***—Homemade meatballs, tomato sauce, Parmesan cheese, and fresh mozzarella
- ***Panino Panzanella***—Grilled portobello mushrooms, Roma tomatoes, red onions, cucumbers, fresh mozzarella, green olives, fresh basil, extra virgin olive oil, and balsamic vinegar

Wood-Grilled Pizzas (Lunch and Dinner)

- ***Pizza Arrabbiata (house specialty)***—Pomodoro Sauce made with browned garlic, chili flakes, extra virgin olive oil, white wine, and parsley. Topped with hot pepperoncini, roasted peppers and onions, artichokes, eggplant, Prosciutto di Parma, and Parmesan cheese
- ***Pizza al Tonno***—Tomato sauce, fresh grilled marinated tuna, Calamata olives, sliced mozzarella cheese
- ***Pizza Picante***—Picante sauce, pepperoni, sweet sausage, mozzarella
- ***Pizza Pomodoro Caprese***—Pizza with Pomodoro sauce, porcini, mushrooms, vine-ripened tomatoes, and fresh mozzarella cheese
- ***Pizza Mare e Monte***—Tomato sauce, grilled marinated shrimp and scallops, black Calamata olives, and fresh mozzarella slices
- ***Pizza Romaneschi***—Sliced artichokes, Prosciutto de Parma, Calamata olives, roasted eggplant, and smoked mozzarella

Entrees (Dinner Only)

- ***Cioppino***—Classic dish with fresh squid, fish, lobster, shrimp, clams, sea scallops, and Gaeta olives, simmered in freshly prepared fish stock
- ***Scallopine di Vitello***—Tender veal scallopine, roasted red peppers, asparagus, and artichoke hearts in a lemon white wine butter sauce
- ***Salmon a la Griglia***—Norwegian salmon marinated in extra virgin olive oil, white wine, garlic, and fresh thyme
- ***Bistecca***—12 oz. N.Y. sirloin grilled to spec
- ***Filetto di Maiale***—Pork tenderloin marinated in honey Dijon mustard and fresh herbs, encrusted with seasoned bread crumbs. Oven-roasted and served with apple brandy cream sauce

- *Costatine D'Agnello*—Oven-roasted rack of lamb with red wine demi-glace
- *Pollo con Carciofini e Limone*—Grilled chicken breast served in a lemon butter sauce, with baby artichokes, wild mushrooms, and capers

Pastas (Lunch and Dinner)

- *Farfalle Arrabbiata (house specialty)*—Bowtie pasta served with house specialty Pomodoro sauce, fire-roasted tomatoes and peppers, Calamata olives, fresh button mushrooms, our secret blend of herbs, and grilled shrimp. Topped with fresh Parmesan cheese
- *Spaghetti Bolognese*—Spaghetti tossed with house Pomodoro Sauce, ground veal, pancetta, mushrooms, red wine, and heavy cream
- *Ziti al Tonno Fresco*—Fresh house-prepared ziti tossed with fresh tuna, olive oil, dry white wine, tomatoes, and Calamata olives
- *Gnocchi con Scamorza e Pomodoro*—Freshly prepared gnocchi simmered in Pomodoro sauce. Topped with smoked Scamorza cheese and fresh basil and oregano
- *Penne con Pollo*—Penne pasta tossed with asparagus, chicken tenders, chopped garlic, butter, and white wine
- *Tortellini alla Nero*—Tortellini tossed with sautéed julienne red peppers, red onion, and zucchini. Deglazed with white wine and finished with fire-roasted tomatoes and grilled portobello mushrooms
- *Risotto alla Pescatora*—Arborio rice, littleneck clams, shrimp, scallops, mussels, squid, and fresh fish in a light plum tomato sauce and fresh herbs
- *Spaghetti alla Vongole*—Spaghetti served with chopped littleneck clams sautéed in garlic, olive oil, white wine, and crushed red peppers
- *Fettuccini Fontina*—Fettuccini in a tomato Fontina cream sauce, with porcini mushrooms, sun-dried tomatoes, roasted peppers, and Parmesan

Desserts—(Lunch and Dinner)

- *Crema Fritta con Salsa di Cioccolato (house specialty)*—Fried custard with chocolate sauce
- *Tira Misu*—Mascarpone and cream cheese mix layered between lady finger cookies soaked in Myers dark rum. Topped with slightly bitter powdered cocoa and strawberries
- *Gellato (house specialty)*—Gellato prepared fresh daily, in-house
- *Fresh Fruit of the Day*—Fresh fruit variety. Check with server for daily selection
- *Death by Chocolate*—Prepared in-house for chocolate lovers

farfalle arrabbiata!

Appendix B

Chapter Math Formulas

Chapter 2: About Recipes

Recipe Conversion Formulas:

$$\text{NEW RECIPE YIELD/ORIGINAL RECIPE YIELD} = \text{RECIPE MULTIPLIER}$$
$$\text{RECIPE INGREDIENT QUANTITY} \times \text{MULTIPLIER} = \text{RAW CONVERSION}$$
$$\frac{\text{TOTAL NUMBER OF OUNCES RECIPE PRODUCES}}{\text{NUMBER OF SERVINGS RECIPE PRODUCES}} = \text{PORTION SIZE}$$

Chapter 3: About the Portion Cost

To Cost Recipe and Plate Card Ingredients:

$$\text{QUANTITY} \times \text{UNIT PRICE} = \text{EXTENDED PRICE}$$
$$\text{EXTENDED PRICE/YIELD} = \text{COST PER (UNIT)}$$

Formulas to Extend a Recipe:

$$\text{RECIPE QUANTITY} \times \text{RECIPE UNIT PRICE} = \text{EXTENDED PRICE}$$

or

$$\text{QUANTITY} \times \text{UNIT PRICE} = \text{EXTENDED PRICE}$$

Minimum Menu Price Formula:

$$\text{COST PER PORTION} + \text{Q FACTOR} = \text{COST PER DISH (CPD)}$$
$$\text{COST PER DISH} \times 1.\text{SF \% (Spice Factor Percentage)} = \text{TRUE COST PER DISH (TCPD)}$$
$$\text{TRUE COST PER DISH/STANDARD FOOD COST \%} = \text{MINIMUM MENU PRICE (MMP)}$$

To Calculate the Spice Factor Percentage:

$$\frac{\text{COST OF SPICE FACTOR ITEMS}}{\text{TOTAL FOOD PURCHASES}} = \text{SPICE FACTOR \%}$$

To Find the Yield Percentage:

$$\text{PART/WHOLE} = \text{YIELD \%}$$

To Find the Waste Percentage:

$$100\% - \text{YIELD \%} = \text{WASTE \%}$$

Triangle of Enlightenment Formulas:

$$\text{COST/COST \%} = \text{SALES OR SELL PRICE}$$
$$\text{COST/SALES} = \text{COST \%}$$
$$\text{SALES} \times \text{COST \%} = \text{COST \$\$}$$

Chapter 5: About Purchasing the Right Quantity

To Find the Popularity Percentage:

$$\frac{\text{EACH ITEM'S TOTAL NUMBER SOLD}}{\text{TOTAL NUMBER OF ITEMS SOLD}} = \text{POPULARITY \%}$$

Using the Popularity Percentage with Sales Forecasts:

$$\text{POPULARITY \%} \times \text{ITEM SALES FORECAST} = \text{NUMBER OF ITEMS FORECAST TO BE SOLD}$$

To Determine How Much to Order Using a Par:

$$\text{PAR AMOUNT} - \text{AMOUNT ON HAND} = \text{AMOUNT TO ORDER}$$

Using Formulas to Calculate How Much to Order:

$$\text{AMOUNT TO ORDER} = \frac{\text{NO. OF SERVINGS DESIRED} \times \text{PORTION SIZE (as a decimal)}}{\text{YIELD \%}}$$

$$\text{NO. OF PORTIONS} = \frac{\text{QUANTITY OF MEAT} \times \text{YIELD \%}}{\text{PORTION SIZE (as a decimal)}}$$

$$\text{PORTION SIZE} = \frac{\text{QUANTITY OF MEAT} \times \text{YIELD \%}}{\text{NUMBER OF SERVINGS}}$$

$$\text{YIELD \%} = \frac{\text{NUMBER OF SERVINGS} \times \text{PORTION SIZE (as a decimal)}}{\text{QUANTITY OF MEAT}}$$

Amount Purchased Equivalency (APE) Formula (to quickly find a new cost per portion when the invoice price has changed):

$$\frac{\text{PORTION SIZE}/16 \text{ (OZ. PER LB.)}}{\text{STANDARD YIELD \%}} = \text{AMOUNT PURCHASED EQUIVALENCY (APE)}$$

$$\text{AMOUNT PURCHASED EQUIVALENCY} \times \text{INVOICE PRICE} = \text{COST PER PORTION}$$

Chapter 6: About the Right Supplier

Supplier Pricing Methods:

$$\text{SUPPLIER CASE COST} \times \text{\% OF MARK-UP} = \text{OPERATOR COST}$$
$$\text{SUPPLIER CASE COST} + \text{\$\$ MARKUP PER CASE} = \text{OPERATOR COST}$$

To Find Edible Portion (EP) Cost:

$$\frac{\text{AP (AS PURCHASED) PRICE}}{\text{YIELD \%}} = \text{EP COST}$$

Chapter 8: About Inventory and Inventory Control

$$\text{TOTAL EXTENDED PRICE}/\text{YIELD} = \text{COST PER POUND}$$
$$\text{QUANTITY} \times \text{UNIT PRICE} = \text{EXTENSION}$$

Book Inventory Variance Formula:

$$\text{OPENING INVENTORY} + \text{PURCHASES} - \text{REQUISITIONS} = \text{BOOK INVENTORY VALUE}$$

$$\text{BOOK INVENTORY VALUE} - \text{PHYSICAL INVENTORY VALUE} = \text{VARIANCE}$$

Inventory Turnover Rate:

1. **To calculate the average inventory value:**

$$\frac{\text{OPENING INVENTORY VALUE} + \text{CLOSING INVENTORY VALUE}}{2} = \text{AVERAGE INVENTORY COST}$$

2. **To calculate the average inventory rate:**

$$\frac{\text{COST OF FOOD SOLD}}{\text{AVERAGE INVENTORY COST}} = \text{INVENTORY TURNOVER RATE}$$

Chapter 9: About Food Production Control

Seat Turnover Formulas:

$$\frac{\text{NO. OF CUSTOMERS} \odot \text{SERVED IN A PERIOD}}{\text{NO. OF SEATS AVAILABLE}} = \text{TURNOVER RATIO}$$

$$\frac{\text{NO. OF CUSTOMERS} \odot \text{SERVED TODAY}}{\text{NO. OF SEATS AVAILABLE TODAY}} = \text{TURNOVER RATIO TODAY}$$

$$\frac{\text{TOTAL NO. OF GUESTS SERVED IN A PERIOD}}{\text{TOTAL NO. OF SEATS AVAILABLE}} = \text{WEIGHTED AVERAGE TURNOVER}$$

Popularity Percentage:

$$\frac{\text{NUMBER OF A SPECIFIC ITEM SOLD}}{\text{NUMBER OF ALL ITEMS SOLD}} = \text{POPULARITY \%}$$

Chapter 10: About Food Cost and Food Cost Percentage

To Calculate the Food Cost Percentage:

FOOD COST/FOOD SALES = FOOD COST %

Cost of Goods Cost Percentage Calculations:

FOOD COST/FOOD SALES = FOOD COST %
BEVERAGE COST/BEVERAGE SALES = BEVERAGE COST %
TOTAL COST OF GOODS/TOTAL SALES = TOTAL COST OF GOODS %

Daily Food Cost in Dollars:

DIRECT PURCHASES
+ STOREROOM REQUISITIONS
+ TRANSFERS IN (Adjustments that Increase Cost)
− TRANSFERS OUT (Adjustments that Decrease Cost)
= COST OF FOOD TODAY

Daily Food Cost Percentage:

$$\frac{\text{COST OF FOOD TODAY}}{\text{FOOD SALES TODAY}} = \text{TODAY'S FOOD COST \%}$$

Accumulated Food Cost Percentage:

$$\frac{\text{COST OF FOOD TO DATE}}{\text{FOOD SALES TO DATE}} = \text{FOOD COST \% TO DATE}$$

Daily Food Cost Using Requisitions & Transfers:

DIRECT PURCHASES
+ STOREROOM REQUISITIONS
+ TRANSFERS IN (Adjustments that Increase Cost)
− TRANSFERS OUT (Adjustments that Decrease Cost)
= COST OF FOOD TODAY

Monthly Cost of Food Calculation:

ADJUSTMENTS THAT INCREASE FOOD COST:
OPENING INVENTORY
+ TOTAL PURCHSES FOR THE MONTH $\Big\}$ (DEBITS)
+ TRANSFERS IN
COST OF FOOD AVAILABLE FOR SALE

ADJUSTMENTS THAT DECREASE FOOD COST:
− TRANSFERS OUT
− STEWARD SALES
− PROMOTIONAL/COMP MEALS $\Big\}$ (CREDITS)
− EMPLOYEE MEALS
− CLOSING INVENTORY
= COST OF FOOD USED THIS MONTH TO GENERATE
DINING ROOM SALES THIS MONTH

Valuing Employee Meals:

NO. OF EMPLOYEE MEALS SERVED × AMOUNT PER DAY = EMPLOYEE MEAL
CREDIT
SALES VALUE OF EMPLOYEE MEALS × FOOD COST % = EMPLOYEE MEAL CREDIT

Calculating Monthly Food Cost Percentage:

$$\frac{\text{TOTAL COST OF FOOD THIS MONTH}}{\text{TOTAL FOOD SALES THIS MONTH}} = \text{ACTUAL FOOD COST \% THIS MONTH}$$

Monthly Cost of Goods Formula:

OPENING INVENTORY
+ PURCHASES
+ TRANSFERS IN
= COST OF FOOD AVAILABLE FOR SALE

COST OF FOOD AVAILABLE FOR SALE
− TRANSFERS OUT
− PROMO/COMP MEALS
− EMPLOYEE MEALS
− CLOSING INVENTORY
= COST OF FOOD SOLD THIS MONTH

Departmental Monthly Cost of Goods Formula:

OPENING INVENTORY
+ TOTAL FOOD REQUISITIONS FOR THE MONTH
+ KITCHEN IN-PROCESS PRODUCTION $\Big\}$ (DEBITS)
+ TRANSFERS IN
COST OF FOOD AVAILABLE FOR SALE

ADJUSTMENTS THAT DECREASE FOOD COST:
- – TRANSFERS OUT
- – STEWARD SALES
- – PROMOTIONAL/COMP MEALS   } (CREDITS)
- – EMPLOYEE MEALS
- – CLOSING INVENTORY
= COST OF FOOD USED THIS MONTH TO GENERATE
   DINING ROOM SALES THIS MONTH

Monthly Departmental Food Cost Percentage:

$$\frac{\text{TOTAL DEPARTMENTAL COST OF FOOD THIS MONTH}}{\text{TOTAL DEPARTMENTAL SALES THIS MONTH}} = \text{DEPT. FOOD COST \%}$$

Chapter 11: About Monitoring Sales

Calculation for Cash Turn-In:

ITEM × NUMBER PRESENT = AMOUNT OF $$ IN DRAWER
ALL CURRENCY + ALL COIN = TOTAL CURRENCY & COIN
ALL CURRENCY + ALL COIN + ALL CHECKS = SUBTOTAL
SUBTOTAL − BANK = TOTAL TURN-IN

Chapter 12: About Menus, Menu Pricing, Sales Forecasts and Sales Analysis

Minimum Menu Price Formula:

EXTENDED PRICE/RECIPE YIELD = COST PER PORTION
COST PER PORTION + Q FACTOR = COST PER DISH (CPD)
COST PER DISH × 1.SF % = TRUE COST PER DISH (TCPD)
TRUE COST PER DISH/STANDARD FOOD COST % = MINIMUM MENU PRICE (MMP)

Menu Pricing Methods:

Food Cost Percentage Method:

TRUE COST PER DISH/STANDARD FOOD COST % = MINIMUM MENU PRICE (MMP)

Contribution Margin Method:

To find Average Contribution Margin:

ALL OTHER COSTS + PROFIT/NUMBER OF GUESTS = AVG. CONTRIBUTION
MARGIN

Contribution Margin Formula:

TCPD + AVERAGE CONTRIBUTION MARGIN = MENU PRICE

Actual Contribution Margin:

ACTUAL MENU PRICE − TCPD = MENU ITEM CONTRIBUTION MARGIN

Ratio Menu Pricing Method:

ALL OTHER COSTS + PROFIT/TOTAL FOOD COST = RATIO
RATIO × TCPD = TOTAL NONINGREDIENT COSTS FOR THE ITEM
TCPD + NONINGREDIENT COST = MINIMUM MENU PRICE

Prime Cost Menu Pricing Method:

Labor Cost per Guest:

PAYROLL + BENEFITS/TOTAL NUMBER OF GUESTS = LABOR COST PER GUEST

Prime Cost per Guest:

TCPD + LABOR COST PER GUEST = PRIME COST PER GUEST

Prime Cost Percentage:

FOOD COST % + LABOR & BENEFIT COST % = PRIME COST %
PRIME COST PER GUEST/PRIME COST PERCENT = MINIMUM MENU PRICE

Menu Pricing for Food Bars/Buffets:

TOTAL COST OF ALL FOOD CONSUMED/NO. OF PEOPLE (☺) = COST OF FOOD
BAR PER PERSON

Forecasting Sales with Guest Counts and Average Check:

NO. OF GUESTS FORECASTED × AVERAGE CHECK = SALES $$

Forecasting Food Cost with Sales and Food Cost Percentage:

FORECASTED FOOD SALES × STANDARD COST % = FOOD COST DOLLARS

Menu Analysis Benchmark Formulas for Popularity and Profitability:

Popularity Benchmark:

TOTAL NUMBER OF ITEMS SOLD/NUMBER OF SELECTIONS IN THIS MENU
CATEGORY = AVERAGE NUMBER SOLD
AVERAGE NUMBER SOLD × 70% = POPULARITY BENCHMARK

Profitability Benchmark:

TOTAL MENU CONTRIBUTION MARGIN/NUMBER OF COVERS = WEIGHTED
AVERAGE CONTRIBUTION MARGIN

Chapter 13: About Beverage Production Control and Service

Calculating Cost per Ounce:

EXTENDED PRICE/YIELD = COST PER OUNCE

Calculating an Extension:

QUANTITY × UNIT PRICE = EXTENDED PRICE

Calculating a Menu Price:

COST PER PORTION/BEVERAGE COST % = MINIMUM MENU PRICE

Chapter 14: About Beverage Cost and Beverage Cost Percentage

Beverage Cost % Menu Pricing Method:

COST PER PORTION/STANDARD BEVERAGE COST % = MINIMUM MENU PRICE

Calculating Beverage Cost Percentage:

BEVERAGE COST/BEVERAGE SALES = BEVERAGE COST %

Calculating Liquor, Beer and Wine Cost Percentages:

LIQUOR COST OF GOODS SOLD/TOTAL LIQUOR SALES = LIQUOR COST %
BEER COST OF GOODS SOLD/TOTAL BEER SALES = BEER COST %
WINE COST OF GOODS SOLD/TOTAL WINE SALES = WINE COST %

Calculating Beverage Cost Percentage:

TOTAL LIQUOR COST OF GOODS SOLD/TOTAL BEVERAGE SALES = BEVERAGE
COST %

Chapter 15: About Bar and Inventory Control

Pour Cost Percentage:

COST OF GOODS SOLD/TOTAL RETAIL VALUE = POUR COST %

Chapter 16: About Controlling Payroll Costs and the Cost of Employee Turnover

Calculating Cost Percentage:

COST/SALES = COST %

Calculating Payroll Cost:

RATE OF PAY × NUMBER OF HOURS WORKED = GROSS WAGES
INDIRECT PAYROLL COSTS + GROSS WAGES = TOTAL PAYROLL

Calculating Indirect Payroll Costs:

INDIRECT RATE + 1 = MULIPLIER
TOTAL DIRECT COSTS × MULTIPLIER = PAYROLL COST OF HOURLY EMPLOYEES

Daily Payroll Cost Calculation:

ANNUAL SALARY/NO. OF HOURS WORKED ANNUALLY = HOURLY RATE OF PAY
$32,000/2,000 = $16.00 per hour
HOURLY RATE OF PAY × NO. OF HOURS PER DAY = PAY PER DAY

Salaried Payroll Cost Calculation:

DAILY SALARIED AMOUNTS × MULTIPLIER = PAYROLL COST OF SALARIED
EMPLOYEES

Payroll Cost Percentage Calculation:

TOTAL PAYROLL COST/TOTAL GROSS SALES = PAYROLL COST PERCENTAGE

Sales per Person per Hour Calculation:

TOTAL GROSS SALES/TOTAL HOURS WORKED = SALES PER PERSON-HOUR

Calculating Employee Turnover Rates:

NO. OF W-2s AT END OF YEAR − NO. OF CURRENT EMPLOYEES = NO. OF PAST
EMPLOYEES
NO. OF PAST EMPLOYEES/AVERAGE NUMBER OF EMPLOYEES = TURNOVER RATE

Chapter 17: About Measuring Staff Performance and Productivity

Mishap Percentage:

MISHAPS PER HOUR/COVERS PER HOUR = MISHAP %
TOTAL NO. OF MISHAPS PER HOUR/COVERS PER HOUR = MISHAP %

Shift Average Figures:

SALES PER HOUR FOR THE SHIFT/# OF HOURS IN SHIFT = SHIFT AVERAGE
FIGURES

Sales per Person-Hour:

SALES PER HOUR/PERSON-HOURS = SALES PER PERSON-HOUR

Covers per Person-Hour:

COVERS PER HOUR/NUMBER OF PERSON-HOURS = COVERS PER PERSON-HOUR

Monthly Average Percentage:

TOTAL AVERAGE SALES PER HOUR/NO. OF DAYS IN MONTH = MONTHLY
AVERAGE SALES PER HOUR

TOTAL COVERS PER HOUR/NO. OF DAYS IN MONTH = MONTHLY AVERAGE
COVERS PER HOUR

TOTAL AVERAGE PERSON-HOURS/NO. OF DAYS IN MONTH = MONTHLY
AVERAGE PERSON-HOURS

TOTAL AVERAGE NO. OF MISHAPS PER HOUR/NO. OF DAYS IN MONTH =
MONTHLY AVERAGE MISHAP %

Chapter 18: About Operating Statements

Income Statement:

SALES − COST OF GOODS − CONTROLLABLE − OCCUPATION = PROFIT/LOSS
EXPENSES   COSTS

Sales Mix %:

DEPARTMENTAL SALES/TOTAL SALES = SALES MIX %

Total Cost of Food:

TOTAL COST OF FOOD + TOTAL COST OF BEVERAGE = TOTAL COST OF GOODS

Cost of Goods Percentage Formulas:

FOOD COST/FOOD SALES = FOOD COST %
BEVERAGE COST/BEVERAGE SALES = BEVERAGE COST %
TOTAL COST OF GOODS/TOTAL SALES = TOTAL COST OF GOODS %

Income Statement Subtotal Lines:

SALES − COST OF GOODS = GROSS PROFIT
GROSS PROFIT − CONTROLLABLE EXPENSES = INCOME BEFORE OCCUPANCY
COSTS
INCOME BEFORE OCCUPANCY COSTS − OCCUPANCY COSTS = PROFIT

Food Cost Budget:

FOOD SALES FORECAST × TARGET FOOD COST % = FOOD COST BUDGET

Finding Variance Dollars:

$$\text{BUDGET \$\$} - \text{ACTUAL \$\$} = \text{VARIANCE \$\$ } (+/-)$$

Finding Variance Percentages:

$$\text{VARIANCE DOLLARS/BUDGET DOLLARS} = \text{VARIANCE \%}$$

Average Check:

$$\text{TOTAL SALES/NUMBER OF GUESTS} = \text{AVERAGE CHECK}$$

Chapter 19: About Preparing Income Statements

Average Check for a Defined Period:

$$\frac{\text{TOTAL \$\$ SALES FOR PERIOD}}{\text{TOTAL NO. OF GUESTS FOR PERIOD}} = \text{AVERAGE CHECK FOR PERIOD}$$

Average Check per Server:

$$\frac{\text{SERVER'S \$\$ SALES PER SHIFT}}{\text{NO. OF GUESTS SERVED PER SHIFT}} = \text{AVERAGE SALES PER SERVER}$$

Average Check—Food:

$$\frac{\text{TOTAL FOOD SALES \$\$}}{\text{TOTAL NO. OF GUESTS}} = \text{FOOD AVERAGE CHECK}$$

Average Check—Beverage:

$$\frac{\text{TOTAL BEVERAGE SALES \$\$}}{\text{TOTAL NO. OF GUESTS}} = \text{BEVERAGE AVERAGE CHECK}$$

Average Check—Food & Beverage Combined:

$$\frac{\text{TOTAL FOOD \& BEVERAGE SALES}}{\text{TOTAL NO. OF GUESTS}} = \text{AVERAGE CHECK}$$

Average Sales per Seat:

$$\text{TOTAL ANNUAL SALES/NUMBER OF SEATS} = \text{AVERAGE SALES PER SEAT}$$

Sales Forecast:

$$\text{WEEKLY SALES FORECAST} \times \text{DAILY PERCENT} = \text{SALES FORECAST FOR THE DAY}$$

Calculating Budget Dollars:

$$\text{ACTUAL TOTAL SALES \$\$} \times \text{\% CHANGE} = \text{NEW SALES DOLLARS}$$
$$\text{ACTUAL TOTAL SALES} + \text{NEW SALES DOLLARS} = \text{SALES FOR NEW OPERATING PERIOD}$$
$$\text{TOTAL REVENUE} \times \text{FOOD SALES MIX\%} = \text{TOTAL BEVERAGE SALES}$$
$$\text{TOTAL REVENUE} \times \text{BEVERAGE SALES MIX\%} = \text{TOTAL BEVERAGE SALES}$$
$$\text{OLD COST PERCENT} +/- \text{\% CHANGE} = \text{NEW COST\%}$$
$$\text{OLD COST \$\$} +/- \text{\$\$ CHANGE} = \text{NEW FIXED COST DOLLARS}$$

Calculating Sales Using Other Operating Data:

$$\text{SEATS} \times \text{TURNOVER} \times \text{AVERAGE CHECK} \times \text{DAYS OPEN} = \text{FOOD SALES}$$
$$\text{FOOD SALES} \times \text{BEVERAGE\%} = \text{BEVERAGE SALES}$$

Glossary

A

ABC Inventory System   A method of identifying inventory items that require the tightest control measures, those that require moderate controls, and those that require only the simplest inventory control measures.

Acceptable Variances   A variance between budget figures and actual figures that is insignificant and requires no management action.

Accounting Period   A standardized time period (e.g., day, week, month) between the tabulation of accounting records.

Actual Budget   Actual sales, actual costs, and profit or loss, as each accrued over the course of the period.

Actual Cost Inventory Pricing Method   The actual unit purchase price of the item is used to value the inventory on hand.

À La Carte Pricing   Menu pricing method in which menu selections are priced separately.

Alcohol Service Training   Certain states require those who serve alcohol beverages to complete an approved training program.

Annual Productivity Report   A report that summarizes the information reported on the monthly productivity chart.

Annual Sales   The total sales for one year for as many years as is desired or is available.

Aperitifs   Types of mixed drinks served from the bottle or used in recipes of multiple alcoholic beverages.

Approved Payee List   Used in conjunction with an invoice payment schedule. This is a list of vendors who are approved as legitimate suppliers for the operation.

Approved Supplier Lists   Suppliers with whom a relationship has been established and agreements put in place regarding products, quality, pricing, delivery, billing, and so on. The purchasing department researches, evaluates, and negotiates terms with suppliers on behalf of the foodservice operation. Approved supplier lists can be created for any size operation.

As Purchased (AP)   An acronym for all products received at the door.

Assumptions   In budgeting, these are the financial directives for a new operating period. They represent management's best estimate as to the economic effect of a change (+/−) in an internal or external environment.

Automated Beverage Control System   An electronic system that automatically counts what has been sold each time a drink is poured. Automated systems are designed to pour amounts that are exactly measured.

Average Contribution Margin Pricing Method   The average amount each item should contribute toward Controllable Expenses, Fixed Costs, and Profit. It is added to an item's True Cost per Dish, to determine a selling price.

Average Inventory Cost   The beginning and ending inventory added together and divided by 2. This average is used to calculate inventory turnover.

Average Sales per Seat   This average measures the annual revenue each seat produces for an operation. Operators compare this figure to the annual seat revenue of other similar operations.

B

Back-of-House (BOH) Functions   All noncustomer contact areas of a foodservice operation.

Back Order   Occurs when a supplier is out of a product and is waiting for shipment from the manufacturer.

Bar   Part of the foodservice operation and located in a separate room that is expressly designed for serving alcohol beverages.

Bar and Inventory Control Report   Provides a comprehensive method for tracking beverage inventory. It tracks use of product by day in the period and for the entire period, the number of drinks that should have been sold, the retail value of those drinks, and the liquor cost percentages by type of beverage.

Bar Cost   See Pour Cost.

Bar Requisitions/Transfers   Forms used to monitor beverage inventory. They have the same appearance as food requisitions and transfers.

Beginning Bank   Records the cash in the drawer at the start of the shift. It is the cash on hand needed to make change during the shift.

Beverage Cost   The cost of goods sold in the preparation of alcohol beverages for a specific accounting period. Like food cost, beverage cost is used to report the total dollar amount spent to generate sales for the period.

Beverage Cost Percentage   The beverage cost reported as a percentage of beverage sales.

Beverage Cost Report   A form used to calculate beverage cost percentage. It indicates the actual cost percentage of liquor, wine, beer, and complements. It is used to determine the cost of goods sold over a specific accounting period.

Bidding   A process businesses use to compare supplier prices, services, and other criteria prior to making purchasing decisions.

Bid Sheet   A form that itemizes each product to be ordered and is used to compare prices among different suppliers.

Bin Card   A smaller version of a perpetual inventory chart. The bin card is attached to each product's shelf location. Every time stock is added to the shelf, the storeroom clerk records the date and the number of units received on the bin card. As product is requisitioned out, the reverse happens.

Blank Requisition   A blank requisition does not have the product items and par amounts preprinted on the form.

Book Inventory Value (Perpetual Inventory Value)   The value of the inventory, calculated from invoices minus what was used during the accounting period.

Bottle Control Systems   Devices used to control the amount of beverage poured from a bottle.

Bottle Exchange System   A method of controlling beverage inventory by exchanging an empty bottle for a full bottle.

Broadline Distributors   Foodservice distributors that carry food, nonfood, nonalcohol beverages, smallwares, large kitchen equipment, and dining room equipment and work with operators to fill just about any need. Some even offer architectural services, installation services, payroll services, advertising and marketing services, training, and much more.

Broker   An independent marketing team contracted to link interested parties together: a processor or manufacturer, a distributor, and an end user. Brokers are marketing specialists.

Browse Sheet   A computer printout of the current prices for products.

Butcher Test   A form used to determine the amount of usable product after trimming. These items may be portioned and cooked to order, or cooked whole.

C

Call Brands   Brand-name liquors carried on the bar that customers may ask to be used in their drink. Call brands automatically trigger a higher drink price.

Call Sheet   See Bid Sheet.

Can Cutting   Yield analysis for canned products.

Cappuccino   A coffee drink that is approximately 10% espresso, 45% steamed milk, and 45% foam.

Captive Audiences   Guests on premises that must be fed because they have no other place to go.

Case-Break Pricing   Special pricing situation triggered when a partial case of a product is ordered. When this happens, the supplier has to "break" the case, and that full unit is no longer available to ship whole. The unit price can be higher than the unit price of the item, had the full case been purchased.

Cash and Carry   The buyer picks up product and pays cash at the time of purchase.

Cash Comparison   Indicates the dollar amount that should be in the cash register. It is calculated by comparing sales to retail value to the quantity of liquor dispensed per shift.

Cash Discount(s)   Discounts given for prompt payment of statements at the end of the accounting period. Typically, this is read as 2%/10 days. This means if the account is paid within 10 days, a 2% discount is earned.

Cash Flow   A description of how cash is used in a foodservice operation.

Cashier's Report   A form used to account for the total revenue collected during a specific period of time, such as a shift.

Cash on Delivery (COD)   The invoice is settled with the driver when the goods are delivered.

Cash Turn-In Report   A form used to account for cash collected during a specific period of time, such as a shift. The purpose of the form is to assist the cashier in counting the cash drawer at the end of a shift.

Charge Receipts   Sales that are charged on credit cards or billed directly. Only those charges in which tips were reported must be included.

Closed Storerooms   Store areas where access is limited to authorized employees only.

Closing Inventory   A physical count of the inventory at the end of the accounting period.

Cocktails   Drinks that use a combination of two or more alcohol beverages. These are sometimes referred to as a blended drink.

Commissaries   A distribution system used by large national chains to supply products to individual stores. Warehouses/plants are regionally located and service stores in a specific area. Commissaries may purchase raw product and produce finished goods in kitchens using company recipes and/or purchase already-processed goods for distribution. These chains use local suppliers for a limited amount of product.

Common Size Analysis   A method of budget analysis that involves analyzing the variance in the percentages between budget and actual results.

Common Usage Pattern(s)   Through observation, experience, and knowledge of the business, the chef or manager establishes how much product is regularly used.

Comparative Analysis   Computes the dollar difference between budget and actual results for each line item. This difference is converted into a percentage. The variance is analyzed.

Competitive Analysis   The process of determining the number of competitors in an area and analyzing the strengths and weaknesses of these competitors in order to discover opportunities.

Competitive Geographic Area or Trading Area   The area defined as that from which most customers originate.

Contribution Margin (CM)   Refers to the contribution that the sale of each menu item makes toward covering raw food cost (TCPD—True Cost per Dish), all other operating costs, fixed costs, and profit.

Contribution Margin (Menu) Pricing Method   The process of setting a menu price by adding the cost and profit associated with each customer to each menu item, except for single food items, such as desserts or appetizers.

Control   To exercise authority over, regulate, verify, or check some function of.

Controllable Expenses   Operating costs incurred as a part of day-to-day operations within the four walls of the business. They are classified as controllable because they tend to vary according to sales, and management has some degree of control over them.

Convenience Products   See Value-Added Products.

Cooking Loss   Measuring what is servable after the cooking process has taken place.

Cordials   Types of mixed drinks that are served from the bottle or used within recipes.

Cost Card(s)   Form(s) used to determine the cost per portion of a single serving of a menu item.

Cost Control   The process of regulating, checking, and exercising authority over income, expenses, and the flow of products and services internal or external to a foodservice operation. Cost-control systems pinpoint responsibility for inefficiency, waste, errors, and fraud.

Cost of Food Available for Sale   All the dollars spent on food for the month.

Cost of Food Sold this Month   An adjusted figure used to compute monthly food cost percentages and analyze financial performance.

Cost of Goods Sold   On the income statement, this line reports all product costs associated with producing the food and beverages served for each revenue center.

Cost per Portion   The raw food cost for one standard serving.

Covers per Person-Hour   An average of how many covers are prepared by each member of the team per hour.

Credit Adjustments   Adjustments that decrease the cost of food available for sale, allowing management to determine just how much money was really spent to generate dining room sales. The credit is an outflow from the food cost account.

Credit Card Discount   A fee paid by foodservice operations to financial institutions for processing credit and debit card transactions.

Credit or Debit Card Voucher   A paper receipt that is used to record a sale made to a customer using a credit or debit card. The receipt is the only record of the transaction.

Credit Memo   A form used to reject all or part of an order. It lists the item(s) name, the quantity refused, the unit price, and the extension.

Criteria   Standard on which judgment may be based.

Customer Comment Card   A card used to ask customers' opinions regarding their dining experience. They provide information after the dining experience has ended.

Customer Count   The number of customers that eat during a designated period of time, such as a meal period, day, week, month, or year.

D

Daily Bid   An informal method of purchasing products used on a daily basis.

Daily Food Cost Worksheet   A report used to track food cost percentage on a daily basis. It is useful because it is a day-to-day indication of how food cost is running.

Daily Incident Log   A form used to record incidents that occurred in serving or denying service to customers.

Daily Sales Report   A report that recaps the entire day's sales activity by each department and shift, including the accompanying totals. It is used for review and analysis and can also be used as a permanent accounting record.

Debit Card   A card that resembles a credit card, but charges made using one are subtracted from the cardholder's checking account at the end of the day's business. A debit card allows the guest to pay for the meal as if writing a check.

Declining Balance Budget   A budgeting system where a department starts an operating period with a budget amount. The account is drawn down (decreased) over the course of the operating period.

Department Food Cost Report   A form used to calculate department food cost percentage.

Diluting Bottles   Water is substituted for liquor and then used to mix drinks. The liquor poured off is sold, and the employee keeps the money for the drinks.

Directs   Direct purchases; purchases that go directly into production.

Discount   The amount of the fee-negotiated arrangement that the foodservice operation has with the bank and the credit card company. This fee is paid by foodservice operations to financial institutions for processing credit and debit card transactions.

Distribution Systems   The system used to deliver products to market.

Drained Weight   Represents what is left after the packing medium is removed.

Dupe Pad   A pad of order checks that are sequentially numbered and issued to the server.

E

Edible Portion (EP)   This acronym represents a food product that has been processed in some way. It has been peeled, trimmed, cooked, and portioned. EP is used to describe the portion of food as served to the guest.

Employee Meals   Cost of meals or food served to employees; considered a form of compensation and therefore part of the payroll costs.

Employee Turnover   The number of times that the total number of positions are filled with employees during an accounting period. Turnover is often expressed as a percentage of the average number of employees needed to operate a foodservice operation.

Equipment Inventory   The total value of all foodservice equipment used by each food preparation area.

Essential Functions   Job tasks that are fundamental and not marginal to job performance.

Evaluation   The process of comparing performance data to established standards.

Expediter   Employee responsible for firing orders to the kitchen and checking that plates match checks (and special requests) as they leave the kitchen.

Expense Detail   All the individual expenses that make up a specific line item in a budget.

External Environment   The external environment includes factors such as government regulations, local market conditions, labor-force demographics, national economic conditions, supplier relations, new technology, and media.

F

Farfalle Arrabbiata   Italian for "the angry bowtie"; the name of the model restaurant designed for the text.

FIFO   An acronym standing for first-in, first-out—a process of rotating inventory so the first items purchased are the first items used in the kitchen; a method of valuing inventory.

Fixed Bid   A buyer prepares very detailed specifications (a Request for Bid—RFB) that are sent only to qualified suppliers. Suppliers submit bids. The buyer will open bids and award a contract to the supplier who best meets the RFB.

Fixed Cost   Costs that remain the same for a period of time.

Food Cost   The actual cost of purchasing raw food products and related ingredients used to generate dining room sales. Food cost is measured for specific periods (daily, weekly, monthly, annually), and it is always expressed in terms of a percentage.

Food Cost Percentage   The proportion of food sales necessary to purchase food products. It is calculated by dividing the cost of food sold by the total food sales and multiplying by 100.

Food Cost Percentage (Menu Pricing) Method   A menu pricing method based on the presumption that costs should be maintained as a fixed percentage of sales.

Food Cost Report   A form used to calculate the food cost percentage.

Food Mishap Report or Void Sheet   A form that accounts for wasted food portions and identifies responsibility and accountability within the production and service staff.

Food Production Schedule   A form that directs the cook's workday and controls the amount of food being prepared in the kitchen.

Food Sales Recap Report   Records the number of menu items sold per day, the total per week, and the current popularity percentage.

Form (Purchasing)   Describes a product in some way other than how it is ordinarily packaged or bought.

Formal Purchasing Method   Involves using a bid system to secure the right quantity and quality of products at the right price.

Free Pouring   When a bartender pours the alcohol beverage straight from the bottle, estimating how much liquid is left in the bottle.

Front Bar   A bar located in a public area of the restaurant in full view of the dining room area.

Front-of-House (FOH) Functions   All the guest contact areas of a foodservice operation.

Full-Line Distributor(s)   Distributors who carry only food, nonfood, and nonalcohol beverages. They may offer limited services.

G

Gross Receipts   Cash sales, charge receipts, and charges to hotel rooms. Gross receipts should not include carryout sales, sales with an added service charge of 10% or more, and state or local taxes.

Guest Check   A form used to record guest food orders and prices, and total sales to guests, and to request food from the kitchen. It is one of the primary FOH tools from which critical operating data is generated.

Guest Check Daily Record   A form used to track the use of customer guest checks by the servers.

H

High Productivity Employees   Employees who meet or exceed performance standards (expected employee performance).

House Brands   See Well Stock.

House Policy   A written policy indicating how employees are to behave in given situations of alcohol beverage service.

I

Income Statement   A report of all income, expenses, and profit for a defined period of time. It reports the financial standing of an operation. Income statements are also referred to as a budget or a Profit and Loss Statement (P & L).

Indirect Payroll Costs   Costs associated with payroll that are mandated by law.

Informal Purchasing Method   A buyer, upon compiling an order, calls the suppliers, receives a verbal price quote, and places the order. The buyer may solicit prices from more than one vendor.

In-Process Inventory   Food that is in the process of getting ready to be sold. In-process inventory can also mean the value of the product in process on the last day of the operating period.

Intermediaries or Middlemen   Businesses that distribute supplies to foodservice operators. Some of these companies are so large they distribute nationally and even internationally. Some are regional businesses. Some distribute product in just a few states or in a specific area, or handle only specialty products.

Internal Environment   Functions carried on within the organization to achieve organizational objectives. It includes front-of-house functions, back-of-house functions, and management functions.

Inventory   The physical quantity of food and nonfood products used in a foodservice operation.

Inventory File/Sheet   A comprehensive list or inventory of all ingredients that need to be purchased. It lists the food and nonfood products by categories, quantities, price, and location within the operation.

Inventory Turnover Rate   The number of times the total inventory is used during a given accounting period.

Invoice A form that accompanies a delivery. It provides an itemized list of what was delivered and serves as a bill or invoice for payment.

Invoice on Account A bill paying procedure. Suppliers send a statement at the end of the month detailing monthly purchases. Operators reconcile invoices on hand and credits with the statement before making a payment.

Invoice Payment Schedule A form used to document all purchases during a given period of time and to ensure that suppliers are paid in a timely fashion.

Invoice Receiving Standard receiving procedure whereby the quantity of product on the truck is verified against the invoice quantity and the Purchase Order quantity.

Invoice Stamp A stamp applied to an invoice by the receiver that ensures that all checks for quantity, quality, and price have been made and that payment of the invoice can move forward.

Issuing A means of tracking the movement of product from the receiving areas to production areas via the storeroom requisition.

J

Job Description A document that describes the job objectives, work to be performed, job responsibilities, skills needed, working conditions, and relationship of the job to other jobs.

K

Kickback Suppliers may offer money to managers to sell their products, rather than offering legitimate discounts for volume purchases. A manager may also be offered a bribe to carry a line of products. Although the bribe is not necessarily stealing from the operation, the practice usually leads to overpricing and other costs to cover the bribe. In addition, this type of collusion is against the law.

L

Lead Time Deadlines for ordering from suppliers.

License Requirements State laws that require food and beverage operations to acquire a license to serve alcohol beverages.

LIFO Last in, first out inventory system. Inventory is valued at its earliest purchase price (starting with beginning inventory cost) first.

Liquor Cost Percentage Also known as the pour cost percentage. It is the proportion of liquor sales necessary to generate liquor sales.

Liquor Storeroom Inventory Report This report tracks the inventory of each beverage item.

Lounge A separate room that is expressly designed for serving alcohol beverages.

Low Productivity Employees Employees who are not producing at established performance standards.

M

Make-or-Buy Analysis (MOBA) A method of analyzing production options for producing a menu item.

Management Controls Methods of comparing and exercising authority over a foodservice operation's performance to attain established operating goals.

Management Functions Planning, organizing, influencing, and controlling all of the internal functions of an operation.

Manufacturers/Processors These businesses process raw product into a more useful form.

Master Budget A budget for the entire operation. A master budget includes all departmental budgets, as well as all other administrative costs.

Master Grocery List A list of every item used in production or in a department.

Measured Pour A pouring method in which the bartender pours the beverage into a glass that has been marked in a way that indicates how much beverage is to be poured into the customer's glass. Most alcohol beverages are measured by the ⅞ ounce, 1 ounce, or 1⅛ ounce.

Menu The first step in the Cycle of Control. It lists all the menu selections, available services, and other marketing information for an operation.

Menu Analysis The process of comparing the popularity and profitability of menu items.

Menu Bank A file of all menu items that work for the operation.

Menu Item Sales Forecast An estimate of what is expected to happen. It gives managers a baseline for sales and costs.

Menu Mix The number of each menu item sold in relationship to the other items sold.

Method of Prep The procedural steps to produce a menu item.

Minimum Menu Price (MMP) Formula   The formula used to determine a sell price based on the standard food cost percentage.

Minimum Order Size   Minimum size an order must be—either in dollars or number of pieces ordered—to qualify for a delivery.

Mishap Percentage   The ratio of mishaps to total covers served. It is calculated by dividing Mishaps per Hour by Covers per Hour and is a measure of efficiency and quality. The percentage, like the other tools, should be used to help set goals and monitor how well employees are performing their jobs.

Mishaps per Hour   An average of the number of mistakes (such as items dropped on the floor, overcooked or undercooked food, and food returned to the kitchen for a variety of reasons) that occur per hour.

Mixed Cost   A cost that has elements of variable costs and fixed costs.

Mixed Drinks   Drinks that use a combination of an alcohol beverage and water or some other nonalcohol ingredient like club soda or ginger ale.

Mixers   Items such as fruit, Bloody Mary mix, Collins mix, and so on, that are used to prepare or flavor alcohol beverages.

Monthly Food Cost Report   A report that indicates the actual cost percentage of food used for all food sales for an identified period of time—usually a 4-week period or a month.

Monthly Productivity Chart   A chart that summarizes the information reported on the shift productivity chart.

Most Recent Purchase Price   A method of valuing inventory that uses the most recent purchase price as the unit price on the inventory form.

N

Neat Drinks   Alcohol beverages poured from the bottle into a glass and consumed—no ice, water, or other additions.

Net Weight   The total weight of a product and the packing medium.

Nonoperating Costs   An expense that is incurred that is not used to generate sales.

O

Occupation Costs   Fixed costs, which do not change for a period of time. They are also referred to as nonoperating costs.

One-Stop Shopping   The practice of ordering all or most products from one supplier.

Open Container Laws   State laws restricting the transfer of open alcohol beverages in an automobile.

Opening Inventory   A physical count of the inventory at the beginning of an accounting period.

Open Storerooms   In an open storeroom environment, access is not restricted and employees remove products themselves.

Operating Costs   Costs that are incurred in order to generate sales. Operating costs are necessary for day-to-day operations.

Operating Cycle of Control (OCC)   A control cycle that divides any food and beverage operation into a series of activities that are necessary to profitably and efficiently supply food and beverage products and services to guests, given an acceptable volume of business.

Order Sheet(s)   Forms used to establish the products needed to be ordered on a particular day and their respective quantities.

Organizational Culture   The shared values, beliefs, attitudes, and norms that help to direct employee behavior by creating a sense of purpose.

Outs   Outs occur when a menu item cannot be provided to a customer because there are not enough raw ingredients to prepare the item.

Outsource   The outsourcing of the production of some "recipe" products to food manufacturing firms that specialize in producing customized restaurant products to restaurant specifications.

Over-Ring   Any time a cashier rings a higher amount than the sale on a cash register or POS terminal.

P

Packing Medium   The fluid in which a product is packed.

Par Amount Requisition   A preprinted requisition sheet with par amounts (a predetermined level or numbers of an item kept in inventory) assigned to each inventory item in regular use.

Par Stock or Amount   The minimum level of inventory needed to carry production between delivery dates.

Payroll Budget   The planned estimate of payroll expenses.

Payroll Budget Estimate/Payroll Cost   A planned estimate of expenses, expressed in dollar amounts or as a percentage of sales. It is an estimate of the cost of labor needed to manage an estimated level of sales.

Payroll Cost Control   The process of meeting cost targets by establishing a payroll budget, properly organizing the workplace, hiring correctly, reducing employee turnover, scheduling properly, and comparing actual costs to projected costs, with the intent of reducing variances.

Payroll Cost Estimate   Calculated by position and person from the Work Schedule.

Payroll Cost Percentage   Shows the relationship between payroll costs and total sales.

Payroll Cost Report   A form used to tabulate payroll cost for all employees.

Payroll Cost Sheet   A form used to tabulate payroll cost for all employees.

Payroll Planning   Involves establishing a payroll budget, properly organizing the workplace, hiring correctly, and reducing employee turnover.

Performance Measurements   Indicates the amount of work produced in a given period of time. Some common production measurements in the foodservice industry are sales per server per hour and the speed at which an order is produced and served.

Performance Standard(s)   The statement of a job task, in terms of activity requirements.

Periodic Inventory System   A system of tracking inventory at the end of an accounting period; an actual physical count of all items on hand at the close of an accounting period.

Perpetual Inventory Chart   Every addition to the existing inventory through purchases is recorded on paper, and, in turn, every item requisitioned for use is subtracted from the chart.

Perpetual Inventory System   Calculates the value of inventory each time an item is either used or added to inventory; a continuous way of tracking inventory; an ongoing physical count.

Personal Performance Review   A formal evaluation of an employee's on-the-job performance.

Physical Inventory   The actual amount of inventory that has been physically counted and that physically exists in storage.

Plate Card   A hybrid form of a recipe. These cards describe one complete menu item as management wishes it to be served; a standard plating guide.

Popularity Percentage   A method of tracking guest's menu preferences. It is defined as the frequency with which each menu item is selected as it competes with other menu items.

Portion Control Chart   A form that shows discrepancies, overages, and shorts in the production. It verifies that the number of portions that should be served were actually served.

Post-Mix System   Carbonated beverage system where the mixer flavor comes in large syrup containers. The syrup is then mixed in a carbonator with water to produce a carbonated beverage; usually packaged as a bag-in-a-box.

Pour Cost   The cost of preparing a single drink.

Pour Guns   Hand-held devices used to control pouring alcohol and nonalcohol drinks.

Pour Systems   Systems used to control the quantity of alcohol beverages used in drinks.

Preemployment Tests   Tests used to prove that the person is capable of performing specific job tasks.

Pre-Mix System   Flavored soda that is ready to serve (premixed with water). It is packaged in stainless steel tanks.

Prime Costs   Food cost, beverage cost, and labor cost (including benefits).

Prime Cost (Menus) Pricing Method   A menu pricing method that factors food cost and labor cost (including benefits) into the menu pricing equation.

Product Specifications   A detailed description of products and services written to assist the buyer and the supplier in getting the right product or service to the operation.

Production Schedule   Used to record ingredients for each menu item needing special attention or instruction, production amounts, and other details. This form controls the back-of-house production, ensuring that menu items will be ready on time.

Productivity   A measurement of how well employees are meeting or exceeding performance standards.

Productivity Measurements   Measures that indicate the amount of work produced in a given period of time. Some common production measurements in the foodservice industry are sales per server per hour and how fast an order is produced and served.

Product or Meat Tags   Special inventory control tools reserved for tracking high-cost products from the point of receipt through production and final sale.

Profit or Loss   Sales minus expenses.

Promotional/Comp(limentary) Meals   Meals given away by the owner/manager for entertainment of friends or professional associates, to accommodate a disgruntled customer, or as a promotional gift.

Prudent Person Rule   A legal standard that compares what a prudent person would do in a situation to the behavior that actually occurred.

Purchase Order (PO)   A Purchase Order is a numbered form that identifies the item(s), the quantity ordered, the price, unit cost, extension, total, and authorization signatures.

Purchasing Units   How items are packaged for delivery.

Q

Q Factor   The Cost per Portion of the surrounding items included in a meal. It is used to address the portion cost of side dishes offered with an entrée.

Quality Standards   Dictate the condition, measure, weight, and count or volume of products used in producing menu items.

Quantity Discount   A discount given when a certain quantity of the same product is ordered.

R

Ratio (Menu Pricing) Method   Uses the relationship between Total Food Cost and all other costs (Controllable Expenses, Occupation Costs, and Profit) to generate a menu selling price.

Receiver's Daily Report/Receiving Report   A daily report of deliveries received.

Receiving   The process of comparing what was ordered against what is being delivered and either accepting or rejecting all or part of the order.

Recipe Cost Card(s)   A form used to calculate the cost of one serving of a specific menu item, using the approved standardized recipe to produce it.

Reconciling Sales   The process of comparing cash register sales with what was actually sold.

Requisitions   Forms used to request that the purchaser order a specific product or service. Requisitions are a means of charging departments for product ordered.

Revenue/Sales   Income earned from all revenue centers. Revenue and sales are interchangeable terms.

S

Sales Forecasts   An estimate of the foodservice operation's sales based on the number of expected customers and the average amount each customer will spend.

Sales History   Operational data about past results used to develop sales forecasts.

Sales per Person-Hour   The amount of sales generated per preparation person.

Sales/Revenue   Income earned from all revenue centers. Sales and revenue are interchangeable terms.

Seat Turnover   The number of times a server is able to meet and greet the guest, secure the order, deliver all food and beverages, present the check, and reset the table for the next customers in a meal period.

Selection Sheet   A form used to compare the prerequisites and competencies of employment applicants.

Semi-à-la-Carte Pricing   A combination pricing method where several courses/selections are grouped together and sold for one price.

Server Education   An educational program for teaching servers of alcohol beverages to control alcohol consumption by bar patrons.

Server Productivity Chart   A form that measures the productivity of each server.

Service Bar   A bar in or next to the kitchen and is used by servers to pick up beverages with meals. It is not in a public area of the restaurant.

Service Standards   The individual actions taken by service personnel that collectively create the service experience provided to the customer, as defined by management.

Service System Chart   A form that lists the service tasks, service standards, and staff member responsible for accomplishing each service task.

Shift Productivity Chart   A form that measures the productivity of food preparation personnel.

Short   Occurs when a different amount appears on the invoice than was actually delivered.

Short Pour   Occurs when less than the recipe amount of alcohol beverages is used to serve drinks.

Shrinkage   Refers to the loss of china and flatware as part of the function of doing business.

Special-Function Bar   A bar set up for functions. It is portable and is used for private parties, catered events, and group functions.

Specialty Product Distributors   Distributors that carry specialty product lines. These businesses specialize in a limited line of specialty products and may offer limited extra services to their customers.

Specifications Detailed descriptions of products and services written to assist the buyer and the supplier in getting the right product (or service) to the operation.

Spice Factor (SF) A percentage added to every menu item to account for things such as spices herbs, garnishes, and waste.

Spoilage Report A form that documents spoiled or damaged items.

Standard The quantity or quality to be operationally achieved or maintained.

Standardized Recipe(s) A recipe that has been tested, adjusted, and retested again and again until it produces a menu item as management wants the item produced.

Standard Operating Procedures (SOPs) Standard methods by which management requires certain processes to be completed.

Steward Sales An adjustment to monthly cost of goods. It is the food sold to an employee, manager, or owner at cost.

Stockouts A term indicating that there is no more of a particular item in stock.

Storeroom Requisitions A form used to issue products. The requisition is then used to charge the cost of the items requested to the department that ordered the products.

Stores Purchases that will be placed into storage areas to be used over a period of time. These items do not go immediately into production areas.

Subrecipes Recipes for products used within a number of other recipes.

Supplier Specification(s) A list detailing the selection criteria a buyer has created for potential suppliers.

T

Tab A form of credit whereby a server does not collect payment for alcohol beverages until the person is through being served.

Table Turnover See Seat Turnover.

Tap Products Beverages poured from a tap, usually beers and ales.

Third-Party Liability A state law that makes those who serve alcohol beverages liable for serving alcohol drinks to people who are considered legally drunk.

Transfer(s) Form(s) used to document the movement of food from one department or unit to the next.

Transfer Form A form that lists the departments involved in the switch, and the items, quantity, unit price, and extensions for those items.

U

Unacceptable Variances The percentage of variance that is considered unacceptable. When unacceptable variances are identified, management is charged with pinpointing the problem and fixing it.

Under-Ring Occurs when a cashier rings a lower amount than the sale on a cash register or POS system.

V

Value-Added Products A food product that has been partially or fully prepared by a manufacturer or processor.

Variable Costs Costs that fluctuate or change with sales.

Variance(s) A deviation from a standard.

Volume A measure of space or capacity. Some examples are gallon, quart, pint, and cup.

Volume Discount(s) Discount given when invoices for all products are over a certain amount.

W

Wages Compensation for employees based on hours worked.

Waste Percentage The percentage of a product that is not servable: 100% − Yield Percentage = Waste Percentage.

Weight A measure of density or heaviness. The standard unit of measure is a pound.

Well Stock Standard house brands of liquor that are used to mix drinks. These are used whenever a customer does not specify a brand name.

Will-Call Order The buyer picks up the order at the supplier's warehouse.

Y

Yield Analysis Calculating the amount of usable food derived from raw products.

Yield Percentage The part of the whole available for sale; the net usable product.

Yield Test See Butcher Test.

Photo Credits

Cover: Burke/Triolo Productions/FoodPix/Getty Images, Inc.

Page 13, Steve Tanner © Dorling Kindersley

Figure 4.3: Dave King © Dorling Kindersley

Figure 4.4: Tony Freeman, PhotoEdit Inc.

Figure 4.9: Dave King © Dorling Kindersley

Figure 4.10: Philip Dowell © Dorling Kindersley

Figure 4.11: © Dorling Kindersley

Figure 4.12: Dave King © Dorling Kindersley

Figure 4.13: Andrew McRobb © Dorling Kindersley

Figure 4.14: Philip Dowell © Dorling Kindersley

Figure 4.15: David Murray © Dorling Kindersley

Figure 4.16: Robb Gregg, PhotoEdit Inc.

Figure 4.17: Brian Yarvin, Photo Researchers, Inc.

Figure 4.18: Colin Walton © Dorling Kindersley

Figure 4.19: Philip Dowell © Dorling Kindersley

Figure 4.20: Stephen Oliver © Dorling Kindersley

Figure 4.21: David Murray © Dorling Kindersley

Figure 7.1: Mark Richards/P. P. O. W. Gallery/Pilkington-Olsoff Fine Arts, Inc.

Figure 8.3: Jeff Zaruba, Corbis/Stock Market

Figure 8.4: Jeff Greenberg, Visuals Unlimited

Figure 11.4A: Clive Streeter © Dorling Kindersley

Figure 11.4B: Matthew Ward © Dorling Kindersley

Figure 16.12: Steve Gorton © Dorling Kindersley

Index